Principle of Architecture, Protocol, and Algorithms for CoG-MIN

Hui Li • He Bai

Principle of Architecture, Protocol, and Algorithms for CoG-MIN

A Sustainably Ecological & Evolutionary Solution for Packet Network System

网络空间命运共同体架构协议体系及应用

一个保障全球网络空间长期法治和平安全的可演进生态系统方案

Springer

Hui Li
School of Electronic and Computer Engineering
Peking University
Shenzhen, China

He Bai
School of Electronic and Computer Engineering
Peking University
Shenzhen, China

ISBN 978-981-96-3595-5 ISBN 978-981-96-3596-2 (eBook)
https://doi.org/10.1007/978-981-96-3596-2

School of Electronic and Computer Engineering, Peking University

This Springer imprint is published by the registered company Springer Nature Singapore Pte Ltd.
The registered company address is: 152 Beach Road, #21-01/04 Gateway East, Singapore 189721, Singapore

To:
All people, nations and organizations who love peaceful, secure, open and cooperative cyberspace.
The coming United Nations of Cyberspace with democracy and rule of law.
献给:
全世界热爱和平安全开放合作网络空间的人们，国家和组织;
多边共管民主透明法治的未来
网络空间联合国。

Foreword I: CoG-MIN—Cornerstone of the Four Networks and Four Flows Theory by Prof. C.C. Chan

In today's rapidly evolving era of information technology, building a Community with a Shared Future in Cyberspace has become a global consensus. As a multilateral co-governance network architecture, the *Co-Governed Multi-Identifier Network* (*CoG-MIN, brief as MIN*) demonstrates immense potential for future network development. Intelligent connected vehicles, as crucial nodes in cyberspace, not only revolutionize transportation modes but also become integral components of the next-generation network architecture. By integrating the *Four Networks and Four Flows Theory* within the framework of a multilateral co-governance network, we can better understand the interactions of intelligent connected vehicles across the four dimensions of information flow, energy flow, material flow, and value flow, as well as their critical roles in the communication network, energy network, transportation network, and value network.

In the realm of cyberspace governance and network architecture, Professor Hui LI's new monograph, *Principle of Architecture, Protocol, and Algorithms for CoG-MIN: A Sustainably Ecological & Evolutionary Solution for Packet Network System*, stands as a beacon of future network development. This comprehensive monograph provides a transformative decentralized co-governance solution based on blockchain technology, namely the MIN architecture, to address the pressing challenges of the current Internet. Embracing the principles of sovereignty, transparency, and collaboration, the MIN architecture enables a more secure, flexible, and efficient network environment that fosters a shared future in cyberspace. This innovative approach not only addresses the limitations of current networks but also paves the way for a new era of cyberspace governance, where the rights and interests of all stakeholders are respected and safeguarded.

Under the *Four Networks and Four Flows Theory*, intelligent connected vehicles achieve deep integration of transportation and communication through dynamic interactions of information flow (real-time data exchange), energy flow (energy management of electric vehicles), material flow (logistics management of vehicles), and value flow (economic and social benefits). The communication network, supported by 5G technology and the Internet of Vehicles (IoV), ensures seamless connectivity between vehicles and the external world; the energy network, through smart grids and charging infrastructure, ensures efficient energy utilization; the transportation network, via intelligent transportation systems (ITS), optimizes traffic flow and enhances transport efficiency; and the value network promotes the commercialization and widespread adoption of intelligent connected vehicles through industrial chain collaboration and innovation.

Crucially, the integration of the *Four Networks and Four Flows Theory* within the MIN architecture significantly strengthens cyberspace's defenses against cyberattacks and enhances the reliability of data transmission. This not only improves the security and privacy of the IoV and other various business scenarios but also boosts operational efficiency and sustainability, offering substantial advantages to all stakeholders in the transportation and communication sectors.

In conclusion, this monograph represents a timely and transformative milestone in the evolution of future network architectures. The innovative MIN architecture offers a visionary roadmap for the integration and advancement of intelligent connected vehicles. I eagerly anticipate the MIN network driving the development of a more secure, efficient, and equitable cyberspace.

Academician, Chinese Academy of Engineering
Beijing, China
Fellow, Royal Academy of Engineering, London, UK
Honorary Professor, University of Hong Kong
Pokfulam, Hong Kong
Distinguished Chair Professor
Hong Kong Polytechnic University
Kowloon, Hong Kong
Founder, World Electric Vehicle Association
Washington, DC, USA
Founder, International Academicians Science
and Technology Innovation Centre
Beijing, China

C. C. Chan

Foreword II by Dr. Peter Janos Major

I am delighted to recommend the book *Principle of Architecture, Protocol, and Algorithms for CoG-MIN: A Sustainably Ecological & Evolutionary Solution for Packet Network System*. In today's digital economy era, the Internet has become one of the most critical global infrastructures. Its role has evolved from simple information exchange to supporting a wide array of novel scenarios and applications.

In the digital economy era, ensuring the security, stability, and sustainable development of networks is a paramount goal. The Co-Governed Multi-Identifier Network (CoG-MIN) provides an innovative and effective solution to achieve this objective. It emphasizes the principles of democracy, inclusiveness, and cooperation in global network governance. By positioning identity identifiers as anchor identifiers, CoG-MIN can support and handle various existing and potential network identifiers, communication semantics, and application scenarios, enabling flexible addressing and routing. It employs an innovative identifier extension mechanism to ensure the continuous evolution of the network. This mechanism establishes a solid foundation for the sustained development of network architecture.

The author of this book is a distinguished expert in the fields of network architecture and network security, with remarkable achievements in both research and practical applications. This book provides readers with valuable insights and inspiration. It not only details the design principles, system architecture, and key technologies of CoG-MIN but also demonstrates its superior performance and broad application potential through rich case studies and experiments. From the history of Internet development to the current state of new network research, and from the design principles of CoG-MIN to its system architecture and various protocols and algorithms, this book offers readers a comprehensive and in-depth understanding. Whether the reader is a researcher in computer networks, an information system planner, or a network security manager, this book will serve as an indispensable reference.

As we look to the future, the CoG-MIN architecture offers a robust solution for addressing the complex challenges of network governance and network security. It embodies a vision of a more secure, democratic, and cooperative cyberspace. I believe that this book will become a milestone in the fields of network management and cybersecurity, contributing significantly to the construction of a peaceful, secure, open, cooperative, and sustainable cyberspace. I hope that countries around the world will actively engage in this multilateral co-governance network and work together to build a secure and trustworthy global cyberspace.

Peter Janos Major

Vice-Chairman of the United Nations
Commission on Science and Technology
for Development (UNCSTD)
Geneva, Switzerland
President of the World Digital
Technology Academy (WDTA)
Geneva, Switzerland
Honorary President of the United Nations
Digital Security Alliance (UNDSA)
Geneva, Switzerland

Foreword III by Prof. Jingan Zhang

The remarkable work by Prof. Hui Li, *Principle of Architecture, Protocol, and Algorithms for CoG-MIN: A Sustainably Ecological & Evolutionary Solution for Packet Network System*, represents an innovative attempt to address one of the most critical challenges of our era—*how to construct a secure, sovereign, and co-governed cyberspace that can support the global Internet system along the trajectory of peace, rule of law, and collaboration.*

Professor Hui Li has proposed CoG-MIN (Co-Governed Multi-Identifier Network), a pioneering architecture that reshapes packet-based network systems through multilateral governance and national sovereignty. CoG-MIN offers a roadmap for co-governance and co-management of global cyberspace. CoG-MIN is not only a technical innovation but also a governance model, striking an ingenious balance between the preservation of national sovereignty and the benefits of international collaboration. It also reflects adaptability and forward-thinking design principles, emphasizing that future network systems must evolve to meet the dynamic demands of a rapidly changing digital era while remaining robust, secure, and shared principles. CoG-MIN is not only an immediate response to current challenges but also a forward-looking and scalable solution for the governance of cyberspace.

I have dedicated my career to the formulation and implementation of science and technology policies. Therefore, I deeply appreciate the significance of this book. CoG-MIN addresses the urgent global need for a multilateral, co-governed Internet system in the digital age. It is not only a major breakthrough in the technological field but also a proactive response to the guiding principles of Internet governance—fairness, inclusivity, respect for national sovereignty, and the promotion of global cooperation. For policymakers, engineers, and researchers alike, this book serves as an indispensable guide to shaping the future direction of the Internet.

Drawing on a multifaceted approach that integrates perspectives from network engineering, governance theory, and policy research, Professor Hui Li has articulated a comprehensive solution to address the complex challenges of cyberspace. CoG-MIN is deeply rooted in the realities of international relations, technological scalability, and the legal foundations of the rule of law. This comprehensive and in-depth consideration ensures that this book not only serves as a valuable reference for technical experts but also provides guidance for global policymakers and governance leaders.

Well-crafted systems and policies have immense power to drive technological innovation and economic development. In the CoG-MIN architecture, technology and governance complement each other, jointly constructing a secure, sovereign, and co-governed digital ecosystem. I firmly believe that CoG-MIN will become a significant force in advancing the transformation of network governance and systems. Therefore, I highly recommend this book to all colleagues who are concerned with science and technology policy, network architecture, and Internet governance.

Let us work together to embrace the grand vision of CoG-MIN and strive to build a secure, sovereign, and co-governed digital future guided by the principles of peace, cooperation, and the rule of law.

Academician of International
Eurasian Academy of Sciences, Helsinki, Finland
Secretary General of the International
Eurasian Academy of Sciences, Beijing, China
Chairman of the China Society for Science and
Technology System Reform, Beijing, China
Former Member of the Leading Party
Group of the Ministry of Science and
Technology of China, Beijing, China
Former President of Science
and Technology Daily, Beijing, China

Jingan Zhang

Foreword IV by Prof. Weimin Zheng

With the rapid development of the Internet, cyberspace has become an integral part of modern society, emerging as the fifth fundamental domain following land, sea, air, and outer space. Over the past fifty years, academia and industry have extensively researched critical technologies related to the architecture and protocols of Internet. The concept of a "Community with a Shared Future in Cyberspace" has gained significant traction, emphasizing the need for a secure, inclusive, and cooperative global internet environment.

In this context, Professor Hui Li's new monograph, *Principle of Architecture, Protocol, and Algorithms for CoG-MIN: A Sustainably Ecological & Evolutionary Solution for Packet Network System*, is both timely and relevant. This book provides a comprehensive introduction to the Co-Governed Multi-Identifier Network (CoG-MIN, shortly as MIN) architecture proposed by Professor Hui Li, offering practical pathways and solutions for the future development of network architecture. Through the blockchain-based global co-governed among top-level domains, endogenous network security, and sustainable evolution, this architecture addresses current challenges faced by the Internet and better meets the evolving needs of network development.

I have a deep appreciation for the theoretical depth and practical breadth exhibited by Professor Hui Li in this book. It begins with a historical overview of Internet development and the current state of related research, highlighting the critical issues and inherent flaws in the existing Internet. The book then delves into how the innovative CoG-MIN architecture addresses these challenges and promotes co-governance in global cyberspace. It provides a detailed exposition of the core technologies and protocol designs of CoG-MIN and their practical applications in key scenarios such as the Internet of Vehicles (IoV), Industrial Internet of Things (IIoT), and Space-Terrestrial Integrated Networks (STIN). This book is not only an in-depth study of technological innovation in cyberspace but also a powerful guide for the future development of the Internet.

In 2019, the MIN architecture and its prototype were recognized as leading scientific and technological achievements at the 6th World Internet Conference. This honor highlights the dedication of Professor Hui Li and his team and fully acknowledges the potential of the MIN architecture in the future development of the Internet. Previous recipients of this honor include prominent technology companies such as Huawei Technologies Co., Ltd., ZTE Corporation, Tencent Holdings Limited, Baidu, Inc., and Alibaba Group Holding Limited, reflecting the high expectations of academia and industry for CoG-MIN.

In my view, through this book, Professor Hui Li has presented us with a hopeful and promising vision of the future network landscape. Three years ago, I had written a Foreword for the introduction version of this MIN architecture, and I believe the publication of this monograph marks an important step for MIN from concept to the practical application of the system. It will inspire more scholars and technical experts to pursue further research, collectively advancing the realization of a community with a shared future in cyberspace. Through continuous exploration and innovation, we can look forward to a more secure, fair, and sustainable global cyberspace, and this book is undoubtedly a significant step towards this goal, guiding us on the path forward.

Academician of the Chinese
Academy of Engineering, Beijing, China
Professor of Tsinghua University, Beijing, China
ACM Gordon Bell Prize Laureate, Beijing, China
10th President of the China
Computer Federation (CCF), Beijing, China

Weimin Zheng

Foreword V by Prof. Yale Li

It is my great honor to introduce this highly innovative and groundbreaking work, *Principle of Architecture, Protocol, and Algorithms for CoG-MIN: A Sustainably Ecological & Evolutionary Solution for Packet Network System*. As the Chairman of Cloud Security Alliance (CSA) Greater China Region and the Executive President of the World Digital Technology Academy (WDTA), I am acutely aware of the importance and profound impact of network technology in today's digital economy era.

Since the emergence of the Internet, human civilization has transitioned from the industrial age to the information age. The advent of IP networks has drastically reduced the cost of information communication, enabling billions of people worldwide to exchange information as freely as they use water or air. This revolutionary change is undoubtedly one of the greatest technological inventions of this century. As the most important global infrastructure in the digital economy era, the Internet has permeated every aspect of human life, work, and entertainment, playing a crucial role in various industries, government management, and services.

However, with the rapid development of the Internet, it also faces many challenges, such as cyberspace management, network security, infrastructure upgrades, and network evolution. Undoubtedly, the Co-Governed Multi-Identifier Network (CoG-MIN) architecture provides a novel solution to address the deficiencies of current networks. The CoG-MIN architecture utilizes a decentralized co-governed scheme based on consortium blockchain technology, achieving multilateral co-governance of cyberspace. Furthermore, it introduces intrinsic network genes and advanced security technologies to ensure communication security and data privacy. Additionally, it proposes a network evolvable scheme that supports smooth network upgrades and various potential communication semantics. Moreover, CoG-MIN has been extensively validated on the networks of global telecommunications operators.

This book systematically introduces the design principles, system architecture, and key protocols and algorithms at various levels of CoG-MIN. It also discusses the practical applications of CoG-MIN in different scenarios. This book not only delves into theoretical discussions but also provides detailed design and implementation introductions, as well as practical validation results, offering readers comprehensive and detailed reference materials. Professor Hui Li's research philosophy and methods not only provide effective solutions to the inherent deficiencies of current networks but also point the way for the future development of networks.

I highly recommend this book. It offers valuable guidance not only to network system researchers, government officials involved in national and local information system planning, and chief information officers, network security managers, and network center managers of enterprises and public institutions, but also to professors, engineers, and students in the fields of computer science and network communication.

I believe this book will become a milestone in the fields of cyberspace management and network security, contributing significantly to the construction of a peaceful, secure, open, cooperative, and sustainable cyberspace. I hope that countries around the world will actively participate in this multilateral co-governed network architecture and work together to build a secure and trustworthy global cyberspace.

Chairman of Cloud Security Alliance
(CSA) Greater China Region
Beijing, China
Executive Chairman of the
World Digital Technology Academy (WDTA)
Geneva, Switzerland

Yale Li

Preface

Undoubtedly, TCP/IP network architecture is the greatest technological invention in this century; it has made human civilization enter the information age from the industrial age. The IP network has made information communication bid farewell to the era of expensive, and billions of people around the world interact with each other's information like cheap tap water or free air. We must pay great respect to its inventors.

The Internet is the most important global infrastructure in the era of digital economy. Human life, work, entertainment, as well as various industries, government management and services are inseparable from the network. Moreover, technological progress continuously drives the Internet to expand the breadth and depth of its applications, evolving from its early roles in information exchange, communication, personal consumption, and e-commerce to more advanced functions such as value creation, low-cost credit provision, and trust development. After the earliest commercial networks, the Internet of Things, the Industrial Internet, the Internet of Vehicles, and the Internet of commercial satellites continue to expand. It can be imagined that it will continue to expand its coverage boundaries with the exploration of the universe and celestial constellation by human beings. As the world moves toward multi-polarity, economic globalization, cultural diversity, and IT application, the Internet will play an even greater role in promoting the progress of human civilization.

The Challenges IP Network Faces

In the era of scarce and expensive communication resources, IP was quickly sought after by users once it appeared. When its cyberspace management, security, upgrade and evolution, and other key issues have not been deeply considered, IP has been rapidly promoted, becoming a global industry de facto standard. Therefore, now looking back, we can find the genetic defects in IP networks.

1. The first defect is unilateral monopoly of cyberspace sovereignty. The top-level domain name and root zone database are centrally managed by a single institution, ICCAN. The current network governance rules are difficult to effectively represent the will and interests of most countries, so decentralized multilateral co-governance is the global demand for domain name space management.
2. The second defect is that IP network lacks the security gene, resulting in continuous security incidents. IP semantic overload refers to the binding of IP addresses and identities. Due to the uniqueness of IP addresses, this semantic overload can cause the flaws in security, mobility, and service quality within IP networks, making them unsuitable for the development of technology and application needs. IP network is lack of protection of data ownership; this poses risks in protecting our data privacy and property rights. Attackers can exploit vulnerabilities of IP network to gain unauthorized access to sensitive user data for profit purposes.
3. The third defect is that the network architecture is severely solidified, and its scalability and evolution are poor. Take the transition from IPv4 to IPv6 as an example. The IP protocol has been deeply embedded in the network protocol stack and application software code, which results in long time and high financial costs for network architecture upgrades.

Sustainable Ecological Evolution Solution of Packet Network: MIN

How to effectively, integrate and completely solve the above defects in IP is the theme of this book. The team of the author's laboratory has spent more than ten years to propose the principle of architecture protocol algorithms for co-governed multi-identifier network (CoG-MIN, shortly as MIN)—a sustainable ecological evolution solution of packet network system.

MIN addresses all the three defects in the IP network architecture. MIN employs the scalable PPoV consensus algorithm to enable multilateral co-management of the cyberspace by all nations. By incorporating advanced security technologies, such as mathematical cryptography, biometrics, and AI, MIN ensures the traceability and security of data privacy. Through extensive scenario testing, we have proven that the security of the MIN network is exponentially enhanced compared to the IP network. We also have taken into consideration the compatibility with the existing IP network and proposed a network evolution scheme based on identity expansion mechanisms. This scheme has been thoroughly validated on the operators' networks of global telecommunications providers.

On the application layer, we have designed the Multiple Identifier System (MIS) to facilitate decentralized identifiers or cyberspace management. On the network layer, we have developed the Multiple Identifier Router (MIR) to enable identifier resolution, packet forwarding, and filtering. In brief, MIN is the combination of MIS and MIR.

The First Feature of MIN: Multilateral Co-governed Cyberspace

MIN supports multiple identifications such as identity, content, services, geographic information, and IP in the network layer. MIN divides the whole network into hierarchical domains from top to bottom. The nodes in the top-level domain are multilaterally co-managed by the countries or regions within the United Nations. The respective regional organizations govern the other domains under the root domain independently. Such hierarchical division allows for the equal and negotiated participation of different countries in the network management, jointly build a secure, trusty, and rule-based cyberspace.

In distributed systems, you may have heard of the "CAP theorem," which says it is impossible to simultaneously achieve full Consistency, Availability, and Partition tolerance. The operation of the bitcoin system since its launch has proved its correctness on the public blockchain. Later on, the "three pick two" formula was proposed. However, this formula can be misleading as it oversimplifies the interrelationships between these properties. To address the challenge of quantifying the classic CAP triangle, we propose a new "impossible triangle" for blockchain. We map the three major properties of the CAP theorem, consistency, partition tolerance, and availability, into quantifiable measures of security, decentralization, and scalability.

On consensus layer, we propose a theoretically optimal and practically efficient consensus algorithm for consortium blockchain—Parallel Proof of Vote (PPoV). It breaks through the sequence limitation of the three phases of the consensus process, and improve the whole throughput. On physical layer, we introduce n-dimensional hypercubes or their variants to build the physical topology of the consortium blockchain nodes. It not only has good partition tolerance property, but also can match well with existing P2P network applications without affecting consistency and scalability. To balance the reliability and cost when deploying the network, we further propose a hierarchical recursive topology based on the n-dimensional hypercube, which uses more short and medium links, and greatly reduces the average minimum repair time while reducing the cost.

For detailed discussion, please refer to the author's monograph: "*Principles and Applications of Blockchain Systems: How to Overcome the CAP Trilemma in Consortium Blockchain*" jointly published by Wiley & IEEE Press.

The Second Feature of MIN: Endogenous Security

The second feature of MIN network is its endogenous security, ensuring end-to-end data traceability throughout the entire communication process. On the network layer, the multi-signature mechanism enables the traceability of network packets. All routers in the MIN network can verify the legitimacy of network packets using signatures. Any illegal packets can be traced back to individuals and user access locations. On the application layer, MIS blockchain system combines real identity and biometric features, such as pupil recognition, and ensures the reliability of user identification and the effectiveness of user management, thereby enhancing the security of the network.

After extensive penetration testing conducted by multiple professional teams using industry-standard attack chains and methods, the results have shown that MIN is highly effective in countering network attacks across various stages of the classic attack chain in both IP-MIN and MIN-MIN scenarios.

The vehicle networking system based on MIN, MIN-V2X, has participated in five network attack-defense competitions with its real vehicle range in 2023, and maintained unbeaten records, which included the World Intelligent Driving Challenge 2023 Network Attack and Defense Competition. The owner can control them remotely through the operators' network and MIN-V2X's customer service app. During the final on-site challenge, all teams tried to take over control of the sweeper and jeep from afar but no one succeeded.

Since 2023, we set standards as our priority, and steadily promoted the release of group and industry standards to advance the development of technological industrialization.

Recently, we proposed a Conjecture Theorem: There might be a guaranteed security solution in MIN network. We also proposed the IP network guarantees security No solution theorem, and proved it by merging the method of contradiction and enumeration.

The Third Feature of MIN: A Sustainable Ecological Evolution System

MIN takes identity identifier as anchor identification, and supports multiple identification addressing, routing, and fallback. MIN makes its physical network system not need to be dismantled and rebuilt when the network layer addressing routing identification mode evolves, but constantly adapt to the future expansion of various identifiers, including the Internet of Things, the Internet of Vehicles, the Industrial Internet, the space-terrestrial integration network, etc. IPv4, IPv6, IPv9, NewIP, NIN, Network 5.0, and known Future Network Identifiers such as content and service can all be integrated on the MIN architecture. The multi-identifier management system based on hierarchical large-scale consortium blockchain and multi-identifier translation algorithms support the above requirements of multiple identifiers translating, addressing, and routing.

MIN will put an end to the requirement of continuous upgrading of network architecture by the continuous evolution of network layer addressing and routing scheme, which is conducive to the coexistence and natural transition of various identification systems. It will greatly save costs and extend the service cycle of existing equipment to the best of its ability. It is expected that MIN to the data packet network architecture is what Signaling No.7 is to the telecommunication system. The support of Signaling No. 7 for basic services and various future intelligent services have made it become the terminator of all previous signaling systems since No. 1.

Application Scenarios of MIN

The application scenarios of MIN can be divided into three levels. In small-scale scenario, MIN can construct the high-security private network for the organizations, like government, web 3.0 finance enterprises. In medium-scale scenario, MIN can support industrial Internet, like the Internet of Vehicles. In large-scale scenario, MIN can ensure a global multilateral co-governed cyberspace for United Nations members. It can also provide DID services to global users and serve as a relay for all DID cross chains.

In terms of its goal to become a truly multilateral co-governing United Nations of Cyberspace globally, MIN is still in its conceptual infancy, with much pioneering work yet to be done by global peers. The purpose of publishing this book now, according to a Chinese proverb, is to "throw a brick and attract jade." We want to contribute and share our ideas and basic design of architecture, protocols, algorithms for building a peaceful, secure, open, cooperative, sustainable, and evolutionary cyberspace governed by the rule of law for all mankind.

In summary, MIN network is a decentralized and multi-lateral co-governed network that tackles the security vulnerabilities and trust issues of the IP network while maintaining perfect compatibility with IP and other network systems.

We would like to invite countries worldwide to engage in this multi-lateral co-management approach and join MIN network to collectively build a secure and trustworthy global cyberspace.

Chapters Arrangement

This book includes 15 chapters. Chapter 1 first introduces the development history of the Internet and the current research state of future networks, and then leads to an overview of Co-Governed Multi-Identifier Network, the theme of this book. Chapter 2 introduces the design principles and system architecture of MIN. Chapter 3 introduces the identifier, identifier semantics, and identifier space defined by MIN. Chapter 4 describes the blockchain-based identifier management technique of MIN. Chapters 5, 6, 7, 8, 9, and 10 provide detailed descriptions of MIN's key technologies such as addressing and routing, Multi-Identifier Router (MIR), data synchronization, cache management and access control, transport protocol, and network control message protocol. Chapter 11 introduces the security mechanisms and large-scale security testing and practical verification of MIN. Chapter 12 focuses on the network evolution and identifier extension in MIN. Chapter 13 describes the secure private network based on MIN, using MIN-VPN as an example. Chapter 14 provides detailed introduction of MIN-Web. Chapter 15 discusses various application scenarios based on MIN.

The readers of this book include officials of the UN World Summit on the Information Society, managers and researchers of the United Nations for a Secure and Peaceable Cyberspace, researchers of the network system, officials and technicians responsible for information system planning of national and local governments, chief information officers of enterprises and public institutions, network security managers, and network center managers, professors, engineers and students from the field of computer science and network communication.

Shenzhen, China

Hui Li
He Bai

Acknowledgments

November, 2024
Shenzhen, China

This book originates from the work of Professor Hui Li's research group at the Peking University. We would like to express our deepest gratitude to all the students, engineers, and teachers who contributed to the CoG-MIN project. Without their invaluable efforts, this book could not have been completed.

The book is divided into 15 chapters. The first author, Prof. Hui Li, was responsible for the overall planning and coordination, ensuring that the book's structure and content aligned with the intended objectives. Prof. Hui Li meticulously wrote Chaps. 1, 2, 3, 4, 5, 6, 7, 11, 12, 13, 14, and 15, covering a wide range of topics with thorough research and insightful analysis. His dedication and expertise were instrumental in shaping the book's comprehensive and cohesive narrative. The second author, Ms. He Bai, oversaw the organization and language refinement of the book and contributed to the writing of Chaps. 8, 9, and 10.

Additionally, we extend our sincere thanks to the students who provided writing materials and contributed to the construction of CoG-MIN. These students include, but are not limited to: Zhuoliang Xiao for material compilation and Tao Liu for partial preliminary research in Chap. 1; Zhengqi Wu for material compilation and related system development and testing, and Zhuoliang Xiao for partial content revision in Chap. 2; Lihong Lin for material compilation, Yuanshao Liang for content revision, and Guohua Wei for related scheme design, development, and testing in Chap. 3; Qi Lv for material compilation, Wuyang Li, Zhenwei Xiao, Yao Yao, Zixian Wang for related system development and testing, and Han Wang for partial scheme design in Chap. 4; Feng Wang for related scheme design, material compilation, and related system development and testing, and Sheng Lan for material compilation and content revision in Chap. 5; Zhengqi Wu, Zhan Guo, Yuhong Chen for material compilation, related development, and testing, and Jianming Que for related scheme design, development, and testing in Chap. 6; Feng Wang for material compilation and related protocol development and testing, Yuhong Chen for material compilation and content revision, Yongxin Song for partial content revision, and Liu Yang for related scheme design in Chap. 7; Zheming Bao for material compilation, and Hongyu Guo for related scheme design, development, and testing in Chap. 8; Lihong Lin, Bin Yin, Mingrui Xiao for material compilation, system development, and testing, and Jiaqing Lv for content revision and figure drawing in Chap. 9; Xin Xiao for material compilation, related scheme design, development, and testing, and Qiufan Wu, Rui Chen for material compilation, content revision, and partial figure drawing in Chap. 10; Bin Wang, Ao Yang, Zhixiong Luo, Xiaozhou You, Xiangzhen Meng, and Hongjian Xing for related scheme design, system development, and testing, and material compilation, Gengxin Li for partial scheme design, development, and testing, Xin Yang, Yunmin Wang for partial scheme design, Zhuoliang Xiao, Yuhong Chen, Rui Chen, and Qiufan Wu for grammar polishing in Chap. 11; Hong Tan and Xiangzhen Meng for material compilation, and Guohua Wei for related scheme design, development, and testing in Chap. 12; Yihang Chen, Zixian Ding, Zhenyuan Yang, Yiwang Le, Yuanshao Liang, Hongyu Guo, and Zhan Guo for material compilation and related system development, and testing in Chap. 13; Feng Zhao and Zhan Guo for material compilation, system development, and testing, Zheming Bao for partial content revision, and Han Wang for partial scheme design in Chap. 14; Xinyuan Pei, Sheng Lan, Yongxin Song, and Zhuoliang Xiao for material compilation and partial scheme design, and Yunmin Wang, Ranran Dang, and Fuli Jiang for partial scheme design in Chap. 15; Shiwei Zhang, Aofan Liu, Xiaopeng Wang, Shibiao Tan, Hang Li, and Guogui Shi for partial content revision. We also express our special thanks to engineers Huajun Ma and Weijuan Yin for their contributions. We are deeply grateful to all others who have made contributions to CoG-MIN.

We also extend sincere thanks to Academician of the Chinese Academy of Engineering, Prof. Jiangxing Wu from NDSC, for his guidance on the development of CoG-MIN Architecture; as well as the following people for their support in the prototype verification: Prof. Ke Xu from Tsinghua University; Mr. Shisheng Chen from the Shenzhen Branch of China Telecom Corporation Limited; Dr. Wei Liang, Director of the Blockchain Laboratory from China Telecom Corporation Limited; Director Jinwu Wei and Senior Engineer Wei Li of the Big Data Research Center of China United Network Communications Limited; Fusheng Zhu, President of Guangdong Communications and Networks Institute; Chairman Kaiyan Tian and General Manager Jiang Zhu of Kingsoft Cloud Network Technology Co., Ltd; Prof. Yiqin Lu from South China University of Technology; Prof. Yijun Liu from Guangdong University of Technology; Prof. Yongxiang Han and Prof. Hanxu Hou from Dongguan Institute of Technology; Prof. Raymond W. Yeung from CUHK; Prof. Wai Ho MOW from the Hong Kong University of Science and Technology; Prof. Zefeng Zheng from Macau University of Science and Technology; Mr. Tao Sun, Director of the Network Information Center of Shenzhen University Town.

We would like to extend our special thanks to Prof. C.C. Chan, Honorary Professor, University of Hong Kong, Academician of the Chinese Academy of Engineering, Fellow of the Royal Academy of Engineering; Dr. Peter Janos Major, Vice-Chairman of the United Nations Commission on Science and Technology for Development (UNCSTD); Prof. Jingan Zhang, Academician of International Eurasian Academy of Sciences (IEAS Europe), and Chairman of the China Society for Science and Technology System Reform; Prof. Weimin Zheng, Academician of the Chinese Academy of Engineering, Professor of Tsinghua University; and Prof. Yale Li, Executive Chairman of the World Digital Technology Academy (WDTA), for their forewords to this book.

We would like to sincerely appreciate the funding support for CoG-MIN research, including but not limited to: PKUSZ-China Mobile Internet Joint Lab. for Sovereign & Trustworthy Internet funded by The China Mobile Internet Co. Ltd. (No. CMIC-202400488); China Environment for Network Innovations (GJFGW[2016]No.2533, [2018]No.775, [2020]No.386, SZFGW[2019]No.261), Shenzhen Key Lab of Information Theory & Future Network Architecture (No. ZDSYS201603311739428), National Key Research and Development Program of China (No. 2020AAA0104203, No. 2017YFB0803204, No. 2016YFB0800101, No. 2012CB315904), National Natural Science Foundation of China (No. 61671001, No. 61179028), Basic Research Enhancement Program of China (No. 2021-JCJQ-JJ-0483), Guangdong Provincial Key Laboratory of Ultra High Definition Immersive Media Technology (No. 2024B1212010006); Key Research and Development Program of Guangdong Province (No. 2019B010137001, No. 2018B010124001), Natural Science Foundation of Shenzhen (No. JCYJ20220531093206015, No. JCYJ20210324122013036, No. JCYJ20190808155607340, No. GXWD20201231165807007-20200807164903001), Huawei Funding (No. YBN2017125, No. TC20201222002), ZTE Funding (No. 2014ZTE03-01-01, No. 2019ZTE03-01), PCL Future Regional Network Facilities for Large-scale Experiments and Applications (No. LZC0019), Inner Mongol Univ. of Technology R&D Fund No.2023-035, Foshan Innovation Team (No. 2018IT100082), and Shenzhen Smart City Tech. Group (No. SZSCG-HT-2021-012); Foshan SaiSiChan Tech. Limited Funding (No.2020IT-008); FuYao Univ.of Sci.& Tech.R&D Funding 2024-018; Huanghe Sci.& Tech. Univ., R&D Funding No.2024-0238; Qinghaiminzu Univ.,Kunlun No.2024-233, China Telecom State Cloud Research Fund R&D No.2025-1026, China UniCom Research Funding No.2024-1056, No.2025-1328; Shenzhen Engineering Lab of Converged Media Networking Technology; Hauwei & PKU Jointly Engineering Lab of Future Network Based on SDN.

Finally, we would like to express our sincere thanks to the dedicated staff at Springer for their invaluable assistance and unwavering support throughout the publication process. Additionally, we extend our heartfelt thanks to each reader for engaging with this book and contributing to the ongoing discourse in this field.

Hui Li
He Bai

Competing Interests The authors have no competing interests to declare that are relevant to the content of this manuscript.

Contents

About the Authors

Hui Li is a Emeritus Professor at Peking University. He is the first scholar in the world who systematically points out the three gene defects of the current IP-based network: (A) IP-based cyberspace sovereignty is a unilateral monopoly. (B) There is a lack of security genes, resulting in frequent security incidents and difficulties in privacy protection. (C) The protocol is solidified, leading to long upgrade times and high costs.

Professor Hui Li first put forward the three conjectural theorems of cyberspace security in the world: (D) There is no deterministic technical solution to ensure security in IP-based cyberspace. (E) By taking IP-based cyberspace as a frame of reference, there are security deterministic technical solutions in future cyberspace that can quantitatively and exponentially improve performance against network attacks. (F) There may be deterministic security solutions in future cyberspace.

Professor Hui Li has led his team for more than 10 years to propose a comprehensive, systematic, and integrated collaborative solution: Co-Governed Multi-Identifier Network (CoG-MIN, briefly referred to as MIN). MIN has been verified through long-term practice and open competitions of offense and defense. Furthermore, the three major gene defects (A), (B), and (C) have been completely solved in theory and practice. The two conjectural theorems (D) and (E) have been rigorously proved mathematically and formally and have undergone verification through long-term practical testing. The conjectural theorem (F) is on the right track, undergoing a rigorous proof process, and holds the potential to be completely resolved in near future.

Major academic and social contributions of Prof. Hui Li include:

(1) He proposed the first co-governed sovereignty network with properties of multilateral governance, independent sovereignty, security, peace, and the rule of law. MIN is based on blockchain technology and the future network. He implemented its prototype on the Operator's Network in the world. MIN obtained the award of the World Leading Internet Scientific and Technological Achievements at the 2019 World Internet Conference in Wuzhen, China. In 2021, the first English monograph on the theme of "Cyberspace UN" in the world, titled "Co-governed Sovereignty Network: Legal Basis and Its Prototype & Applications with MIN Architecture", was published by Springer Publisher. MIN was also awarded the unique Diamond Award among all Golden Awards at the 2022 British International Invention Exhibition.

(2) He put forward a complete set of patent solutions to solve the CAP trilemma of consortium blockchain. The monograph "Principle & Applications of Blockchain Systems: How to Overcome the CAP Trilemma in Consortium Blockchain" was jointly published by Wiley and IEEE Press, providing a solid technical foundation for the security of the community with a shared future in cyberspace and core systems of the digital economy.

(3) He was granted patents for maximum distance separable code for distributed storage systems in both China and the United States. He also proposed practical G(2) regeneration code patents, which have become the de facto global industry standard, saving at least 50% of storage equipment and space investment costs for global IDC centers and achieving significant economic and environmental benefits.

(4) He was the first to apply the theory of stochastic process martingale to the network anti-attack quantitative security analysis model, and the patent was granted in both China and the United States. This provides a mathematical model for

endogenous security and AI-enabled network security.

(5) He has made extensive important social contributions, particularly in the proposal writing and project defense of two major scientific platforms, namely "Cyberspace Technology National Laboratory Construction Plan" and the "National Major Science and Technology Infrastructure Proposal for Future Network", commissioned by the Shenzhen Municipal Government. Prof. Hui Li's efforts have played a significant role in their successful implementation in Shenzhen.

Prof. Hui Li is the Chief Information Scientist of the International Academician Science & Technology Innovation Center, the Foreign Academician of the Russia Academy of Natural Science, the Member of the National Academy of Artificial Intelligence, the Member of the Expert Committee of the World Digital Technology Academy under the guidance of the UN Commission on Sci. & Tech. for Developments, Fellow of IET, the Director of PKU Lab of China Environment for Network Innovations, National Major Research Infrastructure, and the Technology Executive Director of the Sino-EU Intelligent Connected Vehicle and Autonomous Driving Industry Innovation Alliance (SASD). He received his B.Eng. and M.S. degrees from the School of Information Eng., Tsinghua University, Beijing, China, in 1986 and 1989, respectively, and his Ph.D. degree from The Chinese University of Hong Kong in 2000.

Prof. Hui Li has been invited to deliver keynote speeches on the topic of MIN at over 100 conferences, including the 27th Annual Science and Technology Conference of the United Nations Science and Technology Commission at Genewa, the World Internet Conference in Wuzhen, China, Digital Economy Conference, and the Web 3.0 and AI Conference hosted by IEEE, etc.

Prof. Hui Li is the first inventor of 8 US granted patents and more than 50 Chinese granted patents. He is the first author of 9 monographs, with 4 in English (3 published) and 5 in Chinese (4 published). He has also published more than 300 papers in mainstream journals and conferences.

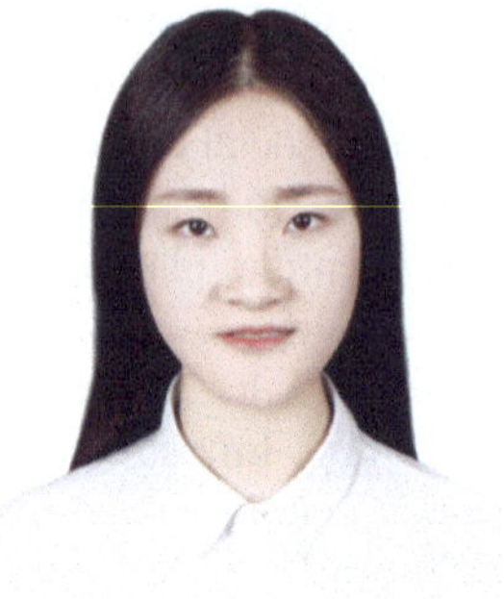

He Bai received her B.Eng. degree from the School of Information Engineering, Zhengzhou University, China, in 2019. She is currently pursuing the Ph.D. degree from the School of Electronic and Computer Engineering, Peking University, China. Her research interests focus on congestion control, transport protocol, and network architecture.

Chapter 1
Introduction

In the twenty-first century, the Internet has become a paramount communication infrastructure, profoundly influencing both production patterns and lifestyles. This chapter offers a systematic exposition on the history of the Internet, with a

particular emphasis on the anticipated trajectory of its future development and the associated technological trends. Meanwhile, it provides an overview of the co-governed multi-identifier network (CoG-MIN), which is the central topic of this book.

1.1 History of Internet

The birth of the Internet can be traced back to the post-World War II era. In the 1940s, the concept of mutual assured destruction (MAD) [1] dominated the confrontation between war participants. The MAD argument states that if one side launches a nuclear attack, the other side will respond with a devastating counterattack, ensuring mutual destruction and thus safeguarding national security. However, if a preemptive strike manages to destroy the enemy's command and control systems, the defensive side would be unable to launch a destructive counterattack. This indicates that the theory may actually favor the aggressor. Therefore, the design of a communication system that can survive a catastrophic nuclear attack becomes imperative.

In 1964, Paul Baran, a distinguished Polish-American engineer affiliated with the RAND Corporation, conceptualized a mesh network characterized by an extensive level of link redundancy, employing a digital communication method known as packet switching [2]. However, during an era dominated by predominantly analog and circuit-switched communication networks, this revolutionary concept was deferred due to prevailing political, economic, and various other considerations. Nevertheless, it should be noted that Paul Baran was not the sole proponent of the packet switching concept. In parallel endeavors, Donald Davies, affiliated with

H. Li, H. Bai, *Principle of Architecture, Protocol, and Algorithms for CoG-MIN*,
https://doi.org/10.1007/978-981-96-3596-2_1

Britain's National Physical Laboratory, sought to establish a novel form of communication network exclusively tailored for civilian applications. Recognizing the limitations of circuit-switching technology, which emulated traditional telephone systems, Davies discerned its inadequacy in facilitating responsive and interactive shared computation across extensive distances. To address these concerns, he endeavored to harness the potential of digital switching, culminating in his pioneering solution utilizing packet switching as an alternative approach [3].

Meanwhile, the Soviet Union successfully launched the "Sputnik 1" satellite on October 4, 1957 (as shown in Fig. 1.1), while previous attempts by the USA to launch artificial satellites had failed. Fueled by deep concerns over national security and a sense of urgency regarding technological advancement, President Eisenhower immediately announced a commitment to increase government funding in the field of technology. With support from the U.S. Congress, the Advanced Research Projects Agency (ARPA) was established within the Pentagon, the U.S. Department of Defense headquarters.

In its early stages, ARPA mainly funded some advanced fundamental research with potential military value. To obtain research contracts from various university departments and institutes, ARPA needed to finance the purchase, operation, and maintenance of dozens of expensive mainframe computers for institutional use. Robert Taylor, the third director of the Information Processing Techniques Office (IPTO) at ARPA, soon found that the funded computers were not compatible with each other and could not be a shared resource for all the institutions funded by ARPA. In addition, these computers are expensive, often costing hundreds of

Fig. 1.1 Sputnik 1 [4]

thousands to millions of dollars, and waste is high. Taylor came up with the idea of building a network where these valuable resources could be shared. Scientists had a similar idea as early as 1945. In 1960, J.C.R. Licklider, IPTO's first director, wrote "Man-Computer Symbiosis," arguing that computer communication was more effective than face-to-face communication. However, it was Taylor who first realized the idea and put it into practice. In the spring of 1966, after just 20 min of conversation, Taylor secured the support of the Secretary of United States Department of Defense for $1 million to build a small experimental network. Then, the Advanced Research Projects Agency Network (ARPANET) was born.

The Network Measurement Center established by Kleinrock at the University of California, Los Angeles (UCLA), an early participant in the theoretical design of packet switching, was selected as the first node on the ARPANET. In September 1969, Bolt, Beranek and Newman Corp. (BBN) installed the first switch and connected the first mainframe computer at UCLA. In December 1970, the Network Working Group (NWG) of the ARPANET project led by Steve Crocker completed the original host-to-host protocol for the ARPANET. This is called network control protocol (NCP). With the completion of the NCP implementation of the ARPANET sites between 1971 and 1972, web users could finally begin to develop applications. In 1972, all 15 of ARPANET's original sites were connected and operating successfully, and the first public demonstration of the system was held in Washington, DC, in October of that year. Figure 1.2 shows a symbolic representation of the Arpanet as of September 1974.

By 1976, ARPANET had a remote international logon across the Atlantic Ocean. But the Internet is like sixteenth century Europe, with different languages, different rules, different standards, and no way to accommodate each other. There is an urgent need for mankind to develop a common set of standards to regulate the connection mode and data transmission of electronic devices. Progress was slow, however, until January 1983, when Robert Elliot Kahn and Vint Cerf invented the transmission control protocol/Internet protocol (TCP/IP) [6]. Figure 1.3 shows the computer network layered architecture. TCP/IP finally wins out among many network communication protocols with their characteristics.

The introduction of TCP/IP protocol has solved the problem of basic rules for data transmission in the vast network of the Internet and determined a set of basic rules for data transmission. To easily determine the location of each computer and find an identifiable destination for data transmission, the IP protocol addresses each node on the network, and this label is often referred to as "IP address." IP addresses are written in four-point decimal notation, such as "211.214.1.XXX." based on the principle of non-duplication, the unordered and complex IP combination imposes a burden on computer operators, and it is difficult for people to easily process a series of unnecessary numbers. In this way, the disorderly and complex IP address indirectly raises the threshold for the use of the Internet and becomes one of the obstacles to the Internet to the general public. To solve this problem, an engineer named

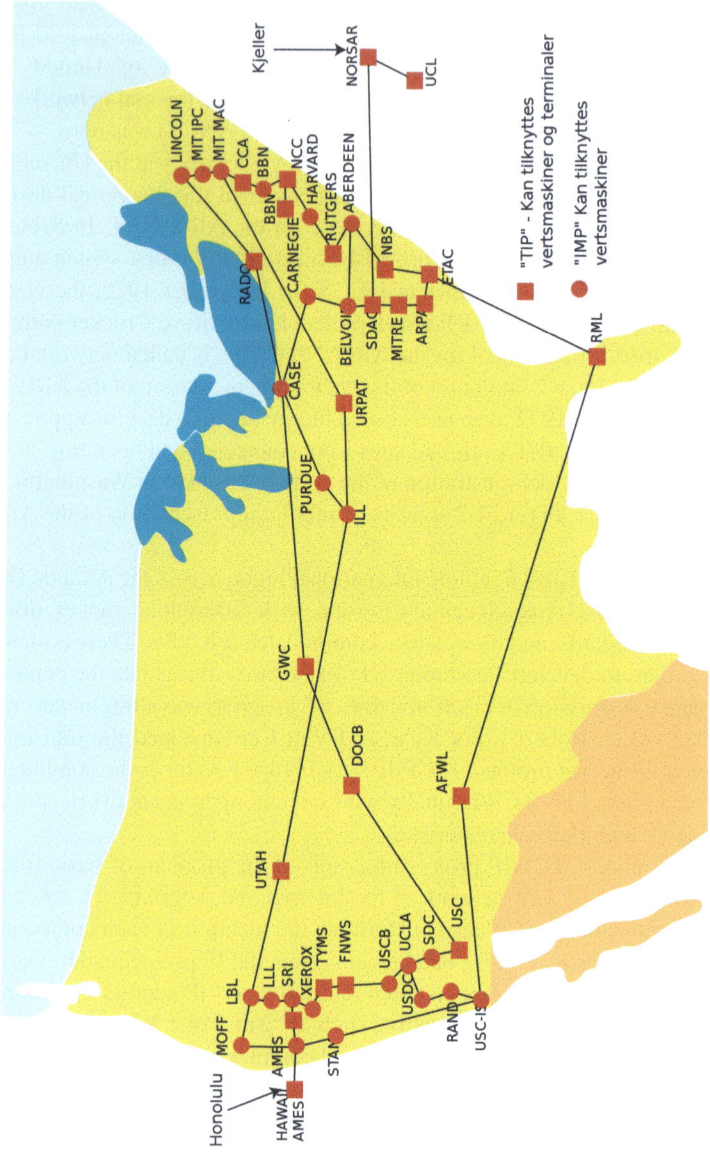

Fig. 1.2 Symbolic representation of the Arpanet as of September 1974 [5]

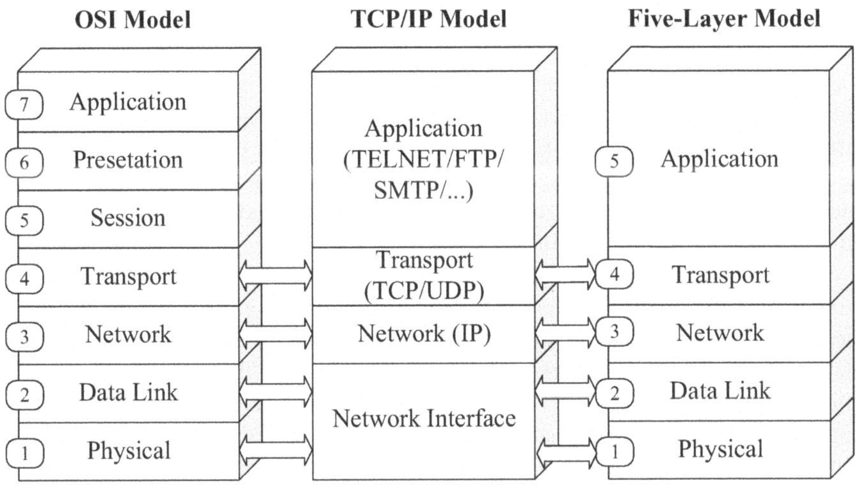

Fig. 1.3 Computer network layered architecture

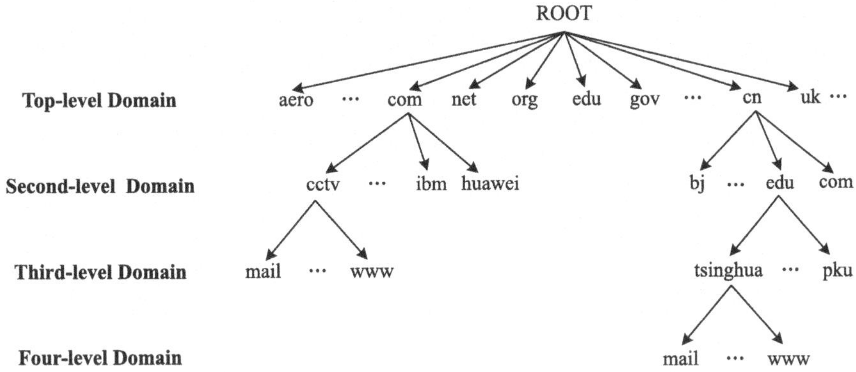

Fig. 1.4 Internet domain name space

Peggy Karp came up with the concept of "Internet names," which led to the successful creation of the domain name system (DNS).

In 1983, Professor Paul V. Mockapetris of the University of Southern California refined the concept of "Internet names" and established the architecture of the domain name resolution system that we use to this day. Figure 1.4 shows the domain name space of the Internet. On March 15, 1985, the first Internet domain name, "Symbolics.com," was registered and is now a relic in the history of the Internet. The DNS is the phone book of the Internet, which can translate host domain names that are easy for humans to remember into computer-friendly IP addresses. In this way, users no longer need to remember complex digital IP addresses, a popular way to access the Internet, but it has laid an important foundation for the civilian use of the Internet.

With the invention and application of domain name, users can easily, accurately, and intuitively find the storage location of the data they need. However, the text, sound, graphics, and other data in the computer world is a string of mutually unknown code, unless there is a professional operation, otherwise ordinary users are difficult to seek information in the "strange" code. Many issues, such as making information more discoverable to a broader audience, standardizing code formats, and providing intuitive visual displays for users, have posed significant challenges on the road to a user-friendly Internet.

Until 1989, a British man named Tim Berners-Lee developed hypertext transfer protocol (HTTP) and hypertext markup language (HTML), which effectively solved these problems. Tim also combined them with the existing Internet to give birth to the "Web." In 1991, Tim worked to promote the idea of the Web widely on the Internet and launched the world's first website. The National Center for Supercomputing Applications also turned its attention to the Web and developed a web browser called Mosaic, which was officially released in April 1993. Soon, the Internet was full of web pages. Tim affectionately referred to this technology as the World Wide Web (WWW).

The technologies and ideas of the World Wide Web set the stage for the Internet's adoption around the world, and then the Internet began to be recognized by society at large. Figure 1.5 shows the graphic representation of a minute fraction of the WWW.

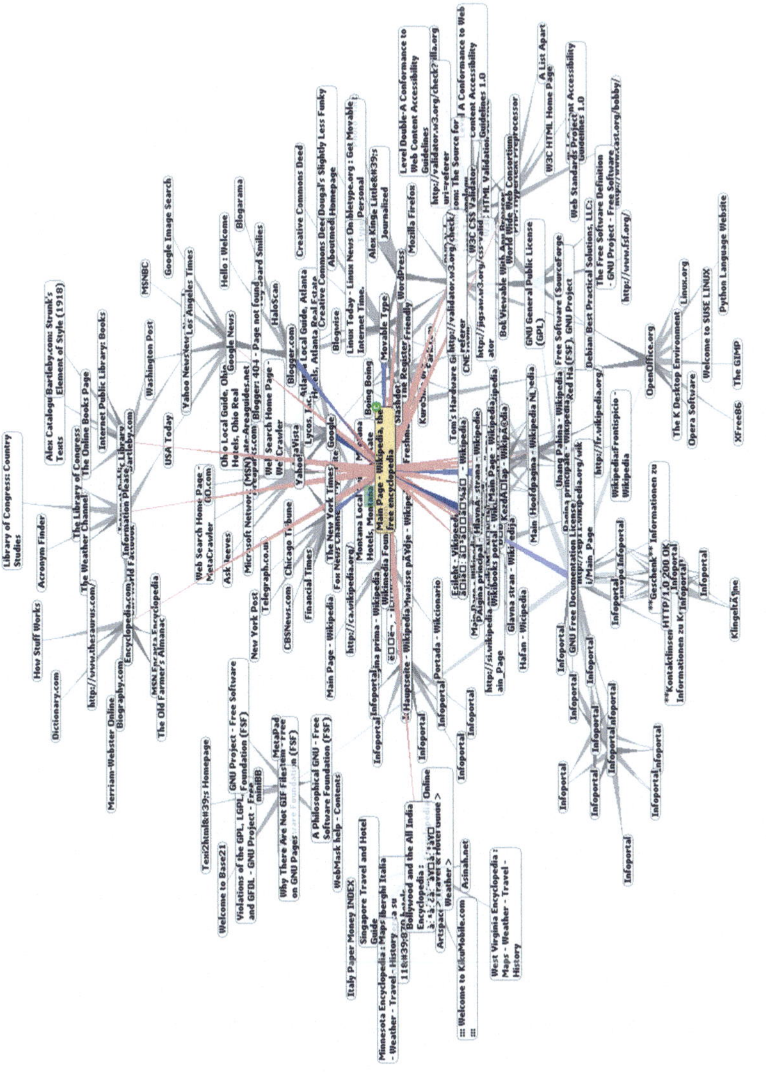

Fig. 1.5 Graphic representation of a minute fraction of the WWW [7]

1.2 Overview of Future Network Architecture

With the rapid development and popularization of the Internet, people pay more and more attention to the openness and freedom of the network, and the demand for security, sharing, trust, and decentralization is increasing. However, the traditional network system is often difficult to fully meet these needs. The emergence of decentralized blockchain technology provides a new solution for future network architecture.

Namecoin is the first project to propose solutions such as distributed domain name storage and merged mining based on the Bitcoin blockchain network [8]. Blockstack further proposes the virtual chain technology to support the migration of the logical layer between different underlying chains and deeply studies the blockchain network architecture, distributed data storage, and infinite ledger technology to improve the overall robustness and reusability of the blockchain domain name system [9].

Although the technical solutions proposed by Namecoin and Blockstack provide an important idea and practical foundation for the development of blockchain domain name systems, the underlying technology of these two projects depends on the Bitcoin system, which restricts their usability and security. In addition, although they can supplement or replace the existing DNS system to a certain extent, they cannot essentially solve the problem of the "narrow waist" structure of the network layer in the traditional TCP/IP network architecture. This problem is a bottleneck that restricts the development of the overall function of the information network, and more effective technical innovation and solutions need to be further explored.

In August 2010, the US National Science Foundation (NSF) released the Future Internet Architecture (FIA) initiative for US national network security, which funded four prospective network studies: Named Data Networking (NDN), Mobility First, NEBULA, and Expressive Internet Architecture (XIA). The NDN project aims to develop a new network architecture and establish a content-centric expressive Internet architecture. The MobilityFirst project treats node mobility as the normal of nodes and uses General Delay Tolerant Network (GDTN) technology to enhance the robustness and availability of the network. With the joint participation of the NSF and 18 top universities and experimental institutions, the FIA project entered the FIA-NP stage in 2015 and plans to build a new Internet covering the world based on the above network architecture.

In 2012, the European Union invested about 25 million euros to continue to fund the theoretical and experimental research on the future Internet system based on the first phase of the original FIRE project on the future network architecture and service mechanism, focusing on the self-knowledge management mechanism in the future Internet to improve the intelligence of the network. In the same year, AKARI in Japan and G-lab in Germany also carried out the second phase of the construction of test beds.

The above projects still use a single identifier management system, which makes it difficult to support the future multi-scenario and high-mobility network requirements. Therefore, there is a lack of a systematic scheme to address the translation and management of potential multiple types of identifier spaces within the network [10].

In 2019, Russia conducted a network blackout test. The test aimed to determine if the country's internal network, Internet of Things (IoT), and communication infrastructure could function independently by relying solely on the self-built RuNet, without relying on global DNS and external network connectivity. The test aimed to verify the integrity and security of the domestic network in the face of an external "network blackout" and ensure the safety of mobile communications, protection of personal information, and prevention of call and message interception. However, the Russia blackout test was primarily based on the self-built national network infrastructure (RuNet). It aimed to establish the world's largest "internal network" by rerouting domestic traffic and using a government-controlled domain system for distribution, eliminating the reliance on root domain servers located overseas. Nevertheless, it still relies on DNS mirror servers and does not fundamentally break free from the unilateral control of the traditional network system.

In China, the government attaches great importance to the development of future networks. There is significant emphasis on theoretical and technological investigations related to future network architecture and domain name resolution system. The Chinese government has made extensive deployments and provided support for fundamental research in the field of next-generation networks.

The Information Engineering University of the People's Liberation Army has conducted research on a novel network architecture for information communication. This innovative architecture addresses the performance limitations observed in the current IP network layer. By constructing a foundational physical network with dynamic reconfiguration and expansion capabilities, it effectively caters to the diverse network demands posed by various services.

The National University of Defense Technology has made notable advancements in the field of network technology by introducing a reconfigurable network router model based on virtualization technology. This model incorporates program control technology to create a standardized operating environment that accommodates diverse components. Consequently, this innovative approach significantly enhances the overall openness and security of the novel network architecture.

Huawei Technologies Co., Ltd. has put forth a pioneering network protocol framework known as "New IP" designed to provide enhanced support for emerging network applications. This framework aims to fundamentally facilitate variable length, multiple semantic addresses, and user-customized networks at the network layer. By adopting the "New IP" protocol, Huawei seeks to address the evolving requirements of modern network infrastructure and enable more efficient and flexible network operations.

1.3 Overview of Co-Governed Multi-Identifier Network

To address the inherent limitations of traditional network systems in terms of service quality, security, and mobility, as well as the issues of monopolistic dominance in the global cyberspace, Professor Hui Li's team at Peking University Shenzhen Graduate School, first proposed and implemented the Co-Governed Multi-Identifier Network (CoG-MIN) [11].

CoG-MIN meets the urgent needs of sovereignty independence, security, peace, order, and future sustainable development of cyberspace, and promotes the construction of a community with a shared future in cyberspace.

CoG-MIN integrates the blockchain technology to realize the decentralized identifier management and resolution and realizes the multilateral co-management of global non-IP top-level identifiers in the future network system (Fig. 1.6).

As shown in Fig. 1.7, CoG-MIN supports a variety of network identifiers such as identity, content, service, IP address, and geographical identifier.

Each country has independent sovereignty over cyberspace at all levels below its top-level identifier. CoG-MIN has implemented the real identity registration for accessing and using the network.

Meanwhile, all network packets in CoG-MIN can be traced to achieve a balance between privacy protection and controllability, which is conducive to the construction of a legal cyberspace.

To achieve the international consensus on the multilateral co-management of cyberspace, CoG-MIN solves the problems such as single organization management of DNS root zone database, semantic overload of IP address, and lack of security gene. It realizes the multilateral co-governed of cyberspace, that is, the top-level multilateral management of the fifth space frontier of mankind to ensure the interconnection of countries, and domestic domain names at all levels mark sovereign autonomy. CoG-MIN allows countries to have independent cyber territories for the first time, that is, the multilateral sovereign Internet—the United Nations of cyberspace.

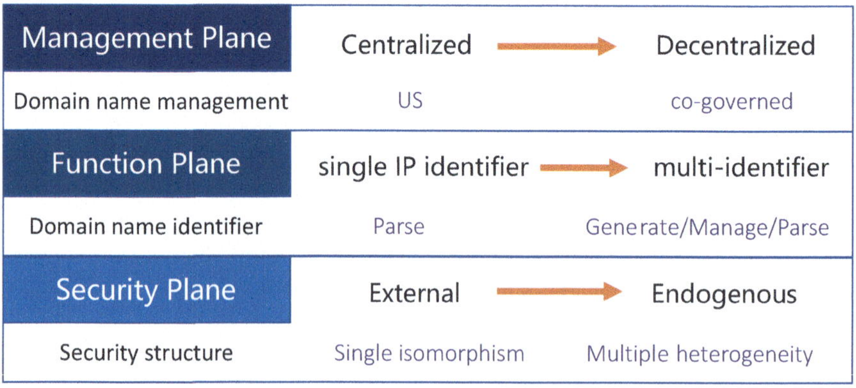

Fig. 1.6 Comparison between the traditional IP system and the novel CoG-MIN system

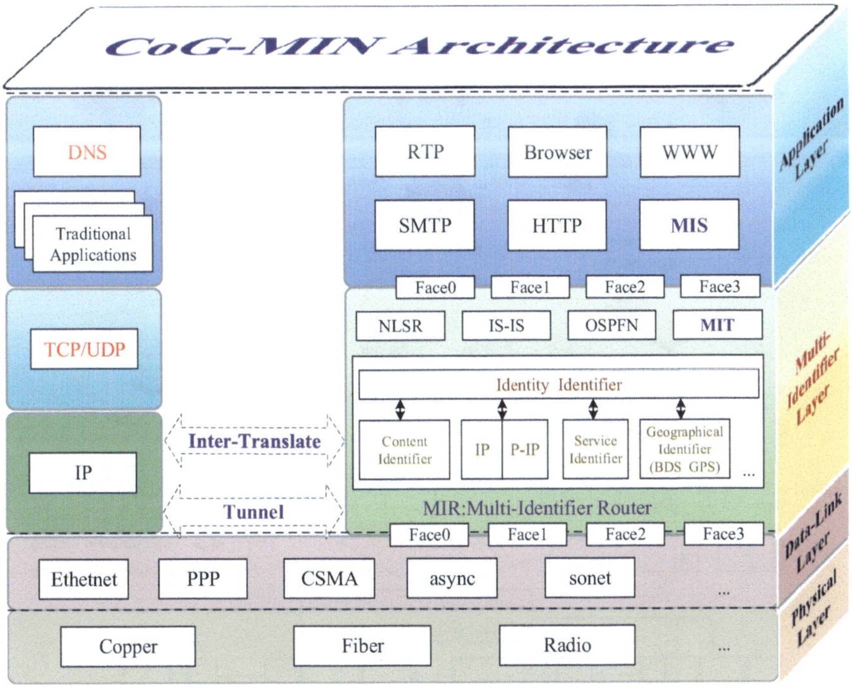

Fig. 1.7 The architecture of Co-Governed Multi-Identifier Network

As shown in Fig. 1.8, the core technology breakthroughs of CoG-MIN are as follows:

A full set of tree-structured decentralized hierarchical consortium blockchain systems, a recursively scalable topology with anti-partition tolerance, and Parallel Proof of Vote (PPoV) consensus algorithm. The top layer of the consortium blockchain supports $n > 250$ countries to jointly manage, the transaction throughput is greater than 500,000 TPS, and the delay is less than 5 s.

A high-speed translation algorithm merging hash table and prefix tree (HPT), an addressing model using HPT for forwarding information base (HPT-FIB) with the support of billions of identifiers, an efficient routing and forwarding algorithm model based on non-Euclidean geometry, which greatly saves storage overhead at the router.

The reverse tunnel protocol for tunneling IP packets over the CoG-MIN networks. Combined with the original IP tunnel protocol, seamless compatibility and progressive deployment with the existing IP network are achieved.

A quantitative analysis model for endogenous security in the network layer, which combines mathematical tools such as Markov chain, stochastic Petri net, and martingale.

An identifier extension mechanism based on identifier back-off, which supports the sustainable evolution of the network architecture.

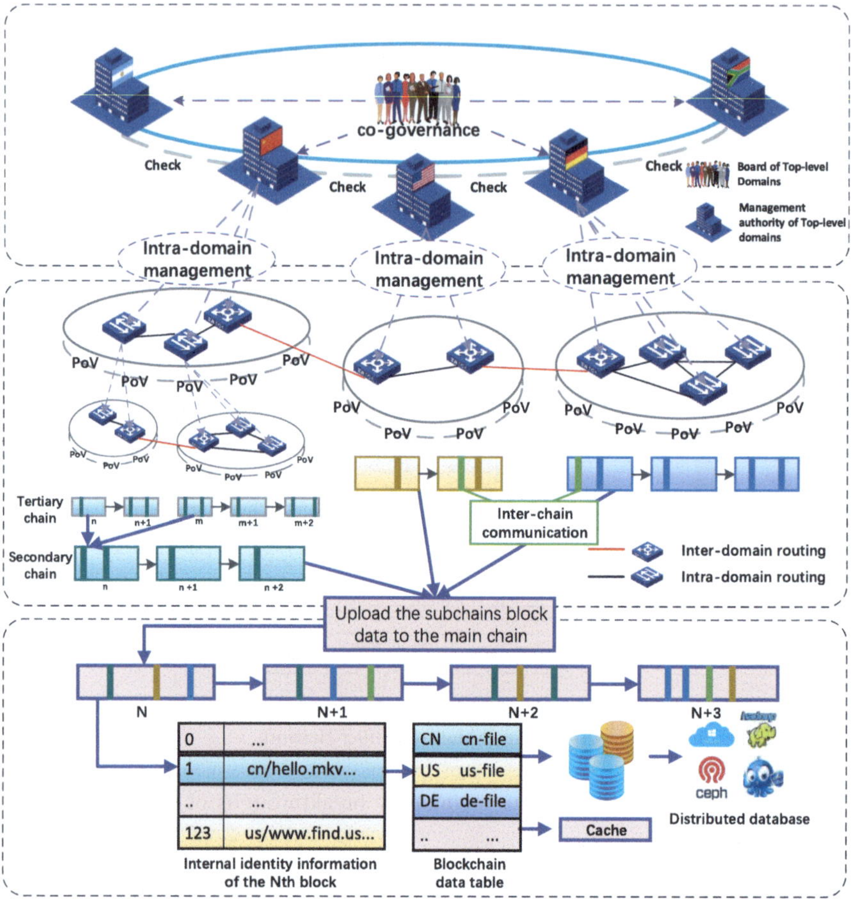

Fig. 1.8 The management plane of CoG-MIN

These technologies ensure the excellent characteristics of CoG-MIN, such as co-governance, high-speed routing, safety, reliability, forward compatibility, backward evolution, and large-scale deployment.

CoG-MIN has successfully defended against the attack tests by multiple professional teams. The test results, as illustrated in Fig. 1.9, demonstrate that various public hazards that exists in the traditional IP network system, such as privacy theft, property rights infringement, cybercrimes, cyber surveillance, cyberattacks, and cyber terrorism, can be eliminated in the CoG-MIN system. Furthermore, the implementation of CoG-MIN paves the way for a cyberspace characterized by peace, security, openness, cooperation, and adherence to the rule of law.

CoG-MIN is committed to building a community of shared future in cyberspace. It offers a progressive and deployable network architecture and application case that aligns with the requirements of all nations seeking a cyberspace based on principles of co-management, co-governance, and independent sovereignty. It safeguards the

Attack phase	Attack means		IP to IP test result	IP to CoG-MIN test result	CoG-MIN to CoG-MIN test result
Reconnaissance	Host discovery		Can be discovered	Discover hosts that are not CUTV's	Nothing found
	Ping scan		Can be detected	Undetectable	Undetectable
	Operating system identification		System fingerprint can be obtained	Nothing found	Nothing found
	Port scan		Can detect all port services	Can't found any port information	Nothing found
Exploitation	Trojan implantation	TCP Trojan	Connected	Can't connect	Can't connect
		UDP Trojan	Connected	Can't connect	Can't connect
		ICMP Trojan	Connected	Can't connect	Can't connect
	Web shell		Connected	Can't connect	Can't connect
Action	ARP poisoning	Sniff	Sniff successfully	Non-intranet	Sniff failed
		Forced disconnected	Disconnected	Non-intranet	Failed

Fig. 1.9 Results of testing experiments under IP to IP-VPN vs. IP to CoG-MIN-VPN, CoG-MIN to CoG-MIN

cyber sovereignty of all countries and, in doing so, contributes to the establishment of a shared and egalitarian "Cyberspace United Nations." CoG-MIN is an important practice of the concept of a community with a shared future for mankind in cyberspace and contributes to the promotion of global network development and governance.

The global deployment of CoG-MIN can be gradually realized starting from small-, medium-, and large-level application scenarios. Small-scale deployments are suitable for sectors like government, military, finance, and other key industries with high-security private network requirements. Middle-scale deployments are versatile and applicable to areas like Internet Information Special Region, Internet of Vehicles [12], Industrial Internet of Things [13], smart city [14], space-air-ground integration information network [15], etc. In large-scale scenarios, CoG-MIN can play a pivotal role by offering top-level identifier registration, management, and analysis services to all countries along the Belt and Road, fostering network sovereignty, and contributing to the establishment of a global Cyberspace United Nations. CoG-MIN aims to create a more secure, interconnected, and globally cooperative digital environment.

Up to now, the main achievements of CoG-MIN are as follows:

In 2011, a research team led by the Chinese academician Jiangxing Wu first proposed a revolutionary system enabling the coexistence of multi-mode addressing in the network layer to break through the bottleneck of IP single identifier in the world. Professor Hui Li, from Peking University Shenzhen Graduate School, spearheaded research in "Addressing and Routing Switching of Reconfigurable Infrastructure Network" as part of this endeavor.

In 2016, Professor Hui Li's team first proposed and implemented the Co-Governed Multi-Identifier Network (CoG-MIN, also known as MIN), which seamlessly integrates blockchain technology with the future network architecture while maintaining compatibility with IP.

In March 2019, the Peking University Shenzhen Graduate School and Guangdong Communications and Networks Institute jointly carried out the large-scale deployment and functional testing of CoG-MIN's prototype system across 12 IDC (Internet Data Center) commercial networks in Beijing, Guangdong, Hong Kong and Macao, as shown in Fig. 1.10. The participating units also include China Unicom Research Institute, China Telecom Strategy and Innovation Research Institute, Southern University of Science and Technology, Chinese University of Hong Kong, Macao University of Science and Technology, etc.

In July 2019, Professor Hui Li's team successfully developed a prototype system for a radio and television sovereign network based on CoG-MIN, which was deployed for enterprises under the National Radio and Television Administration, which passed the test by the Academy of Broadcasting Planning, NRTA, and Radio and Television Measurement and Testing Center.

In October 2019, the project "MIN: Co-Governing Multi-Identifier Network Architecture and its prototype on the Operator Network" was selected as the leading technical achievement of the sixth Wuzhen World Internet Conference (see Fig. 1.11).

It created two histories of the award: (1) the first award for the original and subversive future network system; (2) the first award for a large-scale prototype system rather than mature commercial products.

In February 2020, considering the huge scale of the current IP network, it was not feasible to immediately update the current network architecture to the new CoG-MIN architecture. In response to the specific needs of the high-security network, a high-security special network based on CoG-MIN was developed.

In May 2020, as shown in Fig. 1.12, Professor Hui Li's team teamed up with China Satcom Group Co., Ltd. to build a space-terrestrial integrated network testbed based on the ChinaSat 16 satellite, which verified the feasibility of MIN-based space-terrestrial integrated network.

Furthermore, in May 2020, the expert group in the field of Industrial Internet under the Ministry of Industry and Information Technology of the People's Republic of China adopted CoG-MIN as the technical route for China's independent controllable root service system. Subsequently, Professor Hui Li's team was invited to bid for the "2020 Industrial Internet Innovation and Development Project" funded with 200 million yuan and jointly bid for the "Root Service System Project based on Novel Network identifier Technology" with 23 units such as Zhejiang Lab and Purple Mountain Laboratories.

In July 2020, Professor Hui Li's team deployed the CoG-MIN-based high-security private network, allowing the coexistence of the CoG-MIN network and IP network to meet the practical needs of users such as mobile office, identifier management, rights management, log storage, behavior detection, identifier authentication, and so on. As the first application unit, Shenzhen Media Group deployed the CoG-MIN-based high-security private network in City United Television (CUTV) for its media acquisition, editing, broadcasting, and control management system.

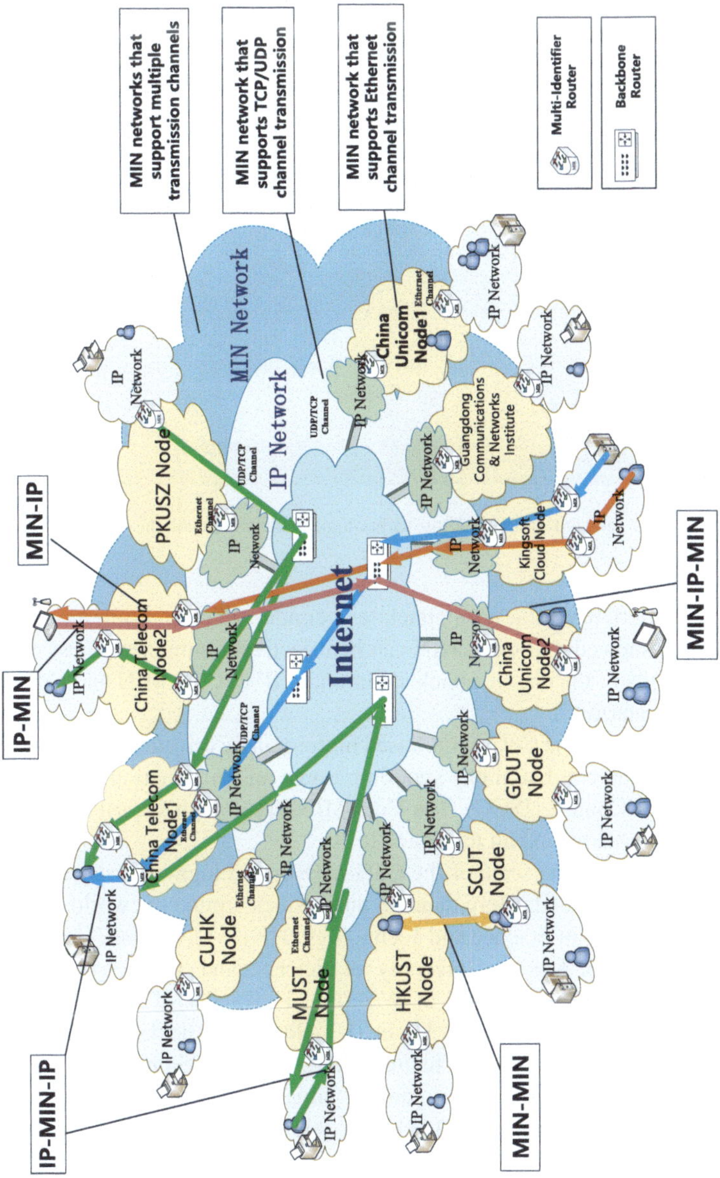

Fig. 1.10 The large-scale testbed of CoG-MIN (also known as MIN) in China

Fig. 1.11 MIN was selected as the leading technology achievement of the 6th Wuzhen World Internet Conference

In December 2020, a long-term attack test, conducted by multiple professional security teams, showed that CoG-MIN can be effectively immune against network attacks in all links of the classic attack chain under IP to CoG-MIN and CoG-MIN to CoG-MIN scenarios.

From 2021 to 2024, the CoG-MIN-based high-security private network had been used as the actual combat topic shooting range of Information Security and Countermeasures Contest (ISCC). The CoG-MIN-based high-security private network successfully withstood all the attack tests.

In September 2021, the scale of the CoG-MIN-based high-security private network was further expanded. More than ten universities around the world, including Hong Kong University of Science and Technology (HKUST), Chinese University of Hong Kong (CUHK), Macau University of Science and Technology (MUST), University of Sheffield, University of Waterloo, University of British Columbia (UBC), Universiti Tunku Abdul Rahman (UTAR), and Auckland University of Technology (AUT), launched transnational deployment. Technical tests such as consensus mechanism, transmission control, situation awareness, and functional tests such as identifier management, video conference, and security supervision were carried out.

From 2021 to 2023, Purple Mountain Laboratory (Nanjing, China) held three consecutive "Qiangwang" International Elite Challenge on Cyber Mimic Defense. The CoG-MIN network was used as the actual combat range, and no failure was achieved. Other advanced driver assistance system (ADAS) of fifteen intelligent

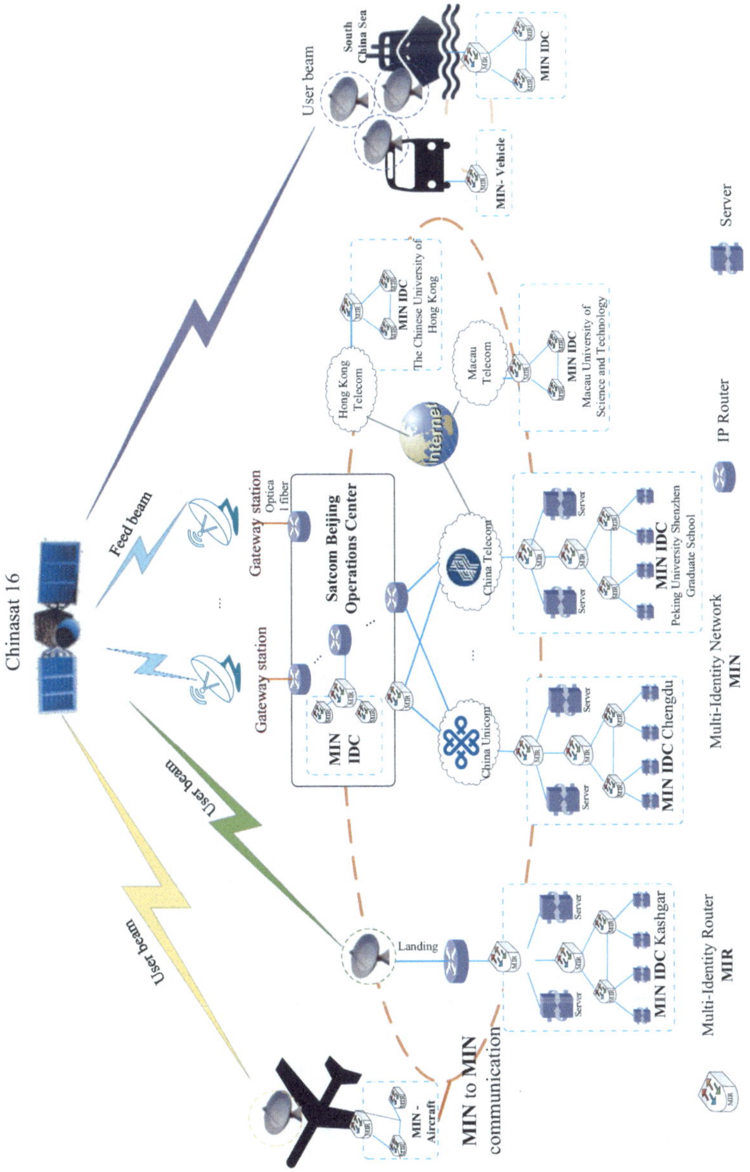

Fig. 1.12 MIN-based space-terrestrial integrated network testbed

connected vehicles (ICVs) from different countries were compromised, and some cars were remotely controlled by the hacker team, including the front wheel direction, door opening, and rear wheel speed and direction.

In December 2021, the patent family about the CAP trilemma of consensus technology for consortium blockchains was awarded the Gold Award for Invention and Entrepreneurship at the 25th National Invention Exhibition.

In 2022, Professor Hui Li's team's a series of invention patents about "Architecture and Application of Sovereignty Network" won the unique diamond award of the 2022 British Invention Show (BIS). This was the first time that Chinese exhibitors have won the highest award since the show began more than 20 years ago.

From July 3 to August 9, 2022, the high-security private network based on CoG-MIN participated in a cybersecurity exercise in Beijing. It encountered 387 attack sources from different countries and regions such as the UK, India, the United States, the Netherlands, and China, and all of them were effectively intercepted. It is verified that the high-security private network based on CoG-MIN has good security and reliability. There was no Hackers can successfully compromise critical equipment.

In February 2023, the Blue Book of Intelligent Connected Vehicle (2022) was finalized, and the part about network security was written by Prof. Hui Li, who proposed an innovative MIN-V2X (Vehicle to Everything) scheme. This part mainly introduces the high-security private network of the high-speed ICV, the exploration of large-scale defense technology of ICV, the security risk analysis of ICV, the mutual recognition and trust security of the identifier authentication system of ICV, and the data security of ICV.

In May 2023, the 2023 World Intelligent Driving Challenge (WIDC) was successfully held at Dongli Lake in Tianjin, China. During its TOPSEC Cup information security attack and defense competition, the high-security private network based on MIN-V2X was employed as an offline actual combat shooting range with a vehicle-cloud collaborative system, involving an unmanned street sweep and an unmanned jeep. Both of these devices could be remotely controlled by drivers using the MIN-V2X client APP through mobile operator networks, enabling control over functions like starting, stopping, steering, and speed adjustments. Remarkably, this shooting range effectively defended against network attacks launched by all participating teams.

In November 2023, CoG-MIN was reported with the topic of "Technology Solution for Jointly Building a Community of Shared Future in Cyberspace: Protocol System and Applications for multilaterally Co-managed Multi-Identifier Network Architecture" at the IEEE International Multilateral Forum of the 2023 World Internet Conference.

In April 2024, Professor Hui Li was elected as the Execute Director of Sino-EU Intelligent Connected Vehicle and Autonomous Driving Industry Innovation Alliance (SASD).

References

1. Getting MAD: a nuclear mutual assured destruction, its origins and practice. Strategic Studies Institute, US Army War College; 2004.
2. Baran P. On distributed communications networks. IEEE Trans Commun Syst. 1964;12(1):1–9.
3. Leiner BM, Cerf VG, Clark DD, et al. The past and future history of the Internet. Commun ACM. 1997;40(2):102–8.
4. Team Mighty. Today in military history: Soviet Union launches Sputnik. (2023-09-28) [2024-01-02]. https://www.wearethemighty.com/mighty-history/today-in-military-history-soviet-union-launches-sputnik/.
5. Yngvar. Symbolic representation of the Arpanet as of September 1974. (2007-01-10) [2024-01-02]. https://commons.wikimedia.org/wiki/File:Arpanet_1974.svg.
6. Cerf V, Kahn R. A protocol for packet network intercommunication. IEEE Trans Commun. 1974;22(5):637–48.
7. Chris 73. WorldWideWeb Around Wikipedia – Wikipedia as part of the World Wide Web. (2004-07-18) [2024-01-02]. https://commons.wikimedia.org/wiki/File:WorldWideWebAroundWikipedia.png#.
8. Kalodner HA, Carlsten M, Ellenbogen PM, et al. An empirical study of name coin and lessons for decentralized namespace design. WEIS. 2015;1(1):1–23.
9. Ali M, Nelson J, Shea R, et al. Blockstack: a global naming and storage system secured by blockchains. In: 2016 USENIX annual technical conference (USENIX ATC 16); 2016, p. 181–194.
10. Pan J, Paul S, Jain R. A survey of the research on future internet architectures. IEEE Commun Mag. 2011;49(7):26–36.
11. Li H, Yang X. Co-governed Sovereignty Network: legal basis and its prototype & applications with MIN architecture. Cham: Springer; 2021.
12. Hbaieb A, Ayed S, Chaari L. A survey of trust management in the Internet of Vehicles. Comput Netw. 2022;203:1–32.
13. Huo R, Zeng S, Wang Z, et al. A comprehensive survey on blockchain in industrial internet of things: motivations, research progresses, and future challenges. IEEE Commun Surv Tutor. 2022;24(1):88–122.
14. Al Sharif R, Pokharel S. Smart city dimensions and associated risks: review of literature. Sustain Cities Soc. 2022;77:1–14.
15. Eiza MH, Raschellà A. A hybrid SDN-based architecture for secure and QoS aware routing in space-air-ground integrated networks (SAGINs). In: 2023 IEEE wireless communications and networking conference (WCNC). Piscataway: IEEE; 2023. p. 1–6.

Chapter 2
Overview of Co-Governed Multi-Identifier Network

The Internet architecture, established in the 1960s and 1970s, addressed the challenge of resource sharing among hosts during an era limited by hardware constraints. With subsequent advances in integrated circuits, network equipment evolved to offer enhanced computing power at a lower cost. This progress fueled the rapid expansion of computer networks, leading to the proliferation of applications like e-commerce, digital media, social networking, and content distribution in the last decade. Today's Internet users care more about the content itself than how and where to get it. Consequently, the current architecture doesn't seamlessly align with modern user needs, prompting researchers to explore new designs for future networks.

2.1 Design Philosophy

The academic community has proposed two main technical approaches to address the problems in the current Internet architecture. The first approach is to use the "progressive improvement" concept to revise and expand the existing network model to adapt to new network requirements. A typical example is using IPv6 to solve the problem of IPv4 address depletion. The second approach is to use the concept of "revolutionary disruption" to reconstruct the existing network architecture and design a content-oriented network architecture, such as information-centric networking (ICN) [1–3].

Named data networking (NDN) [4, 5] was proposed in 2010, and its predecessor was content-centric networking (CCN) [6]. NDN replaces the sender-driven push-based communication semantics in IP networks with receiver-driven pull-based communication semantics. In NDN, content consumers obtain content by sending Interest packets to the network, and any intermediate router or content producer that caches the corresponding content responds with a Data packet. One Interest corresponds to one Data, and NDN uses a pending interest table (PIT) to support a

H. Li, H. Bai, *Principle of Architecture, Protocol, and Algorithms for CoG-MIN*,
https://doi.org/10.1007/978-981-96-3596-2_2

stateful forwarding plane. Each PIT entry records the network interface from which the Interest is received, and all PIT entries along the Interest forwarding path construct a reverse path. The corresponding Data only needs to be returned along the reverse path constructed by the PIT [7]. Through this pull-based interaction, NDN decouples content from producers and better supports content distribution scenarios. To protect content security, NDN requires producers to sign each Data packet, allowing consumers to trust the content without worrying about how and where it is obtained. However, the compatibility of NDN with existing network architectures is still a subject of investigation due to its disruptive architectural design.

Considering the diverse communication requirements, the development trend of the future network should support various addressing methods, such as IP address, identity, service, content, geographical location, and other potential communication modes. Therefore, a co-governed, secure, and evolvable novel network architecture is indispensable. Given this, the CoG-MIN research group at Peking University proposed the co-governed multi-identifier network (CoG-MIN) [8, 9] in 2019. CoG-MIN is a promising future network architecture that provides an ecological solution for the sustainable evolution of packet networks. The design of CoG-MIN follows three main principles: blockchain-based global co-governed among top-level domains, endogenous network security, and sustainable evolution. CoG-MIN has three key designs:

CoG-MIN proposes a decentralized co-governed scheme based on the consortium blockchain technology to achieve hierarchical management of cyberspace. Top-level identifiers are managed through voting using consortium blockchain, which enables global co-governance and connectivity between top-level domains. Sub-domains are independently managed by the owner of the top-level domain, which indicates the sovereignty and independence of cyberspace. Such hierarchical management architecture guarantees the security and flexibility of the whole network system.

Different from the patchy and passive security policies of IP networks, security is the endogenous gene of CoG-MIN since its birth. CoG-MIN proposes a multi-level security architecture to achieve the balance between security and manageability. Such architecture promotes a secure, peaceful, democratic, and transparent cyberspace of CoG-MIN networks.

CoG-MIN supports sustainable network evolution through an identifier extension mechanism based on identifier rollback. It uses identity as the anchor identifier, with the support of addressing and routing of various existing and potential network identifiers. In this way, the network architecture can adapt to the extension of a variety of identifier space, such as Internet of Things, Internet of Vehicles, Industrial Internet of Things, and Space-Air Ground Integrated Network.

For the sake of convenience, in the subsequent chapters of this book, the term "multi-identifier network" is employed to refer to "co-governed multi-identifier network," and the abbreviation "MIN" is used to represent "CoG-MIN."

2.2 System Architecture

The overall architecture of MIN is illustrated in Fig. 2.1.

The physical layer of MIN architecture multiplexes existing protocols and hardware of the current IP-based network, such as Copper, Fiber, and Radio [10].

Similarly, the data link layer of MIN architecture multiplexes existing protocols and hardware of the IP network, such as Ethernet, PPP, CSMA, Async, and Sonet.

The network layer of MIN architecture is the core of any MIN-based system, establishing a set of multi-identifier extension and evolution mechanisms based on the Identity Identifier. The network identifiers currently supported by MIN networks include:

Identity Identifier: The fundamental identifier in the MIN network.
Content Identifier: Compatible with content-centric networks.
IP Address Identifier: Compatible with IP networks.
Hyperbolic Identifier: Used to support the routing algorithm based on hyperbolic coordinates.
Service Identifier: Used to support service-centric networks.

The multi-identifier router [11] is the prototype implementation of routing nodes in the MIN network, responsible for forwarding MIN network traffic. It consists of:

LogicFace module: abstracts the concept of a universal network interface, shielding the differences in underlying communication.
Identifier selector module: selects an identifier from the identifier field of MIN network packets for forwarding.

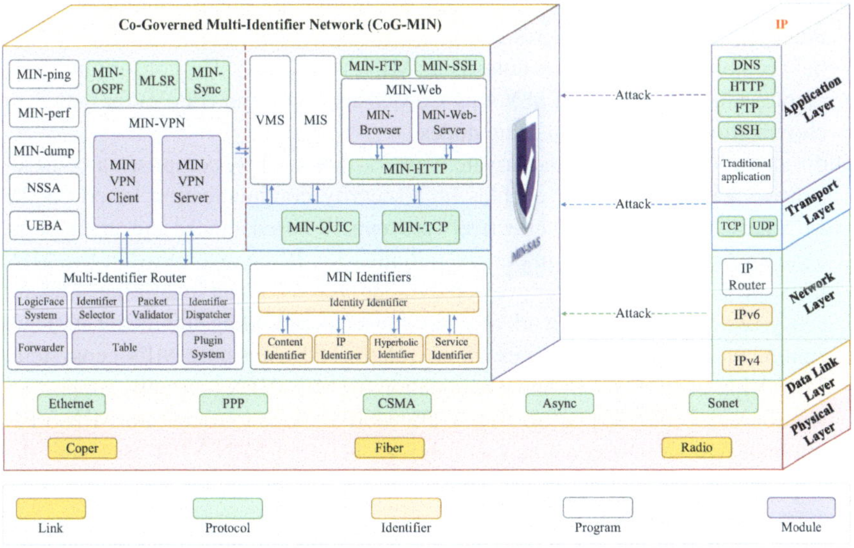

Fig. 2.1 The overall architecture of MIN

Packet validator module: verifies the validity of the signature within MIN network packets.

Forwarder module: performs different processing flows for different types of network packets.

Table module: defines various table structures required for forwarding.

Strategy module: executes forwarding decisions, determining whether, when, and how to forward MIN network packets.

Plugin module: spans across various stages of network packet processing, used for implementing MIR's functional extensions.

The transport layer of the MIN network inherits the excellent designs from IP networks, such as TCP protocol and QUIC protocol, and further proposes the MIN-TCP protocol and MIN-QUIC protocol. These protocols are push-based reliable stream transport protocols implemented on top of the MIN network layer, enabling reliable end-to-end transmission in the MIN network.

The MIN network weakens the concept of the transport layer, allowing application layer protocols and applications to be implemented either on top of the transport layer or directly on top of the network layer. At the application layer of the MIN network, various protocols and applications have been implemented:

Multi-identifier network hypertext transfer protocol (MIN-HTTP) is currently in version 1.0, using MIN-TCP for transport and implementing the specifications of HTTP 1.0, supporting essential web communication.

MIN-web includes MIN-web-server and MIN-browser. MIN-web-server is a basic WebServer development library for developing web backends. MIN-Browser is a MIN-based web browser that supports accessing pure MIN websites.

Multi-identifier system (MIS) is the management plane implementation of the MIN network. It utilizes consortium chain technology to achieve multilateral co-management and mutual resolution of network identifiers. Communication between blockchain nodes is done using MIN-TCP/QUIC. The consortium chain employs the Parallel Proof of Voting Consensus Algorithm (PPoV) for data synchronization between blockchain nodes.

Multi-identifier network virtual private network (MIN-VPN) comprises a comprehensive VPN system that enables high-security communication based on the MIN network. This system effectively prevents IP-based attacks and attack propagation. MIN-VPN is an important initiative for IP compatibility in the MIN network. During the progressive deployment process, it can inherit the software ecosystem from the IP network at a very low cost, providing significant strategic significance in the early stages of the relatively barren pure MIN ecosystem. MIN-VPN-client is the frontend application for MIN-VPN (currently supporting windows and android platforms) that allows IP devices to access the MIN-VPN intranet. MIN-VPN-server acts as a bridge between MIN-VPN users and the intranet, forwarding user traffic to the intranet and returning intranet traffic to the corresponding users.

User and entity behavior analytics (UEBA) is a security module accompanying the MIN-VPN system. It analyzes the access behavior of each VPN user to detect deviations from their normal behavior curve and alerts administrators in case of anomalies.

VPN management system (VMS) is the management backend for MIN-VPN, using MIN-TCP pull-based transmission for communication. VMS and its associated frontend applications are primarily used for VPN user management, rule configuration, etc.

MIN-ping is a tool designed for probing the reachability and communication latency of MIN nodes, similar to the ping network tool in IP networks.

MIN-perf is a tool used to generate MIN traffic for measuring throughput between MIN nodes. It is similar to iperf3 in IP networks and supports both push-based and pull-based traffic generation.

MIN-dump is a command-line tool used to capture and analyze MIN network traffic. It can sniff MIN network traffic passing through network interfaces and parse the traffic into the standard MIN network packet format for subsequent analysis.

Network security situational awareness (NSSA) is typically deployed at the boundaries of the MIN network. It performs full traffic inspection on incoming IP traffic to detect potential attack behaviors and generates analysis reports.

Multi-identifier network file transfer protocol (MIN-FTP) is designed based on MIN-TCP, MIN-QUIC, and pull-based transmission for efficient file transfer. It can make full use of the in-network caching, greatly improving the efficiency of file distribution.

Multi-identifier network secure shell protocol (MIN-SSH) is designed based on MIN-TCP and MIN-QUIC. It is primarily used for secure remote login sessions. It also enables remote login control in a pure MIN environment.

Multi-identifier network open shortest path first dynamic routing protocol (MIN-OSPF) adopts the identity identifier for underlying communication. It exchanges link state advertisements (LSAs) of all types of identifiers between MIN network nodes and reconstructs the network topology based on the collected LSAs to calculate routes.

Multi-identifier network synchronization protocol (MIN-Sync) adopts the pull-based content identifier for underlying communication. It synchronizes data between network nodes, typically used in distributed data synchronization scenarios. It can be used to synchronize routing information (LSAs).

Multi-identifier network link state routing protocol (MLSR) uses MIN-sync to synchronize LSAs and calculates routes based on the collected LSAs from all nodes within the domain during the synchronization phase. It is similar to MIN-OSPF but differs in the method of route synchronization, with one based on push-based communication and the other based on pull-based communication.

Currently, the aforementioned protocols and applications have been implemented and deployed in various scenarios. In order to expand the rich application ecosystem of MIN network, there are many applications are planned.

2.3 Basic Principles

In the management plane of the MIN network, the multi-identifier system (MIS) based on blockchain technology is in charge of multilateral co-governance. In the forwarding plane of the MIN network, the multi-identifier routers (MIRs) is responsible for packet resolving, routing, and forwarding based on various network identifiers. The MIN architecture follows the following design principles:

- Compatibility: The MIN architecture requires excellent compatibility with existing network architectures (mainly IP and NDN), while inheriting the software ecosystem of existing network architectures, facilitating progressive deployment.
- High security: The MIN architecture requires inherent high security at the network layer, supporting packet verification and identity authentication at the network layer, ensuring that only network traffic generated by users with legitimate identities can circulate within the MIN network.
- Easy scalability: The MIN architecture needs to support the scalability of communication semantics. When the new business scenarios and communication requirements arise, the corresponding communication semantics can be customized by simple identifier extensions instead of network architecture reconstruction. It is more sensible to support the evolvability and compatibility of communication paradigms on the existing network architecture rather than redesigning novel network architectures.

Based on the above design principles, the MIN network packet format is defined based on the type–length–value (TLV) format [12]. It supports variable-length fields, enhancing the flexibility and scalability of a network packet. In the forwarding plane, the MIN network supports processing multiple types of identifiers and their corresponding network packets, equipped with a security module to verify the validity of network packets. By embedding digital signatures in each network packet, the integrity of network packets can be ensured, and traceability is supported.

2.3.1 Packet Format

A MIN network packet consists of one or more type/length/value (TLV) triplets. The type field is used to differentiate different types of TLV blocks, while the Length field defines the length of the value portion in 8-bit bytes. The Value field can contain nested TLV blocks or byte arrays. Figure 2.2 shows the general format of a MIN network packet, which includes four regions: the identifier area, signature area, read-only area, and mutable area.

The Identifier area stores one or multiple network identifiers. The MIR distinguishes different types of network packets based on the identifiers stored in this area and selects the appropriate identifier for forwarding.

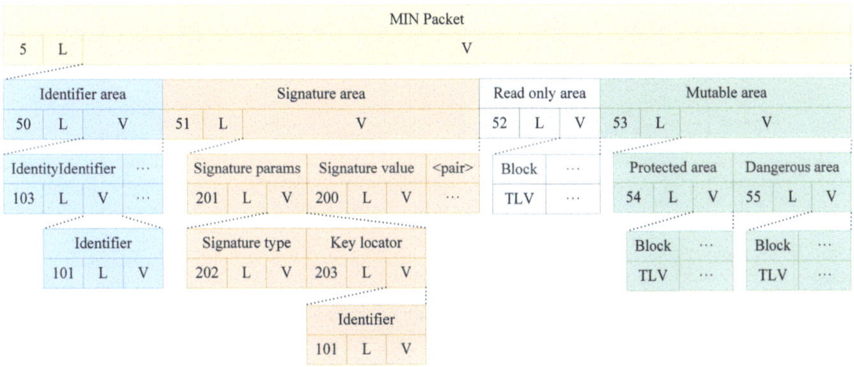

Fig. 2.2 The general format of a MIN network packet

The Signature area contains one or multiple digital signatures. Each digital signature consists of a pair of adjacent TLV blocks. The first TLV block stores the parameters of the signature, including the algorithm used and the location of the certificate required for verifying the signature. The second TLV block stores the signature value.

The read-only area contains zero or multiple TLV blocks, which store fields generated by the sender and do not need to be modified by intermediate routers, such as the payload.

The mutable area is used to store fields that intermediate routers can modify. It consists of two sub-regions: the protected area and the dangerous area. Both sub-regions can contain zero or more TLV blocks. The router signature must be regenerated if an intermediate router modifies the protected area. Instead, the signature regeneration operation is not required if the Dangerous area is modified.

According to the above definition of the packet format, the MIN network defines three types of network packets, namely general push packet (GPPkt), interest packet, and data packet. So far, all communication processes in the MIN network are completed through these three types of network packets. Novel network packets can also be defined if it is necessary to expand new identifiers and communication semantics in the future.

As shown in Fig. 2.3, different types of network packets can be distinguished based on the identifiers stored in the Identifier area.

The GPPkt is used to achieve end-to-end push-based communication semantics, similar to IP packets in the IP network. Each GPPkt contains a pair of identity identifiers: the source identity identifier (sii) and the destination identity identifier (dii). Each identity identifier can uniquely identify a network entity. MIN routers forward GPPkts based on the dii.

Interest and Data packets are used to implement receiver-driven pull-based communication, similar to NDN. A consumer can request content by sending an Interest packet into the network. Any node that has the requested content can respond with

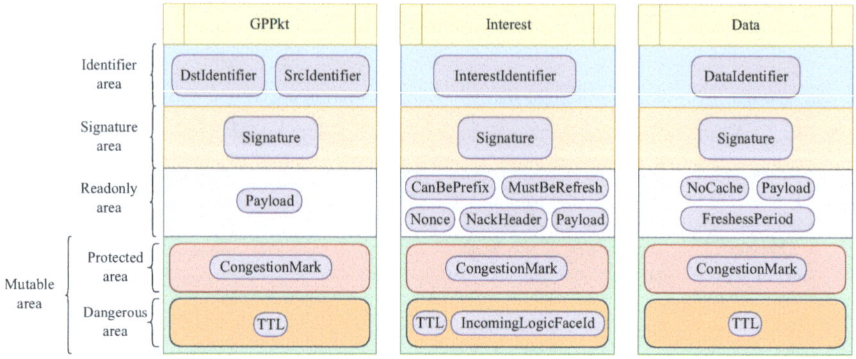

Fig. 2.3 The network packets supported in MIN

a Data packet, whether it is a router caching the corresponding content or a data producer. Most fields inside Interest and Data packets are similar to those in NDN.

In particular, the time to live (TTL) field and CongestionMark field are added to all three types of network packets. The TTL field is used to assist in loop detection. The CongestionMark field stores network congestion information detected by intermediate routers through AQM algorithms. It can be utilized in collaborative congestion control among intermediate routers.

2.3.2 *Packet Processing*

Figure 2.4 illustrates the forwarding process of the MIN router (i.e., MIR). For each received MIN network packet, MIR first verifies the validity of the signature using the Packet Validator module. If the signature is invalid, the packet is discarded. Otherwise, it is passed to the Identifier Selector module.

The Identifier Selector selects an identifier from the Identifier area of the MIN network packet for forwarding. Based on the selected identifier, it distinguishes different types of network packets and executes the corresponding forwarding process:

- For each received Interest, MIR performs the following steps:
  - First, it looks up the content store (CS) to check if there is a matching Data for the Interest. If a match is found, the corresponding Data is returned.
  - If there is no match in the CS, MIR checks the pending interest table (PIT).
  - If there is an entry in the PIT with a matching name (in the MIN network, the name refers to the Interest or Data identifier), the Interest is aggregated, and the ID of the incoming LogicFace is added to the corresponding PIT entry. The forwarding process stops at this point.
  - If there is no matching entry in the PIT, MIR queries the strategy table (ST) to obtain the corresponding forwarding strategy for the network packet.

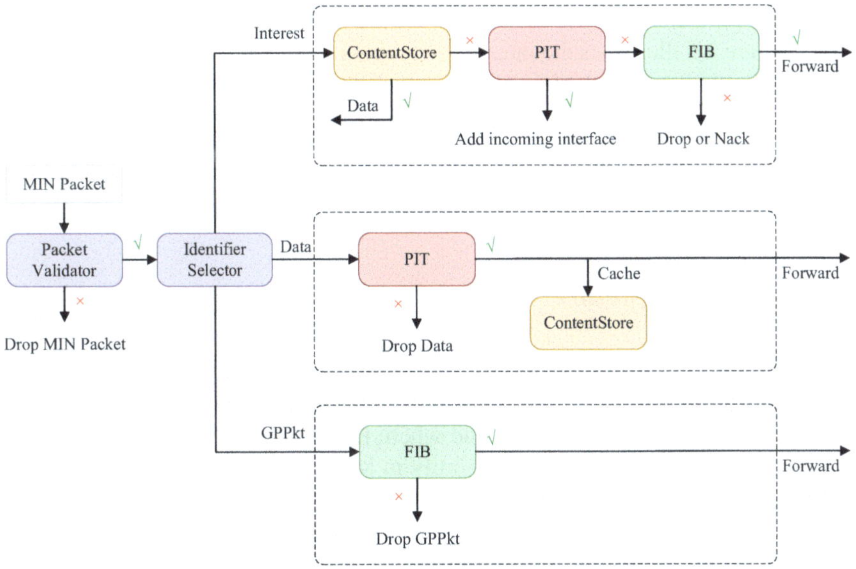

Fig. 2.4 The forwarding process of MIR

- The forwarding strategy then checks the forwarding information base (FIB). If there is no matching FIB entry, it means that MIR is unable to forward the Interest. The forwarding strategy can discard the Interest or return a Nack (negative acknowledgment).
- If there is a matching FIB entry, the forwarding strategy selects one or more LogicFaces to forward the Interest based on demand.

- For each received Data, MIR performs the following steps:
  - First, it checks the PIT. If there is no matching PIT entry, it means that the Data is not requested. MIR can choose to save it in the CS or discard it.
  - If there is a matching PIT entry, MIR caches the Data in the CS and sends a copy of the Data to all the LogicFaces associated with the recorded Interests in the PIT entry.

- For each received GPPkt, MIR uses the destination identity identifier (dii) to query the FIB.
  - If there is a matching FIB entry, MIR forward the GPPkt based on the forwarding strategy and query result.
  - If there is no matching FIB entry, the GPPkt is discarded.

MIR incorporates a built-in packet verification module, which can perform signature verification on each network packet passing through MIR. The packet verification module is based on SM3+SM1 for signature verification. Additionally, MIR adopts a partially parallel architecture design, where the packet signature verification process is parallelized, while the subsequent forwarding process is serialized. Figure 2.5 illustrates the interaction process of parallel signature verification in MIR. For each received MIN network packet, MIR first uses a thread pool to perform parallel signature verification on the network packet. If the verification fails, the packet is directly discarded. The network packets that pass the verification are then passed to the subsequent forwarding processing flow.

2.3.3 Digital Signature

NDN requires data producers to sign each Data packet, protecting the integrity of the data and providing traceability support. As a result, data consumers can trust the Data itself without concerning how and where to obtain it. In MIN, each network entity is required to register a valid identity in MIS, and this identity is associated with a pair of asymmetric keys generated by the SM2 algorithm. This public–private key pair can be used to sign and verify MIN network packets. The private key is kept locally by the network entity, while the public key is stored in MIS and can be accessed by other network entities (e.g., routers). Every MIN network packet sent by a network entity needs to be signed using the private key associated with its legitimate identity.

The signature area of a MIN network packet is of variable length, allowing for one or multiple digital signatures to be stored. Two types of digital signatures have been defined, namely Producer Signature and Router Signature. Additional types of digital signatures can also be supported.

The Producer Signature is generated by the sender of the MIN network packet and is primarily used for traceability and identity authentication. It also serves to protect the integrity of the network packet.

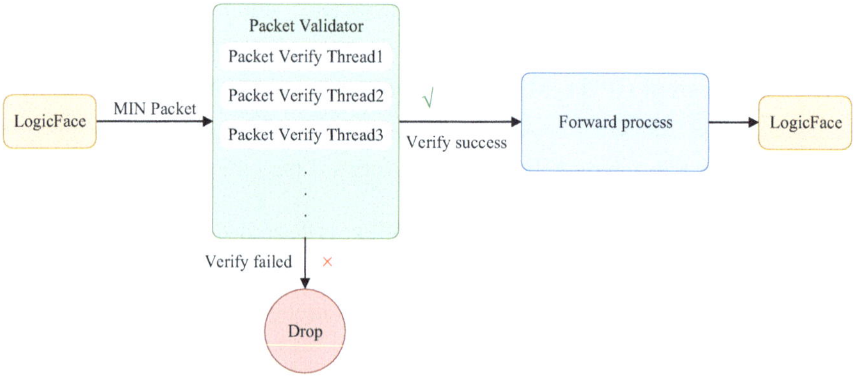

Fig. 2.5 The parallel verification process in MIR

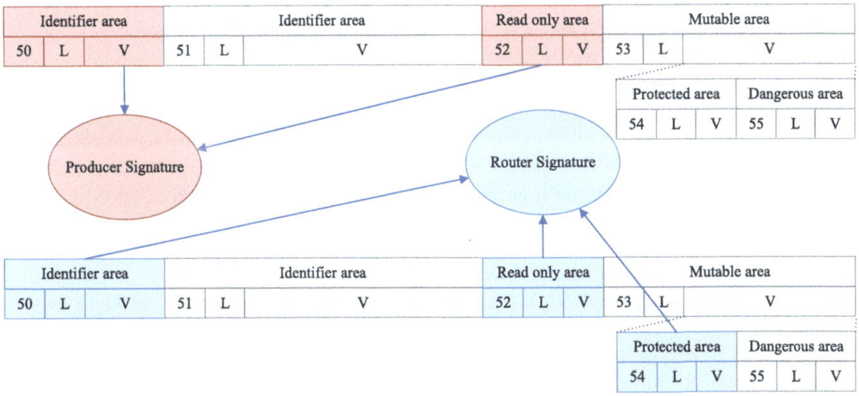

Fig. 2.6 Signatures supported in MIN

The Router Signature is generated by intermediate routers and is primarily used to protect important fields in the variable protection area of the MIN network packet that are allowed to be modified by the router.

Figure 2.6 illustrates the coverage areas of these two types of signatures. The Producer Signature is generated based on the Identifier Area and Read-Only Area, while the Router Signature is generated based on the Identifier Area, Read-Only Area, and Variable Protection Area.

In typical scenarios, the sender of the MIN network packet uses its private key to generate a Producer Signature for each packet. This ensures that the Identifier Area and Read-Only Area are protected, and intermediate routers cannot modify these two areas in any way. If the content of these areas is tampered with by the attacker, the MIN network packet cannot pass the signature verification process. The network traffic from users without legitimate identities is isolated in the signature verification process at edge routers.

In high-security scenarios, network security is more important than transmission performance. The network administrators can choose to enable the high-security mode of MIN. In the high-security mode, the edge router generates the Router Signature for each MIN network packet that passes through this router. For each intermediate router, if there is any modification to the variable protection area of the MIN network packet, the Router Signature inside this packet needs to be verified first, and then a new Router Signature is generated to replace the existing one. Based on this chain of trust, the recipient can reasonably trust that each router in the transmission path is legitimate.

References

1. Xylomenos G, Ververidis CN, Siris VA, et al. A survey of information-centric networking research. IEEE Commun Surveys Tutorials. 2013;16(2):1024–49.

2. Fang C, Yao H, Wang Z, et al. A survey of mobile information-centric networking: research issues and challenges. IEEE Commun Surveys Tutorials. 2018;20(3):2353–71.
3. Nour B, Mastorakis S, Ullah R, et al. Information-centric networking in wireless environments: security risks and challenges. IEEE Wirel Commun. 2021;28(2):121–7.
4. Jacobson V, Smetters D K, Thornton J D, et al. Networking named content. In: Proceedings of the 5th international conference on Emerging networking experiments and technologies; 2009, p. 1–12.
5. Zhang L, Afanasyev A, Burke J, et al. Named data networking. ACM SIGCOMM Comput Commun Rev. 2014;44(3):66–73.
6. Jacobson V, Mosko M, Smetters D, et al. Content-centric networking. In: Whitepaper. Palo Alto: Palo Alto Research Center; 2007. p. 2–4.
7. Yi C, Afanasyev A, Moiseenko I, et al. A case for stateful forwarding plane. Comput Commun. 2013;36(7):779–91.
8. Wang Y, Li H, Huang T, et al. Scalable identifier system for industrial internet based on multi-identifier network architecture. IEEE Internet Things J. 2021;10:1919–32.
9. Li H, Wu JX, Xing KX, et al. Prototype and testing report of a multi-identifier system for reconfigurable network architecture under co-governing. Sci Sinica Inf. 2019;49(9):1186–204.
10. Chen Z, Wang C, Li G, et al. New IP framework and protocol for future applications. In: NOMS 2020-2020 IEEE/IFIP network operations and management symposium. Piscataway: IEEE; 2020. p. 1–5.
11. Zhang X, Chen Q, Li H. MIR: multi-identifier router and its prototype. In: Proceedings of the 8th international conference on computer and communications management; 2020, p. 103–107.
12. Ma X, Afanasyev A, Zhang L. A type-theoretic model on NDN-TLV encoding. In: Proceedings of the 9th ACM conference on information-centric networking. New York: ACM; 2022. p. 91–102.

Chapter 3
Identifier and Identifier Semantics

The evolvability of a network architecture refers to its ability to be designed and implemented in a flexible and scalable manner, allowing it to adapt to changing needs and technological advancements. In MIN networks [1], network evolution can be realized through the extension of network identifiers. Specifically, various types of identifiers are employed to support different network protocols, and routers execute distinct operations on network packets based on the carried identifiers. This realizes the coexistence of various network protocols at the network layer. This chapter introduces the basic network identifier, identifier forms, identifier characteristics, identifier semantics, and identifier space in MIN networks.

3.1 Basic Identifier

Definition 3.1 The network identifier (or identifier in short) carried in a network packet declares how routers should process and forward the packet.

For example, in traditional IPv4 and IPv6 networks, the network identifier is the destination address of the network packet. In MPLS [2], routers process and forward packets based on the labels within the packets. Thus, these labels serve as network identifier. Similarly, the names of Interest and Data packets in named data networking (NDN) [3] are network identifiers, while the hashes used to identify communication subjects in XIA and MobilityFirst networks are also network identifiers. In a network using the hyperbolic routing algorithm [4], the hyperbolic coordinates of network nodes are network identifiers. In summary, the data encapsulated in network packets used in these networks to indicate how routers should handle the network packets is what we refer to as network identifiers (Fig. 3.1).

H. Li, H. Bai, *Principle of Architecture, Protocol, and Algorithms for CoG-MIN*,
https://doi.org/10.1007/978-981-96-3596-2_3

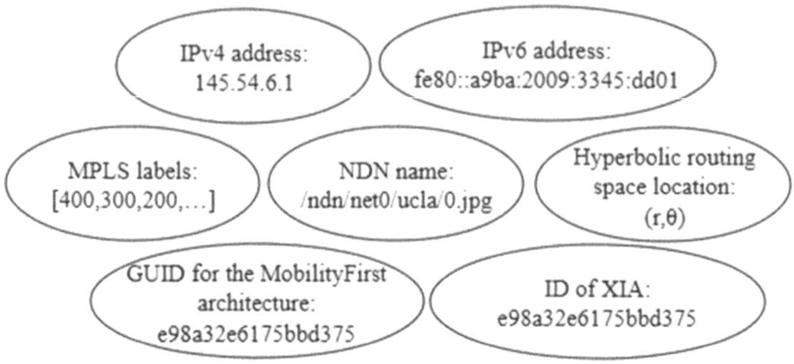

Fig. 3.1 Examples of network identifiers

3.2 Identifier Forms and Characteristics

3.2.1 Concept of Identifier Form

Definition 3.2 The identifier form is the structural characteristics of a network identifier represented by strings.

In different network architectures, the form of a network identifier is not standardized. Additionally, each type of network layer protocol has its own unique processing methods and procedures for handling network packets based on different types of identifiers. Therefore, two key attributes of network identifiers can be abstracted: the structural feature of a network identifier represented by strings, and the processing methods and procedures of a router for handling the network packets carrying the network identifiers. These two attributes are referred to as the identifier form and the identifier semantic. Identifiers can be categorized into different types based on these two dimensions.

3.2.2 Classification of Identifier Forms

The form of a network identifier refers to the structural features of the network identifier displayed by strings. These patterns exhibit certain regularities, such that identifiers with the same pattern have the same structure. In general, regular expressions can be used to describe the morphological characteristics of network identifiers. Based on the identifier form, network identifiers can be classified into the following categories:

Flat identifier: The flat identifier is a type of network identifiers characterized by a less regular feature. It generally consists of a series of irregular numbers, letters, or special characters and cannot be aggregated in the forwarding table. Some network architectures, such as XIA and MobilityFirst, use public keys or hashes of data fragments as network identifiers. These are classic examples of flat identifiers.

Hierarchical identifier: The hierarchical identifier exhibits a pattern where components of an identifier repeat in a structured manner. A typical example is the URL-like identifier used in NDN, such as "/ndn/lab/icon.jpg." IPv4 and IPv6 addresses, when used with address masks, can also be considered hierarchical identifiers.

Spatial coordinate identifier: The spatial coordinate identifier takes the form of geometric spatial coordinates. By mapping network nodes to a geometric space, the coordinates of these nodes are obtained and used directly as network identifiers. An example is the identifier used in the hyperbolic routing model, which looks like (r, θ), representing a typical spatial coordinate identifier type.

Sequential identifier: The sequential identifier consists of a set of forwarding cues, whose dynamic combination directly forms the forwarding path of network packets. The label sequences in MPLS technology and the path fragments in the pathlet routing scheme are typical examples of sequential identifiers.

3.3 Identifier Semantics

3.3.1 Concept of Identifier Semantics

Definition 3.3 The semantics of an identifier refer to the set of processing operations performed by routers on incoming network packets.

For instance, through an analysis of the forwarding characteristics in NDN and IP networks, we can identify the fundamental operations performed by routers on network packets. These operations include looking up the forwarding table, looking up the local cache, looking up the pending interest table (PIT), updating the PIT, caching data in the local cache, and forwarding packets. The set of operations for routers in IP networks is {looking up the forwarding table, forwarding packets}. For Interest packets in NDN networks, the set of operations for routers is {looking up the local cache, looking up the PIT, updating the PIT, looking up the forwarding table (i.e., FIB), forwarding packets}. For Data packets in NDN networks, the set of operations for routers is {looking up the PIT, caching data in the local cache, forwarding packets}. Therefore, in MIN networks that support both IP and NDN communication modes, there also exists their corresponding identifier semantics.

The formal definition of identifier semantics is given below: The operations that routers can perform on a network packet in a network are represented as a set $F = f_0, f_1, f_2, f_3, \ldots$, where f_i can represent an operation such as forwarding packet. The supported operations are extensible. The types of identifiers supported in a network are represented as $I = i_0, i_1, i_2, \ldots, i_k$. Given the above definitions, one type of identifier semantics supported in a network is represented as:

$$\text{Semantics}(i_k) = \{f_k, f_{k+1}, \ldots\} \subseteq F. \tag{3.1}$$

3.3.2 Push-Based and Pull-Based Communication Semantics

Existing network communication semantics mainly includes the push-based and pull-based semantics, which are both supported in the MIN network.

Taking the traditional IPv4 network as an example, the initial design of the IPv4 network was intended for point-to-point communication between two nodes in the network. The two communicating nodes are in a peer-to-peer relationship, without distinguishing which is the data producer and which is the consumer. Consequently, the IPv4 packet has a single structure, as shown in Fig. 3.2. In the packet forwarding process in IP networks, key fields of a IPv4 packet that play a significant role include Identification, Flags, Fragment offset, Time To Live (TTL), Source address, and Destination address.

In the context of push-based network communication semantics, routers perform stateless forwarding. In IPv4 networks, the structure of the forwarding table (routing table) is given in Table 3.1. For each incoming network packet, the router decrements the TTL value by one; if the TTL value becomes zero after decrementing, the network packet is discarded. Then, the destination address is extracted from the network packet, and the router performs a routing table lookup operation to determine the appropriate interface for forwarding the packet, and then performs the packet forwarding operation. If the maximum transmission unit (MTU) value of the outgoing interface is smaller than the size of the network packet, the router is also responsible for fragmenting the IP packet into multiple fragments for forwarding. Irrespective of how the IP network packet is processed within the router, once the

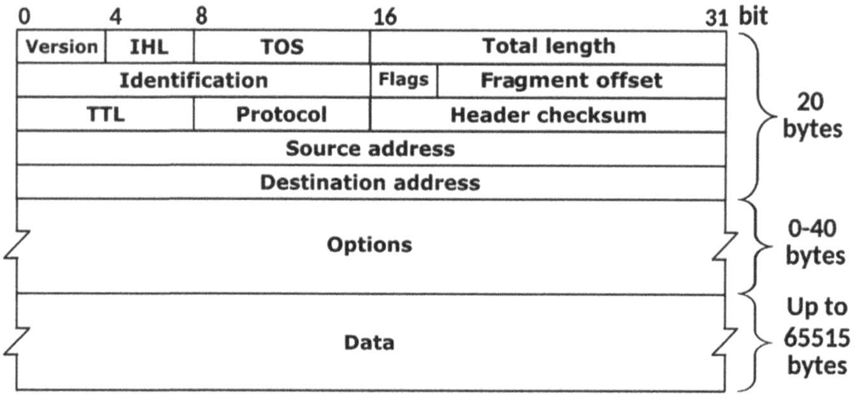

Fig. 3.2 IPv4 packet structure [5]

Table 3.1 Routing table structure of IP routers

Destination	Nexthop	Interface
10.11.0.0/16	10.1.1.2	GE 1/0/0
10.12.0.0/16	10.2.2.2	GE 2/0/0
10.13.0.0/16	10.3.3.2	GE 3/0/0

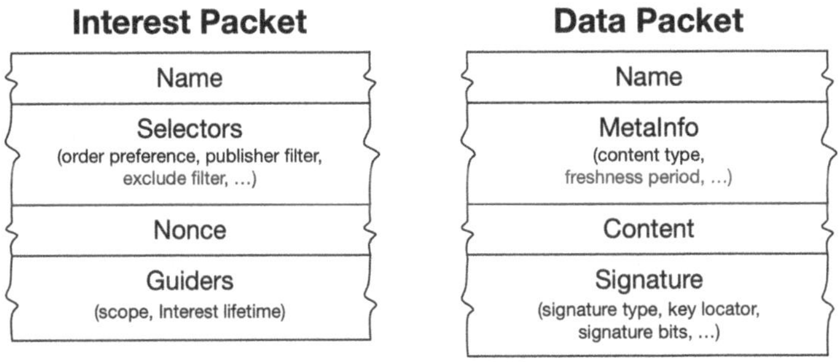

Fig. 3.3 Structure of Interest packet and Data packet in NDN [7]

processing is completed, the packet leaves no trace within the router. This characteristic is the essence of stateless forwarding.

Taking the NDN network as an example, NDN [6–8] is a mainstream implementation of Information-Centric Networking (ICN). In recent years, the communication network has undergone significant evolution, leading to a wide range of upper-layer network applications based on the TCP/IP communication protocol. Internet users primarily focus on retrieving specific content without being concerned about the specific network device from which the content originates.

To align the communication paradigm with the current Internet usage, NDN adopts a pull-based communication semantics. In NDN networks, the data transmission process is driven by data consumers, and any node caching the requested data in the network can be a data producer. NDN defines two different types of packets: Interest Packets and Data Packets. The Interest Packet is sent by the data consumer requesting specific content. The Data Packet, which responds to the Interest Packet, is issued by the corresponding content source in the network. The formats of these two types of packets are shown in Fig. 3.3.

The Name field of a NDN packet plays a major role in packet forwarding. This field functions in addressing and forwarding decisions in NDN networks, similar to the destination address in IP networks. Intermediate routers in NDN networks use the name carried in Interest Packets to look up the forwarding information base (FIB), which serves a similar function to the routing table in IP networks.

In NDN, each router is responsible for managing three primary data structures [7]: a content store (CS), used for temporary caching of received Data packets, a pending interest table (PIT), and a forwarding table (FIB).

These structures play a crucial role in the routing and caching mechanisms of NDN routers, as shown in Figs. 3.4 and 3.5.

For an incoming Interest Packet, the processing steps in an NDN router include [7]:

Check the local Content Store for a Data Packet with the same name as the Interest Packet. If such a Data Packet exists, return it through the ingress interface of the Interest Packet; otherwise, proceed to the next step.

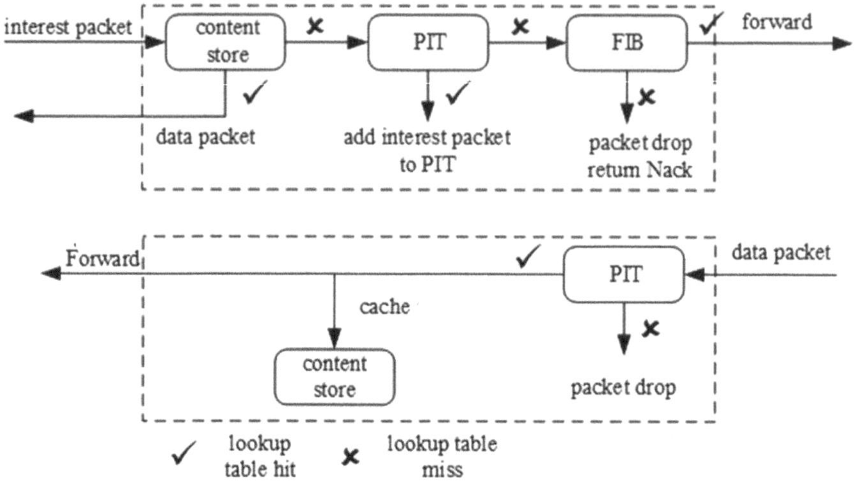

Fig. 3.4 Forwarding process at the NDN node [7]

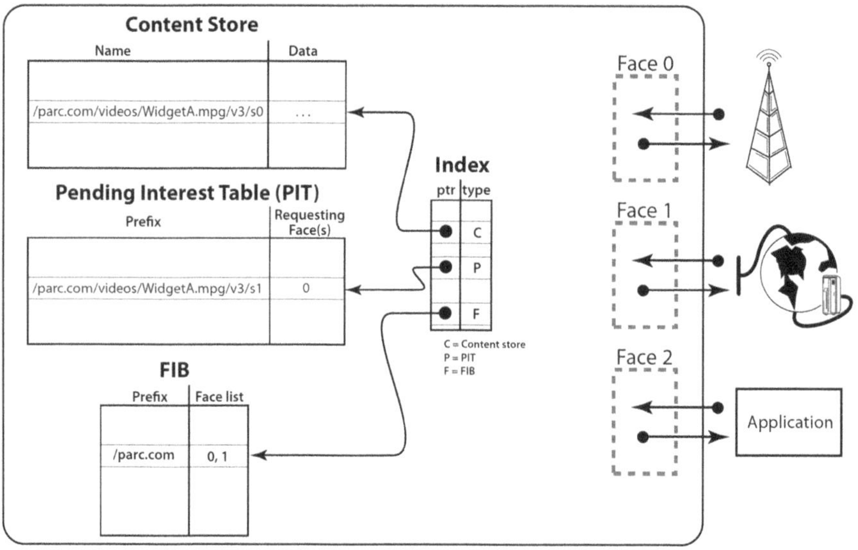

Fig. 3.5 NDN forwarding engine model [8]

Check the PIT for an existing Interest Packet with the same name. If one exists, record the ingress interface of the new Interest Packet in the corresponding PIT entry. In this case, there is no need to forward the Interest Packet further. If there is no existing Interest Packet with the same name in the PIT, proceed to the next step.

Consult the FIB. If a valid entry is found, the router knows the next-hop interface for forwarding the Interest Packet and forward it accordingly, recording the Interest Packet and its ingress interface in the PIT. If no valid entry is found in the FIB, the Interest Packet is discarded.

For an incoming Data Packet, the processing steps in an NDN router include [7]:

Using the name of the Data Packet, search the PIT for waiting Interest Packets with the same name. If a valid entry is found, it records one or more ingress interfaces of the Interest Packets. Forward the Data Packet through these interfaces. If no valid entry is found in the PIT, do not forward the Data Packet.

If the Data Packet is successfully forwarded, cache the incoming Data Packet in the local Content Store and delete the corresponding entries in the PIT.

3.3.3 Examples of Identifier Forms and Semantics

Table 3.2 provides the examples of network identifiers in MIN networks as well as other network architectures, based on their respective identifier forms and semantics.

Table 3.2 Examples of network identifiers

Identifier name	Identifier form	Identifier semantics	Example
Identity identifier	Flat	{lookup the forwarding table, forward packets}	e98a32e6175bbd375
Content interest identifier	Hierarchical	{lookup the local cache, lookup the PIT, update the PIT, lookup the forwarding table (i.e., FIB), forward packets}	/min/pkusz/002.txt
Content data identifier	Hierarchical	{lookup the PIT, cache data in the local cache, forward packets}	/min/pkusz/002.txt
Service request identifier	Hierarchical	{lookup the forwarding table, lookup the PIT, update the PIT, lookup the forwarding table (i.e., FIB), forward packets}	/min/pkusz/web
Service response identifier	Hierarchical	{lookup the PIT, forward packets}	/min/pkusz/web
Geolocation Identifier	Spatial coordinate	{calculate distance, forward packets}	(113.97, 22.59)
Hyperbolic Identifier	Spatial coordinate	{calculate distance, forward packets}	(R_1, Θ_1)
MPLS identifier	Sequential	{check tag, forward packets, join tag, pop tag}	[400, 300, 200, ...]
MobilityFirst-GUID	Flat	{lookup the forwarding table, lookup the local cache, identification resolution, forward packets}	e98a32e6175bbd375

3.4 Identifier Space

In the progressive evolution of networks, older network devices are gradually replaced by newer ones. Different devices exhibit varying sets of operations on network packets and capabilities in interpreting packet forms. Network devices support different types of identifiers. In MIN networks, network devices that support the same type of identifier are divided into a region. These devices can be directly connected through wired or wireless communication or they may not be connected at all. This region is referred to as an identifier space [9].

For MIN networks, the identifier extension mechanism based on identifier rollback technology (introduced in Chap. 12) [9] requires the existence of a fundamental identifier supported by all devices in the network. A unified basic identifier serves as a crucial anchor point in the rollback of network identifiers. For example, all devices in MIN networks have an identity identifier and support the communication semantics associated with it. Meanwhile, the semantics of the identity identifier align with those of a basic identifier. Thus, the identity identifier can be chosen as the rollback basis during the evolution of MIN networks. It is essential for the entire MIN network to support the identity identifier, implying that all devices in the MIN network fall within the identity identifier space. The diagram of identifier space is shown in Fig. 3.6.

The formal definition of the identifier space is as follows [9]:

In the network layer of MIN Networks, the set of all identifiers is represented as $I = i0, i1, i2, \ldots, ik$. Among these identifiers, $i0$ is the basic identifier and is indispensable for each network device. The identifiers $i1$, $i2$, …, ik encompass various types of identifiers such as content interest identifier, content data identifier, service request identifier, service response identifier, geolocation identifier, and IP identifier. It is possible to extend this set to include additional types of identifiers as needed. Ik is a subset of several identifiers in I, such as $Ik = \{i0, i1\}$.

The set of all network nodes, including communication equipment, terminal equipment, and other devices, is represented by V. $V = \{H, R, S, \ldots\}$, where H represents the hosts, R represents the routers, and S represents the switches, and additional types of network devices can be included as well.

$C^{I_k} = \left(I_k, V_{I_k}\right)$ represents the network identifier space, which is a binary group. Ik represents a set of identifier types supported by the identifier space CIk, where Vk represents a subset of network devices V in the identifier space.

Definition 3.4 A set $C^{I_k} = \left(I_k, V_{I_k}\right)$ constitutes an identifier space in a MIN network if and only if the following conditions are met:

Determinism: $I_k \subseteq \mathrm{I}$ and $V_{I_k} \subseteq V$, indicating that the node subset and the identifier subset are selected in the MIN network.

Atomicity: $i_0 \subseteq I_k$, meaning that the identity identifier must be included in the identifier set supported by each identifier space.

Consistency: $\forall v \subseteq V_{I_k} \forall i_j \in I_k$, ij are supported, indicating that all devices in the identifier space support all identifiers in the identifier space.

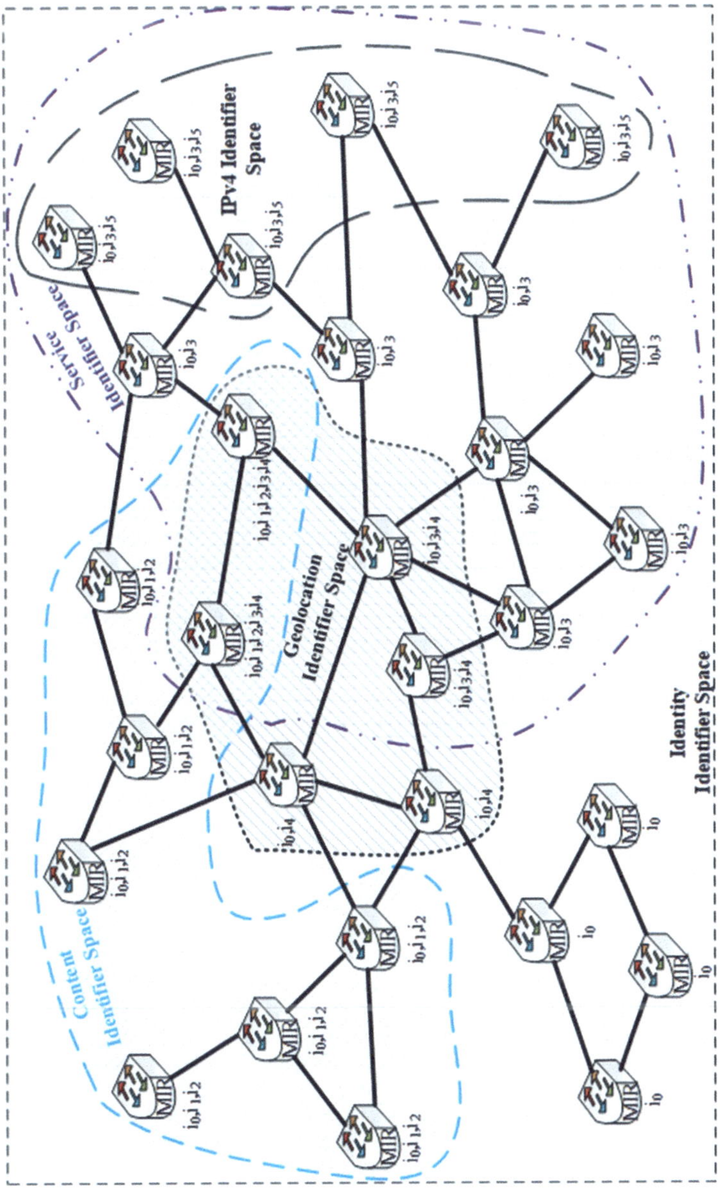

Fig. 3.6 The diagram of identifier space [9, 10]

Closure: if $\exists v \in V$ and for $\forall i_j \in I_k$, v supports i_j, then $v \in V_{I_k}$. This means that any network device that supports all identifiers of an identifier space in a MIN network belongs to that identifiers space.

References

1. Fan B, Jiang Z, Hu S, et al. Attacking identity semantics in DeepFakes via deep feature fusion. In: 2023 IEEE 6th international conference on multimedia information processing and retrieval (MIPR). Piscataway: IEEE; 2023. p. 114–9.
2. Van Der Does T, Galesic M, Dunivin ZO, et al. Strategic identity signaling in heterogeneous networks. Proc Natl Acad Sci. 2022;119(10):e2117898119.
3. Ni L, Gong X, Li J, et al. rFedFW: secure and trustable aggregation scheme for Byzantine-robust federated learning in Internet of Things. Inf Sci. 2024;653:119784.
4. Fonken SJM, Ramaswamy KR, Van den Hof PMJ. A scalable multi-step least squares method for network identification with unknown disturbance topology. Automatica. 2022;141:110295.
5. Postel J. Internet protocol. IETF 1981–1909. https://datatracker.ietf.org/doc/html/rfc791.
6. Saxena D, Raychoudhury V, Suri N, et al. Named data networking: a survey. Comput Sci Rev. 2016;19:15–55.
7. Zhang L, Afanasyev A, Burke J, et al. Named data networking. ACM SIGCOMM Comput Commun Rev. 2014;44(3):66–73.
8. Jacobson V, Smetters DK, Thornton JD, et al. Networking named content. In: Proceedings of the 5th international conference on emerging networking experiments and technologies (CoNEXT'09). New York: ACM; 2009. p. 1–12.
9. Li H, Wu JX, Wei GH, et al. Method and system for general packet network addressing routing and identifier evolution. Sci Sin Inform. 2023;53:1629–44. https://doi.org/10.1360/SSI-2022-0261.
10. Wang H, et al. Mis: a multi-identifier management and resolution system in the metaverse. ACM Trans Multimed Comput Commun Appl. 2024;20(7):1–25.

Chapter 4
Co-Governed Multi-Identifier Management Technology

The existing domain name system (DNS) is non-autonomous and relatively controlled by some countries and institutions. Traditional DNS faces numerous challenges including low efficiency, vulnerability to information tampering, uneven service distribution, and weak resistance against distributed denial of service (DDoS) attacks. These issues pose a potential threat to national information security. Extensive research has demonstrated that the current DNS, along with its alternative approaches, cannot effectively address the problem of DNS centralization or fulfill the Internet's fundamental requirements for equality and openness.

Currently, the prevailing view in the scientific and technological community is that the post-IP era network should be a new multiple-dimensional network system supporting various network identifiers such as identity, content, IP address, and geospatial location. This chapter primarily introduces the co-governed multi-identifier management technology, which plays a crucial role in facilitating the unified management of various network identifiers in CoG-MIN.

4.1 Overview of Blockchain

Blockchain technology is utilized to implement and manage transaction processing in a peer-to-peer network environment [1]. It creates a chained data structure that is immutable, inalterable, and traceable through transparent and trustworthy rules. From a more specific perspective, the blockchain can be described as a sequential arrangement of data blocks that are interconnected in chronological order, safeguarded through cryptographic measures to ensure their immutability and authenticity. In a broader context, the blockchain signifies a revolutionary distributed foundation and computing paradigm. It utilizes a linked data structure to validate and store information, employing distributed consensus algorithms to establish and update data, cryptographic techniques to secure data transmission and access, and smart contracts to automate data manipulation through scripted codes [2].

H. Li, H. Bai, *Principle of Architecture, Protocol, and Algorithms for CoG-MIN*,
https://doi.org/10.1007/978-981-96-3596-2_4

Blockchain has three primary characteristics: decentralization, immutability, and trustlessness.

Decentralization: The blockchain network operates in a peer-to-peer mode, ensuring equal exchange of information among all nodes. All resources and services within the network are collectively maintained by the participating nodes, eliminating the need for intermediate nodes and servers. This decentralized approach enhances network resilience against attacks and faults, while also reducing the costs in data value exchange [3].

Immutability: The organization of blockchain is in a chained structure. It utilizes encryption algorithms to ensure that the data is immutable and unforgeable. The hash information inside each block is contained within the next block, enabling verification of data through this chained structure. Any modification to the data will have a ripple effect on subsequent blocks. This guarantees the accuracy of all stored information [4]. Additionally, the hash algorithm is utilized to prevent the feasibility of forgery attempts based on its irreversible nature. Therefore, once data is confirmed on the blockchain, any unauthorized tampering or forging would disrupt the consensus process, triggering a chain reaction of failed verifications throughout the blockchain.

Trustlessness: The trust mechanism of the blockchain is based on the principle of asymmetric encryption, which eliminates the need for mutual trust or identity verification between nodes during data exchange. Asymmetric encryption is a purely mathematical method that uses a pair of public and private keys for encryption and decryption. For instance, let's consider a transaction where Alice wants to transfer assets to Bob. Alice encrypts the transaction using Bob's public key and broadcasts it to the network. Only Bob's private key can decrypt and access this information. By decrypting the transaction using his private key, Bob verifies himself as the intended recipient of the assets. This verification gains approval and recording across the entire network. The rigorous encryption algorithm and comprehensive authentication mechanism ensure that both parties involved in a transaction within the blockchain network do not need to know or trust each other's identities nor rely on third-party trust guarantees. This enables them to carry out trusted transactions in an unfamiliar mode. All nodes in the network are able to act as supervisors to safeguard the personal privacy for the transaction participants.

4.2 Core Technologies of Blockchain

Blockchain technology encompasses a wide range of technical fields, including distributed systems, cryptography, network protocols, storage, as well as interdisciplinary knowledge from psychology, economics, and game theory. Its core technologies include distributed ledger, consensus algorithm, cryptography, and smart contract [5].

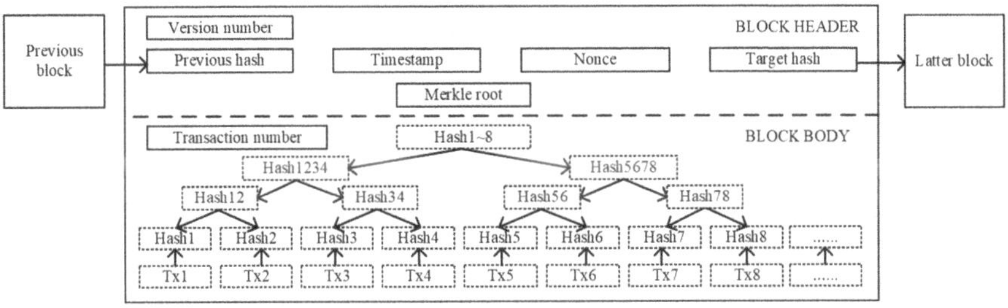

Fig. 4.1 Blocks in a blockchain [1]

As shown in Fig. 4.1, blocks are an essential component of a blockchain. A block in a blockchain comprises two fundamental elements: the block header and the block body.

The block header consists of critical information such as version number, previous block hash, Merkle root, timestamp, target hash, and random number (nonce). This ensures the integrity of data in the blockchain and enables nodes (miners) to solve mathematical puzzles by guessing random numbers to gain bookkeeping rights. Transactions are packaged into blocks and then linked to the blockchain as the latest blocks by nodes that successfully mine them. Each block uniquely points to its previous block through a hash value, forming a distinct chained structure specific to the blockchain. The random number in the block header is derived from solving a mathematical puzzle by miners. The Merkel root is obtained by calculating the hash value of each pair of transaction data hashes in a blockchain system, enabling quick verification of all transaction data within a block. Due to irreversibility of hash functions, if a transaction in the block body is modified, the Merkle root in the block header needs to be correspondingly updated to ensure the integrity of the block data. Additionally, the uniqueness of each block is represented by calculating a unique hash value for each block based on the block header. All transaction data (TX) generated during block creation is stored in the block body where confirmed transactions or spent money are referred to as transaction identifiers (TXID). Unconfirmed transactions are known as unspent transaction outputs (UTXO).

4.2.1 Distributed Ledger

The core of blockchain technology lies in distributed ledger technology, which is a database that allows network nodes to share, replicate, synchronize, and record transactions.

The advantages of distributed ledgers are twofold. Firstly, all nodes can monitor and verify the legality of transactions and can also provide evidence for legitimate data in the ledgers. Unlike traditional centralized bookkeeping schemes, distributed ledgers do not allow any single node to act as a central node for independent bookkeeping. Instead, all nodes collaborate to maintain consistent replica data, thereby preventing malicious manipulation by a single bookkeeping node for fraudulent purposes. Secondly, with a large number of bookkeeping nodes, it is theoretically unlikely for the ledger to be lost unless all nodes are maliciously destroyed. This assumption is so extreme that it is almost impossible to happen in reality. Therefore, it is generally assumed that the redundancy strategy of distributed ledger technology can effectively guarantee the security of ledger data.

4.2.2 Consensus Algorithm

Consensus algorithms are crucial for ensuring the validity and immutability of distributed ledger data. They provide a cooperative way for bookkeeping nodes to verify and confirm transactions quickly. The consensus mechanism solves the problem of block creation and data consistency in a peer-to-peer network. The theoretical basis is the Byzantine fault tolerance problem, and various consensus algorithms exist for different distributed system scenarios.

Consensus algorithms can be divided into two types: one is for non-Byzantine errors with high performance but poor fault tolerance, such as Paxos and Raft. Another class is for Byzantine errors, which tend to be fault-tolerant but have relatively poor performance, includes Practical Byzantine Fault Tolerance (PBFT), Proof of Work (PoW), Proof of Stake (PoS), and Delegated Proof of Stake (DPoS).

Blockchain networks often have Byzantine nodes. There are three approaches to handling Byzantine errors: (1) Increasing the cost of malicious behavior to reduce the likelihood of nodes engaging in malicious activities, which is achieved through proof-based consensus algorithms like PoW and PoS. (2) Attaining consensus among nodes through voting-based consensus algorithms, such as PBFT. (3) Integrating voting-based and proof-based consensus algorithms, which combine the advantages of two types of consensus algorithms, such as proof of vote (PoV) [6, 7], parallel proof of vote (PPoV) [8, 9], and their variants [10].

4.2.3 Cryptography

In blockchain systems, the hash function and asymmetric cryptographic algorithm are commonly used cryptographic algorithms.

The hash function is commonly used for transaction verification and block construction. It can convert data of any size into a fixed-size value, known as the hash value. The hash function is considered unidirectional because it is difficult to determine the original input data from its output.

The hash function used in blockchains possesses several key properties: collision resistance, irreversibility, and unpredictability. The property of collision resistance can be used to detect any tampering or unauthorized modifications in the data. This means that if any modification is made to a piece of data *m*, its corresponding hash value *H*(*m*) will also change. The irreversibility of the hash function ensures that the original input value cannot be derived from its hash value. The hash function in Bitcoin also needs to possess unpredictability. This property means that it is challenging to predict the output hash value based on the input data. The desired hash value can only be found through continuous calculations.

The process of asymmetric encryption involves using a pair of keys for encryption and decryption. The public key, which can be shared with others, is used for encryption, while the private key, which must be kept confidential, is used for decryption. Although there is a mathematical relationship between these two keys, it is not possible to derive one key from the other. The ciphertext encrypted with the public key can only be decrypted by its corresponding private key. Likewise, if the data is encrypted using the private key, only the corresponding public key can decrypt the ciphertext.

In a blockchain network, each user is assigned a unique pair of public and private keys. Similar to the bank card number and password, public keys can be openly shared, while it is crucial for users to securely safeguard their private keys. The private key grants complete access and control over all data in the corresponding account. Transactions in the blockchain network are typically signed and verified using asymmetric encryption algorithms. When a transaction is initiated, the initiator signs the original transaction information using the private key. The signed transaction, along with the initiator's public key, is then broadcasted into the blockchain network. Upon receiving the transaction, the blockchain node verifies its legitimacy using the public key. This mode ensures the secure transmission of confidential transaction data without exposing the initiator's private key.

4.2.4 Smart Contract

Smart contract is an automatically executed protocol based on trusted data on the blockchain [11]. It enables trusted, traceable, and immutable transactions without the need for a third party. Smart contracts were not obtained much attention before the advent of blockchain due to the lack of suitable execution environments and application scenarios. Previously, the focus was primarily on storing data on the blockchain, but the emergence of smart contracts allows for the execution of logic, opening up new possibilities for utilizing blockchain technology [12].

In a blockchain system, the establishment and execution of smart contracts consist of the following three steps.

Step 1: Users from multiple parties collectively create and sign a smart contract. First of all, the relevant parties collaborate to draft a contract that outlines their respective rights and obligations based on their transaction requirements. Next, these rights and obligations are programmatically encoded in electronic form, including the conditions that trigger the execution of the contract. Finally, participants use their private keys to sign the contract to ensure its validity. In this way, a smart contract becomes an electronic agreement with legal force.

Step 2: The smart contract is propagated to each node through the P2P network and waits to be packaged into blocks and written into the blockchain. The contract is disseminated to each node through the P2P network, and the node that receives the contract verifies its validity and waits for a new round of consensus [13, 14]. At the consensus moment, the mining node packages the valid contracts generated in the recent consensus interval into a set of contracts and encapsulates them into blocks and writes them into the blockchain, as shown in Fig. 4.2.

Step 3: Smart contracts are automatically executed, periodically checking their encapsulated state machines, transactions, and trigger events. The schematic diagram of smart contract blocks is shown in Fig. 4.3. Transactions that meet the trigger events are placed into a queue to be verified and wait for consensus. After the consensus is completed, the smart contract is automatically executed and transferred to the users. The results of the execution of the smart contract are written into the blockchain and cannot be tampered with or revoked [15].

Once all transactions within the contract have been executed in a certain order, the state machine marks the contract as completed, and the contract is removed from the latest block. Instead, the contract is marked as in progress and continues to be stored in the latest block for the next round until all transactions in that contract are processed.

The automatic execution of smart contracts enables blockchain systems to implement more complex business logic beyond simple data storage. Smart contracts can also interact with other smart contracts to form larger business networks. Smart contracts have a wide range of applications, including finance, supply chain, Internet of Things, digital identity, and other fields [16, 17].

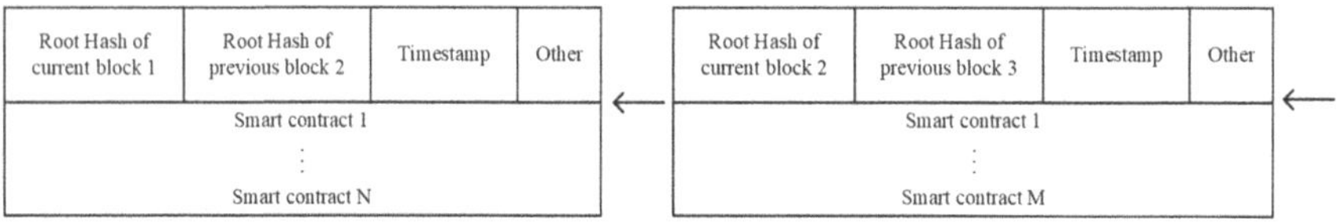

Fig. 4.2 Contract block [1]

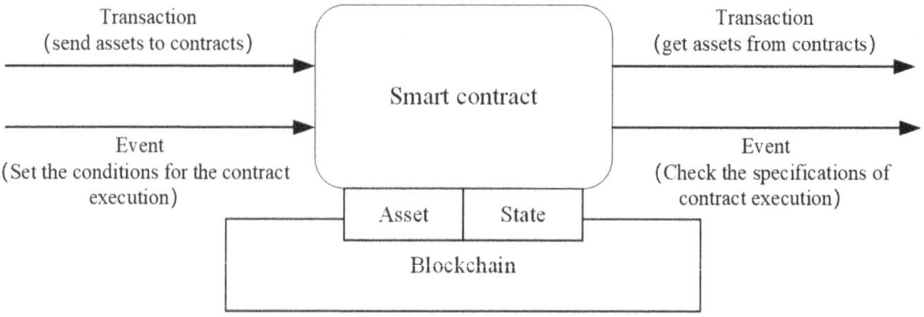

Fig. 4.3 Smart contract block [1]

4.3 Blockchain-Based Identifier Management

The Internet should be a distributed, equal, and globally accessible system. However, the current domain name system (DNS) lacks autonomy, resulting in certain countries and institutions having relative control over it. Additionally, the traditional DNS faces numerous issues, including low efficiency, uneven service distribution, vulnerability to information tampering, and weak resistance to distributed denial of service (DDoS) attacks. These problems pose threats to national information security. Extensive research and practical experience have demonstrated that the existing DNS, along with its optimizations and alternative solutions, cannot fundamentally address the centralization problem [18].

There is a growing desire among various organizations and entities to participate in domain name services and promote net neutrality. In recent years, blockchain technology has gained popularity due to its characteristics of decentralization, immutable timing data, and high security. Leveraging blockchain technology, the development of an autonomous, controllable, open, and shared distributed domain name system holds great significance in driving the advancement of emerging network technologies [19].

There are some challenges to building the DNS using blockchain technology, including:

Data storage limitations: The blockchain's log structure requires all state changes to be recorded on the chain, and all participating nodes must maintain a full copy of the block record. This limits the scalability of the blockchain, as existing hardware technology may not support large-scale storage requirements.

Slow write speed: The processing rate of transactions is affected by the consensus algorithm employed. Typically, it takes several minutes to several hours for new transactions to be accepted, which can result in slower write speeds compared to traditional systems.

Bandwidth limitations: The total transaction volume per block is determined by the block size. In order to maintain fairness, all nodes should accept newly published blocks at roughly the same time. Therefore, the block size is usually limited by the uplink bandwidth of the node. For example, with the current bandwidth of Bitcoin, the block size is 1 MB (approximately 1000 transactions).

To promote equal participation among different countries, organizations, and research institutions in the domain name management system and address the above challenges, the research group of the MIN network has proposed a novel multi-identifier system (MIS) based on blockchain technology [20–27]. Please refer to [27] for a detailed introduction to MIS.

MIS offers support for diverse addressing modes based on multiple identifiers such as identity, content, service, spatial location, and IP address. It enables decentralized management, multi-stakeholder participation, multilateral governance, and equal openness in domain name resolution. It also promotes the construction of a community with a shared future in cyberspace. The architecture of MIS is shown in Fig. 4.4.

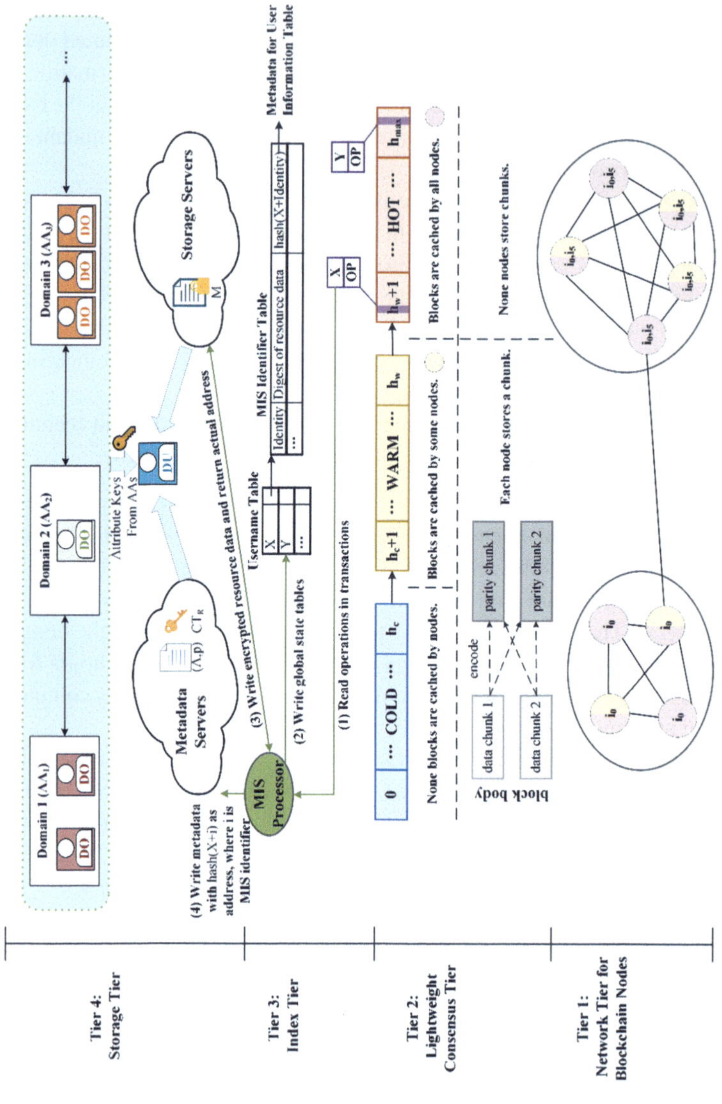

Fig. 4.4 The overall architecture of MIS [23]

In MIS, the steps for identifier registration are as follows:

Step 1: Any identifier that requires routing and addressing needs to be registered in advance with the network. The resource can be accessed by other nodes on the network only after the identifier is authenticated by the consortium blockchain and assigned to it. If a user applies for the registration of an intra-domain identifier, the user only needs to complete the consensus authentication in the local domain, and its detailed data is stored in the local database of the global node in the domain. If a user applies for the registration of an inter-domain identifier, consensus authentication must be conducted in both relevant domains. The detailed data information is stored in the local databases of the respective global nodes after receiving signatures from both parties.

Step 2: After the local consortium blockchain receives the identifier registration request transmitted by the user, the consortium blockchain node reviews its content and reaches a consensus within the domain. Subsequently, the locally generated identifier registration block is uploaded to the upper-level consortium blockchain with the local identifier prefix attached.

Step 3: After receiving the identifier registration block, the upper-level blockchain node uses a routing protocol to transmit the registration message to the controller in the respective domain for further authentication and registration operations.

Step 4: Upon receiving the identifier registration block from the first-level blockchain, the top-level consortium blockchain node verifies the data in the block and returns the corresponding confirmation signal to the original node. Due to the separation of the blockchain database from the block content in the system, the original identifier information is stored in the blockchain database of the top-level domain. Whenever a request is completed, the whole network carries out the synchronization of corresponding blockchain databases to ensure the equivalence and unity of the resource identifier information among the top-level domain servers.

In MIS, the process for requesting network resources is as follows [24]:

Step 1: When the requested content has been registered the network, the user can utilize the corresponding uniform resource identifier to send the content request to the network.

Step 2: When the nearest router receives the request sent by the user, it queries the forwarding table to determine whether to forward the request to the upper-level server. If the corresponding identifier content is stored in the local consortium blockchain, the router returns the content. Otherwise, it proceeds to Step 3.

Step 3: If the corresponding identifier is not available in the local consortium blockchain database, the request is uploaded to the upper consortium blockchain node. After receiving the request from the lower-level node, the node of the upper-level consortium blockchain performs the query according to Steps 1 and 2. If the corresponding identifier is found, it is returned to the lower-level consortium blockchain node. Otherwise, the request continues to be forwarded to the upper-level consortium blockchain node until it reaches the top-level consortium blockchain node.

Step 4: If a top-level consortium blockchain server finds a registered identifier, it automatically issues the shortest path based on the dynamic topology of the existing network. The related routers on the forwarding path receive the new forwarding path table and establish the data transmission path through the multi-hop route. If no corresponding identifier is found at the top-level consortium blockchain node, proceed to Step 5.

Step 5: The top-level consortium blockchain node forward the request to the specific consortium blockchain according to the first prefix of the identifier until the lowest consortium blockchain node specified by the request is reached for performing local query. If the corresponding identifier content is successfully queried, the corresponding content is passed to the requester; otherwise, an error message is returned.

In the implementation of identifier registration, top-level identifiers are registered using the short encoding format, while second-level identifiers and subsequent levels of domain names are required to conform to the long encoding format. The levels of identifiers are separated by "/". All identifiers registered on the blockchain must obtain the signature of the server node from the top-level domain within their respective domains. Additionally, the short encoding of the top-level domain server is automatically appended to the URL path, enabling the top-level domain server to facilitate resolution and oversight functions for the different levels of domains within the respective domain [25, 26].

References

1. Li H, Wang H. Principle and application of blockchain consensus algorithm. Beijing: Science Press; 2019.
2. Yuan Y, Wang FY. Current status and prospects of blockchain technology development. Acta Automat Sin. 2016;42(4):481–94.
3. Murray A, Kim D, Combs J. The promise of a decentralized internet: what is Web3 and how can firms prepare? Bus Horiz. 2023;66(2):191–202.
4. Thyagarajan SAK, Bhat A, Magri B, et al. Reparo: publicly verifiable layer to repair blockchains. In: International conference on financial cryptography and data security. Berlin: Springer; 2021. p. 37–56.
5. Ahmadjee S, Mera-Gómez C, Bahsoon R, et al. A study on blockchain architecture design decisions and their security attacks and threats. ACM Trans Softw Eng Methodol. 2022;31(2):1–45.
6. Li K, Li H, Wang H, et al. PoV: an efficient voting-based consensus algorithm for consortium blockchains. Front Blockchain. 2020;3:11.
7. Li H, Li KJ, Huang JS, et al. A consensus method based on voting. CN109964446B,2022-03-25.
8. Bai Y, Zhi Y, Li H, et al. On parallel mechanism of consortium blockchain: Take pov as an example. In: 2021 the 3rd International Conference on Blockchain Technology, 2021, p. 147–154.
9. Li H, Huang JS, Wang H, et al. A consensus method based on parallel voting. CN112104482B,2021-06-29.
10. Xiao Z, Li H, Wang H, et al. Optimizing parallel proof of vote consensus based on mimic security in consortium blockchains. In: 2022 IEEE international conference on big data (big data), vol. 2022. Piscataway: IEEE. p. 3215–24.

11. Liwei O, Shuai W, Yong Y, et al. Smart contracts: architecture and progress. Acta Automat Sin. 2019;45(3):445–57.
12. Szabo N. Smart contracts: building blocks for digital markets. Extropy. 1996;18(2):28.
13. Mueller B. Smashing ethereum smart contracts for fun and real profit. HITB SECCONF. 2018;9:54.
14. Beksultanova AI, Tkachenko AL. Analysis tools for smart contract security. In: 2nd international conference on computer applications for management and sustainable development of production and industry (CMSD-II-2022), vol. 12564. Bellingham: SPIE; 2023. p. 221–8.
15. Yao Y, Li H, Yang X, et al. An improved vulnerability detection system of smart contracts based on symbolic execution. In: 2022 IEEE international conference on big data (big data), vol. 2022. Piscataway: IEEE. p. 3225–34.
16. Shou C, Tan S, Sen K. Ityfuzz: snapshot-based fuzzer for smart contract. In: Proceedings of the 32nd ACM SIGSOFT international symposium on software testing and analysis, 2023, p. 322–333.
17. Babel K, Daian P, Kelkar M, et al. Clockwork finance: automated analysis of economic security in smart contracts. In: 2023 IEEE symposium on security and privacy, vol. 2023. Piscataway: IEEE. p. 2499–516.
18. Wang Y, Li H, Huang T, et al. Scalable identifier system for industrial internet based on multi-identifier network architecture. IEEE Internet Things J. 2021;10(3):1919–32.
19. Wei GH, Li H, Bai YJ, et al. Space-terrestrial integrated multi-identifier network with endogenous security. Space Integrated Ground Inf Netw. 2020;1(2):66–72.
20. Li H, Li KJ, Chen YL, et al. A consensus method for decentralized domain name system. CN109792437B,2021-01-12.
21. Li H, Wu JX, Xing KX, et al. Prototype and testing report of a multi-identifier system for reconfigurable network architecture under co-governing. Sci Sin Inf. 2019;49(9):1186–204.
22. Li H, Wang XG, Lin ZL, et al. A method and system of top-level domain name management based on consortium chain. CN108124502A,2018-06-05.
23. Wang H, Li H, Smahi A, et al. MIS: a multi-identifier management and resolution system in the metaverse. In: ACM transactions on multimedia computing, communications and applications. New York: ACM; 2023. p. 1–28.
24. Li H, Ma HJ, Li HP et al. A domain name resolution system based on blockchain. CN108064444B,2020-05-19.
25. Wang H, Li H, Ye Q, et al. A physical topology for optimizing partition tolerance in consortium blockchains to reach CAP guarantee bound. Trans Emerg Telecommun Technol. 2023;34:e4820.
26. Wang H, Li H, Smahi A, et al. GBT-CHAIN: a system framework for solving the general trilemma in permissioned blockchains. Distrib Ledger Technol Res Pract. 2023;3:1–16.
27. Li H, Wang H. Principle & applications of blockchain systems: how to overcome the CAP trilemma in consortium blockchain. Hoboken: Wiley; 2024.

Chapter 5
Addressing and Routing

At present, the design and implementation of CoG-MIN [1] are undergoing continuous evolution. In comparison to IP networks and NDN networks, the addressing and routing mechanisms in CoG-MIN require adaptation to its unique characteristics in order to ensure optimal performance [2]. This chapter provides an introduction to the addressing and routing mechanisms within CoG-MIN, covering existing research studies, advanced hyperbolic routing algorithms, and the dynamic routing protocol in CoG-MIN.

5.1 Overview of Addressing and Routing

Addressing and routing are indispensable components in network communication. Addressing refers to finding network devices through given addresses, while routing is the process of selecting suitable paths to reach those network devices. They are complementary and mutually dependent, aiming to transmit data to specified addresses through interconnected networks.

Routing can be classified into two categories based on how routing table entries are generated: static routing and dynamic routing. Static routing involves manually configuring routing table entries, and nodes forward data based on these entries. Static routing is not suitable for larger networks with complex or frequently changing topologies. On the other hand, dynamic routing calculates paths through specific routing protocols and generates routing table entries based on the computed results.

Dynamic routing protocols can be broadly classified into two types: distance-vector routing protocols and link state routing protocols.

Specifically, distance-vector routing protocols determine the path for packet exchange using distance-vector algorithms, such as Bellman-Ford, Diffusing

H. Li, H. Bai, *Principle of Architecture, Protocol, and Algorithms for CoG-MIN*,
https://doi.org/10.1007/978-981-96-3596-2_5

Update Algorithm Finite State Machine (DUAL FSM), and Ford-Fulkerson. In these protocols, routers periodically exchange routing updates with neighboring routers and dynamically build routing tables to determine the shortest path. In networks that use distance-vector algorithms, each router only knows the network topology directly connected to itself and the routing information provided by its neighbors, updating its routing table accordingly. Distance-vector algorithms are widely used in many protocols, such as Routing Information Protocol (RIP), Interior Gateway Routing Protocol (IGRP), and Border Gateway Protocol (BGP).

Link state routing protocols use Dijkstra's shortest path first (SPF) algorithm, also known as the distributed database protocol or shortest path first protocol. Compared to distance-vector routing protocols, link state routing protocols have more complex functions and configurations, but their algorithms are easier to understand. Link state routing protocols gather information from all other routers in the network or a limited area of the network, and eventually, each link state router has the same information about the network. Each router calculates its optimal path independently.

Distance-vector routing protocols are relatively simple in terms of implementation and management, but they have slow convergence speed, generate large amounts of network traffic, consume significant network bandwidth and computational resources, and require special handling to avoid routing loops. In contrast, link state routing protocols are more complex but exhibit better scalability and convergence, and they react faster to changes in network state. Unlike distance-vector routing protocols, which transmit the entire routing table of a node to neighboring nodes, link state routing protocols only need to transmit the node's adjacent link information, resulting in less network resource utilization. However, the drawback is that link state routing protocols require more storage space and better computational capabilities.

Based on different communication semantics, network architectures can be divided into three categories. The first category is network architectures that use push-based semantics, such as IP architecture. The second category is network architectures that use pull-based semantics, such as NDN. The third category is network architectures that combine push-based and pull-based semantics, such as the MIN architecture. The IP architecture uses push-based semantics for data transmission, where end-to-end communication relies on IP addresses, and data transmission occurs after establishing a connection between two communicating hosts. NDN and similar content-centric architectures use pull-based semantics for data transmission, with routing and addressing based solely on the content name. MIN is designed as a hybrid push–pull transmission mode [3]. In the routing schemes of MIN, both push-based and pull-based communication semantics are utilized [4]. First, the link states are synchronized within the nodes, and then the available paths are calculated using the shortest path algorithm. To support multipath forwarding, the available paths are sorted based on path costs. This can reduce the frequency of routing table updates.

5.2 Development of Addressing and Routing Technologies

5.2.1 Traditional Network Routing Algorithms

Routing calculations can be performed using two common methods: the link state routing algorithms and the distance-vector routing algorithms. These algorithms differ in how they gather routing information and perform calculations. A common method for routing calculation involves determining the shortest path based on network topology. The shortest path algorithm plays a crucial role in generating routing table information by calculating the shortest paths between nodes within the network topology. This information is then utilized to guide packet forwarding in routing. Several widely used algorithms for determining the shortest path such as Dijkstra's algorithm, Johnson's algorithm, and Bellman-Ford algorithm this section introduces the fundamental operational principles of the link state routing algorithms and the distance-vector routing algorithms. It also includes dedicated explanations for the shortest path algorithms employed in these methods.

Link State Routing Algorithm

The link state involves information about the connections between routers, such as network interface addresses, link costs, and network types. In link state routing algorithms, each router collects link state information sent by other routers in the network and maintains this information locally. Based on this information, routers can perform routing calculations and make forwarding decisions. Assuming the network topology remains constant, all link state routers in the network eventually obtain consistent link information about the network. The link state routing algorithm involves the following basic processing steps:

Routers acquire network addresses of neighboring routers and other related information, measure the latency to the neighboring router's link as a routing metric, and maintain the link information with the neighboring routers.

The router constructs a link state packet based on the link information with all neighboring routers and includes information about all adjacent links in this packet.

The routers propagate link information packets to each other through network packets (constructed using the next-layer network protocol of the routing protocol), synchronizing the collected link information packets into router storage.

Each router constructs a network topology graph $G(V, E)$ by collecting link state information packets from neighboring routers, where nodes V represent all router nodes, and edges E represent the link relationships between different nodes.

Each router uses a shortest path algorithm to calculate the shortest paths between itself and all other routers in the network topology graph $G(V, E)$, updating its local routing table based on this information.

Distance-Vector Routing Algorithm

The term "distance vector" in the context of routing algorithms literally means "distance in a certain direction." In distance-vector routing algorithms, it refers to two key pieces of information: the route cost (distance) and the next hop (vector). Unlike link state-based routers, distance-vector-based routers can only calculate and update their own routes based on routing table information obtained from neighboring routers. As a result, they do not have knowledge of the entire network topology. The distance-vector routing algorithms involve the following basic processing steps:

The routers initialize and construct routing tables by setting the route cost to default values (usually 0 or 1) for neighboring routers.
The routers exchange their routing table information with each other.
Based on the received routing table information from other routers, the routers use a shortest path algorithm to calculate the shortest paths. Then, they update the routing table with any changes to these shortest paths.

Compared to the link state routing algorithm, the distance-vector routing algorithm is simpler and requires less storage and computational capacity. However, the distance-vector routing algorithm also has several drawbacks. For example, it necessitates the continuous propagation of network updates to neighboring routers following routing table calculations and updates, leading to slower convergence speeds. Additionally, it disseminates entire routing table information rather than just the differences in network topology information between two routers, resulting in higher network overhead. Furthermore, to avoid routing loops, special mechanisms need to be designed and implemented.

5.2.2 Traditional Network Routing Protocols

In IP networks, routing protocols are further divided into Interior Gateway Protocols (IGPs) and Exterior Gateway Protocols (EGPs) based on their operational scope. An Autonomous System (AS) refers to a collection of networks and routers managed by a single entity that implements common routing strategies. In the Internet, the EGP protocols (e.g., BGP) operate between different ASs, while the IGP protocols (e.g., RIP, OSPF, and IS-IS) function within a single AS. In IP networks, different routing protocols may utilize various underlying network protocols, which can be either network layer protocols (such as the IP protocol) or transport layer protocols (such as UDP and TCP protocols). Table 5.1 compares four routing protocols in IP networks.

The Routing Information Protocol (RIP) is a routing protocol based on the distance-vector routing algorithm. It uses the User Datagram Protocol (UDP) as the underlying network protocol. RIP calculates routes using the Bellman-Ford algorithm and is primarily suitable for small-scale networks. However, it has some drawbacks, such as slow convergence and limited network scale.

Table 5.1 Comparison of routing protocols in IP networks

Routing protocol	Routing algorithm adopted	Underlying network protocol	Operation scope
RIP	Distance vector	UDP	IGP
OSPF	Link state	IP	
IS-IS	Link state	IP	
BGP	Distance vector	TCP	EGP

The Open Shortest Path First (OSPF) protocol and Intermediate System to Intermediate System (IS-IS) protocol are both link state routing protocols that use IP as the underlying network protocol. These protocols use the shortest path first (SPF) algorithm to calculate routes, maintain neighboring relationships using the Hello protocol, and divide the network into areas for deployment in large-scale networks. The IS-IS protocol was initially specified by ISO standards and not directly applicable to IP networks. The IETF developed an Integrated IS-IS protocol that enables its operation in the TCP/IP environment.

The Border Gateway Protocol (BGP) is an external gateway protocol with decentralized autonomous characteristics, unlike the previous three internal gateway protocols. BGP uses the Transmission Control Protocol (TCP) to propagate routing information. Similar to Distance-Vector protocols, BGP provides next hop node information for the destination network. BGP publishes routing information containing a list of all autonomous systems that the IP network packets should traverse, which differs from the standard distance-vector protocol.

5.2.3 Emerging Technologies for Addressing and Routing

In NDN, routing protocols can be categorized into three types based on their design characteristics: (1) Enhanced IP routing, which refers to NDN routing schemes that extend the IP routing mechanism. (2) Geometric routing, which involves assigning coordinates to each node and then calculating the routes based on these coordinates. (3) Centralized routing, which draws on the concept of Software Defined Networking (SDN) and establishes a centralized control plane, with regular network nodes being responsible only for data forwarding. Table 5.2 introduces typical routing protocols in NDN.

The OSPFN protocol (OSPF for Named data) [5] is a preliminary link state routing protocol designed for Named Data Networking (NDN). It defines a new type of opaque link state advertisements (LSA) to announce name prefixes and supports the advertisement of name prefixes from multiple sites, whether they are the same or different. Additionally, OSPFN incorporates a configured multipath feature to address the limitation of OSPF in providing only a single best path to each destination.

The Named data Link State Routing protocol (NLSR) is an improved version of the OSPFN protocol. NLSR adopts a hierarchical naming scheme for routers, route

Table 5.2 Comparison of routing protocols in NDN

Routing protocol	Network environment	Category	Design features
OSPFN [5]	NDN overlay IP	Enhanced IP-based routing	A link state routing protocol (reserved IP)
NLSR [6]	NDN	Enhanced IP-based routing	A link state routing protocol without IP; and support multipath forwarding
MUCA [7]	NDN	Enhanced IP-based routing	Combine the advantages of link state algorithm and distance-vector algorithm; and support multipath forwarding and in-network caching
N-BGP [8]	NDN	Enhanced IP-based routing	A distance-vector routing protocol (reserved IP)
HR [9]	NDN	Geometric routing	Based on the hyperbolic coordinates of nodes, and the greedy algorithm is used to calculate routing paths
SDAR [10]	SDN-based NDN	Centralized routing	Maintain a centralized network control plane
SRSC [11]	SDN-based CCN	Centralized routing	Maintain a centralized network control plane

updates, and keys. It operates within NDN and uses a pull-based communication model. NLSR delegates the routing information dissemination to synchronization protocols such as ChronoSync [12] and PSync [13].

The MUltipath forwarding and in-network CAching protocol (MUCA) is similar to the link state routing protocol, MUCA collects network topology information and calculates the shortest paths to content producers. Additionally, routers running MUCA learn multiple alternative paths from neighboring routers, resembling distance-vector routing protocols. MUCA improves the caching hit ratio by enabling internal routers to select the same edge-router for the same name prefix.

Hyperbolic Routing (HR) is a coordinate-based geometric routing solution that can address the routing scalability issue in NDN. In this scheme, nodes propagate coordinate information containing characteristics of the network topology. Routers utilize these coordinates to compute routes and forward network packets to the neighboring node that is closest in terms of the target node's coordinate.

Software Defined Intra-Domain Routing in NDN (SDAR) and the SDN-based Routing Scheme for CCN (SRSC) are two centralized routing solutions. By employing a centralized network control plane, these approaches offer advantages in terms of simplified route configuration and enhanced network control capabilities compared to distributed routing protocols. In centralized routing, route updates are exclusively sent to the controller, which performs route calculations. However, centralized routing also presents certain challenges, such as convergence delays due to ordinary router failures and the risk of a single point of failure for the controller.

Named Data Border Gateway Protocol (N-BGP), similar to the OSPFN protocol, can efficiently propagate, receive, process, and store both IP-based and name-based routing information. N-BGP supports various routing policies. It achieves superior routing efficiency and lower network overhead compared to other routing protocols while maintaining good network stability.

5.3 Hyperbolic Routing Algorithm

5.3.1 Overview of Hyperbolic Routing

In the information era, the Internet has become a ubiquitous infrastructure, with extensive interconnections of large-scale Autonomous Systems (ASs) forming a global network. However, as the network scale continues to expand and the number of network devices increases, the routing costs for networks are exhibiting an exponential growth trend.

Hyperbolic routing draws inspiration from the observation that computer networks exhibit a scale-free property, wherein the degree distribution of nodes follows a power law. This distribution signifies that most nodes are connected to only a few others, while a small fraction of nodes possess high connectivity. The probability of two nodes being connected has a form similar to Newton's Law of Universal Gravitation. Building upon this observation, the expected connectivity degree of each node can be considered as its weight, resulting in the bending of space. In this way, the expected degree of nodes can be viewed as a geometric property. Furthermore, the computer network can be mapped onto a curved hyperbolic geometry space with a non-zero curvature. This allows for a deeper exploration of the network's fundamental characteristics and provides a theoretical foundation for distance-based greedy routing strategies.

In early research, Boguná et al. [14] introduced the Einsteinian model, a hyperbolic geometric space network model. This model effectively captures the scale-free nature of complex network topologies.

As depicted in Fig. 5.1, all nodes are situated within a two-dimensional hyperbolic disc with radius R. The radial node density exponentially increases as the distance from the origin O grows, while the average degree of nodes exponentially decreases. This follows a power law degree distribution. The red lines show triangle Oab made of the hyperbolic geodesics (that is, shortest paths in the hyperbolic space) connecting origin O and two nodes a and b. Geodesics $\overline{Oa}$ and $\overline{Ob}$ are the solid red lines. Geodesic $\overline{ab}$ is the dashed curve. The thick blue links depict the shortest path from node a to node b.

Similar to the synthetic Einsteinian network in Figs. 5.1 and 5.2 illustrates the Internet's hyperbolic map. The size of AS nodes is proportional to the logarithm of their degree. To enhance clarity, only AS with a degree larger than 3 and connections with a probability $p(x) > 0.5$ are displayed. The font size of the country name is proportional to the logarithm of the number of ASs in the country. Only countries with more than ten ASs are labeled. In densely connected regions, there is a mutual attraction between ASs, leading to their clustering. Conversely, in sparsely connected regions, ASs tend to repel each other, resulting in a more dispersed

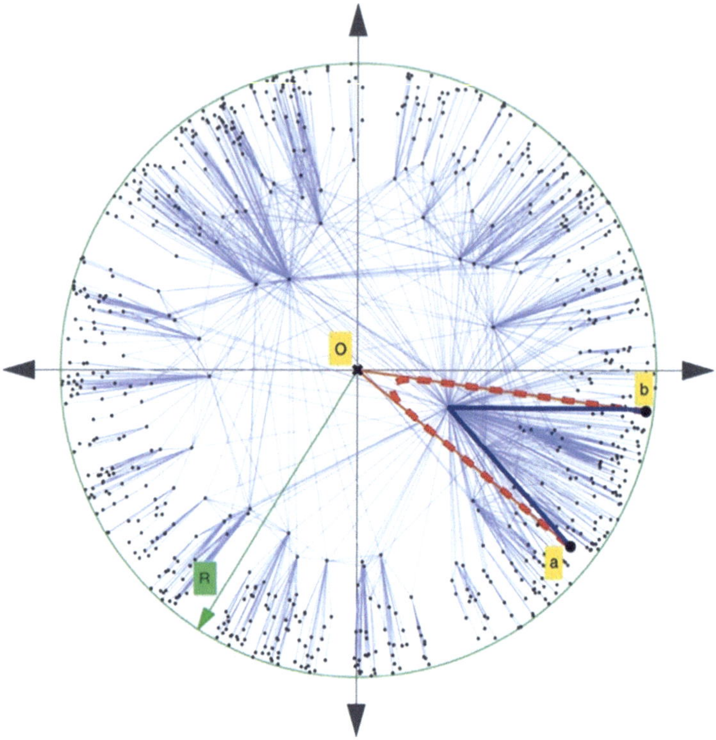

Fig. 5.1 Synthetic network in the Einsteinian model [14]

arrangement. This mapping method effectively captures the characteristics of the actual Internet structure and can be applied to analyze structural features in other complex networks as well.

5.3.2 Hyperbolic Routing Model

Hyperbolic Space

Hyperbolic geometry [15] is also referred to as Lobachevskian geometry. It was developed by the Russian mathematician Nikolai Lobachevsky in the nineteenth century. One of the key postulates of Lobachevskian geometry is that through a given point, more than one parallel line can be drawn to a given line, which contradicts Euclid's parallel postulate. This postulate forms the basis for the exploration and study of hyperbolic geometries and their applications in various fields, including physics, computer science, and network analysis.

In hyperbolic geometry, the sum of the angles in a hyperbolic triangle is always strictly less than π radians (180°). This property distinguishes hyperbolic geometry

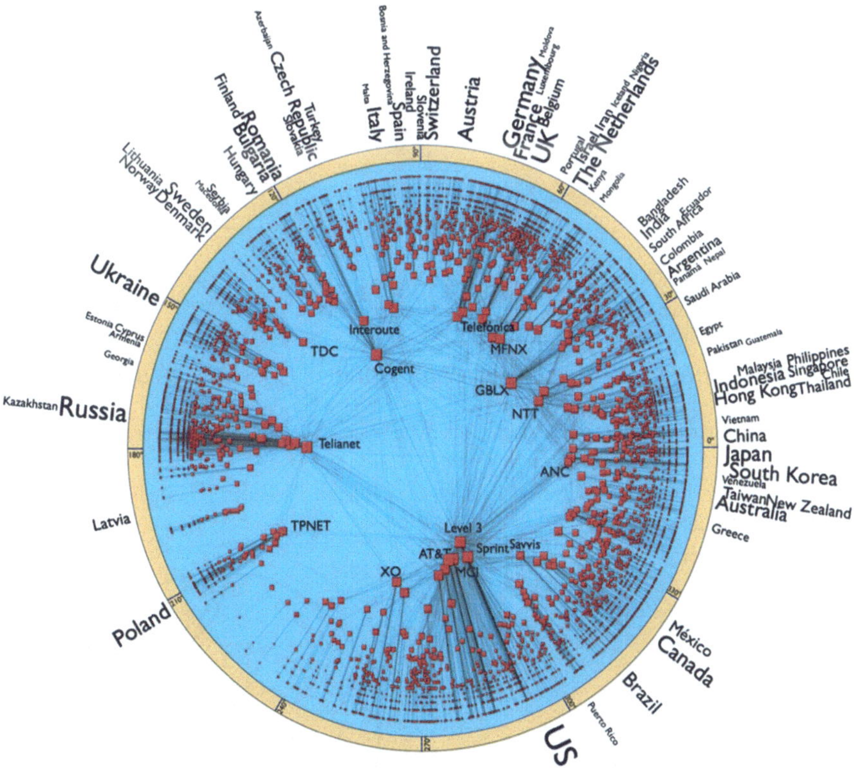

Fig. 5.2 Hyperbolic atlas of the Internet [14]

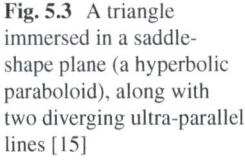

Fig. 5.3 A triangle immersed in a saddle-shape plane (a hyperbolic paraboloid), along with two diverging ultra-parallel lines [15]

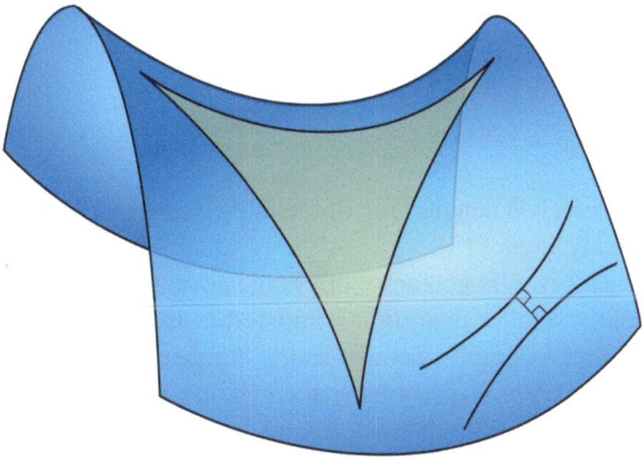

from Euclidean geometry, where the sum of the angles in a triangle is always equal to π radians (Figs. 5.3 and 5.4).

The difference between the sum of the angles in a hyperbolic triangle and π radians is referred to as the "defect." The area of a hyperbolic triangle is proportional to

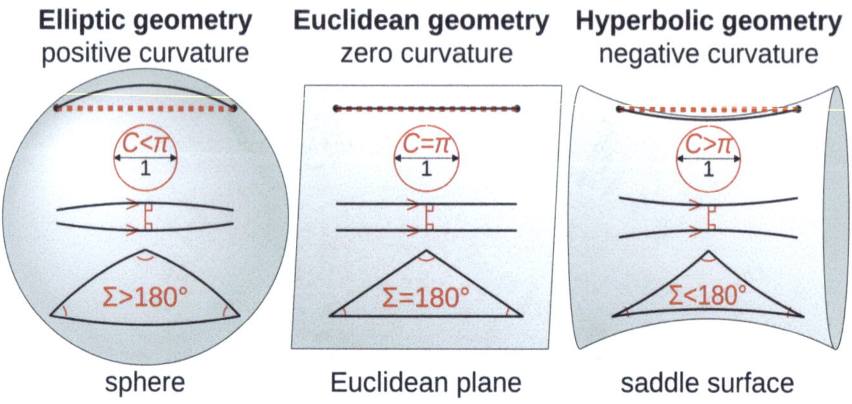

Fig. 5.4 Comparison of elliptic, Euclidean and hyperbolic geometries in two dimensions [15]

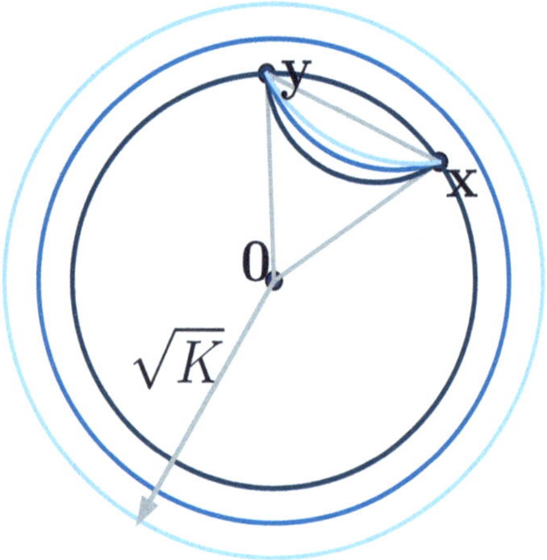

Fig. 5.5 The volume of hyperbolic geometry space grows exponentially with the radius [16]

its defect. When the sum of the internal angles of a hyperbolic triangle is smaller, its area is larger [15].

Hyperbolic geometry offers the advantage of enabling embeddings with significantly smaller distortion compared to Euclidean geometry. When considering the volume in graphs, defined as the number of nodes within a certain distance from a central node, hyperbolic space exhibits exponential growth in volume with respect to the radius. In contrast, Euclidean space shows only polynomial growth, leading to higher distortion in embeddings. The curvature of the hyperbolic space also plays a key role. As the curvature becomes more negative, the distance between the points with the same coordinates increases. This allows for more efficient and effective representations of data in hyperbolic space, particularly in capturing hierarchical and tree-like structures (Fig. 5.5).

Hyperbolic Model

In geometry, the Poincaré disk model is a model of 2-dimensional hyperbolic geometry. As shown in Fig. 5.6, this is an example of a two-dimensional hyperbolic surface in three-dimensional space. Rays are emitted from the bottommost point, passing through the gray Poincaré disk to reach the green hyperbolic surface. The red arc represents a geodesic on the gray Poincaré disk model, which projects to the brown geodesic in the hyperbolic surface model in Poincaré disk space [17].

In the Poincaré disk model, all points reside within the unit disk, and straight lines are either circular arcs that lie completely inside the disk and are perpendicular to the unit circle, or they are diameters of the unit circle [18] (Fig. 5.7).

The Poincaré ball model is the similar model for 3 or n-dimensional hyperbolic geometry, where the points of the geometry are located within the n-dimensional unit ball [19] (Fig. 5.8).

Hyperbolic Distance

In the Poincaré disk model, let the complex numbers corresponding to any two nodes be w and w′, respectively. Then, the distance formula between these two points is shown in Eq. (5.1).

$$x = \log \frac{1+s}{1-s}. \tag{5.1}$$

$$s = \frac{|w - w'|}{1 - w\overline{w'}}. \tag{5.2}$$

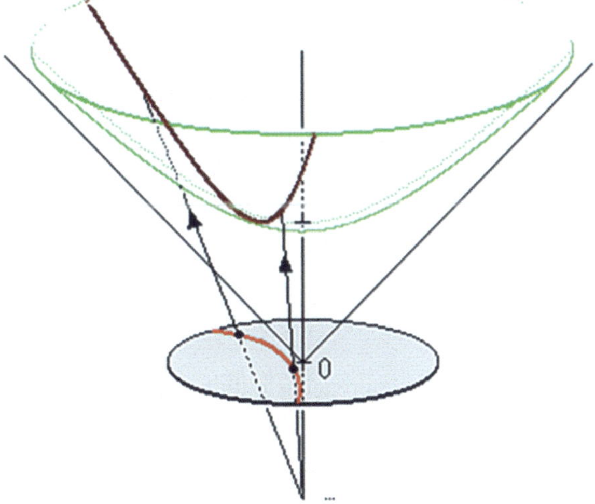

Fig. 5.6 Projective relation of hyperboloid and Poincaré models [17]

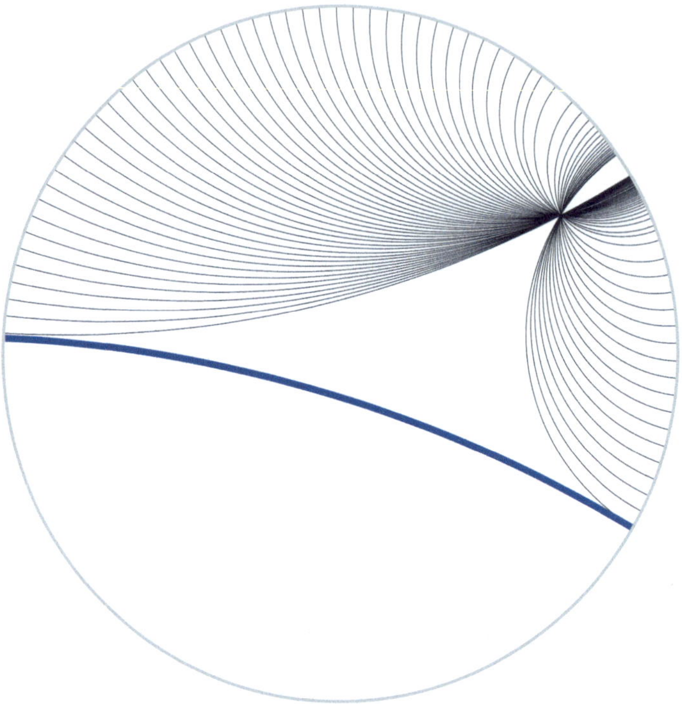

Fig. 5.7 Poincaré disk with hyperbolic parallel lines [18]

In the Poincaré disk model, the relationship between Euclidean distance and hyperbolic distance is expressed by Eq. (5.3). In this equation, r_e represents the Euclidean distance, and r_h represents the hyperbolic distance.

$$r_e = \tanh\left(\frac{r_h}{2}\right). \tag{5.3}$$

The purpose of establishing the Extended Poincaré model is to align the visually perceived distances with the actual hyperbolic distances. As the angles remain unchanged, let (R, θ) and (r, θ) represent the polar coordinates of any point in the Poincaré disk and the Extended Poincaré disk, respectively. The relationship between R and r is expressed by Eq. (5.4).

$$r = \tanh\left(\frac{R}{2}\right). \tag{5.4}$$

For $\tanh(x)$, as the value of x approaches infinity, the function value tends to 1. The Poincaré disk has a radius of 1 unit, so the Extended Poincaré disk corresponds to a space with an infinite radius.

For any two points in the Extended Poincaré disk, with polar coordinates (r, θ) and (r', θ'), the hyperbolic distance [15] between them is denoted as x and is given by Eq. (5.5).

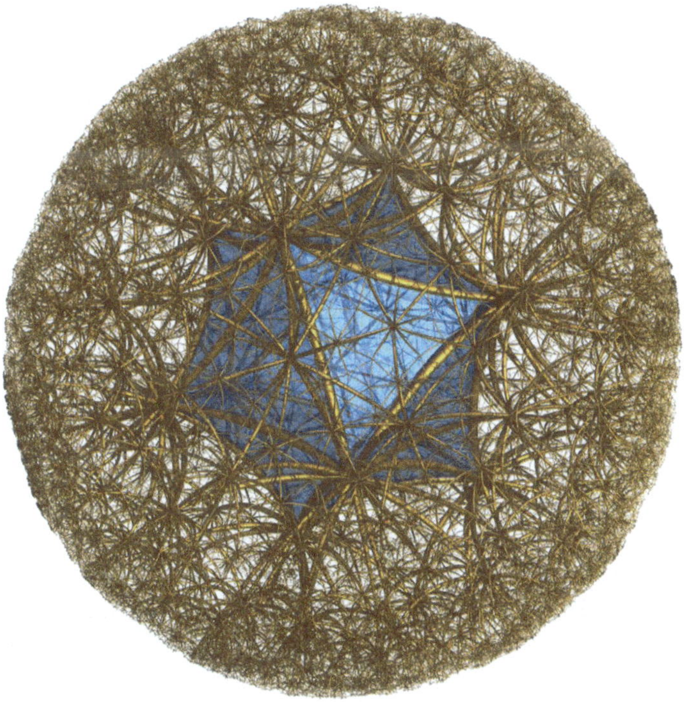

Fig. 5.8 Poincaré sphere model [18]

$$\cosh x = \cosh(r)\cosh(r') - \sin(r)\sinh(r')\cos(\Delta\theta). \tag{5.5}$$

Hyperbolic Routing

Hyperbolic routing employs a simple greedy strategy. It relies on minimal routing information, whereby each current node only needs to compute the hyperbolic distance to the destination node for each of its neighboring nodes and then prioritize the forwarding of the packet to the node with the smallest distance. Network topologies of any scale and node degree can be embedded in a hyperbolic plane without the need for dimension reduction and high-dimensional calculations. For scale-free networks, greedy routing paths based on hyperbolic coordinates are close to optimal routing paths.

The greedy routing based on hyperbolic coordinates includes the following steps:

We assume that the hyperbolic coordinate of source node is (r_s, θ_s) and the hyperbolic coordinate of destination node is (r_d, θ_d). The hyperbolic coordinate of destination node is encapsulated in the packet. Then, the source node forward the packet toward destination node.

Upon receiving the packet, the intermediate node calculates the hyperbolic distance from its neighboring nodes (r_i, θ_i) to the destination node (r_d, θ_d) using the distance formula (Eq. (5.5)). The calculation involves Eq. (5.6), where θ_{id} is the difference in angles between the two points, i.e., $\theta_{id} = \pi - |\pi - |\theta_i - \theta_d||$. The intermediate node then forward the packet to the neighboring node that is closest to the destination node. This process is repeated hop by hop until the packet ultimately reaches the destination node (r_d, θ_d).

$$x_{id} = \operatorname{arccosh}\left(\cosh r_i \cosh r_j - \sinh r_i \sinh r_j \cos\theta_{id}\right) \tag{5.6}$$

5.3.3 Hyperbolic Embedding Algorithm

The essential prerequisite for hyperbolic routing is obtaining the hyperbolic coordinates of nodes in the hyperbolic space based on the hyperbolic embedding algorithm. For the Internet, the hyperbolic embedding algorithm can be used to obtain the hyperbolic coordinates of each AS node. In theory, a good hyperbolic embedding algorithm can achieve nearly 100% routing success rate.

The classic hyperbolic embedding algorithm is HyperMap algorithm proposed by Papadopoulos et al. in 2015 [20]. It can embed any network topology $G(V, E)$ into the hyperbolic space and compute the hyperbolic coordinate (r, θ) of each mapped node. The process of the HyperMap algorithm is as follows (Algorithm 5.1):

Step 1: Arranging the nodes of the input network topology $G(V, E)$, with a scale of t, in the decreasing order of their degrees. Define node i, $i = 1, 2, \ldots, t$, as the node with degree k_i, where $k_1 > k_2 > \ldots > k_t$.

Step 2: Simulating the growth process of the network. Starting by selecting the node with the highest degree as the origin in hyperbolic space, setting its initial radial coordinate as $r_1 = 0$ and the initial angular coordinate θ_1 as any value in $[0, 2\pi]$.

Step 3: Following the descending order of nodes as arranged in Step 1, starting from the second node, proceed by taking a node i $(2 \le i \le t)$ each time. Initialize its radial coordinate as $r_i = \frac{2}{\zeta} ln i$, where ζ is the curvature parameter. Based on the newly added node's radial coordinate, modify the radial coordinates of all previously existing nodes $j()$ as $r_i(i) = \beta r_j + (1 - \beta) r_i$. Then, by solving the maximum likelihood estimation for the formula $L = \prod p\left(x_{ij}\right)^{\alpha_{ij}}\left[1 - p\left(x_{ij}\right)\right]^{1-\alpha_{ij}}$, determine the angular coordinate θ_i for node i. Here, x_{ij} represents the hyperbolic distance, w h e r e $x_{ij} = \frac{1}{\zeta}\operatorname{arccosh}\left(\cosh\zeta r_i \cosh\zeta r_j - \sinh\zeta r_i \sinh\zeta r_j \cos\theta_{ij}\right) \approx r_i + r_j + \frac{2}{\zeta}\ln\left(\frac{\theta_{ij}}{2}\right)$; $p(x_{ij})$ represents the connection probability, where $p\left(x_{ij}\right) = \frac{1}{1 + e^{\frac{\zeta}{2T}\left(x_{ij} - R_i\right)}}$.

Step 4: Repeating the calculation process in Step 3 until every node is assigned unique hyperbolic coordinate.

Algorithm 5.1: HyperMap embedding algorithm

Input: Undirected connected Graph $G = (V, E)$

Output: Hyperbolic coordinates $(r_i, \theta_i)_{i=1}^{t}$ $(t = |V|)$

1: Sort node degrees in decreasing order $k_1 > k_2 > \ldots > k_t$ with ties broken arbitrarily.
2: Call node i, $i = 1, 2, \ldots, t$, the node with degree k_i.
3: Node $i = 1$ is born, assign to it initial radial coordinate $r_1 = 0$ and random angular coordinate $\theta_1 \in [0, 2\pi]$
4: **for** $i = 2$ to t **do**
5: Node i is born, assign to its initial radial coordinate $r_i = \frac{2}{\zeta} \ln i$.
6: Increase the radial coordinate of every existing node $j < i$ according to $r_j(i) = \beta r_j + (1 - \beta) r_i$.
7: Assign to node i angular coordinate θ_i maximizing the likelihood $L = \prod p(x_{ij})^{\alpha_{ij}} \left[1 - p(x_{ij})\right]^{1-\alpha_{ij}}$.
8: **end for**

The computational complexity of the HyperMap algorithm for hyperbolic embedding is $O(n^3)$. In recent years, some scholars, including Bläsius et al. [21], have made improvements to the method of solving maximum likelihood estimation in the HyperMap algorithm, reducing the computational complexity of hyperbolic embedding to $O(n)$. The pseudocode for the fast embedding algorithm [21] is shown in Algorithm 5.2.

Algorithm 5.2: Fast embedding algorithm

Input: Undirected connected Graph $G = (V, E)$

Output: Hyperbolic coordinates $(r_i, \theta_i)_{i=1}^{\hat{n}}$ $(\hat{n} = |V|)$

1: Estimate global parameters n, R, α, T
2: Estimate radial coordinates r_i
3: **for** all nodes $v \in V$ **do**
4: Place v in layer L_i if $\deg(v) \in [2^i, 2^{i+1} - 1]$.
5: Embed all nodes in layers $\geq \frac{\log n}{2}$
6: **for** $i = \frac{\log n}{2} - 1 \ldots 0$ **do**
7: **for** $\log n$ times **do**
8: **for** all $v \in \bigcup_{j \geq i} L_j$ **do**
9: Embed v by optimizing its log-likelihood
10: **end for**
11: **end for**
12: **end for**

5.4 Dynamic Routing Protocol

5.4.1 Overview of Dynamic Routing Protocol for CoG-MIN

The dynamic routing protocol in CoG-MIN [22] is based on the link state routing protocol. It utilizes Link State Advertisement (LSA) to propagate information and employs the graph's shortest path algorithm to generate a routing information table and a name prefix table, guiding the forwarding of network packets [23].

Overall Architecture

Figure 5.9 illustrates the overall architecture of the dynamic routing protocol in CoG-MIN [22]. It comprises several key modules, including the Neighbor State Maintenance Protocol (NSMP), the Synchronization Protocol (Sync), the Link

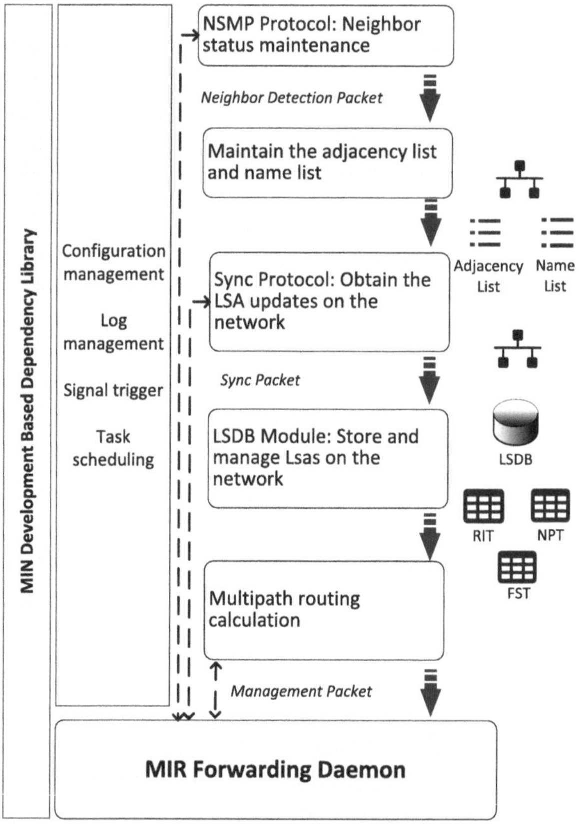

Fig. 5.9 Overall architecture of the dynamic routing protocol in CoG-MIN [22]

State Database (LSDB) Module, and the Routing Calculation Module. These modules support various functionalities such as neighbor discovery, adjacency and name list maintenance, LSA acquisition and storage, and multipath route calculation. Together, these modules maintain and utilize the following data structure information:

Adjacency list: Specifies information about all active neighbors of the router.

Name list: Contains the names currently accessible to the router. This refers to the reachable names of data and services stored by the Multi-Identifier Router (MIR) in the network. The MIR can respond to network packets containing the name information.

Link state database (LSDB): Stores all collected link state advertisements.

Routing information table (RIT): Stores the calculation results of routes to other routers in the network.

Name prefix table (NPT): Stores the calculation results of routes to other routers and their names.

Forwarding strategy table (FST): Stores forwarding policies with different name prefixes.

The MIR Forwarding Daemon serves as the core processor of MIR. It is responsible for packet capture, processing, and forwarding of network packets. In most cases, the MIR forwarding daemon operates on a server running the Ubuntu operating system, functioning as a software implementation of the MIR. The basic dependency library for MIN development offers essential functionalities for all programs within MIN, such as packet construction, identity certificate management, signature verification, and packet forwarding.

The supporting functions in the dynamic routing protocol of the MIN network include configuration management, log management, signal triggering, and task scheduling. Configuration management handles the parameter configuration for the entire dynamic routing protocol. Log management supports the input of logs into log files and command line interfaces. It also provides the ability to filter and output logs based on modules or log levels. Signal triggering involves the occurrence of an event that triggers subsequent events through semaphores during the operation of the dynamic routing protocol. For example, a change in the state of a neighboring node may trigger the modification of Link State Advertisements (LSAs), which in turn triggers the recalculation of the routing information table and name prefix table. Task scheduling enables the execution of tasks at specified times or based on specific events. For instance, it can be used to schedule the expiration event of LSAs.

This protocol ensures scalability through three key approaches:

Protocol layering: The design incorporates protocol layering, specifically by decoupling the Sync protocol from route update acquisition. This allows for flexibility and cooperation between the Sync protocol and other components of the routing protocol. By implementing Sync protocol adaptation code, route updates can be propagated in various ways without requiring modifications to other modules.

Configuration management: The dynamic routing protocol supports multipath calculation and single-path calculation, with the Dijkstra algorithm being the default choice. Additionally, it provides support for other shortest path algorithms. Through configuration management, administrators can manually switch between these algorithms based on specific network requirements. This flexibility in algorithm selection enhances scalability and allows for customization based on network conditions.

Forwarding strategy management: The dynamic routing protocol incorporates a forwarding strategy table (FST) that enables the setting of different forwarding strategies for different prefixes. This enables administrators to define specific strategies based on prefix-based routing, accommodating diverse routing requirements and providing scalability and customization options for strategies.

Key Data Structure

The routing information is disseminated through link state advertisements. Each router (i.e., MIR) in a MIN network supports both push and pull communication semantics. The routing information includes the network topology information and reachability information for name prefixes. Consequently, link state advertisements in MIN network are categorized into two types:

Adjacency Link State Advertisement (ALSA): This type of advertisement contains information about all the neighboring routers that are reachable from the router generating the LSA.

Name Link State Advertisement (NLSA): This type of advertisement records all reachable name prefixes of the router that generates the LSA.

Table 5.3 presents the fields and their meanings for these two types of link state advertisements. Each field is encoded in the type-length-value (TLV) format, and then collectively assembled into a TLV format link state advertisement.

Figure 5.10 shows the structure design of the two types of link state advertisements. The link state advertisement consists of an LSA Header and an LSA Body. LSA headers of different types of LSAs are consistent, and contain the Source MIR Identifier, LSA Sequence Number, and LSA Expiration Time. In ALSA, the LSA Body is a list of Adjacency Information, which contains the Neighbor MIR Identifier, logical interface Uniform Resource Identifier (LogicFace URI), logical interface ID, and Link Cost. In NLSA, the LSA Body is a list of multiple name information, each of which contains Name Identifier information.

The adjacency list and name list store the adjacency information and name information of the local router respectively. The link state database stores all link state advertisements generated by the router itself and collected from the network. The routing information table (RIT) and name prefix table (NPT) store the next hop list to the specified router or name prefix after route calculation. The information is synchronized to the forwarding information base (i.e., FIB) to guide the forwarding of network packets. The forwarding strategy table (FST) stores the forwarding

Table 5.3 The fields of link state advertisements

Type	Field	Field meaning
ALSA	Source MIR identifier	The identity identifier of the source MIR that generates the LSA
	LSA sequence number	The freshness of the LSA
	LSA expiration time	The expiration time of the LSA
	Neighbor MIR identifier	The identity identifier of the neighbor MIR
	LogicFace URI	The unified resource identifier for LogicFace used in the link
	LogicFace ID	The unique ID of the LogicFace used by the link
	Link cost	The link cost
NLSA	Source MIR identifier	The identity identifier of the source MIR that generates the LSA
	LSA sequence number	The freshness of the LSA
	LSA expiration time	The expiration time of the LSA
	Name identifier	The name identifier on the source MIR

strategies used to forward network packets. Table 5.4 lists the fields and corresponding meanings of RIT, NPT, and FST.

Hierarchical Naming Scheme

The dynamic routing protocol uses a hierarchical naming scheme to name elements. The hierarchical naming scheme has three design conventions:

Hierarchical names: The name of an identifier or a MIR is separated by "/". For example, /min/school/fly.jpg.

Minimum three levels: The name contains at least three "/".

Ascending sequence number: To simplify the determination of old and new LSAs, the name of the LSA includes a monotonically increasing sequence number, with larger numbers indicating newer LSAs.

The design of the hierarchical naming scheme is mainly based on two considerations: one is to align with the implementation of MIR, and the other is to keep simplicity and usability of the dynamic routing protocol itself. Hierarchical names facilitate the longest name prefix match lookup, allowing for efficient routing decisions. Additionally, the hierarchical structure of the names automatically signifies the dependency relationships among different elements within the routing protocol. For example, /min/pku/router/info belongs to /min/pku/router. The convention of the number of levels in the name is to adapt the parallel design of the parallel MIR. In the parallel scheme, the hash calculation of the first three prefixes is utilized to assign network packets to different coroutines, ensuring efficient packet processing. The design of increasing sequence number simplifies the logic of judging the age of the LSA. In addition, LSAs generated by the same MIR but with different serial numbers, yet sharing the same name prefix, can be easily recognized. This

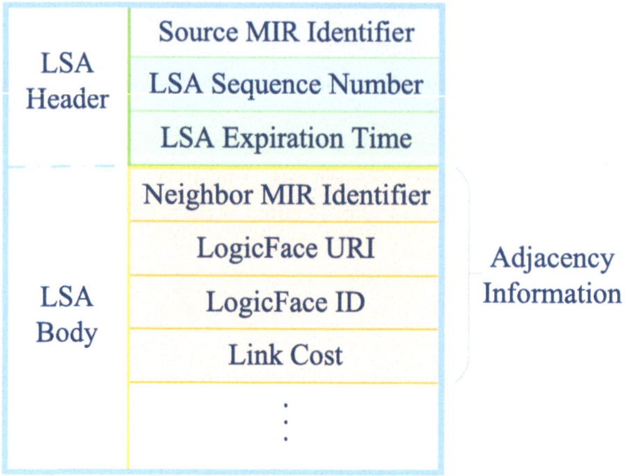

(a) Adjacency Link State Advertisement

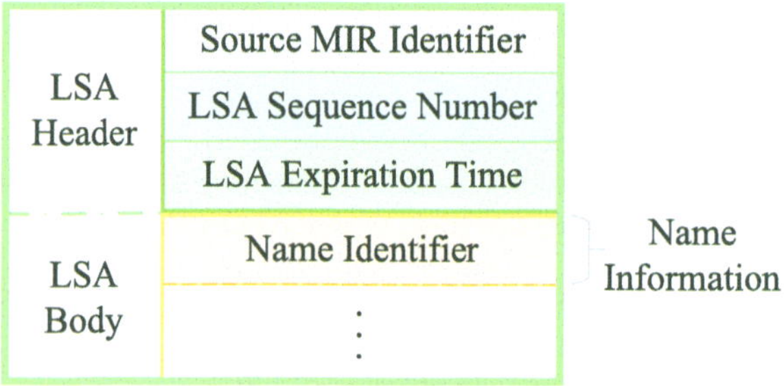

(b) Name Link State Advertisement

Fig. 5.10 The structure of the link state advertisement

Table 5.4 The design of RIT, NPT, and FST

Type	Field	Field meaning
RIT	Destination MIR identifier	The identifier of the destination MIR
	LogicFace URI	The unified resource identifier for LogicFace used in the next hop link
	Route cost	The route cost
NPT	Name identifier	The name identifier on the MIR
	LogicFace URI	The unified resource identifier for LogicFace used in the next hop link
	Route cost	The route cost
FST	Name identifier	The name identifier on the MIR
	Strategy name	The strategy name
	Strategy	The strategy structure, searching for forwarding entries in FIB table according to specified rules

Table 5.5 Naming rules of the dynamic routing protocol in MIN networks

Types of name prefix	Naming rules
MIR name prefix	/<Network Field>/<Site Field>/<Router Field>
Sync protocol notification prefix	/min/sync/notification
Sync protocol name prefix	/min/sync/<uuid>/<IBF>/<fragId>
LSA request name prefix	/localhop/<Network Field>/mlsr/LSA/<Site Field>/<Router Field>/<LSA Type>/<LSA Sequence Number>
NSMP protocol probe name prefix	/<Network Field>/<Site Field>/<Router Field>/mlsr/INFO

facilitates the replacement of older LSAs with newer ones, allowing for efficient updates and maintenance of routing information.

Table 5.5 shows the naming rules for several important name prefixes. The Network Field and Site Field refer to the network and website where the router is located. The Router Field refers to the identification string assigned by the website to which the router belongs. In the name prefix of the Sync protocol, the unique identifier (uuid) field refers to the globally unique string randomly generated by the router during the synchronization process. This uuid field is designed to be located at the third layer of the prefix. Each data set's synchronous network packet, distinguished by its unique identifier, will be assigned to different coroutines in the router for processing. This design leverages the parallelism inherent in the parallel MIR, thereby enhancing the forwarding efficiency of the router. The Invertible Bloom Filter (IBF) field refers to the IBF that stores the entire LSA namespace. The IBF plays a crucial role in the routing information synchronization of the MIN network. The fragId field indicates that when the difference between the LSA namespaces of two router nodes is large, the fragment mechanism of the Sync protocol is automatically triggered to synchronize all the different LSA names. The LSA Type field indicates the type of the LSA. The LSA Sequence Number field indicates the sequence number of the LSA. All other fields are fixed strings as agreed in the naming convention.

5.4.2 *Routing Information Synchronization*

Namespace Representation

In the dynamic routing protocol, the namespace represents a set of LSA name prefixes. To encode this set of LSA name prefixes, the protocol employs the use of an Invertible Bloom Filter (IBF) as the data structure. The resulting encoded representation is referred to as the namespace representation. With the namespace representation replica, each MIR can synchronize routing information changes with other routers. Synchronization nodes are also supported to detect differences between the sets of LSA name prefixes by comparing the encoded states.

Synchronization Process

In MIN networks, the synchronization of routing information involves the synchronization of LSAs stored in the LSDB module. With the Sync protocol, the synchronization process consists of two phases:

Route Update Detection: The Sync protocol passively identifies route updates by comparing the differences between local LSAs and those received from the network.

Route Update Acquisition: After the LSDB module receives route updates through the Sync protocol, it actively pulls the route updates.

The modular design of the Sync protocol enhances scalability. Notably, modifications in the Sync protocol do not require alterations in other components of the dynamic routing protocol. This ensures a seamless integration of updates.

The interaction between the LSDB module and the Sync protocol is characterized as follows: The LSDB module maintains and archives LSAs that cover the entire network. The name prefix set of these LSAs encapsulates the current network state as perceived by MIRs, which is encoded and represented via the IBF within the Sync protocol. When there is an update in the LSAs within a MIR's LSDB module, the Sync protocol is activated to encode this updated state and disseminate it to other MIRs. Subsequently, LSDB modules in these routers retrieve the newly identified route updates.

Figure 5.11 shows the process of routing information synchronization between neighboring nodes.

Step 1: The LSDB module of MIR B refreshes the LSAs and triggers the namespace synchronization process of the Sync protocol.

Step 2: The Sync protocol encodes the latest state and actively pushes the IBF containing the state information to all neighboring routers, including MIR A.

Step 3: After receiving the notification, MIR A immediately sends the Sync Interest packet to MIR B without waiting for the next synchronization period, and pulls the updated names. The uuid1 field in the name field of the Sync Interest packet is as the unique identifier to avoid confusion between different pull processes. The IBFrouterA field is the namespace representation on MIR A encoded in the form of an IBF.

Step 4: After receiving the Sync Interest packet, MIR B calculates all the name prefixes that MIR B has and MIR A does not through the set difference calculation of the IBF, and sends these name prefixes to MIR A using Sync Data packet. If the number of route updates is too large and the set of name prefixes is large, the fragmentation transmission is executed to transmit the routing information difference. Then, the namespace synchronization process carried by the Sync protocol is complete.

Steps 5, 6, and 7: After receiving the route updates from MIR B, MIR A uses the LSA Interest packet to pull the route updates. These updates are then installed in the LSDB module. If there are too many route updates or if the length of an LSA

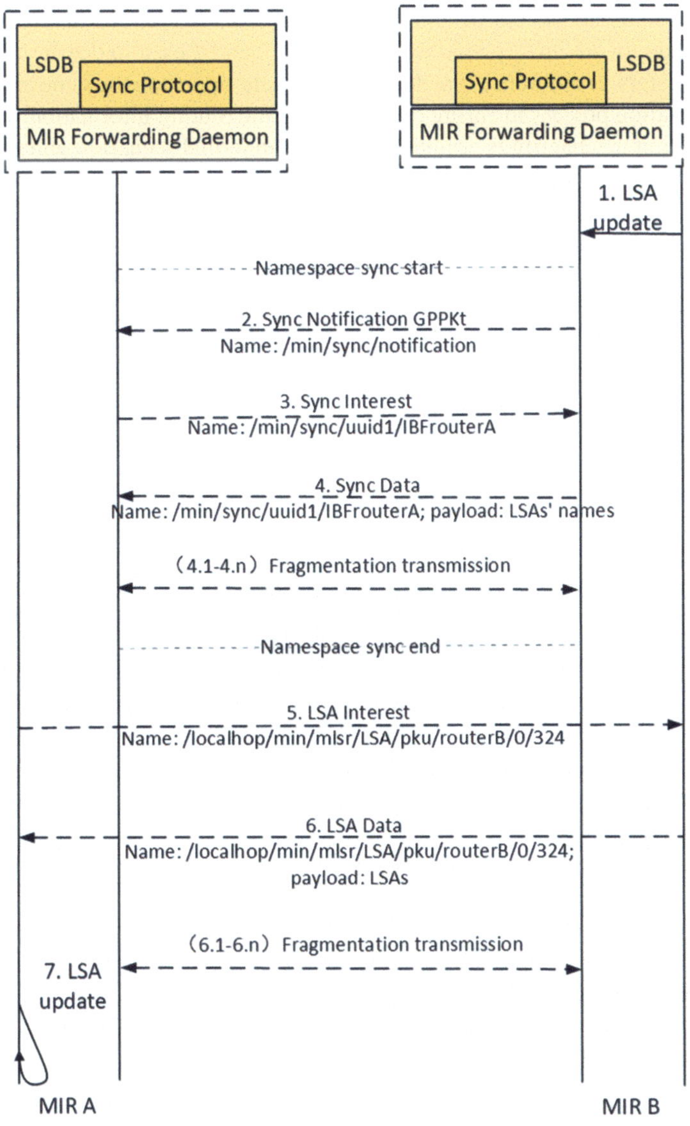

Fig. 5.11 An example of routing information synchronization between neighboring nodes

exceeds the maximum packet size, fragmentation transmission is required to transmit the data in smaller segments.

During the data transmission between neighboring routers, packet loss may occur due to network congestion or program errors. This may lead to the failure of route update notification. In such cases, the routing information synchronization in the MIN network supports data recovery.

When a route update notification fails, the subsequent update will overwrite the failed update. In addition, periodic probe packets can be used to detect differences between routers. If differences are detected, the routers perform the same namespace synchronization process to ensure consistency in the routing information. The periodic detection mechanism is designed to handle abnormal scenarios, and the detection period is generally set to a longer duration to reduce bandwidth consumption caused by frequent detection packets.

In cases where IBF decoding fails, the data producer directly returns the entire namespace to the data consumer, who can then select the appropriate name for subsequent data retrieval.

Fragmentation Transmission

Figure 5.12 depicts a single instance of the fragmentation transmission process.

During the process of routing information synchronization, fragmentation transmission is employed when the namespace or the LSA is large. This process involves the following steps:

The data producer initially sends key fragment information, including data name, data length, and data segment length, to the data consumer.

Then, the data consumer and data producer utilize the ConsumerFetcher and ProducerPublisher, respectively, to transmit the data fragments.

The ConsumerFetcher generates and sends fragment Interest packets based on the fragment information. These Interest packets are processed via the logical network interfaces (ConsumerLogicFace and ProducerLogicFace) of the respective MIRs.

Upon receiving the fragment Interest packet, the ProducerPublisher responds by sending fragment response data packets to the ConsumerFetcher.

If the ConsumerFetcher receives a Nack, indicating packet loss during propagation, it records the loss and performs retransmission. Otherwise, it stores the fragment response Data packets in a collection.

The fragmentation transmission process concludes once all the fragment response Data packets have been received by the data consumer.

During namespace synchronization via the Sync protocol, the fragment data segment is designated in the format: /min/sync/<uuid>/<IBF>/<fragId>. Here, the uuid field represents a unique identifier generated by the data producer for the fragmentation transmission, initiated upon receiving a namespace request from the data consumer.

Figure 5.13 illustrates the network packet processing in a parallel MIR. By default, this router hashes the first three fields of the name of the network packet, divides the hash result by the number of thread pools (n), and obtains a remainder (e.g., 4, as indicated in Fig. 5.13). Subsequently, the network packet is distributed across different processing threads (e.g., the example in Fig. 5.13 distributed to thread 4). The design of the uuid field effectively leverages the parallel processing

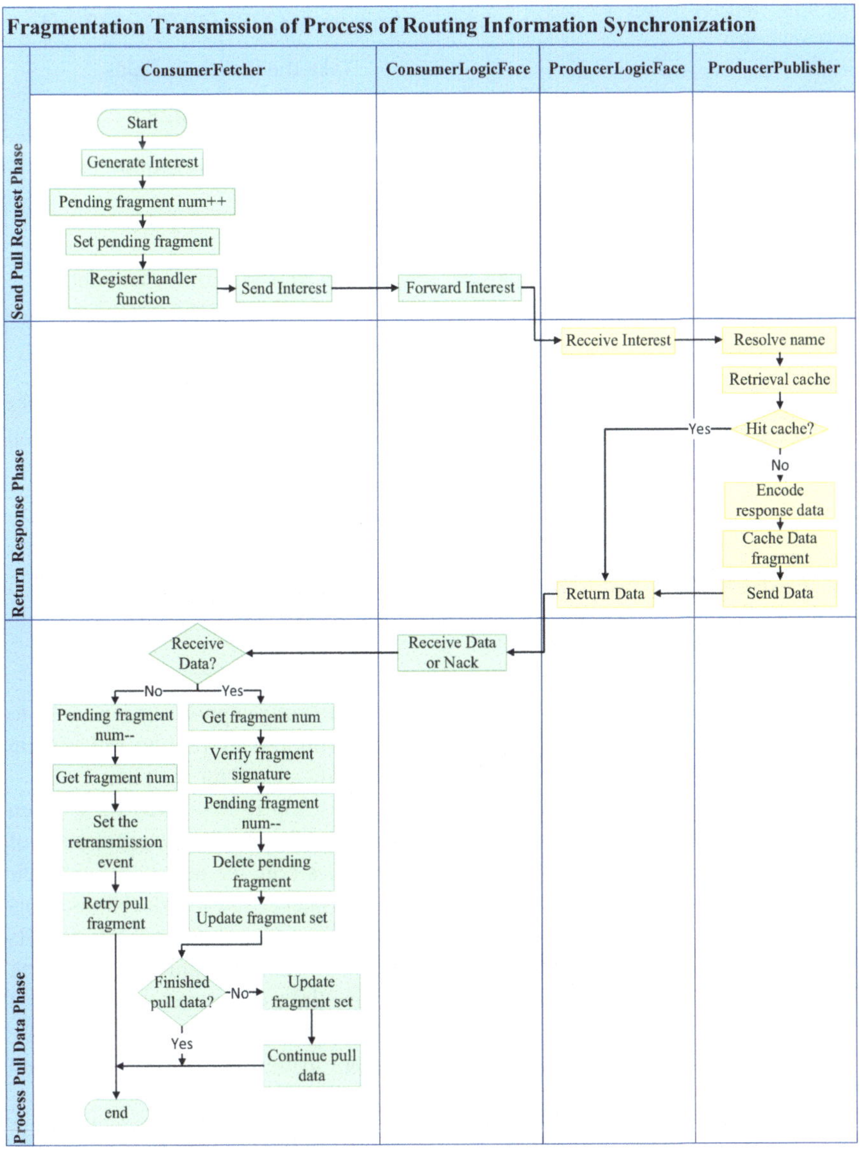

Fig. 5.12 Fragmentation transmission process of routing information synchronization

capabilities of the parallel MIR, thereby reducing the synchronization delay. The IBF field employs an invertible Bloom filter to encode the data consumer's namespace state, enabling the data producer to identify and communicate the set of data names absent in the data consumer. The fragId field, a monotonically increasing positive integer, identifies the relative positions of data fragments. In summary, the naming convention for fragment data segments in routing information

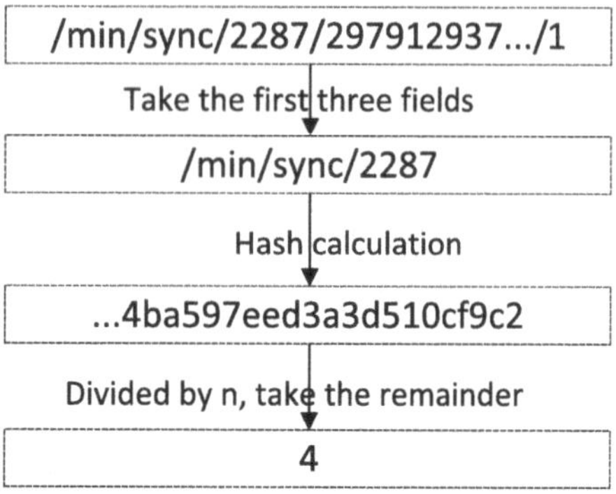

Fig. 5.13 Network packet processing on a parallel MIR

synchronization not only aligns with the parallel processing design of parallel MIRs but also addresses the practical requirements of the fragmentation transmission process.

5.4.3 Routing Calculation and Forwarding

Multipath Routing Calculation

The dynamic routing protocol in MIN networks inherently supports and defaults to multipath routing calculation, while traditional single-path routing calculation remains an optional feature that can be configured via a configuration file.

In single-path routing calculation, a unique next hop is calculated for a given identifier. In contrast, multipath routing calculation allows for the determination of multiple next hops for the same identifier. It provides both the next hops and their respective path costs to the forwarding plane for packet routing decisions. This approach not only offers diverse next hop options for forwarding network packets but also enhances the robustness of the network. For instance, in unicast forwarding scenarios, the router can swiftly identify alternative links in the event of a next hop link failure. Similarly, under multicast forwarding scenarios, the router can simultaneously request data from one or more producers using the results of multipath routing calculations.

The dynamic routing protocol in MIN networks employs the Dijkstra algorithm for shortest path calculations. For example, $C_{A,k}^{B}$ denotes the link cost between MIR A and MIR B, with $L_1 \ldots L_n$ representing all adjacent links of MIR A, and k indicating a specific adjacent link. The multipath calculation process unfolds as follows: During a routing calculation process, all adjacent links $L_1 \ldots L_n$ of MIR A are traversed. For a link L_k, it runs the Dijkstra algorithm, and appends the calculation result to the next hop list in the routing information table. This next hop list is continuously modified and sorted, culminating in the final routing calculation results.

After the routing information table is updated, the name prefix table is also updated, thereby generating the corresponding next hop list for each name prefix. The dynamic routing protocol in MIN networks conveys this next hop list information to the forwarding daemon on MIR via the management packet. The forwarding daemon then determines the appropriate next hop for packet forwarding based on the established forwarding strategy.

Scalable Forwarding Strategy

The dynamic routing protocol in MIN networks supports configurable forwarding strategies based on name prefixes. It includes three basic forwarding strategies: Unicast Forwarding Strategy (UFS), Multicast Forwarding Strategy (MFS), and Broadcast Forwarding Strategy (BFS). Name prefixes can be associated with a certain forwarding strategies. Name prefixes that are not associated with forwarding strategies are forwarded using the default strategies. If a network packet matches a name prefix based on the Longest Prefix Match (LPM) principle, the network packet is forwarded according to the forwarding strategies associated with the name prefix. The name prefix and its corresponding forwarding strategies are stored in the Forwarding Strategy Table (FST), which is searched using a Two-Stage Parallel Binary Search algorithm (TSPBS) to enable high-performance parallel lookup.

When a network packet reaches a MIR, the MIR parses the identifier of the network packet, lookups the entry in the FIB table and FST table according to the LPM principle, and finds the next hop list and forwarding strategies of the identifier. Then, the network packet is processed according to the implementation logic of the forwarding strategies. The processing logic of the three forwarding strategies is different as follows:

Unicast Forwarding Strategy (UFS): The MIR searches for the next hop with the lowest cost in the next hop list and forward the packet to the next hop.

Multicast Forwarding Strategy (MFS): The MIR forward the network packet to all next hops in the next hop list.

Broadcast Forwarding Strategy (BFS): The MIR forward the network packet to all neighboring routers.

The scalability of a forwarding strategy is necessary for the dynamic routing mechanism of MIN networks. During information synchronization, to enable the MIR to send the same notification packet to all their neighbors or request link state advertisements from all their neighbors, the related name prefixes (such as SyncPrefix and LsaPrefix) on MIRs as the broadcast forwarding strategy. The design of the broadcast forwarding strategy can support the routing process running on the MIR to propagate routing information conveniently. For common name prefixes, the default forwarding strategy can be optionally set to the unicast forwarding strategy or multicast forwarding strategy. In the unicast forwarding strategy, all name

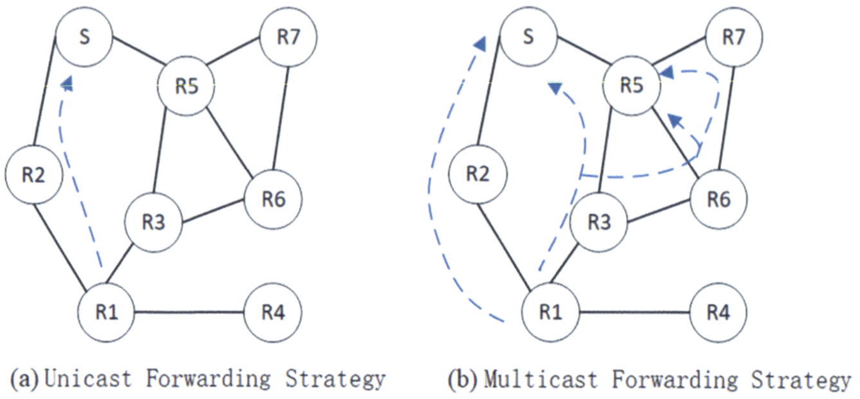

Fig. 5.14 Forwarding paths of network packets in different forwarding strategies

prefixes that do not find the associated strategy are forwarded to the next hop with the lowest routing cost, while in the multicast forwarding strategy, they are forwarded to all logical network interfaces in the next hop list.

Generally, the default forwarding strategy of the name prefix is set to the unicast forwarding strategy or multicast forwarding strategy. The broadcast forwarding strategy does not depend on routing calculation, and it is easy to cause large network traffic overhead. Figure 5.14 shows the forwarding paths of network packets based on different forwarding strategies. *S* indicates the router where the requested content is located, and the dashed line indicates the routing path. The multicast forwarding strategies in MIN networks does not cause network loopback. When the same network packet is sent to the same router again, it is discarded or aggregated. The multicast forwarding strategy can make better use of the forwarding guidance information obtained from multipath routing calculation.

In certain special cases, the dynamic routing protocol may require the network packet that matches the multicast forwarding strategy to be forwarded only to a specific network interface, rather than all the available next hops.

For instance, consider the case where MIR B notifies MIR A about new routing information. In response, MIR A needs to send a prefix request for routing information. Meanwhile, MIR A wants to avoid multicasting the prefix request to all neighboring routers. Instead, it specifically forward the request only to MIR B. This can reduce unnecessary network overhead.

To address the above issue, the dynamic routing protocol for MIN networks introduces a Hint forwarding mechanism, as shown in Fig. 5.15. Since the MIN network packet uses an extensible coding structure, the network packet can carry a network logical interface number by adding a prompt field to the MIN network packet. If the value of the prompt field is null, the packet is forwarded based on the strategy search result. If the value of the prompt field is not null, the logical network interface number is extracted from the field. If the logical network interface

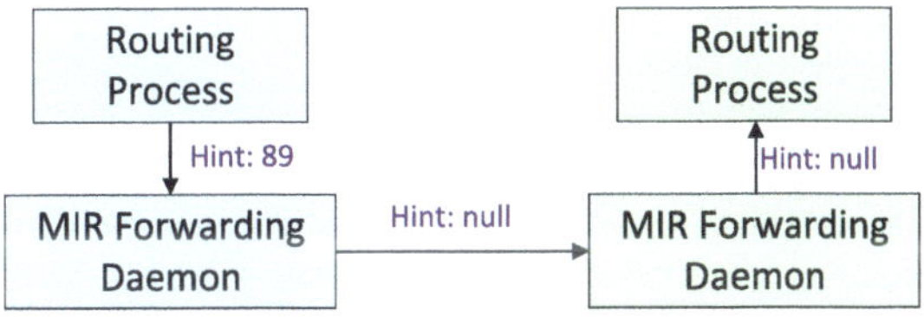

Fig. 5.15 Hint forwarding mechanism

corresponding to the number is successfully queried, the network packet is forwarded through the interface. Otherwise, the network packet is forwarded based on the strategy search result. In the Hint field, the number of the logical network interface (89 in Fig. 5.15) can only be obtained from the record of the incoming interface of a network packet, which is performed by the routing process or other upper-layer process. After being queried by the MIR forwarding daemon, the Hint field in a MIN network packet is set to null before the packet is forwarded. This prevents processing errors when the MIR forwarding daemon on the peer router queries the same logical network interface number.

Dynamic Routing Management

Multi-Identifier Network Dynamic Routing Command Line Tool (MIN-DRC) is a command line tool specifically developed for the dynamic routing protocol in MIN networks. It provides a debug function for the dynamic routing protocol at the management level.

Figure 5.16 shows the overall design of the management module of the dynamic routing protocol in MIN networks. The MIN-DRC process exchanges data with the Multi-Identifier Network Dynamic Routing (MIN-DR) process to obtain or change routing information in MIRs. The specific process is as follows: The MIN-DRC process obtains the command line parameters entered by the user. According to the certain parameters, MIN-DRC generates the routing management interest packet with different command information. The routing management interest packet is sent to the MIR forwarding daemon of the local router through the network logical interface. MIN-DR registers the default prefix of the routing management interest packet. Therefore, all routing management interest packets are forwarded to the MIN-DR process according to the longest prefix matching rule. The Management System module (MgmtSystem) in the MIN-DR process analyzes and processes the routing management interest packet and returns the corresponding data packet to MIN-DRC. The MIN-DRC process receives and parses the data packet, gets the response information, and then prints the response information to the command line interface.

The MIN-DRC process receives the command line and builds a routing management interest pack carrying the corresponding information. The command line design in MIN-DRC includes: Basic Command, Topology Management, Neighbor

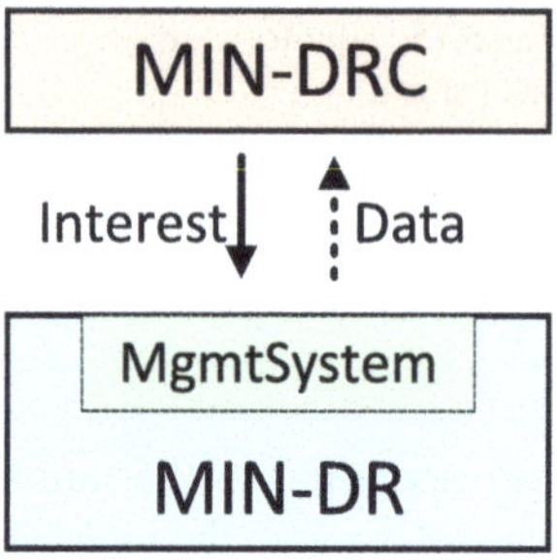

Fig. 5.16 The management module of the dynamic routing protocol in MIN networks

Table 5.6 The command line design in MIN-DRC

Management module	Command line	Function
Basic command	Clear	Clear command line
	Help	Check the command line help
	Exit	Exit command line
Topology management	Topology help	View the topology management command line help
	Topology state	Viewing the topology state
Neighbor management	Neighbor help	View the neighbor management command line help
	Neighbor state	Checking the neighbor state
	Neighbor cost <neighbor name> <cost>	Modify the adjacency link cost
Prefix management	Prefix help	See the prefix management command line help
	Prefix state	View the prefix state
	Prefix insert <prefix>	Publish the prefix
	Prefix remove <prefix>	Delete the prefix
Sync management	Sync help	View the sync management command line help
	Sync state	View the synchronization state
LSDB management	lsdb help	Check the LSDB command line help
	lsdb state	Check the LSDB state
	lsdb build name	Build the name link state advertisement
	lsdb build adj	Build an adjacent link state advertisement

Management, Prefix Management, Sync Management, and LSDB Management. Table 5.6 describes the detailed command line design.

The detailed implementation of the management system module (MgmtSystem module for short) in the MIN-DR process is relatively complex. As shown in Fig. 5.17, the MgmtSystem module receives interest packets through the network

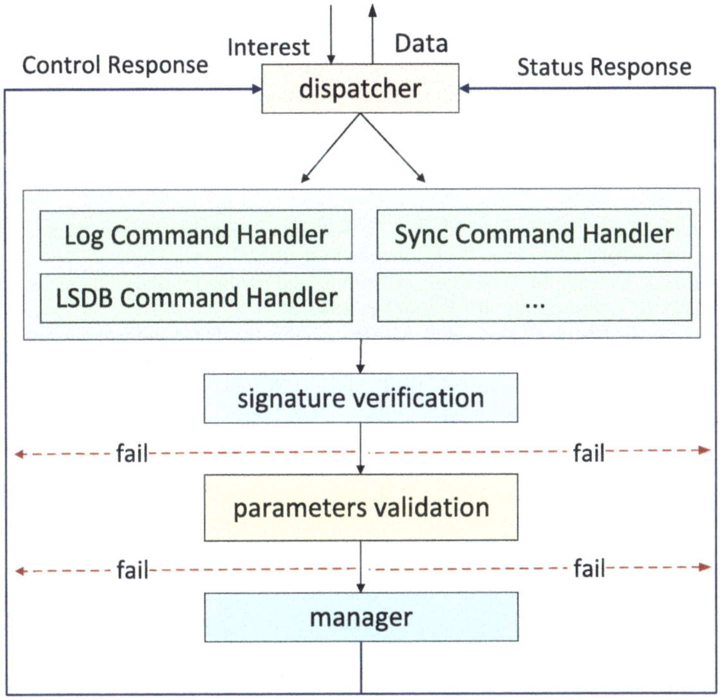

Fig. 5.17 The architecture of the MgmtSystem module

logic interface. The dispatcher parses the interest packets and sends them to different command handlers based on the specific command information. Then, the signature verification and parameter verification are executed. If both verifications are successful, the corresponding control commands can be executed or the route state is returned.

References

1. Li H, Yang X. Co-governed sovereignty network: legal basis and its prototype & applications with MIN architecture. Cham: Springer; 2021.
2. Li H, Wu JX, Xing KX, et al. Prototype and testing report of a multi-identifier system for reconfigurable network architecture under co-governing. Sci Sin Inf. 2019;49(9):1186–204.
3. Zhang XC, Chen QS, Li H. MIR: multi-identifier router and its prototype. In: Proceedings of the 8th international conference on computer and communications management; 2020, p. 103–107.
4. Wand YM, Li H, Xing KX, et al. Identifier management of industrial internet based on multi-identifier network architecture. ZTE Commun. 2020;18(1):36–43.

5. Wang L, Hoque A, Yi C, et al. OSPFN: an OSPF based routing protocol for named data networking. Technical Report NDN-0003, 2012.
6. Hoque AKMM, Amin SO, Alyyan A, et al. NLSR: named-data link state routing protocol. In: Proceedings of the 3rd ACM SIGCOMM workshop on information-centric networking. New York: ACM; 2013. p. 15–20.
7. Ghasemi C, Yousefi H, Shin KG, et al. Muca: new routing for named data networking. In: 2018 IFIP networking conference (IFIP networking) and workshops. Piscataway: IEEE; 2018. p. 289–97.
8. Aldaoud M, Al-Abri D, Awadalla M, et al. N-BGP: an efficient BGP routing protocol adaptation for named data networking. Int J Commun Syst. 2022;35(14):e5266.
9. Cvetkovski A, Crovella M. Hyperbolic embedding and routing for dynamic graphs. In: IEEE INFOCOM 2009. Piscataway: IEEE; 2009. p. 1647–55.
10. Boukerche A, El-Khatib K, Xu L, et al. SDAR: a secure distributed anonymous routing protocol for wireless and mobile ad hoc networks. In: 29th annual IEEE international conference on local computer networks. Piscataway: IEEE; 2004. p. 618–24.
11. Aubry E, Silverston T, Chrisment I. SRSC: SDN-based routing scheme for CCN. In: Proceedings of the 2015 1st IEEE conference on network softwarization (NetSoft). Piscataway: IEEE; 2015. p. 1–5.
12. Wang L, Lehman V, Hoque AKMM, et al. A secure link state routing protocol for NDN. IEEE Access. 2018;6:10470–82.
13. Li T, Shang W, Afanasyev A, et al. A brief introduction to ndn dataset synchronization (ndn sync). In: MILCOM 2018-2018 IEEE military communications conference (MILCOM). Piscataway: IEEE; 2018. p. 612–8.
14. Boguná M, Papadopoulos F, Krioukov D. Sustaining the internet with hyperbolic mapping. Nat Commun. 2010;1(1):62.
15. Hyperbolic geometry (2021-01-16) [2023-12-07]. https://en.wikipedia.org/wiki/Hyperbolic_geometry.
16. Chami I, Ying Z, Ré C, et al. Hyperbolic graph convolutional neural networks. Adv Neural Inf Proces Syst. 2019;32:438.
17. Poincaré ball model (2020-06-25) [2023-12-23]. https://lccurious.github.io/2020/06/25/Poincare-Ball-Model/#fnref3.
18. Poincaré disk with hyperbolic parallel lines (2008-04-26) [2023-12-26]. https://en.wikipedia.org/wiki/Poincar%C3%A9_disk_model.
19. Regular icosahedron [EB/OL] (2019-02-21) [2023-12-27]. https://en.wikipedia.org/wiki/Regular_icosahedron.
20. Papadopoulos F, Psomas C, Krioukov D. Network mapping by replaying hyperbolic growth. IEEE/ACM Trans Networking. 2014;23(1):198–211.
21. Bläsius T, Friedrich T, Krohmer A, et al. Efficient embedding of scale-free graphs in the hyperbolic plane. IEEE/ACM Trans Networking. 2018;26(2):920–33.
22. Wang F, Li H, Wu ZQ, et al. ALRP: an adaptive link state routing protocol for multi-identifier network. In: 2022 IEEE 8th international conference on computer and communications (ICCC). Piscataway: IEEE; 2022. p. 677–84.
23. Que JM, Li H, Bai H, et al. A network architecture containing both push and pull semantics. In: 2021 7th international conference on computer and communications (ICCC). Piscataway: IEEE; 2021. p. 2211–6.

Chapter 6
Multi-identifier Router

In MIN networks, the multi-identifier router (MIR) plays a crucial role as the forwarder responsible for processing and forwarding incoming network packets. This chapter provides a comprehensive introduction of the design and implementation of the MIR.

6.1 Overview of Multi-identifier Router

The multi-identifier router (MIR) serves as a network forwarder within the MIN architecture. MIR is purposefully designed to prioritize modularity and extensibility, making it conducive for conducting experiments involving new protocol features, algorithms, and applications within the MIN.

The overall architecture of MIR is depicted in Fig. 6.1. MIR comprises the following primary modules: LogicFace module, Packet Validator module, Table module, Forwarding Pipeline module, Strategy module, and Plugin module.

When a MIN network packet arrives at the MIR via the LogicFace module, it undergoes verification by the Packet Validator module to authenticate the embedded digital signature. If the verification fails, the packet is promptly discarded. Conversely, if the verification succeeds, the packet is passed on to the Forwarding Pipeline module for subsequent processing. The Forwarding Pipeline module collaborates with the Table module to regulate the forwarding procedure of the network packet [1]. Ultimately, the Strategy module assesses the forwarding decision, determining whether and how the MIN network packet should be forwarded. Additionally, the Plugin module is available to expand the functionality of MIR. A detailed description of each module is as follows.

H. Li, H. Bai, *Principle of Architecture, Protocol, and Algorithms for CoG-MIN*,
https://doi.org/10.1007/978-981-96-3596-2_6

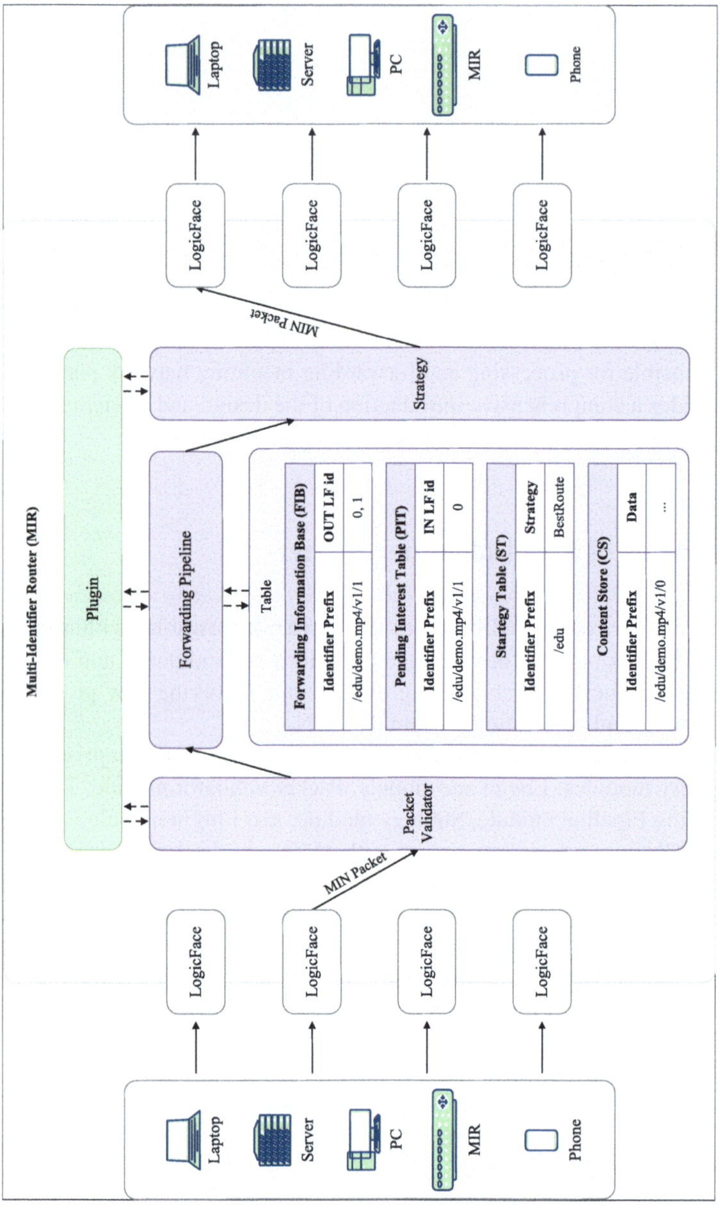

Fig. 6.1 The overall architecture of Multi-Identifier Router

6.1.1 LogicFace Module

In order to ensure portability and compatibility, MIR introduces the concept of logical interface (LogicFace) as the generalized network interface, which facilitates the interconnection between network nodes. Similar to physical network interfaces, LogicFace is primarily responsible for sending and receiving MIN network packets. The advantage of this unified abstraction is that upper-layer modules in MIR, such as the forwarding module, can focus on processing standardized MIN network packets, without needing to consider the variations in underlying communication protocols. The underlying LogicFace can utilize different communication channels, including physical network interfaces, Unix sockets, TCP tunnels, and UDP tunnels [2].

Figure 6.2 illustrates the structure of LogicFace, comprising a Link Service and a Transport. The transport component provides heterogeneous low-level communication capabilities, while the link service implements unified packet fragmentation and packet reassembly functions. The LLPacket is defined as a virtual link layer packet, accommodating the maximum transmission unit (MTU) of different links. It includes two header fields, FragSeq (fragment sequence) and FragNum (fragment number), which facilitate the segmentation and reassembly of packets. Each LLPacket carries either a complete MIN network packet or a fragment of a MIN network packet.

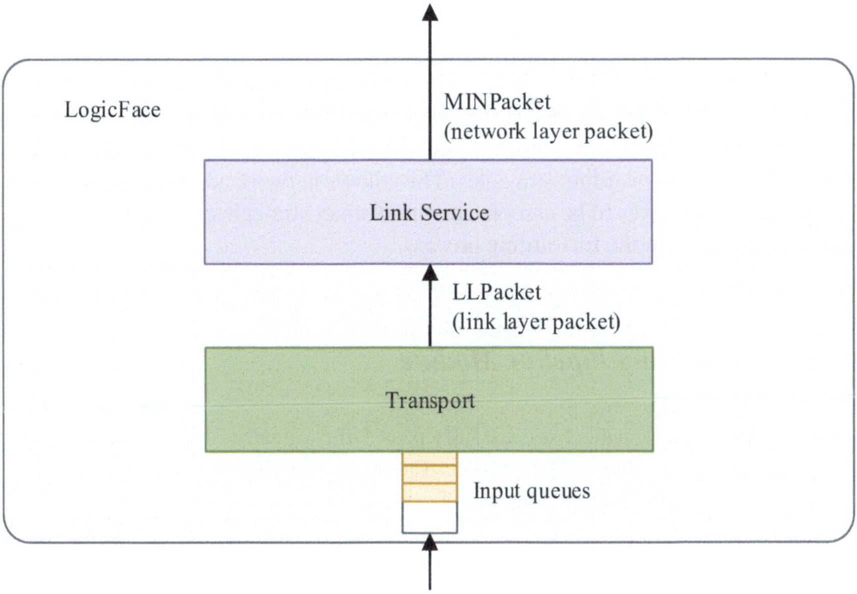

Fig. 6.2 LogicFace

6.1.2 *Packet Validator Module*

Each MIN network packet can be embedded with one or more digital signatures, which serve to ensure data integrity and traceability. Each digital signature consists of signature parameters and a signature value. When a MIN network packet is received, the packet validator module first determines whether the digital signature of the network packet requires verification. For each digital signature that needs to be verified, the packet validator module retrieves the corresponding certificate from the network based on the signature parameters. Subsequently, it verifies the validity of the digital signature. If the authentication fails, the packet is immediately discarded. On the other hand, if the authentication succeeds, the packet is forwarded to the subsequent forwarding pipeline module for further processing [3].

6.1.3 *Table Module*

The table module in MIR encompasses four crucial data structures: a content store (CS) for temporary data caching, a pending interest table (PIT) for Interest aggregation and recording incoming Interests, a forwarding information base (FIB) used for guiding forwarding, and a strategy table (ST) used for storing forwarding strategies. In MIN networks, FIB and ST offer additional support for forwarding to GPPkt. The PIT is responsible for recording the LogicFace of incoming Interests, enabling data to be returned hop-by-hop along the reverse path established by the PIT. The FIB facilitates longest prefix matching queries to determine the appropriate forwarding path for Interests and GPPkt packets. Each FIB entry may correspond to one or more LogicFaces available for forwarding, with the specific LogicFace chosen depending on the forwarding strategy. The ST maintains the mapping between identifier prefixes and forwarding strategies. This allows network administrators to configure different prefixes to be associated with distinct strategies, ensuring flexibility and customization in the forwarding process.

6.1.4 *Forwarding Pipeline Module*

Once a MIN network packet successfully passes the signature verification, the forwarding pipeline module of MIR initiates the forwarding process. Firstly, an identifier selector is employed to select a network packet from the identification area of the MIN network packet for forwarding. This selection process is crucial in determining the specific packet to be forwarded [4]. Subsequently, based on the chosen identifier, the type of the MIN network packet is determined. This step involves classifying the packet into its appropriate category. Finally, the forwarding pipeline module executes a specific forwarding process based on the identified type of the network packet. This process entails forwarding the packet according to the predefined rules and protocols associated with its type.

6.1.5 Strategy Module

MIR incorporates a Strategy module to enable intelligent decision-making within the forwarding plane. This module plays a pivotal role in determining the appropriate forwarding actions for each MIN network packet, including whether, when, and how it should be forwarded. By leveraging the information stored in the FIB and PIT, the Strategy module dynamically adapts the forwarding decisions based on the prevailing network conditions [5].

6.1.6 Plugin Module

The Plugin module provides a standardized set of interfaces and extension specifications, simplifying the task for system developers. By understanding the impact of each interface within the Plugin module on the behavior of the original system, developers can create plugins to extend the functionality of the system without concerning themselves with the underlying implementation details. This separation allows for a more modular approach, enabling developers to focus on the specific requirements of their plugins and seamlessly integrate them into the original system.

In the remaining part of this section, a detailed introduction to the design and implementation of MIR are being provided.

6.2 LogicFace

LogicFace is a comprehensive concept that encompasses various types of network interfaces for efficient packet transmission and reception. It offers flexible communication service in several forms, including Ethernet, Overlay, and Linux/Unix Inter-Process mechanisms, etc.

LogicFace plays a pivotal role in efficient data delivery by facilitating the transmission of Interests, Data, and Nacks. Moreover, it offers support for traditional data pushing behaviors by handling GPPkts [6]. By leveraging the underlying communication mechanisms, LogicFace ensures a seamless and dependable delivery service for MIN packets, thereby promoting a clean and reliable data exchange process.

Inside the LogicFace, two primary components, namely the Link Service and the Transport, play integral roles. Transport is responsible for offering a consistent and high-level programming interface for the underlying communication mechanisms employed. On the other hand, the Link Service component provides essential functionalities for MIN Packets, such as Packet Fragmentation, Packet Reassembly, and Packet Retransmission. Depending on the type of LogicFace, the Link Service interacts with the specific Transport by invoking the corresponding interface.

6.2.1 Transport

The Transport provides best-effort packet delivery service to the Link Service. The detailed implementations of each type of the Transport are as follows.

Unix Stream Transport

The Unix stream transport (UnixStreamTransport) is a type of transport for local communication between MIR and other OS processes. The MIR listens for incoming connections through the Unix Domain Socket, which was created at the initialization of the MIR. Upon each incoming connection, a UnixStreamTransport is created.

The Unix stream transport has the following attributes. The LocalUri attribute, denoted as "unix://path," is responsible for specifying the socket path required to establish a connection. Similarly, the RemoteUri attribute, represented as "fd://file-descriptor," corresponds to the file descriptor associated with the accepted socket within the MIR process. Operating within a localized scope, this transport ensures that its functionality is limited to the local network. Persistency is set to "on-demand," allowing any other persistency settings adapting to the network. The LinkType attribute signifies a point-to-point connection, establishing a dedicated link between two endpoints. Moreover, the transport offers an unlimited maximum transmission unit (MTU), while the actual MTU value for all relevant LogicFace is provided by MIR. Following each successful receive operation, the Transport places all valid packets within the buffer.

TCP Transport

The TCP transport (TCPTransport) is a type of transport that facilitates communication over TCP tunnels overlaying IP protocols, either IPv4 or IPv6.

The MIR listens for incoming connections through the listening socket, which is configured with an appointed port number. Upon each incoming connection, a TCPTransport is established. Additionally, MIR has the capability to establish outgoing TCP connections with other MIRs.

The TCP transport has the following attributes that define its behavior. The LocalUri and RemoteUri attributes adapt depending on the IP version utilized. In the case of IPv4, the LocalUri is structured as tcp4://ip:port, where "ip" represents the IPv4 address and "port" denotes the port number. Similarly, for IPv6, the LocalUri format is tcp6://[ip]:port, enclosing the IPv6 address within square brackets and utilizing lowercase representation. The Scope attribute is determined as "local" when the remote endpoint possesses a loopback IP, while it is classified as "non-local" otherwise. Persistency settings differ depending on whether the transport is established from an accepted socket or for an outgoing connection. For accepted sockets, the Persistency attribute is set to "on-demand," whereas for outgoing connections, it can be configured as either "persistent" or "permanent," with the flexibility to modify this setting using the Update Command. The LinkType attribute consistently signifies a point-to-point connection, establishing a direct link between two endpoints. Moreover, the transport offers an unlimited maximum transmission unit (MTU), while the actual MTU value for all relevant LogicFace is provided by MIR.

UDP Transport

The UDP unicast transport (UnicastUdpTransport) is a type of transport that facilitates communication through UDP tunnels overlaying IP protocols either IPv4 or IPv6.

The UDP unicast transport is characterized by a set of specific static attributes. The LocalUri and RemoteUri attributes vary depending on the IP version utilized. In the case of IPv4, the LocalUri follows the format udp4://ip:port, where "ip" represents the IPv4 address, and "port" denotes the port number. Similarly, for IPv6, the LocalUri format is udp6://[ip]:port, with the IPv6 address enclosed in square brackets and represented in lowercase. The Scope attribute is classified as "non-local," indicating a broader network scope beyond the local environment. Persistency settings differ based on whether the transport is created from an accepted socket or for an outgoing connection. For accepted sockets, the Persistency attribute is set to "on-demand," while for outgoing connections, it can be configured as either "persistent" or "permanent," offering flexibility through Update Command. The LinkType attribute consistently signifies a point-to-point connection, establishing a direct link between two endpoints. Additionally, the MTU attribute represents the maximum length of an IP packet minus the IP and UDP headers, with the actual MTU value provided by MIR for all relevant LogicFace.

Ethernet Unicast Transport

The Ethernet unicast transport (UnicastEthernetTransport) is a type of transport that enables direct communication over Ethernet.

The MIR listens for incoming Ethernet frames through the interface provided by libpcap library on each Ethernet-compatible network interface, excluding interfaces such as the loopback interface, PPP links, GRE tunnels, IPIP tunnels, etc. Upon the arrival of data from new remote endpoint, a UnicastEthernetTransport is created.

The Ethernet unicast transport possesses specific static attributes that define its behavior and configuration. The LocalUri attribute takes the form of dev://ifname, where "ifname" represents the network interface name. On the other hand, the RemoteUri attribute is structured as ether://[ethernet-addr], where "ethernet-addr" indicates the MAC address of the remote endpoint. The Scope attribute is classified as "non-local," indicating a broader network scope beyond the local environment. The Persistency attribute varies based on whether the transport is created from incoming connections or outgoing connections. For incoming connections, the Persistency attribute is set to "on-demand," while for outgoing connections, it can be configured as either "persistent" or "permanent," with the option to modify this setting using the LogicFace/update management command. The LinkType attribute consistently signifies a point-to-point connection, establishing a direct link between two endpoints. Additionally, the MTU attribute represents the maximum transmission unit (MTU) of the network interface, which can currently only be set during LogicFace creation.

6.2.2 Link Service

The Link Service, implemented by LinkService base class, collaborates seamlessly with the transport and provides network layer packet delivery service. It undertakes the intricate task of converting network layer packets—such as GPPkts, Interests, Data, and Nacks—into the link layer packets. The functions of the Link Service are shown as follows:

- **Packet Encoding and Decoding**: The Generic Link Service is responsible for encoding and decoding GPPkts, Interests, Data, and Nacks by encapsulating them within LLPackets. This service accommodates a singular network layer packet or fragment per LLPacket.
- **Packet Fragmentation and Reassembly**: To enable seamless traversal of links with varied MTUs, the service supports packet fragmentation and reassembly.

In packet fragmentation, the link service implements the process of forwarding network layer packets encapsulated in link layer packets to the fragmenter. Subsequently, each packet fragment starts forwarding. In the absence of fragmentation, a packet receives a specified sequence and is then handed to the transport for subsequent forwarding.

When the link layer packet is received, the transport delivers it to the link service. In the case that the link service supports fragmentation, the received packet is carefully checked for the presence of the FragIndex and FragCount fields. They indicate the fragment index and number of fragments, respectively. Fragment reassembly follows, and the reassembler returns the reassembled complete group only when all fragments have been received in their entirety.

6.3 Data Structure

The data structures in MIR include FIB, CS, PIT, and ST (Fig. 6.3).

6.3.1 *Forwarding Information Base*

The FIB is similar to the FIB in an IP or NDN router. It contains identifier prefixes instead of IP address prefixes or NDN name prefixes [7].

Each entry in the FIB consists of an identifier prefix and a set of NextHop records, each of which defines the LogicFace to the next-hop and the associated routing overhead. The NextHop records are sorted in ascending order according to the routing cost. When the identifier carried by the Interest packet or GPPkt matches the identifier prefix in the FIB entry, the next-hop routing node can be accessed through the LogicFace of NextHop record in FIB.

6.3.2 *Content Store*

The CS selectively stores data duplicates at intermediate nodes, which can improve content retrieval efficiency. When subsequent interest packets requesting the same content arrive, the duplicate data can be directly obtained from the CS [8].

The cache placement strategy and cache replacement strategy enable CS to store more useful data, improve the cache hit rate, and reduce the waste of cache space. The capacity constraint of CS should be also considered. The cache replacement strategy should ensure that the CS stays within its specified capacity limits.

6.3.3 *Pending Interest Table*

The PIT records the information about the interest packets that have not yet received the corresponding data packets. It also records the upstream and downstream LogicFace information of the interest packets. When the corresponding data packet arrives, it can be returned to the corresponding original upstream LogicFace recorded in PIT.

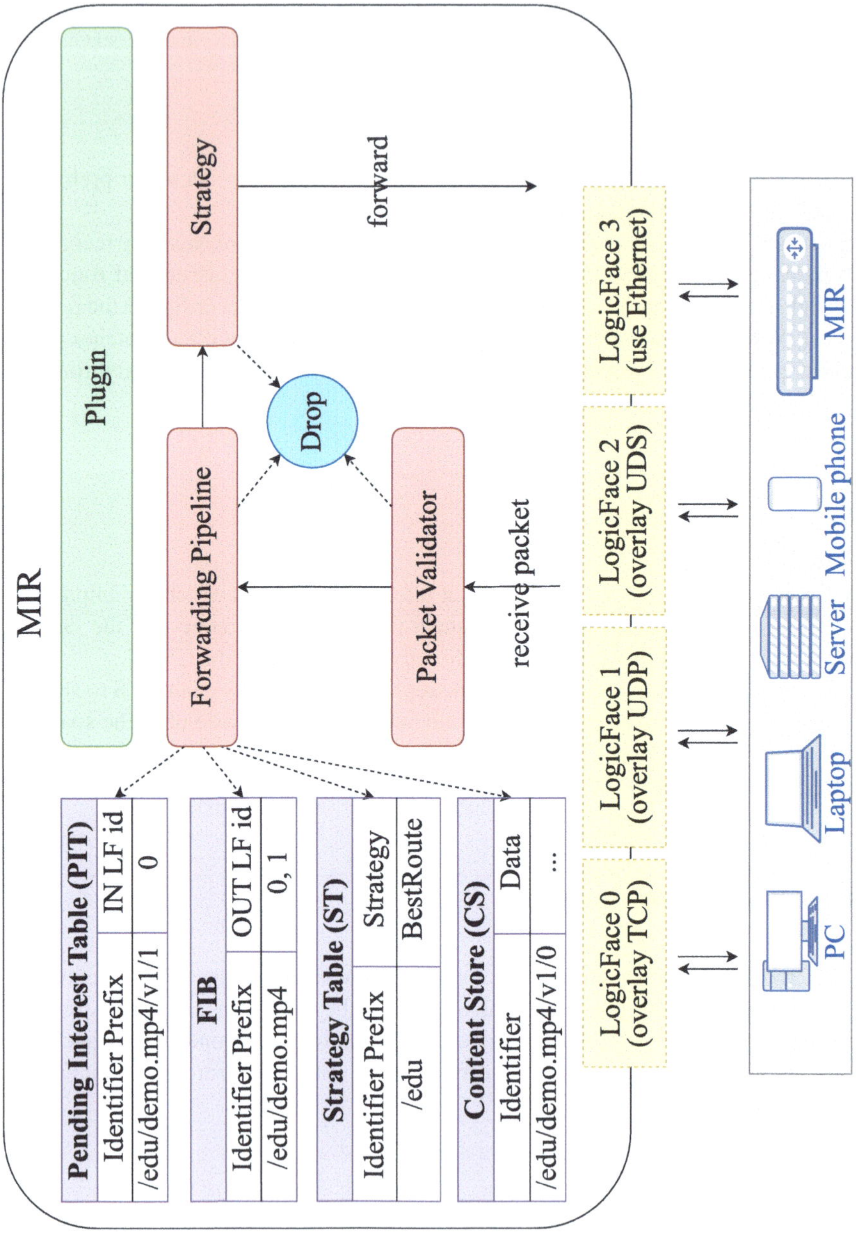

Fig. 6.3 The key data structures in MIR [6]

6.3.4 Strategy Table

Each namespace has its specific forwarding strategy, which is stored in the ST. Each strategy entry in the ST consists of the identifier prefix and the associated forwarding strategy of the namespace. The strategy selection algorithm determines the appropriate forwarding strategy to be adopted in a specific situation.

6.4 Packet Processing

The five stages of processing MIN network packets by MIR, as shown in Fig. 6.4, are as follows [9]:

- Input Stage: The input stage is primarily carried out by the LogicFace module. Its main responsibility is to receive data from the link, decode it, and extract individual MIN network packets. These packets are then forwarded to the subsequent stages of the processing pipeline.
- Pre-processing Stage: The pre-processing stage occurs prior to the MIN network packets received by the LogicFace module being processed by the forwarding thread. This stage encompasses several key tasks, including identifier selection, digital signature verification, and packet distribution.
- Forwarding Stage: The forwarding stage is the central phase of network packet processing and takes place within the forwarding thread. At this stage, MIR employs distinct processing flows based on the type of identifier associated with the network packet. The primary objective is to determine whether and how the network packet should be forwarded.
- Post-processing Stage: The post-processing stage primarily focuses on aggregating and forwarding the network packets that have been selected for forwarding by the forwarding threads. This stage involves performing certain uniform processing tasks on all MIN network packets that are to be sent out.
- Output Stage: The output stage is primarily executed by the LogicFace module. Its main role is to handle the MIN network packets in the sending queue and prepare them for transmission over the link.

6.4.1 Input Stage

The input stage of MIR takes place within LogicFace, which comprises two essential components: the Transport module and the Link Service module. The Transport module is responsible for establishing communication links between routers and implementing the necessary communication logic. Its primary role is to facilitate the establishment of seamless connections between routers. On the other hand, the Link Service module manages network packet fragmentation and reassembly. It

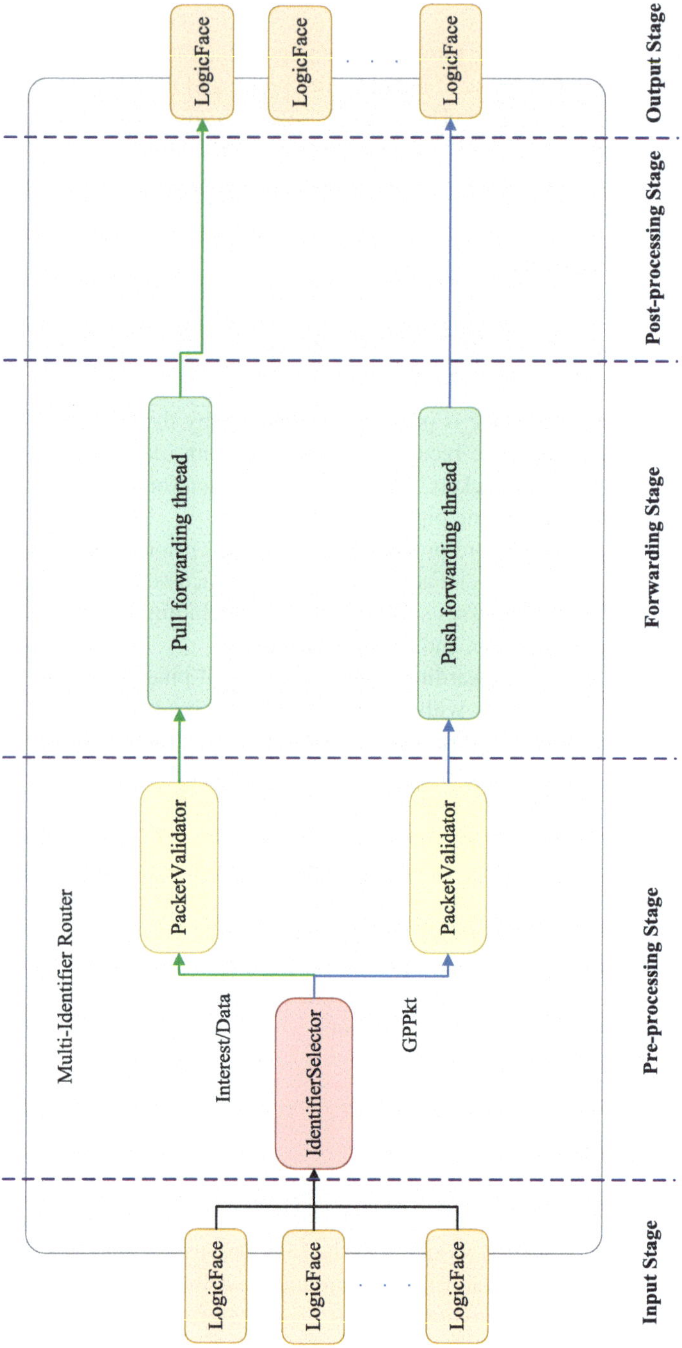

Fig. 6.4 The overall packet processing stages of MIR

offers a unified interface for packet transmission and reception to the upper layers, effectively abstracting the variations in underlying communication channels.

According to the definition of the MIN network packet format, in theory, a MIN network packet can be of infinite size. However, practical considerations such as the maximum transmission unit (MTU) of network links necessitate the establishment of an upper limit for the size of MIN network packets. Currently, MIR sets this limit at 8800 bytes. Any MIN network packet exceeding this size will be rejected for transmission and fail to undergo encoding.

The decision to set the upper limit at 8800 bytes is based on the MTU of commonly used network cards, which is typically 9000 bytes. In a pure MIN scenario, 200 bytes are reserved for the MIN virtual link layer header and Ethernet packet header. By setting the limit to 8800 bytes, fragmentation can be avoided when all network cards have an MTU of 9000 in a pure MIN environment.

However, it is not practical to assume that all network cards in actual deployments will have an MTU of 9000. Furthermore, MIN supports various types of communication links, and the MTU value cannot guarantee a specific minimum value. Therefore, MIR incorporates a virtual link layer packet called LLPacket, primarily utilized for fragmentation, reassembly, and fault detection of MIN network packets.

Figure 6.5 illustrates the format definition of LLPacket, which consists of two main fields: LLPacketHeader and Payload.

LLPacketHeader comprises three fields dedicated to packet fragmentation and reassembly, while the Payload carries either a complete MIN network packet or a fragment of a MIN network packet. The FragId field stores a monotonically increasing integer value to identify the packet to which the fragment belongs. The FragNum field indicates the total number of fragments, while the FragSeq field indicates the sequence number of the current fragment.

The forwarder in MIR does not transmit MIN network packets directly, but rather encapsulates them into LLPackets for transmission. This encapsulation process applies even to MIN network packets that are small enough and do not require fragmentation. The purpose of encapsulating MIN network packets into LLPackets is to ensure consistent handling and compatibility throughout the network system.

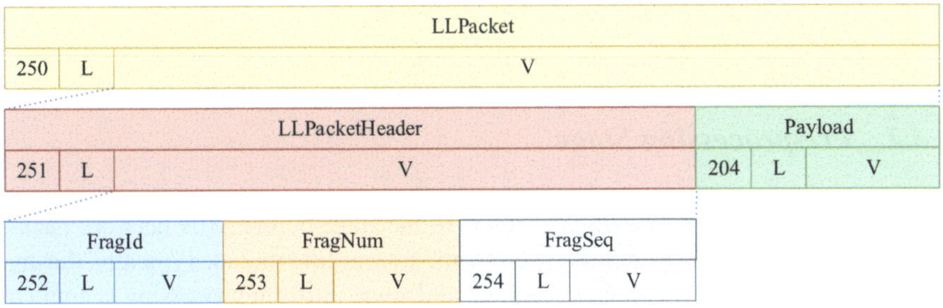

Fig. 6.5 LLPacket format

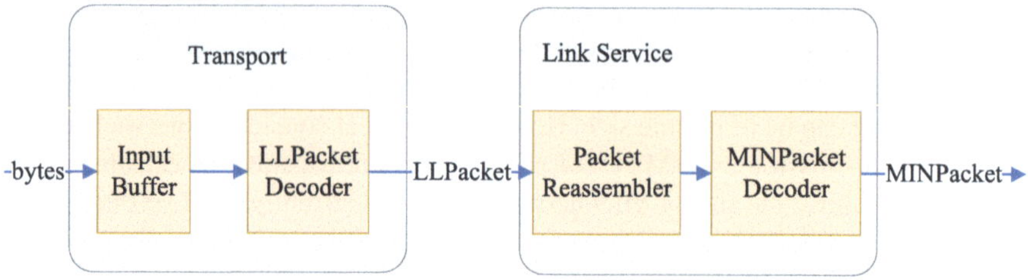

Fig. 6.6 The input stage of MIR

To facilitate transmission, the transporter in MIR defines two generic interfaces: send and receive. The send interface is responsible for sending LLPackets to the underlying link, while the receive interface handles the reception of LLPackets from the underlying communication link. These interfaces provide a standardized approach for transmitting LLPackets and receiving them from various communication links.

To ensure compatibility with different types of communication links, MIR allows router developers to implement different types of transporters. Currently, MIR has defined five types of transporters: InnerTransport, UnixTransport, EthernetTransport, TCPTransport, and UDPTransport. These transporters serve to bridge the gap between MIR's internal LLPackets and the specific characteristics and requirements of different communication links.

As shown in Fig. 6.6, the schematic diagram illustrates the processing flow of LogicFace in the input stage of MIR:

- Firstly, the transporter of LogicFace receives byte data from the underlying transport link and saves it into the input buffer.
- Then, the LLPacket decoder in the transporter reads the byte data from the input buffer and decodes them into individual LLPackets, which are then passed to the link service.
- Next, the packet reassembler in the link service reassembles the input LLPacket sequence into LLPackets containing complete MINPackets.
- Finally, the MINPacket decoder in the link service extracts the payload of the LLPacket and decodes it into MINPackets, which are then passed to the subsequent pre-processing stage for further processing.

6.4.2 Pre-processing Stage

The pre-processing stage specifically refers to the stage before MIN network packets received by LogicFace are processed by the forwarding thread. Typically, during this stage, identifier selection is performed, and some uniform processing is applied to network packets belonging to different types (e.g., digital signature verification, static data statistics, and so on).

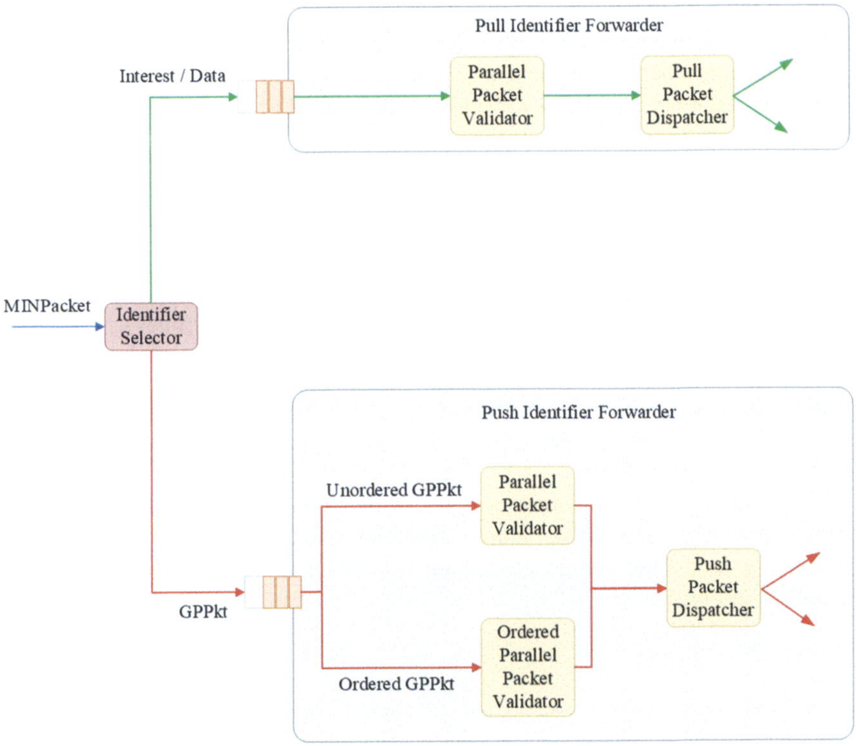

Fig. 6.7 The pre-processing stage of MIR

The processing flow of the pre-processing stage of MIR is shown in Fig. 6.7.

- For each received MIN network packet, the identifier selector is first used to select an identifier from its identifier field for forwarding. The identifier selector selects the first identifier supported by MIR for forwarding from the identifier field, starting from the front. Then, based on the selected identifier, the packet is classified as an Interest, Data, or GPPkt. Finally, the packet is placed into the receiving queue of the corresponding identifier forwarder. If it is an Interest or Data packet, it is placed into the receiving queue of the pull identifier forwarder. If it is a GPPkt, it is placed into the receiving queue of the push identifier forwarder.
- Inside the pull identifier forwarder, individual Interest and Data packets are retrieved from the receiving queue. First, the parallel packet validator is used to perform parallel signature verification. Packets that fail the verification are discarded, while those that pass the verification are passed on to the pull packet dispatcher for further processing. The pull packet dispatcher uses its internal distribution algorithm to assign the Interest and Data packets to a specific pull forwarding thread for processing.

- Inside the push identifier forwarder, individual GPPkt packets are retrieved from the receiving queue. The KeepInOrder field in the GPPkt's read-only area is used to determine whether the packets need to be kept in order (as shown in Fig. 6.8, the KeepInOrder field is a newly added field by MIR to differentiate whether the GPPkt needs to be ordered). If the KeepInOrder field of the GPPkt is True, it is passed to the ordered parallel packet validator for processing. Otherwise, it is passed to the parallel packet validator for processing. Both types of packet validators verify the digital signature in the GPPkt for validity. If the verification fails, the packet is discarded. If the verification is successful, the packet is passed on to the push packet dispatcher for further processing. The push packet dispatcher uses its internal distribution algorithm to assign the GPPkt to a specific push forwarding thread for processing.

In the pre-processing stage, several components play essential roles in MIR: the parallel packet validator, ordered parallel packet validator, pull packet dispatcher, and push packet dispatcher.

The parallel packet validator is designed with simplicity in mind. It incorporates a thread pool that treats the signature verification process of an individual network packet as a task. The internal processing flow of the parallel packet validator is illustrated in Fig. 6.9.

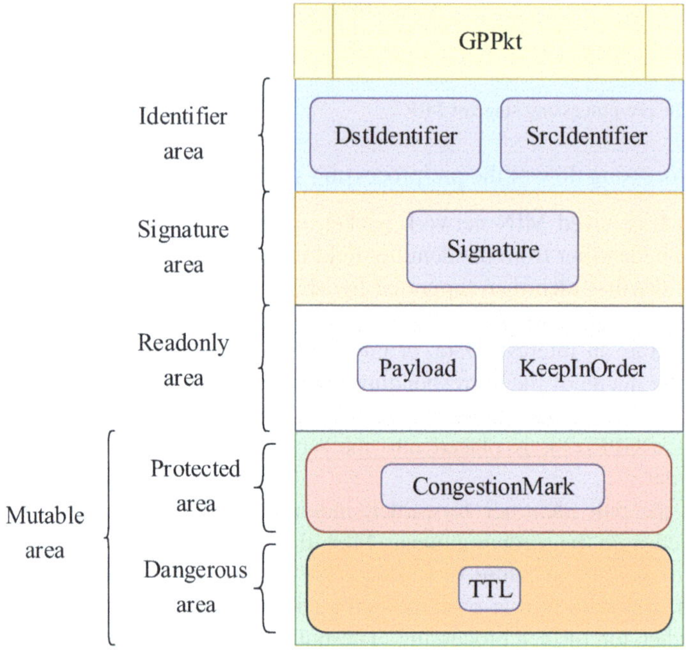

Fig. 6.8 KeepInOrder field in GPPkt

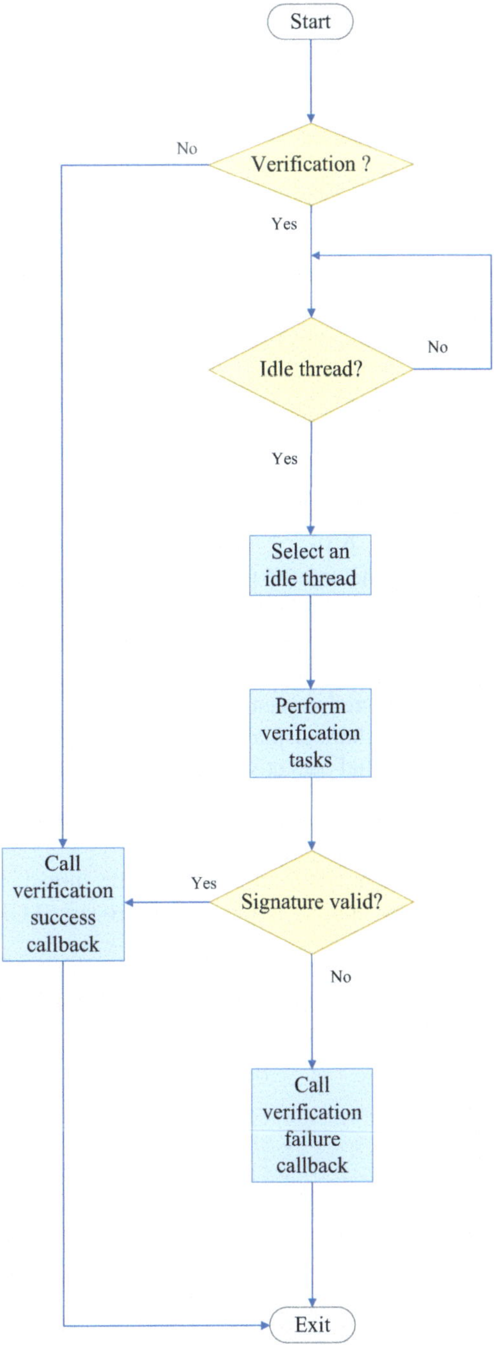

Fig. 6.9 The processing stages of parallel packet validator

- Initially, it checks whether signature verification is enabled. This enables the network administrator to specify in the MIR configuration file whether to enable signature verification. If signature verification is disabled, it triggers a successful verification callback directly, assuming the verification is considered successful.
- Next, it examines the availability of idle threads in the current thread pool. If no idle threads are available, the validator blocks and waits until an idle thread becomes available. However, if there are idle threads, it selects one of them to handle the upcoming task.
- Subsequently, it assigns the selected idle thread to execute the signature verification task. Upon successful verification, it triggers a successful verification callback. Conversely, if the verification fails, it triggers a failed verification callback.

The ordered parallel packet validator builds upon the parallel packet validator by adding packet order preservation. It can perform parallel signature verification while ensuring that the input and output order remains consistent. However, due to the additional requirement of maintaining packet order, its processing capacity may be slightly reduced. The internal structure of the ordered parallel packet validator is shown in Fig. 6.10.

In MIR, the ordered parallel packet validator enhances the signature verification process by utilizing a thread pool for parallel execution. The validated packets are subsequently sent to the sliding window module, where they are arranged in a sequential order. Finally, the packets that pass the signature verification are filtered from the ordered sequence of GPPkts by the verify success filter and outputted.

The flowchart displayed in Fig. 6.11 illustrates the internal processing of the ordered parallel packet validator.

- The processing of the initial steps aligns with the processing approach employed by the parallel packet validator.
- Upon identifying an available idle thread, the first step involves assigning a sequence number to the current processed GPPkt. This sequence number serves

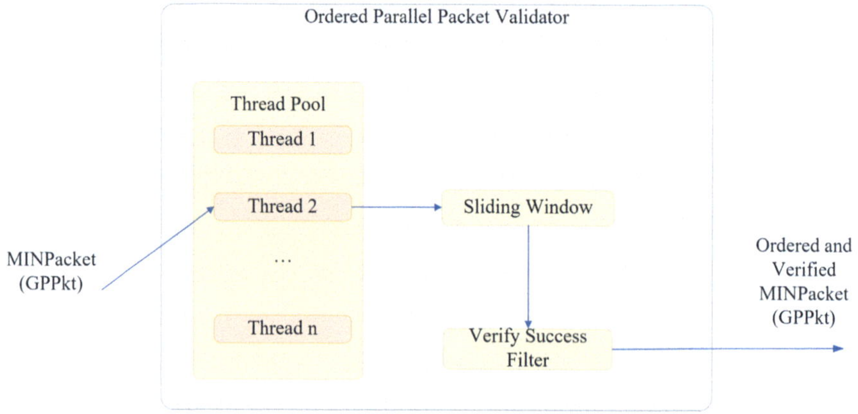

Fig. 6.10 Ordered parallel packet validator structure

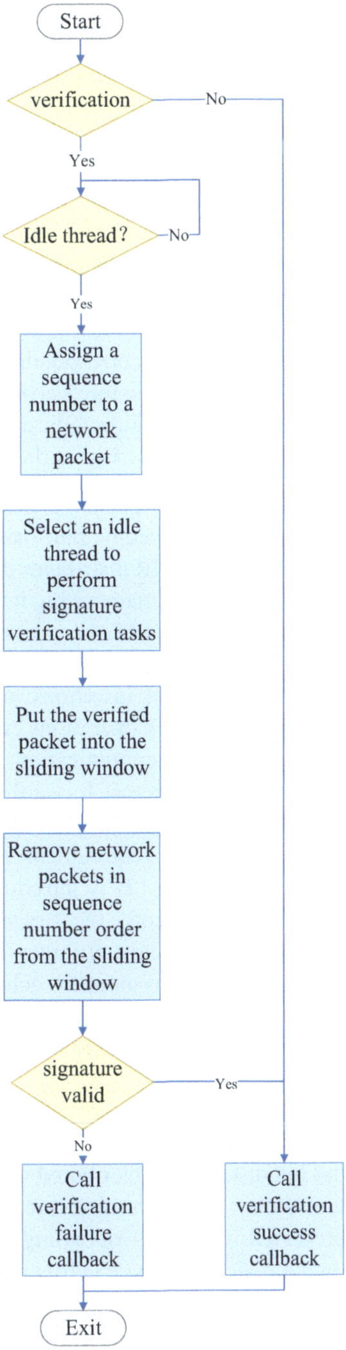

Fig. 6.11 The processing stages of ordered parallel packet validator

as the purpose of indicating the order of packet arrival within the ordered parallel packet validator and is only applicable within the module.

- Subsequently, an idle thread is selected from the thread pool to execute the digital signature verification of the GPPkt. The verification result is then stored in the context object associated with each packet in the MIR. The context object facilitates data sharing between modules.
- Following verification, the GPPkt is inserted into the sliding window module. The sequence number is assigned prior to verification to ensure that the sliding window module can output packets in the correct order. Even GPPkts that fail the verification process are inserted into the sliding window module.
- Next, GPPkts are retrieved sequentially from the sliding window module. For each GPPkt, the corresponding context is examined to determine the success or failure of the signature verification. In the case of failed verification, the corresponding verification failure callback is triggered. Conversely, successful verification of GPPkts triggers the corresponding verification success callback.

The pull-based packet distributor serves the primary purpose of allocating Interests/Data to specific pull-based forwarding threads for processing. To optimize parallelism, the MIR distributes the PIT table within each forwarding thread, resulting in each thread maintaining its own separate PIT table. This design enhances the query speed of the PIT, as concurrent operations by multiple forwarding threads on a single PIT would introduce significant concurrent access overhead. The PIT undergoes frequent insertions, deletions, and modifications, making the parallel optimization of PIT operations crucial.

In pull-based communication, Data is returned along the reverse path recorded in the PIT during Interest forwarding. Consequently, Interests associated with Data must be processed by the same forwarding thread.

To address this requirement, an Forward Thread Id Token (FTIToken) field (as depicted in Fig. 6.12) is introduced in the mutable danger zone of Interests and Data. This field records the forwarding thread responsible for processing the Interest as it traverses the current router. It operates on a hop-by-hop basis, and when Data is returned hop-by-hop, it echoes the corresponding field from the Interest. Consequently, when an intermediate router receives a Data packet, it can determine the appropriate forwarding thread for forwarding based on the FTIToken carried by the Data.

The internal structure of the pull-based packet distributor is illustrated in Fig. 6.13. Upon receiving Interests, a thread ID is computed based on the name, and the Interest is then distributed to the corresponding forwarding thread for processing. Within the forwarding thread, the original FTIToken value from the Interest is preserved in the corresponding PIT entry, while the ID of the current forwarding thread is stored in the FTIToken field of the Interest. For received Data packets, the FTIToken field value is directly extracted as the selected thread ID, and the packet is distributed to the corresponding thread for further processing. Within the forwarding thread, the FTIToken stored in the PIT entry is replaced with the corresponding field in the Data packet.

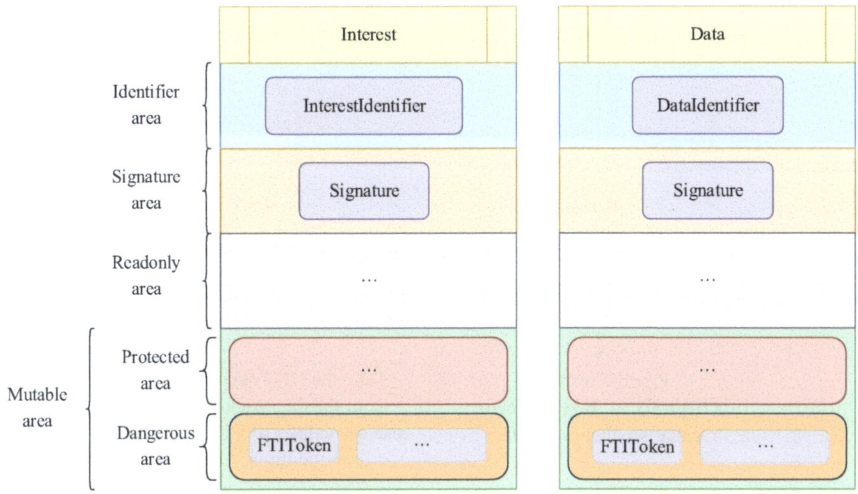

Fig. 6.12 FTIToken field in Interest and Data

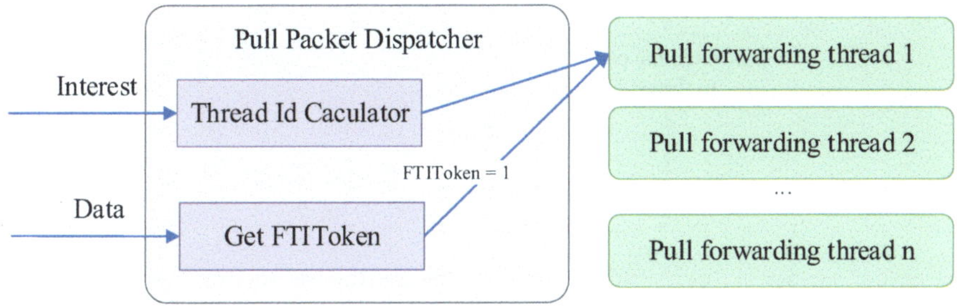

Fig. 6.13 The structure of pull-based packet dispatcher

Figure 6.14 illustrates the flowchart depicting the internal processing of the pull-based packet distributor:

- Initially, the network packet type is determined, and distinct processing steps are executed for Interests and Data packets.
- In the case of an Interest packet, the first m components of the name (where m is a configurable parameter) are extracted to create a prefix. The xxh3 algorithm is employed to map this name prefix to a 64-bit integer value. Subsequently, the lower 16 bits of the hash result are taken modulo the total number of pull-based forwarding threads, denoted as n, to calculate the selected thread identifier, i.
- For Data packets, the value of the FTIToken field is directly utilized as the thread identifier, i.
- Finally, the Interest or Data packet is dispatched to the ith pull-based forwarding thread for processing.

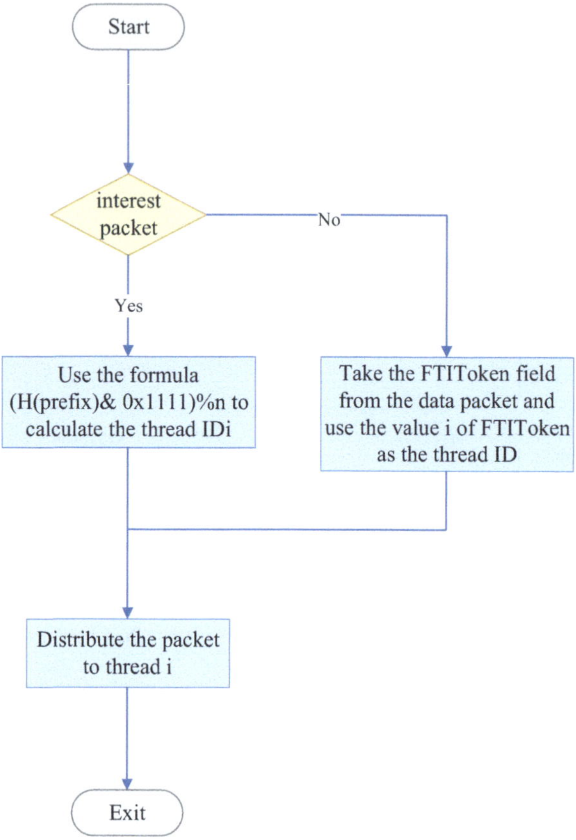

Fig. 6.14 The processing stages of pull-based distributor

The push-based packet distributor plays a crucial role in allocating GPPkts to specific push-based forwarding threads for processing. As previously mentioned, packet reordering can significantly impact transmission performance in certain push-based communication scenarios. Thus, MIR addresses the issue of packet reordering during the parallel signature verification phase by introducing an ordered parallel packet validator. However, at the forwarding phase, where MIR utilizes multiple push-based forwarding threads for parallel forwarding, packet reordering can still occur.

To overcome this challenge, MIR requires the push-based packet distributor to direct all GPPkts belonging to the same data stream and requiring ordering to the same forwarding thread during packet distribution. For instance, in a TCP communication between entities A and B, all packets sent from A to B should be processed by the same forwarding thread, and likewise, all packets sent from B to A should be processed by another designated forwarding thread. However, it is not necessary for packets in both directions to be processed by the same forwarding thread.

Introducing complex and invasive designs to decode business fields above the network layer at the router level would be cumbersome and increase decoding overhead. Consequently, MIR exclusively decodes the fields at the network layer and does not concern itself with the specifics of the upper-layer business. To differentiate packets belonging to different push-based flows at the network layer, MIR introduces a new FlowId field in the read-only area of the GPPkt (as depicted in Fig. 6.15). This field comprises a variable-length integer value randomly generated by the endpoint. By considering GPPkts with the same FlowId as belonging to the same flow, MIR can allocate them to the appropriate forwarding thread for processing.

The flowchart of the internal processing of the push-based packet distributor is shown in Fig. 6.16:

- First, extract the KeepInOrder field of the GPPkt to determine if ordered processing is required.
- If ordered processing is not required, randomly select a thread identifier, i, from the range [0, n).
- If ordered processing is required, extract the FlowId field of the GPPkt, apply the xxh3 algorithm for hashing, and use the low 16 bits to modulo the total number of push-based forwarding threads, n, to calculate the selected thread identifier, i.
- Finally, distribute the GPPkt to the ith push-based forwarding thread for processing.

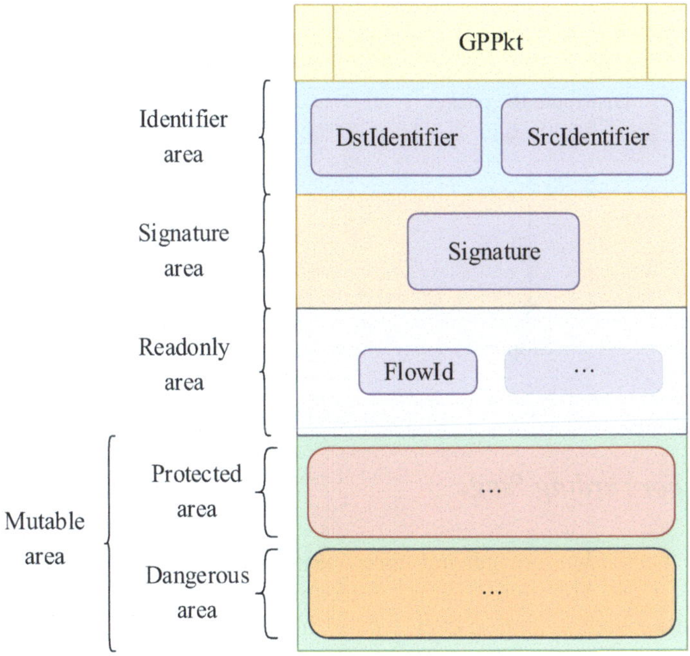

Fig. 6.15 FlowId field in GPPkt

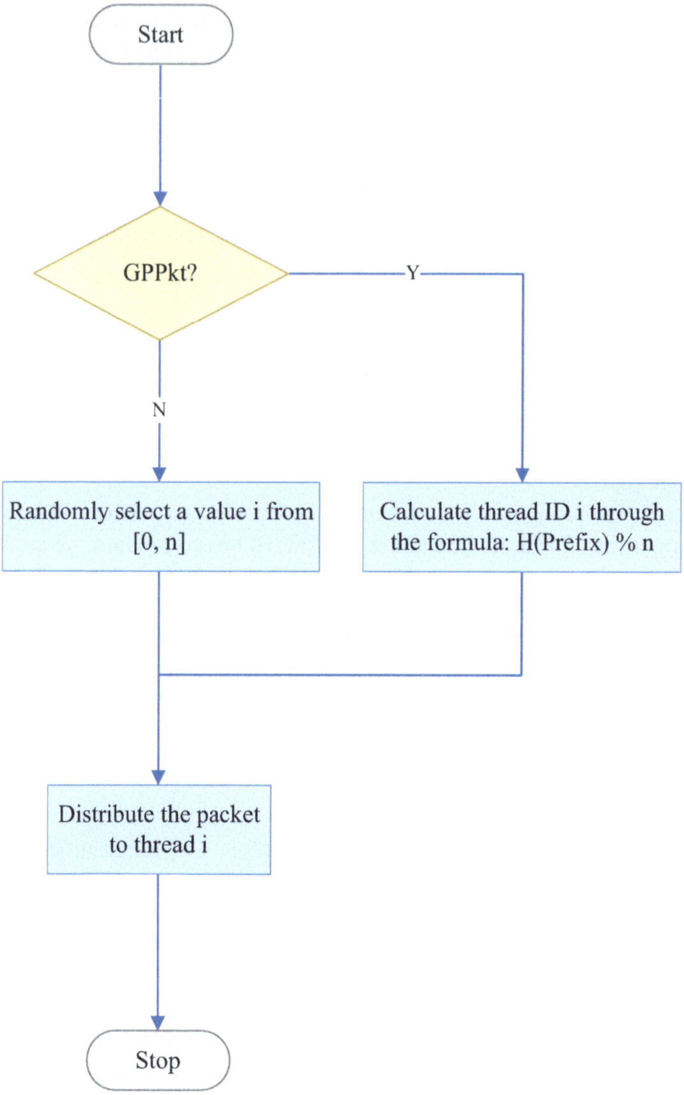

Fig. 6.16 The processing stages of push-based distributor

6.4.3 Forwarding Stage

Identifier Forwarders are integral components within MIR that handle network identifiers. Upon MIR initialization, an Identifier Forwarder is registered for each supported network identifier. Each type of Identifier Forwarder encapsulates the processing logic specific to a particular communication paradigm. Currently, MIR defines two types of forwarders: Pull Identifier Forwarder and Push Identifier Forwarder (Fig. 6.17).

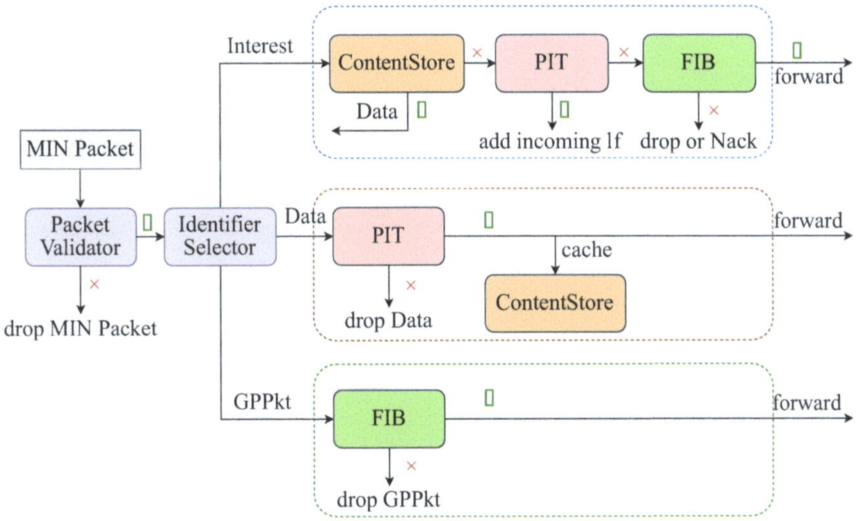

Fig. 6.17 Packet processing in MIR [6]

The Pull Identifier Forwarder is responsible for managing Content Identifiers, which are utilized by Interests and Data packets for communication. It comprises a parallel packet validator, a pull packet distributor, and m pull forwarding threads, where m represents the number of pull forwarding threads.

On the other hand, the Push Identifier Forwarder is designed to handle Identity Identifiers, which are employed by GPPkt for communication. It consists of a parallel packet validator, an ordered parallel packet validator, a push packet distributor, and n push-based forwarding threads (where n represents the number of push-based forwarding threads).

The forwarding stage in MIR takes place within the pull-based forwarding threads and push-based forwarding threads.

Figure 6.18 illustrates the internal processing flow diagram of the pull-based forwarding thread.

- Initially, a MIN network packet is retrieved from the receive queue, and its network packet type is determined.
- In the case of an Interest packet, the processing flow for Interests is executed as follows: The name of the Interest is extracted, and a lookup is performed in the CS table using an exact match rule. If a matching Data packet is found, it is forwarded to the LogicFace where the Interest arrived. If no matching Data packet is found, a lookup is conducted in the PIT table using an exact match rule. If a matching entry is present in the PIT table, the receiving LogicFace of the Interest is added to the PIT entry, and the Interest is discarded. Otherwise, a lookup is performed in the ST table using the longest prefix match rule. If a matching ST entry is found, the corresponding forwarding strategy is applied. If no matching entry is found, the default strategy is applied. Within the selected forwarding strategy, a lookup is executed in the pull forwarding table (Pull FIB) using the

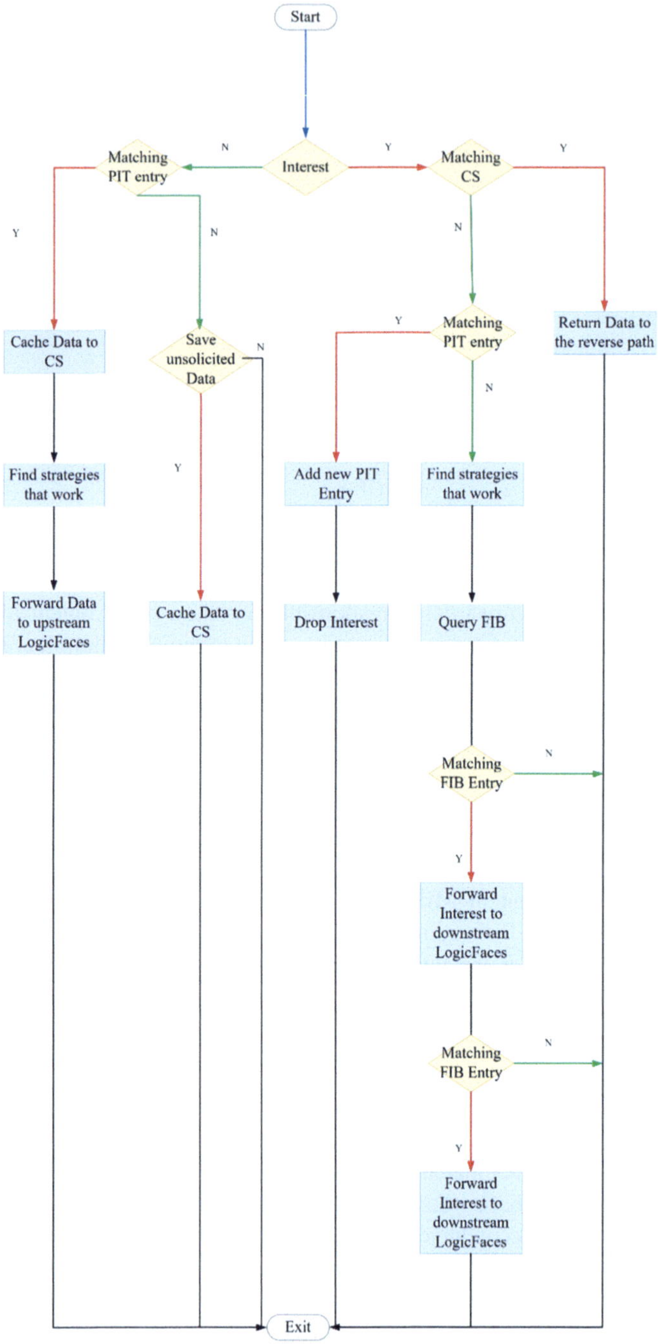

Fig. 6.18 The processing stages of pull-based forwarding thread

Interest's name. If no matching entry is found, the Interest is discarded. Otherwise, one or more LogicFaces are selected based on the forwarding strategy definition (different strategies may choose different LogicFaces; for example, the best route strategy selects the next hop with the lowest cost, while the broadcast strategy selects all available next hops). The Interest is then forwarded to all selected LogicFaces.
- In the case of a Data packet, the processing flow for Data is executed as follows: The name of the Data packet is extracted, and an exact match lookup is performed in the PIT table. If no matching entry is found, it indicates that the received Data packet is unsolicited. The decision to cache or discard the Data packet is based on the network administrator's configuration. If a matching PIT entry is found, the Data packet is cached in the CS, and a lookup is performed in the ST table using the longest prefix match rule. If a matching ST entry is found, the corresponding forwarding strategy is applied. If no matching entry is found, the default strategy is applied. Within the selected forwarding strategy, one or more LogicFaces are selected from the PIT entry that received the corresponding Interest (typically, the implementation of the strategy selects to forward a copy of the Data packet to all LogicFaces where the Interest arrived), and the Data packet is forwarded to all selected LogicFaces.

Figure 6.19 displays the internal processing flow diagram of the push forwarding thread:

- Initially, a GPPkt is retrieved from the receive queue, and a lookup is performed in the ST table using its destination identity identifier (dii). If a matching ST entry is found, the corresponding forwarding strategy is applied. If no matching entry is found, the default strategy is applied.
- Within the selected forwarding strategy, a lookup is conducted in the push forwarding table (Push FIB) using the dii of the GPPkt. If no matching entry is found, the GPPkt is discarded. If a matching entry is found, one or more LogicFaces are selected based on the definition of the forwarding strategy. The GPPkt is then forwarded to all selected LogicFaces.

6.4.4 Post-processing Stage

The post-processing stage refers specifically to the phase that occurs after the forwarding stage but before the MIN network packets are transmitted to the LogicFace for output. During this stage, all MIN network packets intended for forwarding are aggregated, enabling unified post-processing. As the output stage takes place within the LogicFace and the processing among LogicFaces is independent, achieving a unified post-processing approach becomes feasible solely in this stage.

At present, MIR incorporates static statistics of MIN network packets as part of the post-processing stage. It is worth noting that future enhancements can introduce additional functionalities to this stage as well.

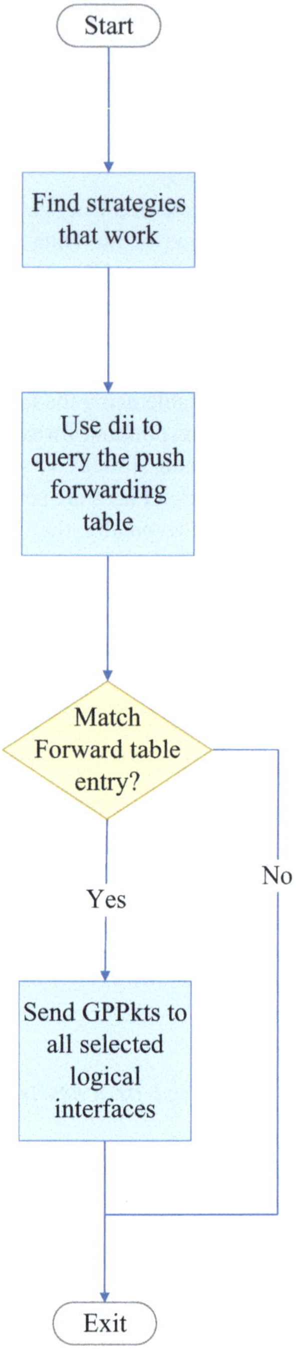

Fig. 6.19 The processing stages of push-based forwarding thread

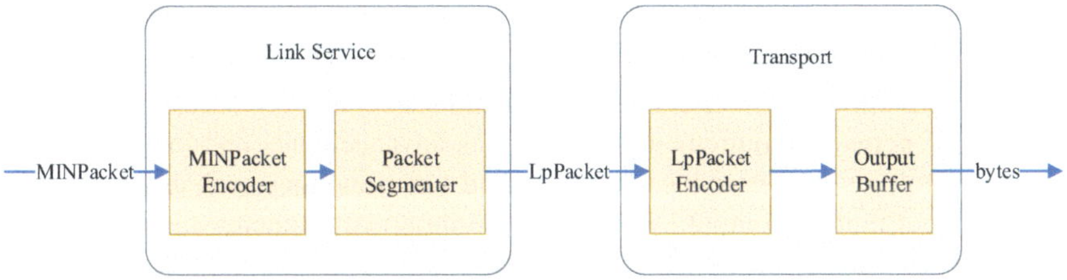

Fig. 6.20 The processing stages of output stage

6.4.5 Output Stage

Figure 6.20 presents the processing flow diagram of the LogicFace during the output stage of MIR.

This stage primarily involves fragmenting and packaging the MIN network packets as necessary and transmitting them through the underlying communication link.

The processing flow in this stage is as follows:

- Initially, the Link Service module of the LogicFace sequentially retrieves MINPackets from the output queue and utilizes the MINPacket Encoder to encode them into byte arrays.
- Subsequently, the Packet Segmenter within the Link Service checks if the encoded byte array exceeds the MTU of the underlying communication link (obtained from the Transport). If the byte array size does not exceed the MTU, a single LLPacket is created, and the encoded byte array is placed in the payload of the LLPacket. However, if the size exceeds the MTU, multiple LLPackets are constructed, with each LLPacket containing a segment of the data. These LLPackets are then passed to the Transport module.
- The LLPacket Encoder in the Transport module encodes the LLPacket into a byte array, which is subsequently passed to the Output Buffer.
- Finally, the Transport module utilizes the appropriate underlying communication mechanism (such as a network card, TCP tunnel, UDP tunnel, or Unix tunnel) to transmit the data stored in the Output Buffer onto the network.

6.5 Wireless Extension

6.5.1 Overview of Wi-Fi Technology

Wireless Fidelity (Wi-Fi) represents a local area network (LAN) communication technology that wirelessly interconnects electronic terminal devices [10]. The technology is grounded on the IEEE 802.11 standard, a wireless LAN communication standard delineated by the Institute of Electrical and Electronics Engineers (IEEE). This standard establishes a wireless connection for portable and mobile terminal devices by defining a Media Access Control layer (MAC) and several Physical layers [11].

Wi-Fi technology offers users high-speed and stable network access, catering to a variety of network requirements. Continuous advancements and innovations in Wi-Fi technology have introduced features and functionalities such as Multi-User multiple input multiple output (MU-MIMO), orthogonal frequency division multiple access (OFDMA), and target wake time (TWT). These technologies enhance the transmission rate, network capacity, and energy efficiency of Wi-Fi, bolstering its performance and advantages.

Currently, Wi-Fi technology provides flexible underlying communication support for various scenarios. For example, it can support the connectivity and control of diverse smart devices, such as smart TVs, smart speakers, smart bulbs, and smart locks [12]. Beyond conventional communication scenarios, Wi-Fi technology also caters to specialized environments by offering tailored network solutions. It supports the connectivity and application of specialized devices such as drones, virtual reality (VR) headsets, and medical equipment [13].

6.5.2 Wireless Extension for MIR

To better adapt to diverse application scenarios, MIR supports the wireless transmission of MIN network packets, enabling devices to join the network easily and conveniently. Raspberry Pi 4b [14] is a single-board computer based on the ARM architecture. It boasts high performance and flexibility, capable of running various operating systems and applications. By utilizing the Raspberry Pi 4b as a device for the wireless access point (AP), it can convert wired network signals into wireless signals, allowing other devices to access the internet via Wi-Fi technology. The wireless extension is realized by activating the wireless access point (AP) function on the Raspberry Pi 4b and running MIR and other MIN architecture support codes to complete the wireless forwarding of MIN network packets.

To construct a network packet transmitted in the Wi-Fi environment, an Ethernet header must be added to the front of the MIN network packet, including the source MAC address, destination MAC address, and type field. When the Ethernet frame is sent to the wireless network card, it is encapsulated into an 802.11 frame and sent to the AP via Wi-Fi. The header of the 802.11 frame includes information such as the source MAC address, destination MAC address, and frame control field. The frame control field is used to identify the type of frame, such as a data frame or management frame. After the AP receives the frame, it determines whether it belongs to itself based on the destination MAC address. If it does, it will be decapsulated. Figure 6.21 illustrates the forwarding process of the MIN network packet in the Wi-Fi environment.

Figure 6.22 shows the Ethernet frame format and 802.11 frame format encapsulating the MIN network packet.

The meanings of the fields in the 802.11 frame are as follows:

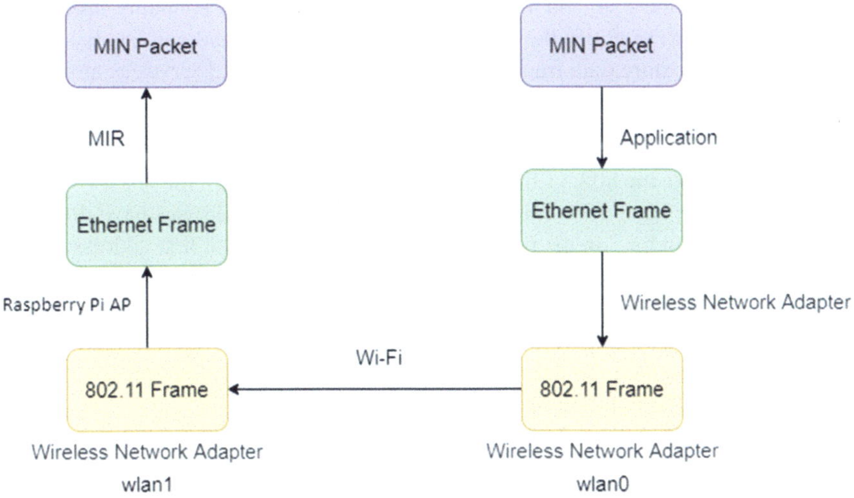

Fig. 6.21 The forwarding process of the MIN network packet in the Wi-Fi environment

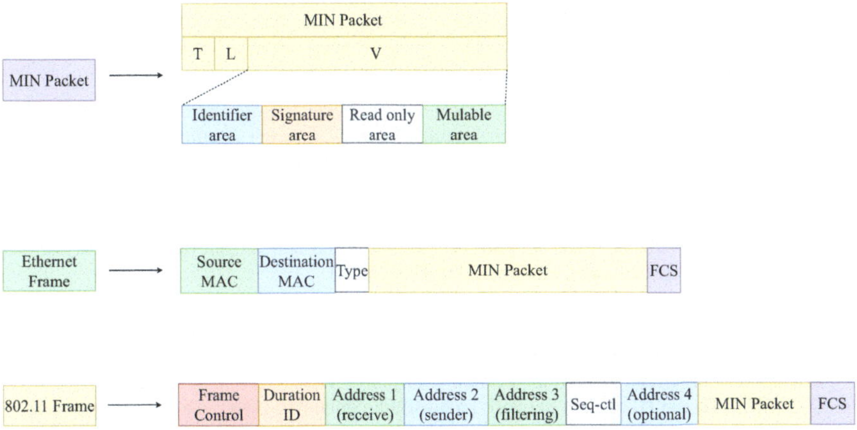

Fig. 6.22 Frame formats in the Wi-Fi environment

- Frame Control: This field contains some flags, indicating the information for this frame.
- Duration ID: This 16-bit field has three types of meanings based on the values of the 14th and 15th bits.
  - When the 15th bit is set to 0, this field indicates the time required for the transmission of this data frame, in microseconds.
  - When the 15th bit is set to 1 and the 14th bit is also 0, this field is used to announce the no-contest time when no new Beacon frame (a type of Management frame) has been received.

  - When both the 15th and 14th bits are set to 1, this field is mainly used for a STA(Station) to notify the AP that it is going to sleep and entrusts the AP to temporarily store data frames sent to this STA. This field serves as an identifier so that the STA can obtain the temporarily stored frames from the AP after waking up.

- Address: Unlike the 802.3 Ethernet transmission mechanism, the 802.11 WLAN data frame can have up to four MAC addresses. These addresses have different meanings depending on the type of the frame. Typically, the first address represents the MAC address of the receiver, the second address represents the MAC address of the sender, and the third address represents the filtering address.
- Seq-ctl: Sequence control bit. This field is used for reassembling data frame fragments when fragmenting data frames and discarding duplicate frames.
- Frame Body: The network packet contained in the frame.
- FCS: Frame Check Sum. It is mainly used to check the integrity of the frame.

In conclusion, the wireless extension of MIR is still being continuously upgraded to provide rich functionality and better user experience and cater to a broader range of application scenarios.

References

1. Diao W, An J, Li T, et al. Low delay fragment forwarding in LEO satellite networks based on named data networking. Comput Commun. 2023;211:216–28.
2. Dhara S, Majidi A, Clarke S. Revving up VNDN: efficient caching and forwarding by expanding content popularity perspective and mobility. Comput Commun. 2023;212:342–52.
3. Man D, Lu Q, Wang H, et al. On-path caching based on content relevance in information-centric networking. Comput Commun. 2021;176:272–81.
4. Xue K, He P, Yang J, et al. Scd2: secure content delivery and deduplication with multiple content providers in information centric networking. IEEE/ACM Trans Netw. 2022;30(4):1849–64.
5. Wang X, Zhang R. Learning automata based content forwarding for information-centric IoT. IEEE Trans Green Commun Netw. 2023;8(1):402–12.
6. Que JM, Li H, Bai H, et al. A network architecture containing both push and pull semantics. In: 2021 7th international conference on computer and communications (ICCC). Piscataway: IEEE; 2021. p. 2211–6.
7. Rosa EC, de Oliveira SF. A review on recent NDN FIB implementations for high-speed switches. In: International conference on advanced information networking and applications. Cham: Springer International Publishing; 2022. p. 288–300.
8. Silva ET, Macedo JMH, Costa ALD. NDN content store and caching policies: performance evaluation. Computers. 2022;11(3):37–53.
9. Xu Q, Su Z, Fang D, et al. Hierarchical bandwidth allocation for social community-oriented multicast in space-air-ground integrated networks. IEEE Trans Wirel Commun. 2022;22(3):1915–30.
10. Niehenke EC. Wireless communications: present and future: introduction to focused issue articles. IEEE Microw Mag. 2014;15(2):26–35.
11. Ramezanpour K, Jagannath J, Jagannath A. Security and privacy vulnerabilities of 5G/6G and WiFi 6: survey and research directions from a coexistence perspective. Comput Netw. 2023;221(109515):1–14.

12. Kumar V, Yadav P, Indrusiak LS. Resilient edge: building an adaptive and resilient multi-communication network for IoT edge using LPWAN and WiFi. IEEE Trans Netw Serv Manag. 2023;20(3):3055–71.
13. Zhang D, Niu K, Xiong J, et al. WiFi/4G/5G based wireless sensing: theories, applications and future directions. In: Integrated sensing and communications. Singapore: Springer Nature Singapore; 2023. p. 387–417.
14. Karthikeyan S, Aakash R, Cruz MV, et al. A systematic analysis on Raspberry Pi prototyping: uses, challenges, benefits, and drawbacks. IEEE Internet Things J. 2023;10(16):14397–417.

Chapter 7
Data Synchronization

Distributed applications involve data synchronization between one and multiple objects. This chapter introduces the design patterns, advantages and disadvantages of the existing data synchronization protocols, as well as the specific design of the two data synchronization protocols in MIN networks.

7.1 Overview of Data Synchronization

Data synchronization is the basic requirement of distributed applications. Different scenarios and applications may require different synchronization modes, and each mode focuses on a different range of synchronized data. For some applications, such as group chats, each node needs to retrieve newly published data from any participant. The data synchronization pattern in this type of application is called full data synchronization. For subscription-based applications, each node is often required to retrieve only a subset of the newly published data from the data producer. For example, users of a weather application may only follow the weather conditions in a specific city or region. The data synchronization pattern used in such applications is often referred to as partial data synchronization.

As the key of network transport, data synchronization faces the challenges of network overhead and transmission efficiency [1]. In the pull-based communication process of MIN networks [2, 3], after the data producer generates the data, the data consumer needs to send the request to obtain the data, and then the data producer sends the data to the data consumer. Data producers publish data with unique hierarchical names. The data consumer sends the Interest packet containing the data name to request the data. Intermediate nodes forward Interest packets from data consumers based on data names and selectively cache Data packets from data producers for the same requests from other data consumers. In the process described above, data consumers constantly send Interest packets to data producers to obtain data. The data synchronization protocol can let the data consumer know when to get

H. Li, H. Bai, *Principle of Architecture, Protocol, and Algorithms for CoG-MIN*,
https://doi.org/10.1007/978-981-96-3596-2_7

the data and what data to get, so that the whole communication process is simple and orderly.

At present, there are many studies on data synchronization protocols based on pull-based communication semantics, but they still face many challenges. For example, in the ChronoSync protocol [4], each synchronous node publishes data with its own unique name prefix. Data is named sequentially, and data names are stored using a Merkle tree structure, with each leaf node storing only the most recent data name, significantly reducing the amount of encoding required for data set representation. However, the ChronoSync protocol requires that each node periodically publishes a synchronization Interest packet to all other nodes to get information about the data generated by the other nodes. This generates a large number of synchronous Interest packets in the network. The iSync protocol [5] uses the Invertible Bloom Filter (IBF) to realize efficient data encoding and fast difference detection. However, the synchronization process requires more round trips and the synchronization delay is high. In addition, the ChronoSync protocol and iSync protocol have limitations in adequately supporting scenarios such as publish-subscribe. This limitation stems from the fact that their design focuses on full data synchronization scenarios and ignores the application requirements for partial data synchronization. The Psync protocol [6] addresses the application requirement of partial data synchronization by naming data sequentially and encoding only the name of the latest data in IBF. However, the Psync protocol also faces the same divergence problem.

For the data transmission based on the pull-based communication semantics in MIN networks, two data synchronization protocols are commonly used: the MINSync protocol and the MINGroupSync protocol [7].

MINSync protocol effectively mitigates the issue of introducing a large number of synchronization Interest packets. Meanwhile, it improves the data recovery mechanism and enhances the security of the synchronization network through identity authentication. However, the MINSync protocol relies on Interest multicast to deliver state change notifications to every node in the group, posing challenges to routing scalability in the network.

To address this issue, the MINGroupSync protocol adopts the idea of group synchronization. It selects the leading node within the group to manage and synchronize the synchronization group and combines the notification of Interest packets to further reduce the number of Interest packets. In addition, each synchronization group adopts distributed management, which can realize full data synchronization and partial data synchronization at the same time. This approach ensures good routing scalability. This chapter introduces the design of these two protocols in detail.

7.2 MINSync

7.2.1 Overview of MINSync

Figure 7.1 shows the overall architecture of MINSync. Each synchronization node maintains three data structures:

Sync Dataset

It stores data published locally or received from other nodes via MINSync for access by local applications.

Dataset State IBF

It represents the namespace that denotes the latest state of the shared dataset in the synchronization network. It is encoded using an IBF and contains the names of all the latest data published in the synchronization network known to the synchronization node. The IBF is updated whenever a node generates new data or receives new data from other nodes.

Dataset State Log

Each node keeps a log that records changes in the synchronized content. As given in Table 7.1, this log is a list of key-value pairs in chronological order. The key is the count representing the number of updates to the IBF, incremented by 1 for each update (starting from 1). The value is the data producer state, containing the producer's prefix and message serial number. The log can be used for data recovery. For example, when a node reconnects after disconnection, it sends a log request to other

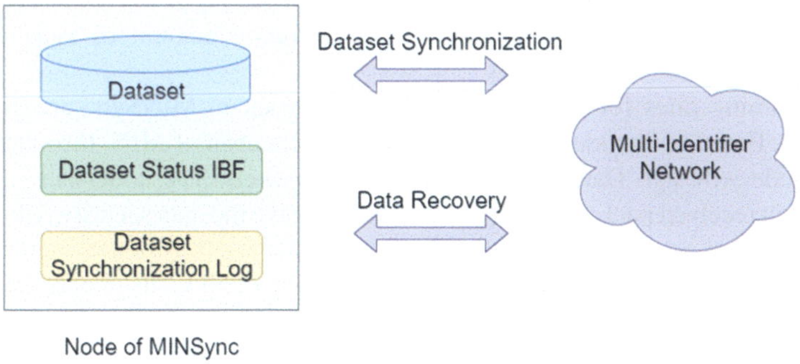

Fig. 7.1 MINSync architecture

Table 7.1 Dataset synchronization log for MINSync

Count	Data producer state
1	/nodeA/1
…	…
20	/nodeA/18, /nodeB/16
21	/nodeB/17, /nodeC/15

Table 7.2 Naming rules for each type of network packet in MINSync

Packet type	Naming rules
Data Publishing Interest Packet	/min/producer-name/minsync/publish/app-name/seq#
Data Requesting Interest Packet	/min/consumer-name/minsync/request/producer-name/app-name/seq#
Node Data Packet	/min/producer-name/minsync/app-name/seq#
Data Recovering Interest Packet	/min/node-name/minsync/recover/count

nodes, including information about the update count of the node. Upon receiving the log request, other nodes compare the count values and directly reply to the missing data. To prevent the log size from increasing indefinitely, MINSync can set the log size based on the available resources and reserve only the latest n records.

7.2.2 Naming Scheme

MINSync adopts the naming rule used in ChronoSync [4] and Psync [6], where data names are named in a "node prefix + sequential name" structure. Each node has a unique routable prefix, the data it publishes is numbered from zero, and the data it publishes is assigned a sequential numbering starting from zero. As new data is generated, the serial number of the data is incremented by 1. In this naming convention, the data generated by the same data producer can be represented with the highest sequence number. The synchronization protocol only needs to close the latest sequence number of the same node prefix, without paying attention to the entire namespace. This can effectively reduce the encoding amount of synchronization state.

The naming rules for each type of network packet in MINSync are given in Table 7.2. Based on the identity authentication mechanism of MIN, the synchronization node will sign Data packets and Interest packets. The node will sign and verify each received packet, which can effectively solve the data security risks of the synchronization protocol.

In the data synchronization process, the processing of all kinds of network packets can be summarized as follows.

Data Publishing Interest Packet

When the data producer node generates new data, it will send the Data Publishing Interest Packet to other nodes in MINSync.

The name of this packet is "/min/producer-name/minsync/publish/app-name/seq#".

- "/producer-name" indicates the name of a node that publishes new data.
- "/publish" indicates that new data is published.
- "/app-name" indicates the name of an application program that generates new data.
- "seq#" indicates the serial number of the node that generates data.

The data producer node uses the private key to sign the Data Publishing Interest Packet to prevent tampering by malicious nodes and ensure the security of data synchronization.

Data Requesting Interest Packet

When other nodes in the synchronous network receive the Data Publishing Interest Packet, they send the Data Requesting Interest Packet to the data producer node.

The packet is named as "/min/consumer-name/minsync/request/producer-name/app-name/seq#".

- "/consumer-name" indicates the name of the node that requests new data.
- "/request" indicates that new data is obtained.
- "/producer-name/app-name/seq#" indicates that new data is requested.

The data consumer node signs the Data Requesting Interest Packet with the private key. Since the MIR does not need to query the forwarding table when processing the Data Requesting Interest Packet and only needs to return packets along the path of the Data Publishing Interest Packet.

In order to further shorten the synchronization process and reduce the number of packets generated in the network, the identifier field is added to the Data Requesting Interest Packet. It has the function of replying to the Data Publishing Interest Packet and obtaining data at the same time.

Node Data Packet

When the data producer node receives the Data Requesting Interest Packet from the data consumer node, it sends the Node Data Packet to the node that requests the data.

The Node Data Packet is named as "/min/producer-name/minsync/app-name/seq#".

- "/producer-name" indicates the name of the node that publishes new data.

- "/app-name" indicates the name of the application that generates new data so that applications of other synchronization nodes can retrieve data in the Sync Dataset.
- "/seq#" indicates the data serial number.

The content of the Node Packet contains the new data generated by the data producer node. The data producer node signs the Node Data Packet with the private key.

Data Recovering Interest Packet

When a synchronization node experiences data loss due to events like packet loss or abnormal connections, it sends a Data Recovering Interest Packet to other nodes.

The Data Recovering Interest Packet is named as "/min/node-name/minsync/recover/count".

- "/node-name" is the name of the node which requests data recovery.
- "/count" represents the latest count of the node synchronization Dataset State Log.

The node uses the private key to sign the Data Recovering Interest Packet. After the other node receives the Data Recovering Interest Packet and verifies the identity of the requesting node, it compares the count value and responds by sending a Data packet that contains the missing data to the requesting node.

7.2.3 Namespace Representation

In order to improve space utilization, the Dataset State IBF of MINSync encodes only the name of the latest data element as the synchronization state. When a new sequence number of a node prefix is encoded, the previous encoded sequence number of that node prefix is first removed from the Dataset State IBF, ensuring that the Dataset State IBF always maintains the latest information. Due to the fixed prefix of each node in MINSync, the sequence number (starting from 0) is incremented whenever new data is published. Therefore, the Dataset State IBF of each node is essentially a condensed representation of the namespace containing all previously published data in the group. For example, if the Dataset State IBF encodes a data name with a node sequence number of 99, then the Dataset State IBF has actually encoded the data name with the node sequence number from 0 to 98. The Sync Dataset of this node has stored the data of the prefix from 0 to 98.

For each node, each unit of its Dataset State IBF contains three fields: *idSum*, *hashSum*, and *count*. Each element received by the consumer node is represented as s_i. First, the data element s_i is mapped to a fixed length number ($BitID_i$) by the hash function H_b. Then the data name mapping table is established and associates each $BitID_i$ with the original name, as given in Table 7.3. Finally, $BitID_i$ is used to encode IBF.

Table 7.3 An example of the data name mapping table

Data name	Mapped value (*BitID*)
/nodeA/1	0001
/nodeA/2	0010
/nodeB/1	0011
/nodeC/1	0100
…	…

Specifically, the number of hashes for each data is represented by k. The optimal number of the hashing operation for mapping each data to IBF is 3 ($k = 3$). The four independent hash functions are H_0, H_1, H_2, and H_3. The data elements are inserted into the Dataset State IBF. $BitID_i$ is mapped to $H_0(BitID_i)$ by the function H_0. The three encoding position values j_1, j_2, and j_3 are obtained sequentially using the functions H_1, H_2, and H_3, while $BitID_i$ is the input. *IBF*[*j*]. *idSum* is converted by $BitID_i$ using XOR. *IBF*[*j*]. *hashSum* is converted by $H_0(BitID_i)$ using XOR. The value of *IBF*[*j*]. *count* pluses one. The Pseudocode of IBF Encode algorithm in MINSync is shown in Algorithm 7.1.

Algorithm 7.1 IBF Encode in MINSync
Input: S
Output: *IBF*

function encodeIBF(*S*)
  for $s_I \in S$ **do**
    $I = H_b(I_i)$
  for *j* in HashtoIndicesBitID$_i$, k, n () **do**
    IBF[j]. idSum ^ = BiIID$_i$
    IBF[j]. hashSum ^ = H_0(BitID$_i$)
    IBF[j]. count + = 1
  return IBF
end function

The process of encoding a single data element in the dataset state IBF of MINSync is shown in Fig. 7.2.

The initial *idSum* and *hashSum* values for all units of Dataset State IBF are 0000, and the initial *count* value is 0. First, the data element s_i is mapped to 1001 by function H_b. Encoding positions *IBF*[j_1], *IBF*[j_2], and *IBF*[j_3] are hashed by functions H_1, H_2, and H_3 for 1001 in turn. 1001 is mapped into 1011 by function H_0. *IBF*[j_1]. *idSum* and *IBF*[j_1]. *hashSum* are operated by XOR with 1011. The value of *IBF*[j_1]. *count* pluses one. The rest operations on *IBF*[j_2] and *IBF*[j_3] can be done in the same manner. Thus, the encoding operation of the data element s_i is completed. The process of deleting data elements from the IBF is similar to the encoding process. It involves performing an XOR operation between *IBF*[*j*]. *idSum* and *IBF*[*j*]. *hashSum*, and then subtracting 1 from *IBF*[*j*]. *count*.

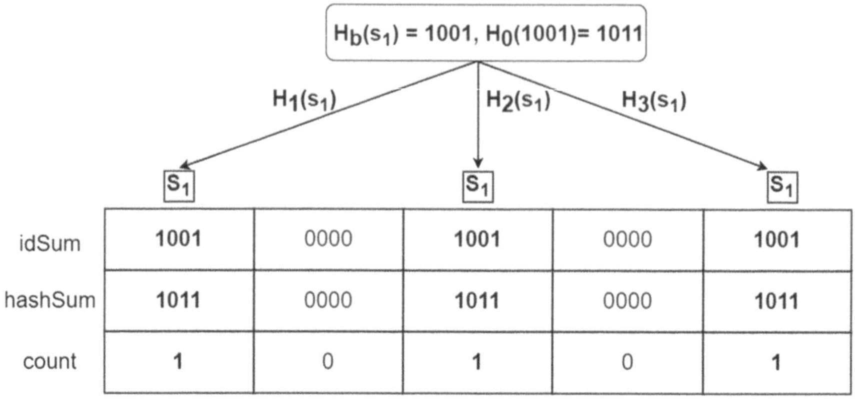

Fig. 7.2 An example of encoding a single data element in the dataset state IBF of MINSync

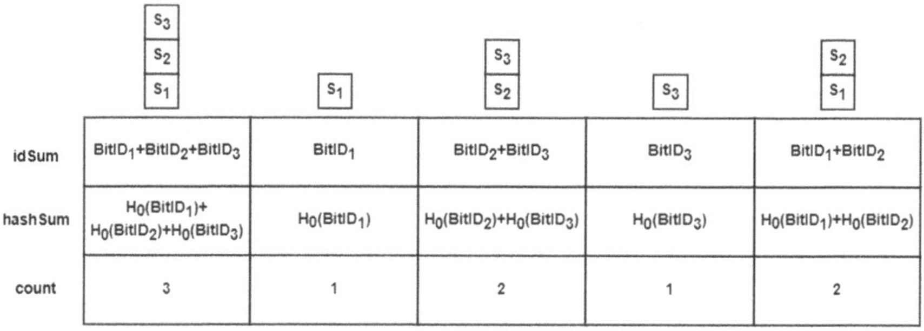

Fig. 7.3 An example of encoding multiple data elements in the dataset state IBF of MINSync

The process of encoding multiple data elements in the dataset state IBF of MINSync is shown in Fig. 7.3.

Dataset State IBF inserts three elements s_1, s_2, and s_3, starting with the element s_1. The process is the same as encoding a single element. Next, the element s_2 is inserted. If s_2 is mapped to the same position as s_1 in the Dataset State IBF, XOR operations are performed on *IBF*[*j*]. *idSum* and *IBF*[*j*]. *hashSum* directly based on s_1 encoding, while increasing *IBF*[*j*]. *count* by 1. The process of inserting element s_3 is the same as s_2. As shown in Fig. 7.3, *IBF*. *idSum* records the XOR sum of all elements inserted into each unit of IBF. *IBF*. *hashSum* records the XOR sum of all element hash values inserted into each unit of IBF, and *IBF*. *count* records the number of elements inserted into each unit of IBF.

7.2.4 Data Synchronization Process

Current pull-based synchronization protocols typically use a long-term Interest mechanism [8, 9]. This method regularly sends Sync Interest to all nodes, generating a high volume of Interest and significantly increasing network overhead.

Unlike traditional methods that use the long-term Interest mechanism, MINSync adopts a more efficient approach. In MINSync, data producer nodes actively send notifications containing data names to other nodes. The data consumer nodes then fetch the data using these names upon receiving such notifications. MINSync solves the problem of high Interest overhead and diverging network status caused by the long-term Interest mechanism.

Figure 7.4 shows the overall synchronization process of MINSync.

Figure 7.5 shows the swimming lane diagram of the synchronization process of MINSync.

In MINSync, when an application deployed on a data producer node publishes new data, the node stores the new data in the Sync Dataset. Then, the node updates its local Dataset State IBF, and updates the Dataset State Log. It sends the Data Publishing Interest Packet to other data consumer nodes, and signs with the private key. After receiving the Data Publishing Interest Packet, other data consumer nodes verify the signature. If the signature verification succeeds, the data sequence number is extracted, and it is checked whether it is sequentially incremented by 1 compared to the last received data sequence number for that node's prefix. If it is incremented by 1, the Data Requesting Interest Packet is issued to retrieve the data. If not, the data recovery process is performed. If the identity verification fails, the received packet will be discarded. After the data producer node receives the Data

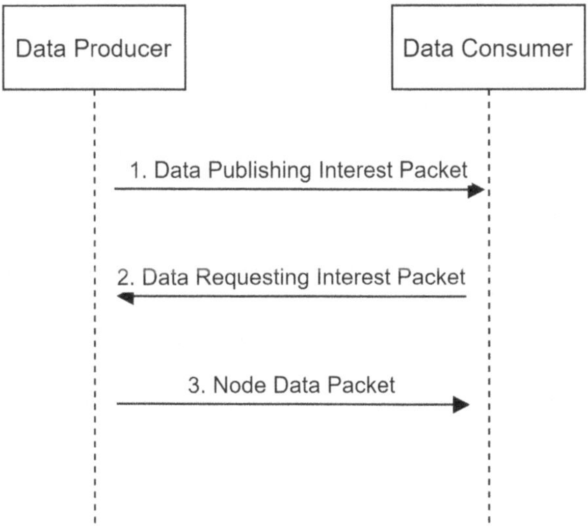

Fig. 7.4 The overall synchronization process of MINSync

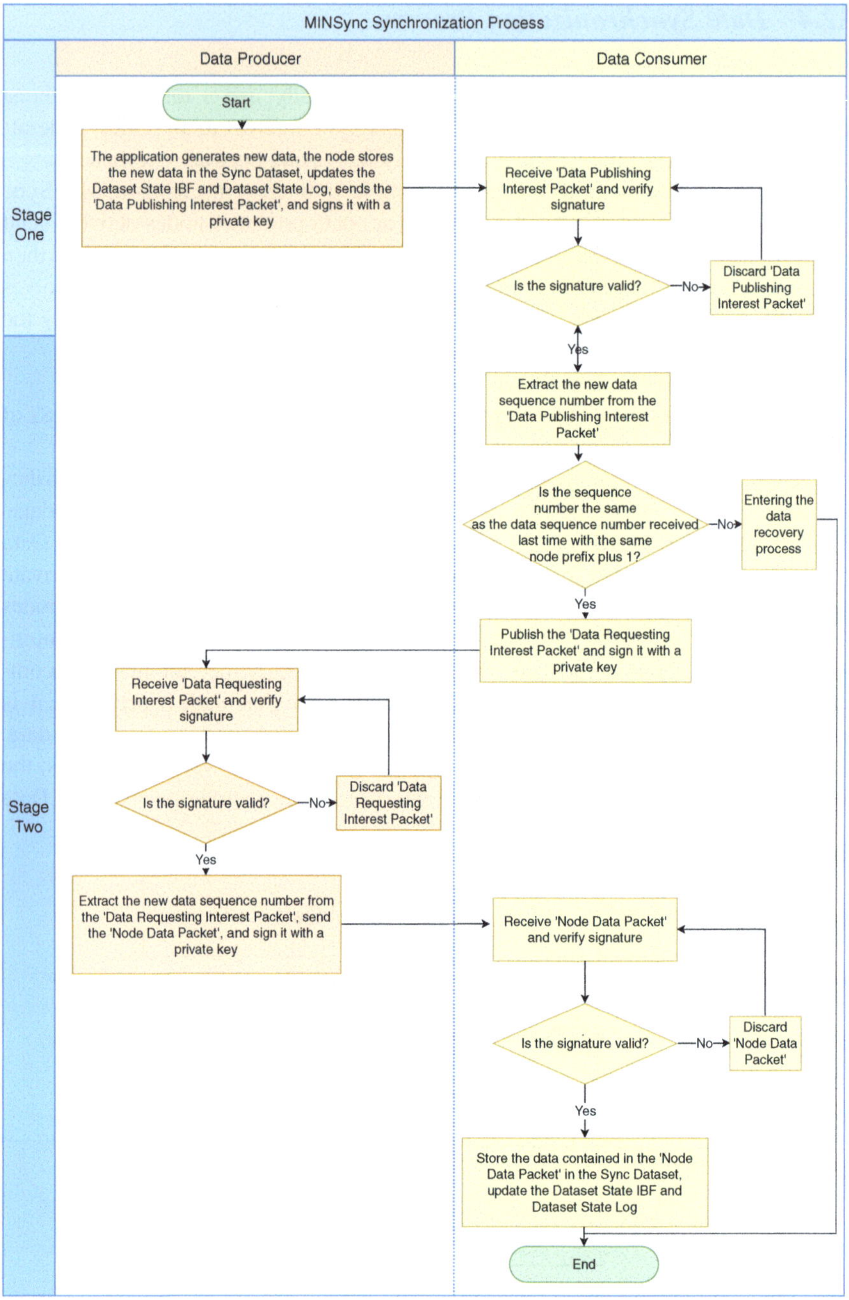

Fig. 7.5 The swimming lane diagram of the synchronization process of MINSync

Requesting Interest Packet, it first performs signature verification. If the signature verification passes, it returns the Node Data Packet containing the new data and signs it with the private key. If the signature verification does not pass, the received packet will be discarded. After receiving the Node Data Packet, the data producer node first performs signature verification. If the signature verification is successful, the data contained in the packet will be stored in the Sync Dataset of this node, and the data name is encoded in the Dataset State IBF. The update is recorded in the Dataset State Log. If the signature verification fails, the received packet will be discarded. Therefore, the data synchronization delay from data producers to data consumers is 1.5*RTT*.

Algorithm 7.2 shows the synchronization process for the data producer node when generating new data and receiving the Data Requesting Interest Packet in MINSync.

Algorithm 7.2 The Synchronization Process for the Data Producer Node in MINSync

Input: The application generates new *data* or *Producer* receives *Data Requesting Interest Packet* from *Consumer*

Output: *Producer* sends *Data Publishing Interest Packet* or *Node Data Packet* to *Consumer*

function minsyncProducerProcess ()
    if application generates new data **then**
        cache *data* in *Sync Dataset*
        update *Sync Dataset IBF*
        update *Sync Dataset Log*
        send *Data Publishing Interest Packet* to *Consumer*
    else if *Producer* receives *Data Requesting Interest Packet* from *Consumer* **then**
        get *Signature* from *Data Requesting Interest Packet*
            if *Signature* is valid **then**
                send *Node Data Packet* to *Consumer*
            else if *Signature* is invalid **then**
                drop *Data Requesting Interest Packet*
            end if
    end if
end function

Algorithm 7.3 shows the synchronization process for the data consumer node when receiving the Data Publishing Interest Packet and the Node Data Packet.

Algorithm 7.3 The Synchronization Process for the Data Consumer Node in MINSync

Input: *Consumer* receives *Data Publishing Interest Packet* or *Node Data Packet* from *Producer*

Output: *Consumer* sends *Data Requesting Interest Packet* to *Producer* or cache *data*

```
function minsyncConsumerProcess (...)
  if Consumer receives Data Publishing Interest Packet from the Producer then
    get Signature from Data Publishing Interest Packet
    if Signature is invalid then
      drop Data Publishing Interest Packet
    else if Signature is valid then
      send Data Requesting Interest Packet to Producer
    end if
  end if
  if Consumer receives Node Data Packet from the Producer then
    get Signature from Node Data Packet
    if Signature is invalid then
      drop Node Data Packet
    else if Signature is valid then
      cache data in Sync Dataset
      update Sync Dataset IBF
      update Sync Dataset Log
    end if
  end if
end function
```

An example of data synchronization in MINSync is shown in Fig. 7.6.

The MIN network shown in Fig. 7.6 consists of six nodes: Node A, Node B, Node C, Node D, Node E, and Node F. After generating new data with sequence number 12, Node C updates the Dataset State IBF and Dataset State Log, and sends a Data Publishing Interest Packet named "/min/nodeC/minsync/publish/app1/12" to the other nodes. After receiving the Data Publishing Interest Packet from Node C, other nodes including Node A, Node B, Node D, Node E, and Node F will send a Data Requesting Interest Packet to Node C, named "/min/consumer/name/minsync/request/nodeC/app1/12". For example, Node A sends "/min/nodeA/minsync/request/nodeC/app1/12". After receiving the Data Requesting Interest Packet from other nodes, Node C will return the Node Data Packet named "/min/nodeC/minsync/app1/12". After receiving the Node Data Packet from Node C, Node A, Node B, Node D, Node E, and Node F store the data contained in this packet in the Sync Dataset, and update the Dataset State IBF and Dataset State Log of this node.

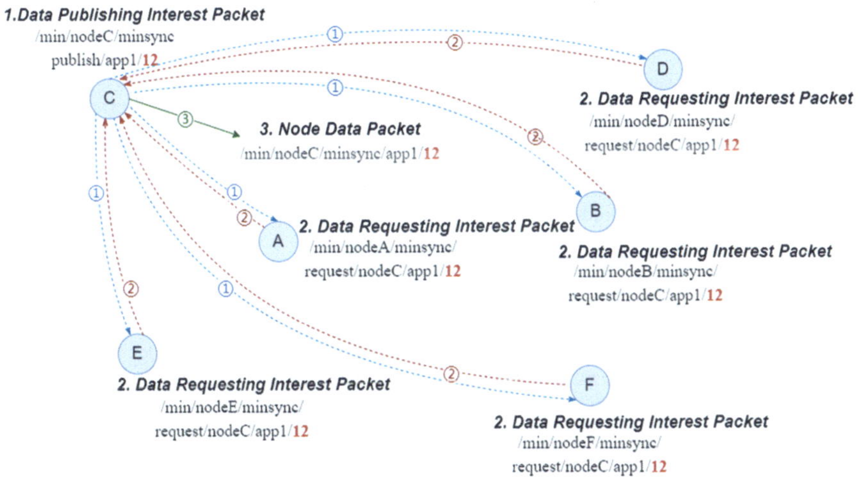

Fig. 7.6 An data synchronization example of MINSync

7.3 MINGroupSync

7.3.1 Overview of MINGroupSync

MINSync relies on Interest packet multicast to deliver state changing notifications to every node in the synchronous network. This poses challenges to routing scalability in the network. Each time a node generates new data, it needs to forward Interest packets to all synchronous nodes of the synchronous network, which is usually not feasible for large networks hosting many synchronization groups.

MINGroupSync [7], another data synchronization protocol for MIN networks, improves the scalability of the data synchronization protocol. MINGroupSync selects the leading node in the synchronous network for management and data synchronization, and each synchronization group adopts distributed management to realize full data synchronization and partial data synchronization at the same time.

MINGroupSync contains several synchronization groups. Each group contains a number of synchronization nodes. In full data synchronization scenarios, each node is both a data producer and consumer. That is, each node needs to synchronize its own new data to other nodes and also needs to obtain synchronization data from other nodes. In partial data synchronization scenarios, some nodes are only data producers and some nodes are only data consumers. In MINGroupSync, nodes are classified into three identities: Leader Node, Assistant Node, and Member Node, as given in Table 7.4.

As shown in Fig. 7.7, the synchronization nodes of MINGroupSync include the following three data structures.

Table 7.4 Functions of each type of node in MINGroupSync

Node type	Node function
Leader Node	1. The Leader Node is responsible for managing the members of each synchronization group, maintaining the Group State, Sync Dataset, and Dataset State IBF of the synchronization group 2. The Leader node aggregates notifications from data producer nodes within a synchronous round and sends them uniformly to data consumers 3. The Leader Node is responsible for managing members within the group, such as adding new nodes and exiting existing nodes 4. The Leader Node is the same as a regular Member Node, serving as both a data producer and data consumer, publishing and retrieving data in a synchronous group
Assistant Node	1. The Assistant Node is the backup node for the Leader Node in this synchronization group, monitoring the connection status of the Leader Node. When the Leader Node fails, it becomes the new Leader Node. The Assistant Node and the Leader Node both have Group State, Sync Dataset, and Dataset State IBF 2. The Assistant Node is the same as a regular Member Node, serving as both a data producer and consumer, publishing and retrieving data in a synchronous group
Member Node	1. In each synchronization group, except for the Leader Node and Assistant Node, all other nodes are Member Nodes. The Member Node has Group State, Sync Dataset, and Dataset State Digest IBF 2. Member Nodes are both data producers and data consumers, publishing and retrieving data in synchronous groups

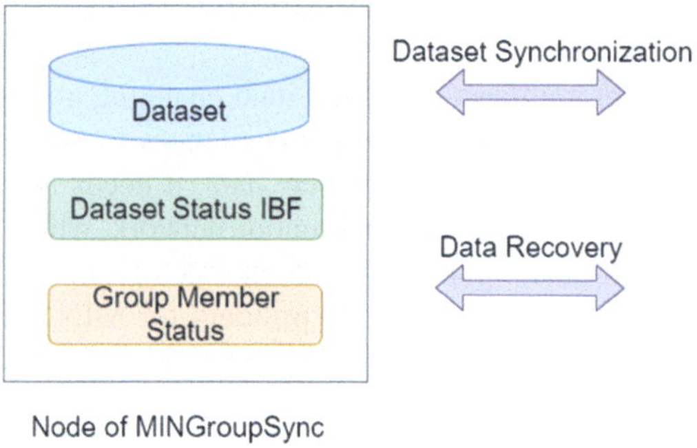

Fig. 7.7 Overview of MINGroupSync

Sync Dataset

Each synchronization node in MINGroupSync possesses this data structure, storing the synchronized content of the respective synchronization group for access and use by applications.

Dataset State IBF

It represents the namespace that signifies the latest state of the shared dataset within the synchronization group. Similar to the MINSync protocol, Dataset State IBF is used for encoding and contains the names of all the most recently published data known to the synchronization group by the local synchronization node. Whenever a node generates new data or receives new data from other nodes, the Dataset State IBF is updated accordingly. Each synchronization node in MINGroupSync possesses this structure.

Group State

It includes the current member status information of the synchronization group, comprising the sequence numbers and node names of all members within the group. Group State serves as a roster of members within the synchronization group, allowing only nodes listed in the roster to participate in data synchronization, data publication, and retrieval within the group. Nodes not listed in the roster are not permitted to engage in data synchronization within the synchronization group. By managing the synchronization group member information, the Leader node effectively maintains the security of synchronized data and prevents attacks from malicious nodes.

During the initialization phase of data synchronization, all nodes in the synchronization group are sequentially numbered, and the identities of nodes are determined. Based on the node importance algorithm, nodes are sorted and numbered from 1 and increasing in order. After being sorted, the No.1 node will be the Leader Node. The No.2 node will be the Assistant Node, and the remaining nodes are Member Nodes. The Leader Node and Assistant Node have the status information of all members in the synchronization group, including the numbers and node names of all members within the group, which is the *Group State* of this group.

7.3.2 Naming Scheme

The naming scheme of MINGroupSync is similar to that in MINSync. Table 7.5 lists the network packets and their naming rules of MINGroupSync.

In the data synchronization process of MINGroupSync, the generation process for each type of network packet is described as follows.

Data Publishing Interest Packet

When generating new data, the producer node will send a Data Publishing Interest Packet to the Leader Node.

The Data Publishing Interest Packet is named as "/min/producer-name/min-groupsync/publish/app-name/seq#".

- "/producer-name" indicates the name of a node that publishes new data.
- "/mingroupsync/publish" indicates that the MINGroupSync protocol is used.
- "/app-name" indicates the name of the application that generates data.
- "/seq#" indicates the serial number of the generated new data.

Table 7.5 Naming rules for each type of network packet in MINGroupSync

Packet type	Naming rules
Data Publishing Interest Packet	/min/producer-name/mingroupsync/publish/app-name/seq#
Data Notification Interest Packet	/min/leader-name/mingroupsync/notify/<new-IBF>
Data Requesting Interest Packet	/min/consumer-name/mingroupsync/request/producer-name/app-name/seq#
Node Data Packet	/min/producer-name/mingroupsync/app-name/seq#
Data Recovering Interest Packet	/min/node-name/mingroupsync/recover/<old-IBF>
New Node Join Interest Packet	/min/node-name/mingroupsync/join
New Node Notification Interest Packet	/min/leader-name/mingroupsync/newmember/node-name
New Leader Notification Interest Packet	/min/node-name/mingroupsync/newleader
New Assistant Notification Interest Packet	/min/node-name/mingroupsync/newassistant

The data producer node signs the Data Publishing Interest Packet with the private key.

Data Notification Interest Packet

When the Leader Node receives the Data Publishing Interest Packet, the data producer node prefix and data serial number are encoded in Dataset State IBF.

After receiving the Data Publishing Interest Packet from multiple nodes in the synchronization group, the Leader Node encodes the prefixes and data serial numbers of all nodes that publish new data in the Dataset State IBF. Then the Leader Node issues Data Notification Interest Packet to all other nodes in addition to the publishing data node.

The Data Notification Interest Packet is named as "/min/leader-name/mingroupsync/notify/<new-IBF>".

- "/notify" indicates that new data is generated.
- "/leader-name" indicates the Leader Node name of the data synchronization group.
- "<new-IBF>" indicates that the Leader Node encode the IBF of the generating new data node prefix and data serial number.

The Leader Node signs the Data Notification Interest Packet with the private key.

Data Requesting Interest Packet

When the data consumer node receives Data Notification Interest Packet, it will request the node that publishes the new data to obtain new data and send a Data Requesting Interest Packet.

The Data Requesting Interest Packet is named as "/min/consumer-name/min-groupsync/request/producer-name/app-name/seq#".

- "/consumer-name" indicates the name of the node that requests new data.
- "/request" indicates obtaining new data.
- "/producer-name/app-name/seq#" indicates the information about the data to be obtained.

The data consumer node signs the Data Requesting Interest Packet with the private key. It should be noted in particular that the Leader node will request the data producer node to obtain new data after receiving the Data Publishing Interest Packet.

As the same as MINSync, MIR does not need to query the forwarding table when processing the Data Requesting Interest Packet and only needs to return packets along the path of the Data Publishing Interest Packet.

In order to further shorten the synchronization process and reduce the number of packets generated in the network, the identifier field is added to the Data Requesting Interest Packet. It can both reply the Data Publishing Interest Packet and obtain data at the same time.

Node Data Packet

When the data producer node receives the Data Requesting Interest Packet, it will send a Node Data Packet to the data consumer node.

The Node Data Packet is named as "/min/producer-name/mingroupsync/app-name/seq#".

- "/producer-name" indicates the name of the new data node that publishes the data.
- "/app-name" indicates the name of the application that generates new data.
- "/seq#" indicates the data series number.

The Node Data Packet contains the new data generated by the node. The data producer node signs the Node Data Packet with the private key.

Data Recovering Interest Packet

When a synchronization node in the network loses data due to network packet loss or abnormal connection, the node will send a Data Recovering Interest Packet to the Leader node of the synchronization group and sign it with the private key.

The Data Recovering Interest Packet is named as "/min/node–name/min-groupsync/recover/<old-IBF>".

- "/node-name" indicates the name of the node whose data is to be recovered.
- "/recover" indicates the name of the node whose data is to be recovered.
- "<old-IBF>" indicates the IBF of the node that requests data recovery.

New Node Join Interest Packet and New Node Notification Interest Packet

When a new node joins the synchronization group, the node will send a New Node Join Interest Packet to the Leader node of the synchronization group and sign it with the private key.

The New Node Join Interest Packet is named as "/min/node-name/min-groupsync/join".

- "/node-name" indicates the name of the node to be added to the synchronization group.
- "/join" indicates the name of the node to be added to the synchronization group.

After verifying the signature, the Leader node will agree the node to join, and send a New Node Notification Interest Packet to all other nodes.

The New Node Notification Interest Packet is named as "/min/Leader-name/min-groupsync/newmember/node-name".

- "/leader-name" indicates the name of the Leader node.
- "/newmember" indicates that a new node is added to the synchronization group.
- "/node-name" indicates the name of the new node.

New Leader Notification Interest Packet and New Assistant Notification Interest Packet

When the Leader node in the synchronization group exits the synchronization group, the Assistant node will act as the new Leader node of the synchronization group.

The node with the next serial number acts as the Assistant node of the synchronization group, and so on. The new Leader Node sends a New Leader Notification Interest Packet to all other nodes and sign the packet with the private key.

The New Leader Notification Interest Packet is named as "/min/node-name/min-groupsync/newleader".

- "/node-name" indicates the name of the new Leader Node.
- "/newleader" indicates the notification of the new Leader Node.

The new Assistant Node will send a New Assistant Notification Interest Packet to all other nodes, and sign the packet with its private key.

The New Assistant Notification Interest Packet is named as "/min/node-name/mingroupsync/newassistant".

- "/node-name" indicates the name of the new Assistant Node.
- "/newassistant" indicates the new Assistant Node notification.

7.3.3 Namespace Representation

Similar to MINSync, MINGroupSync uses Dataset State IBF to represent the namespace of the synchronized dataset. In order to improve space utilization, the Dataset State IBF in MINGroupSync only encodes the name prefix of the data stream and encodes its latest sequence number as the synchronization status. Due to the fixed prefix of each node in MINGroupSync, the sequence number (starting from 0) is incremented sequentially every time new data is published. As a result, the Dataset State IBF of each node is a compact representation of the namespace, encompassing all data previously published within the group. For each node in MINGroupSync, each unit of the Dataset State IBF contains three fields: *idSum*, *hashSum*, and *count*.

7.3.4 Data Synchronization Process

In the data synchronization process of MINGroupSync, each synchronization node acts as both a data producer and consumer. This means that every node is responsible for synchronizing its own newly generated data to other nodes while also retrieving synchronized data from other nodes.

Similar to the MINSync protocol, MINGroupSync does not use long-term Interest mechanism, it employs active notifications to inform nodes about the presence of new data, allowing other nodes to retrieve the data. Since there are nodes joining and exiting the synchronization group, MINGroupSync synchronization nodes only maintain the synchronization dataset within the group after their initial membership in the synchronization group.

MINGroupSync divides the synchronization process into rounds. Each time t is one round. The time t can be adjusted according to the data release rate in the network. The Leader Node of MINGroupSync maintains two types of IBF. One is the Dataset State IBF of the node, and the other is the IBF that encodes only a single synchronization round for notification.

The data synchronization process of MINGroupSync is divided into three stages: initialization stage, data notification stage, and data retrieval stage.

Initialization Stage

During the initialization stage, all nodes in the MINGroupSync synchronization group are numbered in the ascending order, starting from 1. After the sorting is complete, the No.1 node will be the Leader Node, and the No.2 node becomes the Assistant Node. The other nodes are Member Nodes. Each node has the status information (Group State) of all members of the synchronization group, including the numbers and the node names of all members within the group. Group State serves as a member list within the synchronization group. Only nodes listed in the Group State are allowed to participate in data synchronization, data publication, and retrieval within the synchronization group. Nodes that are not listed in the Group State are not permitted to engage in data synchronization within the synchronization group.

Data Notification Stage

In a single synchronization round of MINGroupSync, the synchronization process of the data notification stage is shown in Fig. 7.8.

In MINGroupSync, when an application deployed on a synchronization node generates new data, the node stores this data in its Sync Dataset, updates the Dataset State IBF of this node, and sends a Data Publishing Interest Packet to the Leader Node of this synchronization group. Upon receiving the Data Publishing Interest Packet, the Leader Node checks its presence in the Group State and validates the signature. After verification, it will return the Data Requesting Interest Packet to the data producer node, and then encode the prefix and data sequence number of all received data producers into the new-IBF used for notification. If the Leader node also generates new data, it will be encoded together into the new-IBF used for notification. Then, the Leader node sends Data Notification Interest Packet to Member Nodes, and sends all received information about new data to the Member Nodes. If the data producer node experiences a timeout without receiving the Data Requesting Interest Packet, it will resend the Data Publishing Interest Packet to the Leader node. If the retransmission exceeds the maximum number of times, it will enter the next round of synchronization.

An example of the data notification stage in MINGroupSync is shown in Fig. 7.9.

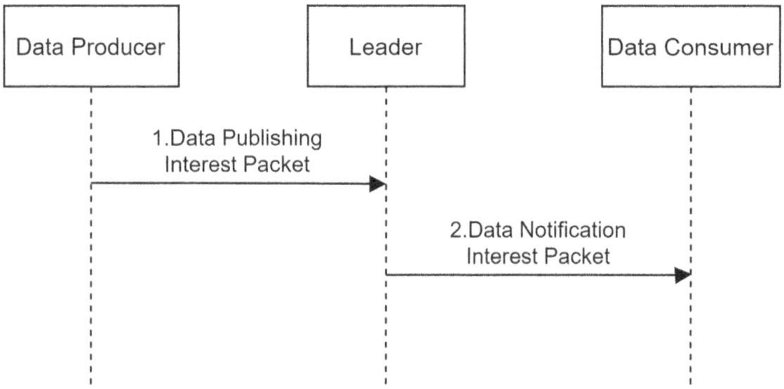

Fig. 7.8 The synchronization process of the data notification stage in MINGroupSync

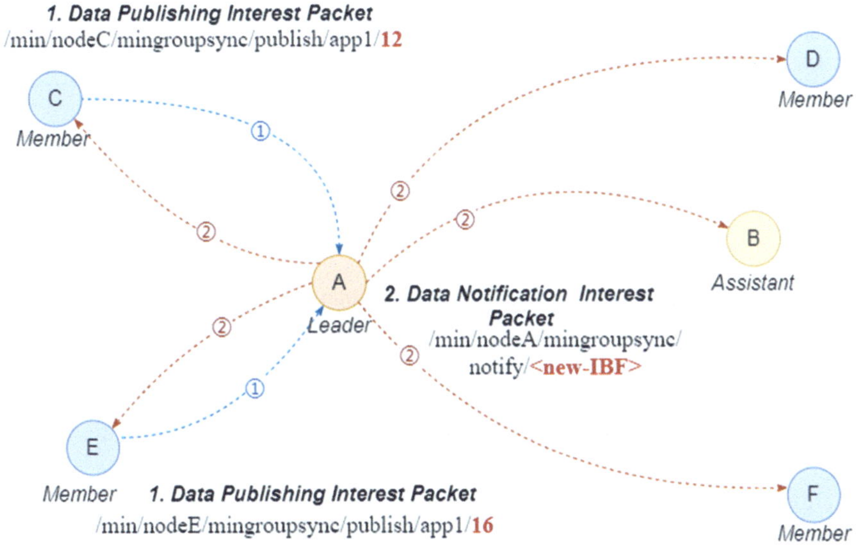

Fig. 7.9 An example of the data notification stage in MINGroupSync

The MIN synchronization network consists of six nodes: Node A, Node B, Node C, Node D, Node E, and Node F. Among them, Node A is the Leader Node, Node B is the Assistant Node. Node C, Node D, Node E, and Node F are Member Nodes.

In one synchronization round, Node C generates new data with sequence number 12, while Node E generates new data with sequence number 16. Node C and Node E update the Sync Dataset and Dataset State IBF and sent Data Publishing Interest Packets named "/min/nodeC/mingroupsync/publish/app1/12" and "/min/nodeC/mingroupsync/publish/app1/16" to Node A. After receiving them, Node A verifies whether it is in the Group State and whether the signature is valid. After verification, the Dataset State IBF of this synchronization group is updated. Node A sends Data Notification Interest Packet named "/min/nodeA/mingroupsync/notify/<new-IBF>" to Node B, Node C, Node D, Node E, and Node F. "/<new-IBF>" is the IBF that only encodes new data names for Node C and Node E.

Data Retrieval Stage

In a synchronization round of MINGroupSync, the synchronization process of the data retrieval stage is shown in Fig. 7.10.

The Leader Node receives the Data Publishing Interest Packet. After signature verification, the Leader Node directly sends the Data Requesting Interest Packet to the node that published the new data to obtain the data. Other nodes in the group, upon receiving Data Notification Interest Packet, conduct signature verification and decode the IBF contained within it. These nodes can obtain the node prefix and sequence number for the newly published data, and then send the Data Requesting

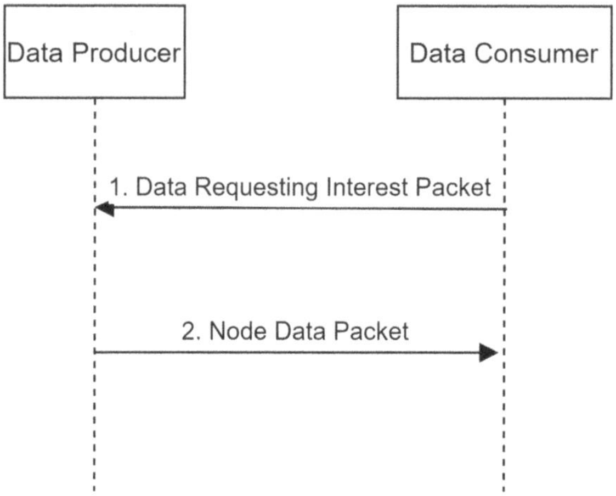

Fig. 7.10 The synchronization process of the data retrieval stage in MINGroupSync

Interest Packet for data retrieval. After receiving the Data Requesting Interest Packet, nodes that publish new data verify whether it is in the Group State and whether the signature is valid. After verification, they return the Node Data Packet according to the original path. Once the Node Data Packet is received, all nodes check its presence in the Group State and the validity of its signature. After verification, the new data contained in the Node Data Packet is stored in the Sync Dataset, and the Dataset State IBF of this node is updated. Therefore, the data synchronization delay between a pair of synchronization nodes in MINGroupSync is $1.5RTT$.

When the Member Node decodes the IBF in Data Notification Interest Packet and obtains the node prefix and serial number for publishing new data, it will send a Data Requesting Interest Packet to retrieve the data from the node that published the new data. The same Data Requesting Interest Packet will be aggregated on the MIR, which can effectively reduce the number of packets in the network link and reduce network overhead.

An example of the data retrieval stage in MINGroupSync is shown in Fig. 7.11.

- As shown in Fig. 7.11a, after receiving the Data Publishing Interest Packet from Node C and Node E, Node A verifies whether it is in the Group State and whether the signature is valid. After verification, Node A will directly send a Data Requesting Interest Packet to Node C and Node E. After receiving Data Notification Interest Packet from Node A, Node C and Node E perform signature verification and send the Data Requesting Interest Packet to the other node. After receiving Data Notification Interest Packet from Node A, Node B, Node D, and Node F perform signature verification and send the Data Requesting Interest Packet to Node C and Node E.
- As shown in Fig. 7.11b, after receiving the Data Requesting Interest Packet from other nodes, Node C and Node E confirm their status in the Group State and validate the signature. After verification, they return the Node Data Packet along the opposite path. After receiving the Node Data Packet, all nodes verify whether it is in the Group State and whether the signature is valid. After verification, the

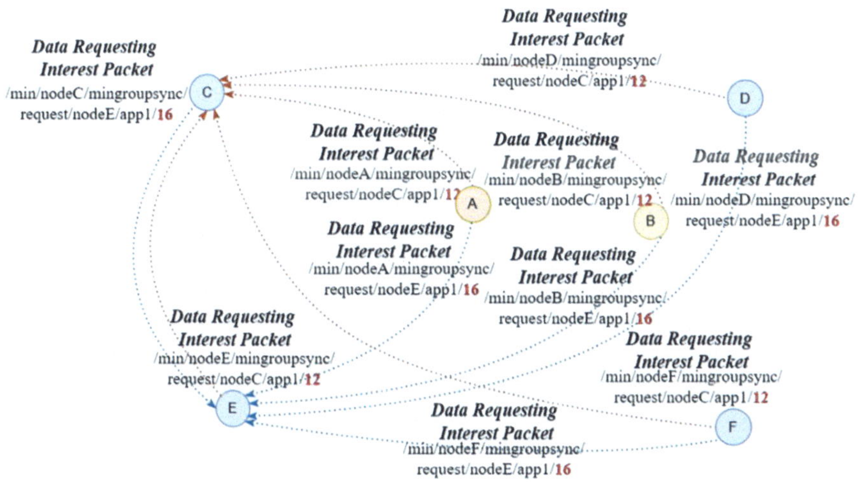

(a) The data consumer node sends a Data Requesting Interest Packet

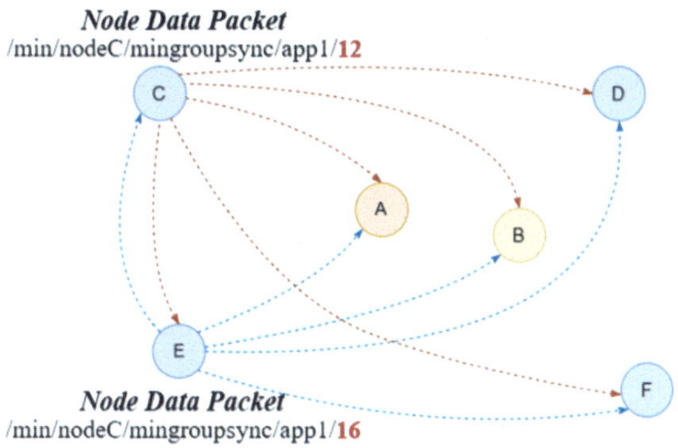

(b) The data producer node sends a Node Data Packet

Fig. 7.11 An example of the data retrieval stage in MINGroupSync. (**a**) The data consumer node sends a Data Requesting Interest Packet. (**b**) The data producer node sends a Node Data Packet

data contained in the packet is stored in the Sync Dataset, and the Dataset State IBF of this node will be update.

In the data synchronization process of MINGroupSync, three kinds of nodes are involved in the data notification stage and data retrieval stage: the data producer node, the leader node, and the data consumer node. The corresponding processing processes of these nodes are shown in Algorithms 7.4, 7.5, and 7.6, respectively.

Algorithm 7.4 shows the synchronization process for the data producer node when generating new data and receiving the Data Requesting Interest Packet in MINGroupSync

Algorithm 7.4 The Synchronization Process for the Data Producer Node in MINGroupSync

Input: The application generates new *data* or the *Producer* receives *Data Requesting Interest Packet* from the other node

Output: *Producer* sends *Data Publishing Interest Packet* or *Node Data Packet* to the other node

function mingroupsyncProducerProcess (...)
  if application generates new data **then**
    cache *data* in *Sync Dataset*
      update *Sync Dataset IBF*
    send *Data Publishing Interest Pakcet* to *Leader*
  else if *Producer* receives *Data Requesting Interest Packet* from the other node **then**
    get *Signature* from *Data Requesting Interest Packet*
    if *Signature* is invalid or the node is not in *Group State* **then**
      drop *Data Requesting Interest Packet*
    else if *Signature* is valid and the node is in *Group State* **then**
      send *Node Data Packet* to the other node
    end if
  end if
end function

Algorithm 7.5 shows the synchronization process for the Leader Node in MINGroupSync when receiving the Data Publishing Interest Packet and the Node Data Packet.

Algorithm 7.5 The Synchronization Process for the Leader Node in MINGroupSync

Input: The *Leader* receives *Data Publishing Interest Pakcet* or *Node Data Packet* from the other node

Output: The *Leader* sends *Data Requesting Interest Packet* and *Data Notification Interest Packet* to the other node or cache *data*

function mingroupsyncLeaderProcess (...)
  if *Leader* receives *Data Publishing Interest Pakcet* from *Producer* **then**
    get *Signature* from *Data Publishing Interest Pakcet*
    if *Signature* is *invalid* or *Producer* is not in *Group State* **then**
      drop *Data Publishing Interest Pakcet*
    else if *Signature* is *valid* and *Producer* is in *Group State* **then**
      send *Data Requesting Interest Packet* to *Producer*
      send *Data Notification Interest Packet* to *Consumer*
    end if

else if *Leader* receives *Node Data Packet* from *Producer* **then**
get *Signature* from *Node Data Packet*
if *Signature* is *invalid* or *Producer* is not in *Group State* **then**
drop *Node Data Packet*
else if *Signature* is *valid* and *Producer* is in *Group State* **then**
cache *data* in *Sync Dataset*
update *Sync Dataset IBF*
end if
end if
end function

Algorithm 7.6 shows the synchronization process for the data consumer node when receiving the Data Notification Interest Packet and the Node Data Packet.

Algorithm 7.6 The Synchronization Process for the Data Consumer Node in MINGroupSync

Input: The *Consumer* receives *Data Notification Interest Packet* or *Node Data Packet* from the other node

Output: The *Consumer* sends *Data Requesting Interest Packet* to the other node or cache *data*

function mingroupsyncConsumerProcess (…)
if *Consumer* receives *Data Notification Interest Packet* from *Leader* **then**
get *Signature* from *Data Notification Interest Packet*
if *Signature* is *invalid* **then**
drop *Data Notification Interest Packet*
else if *Signature* is *valid* **then**
send *Data Requesting Interest Packet* to *Producer*
end if
else if *Consumer* receives *Node Data Packet* from *Producer* **then**
get *Signature* from *Node Data Packet* **then**
if *Signature* is *invalid* or *Producer* is not in *Group State* **then**
drop *Node Data Packet*
else if *Signature* is *valid* and *Producer* is in *Group State* **then**
cache *data* in *Sync Dataset*
update *Sync Dataset IBF*
end if
end if
end function

References

1. Moll P, Patil V, Wang L, et al. SoK: the evolution of distributed dataset synchronization solutions in NDN. In: Proceedings of the 9th ACM conference on information-centric networking; 2022. p. 33–44.
2. Wang YM, Li H, Huang T, et al. Scalable identifier system for industrial internet based on multi-identifier network architecture. IEEE Internet Things J. 2021;10(3):1919–32.
3. Que J, Li H, Bai H, et al. A network architecture containing both push and pull semantics. In: 2021 7th international conference on computer and communications (ICCC). Piscataway: IEEE; 2021. p. 2211–6.
4. Zhu Z, Afanasyev A. Let's chronosync: decentralized dataset state synchronization in named data networking. In: 2013 21st IEEE international conference on network protocols (ICNP). Piscataway: IEEE; 2013. p. 1–10.
5. Fu W, Ben Abraham H, Crowley P. iSync: a high performance and scalable data synchronization protocol for named data networking. In: Proceedings of the 1st ACM conference on information-centric networking; 2014. p. 181–2.
6. Drăgoi C, Henzinger TA, Zufferey D. PSync: a partially synchronous language for fault-tolerant distributed algorithms. ACM SIGPLAN Not. 2016;51(1):400–15.
7. Yang L, Ma J, Li H, et al. GroupSync: scalable distributed dataset synchronization for named data networking. In: 2021 3rd international academic exchange conference on science and technology innovation (IAECST). Piscataway: IEEE; 2021. p. 720–5.
8. Moll P, Shang W, Yu Y, et al. A survey of distributed dataset synchronization in named data networking. Named Data Networking, Tech. Rep. NDN-0053, 2021.
9. Shang W, Yu Y, Wang L, et al. A survey of distributed dataset synchronization in Named Data Networking. NDN, technical report NDN-0053, 2017.

Chapter 8
Cache Management and Access Control

In MIN networks, the in-network caching plays a pivotal role in mitigating overall network traffic. This chapter introduces the cache management and access control schemes deployed on MIRs. The caching scheme includes a cache placement algorithm, a dual-layer caching model, and a cache space reallocation algorithm. Furthermore, the access control policy further achieves fine-grained access control and content privacy protection.

8.1 Overview of In-Network Caching

With the widespread use of the Internet, network traffic is growing exponentially. The demand for multimedia content such as videos, audio, and images is continuously increasing, resulting in significant data transmission requirements and causing network congestion and transmission bottlenecks [1]. In-network caching optimizes data transmission efficiency and improves network response time by storing copies of content at intermediate nodes in the network [2]. It not only reduces redundant content transmission and overall network traffic load, but also effectively reduces network operational costs and transmission delays. Currently, in-network caching has become a key technology for alleviating network congestion and improving the quality of service, especially for bandwidth-intensive applications such as video streaming, social media, and big data analytics.

However, due to the limited storage resources at network intermediate nodes, efficient management of the limited cache space is a crucial challenge [3]. This includes intelligently determining which data should be cached, when to update cached content, and when to release cache space for new content. An efficient caching strategy not only considers the frequency of data access but also predicts future access patterns to optimize the selection of cached data, thereby maximizing network resource utilization [4]. Additionally, with the changing network conditions, the caching management mechanism needs to adapt flexibly to various network environments to achieve accurate and dynamic caching decisions. Therefore, researching and developing more flexible,

H. Li, H. Bai, *Principle of Architecture, Protocol, and Algorithms for CoG-MIN*,
https://doi.org/10.1007/978-981-96-3596-2_8

efficient, and practical in-network caching strategies is an important direction for the development of network technologies.

8.2 Cache Management for CoG-MIN

To achieve efficient management of cache units in MIRs, the MIN research group has proposed a cache management scheme for MIR [5, 6], including a cache placement strategy based on tokens and content popularity, a cache space reallocation algorithm, and a dual-layer caching model based on the bloom filter.

In the cache management scheme for MIN networks, several modules have been introduced in the MIR [7], including the Beta Management Module, Token Management Module, Data Filtering Module, Dual-Layer Cache Architecture, and Space Reallocation Module, as shown in Fig. 8.1. Table 8.1 provides a summary of commonly used symbols in the cache management scheme for CoG-MIN.

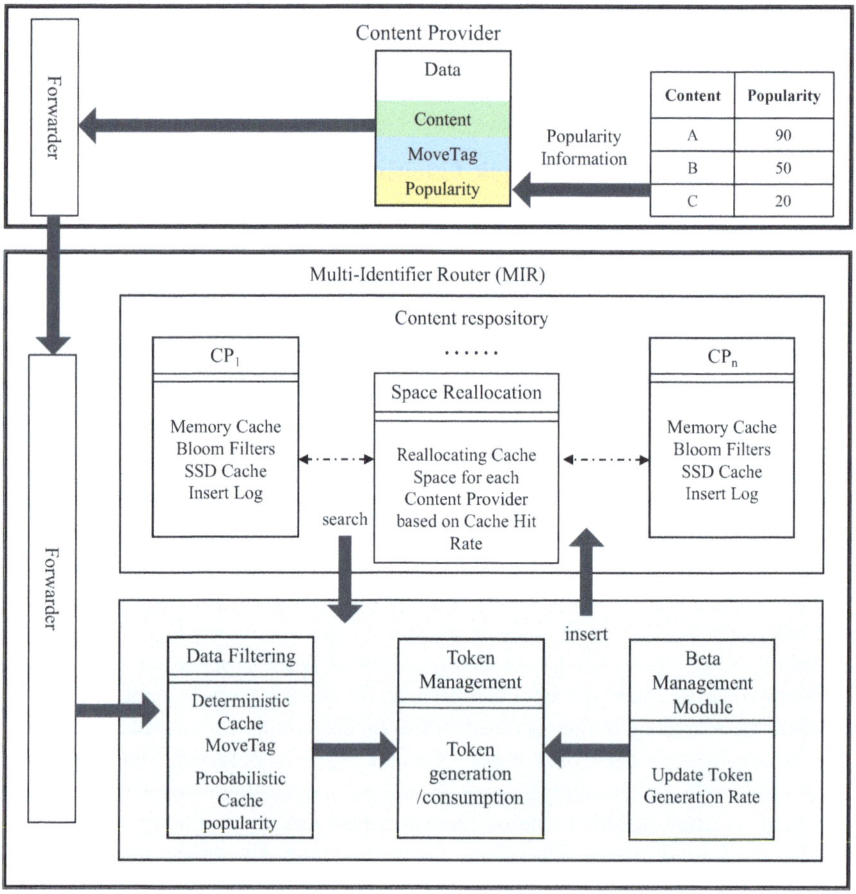

Fig. 8.1 Cache management for CoG-MIN

Table 8.1 A summary of commonly used symbols in the cache management scheme for CoG-MIN

Symbol	Description
$Popularity_c$	The preset popularity level assigned to content c by the content provider, ranging from 0 to 100
β_r	The token generation rate on MIR r
$T_{r,cp}$	The number of tokens held by the content provider cp on MIR r
H_r	The cache hit ratio of MIR r
K_r	The threshold value indicating the number of times that a content is requested on MIR r before it is pushed down
Δt	The time interval of a scheduled task
θ_r	The average time it takes for a content to be evicted from the cache space on MIR r
$\theta_{r,cp}$	The average time it takes for a content from a content provider cp to be evicted from the cache space on MIR r
$\varphi_{r,cp}$	The correction value of the caching probability of a content from a content provider cp on MIR r
$N_{r,op}$	The number of insert and query operations performed on MIR r
$Interest(c)$	The Interest packet sent by consumers when requesting content c
$Data(c)$	The Data packet returned by the content provider when providing content c

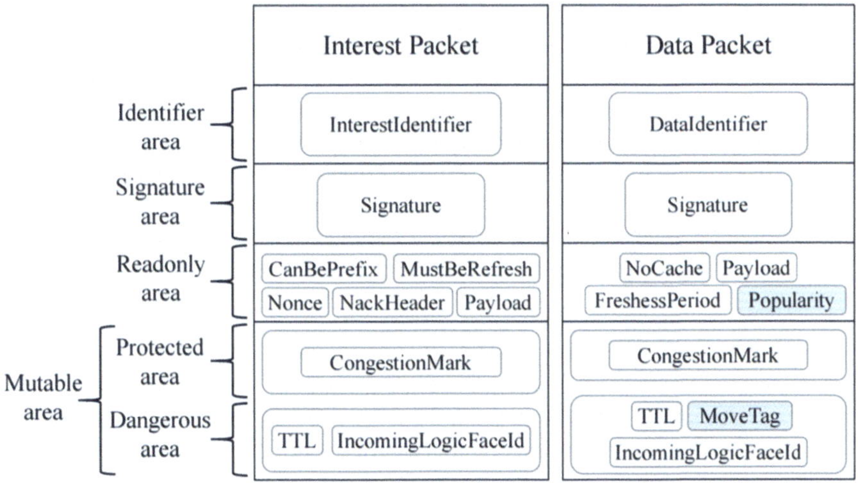

Fig. 8.2 The packet format in cache management scheme for CoG-MIN

In the cache management scheme for CoG-MIN, two new fields are included in the Data packet (Fig. 8.2), namely *MoveTag* and *Popularity*. If the number of requests exceeds the threshold K_r, the content will be pushed to the network edge, and the Boolean value of *MoveTag* is set to *True*; otherwise, it is set to *False*. Popularity is an integer variable that represents the content popularity level ($Popularity_c$).

In the cache management scheme for CoG-MIN, all MIRs in a MIN network are assumed to have the same size of cache space. To simplify the model, all requested contents are considered to have the same size. Considering the content service model of the Internet, the content requesting frequency follows a Poisson distribution, and the content popularity follows a *Zipf*-like distribution with parameter α.

8.2.1 Cache Placement Strategy

The purpose of the cache placement strategy is to determine which data packets should be cached on which intermediate nodes. In MIN networks, the cache placement strategy takes content popularity into consideration. The content published by content providers carries a popularity level, and the scheme supports a push-down mechanism.

In the cache placement strategy, the top-level identifier of the Data packet is used to identify the content provider. For example, the two different Data packets with different content identifiers "/mina/data/file.txt" and "/minb/data/movie.mp4" are treated as coming from two different content providers, namely "/mina" and "/minb". Content providers assign a predefined popularity level for each content, denoted as $Popularity_c \in [0,100]$. Less popular content is assigned a low popularity level, whereas popular content is assigned a high popularity level.

MIR employs a probabilistic caching strategy that takes into account the content popularity level and tokens. Only when the content provider has an adequate number of tokens on a MIR, the content of this content provider is permitted to be inserted into the cache of that MIR. In this context, the token mechanism regulates the insertion rate, ensuring controlled and authorized caching operations. This implies that content providers need to assign a lower preset popularity level to less popular content, reducing the number of tokens consumed. By doing so, more popular content has a greater chance of being cached in MIRs. The number of tokens $T_{r,cp}$ owned by a content provider *cp* on MIR *r* is defined as Eq. (8.1):

$$T_{r,cp} = \sum_{c} f\left(Popularity_c, \beta_r\right). \tag{8.1}$$

Where $f(Popularity_c, \beta_r)$ represents the number of tokens consumed or generated by a single content when it passes through a MIR cache unit.

$$f\left(popularity, \beta_r\right) = -\beta_r \times popularity + 1. \tag{8.2}$$

In Eq. (8.2), the parameter β_r controls the rate at which tokens are generated. If β_r is too large, more non-popular content will be cached, leading to more content replacements in the cache. Similarly, if β_r is too small, only a small amount of content will be added to the cache, causing MIR to be insensitive to changes in cache popularity. Therefore, the caching strategy dynamically adjusts β_r by monitoring the trend of cache hit ratio over a period of time. Additionally, to speed up the convergence, the adjustment frequency is optimized when β_r changes in the same direction. The adjustment algorithm for β_r is given in Algorithm 8.1.

Algorithm 8.1 Adjustment Algorithm of βr
Variable: the change in $\varepsilon \leftarrow \beta_r$
Input: execution interval time Δt
Output: none
Initialization: $cnt \leftarrow 0$, $H_r \leftarrow 0$

function adjustBeta (Δt)
for every Δt **do** // every once in a while
  $h \leftarrow$ *cache hit times* // cache hit count
  $m \leftarrow$ *cache miss times* // cache invalidation times
  if $h/(m + h) > H_r$ **then** //when cache hit ratio increases, β moves in the same direction
    $cnt \leftarrow cnt + 1$
  else //if the cache hit ratio decreases
    $cnt \leftarrow 0$ // then *cnt* is set to 0
    $\varepsilon = -1 \bullet \varepsilon$ // reverse movement
  end if
  $\beta = \beta + \varepsilon \bullet 1.1^{cnt}$ // fast convergence
  $H_r = h/(m + h)$
end for
end function

Since the popularity of content changes over time, it may become more or less popular. It's not enough to just use the initial popularity set by the content provider. Therefore, the cache placement strategy for CoG-MIN also includes a push-down mechanism to ensure that popular content is cached in MIRs closer to the users. When a content is cached, the number of times the content has been requested by consumers ($Cnt_{r,c}$) before being evicted from the cache space is also recorded. If this count exceeds the threshold K_r, $Cnt_{r,c}$ is reset to $Cnt_{r,c}/2$, and the content is pushed downstream. Also, the *MoveTag* of the Data packet carrying this content is set to *TRUE*.

In the push-down mechanism, when a MIR receives a Data packet, it first checks the *MoveTag* of the packet. If it is *True*, it means that the Data packet was obtained from the cache of the previous router using the push-down mechanism. Therefore, the MIR will definitely cache a copy of the data carried by the Data packet. When the *MoveTag* is *False*, MIR will probabilistically cache the Data packet based on the popularity level, but only if there are sufficient tokens available. This probabilistic caching effectively reduces the number of content copies along the path. The *MoveTag* in the Data packet is set to *False* by default. This is because the MIR closest to the content provider typically belongs to the content provider itself, and even if the content provider sets the *MoveTag* to *False*, it does not adversely affect the overall network caching. Algorithm 8.2 shows the processing flow for Data packets and Algorithm 8.3 shows the processing flow for Interest packets.

Algorithm 8.2 The Processing Flow for Data Packets
Input: Package *Data*(*c*) containing content *c*
Output: Boolean value for caching or not

function onProcessData(*Data*(*c*))
cp ← *Data*(*c*). *topLevelIdentifier* // Get content provider name
if *Data*(*c*). *MoveTag* equals to *TRUE* **then**
cache *Data*(*c*) // Push-Down Mechanism
Data(*c*). *SetMoveTag*(*FALSE*) // Reset Move Tag to False
return TRUE // Caching Content
end if
level ← *Data*(*c*). *Popularity*
t← calculate token generation/consumption by (8.2) // Calculate token consumption/generation
if $T_{r,\,cp} + t \leq 0$ **then** // If there are insufficient tokens
return FALSE // do not cache content
end if
$T_{r,\,cp} \leftarrow T_{r,\,cp} + t$ // Calculate the number of tokens processed
$p \leftarrow level + \varphi_{r,\,cp}$ // Add the probability correction value calculated in LRU-ST
success ← cache *Data*(*c*) with probability *p* // Cache content with probability *p*
return success // Return cache results
end function

Algorithm 8.3 The Processing Flow for Interest Packets
Input: Interest packet *Interest*(c) of requesting content c
Output: 1) Boolean value of cache hit or not, 2) A packet that encapsulates content c

function onInterestFindCache(*Interest*(c))
 $cp \leftarrow Interest(c).\ topLevelIdentifier$ // Get the name of the content provider
 $name \leftarrow Interest(c).\ Identifier$ // Getting content identifiers
 $Data(c), exist \leftarrow CachePool.\ get(name)$ // The cache space is searched for the existence of the content
 $N_{op} \leftarrow N_{op} + 1$ // Record the number of cache insert/lookup operations
 if exist **then** // If the content is found in cache space
  $Cnt_{r,c} \leftarrow Cnt_{r,c} + 1$ // Keep track of how many times the content has been requested
  if $Cnt_{r,c} \geq K_r$ **then** // If the preset threshold is exceeded
   $Cnt_{r,c} \leftarrow Cnt_{r,c}/2$ // Reset $Cnt_{r,c}$
   $Data(c).\ SetMoveTag(TRUE)$ // Push the content down
  end if
 else
  return FALSE,*null* // Cache invalidation
 end if
 return TRUE, *Data*(c) // Cache hit
end function

8.2.2 Cache Space Reassignment Algorithm

In the cache space reallocation algorithm, the cache space is divided into multiple partitions based on the number of content providers, and each content provider has an independent cache space.

In the initial state of the system, each content provider has an equal-sized cache space. The cache space reallocation algorithm runs periodically to redistribute the cache space from content providers with lower utilization to those with higher utilization.

After the cache space is reallocated, the previous cache hit ratio is compared with the current cache hit ratio. If the current cache hit ratio is higher, it indicates that the adjustment of the cache space has improved network efficiency, and the cache space reallocation continues based on the cache hit ratios of each content provider. If the current cache hit ratio is lower, it indicates that the previous adjustment of the cache space has led to decreased cache efficiency. In this case, the algorithm compares the cache hit cases of each content provider on the cache space of MIR, and the cache spaces of content providers with significant decreases or insufficient improvements in cache hit ratios are swapped.

Algorithm 8.4 illustrates the specific process of the cache space reallocation algorithm.

Algorithm 8.4 The Processing Flow for Interest Packets
Variable: $\epsilon \leftarrow$ The amount of cache space changed each time

function reallocateCacheSize()
for every n operation **do** // Periodically reallocate the cache space
  $N_{cp} \leftarrow$ *quantity of cp* // Total number of content providers
  $h \leftarrow$ *cache hit times* // Cache hit times
  $m \leftarrow$ *cache miss times* // Cache miss times
  if $H_r < h/(m+h)$ **then** // If this cache hit ratio is lower than the last cache hit ratio
    calculate $H_{r,cp}$ (cache hit ratio for every cp) // The cache hit ratio of each content provider is calculated
    calculate variation between $H^{s}_{r,cp}$ and $H^{s-1}_{r,cp}$, get diff array
    descending sort diff array // The cache hit ratio change value
  of each content provider is calculated and sorted
    for (i = 0; i < $N_{cp}/2$; i++) **do**
      if $diff[i] + diff[N_{cp} - 1 - i] < 0$ **then** // The drop is greater than the rise and the extra space is exchanged
        $Size_{r,cp[i]} = Size_{r,cp[i]} - \epsilon$
        $Size_{r,cp[N_{cp}-1-i]} = Size_{r,cp[N_{cp}-1-i]} + \epsilon$
      end if
    end for
  else
    for (i = 0; i < $N_{cp}/2$; i++) **do** // Reallocate cache space
      $Size_{r,cp[i]} = Size_{r,cp[i]} + \epsilon$
      $Size_{r,cp[N_{cp}-1-i]} = Size_{r,cp[N_{cp}-1-i]} - \epsilon$
    end for
  end if
end for
end function

8.2.3 *Dual-Layer Caching Model*

The MIR can perform packet forwarding and caching. The forwarding function mainly uses CPU resources, while the caching function only uses memory resources as cache space. Memory has the advantage of fast and low-latency access compared to external storage, as it does not require I/O operations for reading. However, due to the relatively high cost of memory per storage unit, the memory capacity of the MIR is typically not very large.

To address this limitation, the cache management scheme for CoG-MIN adopts a dual-layer caching model consisting of memory and external storage. This design allows for an expanded storage space. Additionally, it incorporates a Bloom filter to pre-filter external storage query requests, effectively reducing the number of I/O lookups when cache misses occur.

The dual-layer caching model consists of four main components: memory cache, external storage cache, Bloom filter, and external storage insertion log.

The memory cache refers to the cache space in memory that executes the least recently used (LRU) cache replacement strategy. Although the memory cache has a smaller storage capacity, all operations are performed in memory, resulting in higher efficiency. The external storage cache, on the other hand, refers to the storage space in a hard disk or flash memory. Each read or write operation requires I/O operations, resulting in lower read/write efficiency. However, the external storage cache has a larger storage capacity compared to the memory cache. The contents stored in the external storage adopt a lazy deletion approach. This approach delete removed contents periodically. The memory space utilizes a Bloom filter to facilitate pre-queries by the MIR to check if the content is cached in the external storage, reducing the need for I/O operations. To address potential false positives in the Bloom filter, the lazy deletion algorithm resets the Bloom filter when the false positive rate becomes too high. The external storage insertion log is stored in the external storage and keeps track of every insertion operation. This log employs a linear data structure, where each new insertion operation is appended at the end of the log. The lazy deletion algorithm traverses the entire log, using the LRU algorithm to retain a maximum number of contents. Subsequently, a new external storage insertion log is generated based on the remaining contents.

In the dual-layer cache model, each storage unit serves as a cache for a specific content provider. To simplify the description, only a pair of storage units, namely memory and external memory, is taken as an example below.

Cache Insertion

When caching content, the first step is to insert the content directly into the memory space. If the memory space is not full after insertion, the caching process is complete. If the memory cache is already full, the evicted content needs to be considered for insertion into the external storage. During this insertion process, a log entry is created in the "evicted content inserted into external storage" log. Additionally, the name of the evicted content is added to the Bloom filter as a key.

Figure 8.3 illustrates the cache insertion process.

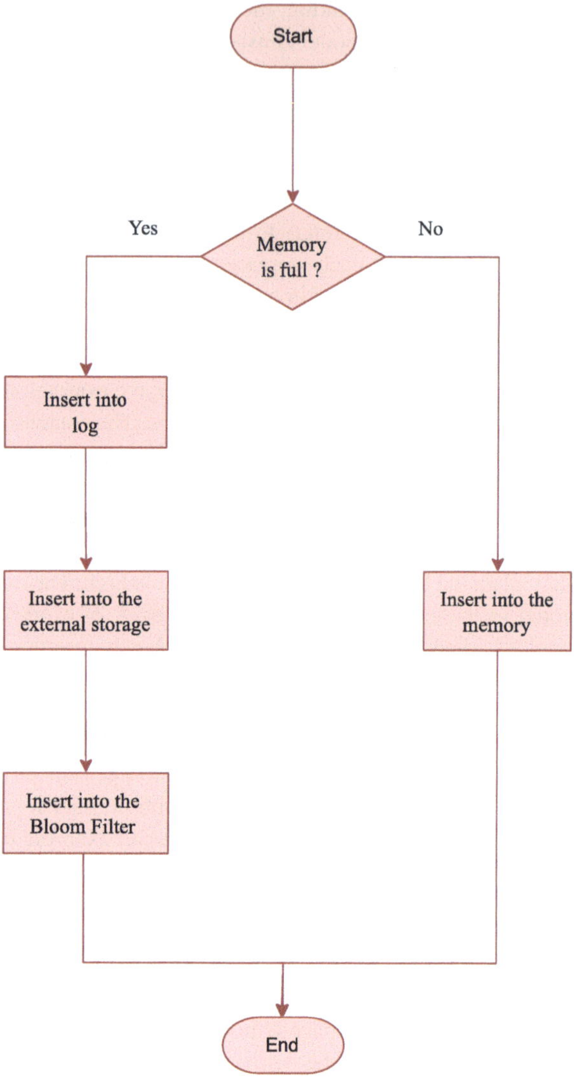

Fig. 8.3 The cache insertion process

Cache Query

In the caching query process, the following steps are followed:

(a) First, based on the content identifier, the memory cache is queried to check if the content exists.

- If it is found in the memory cache, the content is retrieved and directly returned. The caching query process ends.
- If the content is not found in the memory cache, the external storage is considered for further lookup.

(b) To minimize the number of I/O requests, the Bloom filter is queried to check if the content is present in the external storage.

- If the content is not found in the Bloom filter, it indicates that the content is not present in the external storage. The caching query process ends, and the MIR forwards the request to the next hop MIR.
- If the content is found in the Bloom filter, it suggests that the content may be in the external storage. The query continues in the external storage.
  - If the content is found in the external storage, it is inserted into the memory cache, and the evicted content from the memory cache is cached in the external storage (along with writing the insertion log). The found content is then returned.
  - If the content is not found in the external storage, the caching query process ends, and the MIR forwards the request to the next hop MIR.

Figure 8.4 illustrates the cache query process.

Cache Lazy Deletion

In the caching process, the deletion of content from the external storage was not mentioned. This is because a lazy deletion strategy is chosen to handle the removal of expired content.

If a real-time LRU replacement strategy is implemented in the external storage, it will significantly increase the number of I/O operations and decrease system efficiency.

Unlike that approach, the lazy deletion strategy runs in a separate coroutine, ensuring that it does not impact the efficiency of forwarding and caching operations.

Specifically, the cache lazy deletion process is shown below:

The system periodically reads the insertion log of the external storage. It sequentially reads the log file and, using the LRU algorithm, retains only n contents (where n represents the size of the external storage cache), deleting all other content. It then rewrites a new insertion log that contains only those n retained contents, replacing the original log.

Additionally, this strategy includes tracking the false positive rate of the Bloom filter. If the false positive rate exceeds a certain threshold, the Bloom filter is reset to a new filter that contains the current content of the external storage. This helps avoid excessive I/O overhead caused by a high false positive rate.

Figure 8.5 illustrates the cache lazy deletion process.

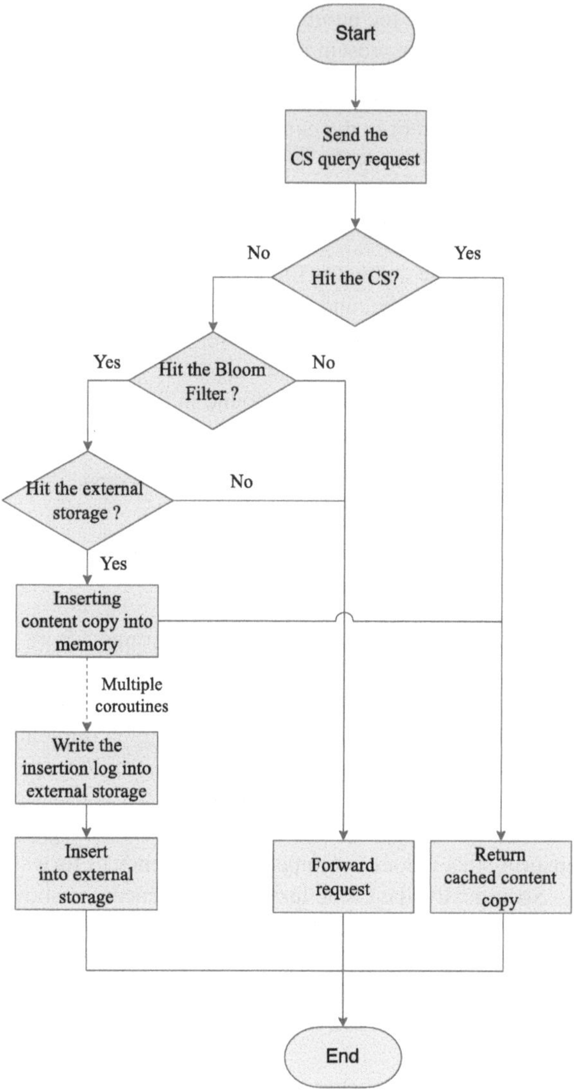

Fig. 8.4 The cache query process

Fig. 8.5 The cache lazy deletion process

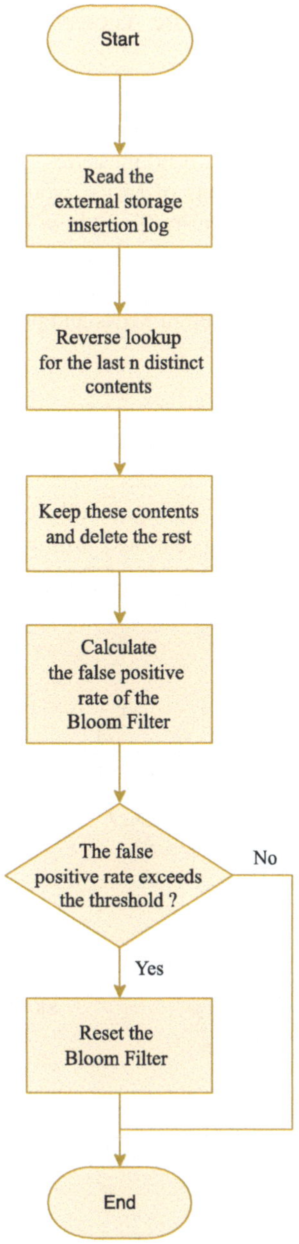

8.3 Cache Access Control for CoG-MIN

In-network caching allows for the decoupling of the location binding between content and content providers. This can significantly enhance network performance. However, if no measures are taken, namely, storing content in plaintext within the cache units of MIRs, would compromise content privacy and greatly reduce network security. To address this issue, the CoG-MIN research group has further proposed a cache access control policy based on the Ciphertext Policy Attribute-Based Encryption (CP-ABE) algorithm [8]. This policy aims to protect the privacy of content cached in MIRs and provide fine-grained access control.

8.3.1 *Cache Access Control Model*

As shown in Fig. 8.6, the cache access control model for CoG-MIN consists of the following entities: Multi-Identifier System (MIS), Attribute Authority (AA), Content Provider (CP), Content Consumer (CC), and Multi-Identifier Router (MIR).

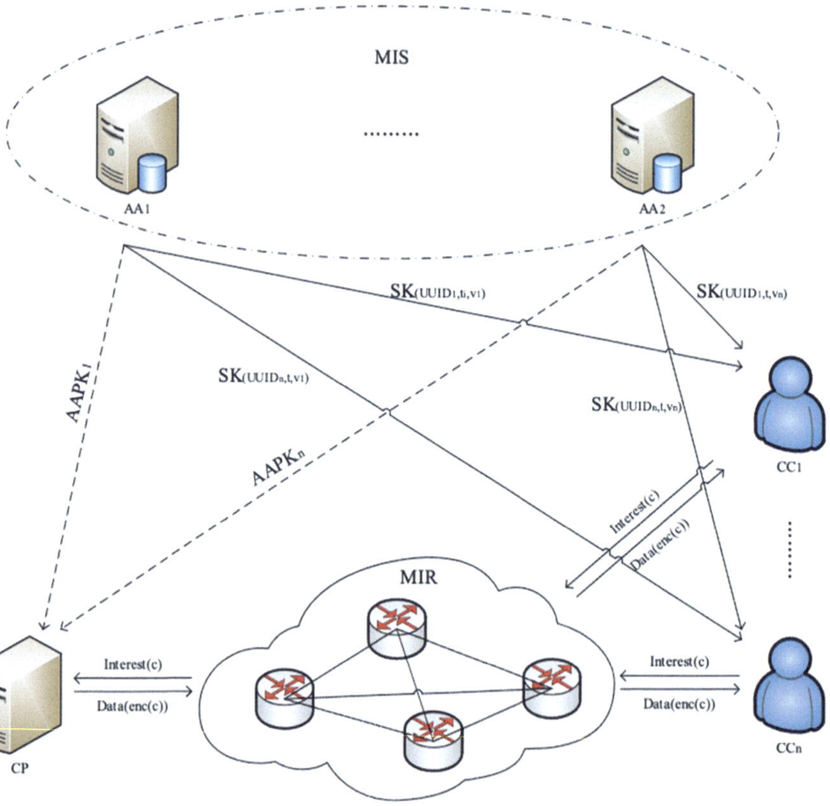

Fig. 8.6 Cache access control model for CoG-MIN

- **Multi-Identifier System (MIS)**: In the cache access control model for CoG-MIN, MIS serves as an Attribute Authority (AA) node to avoid a single point of failure. It stores public parameters and logs of key authorizations on the blockchain to ensure their integrity. Additionally, the MIS provides synchronized time-based identifiers for AAs and content providers.
- **Attribute Authority (AA)**: In the cache access control model for CoG-MIN, there are multiple attribute authorities, and each AA operates within the MIS node. During the initialization phase, AAs on the MIS share the same global public parameters and master key (AAPK). All AAs jointly manage the attribute space. When an AA receives a key generation request, it sends the log of key generation to the blockchain within MIS. The AA sends the generated secret key (SK) to the consumer only after all nodes have synchronized this operation. This can ensure traceability for each attribute authorization. From the perspective of consumers, it can be considered that each AA can provide the same quality of key generation services, which can be regarded as a unified entity.
- **Content Provider (CP)**: The content provider is responsible for setting different access policies for different content and encrypting the content based on the access policy and the identifier corresponding to the current time period. Additionally, when the encrypted content is encapsulated into data packets, the content provider also sets an expiration time for the content.
- **Content Consumer (CC)**: Each content consumer is assigned a globally defined identity identifier (*UUID*) by MIS. Content consumers request attribute private keys from multiple attribute authorities. They use these private keys to decrypt the content obtained from MIRs or content providers. Content consumers can only access the plaintext if their attributes meet the access structure requirements of the content and if the time period when the private key was generated matches the time period when the ciphertext was encrypted. Otherwise, the ciphertext cannot be decrypted.
- **Multi-Identifier Router (MIR)**: The MIRs perform forwarding, routing, and caching functions. When caching the data copy of a data packet, the content provider marks a freshness period field in the packet, which affects the duration of the cache. Content outside this time range will be evicted from the cache. The freshness period field is set as the end time of the current time period to ensure that the MIR does not cache content encrypted in the previous time period.

8.3.2 Cache Access Control Algorithm

Based on the above cache access control model, the cache access control algorithm consists of the following processes:

- **Global System Setup:** $GlobalSetup(\lambda, \mathbb{U}) \rightarrow (GPP, MSK)$. Input is the group generator and attribute set $\mathbb{U}$ with parameter λ, output is the global public parameter *GPP* and master key *MSK*. The algorithm is run by a single AA node within MIS. This node sends the *MSK* to other nodes within MIS through an encrypted communication tunnel and saves the *GPP* in the blockchain.

- **Key Generation:** $KeyGen(GPP, UUID, MSK, attr, time) \rightarrow SK_{UUID,attr}^{time}$. The attribute authority η takes the user's global unique identity identifier *UUID*, its private key *MSK*, global parameters *GPP*, the identifier *time* corresponding to the current timestamp, and the attribute *attr* corresponding to the key to be generated, as inputs of the algorithm. The algorithm outputs the attribute private key $SK_{UUID,attr}^{time}$ corresponding to the attribute *attr* of the consumer identified as *UUID*, and records the consumer's *UUID*.
- **Encryption:** $Encrypt(GPP, M, (A, \rho), time) \rightarrow CT$. The input consists of the global public parameter *GPP*, the plaintext content *M*, the access structure $\mathbb{A}$ associated with the content, and the attribute mapping function ρ. The output is the ciphertext *CT*.
- **Decryption:** $Decrypt\left(GPP, CT, \left\{SK_{UUID,attr}^{time}\right\}\right) \rightarrow M$ or $\perp$. The input consists of the global public parameter *GPP*, the ciphertext *CT*, and the attribute set owned by the user identified as *UUID*. If the decryption is successful, the algorithm outputs the content plaintext *M*. If decryption fails, it outputs $\perp$.
- **Trace:** $Trace\left(GPP, SK_{UUID,attr}^{time}\right) \rightarrow UUID$ or $\perp$. The input consists of the global public parameter *GPP* and the key of a betrayer. If the key is intact, the algorithm outputs the *UUID* of the consumer corresponding to the key. Otherwise, it does not output any result.

The detailed implementations of each process are as follows.

Global System Setup: $GlobalSetup(\lambda, \mathbb{U}) \rightarrow (GPP, MSK)$

When a new time period begins, the algorithm is executed. The input of the algorithm is a group generator with parameter λ. The output of the algorithm consists of the global public parameter *GPP* and the master key *MSK*. Let $N = p_1 p_2 p_3, p_1, p_2, p_3, \mathbb{G}, \mathbb{G}_T, e$, where p_1, p_2, p_3 are distinct large prime numbers, $\mathbb{G}, \mathbb{G}_T$ are cyclic groups of order *N*, *e* stands for the bilinear map, namely $e : \mathbb{G} \times \mathbb{G} \rightarrow \mathbb{G}_T$. $\mathbb{G}_{p_i}$ is a subgroup of $\mathbb{G}$, $\left|\mathbb{G}_{p_i}\right| = p_i$, g_1 is the generator of $\mathbb{G}_{p_1}$. The α, $y \in Z_N$, $h \in \mathbb{G}_{p_1}$ are randomly chosen. A hash function $H(time) \rightarrow Z_N$ is selected and modeled as a random oracle model. All public parameters generated in the algorithm are stored in the blockchain within MIS. The global public parameter *GPP* is as follows:

$$GPP = \left(N, h, g_1, g_1^{\alpha}, e(g_1, g_1)^{y}, \left\{U_{attr} = g^{u_{attr}}\right\}_{attr \in U}\right). \tag{8.3}$$

And the master key is set to:

$$MSK = \left(a, y, X_3\right). \tag{8.4}$$

where $X_3 \in G_{p_3}$.

Key Generation: $KeyGen\left(GPP, UUID, MSK, attr, time\right) \rightarrow SK_{UUID,\mathrm{attr}}^{time}$

This function randomly selects $c \in \mathbb{Z}_N^*$, $t \in Z_n$, $R, R_3, R_3^{'} \in \mathbb{G}_{p_3}$, and for each attribute $attr \in S$, it randomly selects $R_{attr} \in \mathbb{G}_{p_3}$.

The decryption key is defined as follows:

$$SK_{UUID,attr}^{time} = \left(\begin{array}{l} K = g_1^{\frac{a}{c+y}} h^t R,\, K' = c,\, K'' = H\left(time\right),\, L = \\ \qquad g_1^t R_3,\, L' = g_1^{yt} R_3^{'},\, \left\{K_{attr} = U_{attr}^{(c+y)t} R_{attr}\right\}_{attr \in S} \end{array} \right). \tag{8.5}$$

If $gcd(c + y, N) = 1$ or c, the algorithm will randomly select c again. After the calculation is completed, the attribute agency will save the mapping relationship between c and $UUID$ in MIS. The generated key will not be stored in the blockchain. The mapping relationship between c and $UUID$ will be used in the Trace algorithm.

Encrypt: $Encrypt\left(GPP, M, \left(\mathbb{A}, \rho\right), time\right) \rightarrow CT$

The access structure $\mathbb{A}$ is a two-dimensional matrix of $l \times n$, and ρ is the mapping function that maps row $\mathbb{A}_i$ in $\mathbb{A}$ to the attribute $\rho(i)$. The algorithm randomly selects a vector $\vec{\upsilon} = \left(s, v_2, \cdots, v_n\right) \in \mathbb{Z}_N^n$. For each $\mathbb{A}_i$, the algorithm randomly assigns a parameter $r_i \in Z_N$, and calculates the inner product $\lambda_i = \mathbb{A}_i \cdot \vec{\upsilon}$. Finally, the algorithm produces the ciphertext CT:

$$CT = \left(\begin{array}{l} C = M \cdot e\left(g_1, g_1\right)^{as}, C_0 = g_1^s, C_0^{'} = g_1^{ys}, \\ \left\{C_i = h^{H(time)\lambda_i} U_{\rho(i)}^{-H(time)r_i}, C_i^{'} = g_1^{H(time)r_i}\right\}_{i=1}^{l}, \left(\mathbb{A}, \rho\right) \end{array} \right). \tag{8.6}$$

Decrypt: $Decrypt\left(GPP, CT, \left\{SK_{UUID,attr}^{time}\right\}\right) \rightarrow M$ or $\perp$

The algorithm reorganizes the ciphertext CT into several parts, denoted as $CT = \left(C, C_0, C_0^{'}, \left\{C_i, C_i^{'}\right\}_{i=1}^{m}, \left(\mathbb{A}, \rho\right)\right)$. $SK_{UUID,attr}^{time} = \left(K, K', K'', L, L', \left\{K_i\right\}_{i \in S}\right)$. If the attribute set S does not satisfy the access structure $\left(\mathbb{A}, \rho\right)$ of the ciphertext, the algorithm outputs $\perp$. Otherwise, the algorithm calculates the constant $\{\varpi_i \in Z_N\}$. Let $\sum_{\rho(i) \in S} \varpi_i \mathbb{A}_i = \left(1, 0, \cdots, 0\right)$, and then calculate:

$$\begin{aligned} D &= \prod_{\rho(i)\in S}\left(e\left(L^{K'}L',C_i\right)\cdot e\left(K_{\rho(i)},C_i'\right)\right) \\ &= \sum_{\rho(i)\in S} e\left(g_1,h\right)^{(c+y)H(time)t\varpi_i\lambda_i} \\ &= e\left(g_1,h\right)^{(c+y)H(time)ts}. \end{aligned} \tag{8.7}$$

$$\begin{aligned} E &= e\left(K,\left(C_0^{K'}C_0'\right)^{K''}\right)^{\frac{1}{K''}} \\ &= \mathrm{e}\left(g_1^{\frac{a}{c+y}}h^t R,g_1^{H(time)(c+y)s}\right)^{\frac{1}{H(time)}} \\ &= e\left(g_1,g_1\right)^{as} e\left(g_1,h\right)^{(c+y)H(time)ts}. \end{aligned} \tag{8.8}$$

Finally, the plaintext can be calculated according to the formula $M = C \cdot D/E$.

Trace: $Trace\left(GPP,SK_{UUID,attr}^{time}\right) \rightarrow UUID$ or $\perp$

The algorithm first checks the integrity of $SK_{UUID,attr}^{time}$. If it is not complete, the algorithm outputs $\perp$, indicating that it cannot trace back to the user who compromised the key. If $SK_{UUID,attr}^{time}$ is complete, the algorithm first searches $K' = c$ in $SK_{UUID,attr}^{time}$, and then finds the *UUID* of the user in the mapping table *Tab* in MIS, where c is mapped to *UUID*.

Key integrity verification process:

$$K' \in \mathbb{Z}_n, K, L, L', K_x \in G. \tag{8.9}$$

$$e\left(g_1,L'\right) = e\left(g^{\alpha},L\right) \neq 1. \tag{8.10}$$

$$e\left(g_1^{\alpha}\cdot g_1^{K'},K\right) = e\left(g_1,g_1\right)^{y}\cdot e\left(L^{K'}\cdot L',h\right) \neq 1. \tag{8.11}$$

$$\exists attr \in S, makese\left(U_{attr}, L^{K'}\cdot L'\right) = e\left(g_1, K_{atrr}\right) \neq 1. \tag{8.12}$$

References

1. Zahedinia MS, Khayyambashi MR, Bohlooli A. Fog-based caching mechanism for IoT data in information centric network using prioritization. Comput Netw. 2022;213:109082.
2. Zhang Z, Lung CH, Wei X, et al. In-network caching for ICN-based IoT (ICN-IoT): a comprehensive survey. IEEE Internet Things J. 2023;10:14595.
3. Zhang Z, Wei X, Lung CH, et al. iCache: an intelligent caching scheme for dynamic network environments in ICN-based IoT networks. IEEE Internet Things J. 2022;10(2):1787–99.
4. Pruthvi CN, Vimala HS, Shreyas J. A systematic survey on content caching in ICN and ICN-IoT: challenges, approaches and strategies. Comput Netw. 2023;233:109896.
5. Li H, Guo HY, et al. A token and popularity-based information-centric network cache management method and system. CN114448887A, 2022.
6. Guo HY, Li H, et al. Limit-caching: a caching scheme based on limited content popularity in ICN. In: 2021 7th international conference on computer and communications (ICCC). Piscataway: IEEE; 2021. p. 2201–5.
7. Zhang X, Chen Q, Li H. MIR: multi-identifier router and its prototype. In: Proceedings of the 8th international conference on computer and communications management, 2020. p. 103–7.
8. Liu Z, Cao Z, Wong DS. White-box traceable ciphertext-policy attribute-based encryption supporting any monotone access structures. IEEE Trans Inf Forensics Secur. 2012;8(1):76–88.

Chapter 9
Transport Protocol

With rapid advancements in communication technology, network traffic has experienced exponential growth, potentially surpassing the processing capacity of current network devices. When network traffic exceeds the link capacity, network congestion will occur. This may result in degraded transmission performance, such as increased network latency and packet loss. Transport protocols have consistently remained at the forefront of network research.

This chapter primarily introduces transport protocols in MIN networks, including MIN-TCP, MIN-QUIC, and MIN-PTP.

9.1 Overview of Transport Protocol

The hierarchical structure of the computer network involves dividing it into different functional layers, with each level responsible for specific tasks while providing services to the layer above and requesting services from the layer below. This hierarchical structure simplifies network design, implementation, and maintenance, while also promoting standardization and interoperability.

The computer network architecture commonly used today consists of five layers, including the application layer, transport layer, network layer, data link layer, and physical layer. The network layer is responsible for facilitating data transmission between hosts in different networks, selecting routing paths, connecting networks through routers or gateways, and forwarding packets in the network. However, the network layer alone cannot accomplish functions such as connection establishment and flow control. Without a transport layer, the network layer is akin to a road without traffic rules, leading to inevitable chaos. Therefore, the computer network system incorporates a transport layer above the network layer to ensure proper and efficient data transmission.

Traditional transport protocols comprise the Transmission Control Protocol (TCP) [1] and User Datagram Protocol (UDP) [2]. TCP provides a reliable,

H. Li, H. Bai, *Principle of Architecture, Protocol, and Algorithms for CoG-MIN*,
https://doi.org/10.1007/978-981-96-3596-2_9

in-order, byte-stream service to applications [3]. A TCP segment consists of a segment header and a data section. A TCP header contains ten mandatory fields and an optional extension field, such as Source Port, Destination Port, Sequence Number, Acknowledgment Number, Data offset, Control bits (CWR, ECE, URG, ACK, PSH, RST, SYN, FIN, etc.), Window, Checksum, and Urgent Pointer.

UDP is a connectionless transport layer protocol that offers message-oriented datagram services. Although UDP provides integrity verification of both the header and the payload, it does not guarantee message delivery to the upper-layer protocol, and it does not retain the state of the UDP message after transmission [4]. As a result, UDP is commonly referred to as an unreliable datagram protocol. However, UDP is well-suited for real-time data transmission, such as voice and video communications, since occasional packet losses have minimal impact on the received outcome. For instance, missing a few packets while streaming a video does not significantly affect the viewing experience.

With the ongoing advancements of the computer network, the demand for higher performance in data transmission has become increasingly stringent. As a result, transport protocols are constantly evolving to meet various requirements. UDP offers faster transmission speeds than TCP but lacks reliability. On the other hand, TCP provides reliability at the cost of additional overhead due to data acknowledgment on both ends. Additionally, upgrading the TCP protocol often requires upgrading the operating system since it is implemented in the kernel.

To address the aforementioned issues, Google proposes the Quick UDP Internet Connection (QUIC) protocol [5], which implements TCP-like reliable transport over UDP. It was submitted to the Internet Engineering Task Force (IETF) in 2013, and the standard version, RFC 9000, was launched by the IETF in May 2021. QUIC aims to improve the performance of connection-oriented applications that rely on TCP and reduce latency in connection establishment and data transmission. Notably, the congestion control algorithms in QUIC are implemented in the user space rather than the kernel space, enabling more rapid iteration and refinement of these algorithms.

Compared to the conventional TCP/IP protocol stack, the CoG-MIN architecture, as presented in this book, has undergone significant reconstruction and enhancements. This chapter introduces the design of the transport protocols based on CoG-MIN, as illustrated in Fig. 9.1.

The CoG-MIN architecture supports two communication semantics within the network layer for data transmission: push-based and pull-based semantics. Given this, the transport protocols for CoG-MIN consist of the MIN-TCP protocol, which is based on the push-based semantics; the MIN-QUIC protocol [6], which is also based on the push-based semantics; and the MIN-PTP protocol [7], which is based on the pull-based semantics.

- MIN-TCP is designed to provide reliable data transmission service in the MIN network, similar to the TCP protocol in the IP-based network.

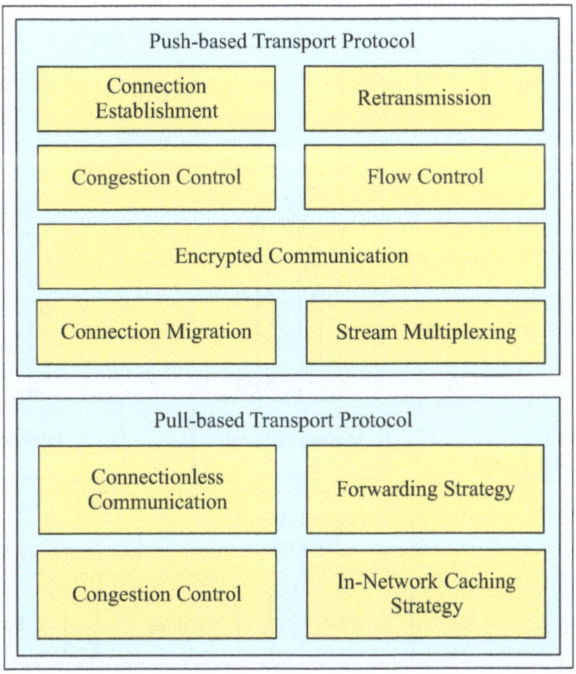

Fig. 9.1 The core designs of the transport protocols based on the CoG-MIN architecture

- MIN-QUIC takes inspiration from the UDP and QUIC protocols and delivers low-delay data transmission services in the MIN network. It is mainly applied to scenarios such as MIN-Web.
- MIN-PTP leverages pull-based semantics to deliver content in the MIN network efficiently. The following sections explain the technical solutions for MIN-TCP, MIN-QUIC, and MIN-PTP.

9.2 MIN-TCP

9.2.1 Overview of MIN-TCP

The overall architecture of the MIN-TCP is illustrated in Fig. 9.2.

The protocol stack of MIN-TCP operates across both the transport and application layers. The application layer primarily provides a general socket layer. The MIN application program utilizes the socket layer's functions to achieve connection monitoring, establishment, and data reading and writing. The transport layer is responsible for actual connection management, state management, and network communication. Communication between the socket layer and the transport layer is facilitated via common socket programming. Unix domain sockets are the preferred

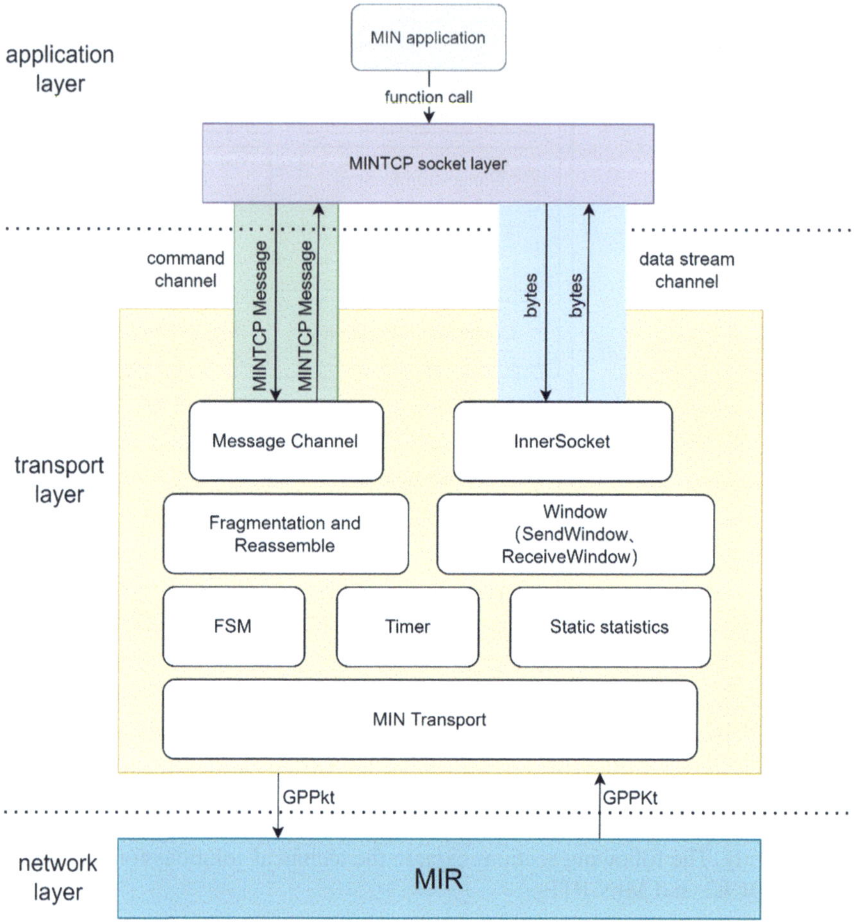

Fig. 9.2 Overview architecture of MIN-TCP

method of communication, while TCP sockets can be used in certain scenarios where Unix domain sockets are not available.

9.2.2 *Packet Format*

The packet of MIN-TCP is carried in the GPPkt packet as the Payload of the GPPkt packet. The format of the MIN-TCP packet is as follows (Fig. 9.3):

```
MINPushTCPPacket = 320 TLV-LENGTH
                   <SrcPort>
                   <DstPort>
                   <Sequence>
                   <ACK>
                   <FINFlag>
                   <SYNFlag>
                   <WindowSize>
                   <CheckSum>
```

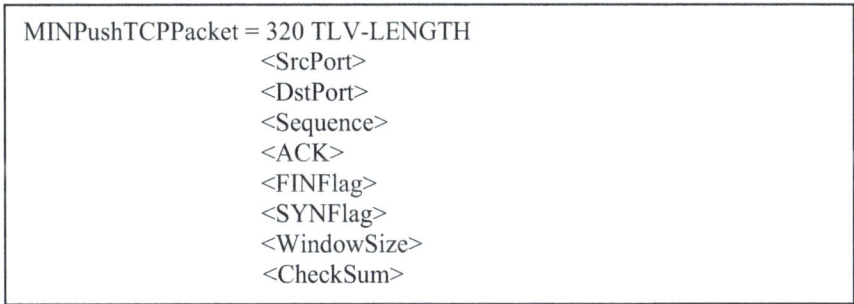

Fig. 9.3 MIN-TCP packet format

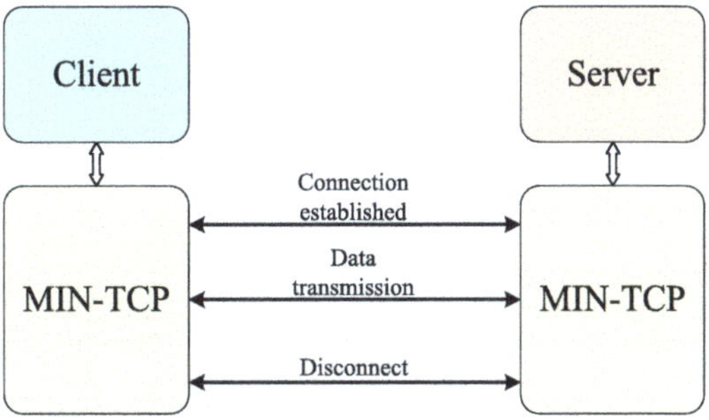

Fig. 9.4 Overview of interaction between Client and Server based on MIN-TCP

9.2.3 Interaction Process

The interaction process of MIN-TCP is primarily divided into three phases: connection establishment, connection disconnection, and data transmission (Fig. 9.4). Client and Server utilize the socket layer interface provided by the MIN-TCP protocol stack to communicate with the protocol stack, while SocketManager handles all protocol stack operations and interacts with MIR.

The connection establishment process begins with the Server side completing the Listen monitoring, followed by the Client sending a Dial request to initiate the three-way handshake for connection establishment. After the creation of InnerListenSocket, it passively receives packets through the OnReceivePacket function. However, it is not actively invoked by InnerListenSocket to initiate the coroutine for packet reception. Instead, MIRTransport triggers this function after registering the listening identifier to MIR and opening a LogicFace's receiving coroutine. This callback-based invocation enables the forwarding of received packets from MIR to InnerListenSocket for further processing.

Figure 9.5 illustrates the process of a three-way handshake in establishing a connection.

The disconnection process in MIN-TCP is a four-way wave-hand process, which handles the Server side and Client side changing to different states after receiving a FIN packet.

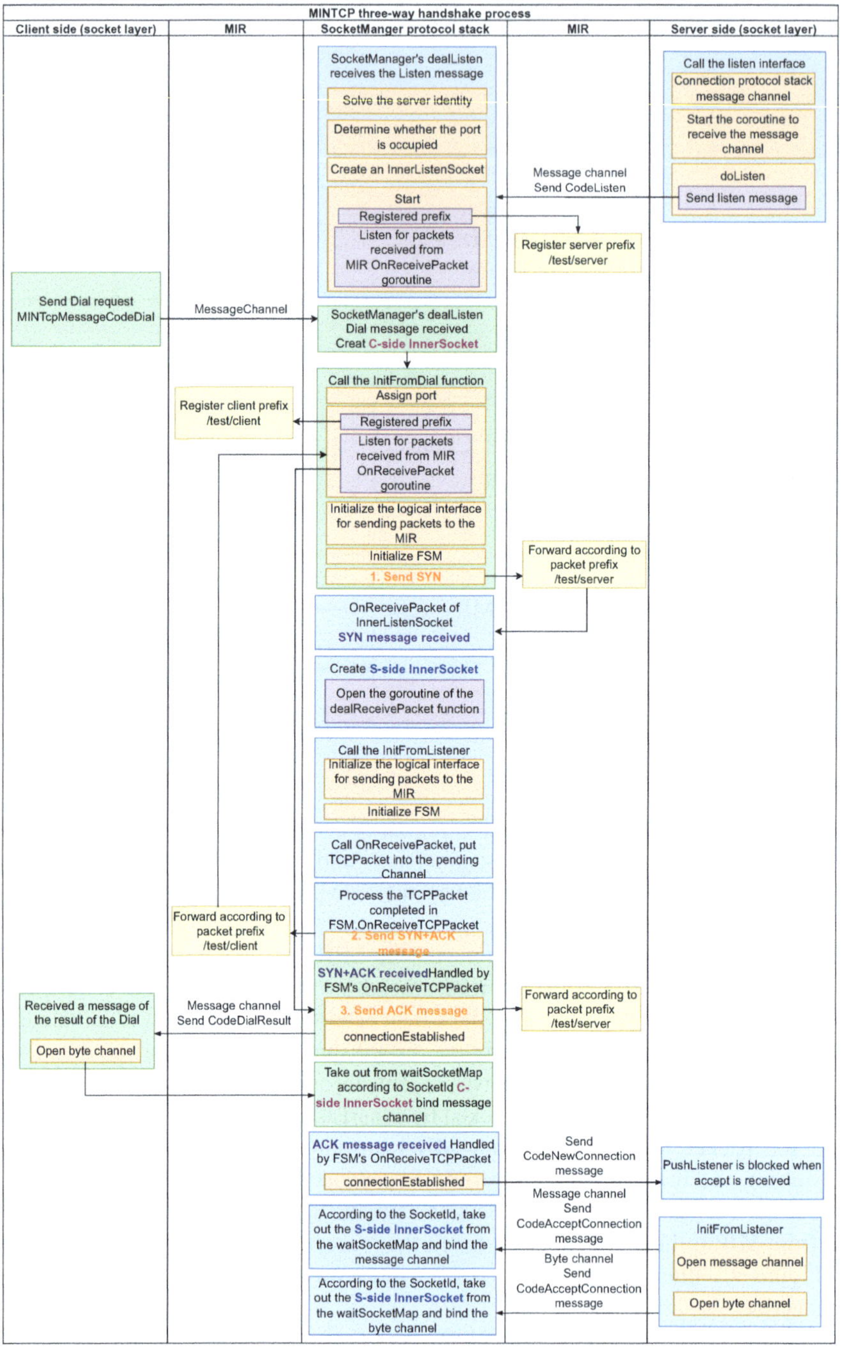

Fig. 9.5 Swimlane flowchart of three-way handshake process in MIN-TCP

Figure 9.6 illustrates the interactive flow for the Client side initiating the disconnection request. The flow for the Server side initiating the disconnection request is the same.

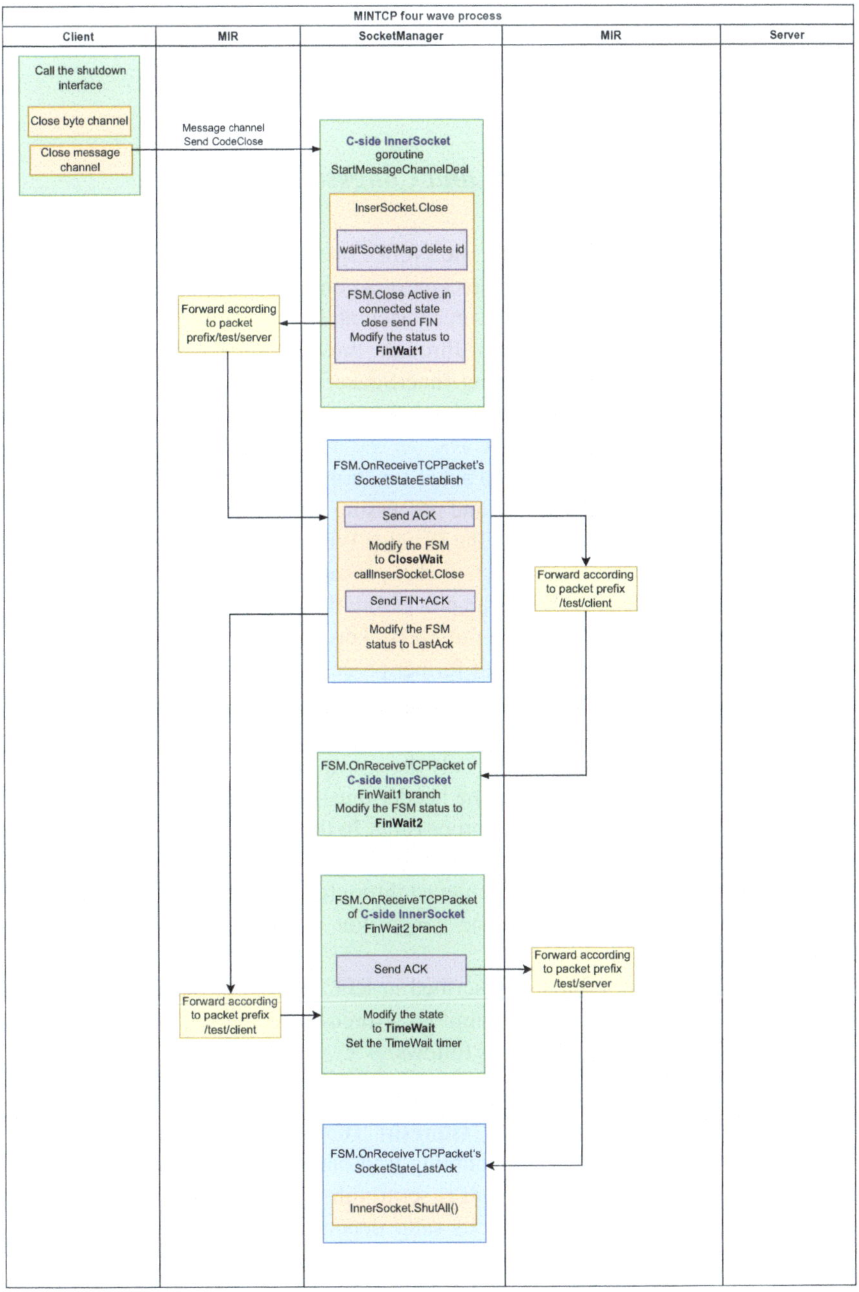

Fig. 9.6 Swimlane flowchart of the four-way wave-hand in MIN-TCP

After a successful dialing process, both the client and server sides establish a Bytechannel through the SocketManager. All data transmission is performed via the Bytechannel. The SocketManager acts as an intermediary, facilitating data transmission between the two ends. During this process, it ensures data reliability and implements congestion control mechanisms.

Figure 9.7 illustrates the swimlane flowchart of the data transmission in MIN-TCP.

9.2.4 Reliable Transmission and Congestion Control

The achievement of reliable transmission relies on the utilization of acknowledgment (ACK), which necessitates the receipt of a confirmation from the recipient to ensure that the transmitted packet has been accurately and completely delivered.

After establishing a connection through three-way handshake, MIN-TCP receives and processes a packet using InnerSocket's dealReceivePacket function. The ACK is calculated by ReceiveWindow's ReceivePacket. The SendAck is called to acknowledge receipt of the packet.

The primary tasks in the ReceivePacket function involve calculating the ACKs, caching packets within the window, and processing them sequentially.

Figure 9.8 shows the structure of the Receive Window, where nextSeq and maxSeq are measured in bytes, while each packet possesses a distinct length:

After receiving orderly packets, the processing flow is as follows: a sliding window operation is performed to take out all packets that have arrived in order and hand them over to the socket layer for further processing (Fig. 9.9).

In actual network scenarios, it is not always guaranteed that packets will arrive in the desired order. This can result in the presence of "gaps" in the sliding window. It should be noted that during this case, only the empty header will be present. This is because any received packet within the header must be in order and will promptly be forwarded to the socket layer for processing. In this state, it responds to the last expected nextSeq (Fig. 9.10).

Congestion control is primarily achieved through the use of window adjustment algorithms. In MIN-TCP, two classic congestion control algorithms, Reno and Cubic, are implemented.

The Reno algorithm, which is described in RFC 5681, was widely used in the early days of congestion control. It employs a three-stage approach to control congestion, which can be summarized as follows:

- **Slow Start Phase**: This stage will continue until the congestion window size reaches the Slow Start Threshold (ssthresh). The slow start algorithm increases the congestion window size by doubling it in one Round Trip Time (RTT) at a time. During initialization, ssthresh is set to infinity (or the maximum value of uint64 in the code), and thereafter its value depends on the occurrence of packet loss events. Once the congestion window size reaches ssthresh, the Slow Start

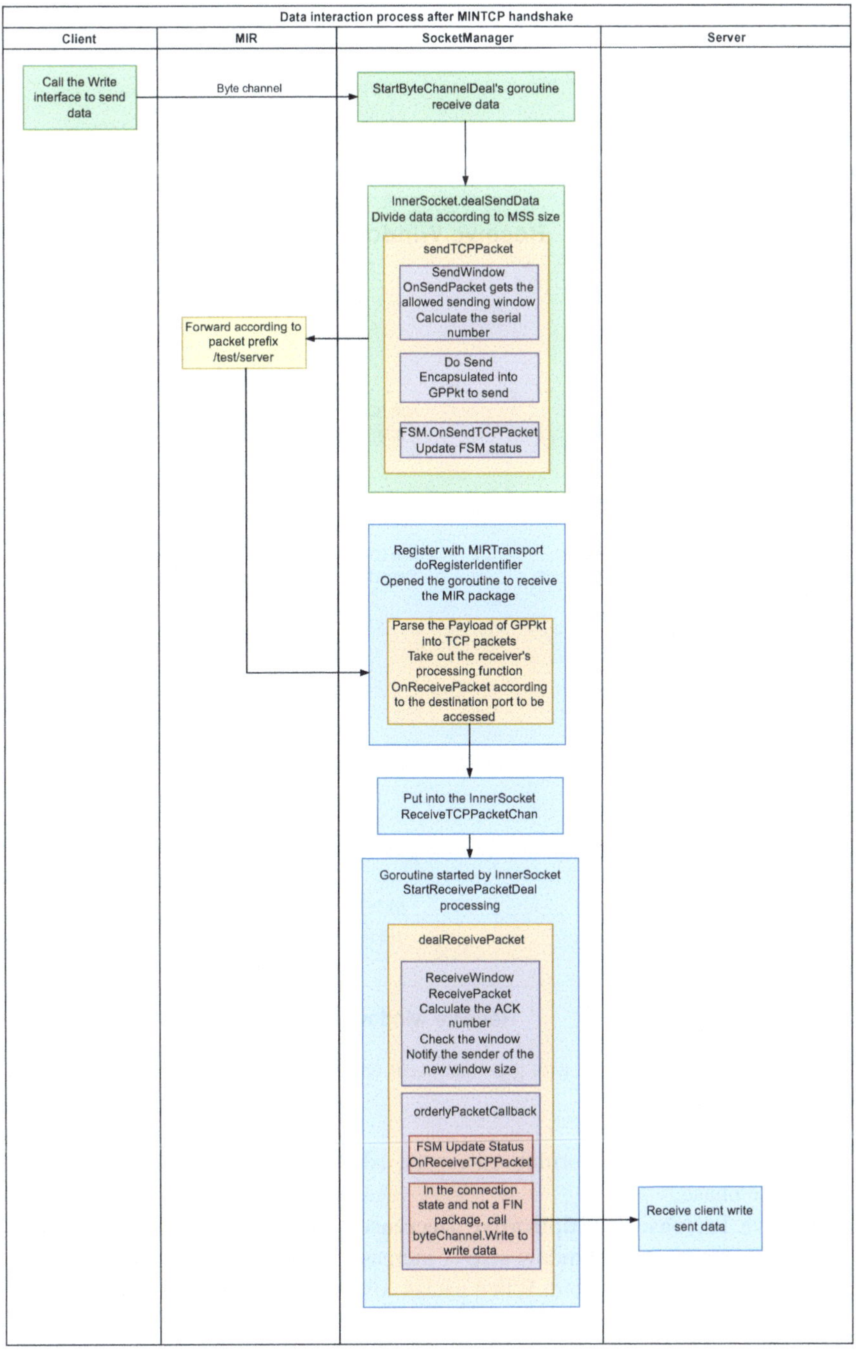

Fig. 9.7 Swimlane flowchart of the data transmission in MIN-TCP

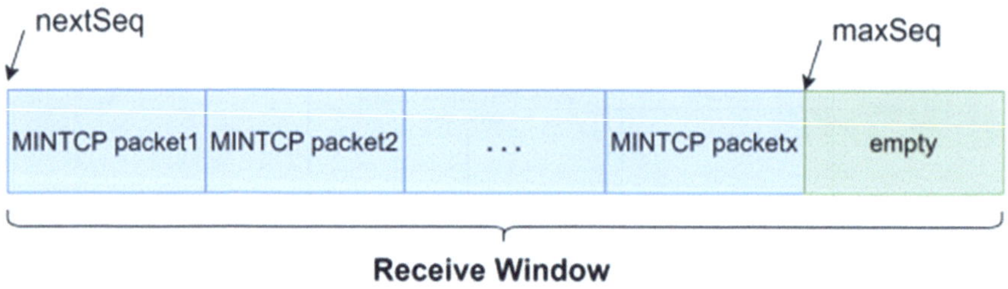

Fig. 9.8 Receive Window in MIN-TCP

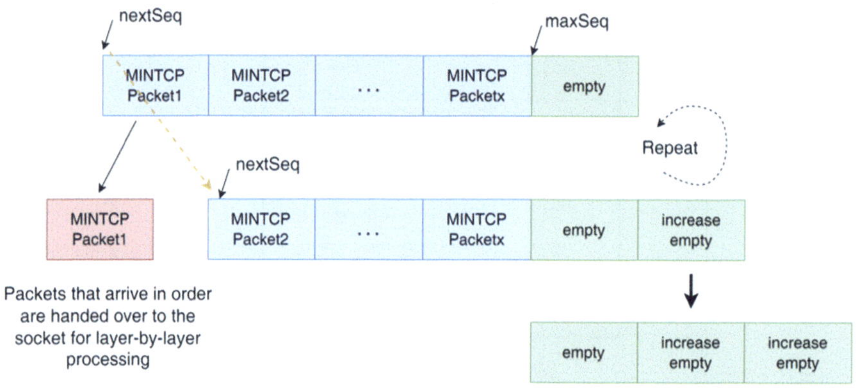

Fig. 9.9 The processing flow for receiving data packets in order

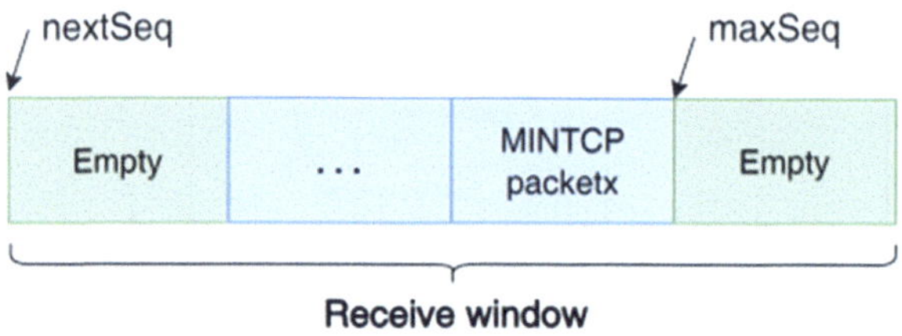

Fig. 9.10 The Receive Window with gaps that occur when data packets are not received in the expected order

phase ends, and the algorithm enters the additive increase and multiplicative decrease phase.

- **Additive Increase Multiplicative Decrease (AIMD) Phase**: During AIMD phase, the congestion window size is increased additively by 1 for every RTT until packet loss is detected. When packet loss occurs, the ssthresh is set to half of the current congestion window size using a multiplicative decrease. Meanwhile, the congestion window size is reset to its initial value, which in the Linux kernel is set to 10.

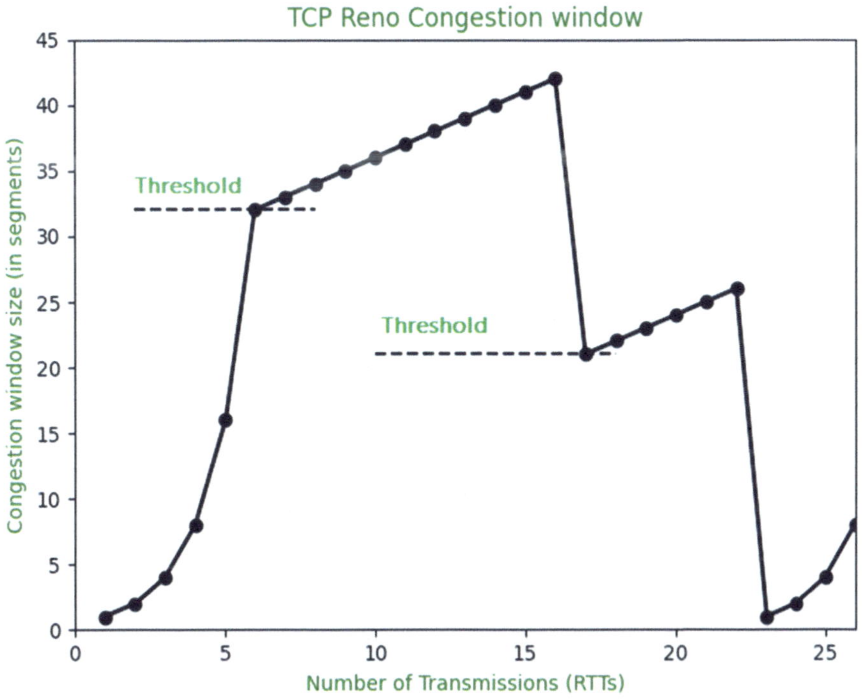

Fig. 9.11 TCP Reno [8]

- **Fast Recovery Phase**: Packet loss is detected by the receipt of three redundant ACKs. Once three redundant ACKs have been received, the ssthresh is set to the current congestion window size, and the congestion window size is reduced to half of its original value. The algorithm then proceeds to the AIMD phase. However, this algorithm has a disadvantage: when packet loss occurs, it always enters the AIMD phase and does not perform the Slow Start phase. As a result, the congestion window size grows slowly when the network environment recovers.

The curve of the congestion window size in TCP Reno is shown in Fig. 9.11.

The implementation of the Cubic algorithm is primarily based on RFC 8312. Serving as the default congestion control algorithm in the Linux kernel, the Cubic algorithm exhibits a robust congestion control process that enhances scalability and stability within high-speed long-distance network environments.

The Cubic algorithm uses a cubic function to increase the window, the specific formula is as follows:

$$W_{\text{cubic}}(t) = C * (t - K)^3 + W_{\max}. \tag{9.1}$$

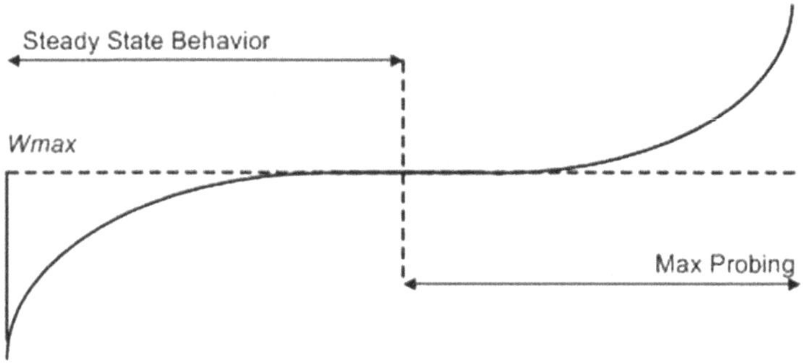

Fig. 9.12 CUBIC window growth function [9]

The CUBIC window growth function is as follows (Fig. 9.12):

Here, C is a constant that determines the aggressiveness of window increase in high Bandwidth Delay Product (BDP) networks, t is the time elapsed since the last congestion event, and K is the time it takes for the above function to increase the current window size to W_{max}.

Where K is calculated by the following formula:

$$K = \sqrt[3]{\frac{W_{max} * (1-\beta)}{C}}. \tag{9.2}$$

Where β is the multiplicative decreasing factor of cubic algorithm.

Based on the value of cwnd (congestion window), Cubic operates in three modes:

- TCP-Friendly Region: The Cubic algorithm operates in TCP mode when cwnd is smaller than the window size reached by TCP at time t after the last loss. To achieve equivalent throughput as standard TCP in TCP-friendly region, Cubic employs the following formula to estimate the window size:

$$W_{est} = W_{max}{}^{*}\beta + 3^{*}\frac{1-\beta}{1+\beta}^{*}\frac{t}{\text{RTT}} \tag{9.3}$$

- **Convex Region**: When the congestion avoidance phase receives an ACK, if the protocol is not in TCP mode and *cwnd* is less than W_{max}, the protocol enters this region, where *cwnd* increment occurs:

$$\frac{W(t+\text{RTT}) - cwnd}{cwnd}. \tag{9.4}$$

- **Concave Region**: When *cwnd* exceeds W_{max}, it suggests potential disruptions in network conditions since the last congestion event, indicating possible fluctuations and departure of contention flows from the network, thereby augmenting available bandwidth.

Due to the highly asynchronous nature of the network, continual fluctuations in available bandwidth persist, resulting in a gradual growth of the concave region at the initial stage. This implies that it becomes challenging to discern whether an increase in bandwidth is attributed to network fluctuations or actual network improvement. Consequently, a cautious and incremental growth rate is adopted.

The process of gradually increasing the network bandwidth is referred to as the maximum probing phase, during which the Cubic algorithm actively seeks a larger W_{max}. As the window growth function in the concave region remains unaltered, both regions maintain their respective window growth functions without any modifications. Consequently, the increment of *cwnd* can be determined as follows:

$$\frac{W\left(t+\mathrm{RTT}\right)-cwnd}{cwnd}. \tag{9.5}$$

9.2.5 State Transition

The state transition of MIN-TCP involves two objects: the Client and the Server. The Server provides services for the Client, transitioning from the CLOSED state to the Listen state through the listen function of the socket layer in order to receive service requests from the Client. On the other hand, the Client initiates a handshake request by calling the Dial function and enters into SYN_SEND state. Upon receiving this handshake request, the Server transitions into SYN_RCVD state. Once it receives an ACK from the Client, indicating successful connection establishment, data communication process commences. After completion of data transmission, both Server and Client enter into connection closing phase. The Server has CLOSE_WAIT and LAST_ACK states. The Client has FIN_WAIT1, FIN_WAIT2, CLOSING, and TIME_WAIT states. The specific state transition process is shown in Fig. 9.13.

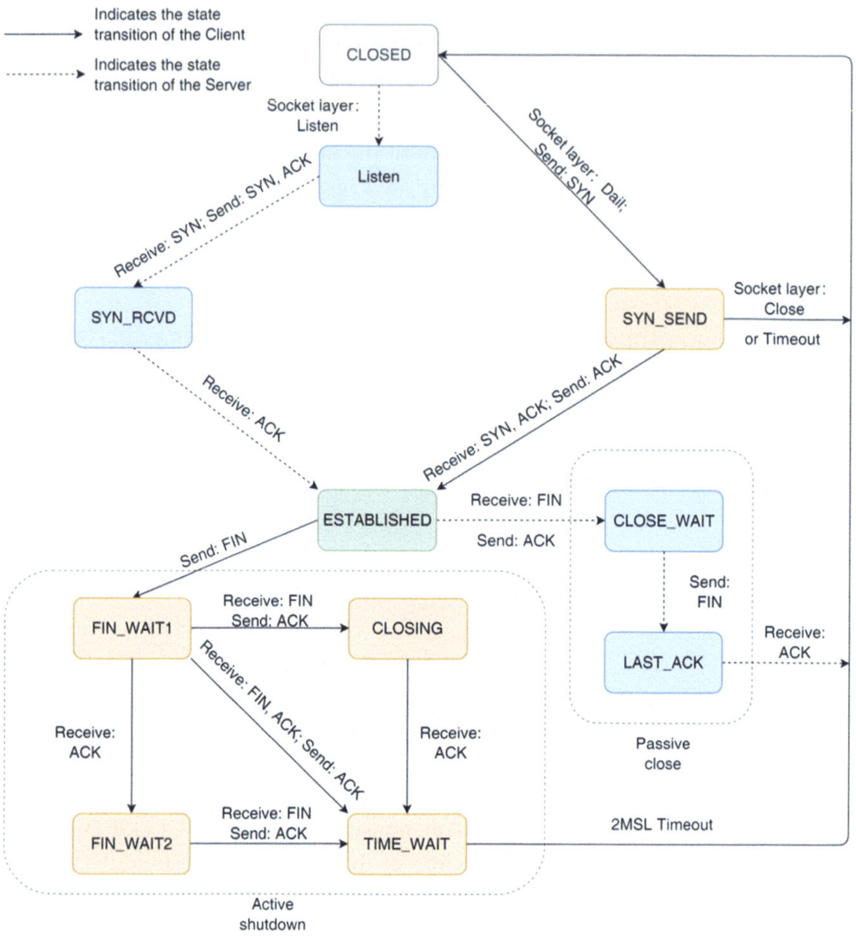

Fig. 9.13 The state transition in MIN-TCP

9.3 MIN-QUIC

9.3.1 Overview of QUIC

Since the emergence of the Internet in the 1990s, the primary protocols used for Internet traffic transmission have been IPv4, TCP, SSL/TLS, DNS, and HTTP. However, the development of these protocols has been relatively slow, with major improvements focused on TCP congestion control algorithms and upgrades to SSL/TLS protocol cipher suites. With the advancement of communication technology, network interaction scenarios have become increasingly complex, and the volume and diversity of transmitted content have grown significantly. There are many contradictions between traditional Internet architecture and the new demands of users.

The rigidity of Internet architecture is a challenging problem, encompassing both the rigidity of intermediate devices and protocol rigidity. The rigidity of intermediate devices is mainly due to the predominance of TCP traffic on the Internet, leading to the specific design of many network devices to handle TCP traffic. For example, some firewalls only allow TCP traffic on ports 80 and 443, while some NAT gateways require modification of the transport layer header during network address translation. These specially designed network devices make it difficult to optimize and modify the TCP protocol, and may also impede the proper transmission of non-TCP traffic. Protocol rigidity arises from the fact that TCP is implemented at the kernel level by operating systems, requiring kernel updates for TCP optimization and improvement. This makes it challenging to update the TCP protocol stack.

For the transport layer protocols, the issues such as the handshake latency during connection establishment and the head-of-line blocking, will impact user experience. Both HTTP/1.0, HTTP/1.1, and HTTP/2 use TCP for transmission and TLS for encryption. However, TCP connection establishment requires three-way handshake, and TLS connection establishment also involves the handshake process. Even with optimization measures, establishing a connection still requires at least 1 RTT, resulting in a delay of 1 RTT. This handshake latency greatly affects user experience, especially in scenarios with short-lived connections, and cannot be eliminated. Head-of-line blocking refers to the situation in TCP, TLS, and other protocols where if a packet is lost or delayed, all preceding packets must wait for retransmission or acknowledgment, causing subsequent packets to be blocked, thus impacting the overall transmission efficiency and performance of the connection. This blocking issue is particularly pronounced in high-latency and high-packet-loss network environments, affecting the timeliness and stability of network transmission.

Quick UDP Internet Connection (QUIC) [10] is a novel transport protocol based on the UDP protocol. It was proposed and promoted by Google. QUIC adopts encryption mechanisms similar to the Transport Layer Security (TLS) protocol. It also incorporates various features such as traffic control, congestion control, and error correction. QUIC can provide more reliable and secure data transmission services without sacrificing connection establishment speed.

QUIC uses the UDP protocol as the underlying transport protocol. Compared to the three-way handshake and connection management of the TCP protocol, the UDP protocol does not need to manage connections and states, thereby avoiding some handshake delays and connection maintenance overhead. QUIC implements reliability similar to the TCP protocol and security similar to the TLS protocol at the application level, while also supporting the concurrent transmission mechanism of the HTTP/2 protocol, effectively enhancing the efficiency and performance of network transmission. Furthermore, QUIC enables efficient network transmission by circumventing limitations imposed by operating systems and intermediate devices. As long as the client and server applications support the QUIC protocol, they can utilize it to achieve efficient data communication.

QUIC adopts multiple innovative technologies [5]. For example, it performs encryption and authentication during connection establishment to reduce RTTs.

Additionally, it multiplexes multiple requests/responses over a single connection through providing each with its own stream to avoid the blocking issue. QUIC encrypts and authenticates packets to prevent tampering by middleboxes. To avoid ambiguity in retransmissions, QUIC uses unique packet numbers and accurate RTT measurements through explicit signaling in ACKs. Furthermore, QUIC uses a Connection ID to identify connections instead of IP/port 5-tuple, enabling connection migration across IP address changes. QUIC also provides flow control to ensure that a single stream does not consume all of the receiver's buffer.

The technical standards of QUIC are defined by a series of RFC documents, mainly including the following:

- RFC 8999: Defines the general attributes of the QUIC protocol, including version number, version negotiation, version compatibility, etc.
- RFC 9000: Defines the details of the QUIC protocol, including connection establishment, data frame format, flow control, congestion control, connection migration, etc.
- RFC 9001: Defines the encryption methods in QUIC, including encryption handshake, key updates, encryption extensions, etc.
- RFC 9002: Defines the packet loss recovery methods in QUIC, including packet loss detection, retransmission mechanism, packet loss recovery, etc.
- RFC 9114: Defines the HTTP/3 protocol based on QUIC, including HTTP/3 frame format, request-response mapping, priority management, etc.
- RFC 9204: Defines the QPACK protocol for compressing and decompressing header fields in HTTP/3 to reduce transmission overhead.
- RFC 9221: Defines the unreliable transport extension in QUIC, supporting application scenarios that do not require reliability guarantees, such as real-time audio and video streaming.
- RFC 9250: Defines the QUIC-DNS protocol for performing DNS queries and responses over QUIC channels, improving DNS performance and security.
- RFC 9287: Defines the QUIC bit-escape extension for embedding additional metadata information in QUIC data frames, enabling additional functionality and optimizations.
- RFC 9308: Defines the application scope of the QUIC protocol, describing its goals, advantages, limitations, and risks of the QUIC protocol.
- RFC 9312 [11]: Defines the manageability of the QUIC protocol, describing the impact and recommendations for network administrators.

These RFC documents collectively define various aspects of the QUIC protocol, ensuring its effective application in modern network environments and providing more efficient and secure network communication services.

QUIC defines two types of packet headers: the long header and the short header. The long header is used for connection establishment, while the short header is used for data transmission.

The format of QUIC long header defined in RFC 8999 is as follows:

Long Header Packet {
  Header Form (1) = 1,

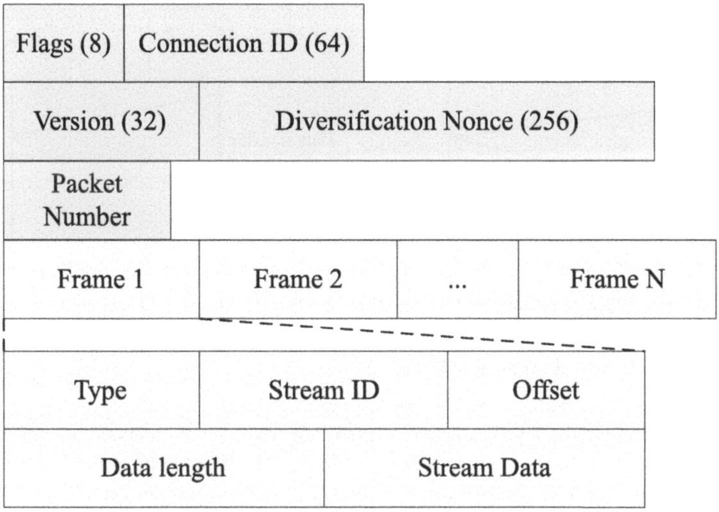

Fig. 9.14 Structure of a QUIC packet

Version-Specific Bits (7),
Version (32),
Destination Connection ID Length (8),
Destination Connection ID (0..2040),
Source Connection ID Length (8),
Source Connection ID (0..2040),
Version-Specific Data (..),
}

The format of QUIC short header defined in RFC 8999 is as follows:

Short Header Packet {
Header Form (1) = 0,
Version-Specific Bits (7),
Destination Connection ID (..),
Version-Specific Data (..),
}

The structure of a QUIC packet is shown in Fig. 9.14.

Several key technologies in QUIC are outlined as follows. For details of other techniques, refer to [5].

Connection Establishment

The QUIC protocol establishes a secure connection when the client sends its first request. Only 1 RTT is consumed during the initial connection establishment when exchanging keys. For subsequent connections, it can be reduced to 0 RTT. As shown in Fig. 9.15, the left diagram represents the cost of the initial connection

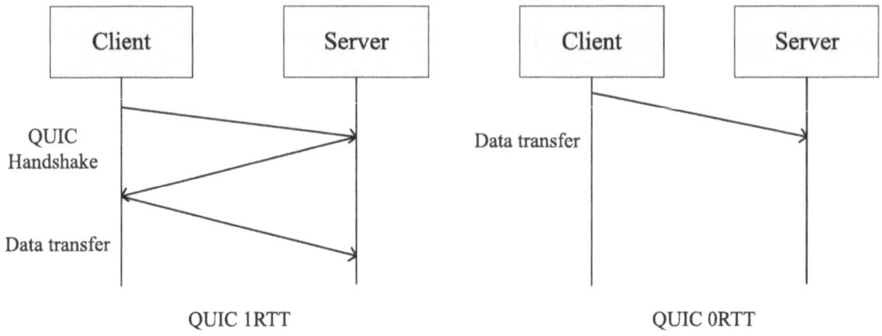

Fig. 9.15 Connection establishment in QUIC

establishment, while the right diagram represents the cost of subsequent connection establishments. This feature significantly reduces the impact of handshake latency on network transmission performance, enhancing the user experience.

Pluggable Congestion Control

According to RFC 9002, QUIC provides a generic signaling mechanism for congestion control, aiming to support different congestion control algorithms. Furthermore, QUIC's congestion control is pluggable, allowing different congestion control algorithms to be configured for different applications and even different connections within the same application. All these algorithms are implemented in user space without the need for modifications to the operating system or kernel.

Moreover, applications can perform hot updates to the congestion control algorithms without downtime or restarts. This means that even during runtime, users can dynamically select and change congestion control algorithms based on the current network environment, optimizing network performance. This dynamic mechanism greatly enhances the adaptability and flexibility of the network, particularly in situations where network quality fluctuates. It also provides network service providers and developers with more choices, allowing them to flexibly address congestion control challenges in various network scenarios.

Smooth Connection Migration

QUIC uses a 64-bit random number called a Connection ID (CID) to identify connections, instead of the IP address/port 5-tuple used by TCP. This design offers several advantages, particularly in the scenario where the user's network environment changes.

When a user switches between mobile networks and Wi-Fi, for example, traditional TCP would require reconnecting and may result in data transmission interruptions and delays. In contrast, QUIC with the random connection ID can avoid this situation because the connection ID remains unchanged and independent of the network. This allows users to smoothly transition between networks while maintaining the connection state without interrupting or delaying data transmission.

Furthermore, the randomness of the QUIC connection ID ensures security. Since the connection ID is generated randomly, it is challenging for attackers to guess or predict it, increasing the difficulty of potential attacks. This design enhances the reliability of the QUIC protocol in protecting user data security.

Stream Multiplexing

QUIC supports stream multiplexing, namely allowing multiple streams to be transmitted within a connection, with each stream being independently processed. An endpoint must decide how to divide available bandwidth between multiple streams [5].

The stream multiplexing in QUIC effectively avoids head-of-line blocking due to TCP's sequential delivery. In traditional TCP, if one stream is blocked, it will block all other streams within the same connection. Unlike it, in QUIC, each stream can be transmitted independently, thus preventing one stream's transmission from being blocked by others.

9.3.2 Overview of MIN-QUIC

MIN-QUIC is a transport protocol based on the CoG-MIN architecture, which enables efficient and secure data transmission in a push-based communication semantics. It draws inspiration from the QUIC protocol and inherits several excellent features. MIN-QUIC also adheres to relevant standards such as RFC 8999, RFC 9000, RFC 9001, RFC 9002, RFC 9114, RFC 9204, RFC 9221. The carrying network layer packet comparison of QUIC and MIN-QUIC is shown in (Fig. 9.16).

In the MIN-QUIC protocol, two identifiers are required to determine the communication endpoints: the local identifier and the peer identifier. The local identifier represents the node's identity in the network, while the peer identifier represents the communication partner's identity in the network.

MIN-QUIC protocol defines the concept of Session ID and Session Stream ID to support session migration and stream multiplexing, similar to the concept of Connection ID and Stream ID in the QUIC protocol.

The Session ID is a randomly generated value used to identify a MIN-QUIC session. The Session Stream ID is an incrementing numerical value used to identify a session stream within a session. Both the Session ID and Session Stream ID are carried as identifier information within the MIN-QUIC packet.

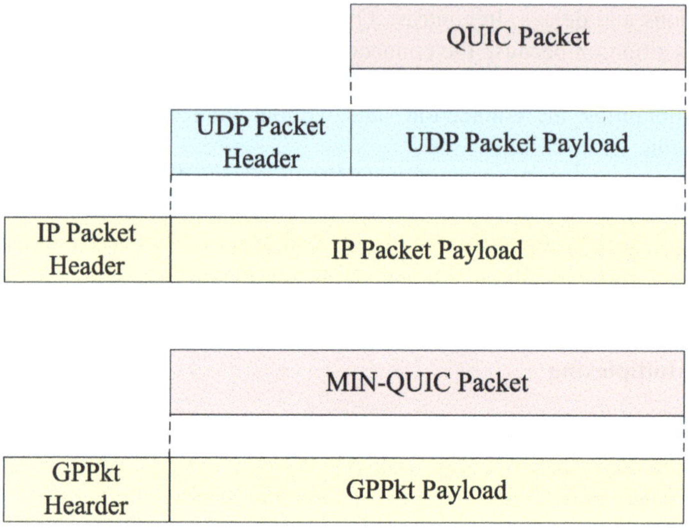

Fig. 9.16 The carrying network layer packet comparison of QUIC and MIN-QUIC

9.3.3 Key Components of MIN-QUIC

The MIN-QUIC protocol incorporates key components from the QUIC protocol, including:

- Stream Multiplexing Module: The stream multiplexing module allows for parallel transmission of multiple data streams over a single transport layer connection. This significantly improves the utilization of network resources and overall data transmission rate. It also reduces latency and the impact of blocking on individual streams, effectively utilizing network bandwidth and meeting the requirements of concurrent transmission.
- Connection Migration Module: The connection migration module enables devices to maintain uninterrupted transport layer connections when switching physical networks. This feature greatly improves user experience and network connection stability. Traditional transport protocols like TCP often require re-establishing connections when switching networks (e.g., from Wi-Fi to cellular), resulting in data transmission interruptions and delays. The connection migration module enhances user experience, particularly in situations where mobile devices frequently switch network environments, ensuring continuous connections. It also improves transmission efficiency by reducing data retransmission and latency caused by network switching, ensuring efficient data transmission.
- Pluggable Congestion Control Module: The pluggable congestion control module allows network developers to choose or customize suitable congestion control algorithms based on specific scenarios, meeting the requirements of different environments. This design enhances the protocol's flexibility and scalability, enabling it to adapt to various network environments and optimize transmission performance.

9.3.4 Encryption Component of MIN-QUIC

QUIC adopts encryption components from TLS 1.3. Unlike QUIC, MIN-QUIC uses a different encryption component to accommodate the characteristics of the MIN network. Specifically, it utilizes the Chinese National Cryptography Standard (known as Guomi) to achieve secure communication.

Guomi encompasses four main algorithms: SM1, SM2, SM3, and SM4. SM1 is a symmetric block cipher with undisclosed implementation details. SM2 is an elliptic curve-based asymmetric public key cryptographic algorithm, including encryption, signature, and key exchange functionalities. SM3 is a hash function used for generating message digests or digital signatures. SM4, also known as SMS4 or WAPI, is a symmetric block cipher.

RFC 8998, titled "Using the SM2 Algorithm Suite with TLS 1.3," defines how to incorporate the Guomi SM2 algorithm suite into the TLS 1.3 protocol. RFC 8998 specifies two complete Guomi algorithm suites:

- TLS_SM4_GCM_SM3: GCM means Galois/Counter Mode. It is a mode of operation for symmetric-key cryptographic block ciphers which is widely adopted for its performance. Utilizes the SM4 block cipher algorithm in GCM mode for encryption/decryption and the SM3 hash function for message authentication and pseudo-random function operations.
- TLS_SM4_CCM_SM3: CCM means counter with cipher block chaining message authentication code. Utilizes the SM4 block cipher algorithm in CCM mode for encryption/decryption and the SM3 hash function for message authentication and pseudo-random function operations. RFC 8998 also defines the usage of the SM2 signature algorithm and curve parameters within the ECDHE handshake process. It relaxes the requirement for client certificates and temporarily eases the dual-certificate requirement.

MIN-QUIC implements the technical specifications outlined in RFC 8998. The default encryption suite in MIN-QUIC is TLS_SM4_GCM_SM3 (0x00c6), the default signature scheme is sm2sig_sm3 (0x0708), and the default curve is curveSM2 (41).

In MIN-QUIC, both communicating parties require identity identifiers, which include public and private keys. The Guomi certificates necessary for MIN-QUIC communication are issued by MIS, and their public and private keys are included in the identity identifiers.

The key differences between MIN-QUIC and QUIC regarding encryption components are as follows:

1. At the handshake layer, MIN-QUIC and QUIC both utilize the ECDHE protocol for key exchange and TLS 1.3 for secure parameter negotiation. The implementation differences are as follows:

   (a) MIN-QUIC uses the Guomi SM2 signature algorithm and curve parameters for authentication, following RFC 8998. It uses Guomi certificates issued by MIS and carries them in MIN packets.

   (b) QUIC uses RSA or ECDSA signature algorithms and curve parameters for authentication, following RFC 8446.

2. At the record layer, both MIN-QUIC and QUIC use session keys for encrypting and decrypting application-layer data and employ authentication tags or message authentication codes for integrity checks. Implementation differences include:

   (a) MIN-QUIC uses the Guomi SM4 block cipher algorithm in GCM or CCM mode for encryption/decryption and the Guomi SM3 hash function for message authentication and pseudo-random function operations. QUIC, on the other hand, uses the AES block cipher algorithm in GCM or CCM mode for encryption/decryption and the SHA-256 or SHA-384 hash function for message authentication and pseudo-random function operations.
   (b) MIN-QUIC uses the MIN packet format as the record layer data packet, which includes fields such as Session ID, Session Stream ID, offset, length, and encrypted payload. QUIC uses UDP packets as the record layer data packet, which includes fields such as Connection ID, packet number, length, and encrypted payload.
   (c) MIN-QUIC employs Session ID and Session Stream ID to identify a MIN-QUIC session and a session stream, participating in the encryption and decryption process. QUIC uses Connection ID and packet number to identify a QUIC connection and a packet, participating in the encryption and decryption process.

In conclusion, MIN-QUIC conforms to the Guomi standards and specifications, utilizing Guomi algorithms and certificates for secure communication. It simplifies the identity identification of communicating parties and data transmission through the use of MIN identity identifiers and MIN packets.

9.3.5 MIN-QUIC and HTTP/3

HTTP/3 is the third major version of the HTTP protocol, complementing the widely used HTTP/1.1 and HTTP/2. Unlike previous versions, HTTP/3 utilizes QUIC to address the head-of-line blocking issue in HTTP/2, improving transmission efficiency and security.

The main features of HTTP/3 include:

- Faster connection establishment: HTTP/3 leverages the QUIC protocol to perform handshake concurrently at the transport and encryption layers, reducing connection latency.
- Zero Round Trip Time (0-RTT): For previously connected servers, clients can bypass the handshake requirement and directly send data.

- Improved resilience to packet loss: HTTP/3 uses the QUIC protocol, enabling multiplexing and avoiding the problem of blocking the entire connection due to the loss of a single packet (i.e., head-of-line blocking).
- Enhanced encryption: HTTP/3 provides default encryption at the transport layer using the QUIC protocol, offering improved security and efficiency compared to HTTP/2.

MIN-QUIC supports HTTP/3 with the following differences:

- MIN-QUIC uses "minhttps" as the protocol name.
- MIN-QUIC replaces slashes ("/") in the host identifier with plus signs ("+"), avoiding ambiguity with slashes in the path.
- MIN-QUIC uses the host identifier as the host name and carries it within MIN packets.

9.3.6 MIN-QUIC Applications

Currently, there are two applications developed based on MIN-QUIC: MQRT and MIN-Web. Both applications utilize the MIN-QUIC protocol to enable data transmission and interaction within the MIN network environment. MIN-Web will be discussed in detail in subsequent chapters.

MIN QUIC Remote Terminal (MQRT) is a command-line execution tool specifically designed for the MIN network. Similar to SSH applications commonly used in IP networks, MQRT allows users to connect to remote servers from a client using a graphical interface or command-line interface, and perform various operating system commands or programs on the server.

MQRT primarily relies on two components: MIN-QUIC and Fyne. Fyne is a cross-platform graphical user interface library written in Go language. It provides clean, aesthetically pleasing, and user-friendly interface elements and layout methods. Essentially, MQRT launches a pseudo terminal (PTY) on the server machine, which is a virtual terminal device that can simulate the behavior of a physical terminal and interact with the Shell process. Users input and output data through the Terminal on the client machine, and the input and output are synchronously transmitted as byte streams through the MIN-QUIC channel between the client's Terminal and the server's PTY in real time. This allows remote control of the server in the MIN network.

Since MIN-QUIC already handles data encryption, MQRT does not require additional encryption processes like SSH. This improves transmission efficiency and security. Additionally, due to the existence of MIN network identity identification and signature verification mechanisms, MQRT does not require additional authentication mechanisms. As long as a trust relationship can be established between the client and the server, communication can take place. If users have higher security requirements, authentication and verification mechanisms related to identity can be added in the future.

9.4 MIN-PTP

9.4.1 Overview of MIN-PTP

MIN-PTP [7] is a pull-based transport protocol in the MIN network. This ensures the transmission efficiency of pull-based communication in the MIN network.

As shown in Fig. 9.17, MIN-PTP consists of four modules: Congestion Detection, Consumer Rate Adjustment, Multipath Forwarding, and Content Popularity-Based Caching Strategy.

9.4.2 Congestion Detection

Motivated by [12], MIN-PTP adopts CoDel algorithm [13], which monitors the sojourn time of Data packets at intermediate nodes, to detect network congestion. MIN-PTP has improved the CoDel algorithm by introducing three states to characterize different congestion situations in the network. Three states, namely NORMAL, LIGHT_NACK, and SERIOUS_NACK, are defined to handle different network congestion situations.

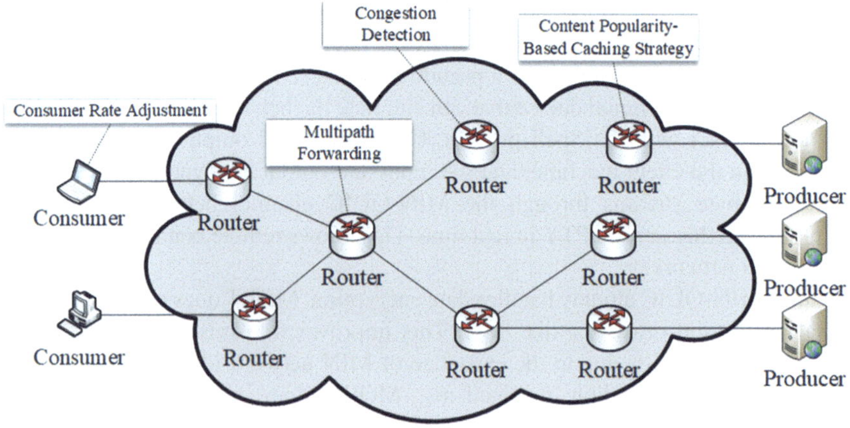

Fig. 9.17 Overview of MIN-PTP [7]

MIN-PTP adopts the commonly used Explicit Congestion Notification (ECN) mechanism to inform the consumer side about the congestion state by explicitly marking Data packets. It extends the Data packet header with an optional field called CongestionMark to carry the congestion state.

Specifically, during each monitoring interval, MIN-PTP measures the queuing delay of each dequeued Data packet. If the recorded minimum queuing delay does not exceed a predefined threshold, the packet is marked as NORMAL. If the minimum queuing delay exceeds the predefined threshold, it indicates mild congestion in the network. The dequeued packets are marked as LIGHT_NACK based on the marking interval. If the duration of the mild congestion exceeds the predefined time threshold, it indicates severe congestion in the network. The dequeued packets during this time are marked as SERIOUS_NACK.

The calculation of the marking interval is defined as:

$$Interval_i = \frac{Interval}{\sqrt{i}}. \tag{9.6}$$

Here, i is the number of marked Data packets. $Interval_i$ represents the next marking time interval. It means that the time interval for marking the next packet will be shortened if congestion persists.

9.4.3 Consumer Rate Adjustment

After receiving a Data packet, the consumer needs to adjust its Interest packet sending rate to adapt to the network conditions through the congestion information carried in the CongestionMark field within the Data packet.

When the CongestionMark value is NORMAL, it indicates a good network condition with available resources. In order to improve link bandwidth utilization and network throughput, the sending window for Interest packets is adjusted using linear increase:

$$Interest_i^{cwnd} = Interest_{i-1}^{cwnd} + \mathrm{sscwnd}, \tag{9.7}$$

where $Interest_i^{cwnd}$ represents the Interest packet sending window at ith time interval, and $sscwnd$ represents the amount of window size change.

When the CongestionMark value is SERIOUS_NACK, indicating network congestion, the receiver needs to decrease its sending rate to mitigate congestion. An exponential decrease approach is used to adjust the sending window:

$$Interest_i^{cwnd} = \frac{Interest_{i-1}^{cwnd}}{2}. \tag{9.8}$$

When the CongestionMark value is LIGHT_NACK, indicating a potential congestion, the receiver adjusts the sending window using linear decrease:

$$Interest_i^{cwnd} = Interest_{i-1}^{cwnd} - \text{sscwnd}. \tag{9.9}$$

9.4.4 Multipath Forwarding

Considering the characteristics of data transmission with multiple sources and multiple paths, the requested content can be provided by multiple content sources, and there may be multiple potential next-hop interfaces for forwarding. Therefore, MIN-PTP designs a multipath forwarding strategy to fully utilize the link bandwidth.

In the multipath forwarding strategy, MIN-PTP incorporates the concept of content popularity to handle requests with different popularity levels.

- Only a small portion of content in the network is frequently requested. By caching these highly popular contents in intermediate nodes, the traffic load in the network can be reduced. Therefore, for highly popular content, it is desirable to transmit this data on the links where it is frequently accessed to improve transmission performance.
- For content with low popularity, MIN-PTP calculates weights for each potential next-hop interface. Each interface's weight represents its level of available capacity. Then, based on these weights, the strategy computes the probability of forwarding through each interface. This allows less popular content to be widely distributed across idle links, maximizing link utilization.

A Request Record Table (RRT) is maintained. When an Interest packet arrives at a router, the router records and updates the following information in the RRT: content identifier, the number of times the corresponding content is requested, request timestamp.

To achieve content popularity estimation, an exponential smoothing updating method is adopted. A simple content popularity estimation formula is designed as follows:

$$P_i' = \alpha * P_i + (1 - \alpha) * N_i. \tag{9.10}$$

where N_i represents the requested number of the content i recorded in RRT during a time period, P_i is the estimated content popularity of the content i, and the parameter α is the smoothing constant.

For highly popular content, a History Path Table (HPT) is introduced to record the historical paths of different content. Each entry in HPT contains three members: content identifier (identifier), forwarding interface ID (faceid), and timeout timer (time).

When an Interest packet that requests the content with a popularity higher than the average content popularity, the HPT is queried based on the content identifier to retrieve its historical interface. The Interest packet is then forwarded to the historical interface.

For content with low popularity, the forwarding process involves calculating a weight for each potential next-hop interface. This weight is determined based on two factors: Pending Interest entries (PI) and available capacity (availBW). The PI indicates the number of unsatisfied Interest packets on a particular forwarding interface. The availBW represents the available capacity of the interface.

The forwarding weight is calculated by the ratio of availBW to PI. A higher value indicates a more idle interface. Based on the calculated weights, each forwarding interface is assigned a forwarding probability. Interfaces with higher weights will forward more traffic.

9.4.5 Content Popularity-Based Caching Strategy

A content popularity-based caching strategy is proposed to improve the cache hit ratio of the Content Store (CS).

When a Data packet arrives, the router compares the popularity of the incoming Data packet with a predefined popularity threshold. If the popularity of the Data packet exceeds the threshold, it is forwarded and cached. However, if the popularity is below the threshold, the router only forward the Data packet without caching.

In order to better adapt to the dynamic changes of network conditions, MIN-PTP proposes a method for dynamically adjusting the popularity threshold. The main steps are as follows:

- At the beginning of the caching decision process, when there are relatively few requests in the network and the overall content popularity is low, it is important to fully utilize the cache space in the intermediate nodes to improve cache hit rate and search efficiency. Therefore, each requested content is cached in the intermediate nodes to effectively utilize the cache.
- When the cache space is full, to make more efficient use of the cache space and adapt to the dynamic content popularity in the network, the average popularity of all contents in the CS is calculated and treated as the current popularity threshold. If the popularity of an incoming Data packet exceeds the average popularity threshold, the cache strategy will forward and cache the Data packet while increasing the popularity threshold with the average value.
- If cache replacement does not occur during a duration, it indicates that the current popularity threshold is set too high, leading to subsequent data packets not being cached and increasing the traffic load in the network. To dynamically adapt to the network state, the router reduces the popularity threshold to half of its original value.

References

1. Cerf V, Kahn R. A protocol for packet network intercommunication. IEEE Trans Commun. 1974;22(5):637–48.
2. Partridge C, Pink S. A faster UDP (user datagram protocol). IEEE/ACM Trans Netw. 1993;1(4):429–40.
3. Eddy W, editor. Transmission control protocol (TCP), STD 7, RFC 9293, 2022. https://doi.org/10.17487/RFC9293. https://www.rfc-editor.org/info/rfc9293.
4. Postel J. User datagram protocol, STD 6, RFC 768, 1980. https://doi.org/10.17487/RFC0768. https://www.rfc-editor.org/info/rfc768.
5. Langley A, Riddoch A, Wilk A, et al. The quic transport protocol: design and internet-scale deployment. In: Proceedings of the conference of the ACM special interest group on data communication, 2017. p. 183–96.
6. Li H, Xiao MR, Bai H, et al. A secure and efficient transmission control method and system in a multi-identifier network architecture. CN115883478A, 2023-09-22.
7. Yin B, Li H, Bai H, et al. An effective pull-based congestion control protocol for multi-identifier network. In: 2022 IEEE 8th international conference on computer and communications (ICCC). Piscataway: IEEE; 2022. p. 452–6.
8. GeeksforGeeks. TCP Tahoe and TCP Reno [EB/OL]. 2024. https://www.geeksforgeeks.org/tcp-tahoe-and-tcp-reno/.
9. Ha S, Rhee I, Xu L. CUBIC: a new TCP-friendly high-speed TCP variant. ACM SIGOPS Oper Syst Rev. 2008;42(5):64–74.
10. Iyengar J, Thomson M, editors. QUIC: a UDP-based multiplexed and secure transport. RFC 9000. https://doi.org/10.17487/RFC9000. 2021. <https://www.rfc-editor.org/info/rfc9000>.
11. Kühlewind M, Trammell B. Manageability of the QUIC transport protocol. RFC 9312. https://doi.org/10.17487/RFC9312. 2022. <https://www.rfc-editor.org/info/rfc9312>.
12. Schneider K, Yi C, Zhang B, et al. A practical congestion control scheme for named data networking. In: Proceedings of the 3rd ACM conference on information-centric networking; 2016. p. 21–30.
13. Raghuvanshi DM, Annappa B, Tahiliani MP. On the effectiveness of CoDel for active queue management. In: 2013 third international conference on advanced computing and communication technologies (ACCT). Piscataway: IEEE; 2013. p. 107–14.

Chapter 10
Network Control Message Protocol

The network control message protocol enables network administrators to accurately obtain the latest network status, in order to repair network failures in time and ensure the quality of data transmission in dynamically changing network environments. There are many applications based on the network control message protocol for detecting and diagnosing network problems on the Internet, such as the path trace tool, i.e., Trace. Path trace tools send control messages through special mechanisms and receive replies to obtain link information and transmission delays between two points. This information is valuable for analyzing network performance, troubleshooting, and optimizing route selection.

The MIN network have flexible communication semantics and support various network identifiers. This chapter introduces the network control message protocol for MIN networks and the multipath trace mechanism based on this protocol. These two work together to achieve efficient and reliable trace of network link status information.

10.1 Overview of Network Control Message Protocol

10.1.1 Internet Control Message Protocol

The Internet Control Message Protocol (ICMP) [1, 2] primarily serves to send ICMP error messages to gateway devices or destination hosts when packet loss and other situations occur during data transmission. In addition to error reporting, ICMP also introduces other control messages, for example, a gateway can guide a host to send IP packets over shorter routes using ICMP messages. Table 10.1 displays the common types of ICMP messages.

The purpose of control messages in ICMP is to provide feedback about the communication environment. As part of the IP protocol, an ICMP message actually

H. Li, H. Bai, *Principle of Architecture, Protocol, and Algorithms for CoG-MIN*,
https://doi.org/10.1007/978-981-96-3596-2_10

Table 10.1 The types and numbers of the common ICMP messages [1]

Type number	Type
0	Echo reply
3	Destination unreachable
4	Source quench
5	Redirect
8	Echo
11	Time exceeded
12	Parameter problem
13	Timestamp
14	Timestamp reply
15	Information request
16	Information reply

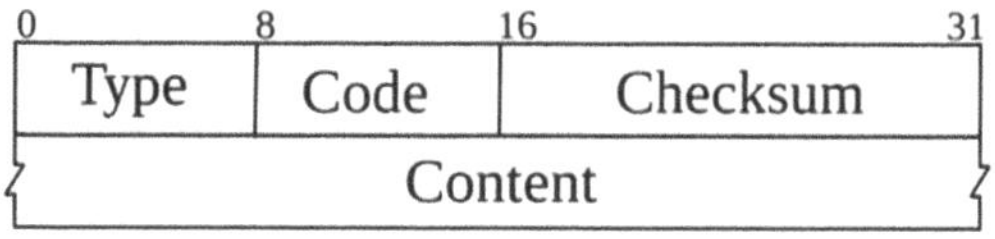

Fig. 10.1 ICMP packet header format [2]

appear as the payload part of an IP packet in network communication. Figure 10.1 illustrates the ICMP packet header format.

Currently, the application of the ICMP protocol is very widespread [3]. For example, the Ping application uses ICMP echo request and echo reply messages to test whether a host is reachable. The Traceroute application uses ICMP error messages to detect paths. The ICMP protocol can also be used to prevent malicious network attacks [4], such as detecting malicious hosts conducting ARP spoofing attacks based on the ICMP protocol, DDoS attack algorithms based on ICMP flooding techniques, detecting and preventing ARP poisoning based on man-in-the-middle attacks using ICMP and Voting [5], and preventing DHCP starvation attacks using the ICMP protocol [6]. Additionally, the ICMP protocol can be utilized for other functions, such as remote fingerprinting, gathering autonomous system information, and implementing reliable multicast technologies.

There are also some related studies on the ICMP protocol in emerging networks, for example, the Named Data Network Control Protocol (NNCP) [7]. The NNCP protocol introduces a new type of packet in Named Data Network (NDN) [8]: the control message, as shown in Fig. 10.2. Control messages are divided into three main categories: Standard Errors, Notification Messages, and Service Messages. The NNCP protocol notifies network information and errors to relevant nodes without disrupting the original communication logic of NDN.

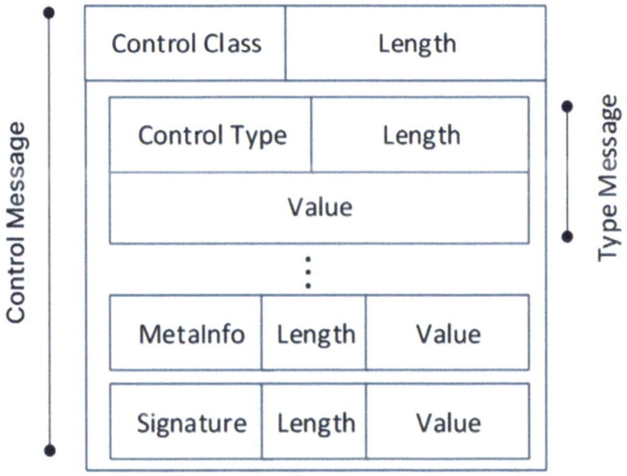

Fig. 10.2 Format of the control message in NNCP [7]

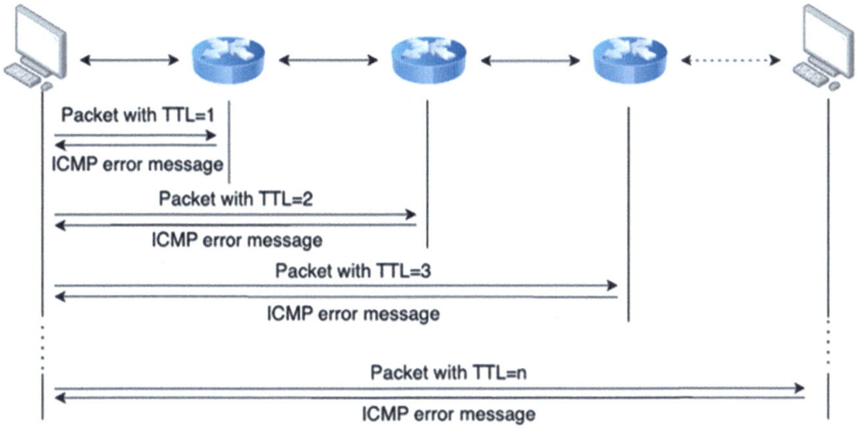

Fig. 10.3 The process of path trace

10.1.2 Path Trace Mechanism

Among the various applications of the ICMP protocol, Traceroute is a major one. Van Jacobson implemented the earliest path trace program under the IP architecture in 1988, known as the Traceroute Tool. Its main process is illustrated in Fig. 10.3. The source host sends network packets with the Time to Live (TTL). When a router receives a packet with an expired TTL, it replies with an ICMP error message of destination unreachable. The packet with TTL of 1 expires at the first hop, and the router sends back an ICMP error message with the current router information. The second packet sent with a TTL of 2 expires at the second router and receives the second ICMP error message with the second router information. This continues until the network packet sent reaches the target host or the network packet with the maximum TTL value has still not reached the target host. The network packets used for path trace can be UDP packets, TCP packets, or ICMP packets, depending on the implementation of different applications.

Currently, the study of path trace mechanisms under the IP-based networks mainly focuses on how to effectively improve path trace efficiency in large-scale networks. In 2020, FlashRoute, an efficient Traceroute tool for large-scale networks, was proposed. This tool initially generates the random source IP address and port number, sending probe packets with the TTL to the destination IP address until reaching the destination host or timing out. For each different TTL value, FlashRoute records the source IP address and port number of the first response packet, ultimately constructing the entire network topology based on the recorded node information. Compared to previous path trace techniques, FlashRoute reduces trace time by approximately 3.5 times.

There are also studies related to path trace mechanisms in NDN. In 2017, Siham et al. proposed NDN-Trace [4], which supports multipath trace in NDN based on Interest packets and Data packets. To distinguish regular network packets from NDN-Trace packets, the name of a NDN-Trace packet starts with "/trace" and includes some parameter information related to multipath trace in other name components. During the multipath trace process, NDN-Trace sends multiple Interest packets into the network and waits for each returned Data packet. These Interest packets travel along different paths to reach the target and return related metrics. NDN-Trace compiles all the gathered information to help users identify the characteristics and performance of available paths.

10.2 Network Control Message Protocol for CoG-MIN

To intuitively probe the network status of MIN networks and the causes of certain abnormal situations in MIRs, the CoG-MIN research team proposed the Multi-Identifier Network Control Message Protocol (MIN-ICMP) [9]. The MIN-ICMP is specifically designed for the diverse communication semantics including push-based semantics and pull-based semantics under the MIN network. The MIN-ICMP defines different types of control messages that provide timely feedback on network conditions, enhancing the transparency of observations of the underlying forwarding processes.

The overall architecture of the MIN-ICMP protocol is illustrated in Fig. 10.4. MIN-ICMP operates as a plugin to monitor abnormal situations on MIRs. When packet loss is detected, it generates control messages and submits them to the logicFace module for forwarding. When the logicFace module receives a control message, the MIR submits that control message to the MIN-ICMP plugin for processing. During this process, the plugin manages the interaction with the table module by managing PIT entries, and the explicit removal of PIT entries also triggers the plugin to send control messages.

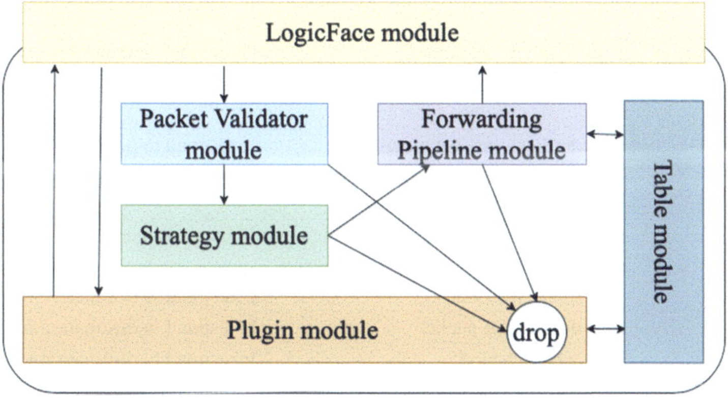

Fig. 10.4 The diagram of MIN-ICMP

10.2.1 Overview of Control Messages

In MIN-ICMP, control messages are special network packets to implement control functions. The MIN-ICMP protocol utilizes control messages to provide feedback on the reasons for packet loss, manage other nodes, and notify other nodes of the current status.

Classification of Control Messages

Control messages can be divided into error messages, management messages, and notification messages, as given in Table 10.2. Error messages are used to transmit information about the causes of packet loss. Management messages are used to check the status of specific nodes and manage them. Notification messages are used to inform neighboring nodes of status changes in the current node.

For a control message, the type number is represented by a three-digit number. The first digit of the three-digit number indicates the major category of the control message: 1 stands for error messages, 2 for management messages, and 3 for notification messages. The last two digits represent the subcategory within the major category, allowing up to 99 subcategories within each major category. Currently, the subcategories have not exhausted the last two digits, leaving ample space for the expansion of subcategories.

Format of the Control Message

The packet format of control messages is shown in Fig. 10.5, and Algorithm 10.1 demonstrates the generating process of control messages. The packet formats of control messages follow the general specification of packet formats in MIN

Table 10.2 Classification of control messages

Control message	Type number and name	Processing rule number
Error message	101: received packet with TTL value of 0	1: respond to destination identifier
	102: duplicate packet received	0: respond to previous hop
	103: signature verification failed for received packet	1: respond to destination identifier
	104: no forwarding route at current node	1: respond to destination identifier
	105: router overload	1: respond to destination identifier
	106: unsolicited packet	1: respond to destination identifier
	107: access denied	1: respond to destination identifier
	108: unsatisfied interest packet	1: respond to destination identifier
	109: packet too large	0: respond to previous hop
	110: other unknown reasons	1: respond to destination identifier
Management message	201: normal response	1: respond to target identifier
	202: content discovery and metadata retrieval	1: respond to target identifier
	203: data control	1: respond to target identifier
Notification message	301: bottleneck notification	2: send to all neighbors
	302: bottleneck recovery notification	2: send to all neighbors
	303: explicit PIT entry removal	1: respond to target identifier
	304: service stop	2: send to all neighbors
	305: service recovery	2: send to all neighbors

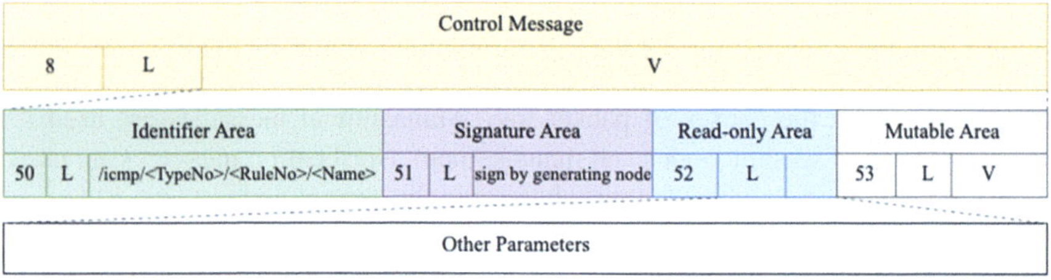

Fig. 10.5 Format of the control message

networks, namely divided into the Identifier area, Signature area, Read-only area, and Variable area.

- Identifier Area: Contains the control identifier. If the control message is a GPPkt packet, the Identifier area may also include a second identifier, representing the source node of the control message.
- Signature Area: Contains the signature of the MIR that generated the control message.
- Read-only Area: The Value part in Type, Length, Value (TLV) stores other parameters of the control message.
- Mutable Area: Reserved area.

Algorithm 10.1 Control Message Generation Algorithm

Input: typeNo, orignalPacket, mir // typeNo is the type number of the control message, orignalPacket is the original network packet of the error message, which can be empty, mir is the current MIR

Output: controlPacket // Generated control message

```
ruleNo = getRuleNoByTypeNo(typeNo)// Get the processing rule number
    corresponding to the type number
identifierString = "/icmp/"+typeNo+"/"+ ruleNo
if ruleNo == "1" then // If forwarding to a specific identifier, add the
    specific identifier after the control identifier
   sender = getSenderIdentifierFromPacket(orignalPacket)
   identifierString = identifierString+"/"+sender
end if
controlPacket = newControlPacketByIdentifier(identifierString)
// Create a new control message according to the control identifier
ControlPacket. SetOtherPara (typeNo orignalPacket)
return controlPacket
```

Control Identifier

In MIN-ICMP, the identifier of a control message can be referred to as the Control Identifier. The Control Identifier consists of a fixed prefix and a type number. It can also include the processing rule and destination identifier. The Control Identifier contains forwarding information of the control message, allowing the logical interface module in router nodes to be aware of it and forward the control message based on the Control Identifier.

The Control Identifier includes the control message processing rule number. The Control Identifier takes the form "/icmp/<TypeNo>/<RuleNo>/<Name>," and the specific components are described as follows:

- icmp: It represents that the network packet is a control message and serves as a fixed string prefix for all control messages.
- TypeNo: It represents the message type number of the control message. Nodes can analyze this component to determine the cause and type of the control message.
- RuleNo: It represents the processing rule number of the control message. Nodes can use this component to determine whether forwarding measures should be taken.
- Name: This parameter exists only when RuleNo indicates forwarding to a specific node. It represents the specific identifier, known as the destination identifier, to which the control message is forwarded. Other routers that receive this control message will use this parameter as a routing basis.

To facilitate faster processing of control messages by MIRs, MIN-ICMP explicitly stores the RuleNo and Name parameters as named components within the Control Identifier. MIN-ICMP also provides alternative ways to include control message forwarding information. Network administrators have the flexibility to place such information in the list of additional parameters within the read-only area of the control message.

Other Parameters of the Control Message

MIN-ICMP introduces the mechanism of additional parameters in the read-only area of control messages to better describe the information carried by control messages. These additional parameters appear as strings, with each parameter separated by a newline character. Each parameter consists of the parameter's English name (case-insensitive) followed by a colon (:), and then the specific value of that parameter.

The specific descriptions of parameter names, introductions, and their existence scopes can be found in Table 10.3. Due to the different purposes of different parameters, their existence scopes also vary. For example, the "Abstract" parameter represents the summary of the raw network packet, and the concept of the raw network packet is relevant only to error messages. Therefore, this parameter exists only

Table 10.3 Other parameters in the control message

Parameter	Description	Control message
Abstract	A summary of the original network packet	Error message
Timestamp	The timestamp when the control message is generated	Error message, management message, and notification message
ManageType	The management types include: "get" (retrieve data), "add" (add data), "del" (delete data), "update" (update data), or "echo" (request response)	Management message
DataName	The name of the data retrieved from the destination node	Management message
Data	The data carried by a management message or notification message	Management message and notification message
ManageToken	The authorization token is stored through this parameter in a management message	Management message
Nonce	The random number of a control message	Error message, management message, and notification message
TypeNo	The category parameter of a control message	Error message, management message, and notification message
RuleNo	The processing rules of a control message	Error message, management message, and notification message

(continued)

Table 10.3 (continued)

Parameter	Description	Control message
Name	When RuleNo equals to 1, the Name parameter represents the identifier of the destination node. It can also serve as a supplementary parameter for "content discovery and metadata retrieval" of management messages, representing a specific content identifier	Management message
LinkCapacity	It represents the link capacity, which can be used as a supplementary parameter in an error message when indicating that a network packet is too large. It serves to explicitly specify the maximum size of packets that can pass through the next-hop link	Error message, management message, and notification message
NumberPara	A supplementary extensible parameter used to store numerical values	Error message, management message, and notification message
BytePara	A supplementary extensible parameter used to store binary data	Error message, management message, and notification message

within error messages. The "Timestamp" parameter represents the timestamp when the control message is generated and can exist in all categories of control messages, including error messages, management messages, and notification messages.

In addition to considering parameters with specific purposes, MIN-ICMP also allows for the inclusion of supplementary parameters for the extensibility of control messages. These supplementary parameters are known as "NumberPara" and "BytePara." These extensible parameters do not have predefined special purposes, making it convenient for developers or network administrators to place the desired data based on its type within these two parameters.

The "Abstract" parameter represents the summary of the original network packet in an error message. The process of generating the summary involves using the SM3 hash algorithm on the Identifier Area and Read-only Area of the raw network packet, resulting in a fixed-length 32-byte string. Subsequently, this string is encrypted using the sender's public key with the SM2 encryption algorithm, yielding the encrypted abstract. Algorithm 10.2 provides a detailed description of the specific steps involved in the generation process.

Algorithm 10.2 Abstract Generation Algorithm
Input: packet, mir // 'packet' is the original network packet that triggered the error, and 'mir' is the current MIR
Output: abstract // Returns a summary of the original network packet

1: IdentifierRawBytes = packet. IdentifierField. GetBytes () / / Obtain the signature of the original network packet
2: ReadonlyRawBytes = packet. ReadonlyField. GetBytes () / / Obtain the Read-only Area of the original network packet

```
digestData = identifierRawBytes + readonlyRawBytes
digest = mir.sm3.sm3_hash(digestData) // Generate the digest
Sender = getSenderIdentifierFromPacket (packet) / / Retrieve the sender's
information from the raw network packet.
if mir.isPubKeyExit(sender) then pubKey = getPubKey(sender) // Obtain
the public key from the node
else pubKey= getPubKeyFromMIS(sender) // Obtain the public key
from the MIS
end if
abstract = mir.sm2.encrypt(digest)
return abstract
```

Table 10.4 Processing rules for control messages

Processing rule number (ruleno)	Initial node	Other nodes
0	Send to the previous hop	Do not forward
1	Send to the target node	Forward based on the target node's identifier
2	Send to all neighboring nodes	Do not forward

Processing Rules for Control Messages

The processing rules for control messages (RuleNo) determines how a node handles the control message. Specifically, it indicates whether a router should forward the control message and, if so, based on which identifier it should be forwarded.

The processing of control messages involves two entities: the originating node that generates the control message and other nodes that receive the control message. For the current node, the processing rules for control messages include options such as sending it to the previous hop, sending it to the target node, or sending it to all neighboring nodes. For other nodes, the processing rules for control messages consist of either not forwarding the message or forwarding it based on the target identifier. Table 10.4 presents the correspondence between rule numbers and these two categories of processing rules.

When the network conditions are poor, packets sent by routers may be discarded for various reasons. The first time a network packet is dropped, it triggers the router to generate an error message. However, due to the same poor network conditions, the error message is also discarded by the next router, resulting in the generation of a new error message. In the case of continuously poor network conditions, router nodes in the network will keep generating error messages until the network conditions improve. This situation is referred to as "infinite hell" for control messages.

To avoid continuously generating control messages, the MIN-ICMP protocol handles the situation of error message packet loss differently. In this case, no error message is generated. However, there is a special case when it comes to the "Echo Reply" management message within control messages. In this case, if the "Echo Reply" management message is lost, an error message will still be sent. This is because this type of management message is designed to probe the connectivity of the path, and receiving error reports for such management messages can provide valuable information about the overall network status. By sending error reports only for this type of control message, the issue of "infinite hell" is avoided.

Figure 10.6 illustrates the specific process of receiving and processing control messages in a MIR. When a MIR receives a network packet, it first analyzes the

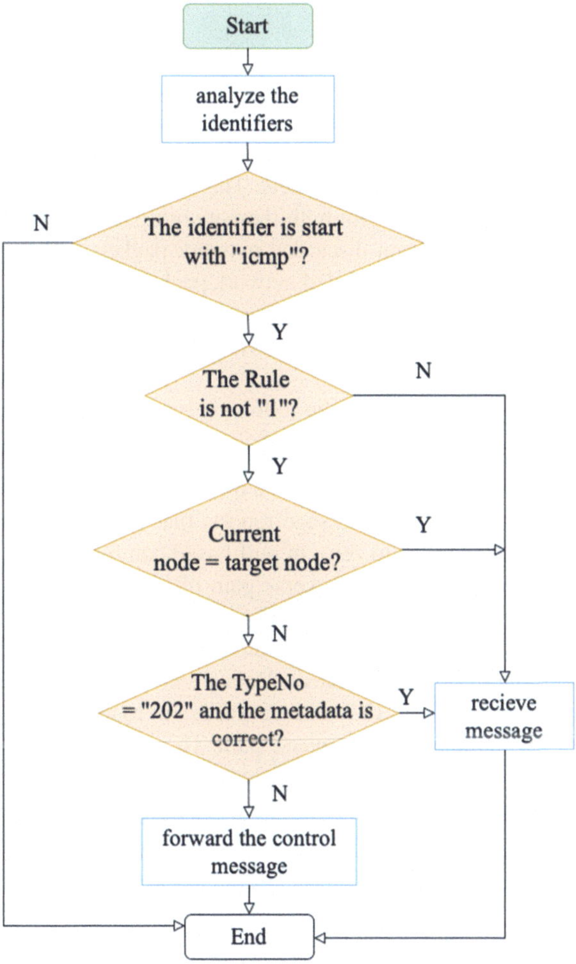

Fig. 10.6 Processing flow diagram of the control message in MIR

identifier of the packet to determine if the first name component is "icmp." If it is not, it means that the packet is a regular network packet, and the process is exited and ended. If the packet is a control message, further processing is performed. The MIR determines the processing rules based on the identifier of the control message. When the processing rule is not 1, it indicates that the control message is intended for the current node, so it is received and processed directly. Even if the processing rule is not 1, if the current node is the target identifier or if the target identifier hits the current node's CS, the control message is also received and processed. If the control message is a management message with type number 202 (i.e., content discovery and metadata retrieval) and the desired metadata is present in the current node's CS, the MIR also chooses to receive the control message and respond with a reply. In other cases, the control message is forwarded based on the target identifier.

10.2.2 Error Message

In MIN-ICMP, an error message is a control message used to provide feedback on the occurrence of errors in network packets. The error message describes various possible errors including issues with both the network packets themselves and the routers. To differentiate between discarded network packets and network packets containing error messages, the discarded network packets are referred to as original packets. The "Abstract" parameter in the error message contains a summary of the original network packet, allowing the receiving node to identify which network packet was discarded.

Error messages are classified into the following types:

- Received Packet with TTL Value of 0: If a received network packet has a TTL value of zero, an error message is generated either by the intermediate router or by the destination node. This message reports that the TTL component in the network packet has changed to zero. In pull-based communication, the forwarding of a Data packet follows the reverse path of the Interest packet. Thus, the number of routing hops remains the same for an Interest packet or its corresponding Data packet. Given this, if the Interest packet can reach the destination node, the destination node generates a Data packet with the same TTL as the Interest packet to reply. This TTL value is sufficient to allow the Data packet to reach the original node along the reverse path. Therefore, under normal circumstances, only GPPkts and Interest packets can trigger this error about "Received Packet with TTL Value of 0." For error messages related to GPPkts, intermediate routers will perform forwarding operations based on control identifiers. For error messages related to Interest packets, intermediate routers will return the error message in the reverse path of Interest packets according to the recorded interfaces in the PIT entry and delete the corresponding PIT entry after forwarding.
- Duplicate Packet Received: This error message is generated by intermediate routers and destination nodes to report the reception of duplicate network pack-

ets. The duplicate network packet is identified based on its packet type, packet identifier, and "Nonce" component. When a MIR detects the same network packet received within a short period, it first generates an error message with the type "Duplicate Packet Received" and forward it to its previous hop while discarding the original network packet. This error message is to prevent network packets from looping in routers in large-scale and complex networks. Both push-based and pull-based network packets can trigger this error message. Unlike other error messages, this error message is only transmitted to the previous hop of the original network packet.

- Signature Verification Failed for Received Packet: This error message is generated by intermediate routers and destination nodes to report the failure of signature verification of the received network packet. Upon receiving a network packet, a MIR first verifies the signature component of the packet. If the verification fails, it generates this error message and forward it to the sender of the original network packet, discarding the original packet. If the original network packet is an Interest packet, the error message is transmitted along the reverse path of the Interest packet and the corresponding PIT entry is deleted after transmission. If it is a data packet, a push-based error message is generated using the identity identifier from the signature section. If it is a GPPkt, a push-based error message is generated using the source identifier from the identifier section.
- No Forwarding Route at Current Node: This error message is generated by intermediate routers. It applies to situations where the current router receives a network packet that should be forwarded but there is no matching forwarding route and no default route, meaning the interface information to forward the packet is uncertain. When a router encounters this situation, it generates an error message and forward it to the sender of the original network packet, discarding the original packet. If the original network packet is an Interest packet, the error message is transmitted along the reverse path of the Interest packet and the corresponding PIT entry is deleted after transmission. If it is a data packet, a push-based error message is generated using the identity identifier from the signature section. If it is a GPPkt, a push-based error message is generated using the source identifier from the identifier section.
- Router Overload: This error message is generated by intermediate routers when the number of received network packets or the processing workload exceeds the capacity of the node, resulting in packet loss. When a router encounters this situation, it generates an error message with the type "Router Overload" and forward it to the sender of the original network packet, discarding the original packet. If the original network packet is an Interest packet, the error message is transmitted along the reverse path of the Interest packet and the corresponding PIT entry is deleted after transmission. If it is a Data packet, a push-based error message is generated using the identity identifier from the signature section. If it is a push-based packet, a push-based error message is generated using the source identifier from the identifier section.
- Unsolicited Packets: This error message is generated by intermediate routers or consumer nodes. It occurs when a received network packet is a Data packet, but

there is no matching PIT entry. The absence of a matching PIT entry can be due to the absence of a corresponding Interest packet being transmitted or the expiration of the matching PIT entry in the router. The router node generates a push-based error message using the identity identifier of the Data packet sender and forward it.

- Access Denied: This error message is generated by intermediate routers or destination nodes. The original network packet triggering this error message can be an Interest packet or a push-based packet. There are several reasons for access denial, such as the network packet being intercepted by an access control filter or the network packet containing a specific prefix that is denied access. If the original network packet is an Interest packet, the error message is transmitted along the reverse path of the Interest packet, and the corresponding PIT entry is deleted after transmission. If it is a GPPkt, a push-based error message is generated using the source identifier from the identifier section.
- Unsatisfied Interest Packet: This error message is generated by the destination node to respond to an unsatisfiable Interest request. Unsatisfiable Interest packets can occur when the content has been deleted by the provider or when the provider has never generated the requested content. The original network packet can only be an Interest packet, and upon receiving an unsatisfiable Interest packet, the destination node generates a Data packet containing the error message. This Data packet is transmitted along the reverse path of the Interest packet created in the PIT entry, and intermediate nodes delete the PIT entry after forwarding.
- Packet Too Large: This error message is generated by intermediate routers or destination nodes. In the traditional MAC layer, the frame size is limited due to physical technology constraints. Although MIN networks can use hop-by-hop fragmentation to address this issue, it can consume significant computational and storage resources in MIRs. The "Packet Too Large" error message serves as a mechanism to explicitly indicate the capacity of the next-hop link, in conjunction with the "LinkCapacity" parameter in control messages. This error message can be generated for Interest packets, Data packets, and GPPkts. If the original network packet is an Interest packet, the error message is transmitted along the reverse path of the Interest packet, and the corresponding PIT entry is deleted after transmission. If it is a Data packet, a push-based error message is generated using the identity identifier from the signature section. If it is a GPPkt, a push-based error message is generated using the source identifier from the identifier section.
- Other Unknown Reasons: This error message is generated by intermediate routers or destination nodes. It can occur due to various reasons such as the TTL (Time to Live) component of the network packet reaching 0, router errors causing restarts, routers inexplicably losing network packets, or fragmentation errors, among others. If the original network packet is an Interest packet, the error message is transmitted along the reverse path of the Interest packet, and the corresponding PIT entry is deleted after transmission. If it is a Data packet, a push-based error message is generated using the identity identifier from the sig-

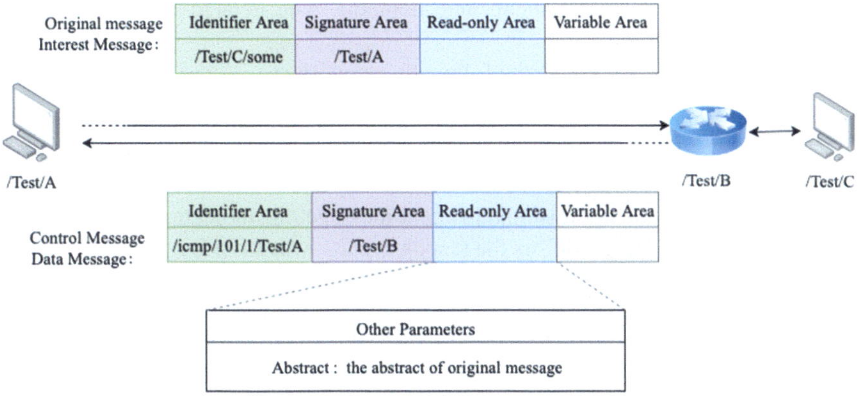

Fig. 10.7 An example of an error message for "Received Packet with TTL Value of 0"

nature section. If it is a GPPkt, a push-based error message is generated using the source identifier from the identifier section.

Figure 10.7 depicts the interaction diagram for error messages. Node A ("/Test/A") initiates an Interest packet with the identifier "/Test/C/some" to Node C ("/Test/C"). However, at intermediate node B ("/Test/B"), the TTL component of the Interest packet reaches 0. In response, intermediate node B generates a control message according to the MIN-ICMP protocol. The control message identifier is "/icmp/101/1/Test/A". Here, "icmp" indicates that it is a control message, "101" signifies that it is an error message for "Received Packet with TTL Value of 0", and the third name component "1" indicates that the control message should be sent to a specific identifier host, which is "/Test/A". Additionally, the "Abstract" parameter of this control message contains the encrypted digest of the original network packet.

10.2.3 Management Message

Management messages are control messages used to manage other nodes. The communication process follows a request/response model, where each management message request corresponds to a response. Management messages consist of Interest packets (request) and Data packets (response). Both the Interest and Data packets of management messages adhere to the naming rules of control identifiers, with the "Name" parameter in the name identifier containing the identifier of the specific node.

To differentiate between the two nodes involved in the management message, the initiating node is referred to as the source node, while the responding node is referred to as the target node. When managing other router nodes, the "ManageToken" parameter in control messages can be used for security purposes. This parameter serves as a security supplement and contains data related to management permissions.

Management messages have the following categories:

- Normal Response: This management message is similar to the echo request and echo reply network packets in ICMP protocol. It is primarily used to probe whether the target node can be reached correctly and if it can respond in a timely manner. Upon receiving this management message, the target node immediately sends a "Normal Response" as the response part, which is a Data packet.
- Content Discovery and Metadata Retrieval: This management message is used to determine whether a specific content identifier exists within a router. If the content identifier exists in the destination router, the router will reply with the metadata (Meta) of the content data packet. Here, metadata refers to data related to the meta-content, such as the size of the meta-content, fragmentation size, and number of fragments. If the content identifier does not exist in the destination router, an empty data packet is sent in response. This management message utilizes the "Name" and "Data" parameters. The "Name" parameter contains the content identifier for which metadata is requested, and the "Data" parameter contains the retrieved metadata.
- Data Control: This management message, in conjunction with the "DataName" parameter representing the data name, the "ManageType" parameter representing the management type, and the "Data" parameter containing the specific data, allows for the management of data in other routers. As introduced in Table 10.3, The management types (ManageType) that can be achieved with management messages include "get" (retrieve data), "add" (add data), "del" (delete data), "update" (update data), or "echo" (request response). The "DataName" of the management message encompasses ACL structures with management permissions, FIB, the identity identifier of the MIR, all policies within a MIR, PIT, and all logical interfaces (LF). The returned Data packet for "Data Control" contains the "Data" parameter in accordance with the control message. It contains the data obtained in the table entry. If it is a modification or other operations, the "Data" parameter contains "success" or "fail" to indicate the success or failure of the operation.

In the illustrated scenario in Fig. 10.8, a Router A ("/Test/A") remotely retrieves FIB from a Router B ("/Test/B"). Router A generates an Interest packet with the identifier "/icmp/203/1/Test/B" and forward it. Here, "203" indicates the message type of the management message is "Data Control," and the third name component "1" indicates that the control message should be sent to a specific router, with the specific node's identifier as "/Test/B". The read-only region of this Interest packet contains other parameters, with the "ManageType" parameter set to "get" to indicate the retrieval of data and the "DataName" parameter indicating the data to be retrieved as "FIB." Router B replies to Router A with a Data packet. The Data packet follows the naming rules of control identifiers, which differ from the Interest packet identifier. Additionally, intermediate routers do not generate PIT entries for Interest

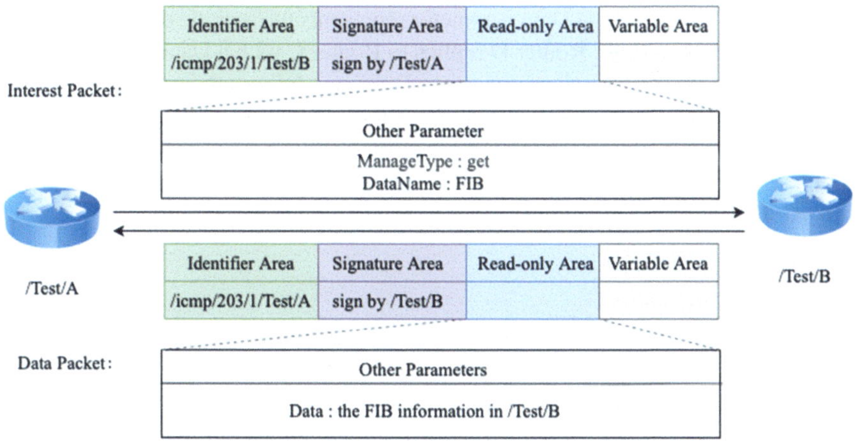

Fig. 10.8 An example of the management message for retrieving data

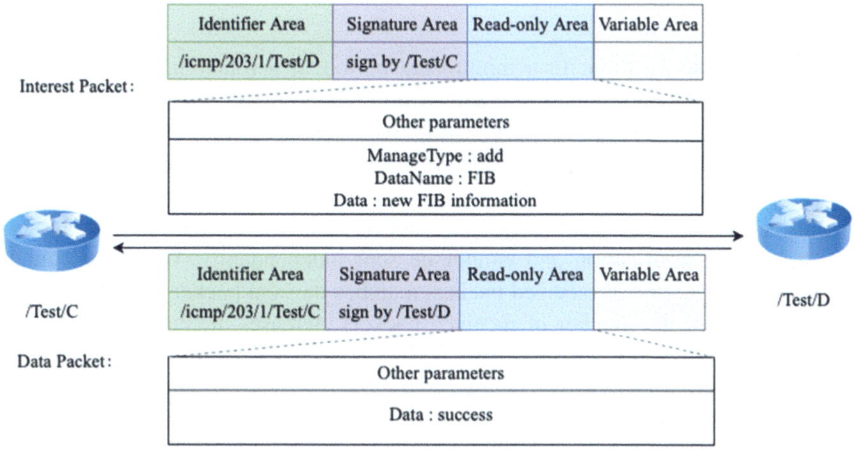

Fig. 10.9 An example of the management message for adding data

packets starting with "icmp." The value of the Data parameter in the response packet is the FIB information within Router B.

The diagram shown in Fig. 10.9 describes the scenario where Router C ("/ Test/C") remotely adds FIB data to Router D ("/Test/D"). Router generates an Interest packet with the identifier "/icmp/203/1/Test/C" and forward it. In the identifier, "203" represents the management message type for "Data Control," and the third name component "1" indicates that the control message should be sent to a specific router node, followed by the identifier of the specific node. The Interest packet includes other parameters in the read-only region. The ManageType parameter is set to "add" to indicate adding data, the DataName parameter represents the target data as "FIB," and the Data parameter represents the specific data to be added as "new FIB information." Router D replies to Router C with a Data packet. Unlike regular Interest and Data packets, the control message follows the naming format of control identifiers, rather than using the same format as the Interest packet. Intermediate routers do not generate PIT entries for Interest packets starting with "icmp." The value of the Data parameter in the response Data packet indicates whether the addition of FIB information in Router D was successful.

10.2.4 Notification Message

Notification messages are control messages used to inform neighboring nodes about the current state of a node. They are primarily used to send information about network state changes to neighboring routers and can only reach neighboring routers without requiring a response.

Notification messages are typically included in GPPkts and consist of the following categories:

- Bottleneck Notification: In a monitoring period, if a router receives network packets larger than it sends, and packet loss has occurred, it becomes a bottleneck router. To maintain network health, the router sends a notification message to its neighboring nodes, asking them to reduce the forwarding of network packets to this router.
- Bottleneck Recovery Notification: This notification is sent after the router issues a bottleneck notification and cannot be sent independently. When the router detects that the rate of received packets matches the sent packets, and both metrics rise when the number of received packets increases, it sends a bottleneck recovery notification to neighboring nodes, asking them to revoke the previous packet reduction measures.
- Explicit PIT Entry Removal: It refers to PIT entry removal due to timeout expiration. Additionally, this notification only targets the ingress interface listed in the PIT entry and is sent one hop.
- Service Stop: When a router stops forwarding network packets due to internal reasons and stops its forwarding services, it sends a service stop notification to all neighboring nodes to prevent packet loss during transmission.
- Service Recovery: This notification can follow a "Service Stop" notification or can be issued as a first-time "hello" notification when a router comes online. It can accompany a "Data" parameter to inform neighboring nodes about the routing information stored in the router.

Figure 10.10 shows a schematic of the "Service Stop" notification message where router node A "/Test/A" sends a "Service Stop" notification to all its neighbors due to hardware failure. This notification is included in a GPPkt packet, originally identified as "/Test/A" with a destination identifier of "/icmp/304/2". In the destination identifier, "icmp" is the fixed prefix for the MIN-ICMP

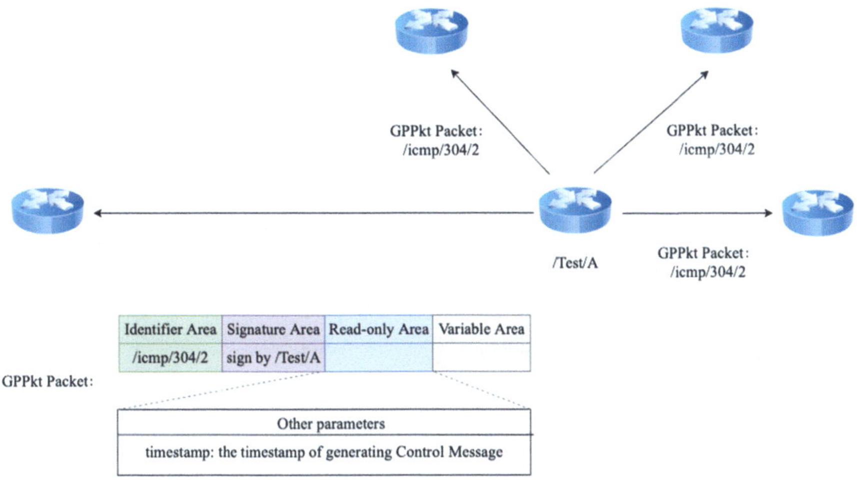

Fig. 10.10 An example of the notification message

protocol indicating that the packet is a control message, "304" denotes the type of control message as "Service Stop," and the third component "2" indicates that the control message's processing rule is to be sent to all neighboring nodes. No further forwarding of this type of control message is required by the receiving router node.

10.3 Multipath Trace Tool for CoG-MIN

10.3.1 Overview of MIN-Trace

The MIN-Trace [9] mechanism is a multipath trace mechanism. It is based on the MIN-ICMP and is used to find multipath information from the current node to others. The path information includes the identifiers of nodes along the paths and the timestamps of their traversal.

The architecture of MIN-Trace, as shown in Fig. 10.11, consists of two parts:

MIN-Trace Client: This client application runs on the user side. It is responsible for sending initial tracing requests and displaying the discovered path information after the tracing session is completed.

MIN-Trace Plugin: This plugin handles tracing Interest packets and reply tracing Interest packets. It processes all network packets with name prefixes starting with "trace" in the local MIRs. It maintains a Pending Trace Table (PTT), which is primarily used in the pull-based path tracing mechanism. The PTT records the forwarding information of pull interest packets and prevents the aggregation of tracing Interest packets.

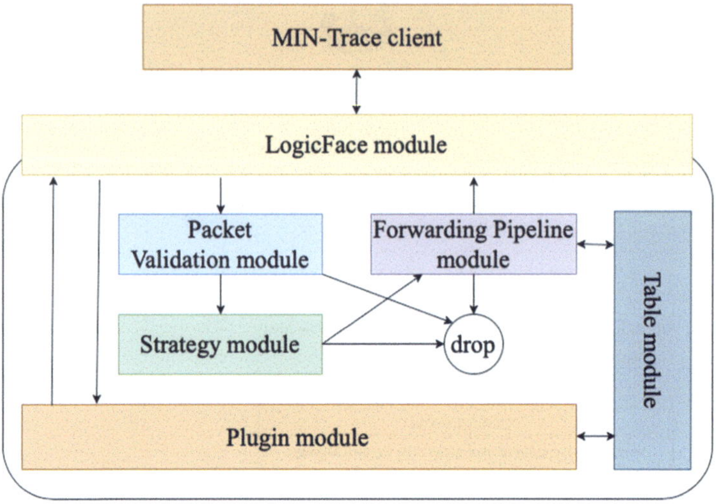

Fig. 10.11 Architecture of MIN-Trace

When the MIN-Trace client initiates a command, it sends a packet to the logical interface module of the router. The router identifies it as a tracing packet and forward it to the MIN-Trace plugin. The plugin utilizes the data structures in the MIR module, such as the FIB and CS, to process the tracing packet. The processing result can be either forwarded by the logical interface module of MIR or submitted to the MIN-Trace client for displaying the result of the path tracing.

10.3.2 MIN-Trace Design

Tracing Session

In MIN-Trace, a tracing session refers to the process from the initial sending of a tracing packet to receiving the path information. For example, Node A, equipped with the MIN-Trace Client, initiates a path tracing with the target "/test/object". The tracing eventually reaches Node B and returns. In this scenario, Node A is the initial node that initiates the path tracing, the target "/test/object" is the target identifier, and Node B is the target node. The identity identifier of the target node is either the target identifier or the target node's CS contains the target identifier. The entire process from initiating the tracing to receiving the path information is considered a tracing session.

Tracing Target

MIN-Trace's tracing targets are classified into Application Type, Content Type, and Any Type. The Any Type refers to an unspecified object type along the path.

- When the tracing target is Application Type, the result of path tracing is all the paths that can reach the specified application.
- When the tracing target is Content Type, the result of path tracing is to find the nearest router nodes that cache the content data packets or the content data packet producer.
- When the tracing target is Any Type, if the closest type to the initiator is Content Type, it is classified as Content; otherwise, it is classified as Application.

The multipath tracing mechanism is divided into pull-based and push-based implementations based on different communication semantics. Pull-based tracing is used for Content Type and Any Type targets, while push-based tracing is used for Application Type targets.

Tracing Identifier

MIN-Trace utilizes special network packets, known as tracing packets, to explore the path information during packet transmission. The tracing identifier is the first identifier of the tracing packet and has the following structure: /trace/<parameters> /<NameToTrace>. The components of the name are explained as follows:

- Trace: This component represents that the network packet will be intercepted and processed by the trace plugin. It is a fixed prefix for all tracing packets and is case-insensitive.
- Parameters (Table 10.5): This component represents all the parameters required for the current tracing. Pull-based tracing packets require three parameters: IsMulti, IsContent, and TraceNonce. Among them, TraceNonce can be generated using different cryptographic methods. Push-based tracing packets require two parameters: IsMulti and IsReply. These parameters can be encoded in different ways within a name component.
- NameToTrace: This component represents the destination of the tracing session, which is the target identifier. When the tracing packet is a push-based packet in the reply phase, this parameter represents the destination of the push-based tracing packet, i.e., the name identifier of the source node that initiated the tracing command.

In MIN networks, pull-based communication follows a request/response model, where data packets serve as the responses to interest packets. Therefore, the pull-based tracing process differentiates between requests and responses based on the tracing packet type. For push-based path tracing, the entire process is divided into two phases: the Search Phase, which involves finding the target node, and the Reply Phase, which involves replying to the initial node.

Table 10.5 Parameters in the tracing identifier

Parameters	Scope of application	Description
Is Multi	Pull-based, push-based	Indicates whether the current path tracing is single-path or multipath tracing
Is Content	Pull-based	Indicates if the tracing object identifier is of content type. This parameter is used only in pull-based tracing. The destination in pull-based tracing can be classified as "cached content" or "any"
Is Reply	Push-based	Indicates if the tracing packet belongs to the reply phase
TraceNonce	Pull-based	Represents a random number for each path tracing process. It helps prevent routers from aggregating interest packets from different tracing sessions. To distinguish it from the random component in the interest packet's packet structure, the random number in the name component is referred to as the tracing nonce
NameToTrace	Pull-based, push-based	Represents the name identifier of the destination in the tracing session, i.e., the target identifier. However, when the tracing packet is a push-based packet in the reply phase, this parameter represents the destination of the push-based tracing packet, i.e., the name identifier of the source node that initiated the tracing command. This parameter is also the only one occupying multiple name components

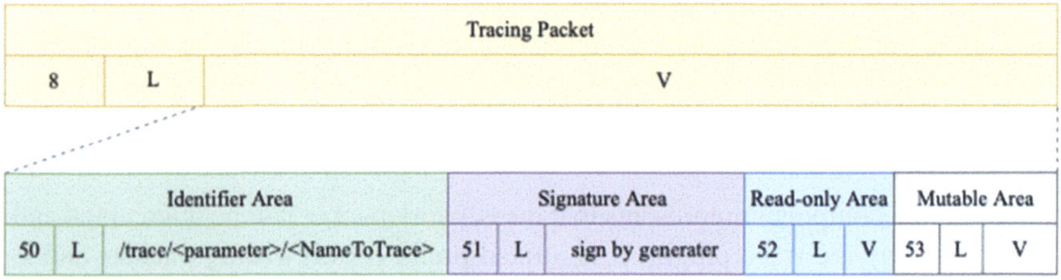

Fig. 10.12 The format of the tracing packet

Tracing Packet

The tracing packet format is illustrated in Fig. 10.12. The tracing packet follows the basic partitioning of network packets in a MIN network: the identifier field, signature field, read-only field, and mutable field. The identifier field stores the tracing identifier, while the signature field contains the node signature for generating the tracing packet. The read-only field holds the path information in pull-based tracing, while the mutable field stores the path information in push-based tracing.

In MIN networks, data can only be inserted into the read-only field when constructing the network packet, while the content of the mutable field can be modified by intermediate router nodes during packet transmission. In the pull-based process, a tracing packet is generated at each hop, allowing data to be inserted during the packet creation. On the other hand, in the push-based process, a push-based tracing packet in the reply phase requires path information to be inserted at intermediate nodes from the target node to the initial node. Therefore, in the push-based process, the data is placed in the mutable field.

Pending Trace Table

In MIN-Trace, a Pending Trace Table (PTT) is introduced, primarily used in the pull-based path tracing mechanism to record the forwarding of pull-based interest packets and prevent aggregation of tracing Interest packets. Its structure is depicted in Fig. 10.13.

The PTT consists of different PTT entries, where each entry represents a tracing session. Each entry has the following attributes: key, inLF, inTime, Paths, and one or more OutRecords.

- key: Used to differentiate each PTT entry and takes the form of "/<parameters>/<NameToTrace>". To save storage space, the key no longer includes the fixed prefix "/trace" for tracing packets.
- inLF: Represents the logical interface where the tracing Interest packet is received.
- inTime: Indicates the timestamp when the tracing Interest packet is received, which is returned as time information when the PTT entry is completed and data packets are returned.
- Paths: Contains the path information obtained during exploration.
- OutRecords: Represents each record forwarded for a tracing session exploring multiple paths. Each OutRecord has the following attributes: outLF and outTime. outLF denotes the logical interface through which the record is forwarded, while outTime represents the timestamp when it is forwarded. By combining outTime with inTime, the total time for the entire tracing session's current routing exploration can be obtained.

MIR explores all possible paths for each tracing session. However, to avoid waiting indefinitely for exploration results, MIR sets an expiration time for each PTT entry. When the PTT entry expires, the current entry's time and path information are packaged into a data packet and forwarded to the previous hop via inLF.

The scenarios where PTT is used primarily involve inserting a PTT entry, deleting a PTT entry, and searching for a PTT entry. PTT data structure is organized using hashing, providing O(1) lookup efficiency.

Pending Trace Table (PTT)					
key	inLF	inTime	Paths	OutRecords	
				outLF	outTime
/11/pku/content/jdsl234j	1	06:16:00	......	2	06:16:02

Fig. 10.13 Pending Trace Table

10.3.3 Pull-Based Multipath Tracing Process

Figure 10.14 depicts the pull-based multipath tracing process. For tracing sessions with target identifiers of content type and any type, it employs the use of Interest packets and Data packets, which adhere to the pull-based communication semantics.

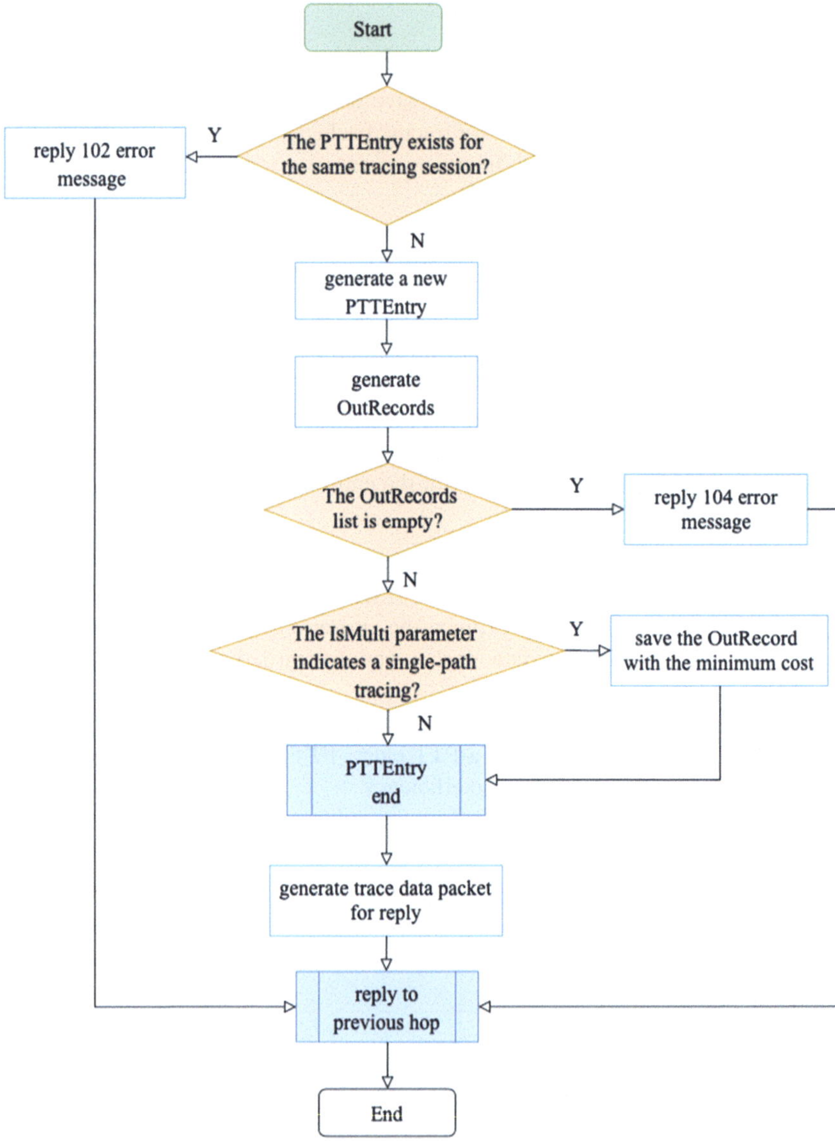

Fig. 10.14 The pull-based multipath tracing process

Upon receiving network packets, the MIR filters out tracing packets starting with "trace" and forward them to the MIN-Trace Plugin within MIR. Once the plugin determines that the packet belongs to an Interest packet, the pull-based tracing process begins with the following steps:

1. The MIN-Trace Plugin first extracts the tracing identifier from the Interest packet and analyzes its parameters to determine if the current router node is the target node. If the current node is the target node, proceed to step 2. Otherwise, proceed to step 3. The target node determination is based on the following criteria: If the current node's content cache includes the target identifier indicated by the NameToTrace parameter, the current node is considered the target node. If the IsContent parameter indicates an Any Type for the tracing target identifier, and the current node's identifier matches the target identifier indicated by the NameToTrace parameter, it also indicates that the current node is the target node. Otherwise, the current node is not the target node.
2. The plugin generates a Data packet with the same identifier and forward it from the receiving interface. The Data packet includes the current router's identifier, the time of receiving the Interest packet, and the time of forwarding the Data packet. The processing of the current tracing packet ends here.
3. The plugin searches for a matching entry in PTT to determine if there is an existing PTTEntry for the same tracing session. The match is based on the tracing purpose identifier, tracing random number, and parameters, which are the key attributes in the PTT data. If a match is found, indicating a looped packet, the plugin sends a MIN-ICMP error message with code 102, indicating "Duplicate network packet received," back to the previous hop and terminates the processing of the tracing packet. If there is no matching PTT entry, continue the process and proceed to step 4.
4. The plugin determines that the current tracing Interest packet belongs to a new tracing session. It generates a new PTTEntry based on the tracing Interest packet, arrival time, and logical interface. Then, the plugin queries the FIB entries in the current router node based on the target identifier in the PTTEntry to obtain all possible next-hop logical interfaces and generates OutRecords belonging to that PTT entry.
5. The plugin retains the OutRecords based on parameters. If the IsMulti parameter in the tracing Interest packet indicates a single-path tracing, only the OutRecord with the minimum cost is retained. If the parameter indicates multipath exploration, all OutRecords are retained. If the OutRecords list is empty, it means that the node does not know how to reach the target identifier. The MIN-Trace plugin sends a MIN-ICMP error message with code 104, indicating "Current node has no forwarding route," back to the previous hop, revokes the PTTEntry, and ends the processing of the current tracing packet. If the OutRecords list is not empty, continue the process and proceed to step 6.
6. The plugin generates a new tracing Interest packet for each OutRecord entry based on the OutRecords. The new Interest packet has a different random component in the immutable area compared to the received tracing Interest packet, while other packet contents remain the same. The new tracing Interest packets

are forwarded based on the logical interface in the OutRecord, and the timer for the corresponding PTTEntry is started. The timer prevents an OutRecord from being left without a response for a long time. After the PTTEntry expires or all OutRecords in the PTTEntry receive corresponding tracing Data packets or error message responses, the plugin determines the end of the PTTEntry. After the end of the PTTEntry, the plugin extracts the contents of all OutRecords' response packets and adds the router's identifier and the forwarding time as the read-only area of the new Data packet. Finally, the plugin forward the Data packet from the interface where the tracing Interest packet was received, and the processing of the current tracing packet ends.

When the client program initiating the MIN-Trace command receives a tracing Data packet in response to the tracing session, it extracts the path information content and displays it to the network administrator.

The processing flow of the MIN-Trace plugin upon receiving a tracing Data packet is simplified. When the MIN-Trace plugin receives a tracing Data packet, it follows the following steps:

1. The plugin extracts the tracing identifier from the packet, analyzes it, and obtains the tracing identifier.
2. The plugin determines the existence of a corresponding PTTEntry and OutRecord records for the tracing session based on the NameToTrace parameter, TraceNonce, and the information of the logical interface where the tracing Data packet was received.
3. If there is no matching record, it returns a MIN-ICMP error message with code 106, indicating an "Unrequested packet," to the previous hop and terminates the processing of the Data packet. The error message is sent back to the target identifier, which is the previous hop in this case. If a matching OutRecord is found, the content of the tracing Data packet is stored in the corresponding PTTEntry.

The pull-based multipath tracing process in MIN-ICMP utilizes detailed error messages to check if a node is the target node before creating a PTTEntry. This approach saves space in the PTT and improves efficiency.

10.3.4 Push-Based Multipath Tracing Process

Figure 10.15 depicts the push-based multipath tracing process. For tracing sessions with target identifiers of application type, it employs the use of GPPkts, which adhere to the push-based communication semantics.

When the MIN-Trace plugin receives a push-based tracing packet (GPPkt), it follows the subsequent process described below.

1. The plugin extracts the trace identifier from the GPPkt and analyses all parameters within the trace identifier to determine if the current node is the target node. The target node is identified when the NameToTrace parameter matches the cur-

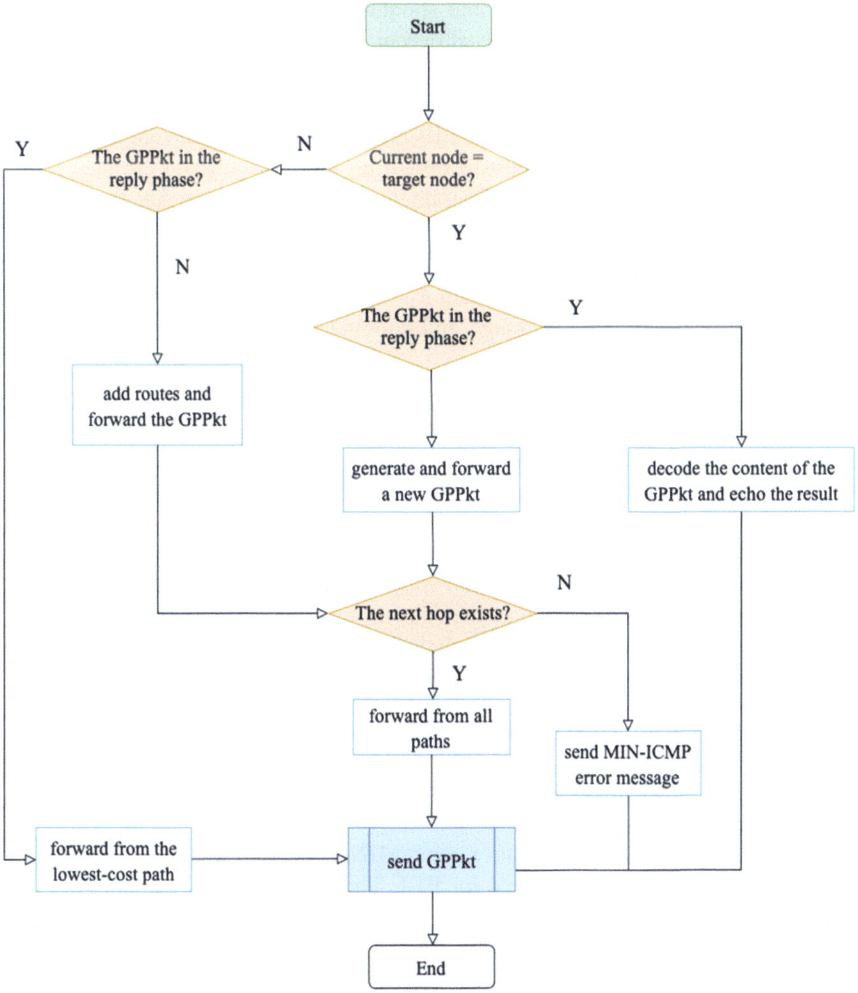

Fig. 10.15 The push-based multipath tracing process

rent router node identifier or when the NameToTrace parameter represents a local application. If it is not the target node, the process jumps to step 5. If it is the target node, the process continues.

2. The plugin determines the phase of the current GPPkt based on the IsReply parameter. If the trace push packet is in the reply phase, indicating that the current node is the source of the MIN-Trace command, the MIN-Trace Client decodes the content of the GPPkt, echoes the result to the network administrator, and concludes the handling process of the trace packet. If it is in the path discovery phase, the process continues.
3. In the path discovery phase, it indicates that the current node is the destination node for the trace session. The plugin generates a new trace GPPkt that is in the

reply phase of the trace session and should be forwarded to the source of the trace session. The new GPPkt has a different trace identifier with distinct IsReply and NameToTrace parameters, where the NameToTrace parameter represents the identifier of the source initiating the trace session.
4. The MIN-Trace plugin queries the FIB table entries of the current node based on the NameToTrace parameter to obtain all possible next-hop logical interfaces. Depending on the IsMulti parameter, it forward the packet through the explored single or multiple paths. If there are no possible next-hop logical interfaces, indicating that the node does not know how to reach the target identifier, the MIN-Trace plugin responds with a "104 No Forwarding Route at Current Node" MIN-ICMP error message and concludes the handling process of the trace packet.
5. If the current node is not the destination node of the trace session, the IsReply parameter is used to determine the phase of the current trace packet. For a trace packet in the reply phase, the current router's name identifier and reception time are added to the mutable area of the packet. The plugin queries the FIB table entries of the current node based on the NameToTrace parameter to obtain all possible next-hop logical interfaces. Depending on the IsMulti parameter, it forward the packet through the explored single or multiple paths and concludes the handling process of the trace packet. For a trace packet in the path discovery phase, it is directly forwarded through the lowest-cost logical interface, concluding the handling process of the trace packet.

When the trace session is complete, i.e., when the MIN-Trace Client, the client initiating the MIN-Trace command, receives a reply trace GPPkt, it parses the content of the GPPkt, obtains the path trace results, and echoes them to the network administrator.

For tracing targets with application type, MIN-Trace utilizes a push-based tracing process that eliminates the need for PTT. This implies that there is no need to wait for PTTEntry expiration to receive a reply. In complex multi-hop network environments, MIN-Trace achieves higher time efficiency. Moreover, the absence of PTT in the push-based process reduces space consumption. Additionally, only two distinct push packets are used throughout the tracing session, significantly fewer than generating new tracing packets at each hop.

10.3.5 MIN-Trace Implementation

MIN-Trace architecture consists of two main components: the MIN-Trace Client program and the MIN-Trace Plugin program.

MIN-Trace Client Program

MIN-Trace Client is a component of MIN-Trace that directly interacts with network administrators. Its main purpose is to initiate a tracing session, send the first tracing packet, and display the tracing results. MIN-Trace Client is implemented as a command line tool. The command line is as follows:

$$trace - n\langle NameToTrace\rangle[-m | - s][-t\ any \| application \| content]$$

Explanation:

- "-n" is a mandatory parameter signifying the destination identifier for the tracing session, essentially representing the NameToTrace parameter.
- "-m" or "-s" are optional parameters. Specifically, "-m" denotes that the tracing session engages in a multipath exploration, while "-s" signifies a single-path exploration. In the absence of this parameter's specification, the session defaults to a multipath exploration.
- "-t" designates the type of the tracing session's destination identifier, which can be "any," "application," or "content." The default value is "any."

The MIN-Trace Plugin Program

MIN-Trace Plugin is implemented as a plugin within MIR, providing advantages such as modularity, ease of deployment, and convenient updates and iterations. When the MIN-Trace Plugin receives an Interest packet, Data packet, or a push-based packet (i.e., GPPkt), it follows the respective processing flow outlined in Algorithms 10.3–10.5.

Algorithm 10.3 OncomingInterest Algorithm
Input: ingress, interest // ingress is the received logical interface, and interest is the trace Interest packet

1: nameToTrace←the nameToTrace of the trace interest
2: isContent←the isContent parameter of the trace interest 3:
3: isMulti←the isMulti parameter of the trace interest
4: current←the name of the current node
5: expireTime ← the expire time of the outRecord
6: **if** (! isContent && current == nameToTrace) **or** (the MIR is cached the data) **then**
7: // If the current node is the destination node, reply with a trace packet
8: payload←current+time
9: generate new Data packet and send it out from ingress

```
        return
    end if
    generate PTTEntry and save it in plugin
    // Create a new PTTEntry to generate OutRecords based on the isMulti parameter
    if isMulti then
        nexthops ← getAllNextHop (nameToTrace)
        else
        nexthops ← getMinCostNextHop(nameToTrace)
    end if
    generate outRecord list based on nexthops
    // Send a new trace interest pack for each OutRecord
    for each outRecord do
        start a time mission for this outRecord
        setExpirtTime(outRecord, expireTime)
        send a new trace interest based on outRecord
    end for
    return
```

Algorithm 10.4 OncomingData Algorithm

Input: ingress, dataPacket// ingress represents the logical interface to receive, and dataPacket represents the trace packet

```
nameToTrace←the nameToTrace of the trace Data packet
current←the name of the current node
// If there are no corresponding PTTEntry and OutRecords, reply to 106 error message and discard the packet
if (there is no PTTEntry for nameToTrace) or (there is no outRecord for ingress) then
    generate a 106 error message and drop this data
    return
end if // Store the contents of the packet into PTTEntry
outRecord ← getOutRecord(nameToTrace, ingress)
pathData ← getPathData (dataPacket)
save pathData in PTTEntry for nameToTrace
setExpireTime(outRecord, 0)
return
```

Algorithm 10.5 OncomingGPPkt Algorithm

Input: ingress, GPPkt // ingress indicates the logical interface to receive, and GPPkt indicates the trace push packet.

```
nameToTrace←the nameToTrace of the trace GPPkt
PTT ← the PTT list of the plugin
isReply←the isCache parameter of the trace interest
isMulti←the isCache parameter of the trace interest
current←the name of the current node
// Generate the next hop according to the IsReply parameter and isMulti parameter
if ! isReply then
    if isMulti then
        nextHops = getAllNextHops(nameToTrace)
    else
        nextHops = getMinCostNextHops(nameToTrace)
    end if
end if
// If the current node is the destination node, it is directly displayed in the reply phase, and a new packet is generated in the pathfinding phase
if nameToTrace == current then
    if isReply then
        pathData = resolvePathDataFromGPPktPacket(GPPkt)
        send pathData to MIRC
        return
    else
        newGPPkt = generateNewGPPkt(current)
        send newGPPkt from nextHops
    end if
else // If not, send the push packet from the next jump
    if isReply then
        send this GPPkt from the min cost next hop
    else
        send this GPPkt from nextHops
    end if
end if
return
```

References

1. Postel J. Internet control message protocol. STD 5, RFC 792, 1981. https://doi.org/10.17487/RFC0792. <https://www.rfc-editor.org/info/rfc792>.
2. Internet control message protocol. Wikipedia. 2024. https://en.wikipedia.org/wiki/Internet_Control_Message_Protocol.

3. Onyema EM, Kumar MA, Balasubaramanian S, et al. A security policy protocol for detection and prevention of internet control message protocol attacks in software defined networks. Sustainability. 2022;14(19):11950.
4. Shah SQA, Khan FZ, Ahmad M. The impact and mitigation of ICMP based economic denial of sustainability attack in cloud computing environment using software defined network. Comput Netw. 2021;187:107825.
5. Arote P, Arya KV. Detection and prevention against ARP poisoning attack using modified ICMP and voting. In: 2015 international conference on computational intelligence and networks. Piscataway: IEEE; 2015. p. 136–41.
6. Yaibuates M, Chaisricharoen R. ICMP based malicious attack identification method for DHCP. In: The 4th joint international conference on information and communication technology, electronic and electrical engineering (JICTEE). Piscataway: IEEE; 2014. p. 1–5.
7. Nour B, Sharif K, Li F, et al. NNCP: a named data network control protocol for IoT applications. In: 2018 IEEE conference on standards for communications and networking (CSCN). Piscataway: IEEE; 2018. p. 1–6.
8. Zhang L, Afanasyev A, Burke J, et al. Named data networking. ACM SIGCOMM Comput Commun Rev. 2014;44(3):66–73.
9. Xiao X, Li H, Bai H, et al. MIN-trace: a multipath traceroute scheme for multi-identifier network. In: 2023 2nd international joint conference on information and communication engineering (JCICE). Piscataway: IEEE; 2023. p. 71–8.

Chapter 11
Network Security

In cyberspace, everything is interconnected, sharing a common destiny. The functioning of society, government operations, and daily necessities like clothing, food, housing, and transportation all rely on software, data, and networks.

Traditional network security mechanisms, such as firewalls, antivirus software, and intrusion detection systems, have long been employed to safeguard networks. However, with the evolving threat landscape, novel network security mechanisms have emerged as the next generation of defense measures to tackle the shortcomings of traditional approaches.

This chapter first introduces relevant research on traditional network security mechanisms and new network security mechanisms. Additionally, this chapter focuses on highlighting the various security measures employed in CoG-MIN, emphasizing its importance and effectiveness in providing advanced protection.

By exploring these topics, readers can gain insights into the evolving field of network security and understand the specific security measures deployed in CoG-MIN, which aims to provide robust and comprehensive protection in cyberspace.

11.1 Overview of Network Security

11.1.1 Challenges of Network Security

The initial design of the IP network was solely for end-to-end transmission, so network security was not a primary concern. Within the TCP/IP network system, each layer has several common malicious attack methods, as illustrated below.

At the **Data Link Layer**, there are attacks like ARP poisoning and MAC address flooding. The ARP spoofing attack exploits the communication mechanism of Ethernet. If an IP host needs to automatically request the MAC of the target host, the ARP protocol must be used. Attackers can impersonate the source host to poison the

H. Li, H. Bai, *Principle of Architecture, Protocol, and Algorithms for CoG-MIN*,
https://doi.org/10.1007/978-981-96-3596-2_11

victim's ARP relationship mapping table, achieving objectives like data theft. MAC flooding attacks involve filling the victim host's MAC table, causing the switch's MAC address table to overflow. As a result, packets entering the switch are broadcast to every port, allowing the intruder to successfully monitor all data from any switch port.

At the **Network Layer**, there are attacks like Smurf flood attacks, IP spoofing attacks, and ICMP route deception attacks. The Smurf flood attack often appears in combination with IP spoofing. Smurf attacks use ICMP echo request (ping) packets with the reply address set to the victim network's broadcast address to overwhelm the victim host. This causes all hosts in that network to respond to this ICMP echo request, leading to network congestion. More complex Smurf attacks change the source address to a third-party victim, eventually causing the third party to crash. The essence of these attacks is the lack of signature and authentication mechanisms.

At the **Transport Layer**, attackers typically use methods like port scanning and UDP flood attacks. The principle behind port scanning is that when a host initiates a connection request to a specific port on a remote server, the server will respond if it has the corresponding service running on that port. If the server does not have the requested service running on that port, it will not respond even if a connection request is sent to that port. To conduct port scanning, an attacker may attempt to establish connections to all well-known ports or a specific range of well-known ports. By analyzing the server's responses or lack thereof, the attacker can gather information about which services are installed and running on the target server.

At the **Application Layer**, it has seen a plethora of network attack methods, such as deception, privilege escalation, identity theft, flooding, and other attack methods.

11.1.2 Limitations of Traditional Network Security Schemes

Traditional network security is a network security family represented by firewalls, antivirus software and intrusion detection, etc. Traditional network security has the following characteristics [1].

- Traditional network security functions at the border. The most obvious feature of traditional cyber security is that it functions on the physical boundaries that exist. Firewalls, antivirus software, Intrusion Detection System (IDS), Intrusion Prevention System (IPS), Data Loss Prevention (DLP), Web Application Firewall (WAF), Endpoint Protection Platform (EPP), and other boundary devices act on the border, according to the behavior at the border for protection and monitoring.
- The lack of specificity of traditional network security protection targets makes it lose its clear direction. It typically aims to protect general targets such as networks and hosts, without specific references. This lack of differentiation in security goals prevents focused support and restricts the approach to external boundaries and behaviors. This limitation is a significant challenge in traditional network security. For critical infrastructure, the business operations and data

running on these servers and networks are critical. Unfortunately, traditional network security often overlooks the unique security requirements of critical infrastructure. Traditional network security typically prioritizes external security measures at the border, assuming that the internal side of the border is inherently secure. However, this assumption is flawed and carries significant limitations. Additionally, relying on default account security, which assumes that all activities performed by verified accounts are trustworthy, poses a considerable security risk, as account theft and hijacking remain prominent and persistent threats.

- Traditional border devices designed for traditional network security have lower processing power. The boundary security device functions at the boundary, and its performance is inherently insufficient. Its processing capability is relatively limited, especially under strict service constraints. Known threats are often the main content of the boundary security device.
- Traditional network security is centered on the features of intrusion behavior. It lacks awareness of the security target and protection subject. Traditional network security neither prioritizes nor verifies the identity of network users. In the absence of accurate perception of both the protection target and access identity, traditional network security primarily revolves around behavior feature-based research and defense. This approach often uses the Feature Store to store extensive feature information.
- Traditional network security excels in detecting known vulnerabilities but falls short in perceiving unknown threats. It possesses robust defenses against recognized vulnerabilities but lacks the capability to effectively identify novel risks. Unknown threats and zero-day vulnerabilities pose significant challenges to traditional network security. When intruders use combination attacks or zero-day attacks, traditional network security often proves ineffective in thwarting such advanced techniques.

11.1.3 Introduction of Advanced Network Security Schemes

Advanced network security is born to address the limitations of traditional network security, mainly in the following aspects to improve the defense [1].

Advanced network security protection can enhance the existing border security products by addressing the limitations of border processing equipment, particularly in association and context analysis. The combination of edge and cloud architecture enables conventional detection at the edge and enhanced detection and analysis at the cloud center to compensate for the deficiencies of traditional border products, such as Endpoint Detection and Response (EDR), Security Information and Event Management (SIEM), situational awareness, and threat intelligence.

Advanced network security enhances human intervention. Security visualization has become a major direction of security development, for example, Security Operations Center (SOC), situational awareness, threat hunting, and Security Orchestration Automation and Response (SOAR).

Advanced network security reconstructs the border after the border disappears. The biggest dilemma of traditional border security lies in the disappearance of borders, not that border security is no longer important, but that the basis for its survival no longer exists. If borders can be reconstructed, the idea of border security can regain its vitality. Software Defined Perimeter (SDP) represents an architectural approach rooted in the principles of zero-trust. This approach encompasses a wide scope, encompassing identity subjects and asset objects [2].

Advanced network security introduces the concept of zero-trust architecture and secure identity. In the zero-trust architecture, identity is regarded as the core element. Even without zero-trust, the secure identity can be a powerful tool for security enhancement. Among the three basic security elements of asset, identity, and behavior, identity has difficulty and relative certainty in distinguishing and has good security enhancement ability. Both the next-generation firewall and User and Entity Behavior Analytics (UEBA) focus on the enhanced identification and analysis of identity. Lightweight Directory Access Protocol (LDAP) and other identity managements are meticulously configured to facilitate seamless integration of identity within the system, mitigating the risk of identity information loss resulting from scenario changes and context switches.

Advanced network security introduces sandboxes and decoys. Both sandboxes and decoys provide a medium for observing behavioral certainty. Sandboxes provide a target-free behavior observation environment and effectively determine the safety of actions by actively monitoring potentially harmful behaviors as they unfold. In particular, due to the operation within a sandbox environment, additional perceptual measures can be employed to aid in assessing the correlation between pre- and post-behaviors. A prominent industry leader in this domain is FireEye. Decoys serve two fundamental objectives: detecting the presence of security incidents and impeding attacks to gain response time. Similar to sandboxes, decoys can incorporate supplementary perceptual measures to gather additional insights into the intruder's activity. Access to greater intrusion-related information and increased response time inherently empower the defense to devise more effective response strategies.

Advanced network security has a cloud security and non-trust environment. The advent of cloud computing has necessitated a comprehensive restructuring of the entire IT infrastructure, consequently demanding a corresponding shift in security measures to align with the cloud environment as a whole. As the cloud transcends conventional boundaries, users often lack awareness of the specific locations where their business operations and data reside. It's a completely non-trust environment for users. Cloud security represents a vast domain of advanced security practices that encompasses almost all aspects of security, ranging from theoretical frameworks to technical implementation. It has undergone significant transformations when compared to traditional security approaches.

Advanced network security focuses on security at the application level and security at the business logic level. There will always be vulnerabilities in any application. It is crucial to acknowledge that hackers consistently manage to discover and exploit vulnerabilities before manufacturers can address them. Ensuring secure usage of applications and business logic in the presence of vulnerabilities, as well as promptly remedying these vulnerabilities through patches, is an ongoing challenge. Numerous security companies are actively engaged in this area, such as the more intelligent Web Application Firewall (WAF).

11.1.4 Evolution Trend of Network Security Protection

To address the security vulnerabilities of traditional networks, the initial approach involves proposing supplementary technologies based on specific problems, such as Cryptographically Generated Addresses (CGA) and TrueIP. These solutions are designed to address specific security vulnerabilities in traditional networks and can be seen as standalone security mechanisms layered onto the network. CGA describes a universal address generation scheme that can be widely applied to various scenarios, binding IPv6 addresses to user public keys. This scheme introduces a hash extension technique to increase the effective hash length, breaking the 64-bit length limit. The focus of this scheme is to eliminate the weaknesses of earlier schemes and is easy to deploy. TrueIP introduces an innovative approach that utilizes identity-based cryptography to counter IP spoofing. By leveraging a novel identity-based signature scheme, TrueIP enables verification of IP addresses without relying on certificates or public key infrastructure. Notably, this solution does not necessitate modifications or limitations to existing internet routing protocols, allowing for incremental deployment. However, it is important to acknowledge that these solutions primarily address specific challenges within traditional network environments and may encounter difficulties when migrating to future network scenarios. Additionally, performance flaws have also been identified as a potential limitation of these solutions.

The current internet system has been widely deployed for nearly half a century, and reforming it could incur significant costs. An alternative approach focuses on incorporating security protection mechanisms while preserving the stability of the original address protocol system and routing system, such as detection mechanisms to ensure routing security. Representative improved IP systems include Locator/ID Separation Protocol (LISP), Host Identity Protocol (HIP), New IP, and MobilityFirst. LISP is a protocol deployed at the network layer, dividing IP addresses into two new numbering spaces: Endpoint Identifier (EID) and Route Locator (RLOC). Differentiating and overlaying the two numbering spaces, packets are addressed and forwarded based on RLOC during public network transmission. When the packet reaches the site edge, the outer IP layer is stripped, and forwarding is based on the inner EID IP. This solution maintains the existing host protocols and internet infrastructure, providing notable benefits in terms of traffic engineering, multi-homing, and mobility. However, its security has not been verified, and it is still in the experimental stage. HIP separates the closely coupled transport layer and network layer in traditional network architecture, inserting a host identity layer as an independent new protocol layer between them. It uses the host ID as the unique identity of each host, establishing a secure, shared host layer for verified hosts. HIP introduces a mutual peer identity verification scheme for key exchange, thereby establishing an encrypted host identity namespace. This approach serves as a defense mechanism against denial-of-service attacks and man-in-the-middle attacks. However, the system is hampered by low compatibility and high deployment costs. New IP separates identity and location, using temporary identifiers for identity hiding; access routers verify the source host identity through asymmetric keys, but inter-domain verification uses symmetric keys. The downside is that there are still systemic differences and low compatibility issues. MobilityFirst focuses on network mobility and reliability, using a flat Globally Unique Identifier (GUID) in its name-based service layer to identify networked objects. It utilizes a global name resolution service to facilitate a rapid, identity-based, and address-based hybrid routing strategy. This approach dynamically associates the target GUID with its most up-to-date routing address. However, unfortunately, MobilityFirst encounters certain performance concerns that need to be addressed.

In contrast to the aforementioned improvement-oriented approaches, innovative network architectures argue that these methods lack fundamental changes and merely offer remedial strategies, thereby falling short of providing comprehensive solutions to security challenges. Therefore, innovative research starts by changing the underlying network protocol, focusing on how to bind security mechanisms in the address system and routing protocol, and trying to use cryptographic means to authenticate the source and destination addresses. The Accountable Internet Protocol (AIP) introduces a novel approach that utilizes the hash value of each network entity's public key as its identity identifier. This methodology effectively binds identity and address, establishing a foundation of trustworthiness for each accessing host through an identity-based self-authentication mechanism. AIP offers initial solutions to combat various types of attacks, including source address spoofing, denial-of-service attacks, route hijacking, and route forgery. By addressing these security challenges, AIP strives to enhance the overall security and accountability of the Internet Protocol. The main disadvantage is that compatibility is relatively poor. The eXpressive Internet Architecture (XIA) supports multiple network entities and can expand its functions over time to adapt to new, unforeseen entities. Building upon the principles of AIP, this solution incorporates a directed acyclic graph mechanism. However, it is important to acknowledge that compatibility poses a significant challenge that XIA must address.

To this end, CoG-MIN is proposed as a new network architecture, and the security defense enhancements and protection mechanisms implemented at each layer of CoG-MIN are shown in Fig. 11.1. A comprehensive explanation of these improvements and mechanisms will be provided later.

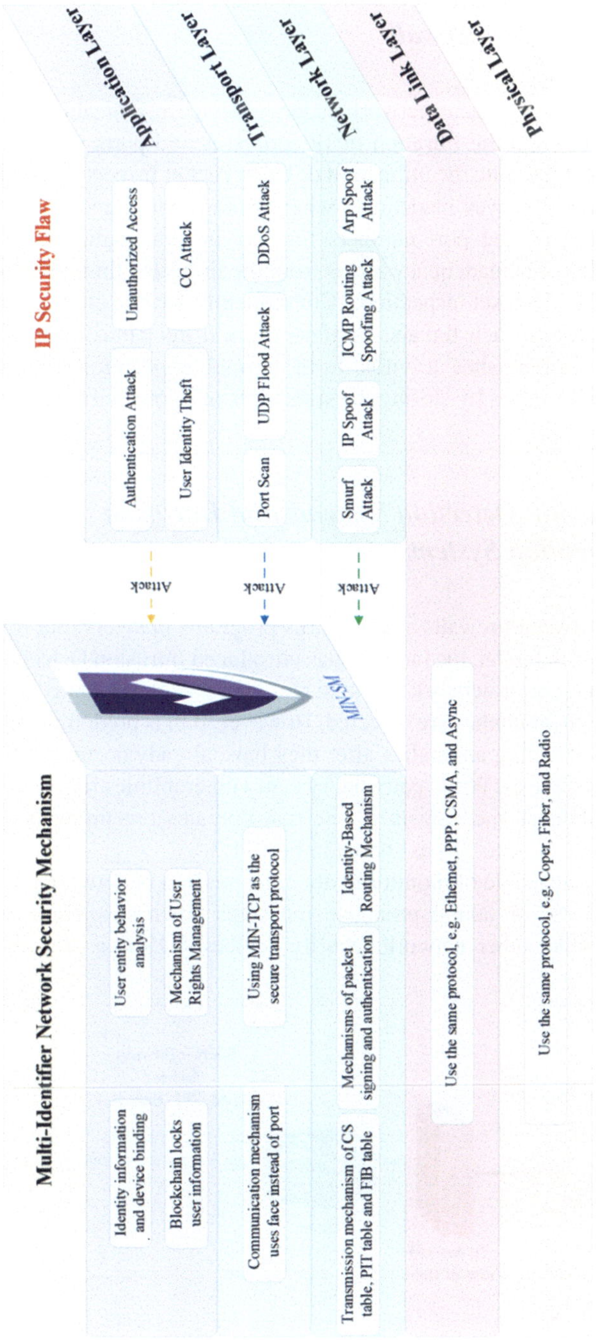

Fig. 11.1 Security protection mechanisms implemented at each layer of CoG-MIN

11.2 Common Network Security Technologies

11.2.1 Traditional Firewall

A firewall serves as a critical network security device responsible for regulating network traffic through the filtration of IP addresses and ports within packets, as shown in Fig. 11.2. Despite the utilization of Deep Packet Inspection (DPI) technology, a firewall often proves inadequate when dealing with attackers who employ genuine IP addresses and port numbers for carrying out malicious activities or launching attacks. This inadequacy stems from the firewall's limited ability to conduct only superficial packet inspections. Consequently, several challenges persist in effectively countering such threats. In general, each malicious attack code has a Signature that distinguishes a virus from normal application code. Antivirus Programs identify viruses by storing the signatures of known viruses.

11.2.2 Intrusion Detection Systems and Intrusion Prevention Systems

To fill the gap between firewalls and antivirus programs in layers four to five of the seven-layer network model, the industry has introduced Intrusion Detection Systems (IDSs). IDS can monitor network traffic in real time and alert managers or firewalls immediately when anomalies are detected. However, IDS is predominantly function retrospectively, detecting anomalies after they have already occurred, often resulting in delayed responses. While patching system vulnerabilities remains crucial, the most effective defense mechanism is one that operates preemptively, preventing damage before it can occur [4] as shown in Fig. 11.3.

IDS is a device capable of monitoring the transmission of network traffic in real-time, issuing alerts, or taking proactive measures when suspicious behavior is detected [6]. Unlike other network security devices, IDS is a proactive security

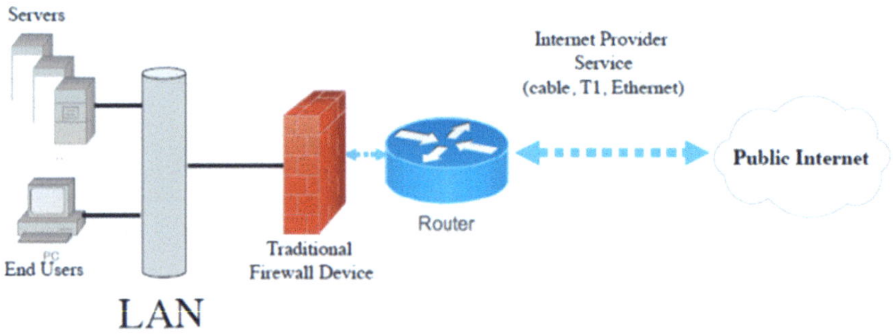

Fig. 11.2 Traditional Firewall [3]

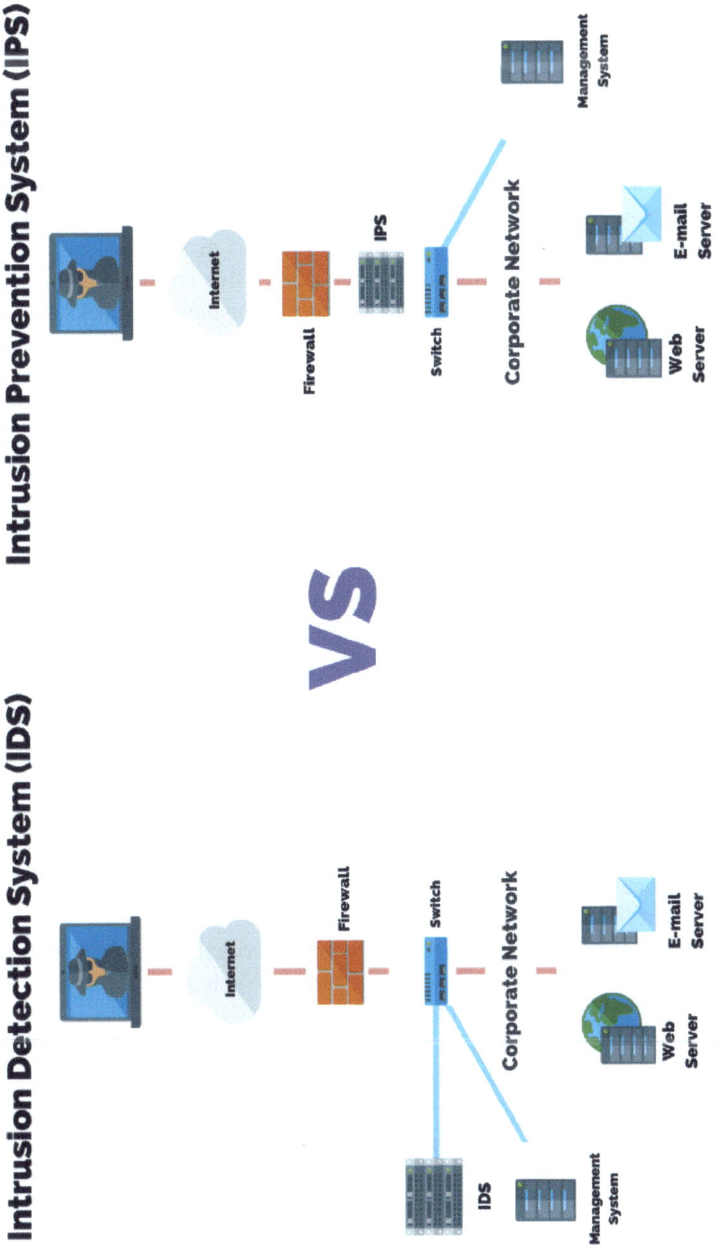

Fig. 11.3 IDS&IPS [5]

protection technology. By monitoring the system in real-time and issuing warnings if anomalies are detected. IDS can be divided into host-based IDS and network-based IDS as well as anomaly IDS and misuse IDS. Anomaly detection involves constructing a model that represents the normal behavior of a system. Any visitor behavior that deviates from this established model is classified as an intrusion. On the other hand, misuse intrusion detection requires developing a model that encompasses all malicious and unacceptable behaviors. When a visitor's behavior aligns with this model, it is identified as an intrusion. In both cases, the detection process relies on establishing comprehensive behavioral models to differentiate between normal and intrusive activities. The security strategies of these two detection modes are completely different, and each has advantages and disadvantages. The false positive rate of anomaly detection is relatively low. But considering that some behaviors inconsistent with normal behaviors are not malicious attacks, the false positive rate of anomaly detection is high. Due to the utilization of direct matching of abnormal behavior patterns, misuse detection exhibits a relatively low false positive rate. However, the malicious behaviors are complex and diverse, and may not be collected in the pre-established behavior pattern library, so the false negative rate is high. These classifications and characteristics of IDS require that users select the detection mode according to their professional requirements and system characteristics. Of course, the two detection modes can also be combined.

The difference between IDS and firewalls is that IDS functions as a passive listening device and does not require a direct connection to any specific link to operate effectively. Consequently, deploying IDS necessitates connecting it across a link through which network traffic must pass. IDS are usually placed as close as possible to the source of the attack or protected resources, such as switches in the server zone and LAN switches in the protected network segment.

With the rapid development of the IDS market, many companies have invested in this field. For example, Venustech Qiming, Internet Security System (ISS), Cisco, and Symantec are among the companies that have launched their products.

Compared to IDS, Intrusion Response Systems (IRS) is a more proactive defense technology. IRS can respond quickly when it detects intrusion behavior and automatically prevent further intrusion.

Intrusion Prevention System (IPS) is a network security device designed to monitor network traffic and data transmission behavior. When abnormal or malicious data transmission behavior is detected, the IPS promptly intervenes by interrupting or isolating the identified behavior. IPS represents an evolutionary advancement over IDS and IRS, combining the strengths and advantages of both technologies. By integrating detection and immediate prevention capabilities, IPS offers a comprehensive solution for identifying and mitigating security threats in real-time.

Similar to IDS, IPS primarily concentrate on safeguarding data by actively searching for attack code signatures and implementing measures such as filtering or discarding malicious packets.

Additionally, IPS solutions often aid in the identification of attacks by examining abnormal behavior in applications or network transmissions. For example, user programs violate security regulations, packets are sent and unpacked during sensitive periods, and application vulnerabilities are exploited. IPS go beyond considering solely the known characteristics of viruses. They focus on identifying attack programs or malicious code, including their clones and variants, and take proactive measures to prevent or minimize the potential harm they can cause. IPS is usually used as a supplement to the firewall and antivirus programs in the usage scenario. When necessary, IPS can also provide effective evidence for holding attackers criminally responsible.

IDS and IPS are two important security products in the field of network security. IDS is mainly used to detect abnormal intrusion behaviors and generate alarms. IPS is used to detect and defend against malicious activities that are judged as attacks and can cause damage to the network. IPS, by contrast, focuses more on risk control.

IDS and IPS are not mutually exclusive. Instead, they cooperate. In the absence of IDS, the decision on which security products to deploy and where to deploy them is primarily based on subjective assessment and intuition. However, the widespread deployment of IDS enables us to gain real-time insight into the current state of the network. This information empowers us to make more informed judgments regarding the appropriate placement of security products, such as IPS. Therefore, the relationship between IDS and IPS is complementary, and together they constitute a complete security solution to deal with different types of network security threats.

11.2.3 Web Application Firewall

Web Application Firewall (WAF) is a device that specifically protects Web applications by enforcing a series of security policies against HTTP/HTTPS. In recent years, with the increasing richness and complexity of Web applications, Web servers have gradually become the main targets of attackers. Security events such as SQL injection, Website Distortion, and Website Malicious Code occur frequently. The traditional firewall and other devices often face limitations in effectively addressing modern security challenges.

The Web application protection system offers a viable solution to overcome these issues [7], as shown in Fig. 11.4.

Unlike traditional firewalls, WAFs work at the application layer. By analyzing the business processes and logic of web applications, WAF is capable of detecting various types of requests originating from web application clients. It verifies the security and legitimacy of the content within these requests and promptly interrupts any illicit or unauthorized requests. The primary objective of employing a WAF is to safeguard the security of websites by effectively identifying and mitigating potential threats and attacks in real time [9].

The primary functions of WAF encompass several key areas, including audit devices, access control devices, architecture design tools, and Web application hardening tools. The audit device is designed to intercept HTTP data or sessions that adhere to specific predefined rules. The access control device is responsible for managing and regulating access to the web application. The WAF package typically

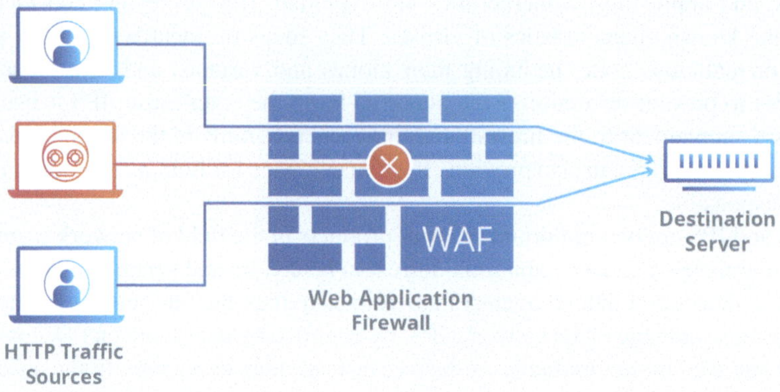

Fig. 11.4 IDS&IPS [8]

offers two security modes: active security mode and passive security mode. Architecture design tools are used to assign functions, centralized control, and virtual infrastructure in the reverse proxy mode. The Web application hardening tool is used to enhance the security of protected Web applications, including anti-attack, anti-vulnerability, anti-hidden links, anti-web crawling, anti-website malicious code, anti-DDoS, and so on.

In general terms, WAF is a specialized product designed to safeguard web applications by incorporating specific detection rules. The WAF examines the content of each incoming request based on these predefined rules and employs defensive measures against those that fail to meet the security criteria. This proactive approach ensures the security and integrity of web applications by filtering out potentially malicious or unauthorized requests. The WAF serves as a highly valuable solution for enhancing the security of web applications, offering comprehensive protection for enterprise-level web application.

The processing flow of WAF can be roughly divided into four parts: preprocessing, rule detection, processing module, and log recording. In the preprocessing stage, when the WAF receives the data request traffic, it performs an initial evaluation. Initially, it identifies whether the request is an HTTP or HTTPS request. Subsequently, the WAF verifies if the URL request is listed in the whitelist. If the URL request is present in the whitelist, it is promptly forwarded to the back-end Web server for further response processing. However, for packets that are not included in the whitelist, they proceed to the rule detection phase after parsing. Each WAF product has its unique detection rule system. The parsed data packets will enter the detection system for rule matching, check whether the data request conforms to the rules, and identify malicious attack behaviors. According to the different detection results, the processing module will make different security defense actions. If the rules are met, it will be sent to the back-end Web server for response processing. For the requests that are not in line with the rules, it will perform related blocking, recording, and alarm processing. In the process of processing, the WAF will also record the log of the interception processing, so that users can view and analyze the log in the future.

Regarding the deployment modes of WAF, there are several options available. WAF can be deployed in series at the network egress of critical devices, such as WEB servers, similar to IPS devices. WAF can be deployed in the following modes: transparent bridge, reverse proxy, mirrored traffic, and routed proxy.

Different WAF products will customize different intercept warning pages. During regular penetration testing, it is possible to identify the specific WAF product being used by a website based on the distinctive intercept pages. This knowledge can be leveraged to intentionally bypass the WAF for specific purposes. The most common approach to bypassing a WAF is through the use of various encoding techniques. However, successful bypassing relies on the prerequisite that the submitted encoded parameter content undergoes relevant decoding before entering the database query statement.

11.2.4 Data Leakage Prevention

Data Leakage Prevention (DLP), also known as Data Loss Prevention (DLP), is a policy that technically prevents the leakage of sensitive enterprise data in a form that violates the provisions of your security policies. DLP is one of the most mainstream means of information security and data protection in the world. It is an effective way of protection that is widely used at present, just like information grade protection/classification protection [10].

DLP is not solely a technical product; it is a process-based management methodology that encompasses various management system-related aspects. It extends beyond being a mere technology, as shown in Fig. 11.5. DLP is a comprehensive concept, and according to the latest Gartner report, it can be categorized into two main types:

- Integrated DLP: DLP is only a part of a product's functionality, and is often used for quick compliance, simple ways to analyze content, and cannot be used to generalize policies in one environment to other environments.
- Enterprise-Level DLP: Focuses on the relevant parts of DLP data content, often with terminal, network, discovery, and cloud components. Enterprise-level DLP has complete and in-depth content inspection capabilities, supports centralized management, and policies can be used across different scenarios.

The general pattern of DLP is to build a policy database that contains all the detection policies and definitions of sensitive data. When an employee performs a certain behavior (such as sending an email to an external network), the system scans and determines whether the behavior conforms to the security policy and takes corresponding actions, such as blocking or warning. In addition, DLP also needs to add permission control, audit, endpoint control, and other functions to finally form a complete set of solutions. Nevertheless, this basic mode of DLP implementation

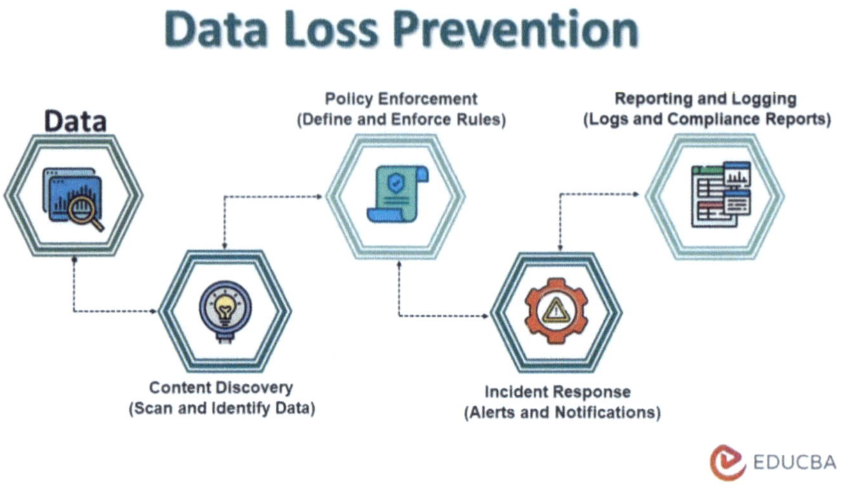

Fig. 11.5 DLP [11]

poses challenges in detecting unstructured data and ensuring effective protection against malicious activities. Therefore, there is a need for more comprehensive and in-depth technical measures to enhance data protection [12].

To effectively mitigate data leakage, DLP systems monitor the flow of data across the network, on employee devices, and within the company's infrastructure. By tracking data movement, DLP systems can identify potential risks and take appropriate actions. This may include generating alerts to notify administrators or security teams, adjusting permissions on sensitive data, or, in certain circumstances, blocking the transmission of data that poses a risk of leaving the company's network [13].

For example, in the face of security threats from insiders such as employees, former employees, contractors, and suppliers, DLP can help stop the unauthorized forwarding, copying, or destruction of sensitive data by tracking sensitive information within the network. In the face of external attacks such as phishing and malware, DLP can help prevent malicious actors from successfully obtaining or encrypting internal data. In the case of accidental data exposure, such as insiders inadvertently sending sensitive data out, DLP can detect and prevent such accidental data breaches by tracking sensitive information within the network in a similar way to how DLP prevents internal attacks. In addition, in some DLP solutions, DLP is combined with strategies such as data fingerprinting, keyword matching, pattern matching, file matching, and exact data matching to detect sensitive data.

11.2.5 Endpoint Protection Platform and Endpoint Detection Response

Endpoint Protection Platform (EPP) and Endpoint Detection and Response (EDR) are two important concepts in enterprise security defense. EPP is often defined as an endpoint security solution whose goal is to protect end devices from various attacks and threats. In contrast, EDR is often defined as a detection and response solution whose goal is to detect and respond to threats that have bypassed other security defenses. EPPs and EDRs are used in different scenarios. EPPs are commonly used to prevent the spread and execution of malicious software, including viruses, trojans, malware, etc. EPP usually includes antivirus software, intrusion prevention, firewalls, and other features that can help businesses protect their end devices from various attacks and threats. EDRs, in turn, focus on detecting and responding to threats that have bypassed other security defenses. EDRs can analyze logs, events, and data on end devices to detect security threats more quickly and take quick response measures [14].

EDR technology typically encompasses the following key functions: real-time monitoring of endpoint devices and network communications, detection of abnormal or malicious behavior such as malware infections, network attacks, and data leaks; prompt delivery of real-time alerts and responses to swiftly mitigate security incidents; and collection, storage, and analysis of logs and events on endpoint devices to facilitate subsequent investigation and analysis.

EDR technology is often used in conjunction with other security technologies such as antivirus software, firewalls, IDS, and security information and event management (SIEM) systems, among others, to improve the security and protection of terminal devices.

The advantage of EDR lies in its ability to provide real-time monitoring and response, which can quickly detect and mitigate security incidents and reduce the duration of security breaches, thereby reducing losses. At the same time, EDR technology has advanced threat detection capabilities and can detect a variety of new malware and attack technologies to ensure the security of terminal equipment. In addition, EDR technology can collect, store, and analyze events and logs on terminal devices, providing valuable security information to help enterprises better understand security events and threats.

With the continuous development of the Internet and cloud computing, the development of EPP and EDR is also evolving, as shown in Fig. 11.6.

The EPP and EDR are no longer simple antivirus software and intrusion detection systems but have more intelligent and automated functions. For example, modern EPPs and EDRs can use techniques such as machine learning and artificial intelligence to detect and respond to threats more accurately, thereby improving enterprise security.

In conclusion, EPP and EDR are very important concepts in enterprise security defense. They can help enterprises protect end devices from various attacks and threats, as well as detect and respond more quickly to threats that have bypassed

Fig. 11.6 EPP&EDR [14]

other security defense measures. In the dynamic landscape of the Internet and cloud computing, the functionalities of EPP and EDR systems are continuously evolving to incorporate intelligent and automated capabilities. This adaptability is essential to meet the ever-changing security requirements of enterprises.

11.2.6 Security Information and Event Management

Security Information and Event Management (SIEM) has significantly evolved from its origins as a log management solution. While initially focused on log management, SIEM has now become a much more robust and powerful technology. Modern SIEM software providers have incorporated advanced techniques such as machine learning, advanced statistical analysis, and other analytical methods to enhance its capabilities. SIEM systems aggregate log data, security alerts, and events into a centralized platform that provides real-time analytics for security monitoring.

SIEM includes Security Information Management (SIM), which involves the collection of all network activities. This includes log data collected from servers, firewalls, domain controllers, routers, databases, and network flows, as well as unstructured data in the network, such as emails. Two techniques can be used to collect log data, agentless collection and agent-based collection. Agent-based log collection methods require an agent to be deployed on each device, which collects logs and then analyzes and filters them before returning them to the SIEM server. This technique is primarily used in closed and secure networks, such as the Demilitarized Zone (DMZ) where communications are limited. Agentless log collection is a more common approach where the SIEM server automatically collects logs generated by the device using a secure communication channel, such as a specific port using a secure protocol [15], as shown in Fig. 11.7.

SIEM addresses the typical application scenario of brute force cracking. For instance, if an individual repeatedly enters an incorrect network access password multiple times within a minute, it may be considered a low-priority attack, possibly due to the user making repeated mistakes. However, if an unusually high number of incorrect password attempts, such as 200 times per minute, is detected, it is highly likely to be a brute force attack. In this case, the hacker is systematically attempting to crack the account password. SIEM can effectively identify and flag such brute force attacks, promptly notifying security administrators. Upon receiving an alert, SIEM can automatically initiate a predefined workflow to respond to the attack [16].

SIEM software provides administrators with a track record of various activities in their network environment. SIEM software collects and aggregates log data generated by all technical infrastructure, from host system applications to network and security devices such as firewalls and soft filters. SIEM software is a tool for security monitoring and event management that identifies, classifies, and analyzes data. The software has two main goals. One is to produce security-related incident reports, including successful/failed logins, malware activity, and other possibly malicious

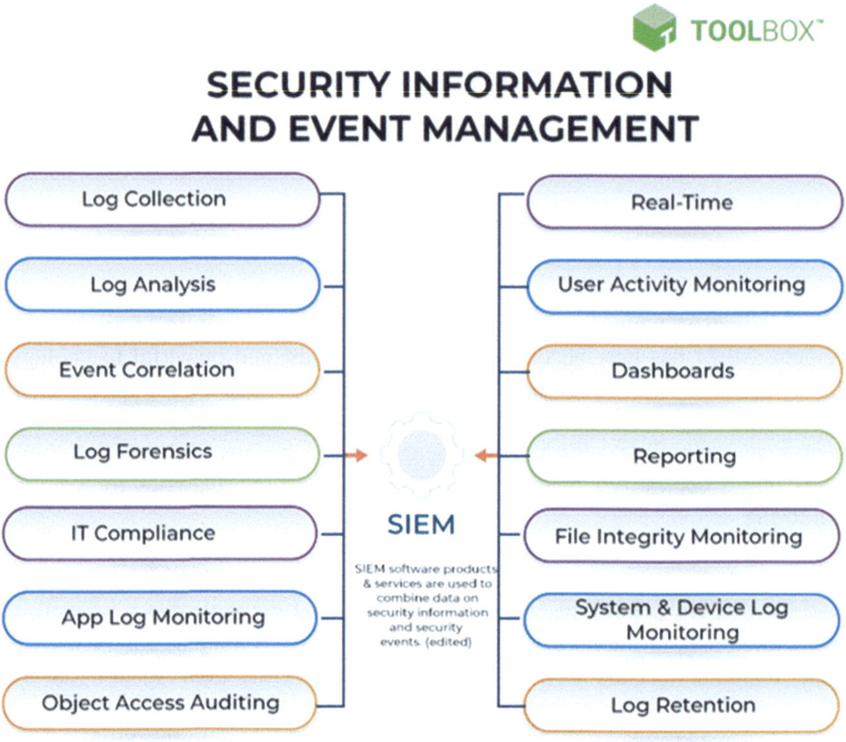

Fig. 11.7 SIEM [17]

activities. Second, if the analysis shows that an activity violates a predefined rule set, it is considered a potential security issue and SIEM will issue an alert.

Large enterprises often view SIEM as the foundation to support a Security Operations Center (SOC). A typical SIEM product is a collection of many other security rules and tools combined under a comprehensive framework. A typical SIEM consists of the following modules: Log Management System (LMS) for traditional log collection and storage; Security Information Management (SIM) for centralized collection and management of security-related data from multiple data sources, such as firewalls, DNS servers, routers; Security Event Management (SEM) provides proactive monitoring and analytics, including data visualization, event correlation, and alerts, analyzing logs and events in real-time to provide threat monitoring, event correlation, and incident response.

SIEM software is a vital part of an enterprise's security defense system, which can help enterprises quickly identify and respond to security incidents, and protect their information security and business operations. In practical applications, SIEM needs to be customized according to the actual situation of the enterprise to better meet the security requirements of the enterprise. At the same time, SIEM also needs to need to undergo continuous upgrades and improvements to keep pace with evolving security threats.

Most SIEMs are usually made up of the following components:

- Security Data Collection: The SIEM system mainly relies on security log data to obtain an accurate picture of events occurring in real-time. This log data can come from a firewall, server, database, or any other process running in a digital environment. The SIEM system collects this data through proxies or applications and stores it in a central data store.
- Security data parsing and standardization: To be able to interpret data efficiently across different sources and event correlations, SIEM systems can normalize logs. This normalization process involves processing the log into a readable structured format, extracting important data from the log, and mapping the different fields contained in the log.
- Security data storage and analysis: The next step for the SIEM system will be to connect the dots and correlate events from different data sources. This correlation work is based on rules provided by various SIEM tools, predefined rules for different attack scenarios, or rules created and tweaked by analysts. Most SIEM systems also provide built-in mechanisms for generating reports. These reports can be used to manage audits. For example, daily reports detailing the triggering of alerts or rules can be embedded in dashboards.
- Security data presentation: The ability to visualize data and events in the SIEM system is another key component. Dashboards contain multiple visualizations, or views, that help identify trends, and anomalies, and monitor the health or safety status of the entire environment. Some SIEM tools will come with pre-made dashboards, while others will allow users to create and adjust their dashboards.

At present, there are many mature SIEM products, including open-source OSSIM, Elastic SIEM, and Opensoc.

11.2.7 Situational Awareness

Situational Awareness was first proposed by the US Air Force in the 1980s and consists of three levels perception, comprehension, and prediction. Endsley's theory defines network security situational awareness as follows: Network security situational awareness is the comprehensive analysis of network security elements, assessment of network security situation, prediction of its development trend, visualization of the user, and corresponding reports and countermeasures [18], as shown in Fig. 11.8.

The situational awareness platform leverages advanced technologies such as big data and machine learning to extract and analyze vast amounts of data from multiple dimensions. Through multi-dimensional correlation analysis, the platform enables the generation of security risk alarms and offers valuable trend prediction capabilities. The four key aspects of the platform include handling massive data, conducting association analysis, facilitating large-screen display, and providing trend

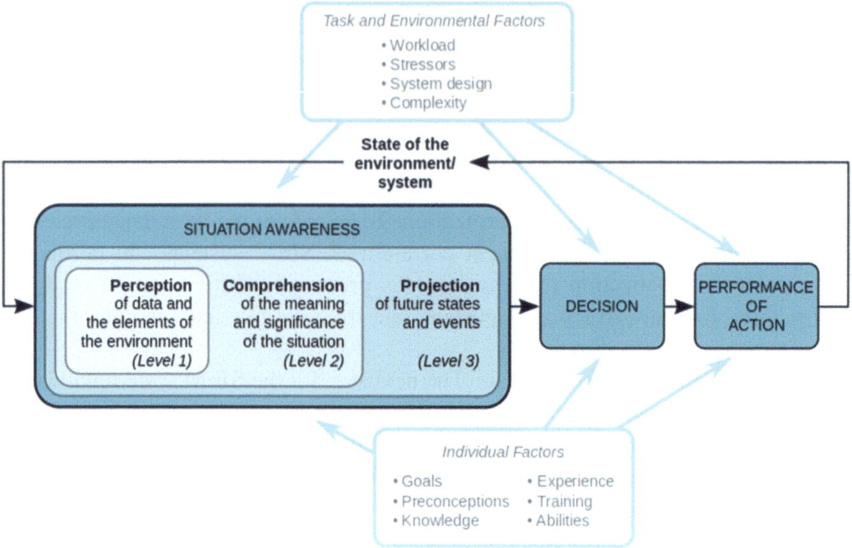

Fig. 11.8 Situational Awareness [19]

prediction. Among these key aspects, trend prediction stands as the core functionality, while also being a challenging task to accomplish effectively in today's context.

Situational awareness focuses on deepening the prediction of security trends through big data, machine learning, and other technologies. At present, the situational awareness products include the following functional modules: asset management, vulnerability management, big data platform, log analysis platform, threat intelligence, sandbox, user behavior analysis, network traffic analysis, forensics traceability, threat capture, and other capabilities.

As the monitoring scope expands, the volume of data also increases significantly. Therefore, the establishment of a comprehensive situational awareness platform relies heavily on a robust big data infrastructure with powerful processing and computing capabilities. In this context, threat intelligence plays a critical role in managing the vast amounts of data and alarms, assisting in the efficient identification of attack behaviors and attackers. The quality of threat intelligence serves as a crucial metric to evaluate the effectiveness of a situational awareness platform.

The core purpose of utilizing platform capabilities such as situational awareness is to monitor complex and advanced attacks, which requires the situational awareness platform to first capture the microstate, and the low-cost and efficient total factor data acquisition capability is the foundation. At present, the cyberspace attack defense is no longer feature-based monitoring but needs to use threat intelligence and expert experience to build a scenario-based analysis system, which is a process of continuous learning and reference in the offensive and defensive confrontation with the times and needs continuous operation of such analysis management.

11.2.8 Security Operations Center

The Security Operations Center (SOC) originated from the Network Operations Center (NOC). With the increasingly prominent problem of information security and the continuous development of security management theory and technology, it is becoming more and more important to manage the whole network and system from the perspective of security. However, the traditional NOC lacks the necessary technical support in this respect, necessitating the emergence of the SOC concept [20].

At the time of SOC 1.0, SOC was usually regarded as an integration of SIEM. Today, SOC have evolved into a more complex system that uses SIEM products to operate and provide services to customers, which is what we call SOC 2.0.

A modern SOC is more than just a simple security incident management system. It is a highly automated system capable of quickly detecting and responding to security incidents, while also providing real-time visualized data and analytics to help businesses identify and respond to threats. The SOC encompasses numerous additional components, including but not limited to vulnerability scanning, malware analysis, network traffic analysis, authentication management, and the implementation of security incident response plans.

The goal of SOC is to improve the security of enterprises and reduce security risks and losses by centrally managing and monitoring their security incidents. This requires the SOC team to have professional security skills and knowledge and to be able to work closely with other departments or teams, including departments such as IT, network, legal, and compliance departments. At the same time, SOC also need to constantly learn and innovate to adapt to changing security threats and technologies. SOC serves as a centralized security management system, with assets at its core and security incident management as a key process. It adopts the concept of security domain division to establish real-time asset risk models, aiding administrators in incident and risk analysis, early warning management, and emergency response. SOC is a sophisticated system that encompasses products, services, and operations and maintenance. It represents the organic integration of technology, processes, and human expertise, as shown in Fig. 11.9.

As the security situational awareness platform gains prominence, SOC will utilize the platform as a means to facilitate intelligent security operations. It will enhance various aspects, including risk monitoring, analysis, and decision-making, notification and collaboration, response and mitigation, as well as traceability and forensics. To support these capabilities, popular technologies and platforms will be integrated, such as big data technology, east-west traffic collection technology, EDR, machine learning, anti-spoofing attack technology, among others. At the same time, the situational awareness platform and the Information Technology Infrastructure Library (ITIL) concept are integrated with the information security management standard. And the security operation is divided into different roles, such as security managers, security experts, security operations and maintenance, security analysts, security emergency response personnel, security researchers, etc.,

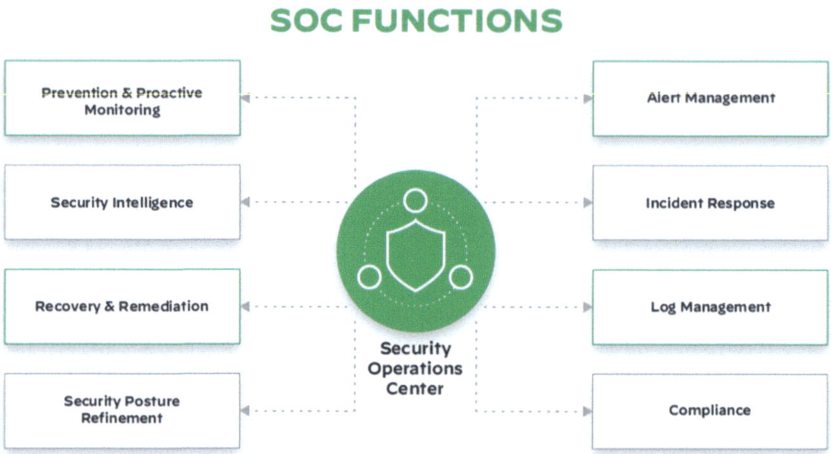

Fig. 11.9 SOC [21]

in the process of integrating the whole life cycle of security incident management. Throughout the integration of the entire life cycle of security incident management, these roles are interconnected through a well-defined workflow, ensuring a more standardized and organized security operation process.

11.2.9 User and Entity Behavior Analytics

User and Entity Behavior Analytics (UEBA) is a new security architecture designed to improve security by analyzing the behavior of people and systems. UEBA is widely used in the context of Big Data, especially in the area of DLP, which has significant advantages [22], as shown in Fig. 11.10.

In the practice of DLP, the elements of UEBA mainly include personnel, data, and operation mode. Traditional UEBA focuses on the aggregation of large numbers of logs, rather than the data itself.

This technical idea makes UEBA have some disadvantages:

1. The collection of massive log data, with volumes that can exceed 100 million per day, poses significant challenges in effectively mining the data.
2. Building and analyzing user behavior models is essential. However, due to variations in cultures and management approaches across different enterprises, there are substantial differences in user behaviors. Consequently, traditional UEBA requires the establishment of separate models for each enterprise, resulting in lengthy modeling periods and limited universality of the models.
3. The collection of broad-scope information is necessary, but it often suffers from low accuracy levels.

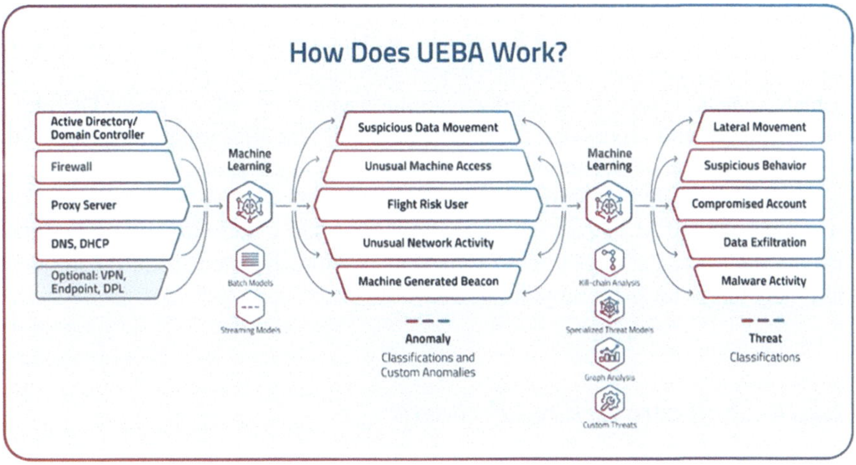

Fig. 11.10 UEBA [23]

The construction cost of traditional UEBA is high, resulting in significant post-analysis expenses and the requirement of a dedicated operations and maintenance team. This leads to increased operating costs, which can be challenging for many enterprises to afford.

Under the premise of taking into account the basic elements of traditional UEBA, the new generation of UEBA shifts its focus from extensive log collection to the log collection of sensitive data, reduces operating costs, and improves efficiency through auxiliary visualization and other analysis and mining means.

The new generation of UEBA can better meet the needs of enterprises, reduce security risks, and improve the security of enterprises. Based on massive data, UEBA technology predicts the abnormal behavior or internal threats of internal users, gives decisions directly from the "human" perspective, catches the "bad guys," takes the initiative to attack, prevents data leaks before they occur, and provides a reliable basis for security analysts. In simpler terms, UEBA aims to detect individuals who have engaged in malicious activities or are likely to do so, using technical means.

The linkage of UEBA and DLP can improve the efficiency and accuracy of detection and reduce false positives. As the last line of defense for APT attacks, data anti-leakage products can effectively prevent the leakage of user data assets. However, the pure DLP solution has the problem that sensitive information is not easy to define, resulting in a high false positive rate and a low detection rate. It can only passively monitor and protect data, but cannot actively defend it. Moreover, DLP has a remarkable effect on the general personnel, but the protection ability of the personnel with ulterior motives is slightly insufficient. An active defense, the defense of others with intentions, is the strength of UEBA. The combination of UEBA and DLP technology allows for more accurate targeting of unusual behavior.

Compared to traditional security devices that primarily analyze external threat systems such as SOC/SIEM, UEBA places greater emphasis on detecting abnormal users, such as instances where privileged accounts are compromised, and user anomalies, such as legitimate users engaging in unauthorized activities. UEBA is less concerned with processing massive amounts of alarm information. UEBA has more advantages in the scenario of enterprise internal threat analysis, focusing more on user behavior, and finding problems from another perspective. Generally, UEBA will work with SIEM to conduct unified reconnaissance and analysis of external data and internal data, realize multi-dimensional anomaly detection of the system, and timely alarm for incoming threats to avoid risks.

11.2.10 Software Defined Perimeter

Software Defined Perimeter (SDP) is a new generation of network security model based on the concept of zero-trust, proposed by the International Cloud Security Alliance CSA in 2013 [24].

The traditional network security model is based on the physical perimeter defense of the firewall, which is also known as the Intranet. With the continuous development of emerging technologies such as cloud computing, mobile Internet, AI big data, and Internet of Things (IoT), traditional security perimeter are gradually disintegrating. In the past, server resources and office equipment were in the Intranet, but now with the popularity of applications such as migration to the cloud, mobile office, and the IoT, network perimeters are becoming increasingly blurred and business application scenarios are becoming more complex, and traditional physical perimeters security can no longer meet the needs of enterprises' digital transformation [25].

SDP technology architecture comes into being, which can protect enterprise networks and applications more flexibly and securely. SDP gradually transforms the network perimeters into a software-based abstraction layer through various technical means, such as authentication, encryption, and access control, to achieve refined network access control and security protection. SDP can not only protect the internal network of enterprises, but also protect emerging application scenarios such as cloud computing, mobile devices, and the IoT, providing a more comprehensive security guarantee for enterprises' digital transformation.

Compared with traditional firewalls, SDP has the following advantages: (1) *Enhanced Flexibility*: SDP provides increased flexibility by allowing network access control to be configured based on specific conditions and requirements. (2) *Heightened Security*: SDP offers more robust security measures through its ability to provide fine-grained access control and encryption protection. (3) *Adaptability to Emerging Technologies*: SDP is designed to be adaptable to emerging technologies, making it an ideal solution for protecting new application scenarios such as cloud computing, mobile devices, and IoT.

In April 2019, the internationally renowned IT consulting agency Gartner published "Zero Trust Network Access Market Guide" industry report. The report pointed out that Zero-Trust Network Access (ZTNA) is also known as SDP, is an identity-based and context-based logical access perimeter created around an application or a group of applications. These applications are hidden, undiscoverable, and restrict access to a specified set of entities through trusted proxies. Before granting access, the agent verifies the identity, context, and policy compliance of the designated visitors. This mechanism will significantly reduce the attackable surface by removing application resources from public view. It also predicts, by 2023, 60% of enterprises will replace VPNs with SDP solutions [26].

Zero-trust security is a concept, and SDP is a technical architecture and solution to implement the concept of zero-trust security. Enterprises can implement the principles of zero-trust security concept by deploying SDP products or solutions. The zero-trust philosophy emphasizes: "Never Trust, Always Verify." The network cloaking technology of SDP effectively realizes the principle of "Never Trust." Unlike traditional TCP/IP networks that default to allowing connections, the server remains completely invisible to end users without proper authentication and authorization, shifting from "By Default Trust" to "Never Trust." In addition, different from the traditional network security authentication, Verify Once, by implementing real-time dynamic trusted authorization authentication on the SDP gateway, you can realize Always Verify the connection authorization. SDP is a fast and efficient technology architecture of zero-trust security practice.

The SDP security model consists of three main components, including Initiating SDP Host (IH), Accepting SDP Host (AH), and SDP Controller (Controller).

Both AH and IH are connected to the Controller, and the connection between them is managed through the Controller's interaction with the security control channel. This structure enables the control plane to remain separate from the data plane for a fully scalable security system. In addition, all components can be clustered for capacity expansion or improved stable uptime.

SDP is an open technology architecture, and its philosophy is very similar to the zero-trust concept. Many security manufacturers are launching zero-trust products based on SDP technology. It can be said that SDP is one of the best technical architectures to realize the concept of zero-trust at present. Before each hacking contest, CSA introduces hackers to the architecture of the SDP. It consists of three components [27]:

- Gateway: responsible for protecting the business system, preventing all kinds of network attacks, and only allowing traffic from legitimate clients to pass through.
- Client: responsible for verifying user identity and forwarding access requests to the gateway.
- Controller: responsible for identity authentication, policy configuration, and control of the entire process.

SDP has five defense mechanisms:

- Single Packet Authorization (SPA): Gateway opens the specified port to the IP address of Client only after receiving and verifying the SPA packet sent by Client. This technology can shield the vast majority of illegal user network attacks, so that vulnerability scanning, DDoS, and other attack methods are ineffective.
- mutual Transport Layer Security (mTLS): The communication between the Gateway and the Client is encrypted, and it is mutual TLS. The Gateway authenticates the user, and the user also authenticates the Gateway. Bidirectional authentication ensures that man-in-the-middle attacks cannot work.
- Dynamic firewall: After SPA, the Gateway will release the specified port. But the port release is temporary, no operation within a few seconds, the port will automatically close. Maximize protection strength.
- Device authorization: SDP not only verifies the user's identity but also verifies the user's device. The verification of the device includes the verification of the health status of the device, such as whether the anti-virus software is installed. Device verification also includes verifying the device certificate. Only legitimate devices can install the certificate. The certificate is involved in the process of encrypting communication data. Ensure that all connections are from legitimate devices.
- App binding: Users can only access authorized apps. This conforms to the principle of "minimizing authorization" and ensures that threats cannot spread horizontally.

SDP is designed to solve the problem of how to plan and refactor networks in real time and dynamically in the Global Information Grid (GIG), as shown in Fig. 11.11. Until SDP fully matures, VPN is still the better solution for remote access. It is the most common solution for providing secure remote access, not only giving remote workers access to an enterprise network but also enabling them to

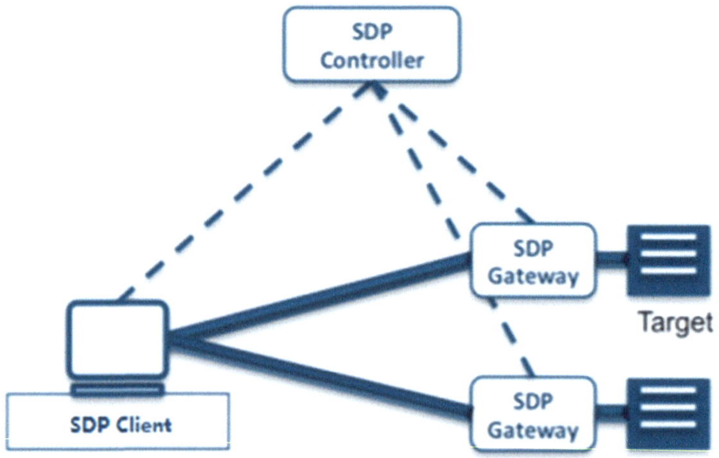

Fig. 11.11 SDP [28]

access applications and data on that network. However, the outdated perception that users are naturally "trusted" on Local Area Networks (LANs) leaves a wide open field for attackers.

The new paradigm of remote access with SDP uses a zero-trust approach to replace extensive network access with identity-based fine-grained access to provide access to critical network resources. SDP protects organizations from a variety of threats and hacking techniques, preventing criminals from successfully penetrating corporate networks.

Common security threats that VPN technology does not protect against reveal the effectiveness of SDP in confronting such threats [29]:

Man-in-the-middle attacks, in which an attacker places himself in the middle of a user's conversation with an app, eavesdropping or pretending to be one of the parties, making it appear as if the exchange of information is still going on normally. Both SDP and VPN solutions protect against man-in-the-middle attacks through encrypted tunnels. But SDP is fully deployed and always online, securing traffic at all times and providing secure access to enterprise networks. Many traditional VPN solutions save money and reduce latency by sending traffic directly through a separate tunnel, putting terminals at risk. SDP solves this problem by protecting open endpoints.

In a DNS hijacking attack, an attacker intervenes in DNS resolution and directs users to a malicious site instead of the legitimate site they intended to visit. This can be accomplished using malicious software or unauthorized modifications to the server. Once an attacker takes control of the DNS, he or she can direct others accessing the Internet through the DNS to fake websites or direct users to pages containing malware or third-party search engines. The always-on SDP solution relies on a network-as-a-service architecture that uses a curated secure DNS service to perform resolution and defend against DNS hijacking attacks.

In DDoS attacks, applications are overloaded by a flood of traffic and cannot respond to normal requests. Because they are distributed, such attacks are very difficult to stop. DDoS attack is characterized by an apparent attempt by the attacker to block legitimate use of the service. SDP solution DDoS attacks are effective because they protect applications rather than end-user devices. In the SDP model, applications and the infrastructure that hosts them are not directly connected to the Internet. The SDP solution acts as a gateway to block all unauthorized access.

In port scanning, an attacker uses port scanning to locate open ports on the network that can be used for attack. Because SDP solutions isolate all network resources from the Internet, attackers cannot use this technique to find a way in.

Similar to DDoS, a brute force attack is one of the ways an attacker can gain access to a network or application through repeated login attempts. SDP solutions immediately detect failed login attempts, while noting suspicious geolocation or login periods, changes in device status, and missing or disabled terminal antivirus software to deny access.

11.2.11 Next Generation Firewall

Next Generation Firewall (NGFW) is a high-performance firewall that can fully address application layer threats. It not only contains all the functions of traditional firewalls, such as basic packet filtering, status detection, NAT, VPN, etc., but also integrates more advanced security capabilities such as the identification and control of applications and users, and IPS. It has faster processing efficiency and stronger external expansion and linkage capabilities. With in-depth insights into users, applications, and content in network traffic and a high-performance processing engine, the NGFW provides integrated security protection, helps users securely conduct services, and simplifies the network security architecture [30].

In 2007, Gartner proposed the concept of NGFW in response to the changes in enterprise business processes and IT architecture and the new trend of security threats. In 2009, Gartner officially released Defining the Next-Generation Firewall, which defines a network firewall as an online security control measure, that is, a network security policy can be executed in real-time across each trusted level network. Gartner uses the term "NGFW" to describe the need to upgrade firewalls in response to changes in the way business processes use IT, and in the way, attacks are launched against business systems.

Early packet-filtering firewalls were initially designed to fulfill network isolation requirements by implementing basic access control. Later, stateful inspection firewalls were introduced, integrating TCP/UDP and application state detection capabilities to provide Layer 3 to Layer 4 protection. These firewalls introduced the concept of policies and shifted their focus from individual packets to data streams, resulting in improved processing efficiency. In 2004, Unified Threat Management (UTM) emerged, combining traditional firewalls with content security features such as antivirus, IPS, and URL filtering, as well as VPN functionality. While each module operated independently, detection required unpacking, leading to limited efficiency gains.

However, UTM simplified security product deployment to some extent and became more suitable for small and medium-sized enterprises. With the proliferation of applications and the increasing complexity of their relationships with ports and protocols, NGFW emerges. It can distinguish applications corresponding to traffic, even if these applications use the same protocol and port. NGFW solves the problem that UTM devices need to process packets module by module, resulting in low performance.

With the development of mobile, social, cloud, and big data, the Information and Communications Technology (ICT) network environment has been reshaped once again.

To address the security challenges in today's network environment, NGFWs must meet the following requirements:

- High Performance: As a real-time protection device, the NGFW's performance is always the first consideration when purchasing an NGFW.

- Comprehensive Threat Prevention Capability: NGFWs should inherit and enhance traditional security functions while providing extensive application identification and protection against application-layer threats and attacks. They should incorporate a user authentication system to handle mobile access and support content security protection, including web page filtering, email filtering, and scanning of various file content. Furthermore, NGFWs should include SSL encryption traffic detection to decrypt SSL traffic and perform subsequent content security checks. Integration with sandboxes allows for the detection and identification of unknown threats by sending suspicious files for analysis.
- Refined Detection Granularity and Real Time Monitoring: NGFWs should offer fine-grained detection capabilities with complete flow-based detection and real-time monitoring. They should support cache-free technology, enabling the detection of applications, intrusion behaviors, and virus files in fragmented and grouped packets using minimal system resources.
- Cloud Computing and Data Center Support: NGFWs should be compatible with cloud computing and data centers, providing comprehensive virtualization capabilities across routing and forwarding, configuration management, and security services. NGFWs should be able to be virtualized into multiple independent virtual firewalls, catering to the needs of cloud computing and data center tenants.
- Simplified Management and Visualization: NGFWs should simplify management tasks by offering a visual management interface and extensive log reporting. They should support intelligent policy optimization and agile cloud management.

With the transition from traditional firewalls to NGFWs, network attacks have evolved from targeting the network layer to focusing on the application layer. In the era of big data and artificial intelligence (AI), NGFWs must adapt and evolve into platform-based and intelligent solutions.

Gartner released the Magic Quadrant Report of Global Network Firewalls in December 2022, as shown in Fig. 11.12.

In the report, firewall products of various security companies are divided into the following four roles:

- Leaders, who execute well under the current vision of changing the rules of the market.
- Visionaries, who understand where the market is going or have a vision to change the rules of the market but have not executed well yet.
- Challengers, who are doing well or may be dominant in a large part of the market but have no understanding of the market direction.
- Niche Players, who are nice market players who have successfully focused on a niche but have yet to leapfrog others.

Here are some examples of NGFW products offered by several mainstream security companies.

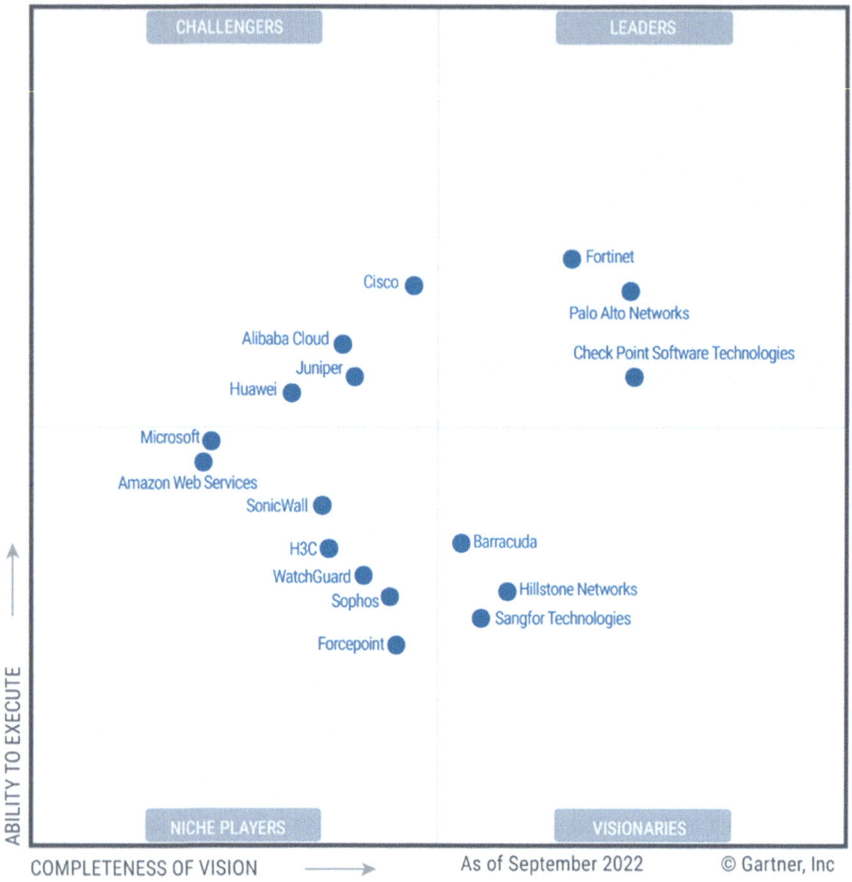

Source: Gartner (December 2022)

Fig. 11.12 Magic Quadrant [30]

Sangfor NGAF

Sangfor Next-Generation Application Firewall (NGAF), as shown in Fig. 11.13, is specifically designed to enhance network perimeter security. It incorporates advanced security defense technologies and user-friendly product design concepts. By leveraging these innovations, Sangfor NGAF not only improves security detection, prevention, and control capabilities at the network perimeter but also enables visual display and swift resolution of network security risks. This streamlines the construction of network border security, resulting in a comprehensive intrusion prevention effect.

Sangfor NGAF integrates three intelligent security detection engines: Intrusion Prevention System (IPS), Sangfor AI-based Vanguard Engine (SAVE), and Web Intelligence Search Engine (WISE). These engines work together to ensure

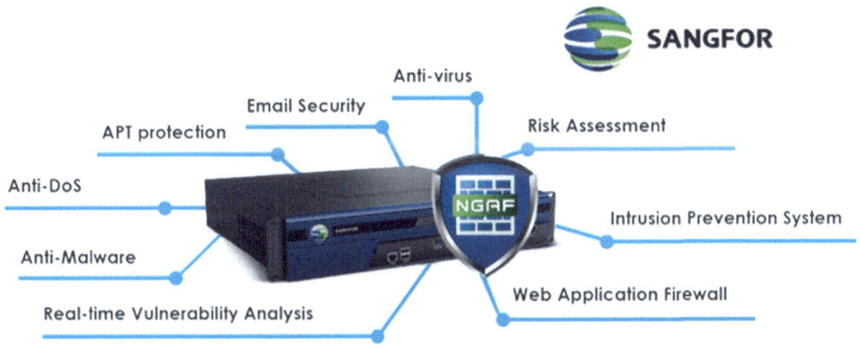

Fig. 11.13 Sangfor NGAF [31]

effective security outcomes. The solution also incorporates innovative cloud honeypot active defense technology, combining local honeypots and cloud honeypot virtual environments. This approach creates realistic and comprehensive simulated business scenarios, effectively reducing the likelihood of detecting camouflage services. Cloud honeypots mitigate the risk of local business disruptions, enable fast traceability forensics, and provide accurate profiles of attackers.

Sangfor NGAF offers a wide range of response methods, including one-click virus search and elimination, file isolation, terminal isolation, and real-time synchronous interception of malicious IP/domain names/file MD5 across the entire network. It can accurately identify compromised hosts and boasts a local rule base of over 1.6 million botnets. Utilizing various means such as rule engines, behavior analysis engines, cloud big data analysis engines, and cloud active detection engines, Sangfor NGAF provides timely, comprehensive, and effective protection against botnets, mining trojans, ransomware, and other threats. It facilitates deep linkage fast response and integrates with Extended Detection and Response (XDR) and System Integrity Protection (SIP) platforms, offering end-to-end visibility into attack propagation and granular traceability down to the process level. Additionally, it enables one-click detection and elimination, as well as one-click terminal isolation through EDR integration. Sangfor NGAF integrates with the ZTA zero-trust platform, enabling dynamic business intelligent access management, and linking with the Security Access Service Edge (SASE) platform. This allows for dynamic expansion of data leak prevention and secures remote office access, ensuring accurate and closed-loop response to threat events [32].

Sangfor NGAF security policy is simple and effective, built-in rich scenario-based security policy templates such as office network, server security, etc., support failure policy, shadow policy, redundancy policy, policy crossover, policy merger and other more than ten kinds of inspection rules to ensure the accuracy of the policy; Security policy optimization and intelligent detection mechanism of redundant policies to ensure the effectiveness of policies. Built-in lightweight visual security operation center, special operation blackmail protection, account security, and business asset security protection, quickly locate business security problems based on the user's perspective.

Topsec Next Generation Firewall

Topsec next-generation firewall integrates AI-driven unified intelligent detection engine and combines multiple security modules such as intrusion prevention, WAF, TVD, URL filtering, DDoS protection, HTTPS traffic detection, advanced threat protection, anomalous behavior analysis, DLP, threat intelligence, linking various network devices of the cloud, management and endpoint, ultimately providing users with an intelligent, proactive and secure "zero-dead-angle" comprehensive protection solution that integrates AI single-point defense, multiple intelligent synergies and cloud detection empowerment.

The Topsec NGF is shown in Fig. 11.14.

Topsec next-generation firewall system has built-in AI-driven integrated intelligent detection engine, which can not only handle traditional security services such as antivirus and intrusion prevention, but also detect DGA domain names, covert channels, malicious encrypted traffic and block its communication process, so as to effectively defend against a variety of advanced threat attacks that were difficult to detect in the past. For data leakage protection, Topsec NGFW is based on keyword data filtering and file filtering. It restores the encrypted traffic of common network application protocols through SSL decryption, and matches the recovered file content to block or release the encrypted data flow. It can effectively prevent malicious visitors from invading website databases and stealing business data or other sensitive information through SQL injection, webpage Trojan horse, and other attacks. Topsec has an independent zombie creep detection and defense engine with zombie

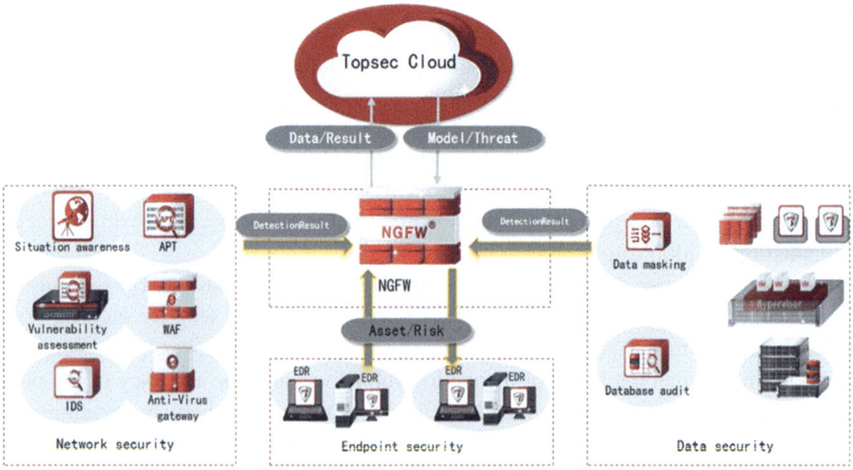

Fig. 11.14 Topsec NGF [33]

creep signature database and botnet signature database, which can not only detect and defend against new types of malicious code such as zombie viruses, Trojan horses, worms, but also detect attacks launched by external botnets in real time, alarm, and intercept botnet attacks according to the configured policies. At the same time, it has built in a variety of advanced threat attack defense solutions, including AI-based advanced threat detection, behavior analysis-based abnormal threat detection, and linkage-based unknown threat detection, enabling multi-directional in-depth detection of and defense against advanced threats.

It adopts self-developed Operating System NGTOS, that is, the Next Generation Topsec Operating System. At the same time, it adopts high-performance processor technology and architecture design and is compatible with many operating systems, which improves the security of the whole system to the greatest extent. It is designed and developed based on the NGTOS platform, a new generation of security system of Topsec, inheriting the advantages of high performance of NGTOS platform. The throughput capacity of a single hardware device is as high as 120 Gbps, hundreds of millions of concurrent connections, and millions of new processing capacity [34].

The multi-task mechanism of NGTOS adopts two mechanisms of Preemptive Priority Scheduling and Round-Robin Scheduling to ensure the reliable real-time performance of tasks. Priority preemption allows high-priority tasks to be executed first to ensure the timeliness of important tasks. The rotation scheduling mechanism can ensure that all tasks can be executed to prevent task hunger. The use of these mechanisms can make the same hardware configuration meet the stronger real-time requirements, leaving more room for application development.

NGTOS adopts a system designed and implemented for packet forwarding. Compared with the general operating system, NGTOS is more concise and contains only necessary functional modules, thus improving the stability and reliability of the system. At the same time, NGTOS adopts a variety of optimization technologies, such as packet preprocessing, zero-copy technology, and so on, which can carry out packet forwarding more efficiently.

Through cooperation with Intel, Topsec uses Intel data layer high-speed processing technology to quickly migrate the packet processing solution to the latest Intel architecture platform to obtain the best performance.

QAX Next Generation Firewall

QAX Next Generation Firewall is an innovative firewall product that can fully cope with traditional network attacks and advanced threats and can be widely used in the business network boundaries of government agencies, various enterprises and organizations to achieve network security domain isolation, refined access control, efficient threat protection and advanced threat detection functions. On the basis of the next generation firewall, the product integrates innovative security technologies such as threat intelligence, big data analysis and security visualization, and through intelligent collaboration with the network threat perception center, security management analysis center, terminal security management system, etc., to build a data-driven new generation threat defense platform for users at the network border [35].

Comprehensive protection against network attacks is achieved by leveraging new technologies such as threat intelligence, security big data, and collaborative interaction. These advancements greatly reduce traditional defense blind spots and effectively prevent mainstream threats like viruses, exploits, malware, and botnets from infiltrating the network perimeter, ensuring comprehensive and efficient business network protection. Timely insight into potential threats, based on accurate advanced threat discovery capabilities and the use of supporting visualization tools and platforms, significantly enhance the global visibility of the network and the perception of network threats, through real-time insight into the threat situation, defense of vulnerabilities and lost assets, and timely detection of latent abnormal risks and advanced threats in the network. Improve response and disposal efficiency, based on intelligent man-machine collaborative design and supporting management and analysis platform, continue to promote the user's safe operation landing, greatly reduce the operation and maintenance management cost of large-scale deployment users, avoid the risk of misconfiguration, and significantly improve the ability to respond and deal with quickly.

QAX Next Generation Firewall supports a variety of flexible deployment modes, including load balancing, VPN, virtual system, high availability, and other functions. At the same time, it can defend against traditional network attacks such as scanning, flooding, abnormal packets, etc., and supports various traditional firewall functions. In addition, the product also has high-performance threat prevention capabilities, with a deeply integrated threat prevention engine built in, which can provide high-performance protection against more than five million popular viruses, more than 5000 types of vulnerability exploitation attacks, and more than 1000 types of spyware behavior.

QAX Next Generation Firewall also has intelligent collaborative defense capabilities, supporting intelligent collaboration with cloud and terminal security systems to achieve advanced security functions such as virus cloud search and kill, real-time threat intelligence handling, emergency response policy push, high-risk terminal management and control. In addition, the product can also carry out visual association analysis, presenting multidimensional information such as application, user, content, threat, and geographical location in a graphical association, and realizing efficient security analysis through progressive data drilling.

In summary, QAX Next Generation Firewall has a variety of flexible deployment methods, can defend against traditional network attacks, and supports a variety of traditional firewall functions. In addition, it has capabilities such as high-performance threat protection, intelligent collaborative defense and visual association analysis to provide users with comprehensive security.

11.3 Intrinsic Security Characteristics of CoG-MIN

11.3.1 Endogenous Security

Endogenous security refers to the security functions or attributes achieved by leveraging the system's internal properties, such as the structures, mechanisms, operating scenarios, and regularities. Systems with endogenous security possess the ability to self-recover and self-protect when a network attack occurs. Traditional defense strategies are more about passively responding to attacks on the system, while endogenous security is about proactively identifying and solving potential security problems.

The key features and concepts of endogenous security include active defense, adaptive defense, dynamic response, and the principle of least privilege. Active defense refers to the use of active defense methods such as machine learning and behavioral analysis, rather than relying on traditional static security methods. Adaptive defense refers to the use of real-time security monitoring records to automatically optimize its own security rules. Dynamic response refers to the dynamic triggering of corresponding response measures when system problems are detected, including isolating unsafe and adjusting security policies to minimize negative impacts. The principle of least privilege refers to ensuring that each user has only the minimum permissions required to perform their tasks, avoiding security risks caused by abuse of permissions.

Additionally, during the research in endogenous security, Mimic Defense (MD) [36] aims to mitigate the problem of generalized uncertainty disturbances in cyberspace through dynamic heterogeneous redundancy construction and mimic camouflage mechanisms. Mimic defense seeks to endow information systems with inherent security capabilities through architectural design. Mimic defense involves the dynamic construction of diverse mimic environments for networks, platforms, software, data, etc., with the purpose of providing dynamism, non-determinism, heterogeneity, and non-persistence in the target environment. By utilizing dynamic heterogeneous redundant architectures and mimic camouflage mechanisms, mimic defense transforms random or non-random disturbances into probabilistically controllable reliability events.

Dynamic Heterogeneous Redundancy (DHR) [37] is the core of mimic defense. The functionality of a computer system can be summarized as "input–process–output (IPO)," which corresponds to the IPO paradigm in structured design. In the "processing" stage, the dynamic heterogeneous redundancy structure utilizes a set of heterogeneous execution units to process the input. The input is replicated into n copies by an input agent and distributed to n heterogeneous execution units in the execution unit set for processing. The processing results are collected by a voter to make a decision and obtain a unique and relatively correct output. Heterogeneous elements form heterogeneous components, and an online execution unit set is composed of selected heterogeneous components using a dynamic selection algorithm.

Based on runtime feedback information, the dynamic selection algorithm generates a new execution unit set to replace the current one.

The foundation of the dynamic heterogeneous redundancy structure lies in heterogeneity. The execution units should strive to be heterogeneous in various attributes or characteristics to avoid the simultaneous occurrence of the same vulnerabilities. On the contrary, when the attack targets non-heterogeneous attributes, the dynamic heterogeneous redundancy structure loses its protective capability. The more heterogeneous levels, or the more heterogeneous attributes of the execution units, the more vulnerabilities can be defended against, and the higher the difficulty of attacks. Heterogeneity can be achieved based on diversity, such as the diversity of applications, operating systems, and programming languages, all of which can contribute to heterogeneity. However, diversity also faces the challenge of "homogeneity," where superficially different implementations are actually different versions or variations based on the same code framework. Therefore, relying solely on the existing diversity of products for heterogeneity is not ideal. On the one hand, achieving heterogeneity requires both research in heterogeneous technologies and enhancing heterogeneity from multiple perspectives. Dynamics, as a temporal dimension gain of heterogeneity, can compensate for the insufficient heterogeneity caused by "homogeneity" issues.

The dynamic selection algorithm imbues the dynamic heterogeneous redundancy structure with dynamism. If the current execution unit set is breached by an attack, the dynamic selection algorithm regenerates a new execution unit set to replace the current one after receiving feedback from the system. This change alters the environment on which the attack relies, making it difficult to maintain or reproduce the same attack. On the other hand, the presence of dynamism causes the system to exhibit different characteristics at different time intervals, presenting uncertainty to the attackers, and further increasing the difficulty of the attacks. Redundancy refers to multiple execution units processing the same request, comparing the processing results of different execution units, and obtaining a relatively correct response through voting, which is then returned to the user. The coordination between redundancy and heterogeneity changes the single environment on which an attack depends, increases the difficulty of attacks, and enhances the system security. In the process of model specification, there should be at least two execution units within the execution unit set to maintain the characteristics of heterogeneous redundancy. When the processing results of the two execution units are inconsistent, it is impossible to determine the relatively correct result.

By incorporating the concept of mimic defense, CoG-MIN is endowed with endogenous security capabilities, which further enhances the security of the network architecture and strengthens the reliability and trustworthiness of the overall system. This facilitates the establishment of a more trustworthy and reliable network security environment.

Based on the idea of mimic defense, the MIN research group designs the Weighted Network Centrality Measure (WNCM) algorithm [38], which ranks network devices based on their centrality and importance and protects a subset of devices that are deemed most important and influential. The Network Centrality

Measure (NCM) is a commonly used centrality-based algorithm in the fields of graph theory and network analysis to identify the roles of specific nodes and their impact on the network. This approach aims to enhance the efficiency of network defense by selectively focusing on nodes based on user security requirements, considering the limited system resources.

Taking the network topology shown in Fig. 11.15 as an example, seven devices in the internal network require prioritization for protection. These devices include two border routers, three servers providing internal network forwarding services, and two servers providing storage functions. The WNCM algorithm compares and selects 2–3 network devices for deploying a specialized protection mechanism. The nodes identified by the WNCM algorithm as requiring enhanced protection are deployed with mimic defense mechanisms.

At the application layer of CoG-MIN, core devices such as firewalls, critical routers, and servers can be implemented using a mimic architecture. For example, the architecture of the Mimic Distributed File Storage System [39] is shown in Fig. 11.16.

The Mimic Distributed File Storage System [39, 40] achieves heterogeneity by employing various Erasure Codes (ECs) for encoding file data. As a fault-tolerant redundancy technology, erasure codes are widely used in distributed storage systems due to its high performance, high utilization, and strong fault tolerance capabilities. The (k,n) erasure code divides the original data into k data blocks, and encodes them into n $(n > k)$ data blocks, which are then stored in multiple distributed nodes. The (k,n) characteristic ensures that any subset of k' $(k' \geq k)$encoded slices can be used to recover the original complete data. Various erasure codes are embedded in the storage system, such as Binary Reed-Solomon (BRS) codes [41], Minimum Bandwidth Regenerating (MBR) codes, Minimum Storage Regenerating (MSR) codes, and so on. Since the parameters of each encoding method are different, the encoded blocks obtained from the same data block can have significant

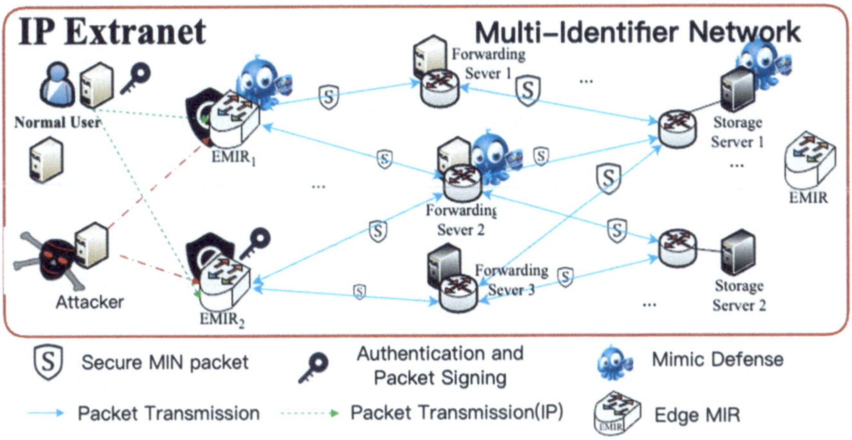

Fig. 11.15 The dynamic protection for CoG-MIN based on mimic defense [38]

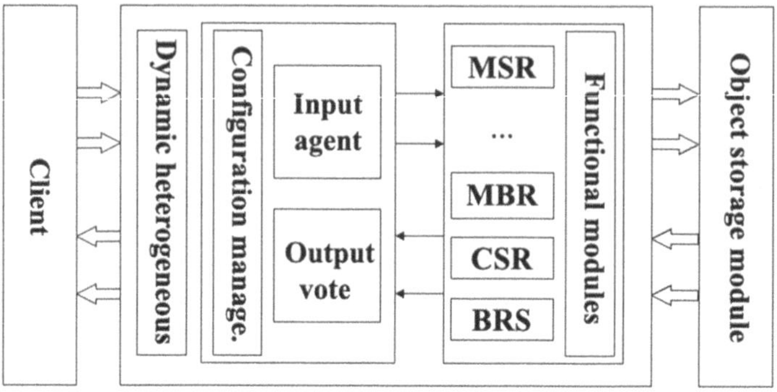

Fig. 11.16 Mimic Distributed File Storage System [39]

differences in size and quantity. This design ensures the heterogeneity between execution units and the dynamic nature of the network.

11.3.2 Access Authentication

In CoG-MIN, each user or network device are required to register true identity information in MIS and obtain a unique identity before connecting to the network [38]. Subsequently, each packet sent by the user or network device needs to be signed with the corresponding private key for forwarding. The node receiving the packet will authenticate the packet. This approach can establish a strong bond between users and content. If there are any issues with the published or requested content, it can be identified by the specific user. This can ensure effective management and control over user actions and resources. Participants involved in the overall identity registration and packet forwarding process include MIN clients, MIS, and MIRs. An example of the above access process is shown in Fig. 11.17.

The user identity registration process is based on asymmetric cryptography. First, the MIN client generates a public key and private key locally for the user. Then, the client submits the public key and the identity information signed with the private key to any node in MIS. When a node receives the request sent by the client, it first checks the format of the request. Then, it searches the user information in the local database and performs simple verification on certain contents, such as the legitimacy of username, whether there is duplication of user information, the validity of the user's public and private keys, etc. If any of the above steps fails, an error message is returned to the user. If all the verifications are successful, a transaction will be generated by the accounting node of the MIS consortium blockchain and sent to all blockchain nodes. When the voting nodes in the blockchain receive a pre-block, they will vote on whether to allow the pre-block to become an official block. The leader node collects the voting results, performs the vote counting, and generates a proof of voting. Identity authentication is reflected in the communication

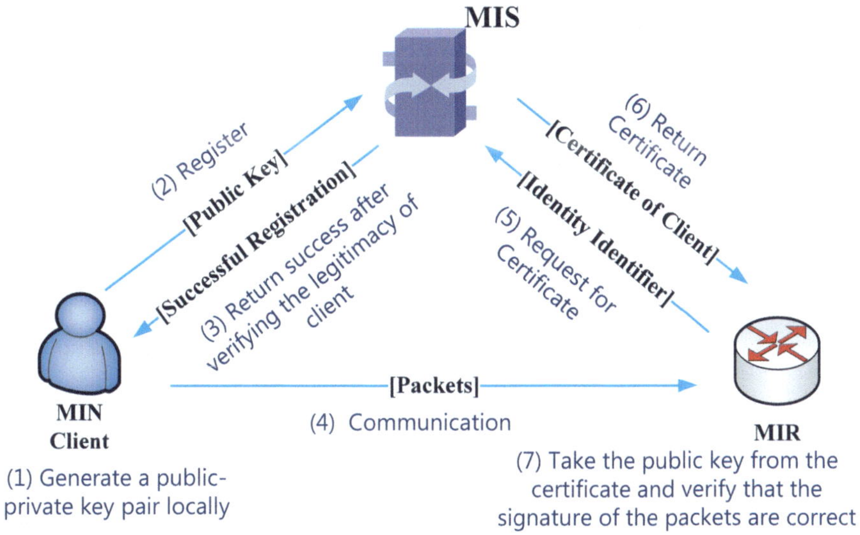

Fig. 11.17 User access process

process. After the registration is completed, users need to sign each packet they publish with their private key, writing it into the signature field of the MIN packet. MIRs regularly maintain the user information table obtained from the MIS. Upon receiving a packet, the router extracts the corresponding user's signature information, and performs identity authentication using the public key information obtained from MIS. The packet format supports embedded digital signatures to ensure the integrity and traceability, as detailed in Chap. 2.

11.3.3 Packet Encapsulation

Considering the completeness of the TCP/IP ecosystem, CoG-MIN is compatible with IP-based networks. In the current IP-based network environment, the most basic application scenario for CoG-MIN is the security private network. In general, MIN serves as a security isolation zone to separate the traditional IP-based external network and the high-security internal network.

On the one hand, the MIN network is centered on the identity identifier. All users entering the MIN network need to undergo identity authentication. Additionally, the packets users send within the MIN network need to be signed, ensuring the reliability and traceability of information.

On the other hand, MIN incorporates multiple identifiers and supports both push-based and pull-based routing and forwarding mechanisms. It can encapsulate IP packets according to user requirements, enabling packet forwarding that is not based on the IP address. This renders attack methods such as port scanning, which

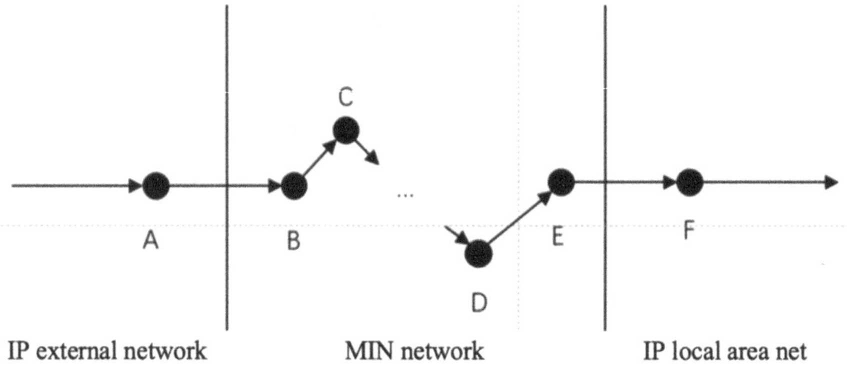

Fig. 11.18 Packet transmission process

rely on the IP system, ineffective. The packet transmission process is shown in Fig. 11.18.

Most users and services still rely on IP networks. The user issues a service request on the IP public network, and the packet travels through the network toward the IP internal network. First, the request packet arrives at the edge MIR (EMIR) (B-point), where identity authentication, packet authentication, and IP packet encapsulation are implemented. The internal MIN network filters and examines the received packets, and forward legitimate packets until they reach the EMIR endpoint (E-point). The E-point decapsulates the packet and forward it into the IP local area network. The process is reversed for outbound traffic.

In this process, CoG-MIN defines packet formats and designs forwarding algorithms based on multiple network identifiers to achieve the coexistence of various types of packets, ensuring network availability. Based on the identity authentication and packet signature mechanism, each packet needs to be authenticated before it can be accessed into the network. The packet encapsulation and decapsulation technologies are used to encapsulate IP packets in MIN network packets. A detailed description is given in Chap. 2.

11.4 Security Situation Awareness System

As the scale and complexity of networks continue to grow, network attack techniques are constantly evolving, and new attack tools are emerging in large numbers. In recent years, various security incidents have been occurring frequently. In enterprises, government institutions, and financial organizations, security devices such as firewalls, Web Application Firewall (WAF), Intrusion Detection System (IDS), and other security devices are independently deployed. The handling of security events is based on the capabilities of these individual devices. However, many security attacks or penetrations nowadays are combinations of normal access behaviors, such as Challenge Collapsar (CC) and Advanced Persistent Threat (APT) attacks. These threats cannot be effectively prevented or identified by relying on a single system alone. It requires the correlation and analysis of multiple systems to achieve unified protection.

Therefore, the focus of network security professionals has shifted from solving individual security issues to studying the overall security state of the network and its changing trends. By utilizing the data generated by all security devices and systems, a security situation awareness platform obtains, understands, evaluates, and predicts the future development trends of various factors that affect network security. This platform provides a quantitative analysis of network security and enables precise measurement of network security. It can achieve early security warnings, early security event handling, security event tracking, and comprehensive management of security situation awareness.

Based on this, CoG-MIN research team has designed a security situation awareness system based on the CoG-MIN architecture. The system collects network traffic data and security device log information across the entire network and utilizes a big data security analysis platform for processing and analysis. By relying on the situation awareness model, it detects threat alerts and provides real-time presentation of the complete network attack situation to users, thus providing a basis for decision-making in security event handling [42].

11.4.1 Overview of System Architecture

The overall architecture of the security situation awareness system is shown in Fig. 11.19.

The security situation awareness system adopts Endsley's security awareness model, which divides situation awareness into three levels: perception, comprehension, and projection. Perception includes information on the status, attributes, and dynamics of important elements in the network environment, as well as the process of classifying and sorting them. Comprehension is the integration and interpretation of information on these important elements, not just the judgment of a single analysis object. The analysis also includes the integration and sorting of multiple related objects. At the same time, comprehension is constantly updated and evolved as the situation changes, and new information is constantly integrated to form new comprehension. Based on comprehending the status and dynamics of the situation elements, the system projects the upcoming status and dynamics of each element in the situation [43].

The security situation awareness system has three main functions as follows:

- **Traffic Detection Function:** The system performs parallel analysis of all traffic through the MIN border router.
- **Host Detection Function:** The system collects and alerts on abnormal behavior or status on the server.

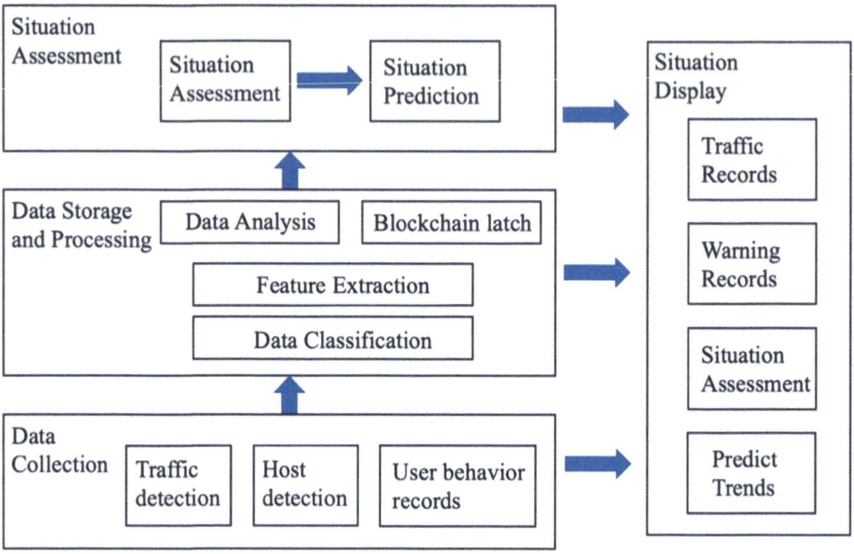

Fig. 11.19 The overall architecture of the security situation awareness system

- **User Behavior Analysis Function:** The system records the access behavior of intranet users, locks and stores it in the blockchain, and then conducts offline user behavior analysis.

The background of the framework is mainly divided into three levels as follows:

- **Real-Time Data Collection Layer:** This layer consists of three sub-modules. The traffic detection module collects real-time network traffic data, including IP traffic and MIN traffic. The host detection module monitors host security and collects data on abnormal host behavior. The user behavior recording module automatically records user behavior and securely stores it in the blockchain. These sub-modules collect real-time data and pass it to the upper layer for analysis.
- **Data Storage and Processing Layer:** This layer analyzes, categorizes, extracts, and stores the previously collected data, such as quintuple extraction of IP traffic and TLV analysis of MIN traffic. It utilizes artificial intelligence algorithms to detect anomalies in real-time and generate reports on abnormal traffic or events.
- **Situation Assessment and Prediction Layer:** This layer integrates all types of abnormal events from the alarm log, assesses the system's security in real-time, predicts future system trends, and provides key security information to professional experts. Security operation and maintenance personnel use this information for further policy control and system maintenance.

11.4.2 *Traffic Collection*

The flowchart of traffic detection is shown in Fig. 11.20.

In Fig. 11.20, the first route is a real-time analysis of IP traffic, while the second route is real-time analysis of MIN traffic.

IP Traffic

Real-time performance and minimal packet loss rate are crucial factors in traffic collection. Therefore, utilizing Netflow tools undoubtedly presents an excellent choice in achieving these objectives. Netflow utilizes seven attributes of IP packets, including source IP address, destination IP address, source port number, destination port number, type of third layer protocol, type of service (ToS) field, and logical port for network device input/output, to quickly distinguish various types of business data flows transmitted in the network.

The security situation awareness system uses the Netflow tool Pmacct for real-time traffic collection. Pmacct is a network monitoring library based on libpcap that allows users to export, measure, classify, and summarize traffic for IPv4 and IPv6. Pmacct supports fully customized historical data crashes, stream sampling, filtering and labeling, recovery operations, and triggers. Pmacct allows the system to implement behaviors such as classification, aggregation, replication, and export of network traffic data. It also supports exporting to relational databases, NoSQL databases, RabbitMQ, Kafka, memory tables, files, and more.

Figure 11.21 shows the partial traffic feature information filtered by Pmacct.

It can be seen that Pmacct not only captures traffic in real time but also performs preliminary feature extraction. It provides great convenience for subsequent data processing and analysis.

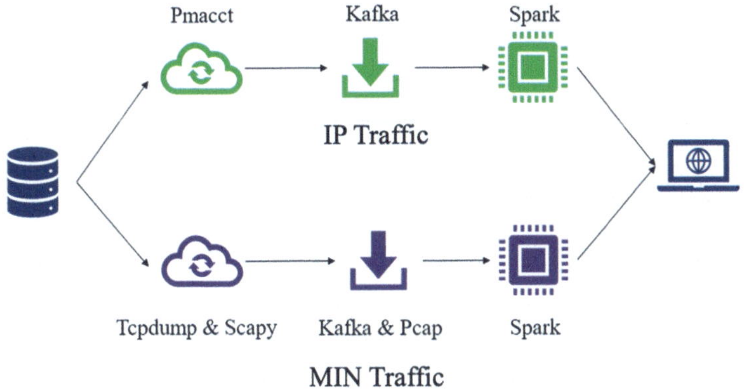

Fig. 11.20 Schematic diagram of the traffic detection of the security situation awareness system

id	client_mac	ip_src	ip_dst	port_src	port_dst	time_start	time_end	len	pkt_list
1	3c:06:30:4c:21:bd	10.113.36.86	8.8.8.8	54772	443	1667208130	1667208130	0	[{"d": 1, "l": 0, "f": "S", "t": 0}]
2	3c:06:30:4c:21:bd	10.113.36.86	8.8.8.8	54773	443	1667208131	1667208131	0	[{"d": 1, "l": 0, "f": "S", "t": 0}]
3	3c:06:30:4c:21:bd	10.113.36.86	221.181.99.29	54866	443	1667208146	1667208162	4260	[{"d": 1, "l": 0, "f": "S", "t": 0},
4	3c:06:30:4c:21:bd	10.113.36.86	8.8.8.8	54772	443	1667208147	1667208147	0	[{"d": 1, "l": 0, "f": "S", "t": 0}]
5	3c:06:30:4c:21:bd	10.113.36.86	8.8.8.8	54773	443	1667208147	1667208147	0	[{"d": 1, "l": 0, "f": "S", "t": 0}]
6	3c:06:30:4c:21:bd	10.113.36.86	221.181.99.44	54934	443	1667208172	1667208187	4260	[{"d": 1, "l": 0, "f": "S", "t": 0},
7	3c:06:30:4c:21:bd	10.113.36.86	8.8.4.4	54973	443	1667208187	1667208187	0	[{"d": 1, "l": 0, "f": "S", "t": 0}]
8	3c:06:30:4c:21:bd	10.113.36.86	8.8.4.4	54974	443	1667208187	1667208187	0	[{"d": 1, "l": 0, "f": "S", "t": 0}]
9	3c:06:30:4c:21:bd	10.113.36.86	8.8.4.4	54973	443	1667208188	1667208188	0	[{"d": 1, "l": 0, "f": "S", "t": 0}]
10	3c:06:30:4c:21:bd	10.113.36.86	8.8.4.4	54974	443	1667208188	1667208188	0	[{"d": 1, "l": 0, "f": "S", "t": 0}]
11	3c:06:30:4c:21:bd	10.113.36.86	8.8.4.4	54973	443	1667208189	1667208189	0	[{"d": 1, "l": 0, "f": "S", "t": 0}]
12	3c:06:30:4c:21:bd	10.113.36.86	8.8.4.4	54974	443	1667208189	1667208189	0	[{"d": 1, "l": 0, "f": "S", "t": 0}]
13	3c:06:30:4c:21:bd	10.113.36.86	8.8.4.4	54973	443	1667208190	1667208190	0	[{"d": 1, "l": 0, "f": "S", "t": 0}]
14	3c:06:30:4c:21:bd	10.113.36.86	8.8.4.4	54974	443	1667208190	1667208190	0	[{"d": 1, "l": 0, "f": "S", "t": 0}]
15	3c:06:30:4c:21:bd	10.113.36.86	8.8.4.4	54973	443	1667208191	1667208191	0	[{"d": 1, "l": 0, "f": "S", "t": 0}]
16	3c:06:30:4c:21:bd	10.113.36.86	8.8.4.4	54974	443	1667208191	1667208191	0	[{"d": 1, "l": 0, "f": "S", "t": 0}]
17	3c:06:30:4c:21:bd	10.113.36.86	8.8.4.4	54973	443	1667208192	1667208192	0	[{"d": 1, "l": 0, "f": "S", "t": 0}]
18	3c:06:30:4c:21:bd	10.113.36.86	8.8.4.4	54974	443	1667208192	1667208192	0	[{"d": 1, "l": 0, "f": "S", "t": 0}]
19	3c:06:30:4c:21:bd	10.113.36.86	219.223.222.230	55000	443	1667208197	1667208197	0	[{"d": 1, "l": 0, "f": "S", "t": 0}]

Fig. 11.21 Database storage example

MIN Traffic

For the collection of MIN traffic, the security situation awareness system uses tcpdump based on libpcap for crawling and then uses the Scapy library for preliminary packet analysis and feature extraction. Scapy is a very powerful third-party library that relies on libpcap and can be used for network sniffing. It implements a large number of protocols internally, such as DNS, ARP, IP, TCP, and UDP. It can forge or decode a large number of network protocol data packets and can send, capture, and match request and response packets. Since MIN traffic needs to be saved as offline pcap traffic packets for subsequent analysis, the system mainly uses the Scapy library for sniffing MIN network traffic.

Due to the Type–Length–Value (TLV) encoding of the MIN packet, the system needs to perform corresponding TLV decoding on it.

An example of TLV encoding is shown in Fig. 11.22.

Correspondingly, referring to this instruction document, the values of the required key fields are extracted and passed to the next layer of modules for processing.

Figure 11.23 shows the logical structure of host detection system.

11.4.3 Host Detection

The Host-Based Intrusion Detection System (HIDS) deployed within the MIN network focuses on the host system itself and local users as the primary targets for detection. It operates in a client/server mode, requiring the installation of an agent program (agent) on each protected end system (host). The HIDS leverages various data sources such as audit data, system logs, application logs from the host to

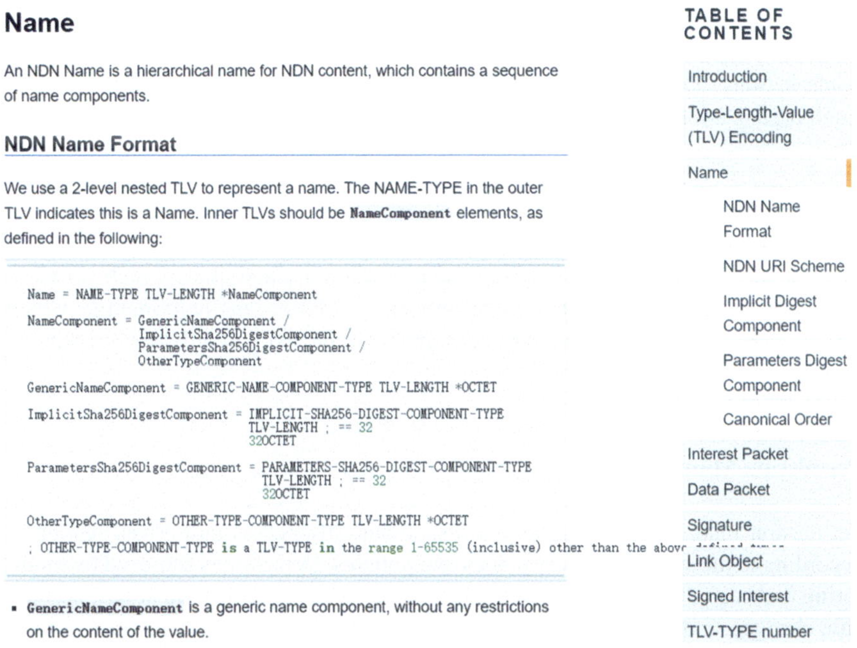

Name

An NDN Name is a hierarchical name for NDN content, which contains a sequence of name components.

NDN Name Format

We use a 2-level nested TLV to represent a name. The NAME-TYPE in the outer TLV indicates this is a Name. Inner TLVs should be **NameComponent** elements, as defined in the following:

```
Name = NAME-TYPE TLV-LENGTH *NameComponent

NameComponent = GenericNameComponent /
                ImplicitSha256DigestComponent /
                ParametersSha256DigestComponent /
                OtherTypeComponent

GenericNameComponent = GENERIC-NAME-COMPONENT-TYPE TLV-LENGTH *OCTET

ImplicitSha256DigestComponent = IMPLICIT-SHA256-DIGEST-COMPONENT-TYPE
                                TLV-LENGTH ; == 32
                                32OCTET

ParametersSha256DigestComponent = PARAMETERS-SHA256-DIGEST-COMPONENT-TYPE
                                  TLV-LENGTH ; == 32
                                  32OCTET

OtherTypeComponent = OTHER-TYPE-COMPONENT-TYPE TLV-LENGTH *OCTET

; OTHER-TYPE-COMPONENT-TYPE is a TLV-TYPE in the range 1-65535 (inclusive) other than the above defined types
```

- **GenericNameComponent** is a generic name component, without any restrictions on the content of the value.

TABLE OF CONTENTS

Fig. 11.22 An example of TLV encoding in NDN name format [44]

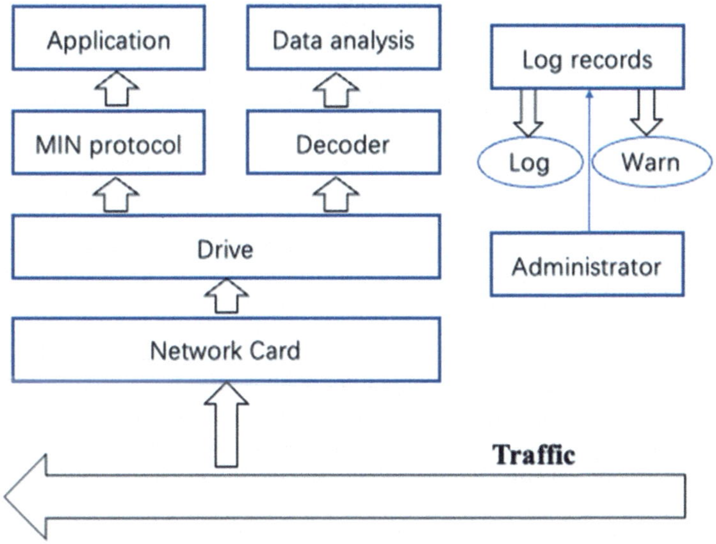

Fig. 11.23 Logical structure diagram of host detection system

analyze and evaluate real-time connections within the host network and host files. By identifying suspicious events, the system can promptly respond and take appropriate actions. This mode of operation is cost-effective for both enterprises and small organizations. The main logical structure of the system is as follows.

Port Monitoring

Port monitoring involves monitoring for port scanning activities, which refers to scanning individual or specified ports one by one. Port scans help identify which services are available on a computer and can be exploited based on known vulnerabilities.

Permission Management

Permission management ensures that users can only access authorized resources according to the system's security rules and policies. Detection is achieved by monitoring and recording abnormal activities such as unusual user login states, permission changes, and modifications or deletions of restricted-access directories or files. Relevant logs include:

- /var/log/auth.log: Login authentication log.
- /var/log/btmp: Records all failed boot information.
- /var/log/faillog: Contains user login failure information, including erroneous login attempts.
- /var/log/lastlog: Records recent information for all users. It is not an ASCII file and requires the "lastlog" command to view its contents.
- /var/log/wtmp: Contains login information, which can be used to track who is logging into the system and who is accessing this file or information.

System Information

The main system information detected includes the addresses of each host, CPU usage, memory usage, and more. A set of "normal" values for system conditions is established, which can be defined manually or determined through system observation and statistical analysis. By comparing the runtime values with the defined "normal" conditions, signs of attacks can be detected. Relevant logs include:

- /var/log/syslog: System log.
- /var/log/messages: Records common system and service error messages in Linux operating systems.
- /var/log/secure: Linux system security log, recording user and group corruption, as well as user login authentication information.

Process Monitoring

Various applications, including different service programs, run on host systems. Each running program consists of one or more processes, which exist within specific system environments, have limited access to system resources and data files, and communicate with specific processes.

The alert information generated by the data analysis engine is organized into the Alarm Log in the format shown in Fig. 11.24.

Figure 11.25 provides an example of an Alarm Log that is locally generated on the server.

The fields in the Alarm Log are stored in a MariaDB database and provided to the frontend interface for display.

11.4.4 Functional Testing

System Registration and Login

The administrator installs the client installation program of the security situation awareness system, which is provided by the technical personnel, and waits the successful completion of the installation process. After successful installation, the program generates a shortcut icon on the computer desktop and automatically starts. Enter the registration and login page of the security situation awareness system (as shown in Fig. 11.26).

Fig. 11.24 The format of an Alarm Log

```
** Alert xxxxxxxxx
Event location    Event Time
User: Time Event
Event Source: User: Computer: Event Description
Secure ID:
Description :
```

Fig. 11.25 An example of an Alarm Log

```
**Alert
2020 Apr 26 03:49:36 ubuntu->/var/log/auth.log
Rule: 10100 (level 4) -> "First time user logged in."
Src IP: 27.17.223.218
User: minuser
Apr 26 03:49:36
```

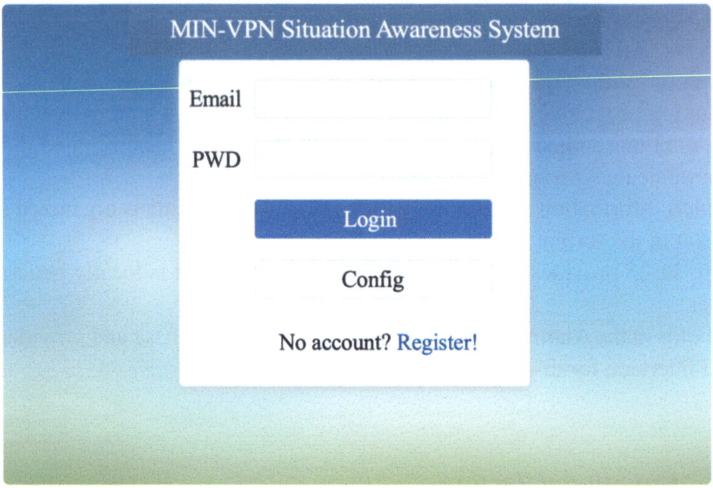

Fig. 11.26 Login page

Click register to enter the registration page (as shown in Fig. 11.27), and enter relevant information to register.

Select the server configuration, click the server configuration button, and configure the corresponding server information (as shown in Fig. 11.28).

After successful registration according to the prompt, the dialog box will pop up. Enter the registered account and password to enter the main page of the security situation awareness system (as shown in Fig. 11.29).

Traffic Detection

Click on "Situation Display" to enter the "Comprehensive Situation Awareness" large screen information page (as shown in Fig. 11.30).

The modules on the situation page include a security map of the entire network and threat rating.

The security map of the entire network dynamically displays the threats to protected networks in a regional dimension. By concretizing the attack source and target, users can intuitively understand the security status of assets. The dots in Fig. 11.31 represent a server equipped with a security situation awareness system. The alarm sources of each server are represented on the map through attack lines and are displayed in a scrolling display box below. This information encompasses attack source details, attack target information, attack types, timestamps, and more.

The right column in Fig. 11.31 displays the threat scoring module, which reflects the overall security status of the network. The information presented in the figure mainly includes host security threat value and network security threat value. A higher value indicates a higher threat.

Click on the "Situation Threat Value Curve" to view the network and host security situation value curves. The horizontal axis of the security threat value curve

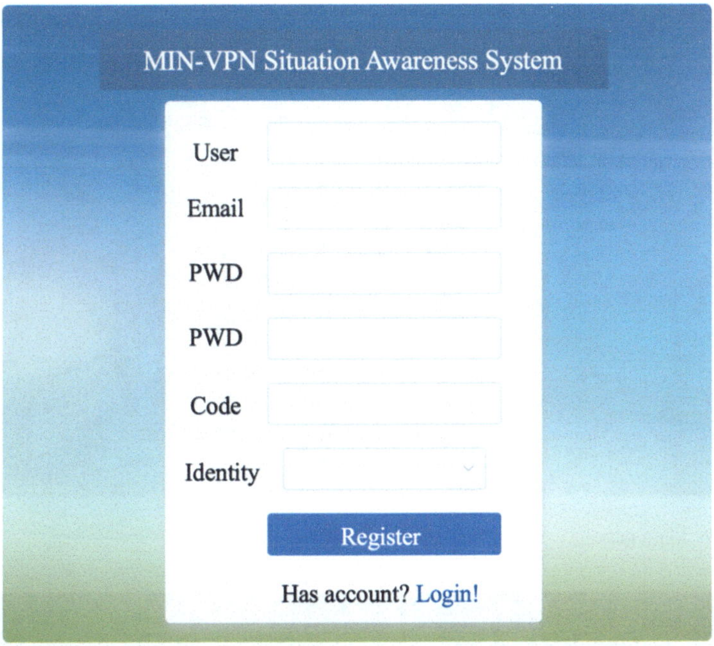

Fig. 11.27 Registration page

Fig. 11.28 Configuration page

represents time, while the vertical axis represents the security threat value. A higher threat value indicates a higher level of threat received. Place the mouse arrow at a certain point in time to see the security threat value at that time (as shown in Fig. 11.31).

The network security threat value is automatically updated every 3 s, and the host security threat value is automatically updated every 3 min.

After clicking on "firewall," three modules will be displayed: network security situation threat awareness, attack source statistics, and attack situation display and processing.

Network security situation threat awareness displays real-time network security situational threat situations. A higher threat value indicates a greater level of threat being encountered. Attack source statistics is a statistical analysis of the attack

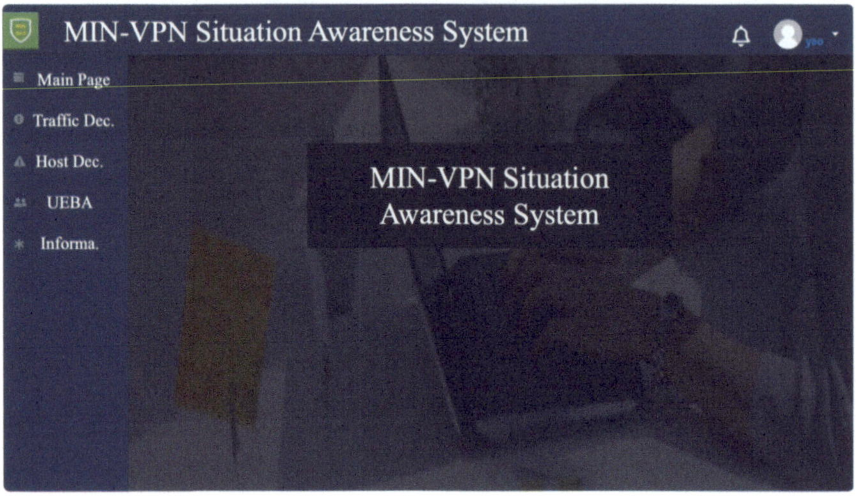

Fig. 11.29 Main page

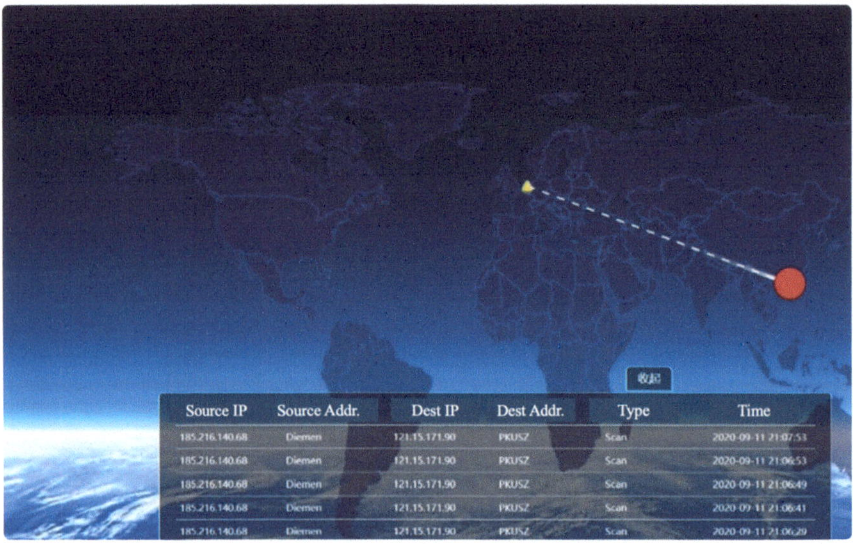

Fig. 11.30 Situation page

source and its related information, including the IP address of the attack source and the number of attacks (as shown in Fig. 11.32).

The attack situation displays and processing module presents the latest 100 network attack warnings perceived in the following list. This includes pertinent details such as attack source information, attack target information, attack type, timestamps, and more. Administrators have the capability to delete a certain alert based on the actual situation if it is determined to be a false alarm. Conversely, if it is confirmed to be a hacker attack, the corresponding attack source can be blacklisted for further preventive measures (as shown in Fig. 11.33).

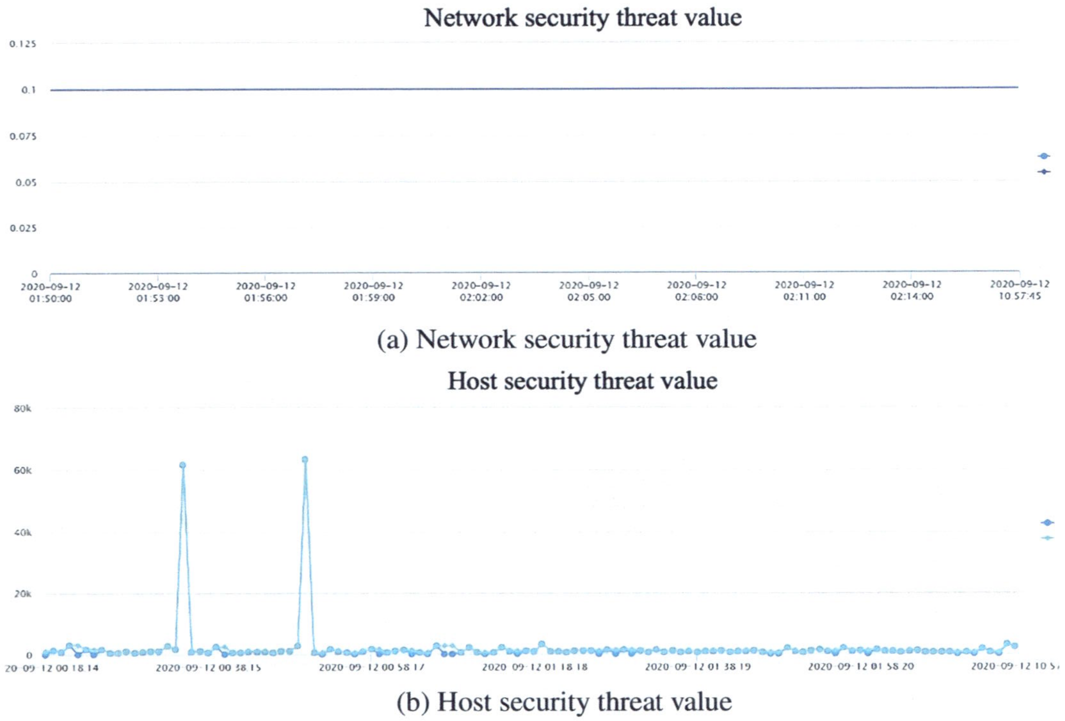

Fig. 11.31 Situation threat value page. **(a)** Network security threat value. **(b)** Host security threat value

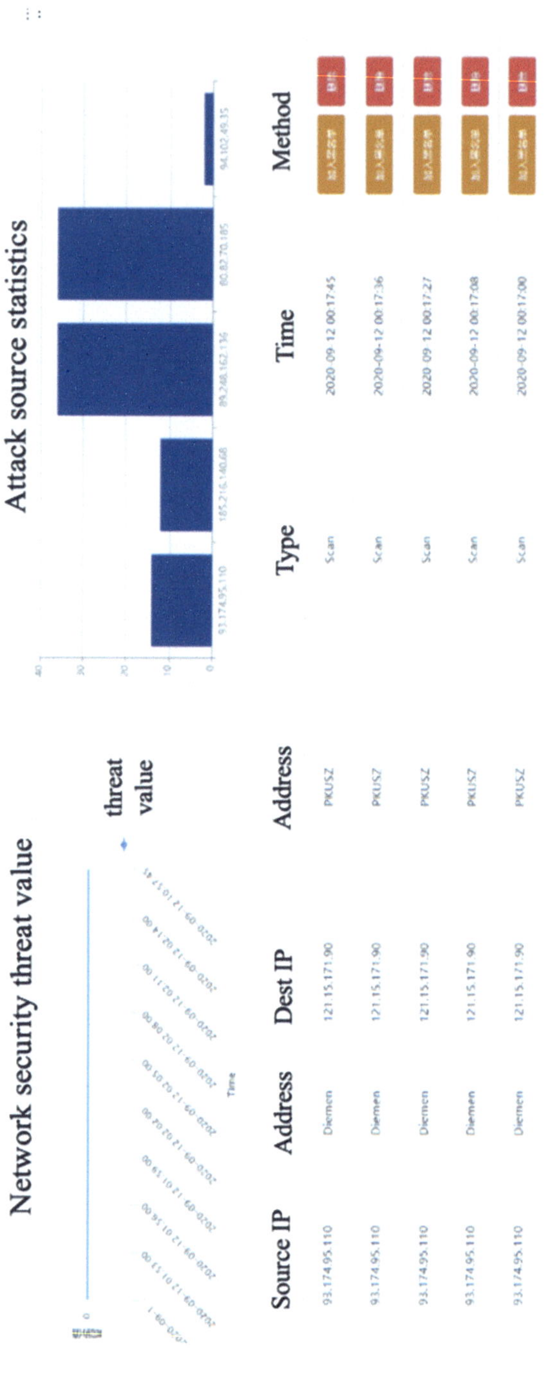

Fig. 11.32 Situation threat display page

Source IP
Address
Dest IP
Address
Type
Time
Method
93.174.95.110
Diemen
121.15.171.90
PKUSZ
Scan
2020-09-12 00:17:45
93.174.95.110
Diemen
121.15.171.90
PKUSZ
Scan
2020-09-12 00:17:36
93.174.95.110
Diemen
121.15.171.90
PKUSZ
Scan
2020-09-12 00:17:27
93.174.95.110
Diemen
121.15.171.90
PKUSZ
Scan
2020-09-12 00:17:08
93.174.95.110
Diemen
121.15.171.90
PKUSZ
Scan
2020-09-12 00:17:00

Fig. 11.33 Blacklist page

After clicking on “Firewall Rule Configuration,” two modules will be displayed: “Add inbound direction rules” and “Add outbound direction rules.” This module provides administrators with a convenient interface to efficiently view, add, and delete firewall rules for hosts on the front end. The page displays the firewall rules that have been added so far. Click the “Delete” button to delete the rule, and click “Add rules” to manually add a custom firewall rule just like the picture as shown in Fig. 11.34).

Click on “Threat Event” to view the malicious IP attempting to establish a connection with the host, the geographical location of the IP, and the time of the attempt to connect. Click on this item to further view the “black history” of the IP (as shown in Fig. 11.35).

Click on “Threat Warning” to view the suspected malicious IP of the host, the geographical location of the IP, and the time of attempting to connect. When new data is available in the “Threat Warning” section, the small bell in the top bar will display a red numerical prompt. This serves as a reminder for the administrator to promptly review the relevant information. If necessary, it is advisable to check the system log on the host to verify whether the malicious IP has penetrated the host (as shown in Fig. 11.36).

Host Detection

After clicking on the “Warning List” under the host detection column, 1000 latest security warning records recorded by the security situation awareness system will be displayed. Administrators can view details and delete a record (as shown in Fig. 11.37).

When the backend process of the security situation awareness system on port 9002 is killed: (Fig. 11.38 shows the backend process).

The security situation awareness system will detect a change in port status and issue a warning: (as shown in Fig. 11.39).

Click on the details to view the full log: (as shown in Fig. 11.40).

Add inbound and outbound direction rules
Protocol
Source
Source IP
Dest IP
Method
Method
1 TCP 219.223.199.162 DROP
2 TCP 81.68.88.208 DROP
3 TCP 125.71.212.99 DROP
Add rules

Fig. 11.34 Firewall rule configuration page

71.6.135.131	San Diego	2021-03-05 17:45:42
192.241.220.26	Palo Alto	2021-03-05 17:45:42
188.124.36.161	Dzerzhinsky	2021-03-05 17:45:41
71.6.135.131	San Diego	2021-03-05 17:45:40
74.120.14.31	Ann Arbor	2021-03-05 17:45:36
188.124.36.161	Dzerzhinsky	2021-03-05 17:45:38
89.248.165.44	Diemen	2021-03-05 17:45:35
89.248.165.44	Diemen	2021-03-05 17:45:34
74.120.14.31	Ann Arbor	2021-03-05 17:45:33
162.142.125.82	Ann Arbor	2021-03-05 17:45:29

Fig. 11.35 Threat event page

Host Asset Details

The security situation awareness system provides the capability to query host asset details, including host information and database information. The host information records the host asset ID, asset type, label information, IP address (public or private), MAC address, region, operating system, CPU, memory size, kernel version, hard disk space usage, and more. On the other hand, the database information records the space occupied by the database, the databases contained (collections), the ports used, database user information, user permission information, and other pertinent data.

All collected data information is stored in the MongoDB database, specifically in the Assets collection under the Situation_Awareness database.

Warning

195.54.160.85	Saint Petersburg	2021-03-18 22:11:20
5.252.230.56	Unknow	2021-03-18 22:06:43
58.60.1.46	Shenzhen	2021-03-18 21:44:19
58.60.1.46	Shenzhen	2021-03-18 21:29:55
200.195.136.12	Unknow	2021-03-18 16:10:58
106.53.31.34	Beijing	2021-03-18 02:40:54
106.53.31.34	Beijing	2021-03-18 02:40:54
114.67.108.60	Beijing	2021-03-17 01:59:38
101.32.23.147	Beijing	2021-03-16 17:23:54
106.54.92.214	Beijing	2021-03-08 16:18:42

Fig. 11.36 Warning page

To directly search for host information in the database, the following commands can be used:

```
db.Assets.find ({"asset_type": "server"})
```

Obtain the host information in the database as shown in Fig. 11.41.

```
db.Assets.find({"asset_type":"database"})
```

Obtain the database information in the database as shown in Fig. 11.42.

The homepage of the Asset Center is displayed as shown in Fig. 11.43.

Click on the database assets to expand the details and view the specific information of the database: (as shown in Fig. 11.44).

Click on the host assets to expand the details and view the specific information of the host: (as shown in Fig. 11.45).

Asset updates can be performed by navigating to the SA_server/dist/AssetInfo directory and executing the respective AssetInfo program. "./AssetInfo -h" can be used to query how the program is used: (as shown in Fig. 11.46).

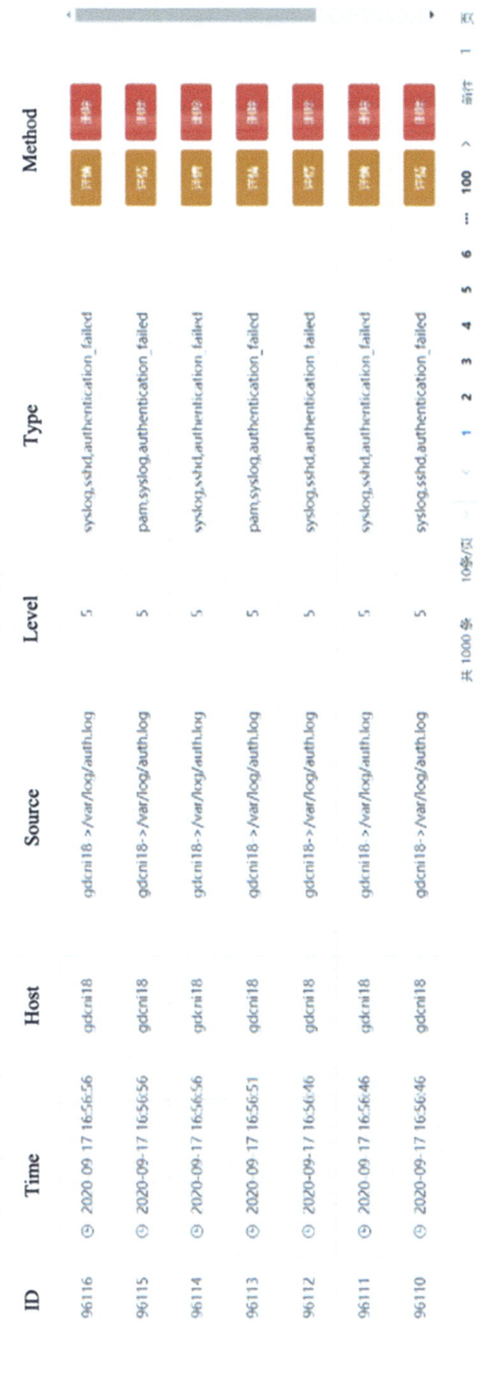
ID
Time
Host
Source
Level
Type
Method
96116 2020-09-17 16:56:56 gdcni18 gdcni18->/var/log/auth.log 5 syslog,sshd,authentication_failed
96115 2020-09-17 16:56:56 gdcni18 gdcni18->/var/log/auth.log 5 pam,syslog,authentication_failed
96114 2020-09-17 16:56:56 gdcni18 gdcni18->/var/log/auth.log 5 syslog,sshd,authentication_failed
96113 2020-09-17 16:56:51 gdcni18 gdcni18->/var/log/auth.log 5 pam,syslog,authentication_failed
96112 2020-09-17 16:56:46 gdcni18 gdcni18->/var/log/auth.log 5 syslog,sshd,authentication_failed
96111 2020-09-17 16:56:46 gdcni18 gdcni18->/var/log/auth.log 5 syslog,sshd,authentication_failed
96110 2020-09-17 16:56:46 gdcni18 gdcni18->/var/log/auth.log 5 syslog,sshd,authentication_failed
共 1000 条
10条/页
1 2 3 4 5 6 ... 100
前往 1 页

Fig. 11.37 Warning page

```
tcp6        0      0 :::9002                 :::*                    LISTEN      15816/node
```

Fig. 11.38 Background processes

17487	2020-08-14 15:01:42	gdcni19	gdcni19->netstat -tan |grep LISTEN |egrep -v '(127.0.0.1| //1)' | sort	7	ossec	详情 删除

Fig. 11.39 Warning

```
ossec: output: `netstat -tan |grep LISTEN |grep -v 127.0.0.1 | sort`: tcp 0 0 0.0.0.0:22 0.0.0.0:* LISTEN tcp 0 0 0.0.0.0:27017 0.0.0.0:* LISTEN tcp 0 0 0.0.0.0:6363 0.0.0.0:* LISTEN tcp 0 0 0.0.0.0:9005 0.0.0.0:* LISTEN tcp 0 0 0.0.0.0:9696 0.0.0.0:* LISTEN tcp 0 0 0.0.0.0:9748 0.0.0.0:* LISTEN tcp6 0 0 :::22 :::* LISTEN tcp6 0 0 :::5010 :::* LISTEN tcp6 0 0 :::6363 :::* LISTEN tcp6 0 0 :::9000 :::* LISTEN tcp6 0 0 :::9001 :::* LISTEN tcp6 0 0 :::9003 :::* LISTEN tcp6 0 0 :::9696 :::* LISTEN Previous output: ossec: output: `netstat -tan |grep LISTEN |egrep -v `(127.0.0.1| //1)` | sort`: tcp 0 0 0.0.0.0:22 0.0.0.0:* LISTEN tcp 0 0 0.0.0.0:27017 0.0.0.0:* LISTEN tcp 0 0 0.0.0.0:6363 0.0.0.0:* LISTEN tcp 0 0 0.0.0.0:9005 0.0.0.0:* LISTEN
```

Fig. 11.40 Full log

```
> db.Assets.find({"asset_type":"server"})
{ "_id" : ObjectId("5f9ac758deefbcfe34beb81f"), "asset_id" : "SERVER-01", "asset
_type" : "server", "asset_tag" : "", "asset_name" : "gdcni18", "asset_security"
: "未受保护", "asset_server" : { "system" : "Ubuntu 16.04 xenial", "cpu" : "Inte
l(R) Xeon(R) Silver 4114 CPU @ 2.20GHz", "kernel" : "4.15.0-115-generic GNU/Linu
x", "memory" : "128GB", "disk" : { "total" : "314G", "used" : "46G" }, "net" : {
 "public_ip" : "[illegible]", "private_ip" : "[illegible]", "mac" : "[illegible]" } }, "asset_location" : "China, Shenzhen" }
>
```

Fig. 11.41 Host information

```
> db.Assets.find({"asset_type": "database"}){
 "_id": objectId("5f9aa964165dc7472590d2fa"),
 "asset_id",
 "DATADASE-S01-01",
 "asset_type": "database",
 "asset_tag": "",
 "asset_name": "Mongo",
 "asset_security": "未受保护",
 "asset_databases": {
  "databases"[{"name": "Situation_Awareness","size": "14.75MB"},
   {"name": "admin","size": "0.07MB"},
   {"name": "blockchain","size": "4739.13MB"},
   {"name": "local","size": "0.04MB"},
   {"name": "packet_flow","size": "68.15MB"},
   {"name": "local","size": "0.04MB"}
  ],"users": [{"name": "pkusz","dbs": "admin"}],"port": "27017"
 },"asset_location": "China, Shenzhen"}
```

Fig. 11.42 Database information

Fig. 11.43 Asset Centre page

Fig. 11.44 Database information

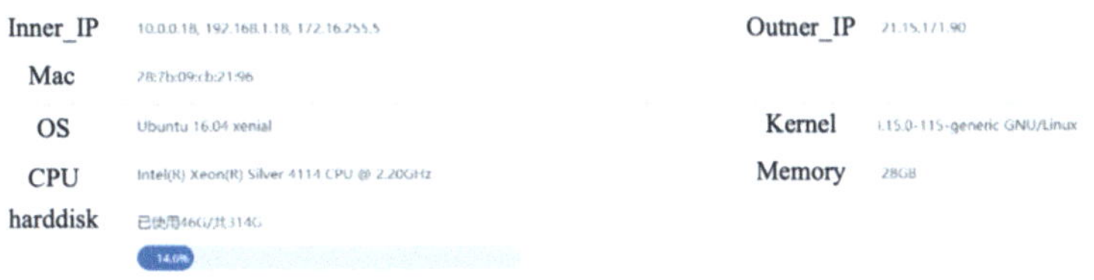

Fig. 11.45 Host information

```
smct5@smct5:~/Downloads/SA_server/dist/AssetInfo$ ./AssetInfo -h
usage: AssetInfo [-h] [-u {server,databases}]

optional arguments:
  -h, --help            show this help message and exit
  -u {server,databases}, --update {server,databases}
                        update asset information
```

Fig. 11.46 Command information

11.5 Dual-Defense Strategy

In recent years, there have been frequent security incidents in industrial control systems [45]. These systems store a large amount of sensitive industrial data and valuable commercial information. However, their own protection capabilities are relatively weak. During the processes of data collection, conversion, and transmission, they are vulnerable to eavesdropping, interception, and tampering, leading to cyber security incidents in industrial control system networks. The massive amount of network data generated by numerous sensor devices comes in various formats, making the storage and distribution of data complex and imposing higher demands on network security. During the process of data analysis and utilization, there is a risk of network infiltration attacks and data privacy breaches. Attackers often exploit vulnerabilities to launch network attacks, starting with port scanning to identify the weakest links and vulnerabilities in security defenses. Once they gain system access or control privileges, they proceed with network attacks, extending their reach to other network nodes. Figure 11.47 illustrates the process of a network attack.

To address the network security issues in industrial control systems mentioned above, CoG-MIN research team proposes a dual-defense strategy [46]. In the design, it utilizes key encryption techniques, blockchain technology, and trusted computing whitelist strategies to achieve static network security defense. By dynamically collecting data traffic and access logs, the strategy detects system vulnerabilities, comprehends and predicts the situation, and achieves situation awareness of network attacks. Additionally, taking inspiration from immunology, the strategy cultivates immune vaccines to counter unknown network attacks, enabling proactive and dynamic network security defense.

11.5.1 Static Defense Strategy

Identity Authentication and Blockchain Protection

To safeguard the security of industrial control network devices and information, the identity authentication mechanism is based on lightweight elliptic curve cryptography (ECC) for digital signatures. Apart from the identity registration phase, subsequent authentication phases do not require third-party involvement, ensuring communication security while reducing computational and communication overhead. Data transmitted in industrial networks [45] is encrypted at the packet level rather than the channel level, utilizing asymmetric encryption techniques and hash hashing for security protection, preventing sensitive information from being eavesdropped, intercepted, or tampered with.

In MIS, the nodes are divided into committee nodes, accounting nodes, and ordinary user nodes. Committee nodes are elected by members who volunteer to jointly maintain the consortium blockchain, and they have equal voting rights. The accounting node is a node with the authority to produce blocks voted by the committee nodes.

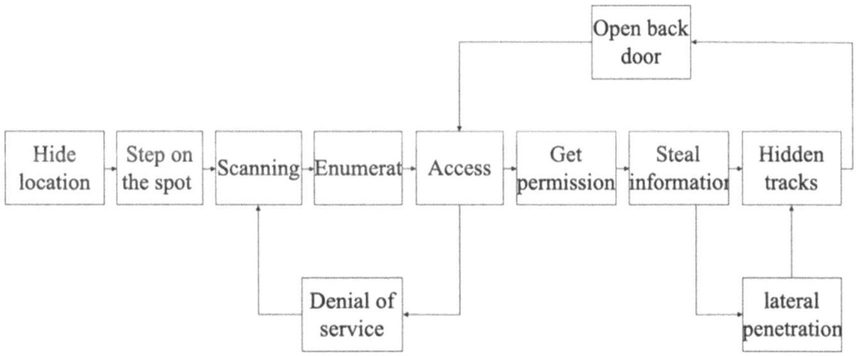

Fig. 11.47 Network attack process [46]

During user registration, users generate their own public–private key pairs and submit their public key and their real identity information, signed with their private key, to any blockchain node in MIS. The node checks the format of the registration request and queries its local database to avoid duplicate registrations. Subsequently, the node performs preliminary verification of the registration information and packages it into a blockchain transaction, submitting it to the consensus nodes in the MIS consortium blockchain, which are selected by regular node rotation. The transaction information is stored in the transaction pool.

The PoV consensus algorithm is employed to accelerate the blockchain consensus process. At the beginning of the blockchain consensus, the accounting node will take out several pieces of transaction information from the transaction pool to generate a pre-block and send it to all committee nodes in the blockchain to request their verification signature for the pre-block. The committee node will verify the pre-block header and each transaction content. Verification methods include probability-based methods or custom keyword filtering lists. After passing the verification, the pre-block is signed and the signature information is sent back to the accounting node.

If signature verification from more than half of the committee nodes is received within a given time threshold, the accounting node will store the signature information in the block header, and write the pre-block to the main consortium chain. On the chain, it becomes an official block. Otherwise, when the accounting node does not receive more than half of the signatures within the time range, it will delete this pre-block, rotate to the next accounting node, and restart the pre-block generation and verification process.

When users engage in network data transmission, the data packets contain their valid signature information, thereby documenting the users' access paths within the multi-identity network. This process enables the tracking and traceability of network security. When abnormal access is detected, the user's reserved registration identity information will be retrieved from the blockchain database, and the user will be warned or banned.

Trusted Computing

The static defense strategy involves deploying Trusted Computing Modules (TCMs) within the client host hardware to store the encryption keys used during the consensus process of the blockchain nodes. The private keys are stored within the TCM module and cannot be accessed or leaked externally, while the public keys are used to identify node identities and verify signatures. Additionally, the Trusted Computing Module can provide trusted signatures for various data generated in the MIN network. By protecting sensitive data such as keys, through the trusted chain transmission of various levels of chips, the integrity, confidentiality, and security of industrial control network data are ensured. The identity verification and key mechanisms guarantee the trustworthiness of the computing environment.

The trusted goal is to ensure the integrity of systems and applications, thereby ensuring that they run in the expected trusted state. The identification and protection of applications uses whitelist mechanisms, and only needs to ensure that a small number of trusted applications are running in the current network system. This mechanism realizes the supervision and protection of the entire cycle of applications from startup, loading, and running, reduces system load, and improves system availability. Application developers use their private keys to issue application signatures and register them with MIS, or MIS trusted services provide verification benchmarks and establish an application whitelist database. For applications listed on the whitelist, it is crucial to conduct an in-depth analysis of their critical behaviors during normal operations and then establish a comprehensive whitelist behavior rule library specific to each application. When the application starts, the hash metric value of the application is obtained and compared with the expected baseline value taken out from the TCM to complete the integrity measurement of the application. Execution of an application will only be allowed if it is intact and has not been tampered with. At the same time, during the running process of the application, the running status of its key behaviors is monitored in real time and compared with the pre-established application behavior rule library to detect abnormal behaviors in time and record the operations in the log. In this way, it balances security and availability and ensures the orderly operation of applications. Figure 11.48 shows the remote attestation of trusted computing.

At the same time, the security of TCM also needs to be guaranteed. Each TCM module has an Endorsement Key (EK) certificate that uniquely identifies its identity. Through Direct Anonymous Attestation (DAA) technology of trusted computing remote proof, the feasibility of trusted computing storage and computing environments can be remotely confirmed. DAA uses the Carmenisch-Lysyanskaya signature mechanism to sign the certificate with the member public key generated by TCM to ensure the legitimacy of the TCM.

Identity authentication, blockchain, and trusted computing, among other static defense measures, provide sufficient external barriers for network security. They ensure a balanced combination of confidentiality, integrity, and availability, safeguarding the security of network nodes. These measures effectively prevent and trace security issues related to network node individuals.

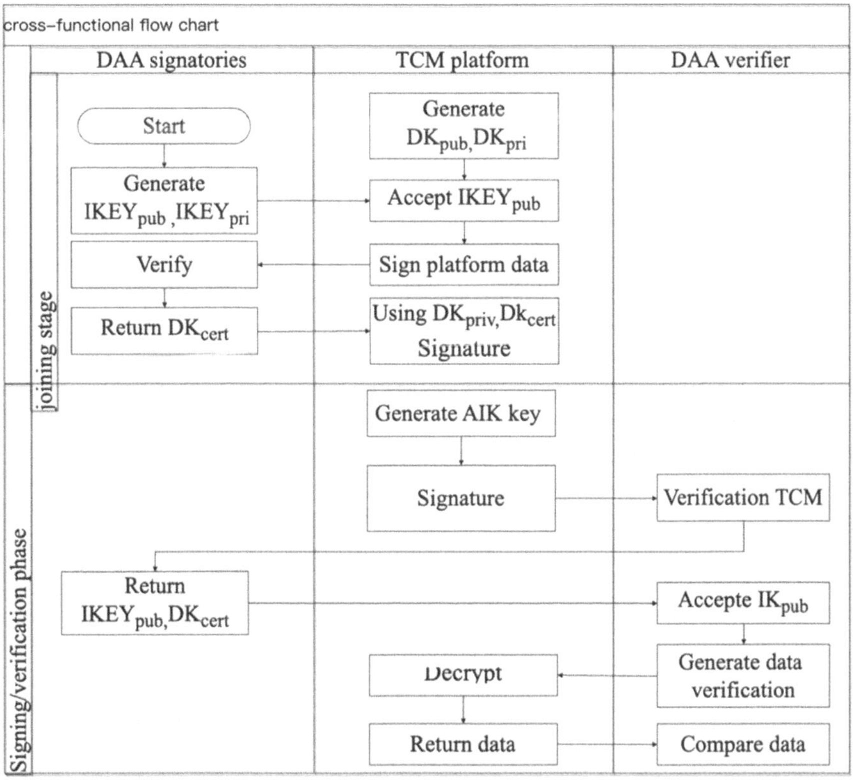

Fig. 11.48 The remote attestation of trusted computing [46]

11.5.2 Dynamic Defense Strategy

In an industrial control network, nodes are not isolated entities and may face collective network issues as well as new and severe types of unknown network attacks. Furthermore, attack methods are becoming increasingly diverse, and attackers are becoming more specialized in their techniques. Therefore, it is necessary to establish effective dynamic defense strategies. The measures adopted in dynamic defense strategies include network security situation awareness and network security vaccine cultivation.

Network Security Situation Awareness

Network situation awareness involves the perception of massive behaviors occurring within a network, the extraction of elements causing changes in the situation, and the tracing and analysis of attack threats and abnormal network behaviors, including their trajectories, sources, destinations, as well as predicting and understanding the development trends of the network. It also involves reporting early warnings and handling emergencies related to network risks.

During static defense measures, network entities generate a large amount of dynamic backbone network traffic data and raw log files, including user activity logs and alert information. These diverse and heterogeneous data sources provide ample training material for dynamic defense situation awareness in network security. Therefore, it is necessary to implement unified and effective management and analysis of log files.

As shown in Fig. 11.49, the situation awareness system constructs a decision tree containing either all or a subset of the security policy rule set based on the log files.

It involves parsing, filtering, handling omissions, and normalizing the entries in the log files. The initial preprocessing of raw data generated by network monitoring devices and management systems includes data cleansing, noise reduction, dimensionality reduction, normalization, merging or transformation, and data validation. This process yields standardized datasets of industrial control network assets, threat data, and vulnerability data. Next, correlation analysis is performed on the data, utilizing prior knowledge to model network activities, patterns, and characteristics. Through protocol reconstruction, the presence and forms of various entities within the network are identified. By employing machine learning decision tree classification algorithms, three different types of network behaviors can be distinguished:

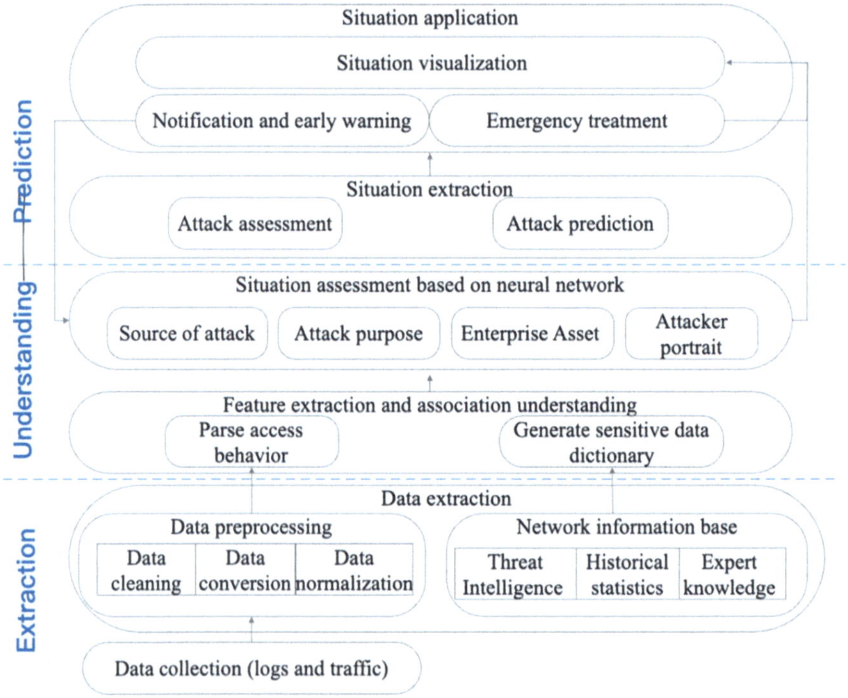

Fig. 11.49 Overall framework diagram of the situation awareness system [46]

malicious attack behaviors, abnormal risk behaviors (including weak passwords, risky logins, and remote control), and normal access behaviors. Behaviors that deviate from the baseline trigger behavior alerts, allowing for timely risk detection and better identification of covert attacks. The system can also analyze and establish patterns and correlations between unauthorized activities of illegal and legitimate users to anticipate potential attack behaviors. Additionally, the system analyzes the frequency of content access, strengthening the defense against high-frequency access to popular data and high-value business information within the industrial control network.

Based on the network attack chain, the situation awareness system detects traffic anomalies and malicious attack behaviors such as external attacks, internal malicious scans, Address Resolution Protocol (ARP) spoofing attacks, and internal policy violations. It creates a network security situation map from different perspectives, including external attacks on internal systems, lateral movement within the internal network, and internal connections leaking to external networks. This map provides an understanding of the overall security situation in the industrial control network, facilitates the detection and discovery of security events, and analyzes and evaluates network vulnerabilities and the impact of attacks. Through deep modeling and analysis of massive logs and traffic information from historical attack behaviors, the system obtains the identity of attackers, their preferred attack methods, and attack paths. It creates profiles of attackers and their behaviors, including individual and collective behavior profiles, to analyze the intent of network attackers. Furthermore, it constructs a network attack knowledge map, providing visual reference for understanding the capabilities, objectives, and potential future attack behaviors of network attackers.

Additionally, the situation awareness system analyzes the vulnerabilities and weak points within the enterprise assets and control systems in the industrial control network. To achieve situation awareness of security attacks, it is necessary to first examine the security status and understand the various assets and stakeholders present in the industrial control network, as well as potential security vulnerabilities. This process involves creating visual depictions of the network's own assets and security vulnerabilities to gain a comprehensive understanding of the enterprise's security status.

After acquiring comprehensive network threat status data, the system utilizes techniques such as convolutional neural networks (CNNs) to predict the behavioral patterns and resulting harm of potential attack activities based on the current network status and identified attack activities, combined with the vulnerabilities of industrial control network assets.

Network Security Vaccine Cultivation

The immune system of living organisms develops immunity against viral infections through physical barriers, innate immune systems, and adaptive immune systems. It achieves collective immunity by coordinating with heterogeneous nodes, cultivating and administering vaccines to counter uncertain environments.

Immunity is the process by which organisms recognize and differentiate between their own tissue systems (self) and non-self-systems (non-self) and respond to and develop tolerance against pathogenic invasions from non-self-entities. In the context of vaccine cultivation, the "self" represents normal and legitimate network behavior. Vaccines applied within living organisms generally involve selecting highly immunogenic pathogens and modifying them through processes such as artificial attenuation, physical and chemical inactivation, genetic modification, or animal cell passaging, to eliminate their inherent toxicity while retaining their immunogenicity. Antigens can stimulate and induce immune responses. Vaccines administered to living organisms are typically injected to stimulate the production of antibodies in the recipients, promoting the development of their own immune tolerance. The immune system of living organisms recognizes antigens and produces antibody proteins that specifically bind to the antigens. The degree of match and structural similarity between antigens and antibodies is referred to as affinity. If the affinity exceeds a specified threshold, antibodies are massively replicated; otherwise, their production is inhibited.

The proactive immunity provided by trusted computing techniques in static defense empowers network information systems with static immunization capabilities. Network vaccines used for artificial immunity differ from biological immune systems as they focus on detecting network intrusion behaviors and providing real-time dynamic network defense. They involve perceiving and recognizing abnormal network behaviors as well as responding to and countering them. The antigens used in artificial immunity represent the objective functions for defending against network attacks and various constraints within the network. Network vaccines enhance the resilience and elasticity of the network while mitigating the risk of network attacks, ensuring the stable operation and eventual recovery of industrial control systems when faced with network attacks. Therefore, the cultivation of network defense vaccines needs to be conducted dynamically in the network environment, undergoing sandbox testing and simulated confrontations, and constructing a genetic map library of attacks to continuously enhance the construction of attack behavior pattern libraries, better addressing unknown network threats.

Network security immune vaccines are strings extracted from the features of transmitted network packets. Antibodies, on the other hand, are the measures taken in static defense and the rules generated in dynamic defense. To detect network intrusions, it is necessary to establish a rule library for network attacks. Initially, preprocessing operations such as completing missing features and eliminating redundant attributes are performed on feature data such as logs and traffic information. Clustering analysis is conducted using K-means to extract the rule library of self and non-self, generating preliminary antibody rules, which are the embryos of antibody cells. During the matching process between antigens and antibodies, immune antibody cells continuously defend against network attacks, undergo clonal regeneration, and evolve into network security memory cells. Memory cells accurately record past network intrusion behaviors and their attack methods. They are encapsulated as vaccine cells after being stamped with timestamps according to the defined vaccine format. These vaccine cells, serving as excellent antibodies, are

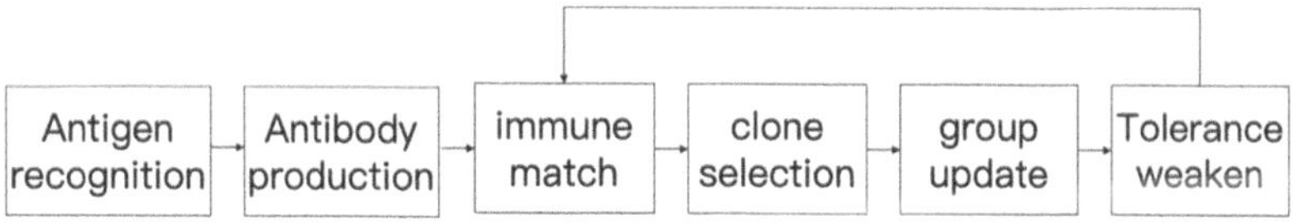

Fig. 11.50 Immune process against network attacks [46]

added to the antibody rule library, enabling the detection and defense against network intrusions. Simultaneously, synergistic collaboration with the external defense system constructed in static defense forms a combined force, providing proactive network defense capabilities. The immune process is shown in Fig. 11.50.

The encapsulated network security vaccines are forwarded to neighboring vaccine defense centers by looking up the local routing table and eventually distributed to network nodes within the industrial control network, completing the vaccination of network vaccines. Once network nodes are vaccinated, if the affinity between antigens and antibodies can be increased, their own resistance to attacks is enhanced. Once a vaccinated network vaccine matches the antigens it contains, immune cells can undergo clone regeneration under antigen stimulation, leading to activation and detection of network attack behaviors. Otherwise, the network state before vaccination needs to be restored.

As attacks progress, new attack methods and strategies continuously emerge, causing the immune function of network vaccines to weaken. Network nodes can also serve as training and cultivation nodes for network vaccines. When new attack behaviors are discovered, these nodes continuously train and learn to evolve, collaborating between different nodes during the process of countering attack behaviors. By improving their own immune capabilities, they enhance the antibody vitality within vaccine cells.

During the cultivation process of network security vaccines, dynamic analysis of network logs and traffic is conducted, without affecting the availability of the industrial control network system, ensuring the unity of availability and security.

11.6 Adaptive Active Query Mechanism Based on Information Entropy

In the IoT environment, random number generation will serve as an important input for many functions [47]. However, the current access control method used in the IoT environment is still token-based, and one-time verification is valid for a long time. This static management method has security defects and poses a continuous threat to the IoT environment. Therefore, facing the challenges of limited IoT device resources, lack of trusted authority, and frequent changes in permissions, the CoG-MIN research team proposed an adaptive active query mechanism based on information entropy. By combining the idea of adaptive defense, it can realize active tracing of permission changes and break the static control deadlock.

The adaptive active query mechanism based on information entropy mainly includes two aspects: a random number generation algorithm based on a historical information entropy pool and an adaptive active query mechanism. The adaptive active query mechanism can realize active tracing of changes in permissions of connected users, while the random number generation algorithm based on a historical information entropy pool can be used to ensure the efficiency and reliability of a single query. The two are introduced below.

11.6.1 Random Number Generation Algorithm Based on a Historical Information Entropy Pool

The random number generation algorithm based on a historical information entropy pool takes the Fortuna [48] algorithm as the basis and adds the multi-identifier entropy source mechanism in a MIN network. The algorithm consists of three parts: entropy compressor, generator, and seed. First, a total of 32 entropy pools are set as P0, P1, …, P31. In theory, each entropy pool contains an infinite string, but, because the string in the entropy pool is only used as input to the hash function, in the implementation, there is no need to store this infinite string, and only add events to the entropy pool at the same time to calculate the hash value, each entropy source cycle to add random events to the 32 entropy pools. This ensures that the entropy generated by each entropy source is evenly distributed to each entropy pool. Each event, when placed in the entropy pool, appends the random information that the event contains to the original string in the entropy pool.

When the string length in the P0 pool is sufficient, the generator's seeds are updated. Each seed is marked with the sequence numbers 1, 2, 3, …, based on its sequence number. Strings from one or more pools are then used to generate the seed. When generating the r-th seed, if 2^i is a multiple of r, then the string from the i-th entropy pool will be used, so P0 will be used every time a seed is generated, P1 will be used every two seeds, and P2 will be used every four seeds. Once one of the entropy pools is involved in generating a new seed, the contents of the entropy pool are reset to an empty state.

The random number generation system in the adaptive active query mechanism based on information entropy can automatically adapt to the environment. If the attacker knows very little about the source of entropy, then they cannot predict the entropy in P0 before updating the seed. The attacker can capture events generated by a partial entropy source. Assuming that the attacker controls certain entropy sources and can determine when and what events these sources will produce, and that the attacker can request random data from the pseudo-random number generator at any time, then the attacker may possess significant information about the entropy source or be capable of simulating numerous random events. In such a scenario, the attacker will have sufficient information about the entropy in P0 to calculate the new state of the generator based on the generator's previous state and its output. Since P1 contains twice as much entropy as P0 and P2 contains four times as much as P0, regardless of how many random events an attacker can manipulate or fabricate, as long as they cannot predict the events from a specific entropy source, there will always be an entropy pool with sufficient entropy to withstand the attack.

Generators are responsible for converting fixed-length internal states into output of any length. When using block ciphers such as AES as generators, the generator can also be implemented with algorithms like Advanced Encryption Standard (AES), Serpent, or Twofish. The internal state of the generator consists of a 256-bit block cipher key and a 128-bit counter. The generator can be thought of as a block cipher operating in counter mode, where CTR(Counter) mode can produce a random stream of data.

When a random number is requested, the generator executes an algorithm to generate pseudo-random data. After each request, an additional 256-bit pseudo-random data is generated and used as a new key for the block cipher. The old key is then wiped away, eliminating the possibility of leaking the previously requested information.

If one of the generator's states is compromised, the speed at which it can return to a safe state depends on the rate at which the portion of entropy that the attacker cannot predict flows into the pool. Assuming that entropy flows into the entropy pool at a fixed rate p, a total of pt. bits of entropy are generated after time t. Therefore, approximately $pt/32$ bits of entropy are added to each entropy pool. If an entropy pool that stores more than 128 bits of entropy is used when the generator updates its seeds, the attacker cannot obtain the new state of the generator. There are two scenarios here. In the first scenario, if P0 can gather 128 bits of entropy before the next seed update, then the generator returns to a secure state. However, this outcome hinges on the amount of entropy P0 will accumulate before the seed update. In the second scenario, when the random event is known to the attacker (or generated by the attacker), P0 updates the seed too rapidly to gather sufficient entropy before the next seed update. Let t represent the time interval for updating the seed. Then, every 2^{i*t} times Pi will be involved in generating the seed. During this time, Pi can collect $2^{(i*pt)}/32$ bits of entropy when $128 \leq 2^{(i*pt)}/32 < 256$ (the upper limit is to ensure that PI-1 cannot collect 128 bits of entropy during this time). Once Pi is involved in a new seed, the generator can return to a safe state. From the above inequality, then get:

$$2^{i}t < \frac{8192}{\rho} \tag{11.1}$$

In other words, the upper limit on the time it takes to return to the safe state is the time it takes to obtain the 2^{13} bit entropy ($8192/p$) [49]. This is a constant, so even if the generator is breached at some point, it will eventually be able to return to a secure state. This is the most significant enhancement of Fortuna [48] compared to Yarrow [50]. The generator can automatically restore to a safe state. If the entropy source provides entropy quickly, the recovery will be completed swiftly. However, if the entropy source provides entropy slowly, the recovery process will take a longer time.

Pseudo-random number generators have been successful in collecting entropy and generating random numbers after obtaining the initial seed. After each computer reboot, the entropy source must provide sufficient events before the first seed can be obtained to generate random data. Additionally, there is no guarantee that the state after the first seed is unpredictable. The solution is to use a seed file. The pseudo-random number generator maintains an entropy file known as a seed file that only the pseudo-random number generator can access. After each restart, the pseudo-random number generator reads the seed file and uses the file contents as an entropy source to obtain an unknown state. Of course, the seed file needs to be rewritten after each use. The pseudo-random number generator needs to update the seed file periodically. Just make sure that the pseudo-random number generator can update the entropy regularly once it has collected a sufficient amount, and a practical approach is to update the entropy every time the system is shut down and approximately every 10 min.

The entropy source information is composed of seed files and historical valid traffic entropy packages. Entropy information is extracted according to interactive traffic through the entropy compressor, and hash processing is performed through the hash function for privacy protection and compression. The generator is based on block cryptography algorithms, such as AES, Serpent, Twofish, etc. The basic idea is to run the block cryptography algorithm in counter mode to process the information entropy package. Depending on the service object, the proposed algorithm includes two working modes: pure random number generation mode, using a large amount of entropy pool information to provide random numbers for GK itself; query mode, using the independent entropy pool of each device, participating in the query link of the corresponding device, generating random numbers and providing access control query credentials that can participate in traceability. The random number generation algorithm used in these two modes is the same.

In the strong random number mode, the entire entropy pool is divided into k sub-entropy pools. The entropy accumulator evenly distributes the information entropy among these sub-entropy pools. During the nth reseeding of the generator, if n is an integer multiple of 2^k, the subpool k is selected. Then, the sub-entropy pool k is used in the $1/2^k$ reseeding time cycle. This rotating selection strategy ensures that the lower-numbered entropy pool contributes available information entropy more frequently for the reseeding operation, while the higher-numbered entropy pool collects richer information entropy over longer intervals. Each reseeding operation involves hashing the specified entropy pool into the key of the block cipher, using two iterations of SHA-256. As long as the attacker cannot control all the entropy sources flowing into the system, there will always be some sub-entropy pools that can gather enough entropy between reseeding operations. This ensures that the pool can generate sufficiently secure random numbers. Additionally, because the interval between the usage of the entropy pool is proportional to the amount of correlated entropy, the system can always recover from an injection attack at a constant time cost.

In query mode, the entropy pool is divided based on the interaction object. Both the interrogator and the responder maintain symmetric records of historical information, resulting in the construction of the same entropy pool. The responder selects the appropriate entropy information from the entropy pool based on the query rules, which are then used by the generator to generate random numbers.

11.6.2 Adaptive Active Query Mechanism

Adaptive active query mechanism actively verifies and dynamically adjusts access rights in IoT environments. It actively tracks and adjusts the legitimacy and changes of permissions in a "query and response" manner. A single query is generated based on the private history data packets of both parties during communication, enhancing the reliability and efficiency of the query while preventing attackers from identity forgery or man-in-the-middle attacks.

On this basis, combined with adaptive defense concepts, the adaptive active query mechanism can disrupt the static attack surface by implementing the query after establishing a connection between the server and the access point.

Furthermore, the adaptive learning mechanism can be designed based on the security evaluation scheme. It dynamically adjusts the query frequency, balancing defense costs and security gains, and preventing unknown attacks, as shown in Fig. 11.51.

Adaptive active query mechanism reliably generates random numbers by leveraging the entropy pool of both communication parties. Subsequently, it constructs a reliable single query-response scheme. Random numbers play a crucial role in enhancing security and unpredictability during each query. Typically, their generation relies on random number generators. However, most existing true random number generators require an extensive collection of external information, resulting in an excessive resource burden. In this context, two random number generation modes were established based on the entropy and query mechanism of the traffic packet. A random number generation algorithm that utilizes historical information entropy was proposed. This algorithm is seamlessly integrated into the Internet of Things access control system without imposing a significant additional resource burden. By constructing a true random number generator capable of consistently and securely generating a large number of random numbers without depletion, the requirements of high-speed interactions on the Internet of Things environment can be addressed.

During the communication process, the involved parties record the communication information and process their respective historical information. This information is compressed into entropy packets. The resource visitor user S stores the generated entropy packet locally, while the resource owner user O sends its entropy packet to the trusted guard GK and stores it in the entropy packet database.

As the behavior and information exchange between the communication parties progresses, the generated information from the interaction between GK and user S continues to accumulate and become more intricate. This accumulation leads to the

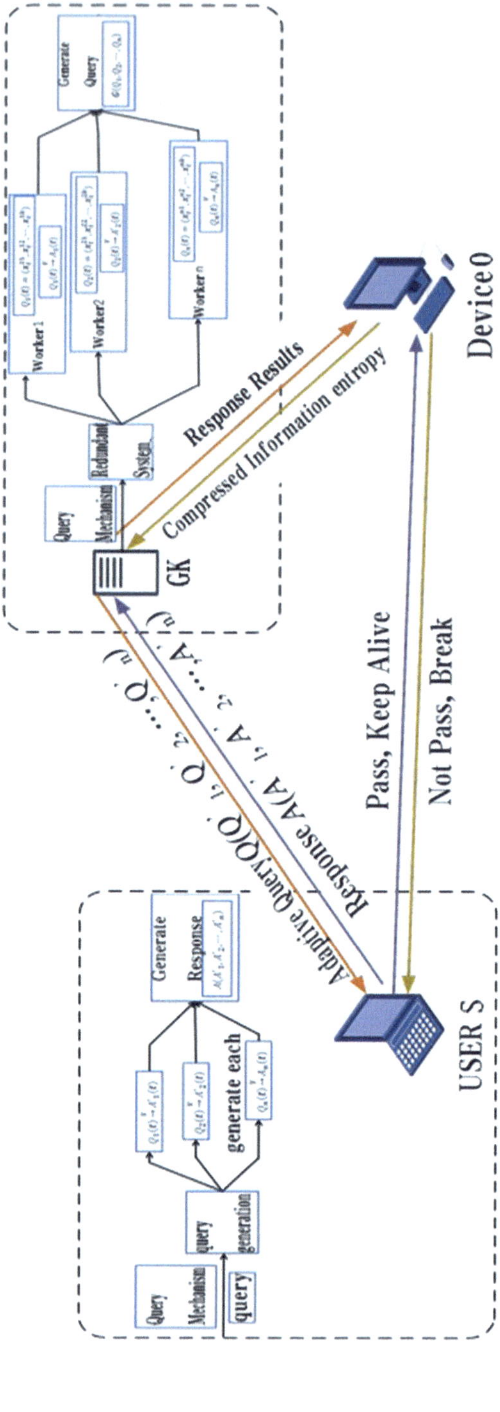

Fig. 11.51 Schematic diagram of the adaptive active query mechanism

generation of more entropy packets, deepening the entropy pool and increasing the information entropy. The random number generation algorithm based on historical information entropy exhibits the characteristic of exponentially increasing security as the depth of the entropy pool grows. Therefore, as the communication deepens, the query results become more reliable. Attackers, whether attempting a man-in-the-middle attack or introducing entropy pool pollution inputs, are unable to obtain complete information about the entropy pool.

After the resource owner completes the power token verification of the resource visitor and establishes a connection relationship, an initial trust value, and intermediate trust level are established between the two parties. Once the connection is established, the guard node GK initiates a heterogeneous redundant query to the user S, who is the resource visitor. Within GK, multiple query generators are constructed, and each generator functions as an executive body. These executors independently generate queries and responses for GK based on different configurations, reflecting a consistent function with a heterogeneous structure among the executors. During each fixed query period T, GK randomly selects N query generators to generate questions and sends them to users based on the communicated information pool. The correct response results are generated by the users based on the queried content and the historical information pool shared between the communication parties. This is achieved using a symmetric random number generation algorithm based on historical information entropy. For the response sent back by the user, a threshold decision method is employed to determine its legitimacy. Only by providing enough correct responses can user S maintain their trust value and trust level, thus preserving the authorization relationship. Failure to provide correct responses or falling below the judgment threshold results in a reduction in trust value and trust level. This continues until reauthentication becomes necessary. If the response from the query object is not entirely correct or falls below the judgment threshold, the trust value will be decreased to varying degrees. Once it falls below a specific trust threshold, GK considers the user untrustworthy. Consequently, GK can send a request to the blockchain management node to revoke or modify the user's permissions.

Based on the characteristics of the query algorithm described above, an adaptive learning mechanism can be further designed. This mechanism involves learning and dynamically adapting to the behavior of subjects through continuous interactive access and feedback within the system. During the system's continuous interactive access, the mechanism learns from the interactive traffic and behavior of the subjects. Over time, certain familiar nodes tend to perform fixed functions and adopt similar behaviors. Through long-term monitoring and learning, the mechanism establishes data access relationships between nodes and learns trusted operational behaviors. This enables the system to dynamically identify unknown abnormal access behaviors and malicious operations, thereby preventing unknown network attacks and abnormal authorization behaviors. It helps mitigate security risks within the internal environment caused by trusted nodes being compromised. The feedback obtained from this learning process serves as important evaluation factors that are input into the security evaluation model. These factors include historical behavior and trust value, among others. They are combined with the security requirements of defenders, such as query frequency, redundancy coefficient, and other parameters, to actively and dynamically adjust the defense strategy. This ensures a balance between system security, efficiency, and defense costs, allowing for effective combat against unknown security threats in the open environment of the Internet of Things.

The introduced algorithm for random number generation based on historical information entropy offers increased security compared to simple pseudo-random number generators. It generates random numbers that are more difficult to decipher, providing higher security levels. The method utilizes multiple entropy accumulators to collect a variety of random data from historical chat data, increasing the quality and quantity of entropy. High-quality random numbers are then generated by encrypting the state machine. In terms of encryption algorithms, the introduced method employs two layers of encryption algorithms. The first layer uses AES-256 as a pseudo-random function, while the second layer uses SHA-256 as a hash function. Both AES-256 and SHA-256 are recognized as secure and efficient encryption algorithms. By using counters and encryption algorithms, the algorithm ensures that the output is different each time and periodically updates the internal state through reseeding. Even if an attacker gains access to the internal state at a particular moment, it is not possible to reverse-engineer the previously generated random numbers, thus resisting state leakage attacks. Furthermore, the algorithm automatically resets and exploits the seed. After generating a certain number of random bytes, it employs a reseeding algorithm to replace the old seed with a new one. This prevents the repetition of the same random number sequence and increases the difficulty for attackers attempting to crack the seed, effectively combating entropy depletion attacks. Overall, unless the attacker can control all the entropy sources flowing into the system, they cannot obtain complete entropy information and pass the active questioning examination. Therefore, even if an attacker succeeds in a man-in-the-middle attack or entropy injection attack within a certain period, they will not go undetected. Trusted nodes on the edge are dynamically classified as untrusted nodes because they are unable to pass the query authentication.

After ensuring the credibility of each query through the random number generation algorithm based on historical information entropy, an active query mechanism is established. In this mechanism, the guard node GK initiates multiple queries to users who have established a connection relationship at fixed intervals. The query results are evaluated using a threshold judgment to determine whether the user still possesses a legal identity. This active defense approach helps address the imbalance between attack and defense brought about by static defense measures. The process can be divided into the attack and defense process within a single query cycle and the process of maintaining illegal access rights throughout the entire system.

The adaptive active query mechanism achieves dynamic adjustment of defense levels and parameters from multiple dimensions such as heterogeneous redundant construction, policy scheduling, and parameter configuration, breaking the unequal offense and defense situation in static defense, and realizing active permission tracing and adaptive policy changes, thereby ensuring the efficiency and reliability of the system.

11.7 Quantitative Evaluation Model for Network Security

11.7.1 Overview of Quantitative Evaluation for Adaptive Cyber Defense

Adaptive Cyber Defense (ACD) is a cyber defense technology, which can continuously change the attack surface that can be exploited by spontaneously reconfiguring the network environment randomly. The dynamic nature of active defense reverses the unequal attack and defense of traditional static networks, providing defenders with a tactical advantage in the offensive and defensive game. However, the dynamic nature of ACD also introduces complexity into the attack and defense process, making it challenging to quantitatively evaluate the effectiveness of ACD mechanisms.

The existing studies for the quantitative evaluation of ACD mechanisms can be divided into experimental evaluation methods that focus on microscopic research and theoretical evaluation schemes that pay more attention to macroscopic laws.

Experimental Evaluation Methods

On the one hand, the experimental schemes based on real experiments involve applying specific ACD technologies to specific scenarios, such as address space randomization, data randomization, dynamic control strategy, and more. These methods build specific systems or real test beds, where code injection, denial of service attacks, and other attacks are carried out within the constructed real system environment. The effectiveness of the security mechanism is then assessed from various perspectives, including its anti-attack ability, network resource occupation, network scale consumption, and system performance [51].

These schemes are generally considered to have the highest confidence as they replicate the most realistic scenarios and rely on fine-grained information collection. By building a specific system, multiple aspects and indicators can be tested, enabling a more comprehensive evaluation. However, this approach has drawbacks such as high development and deployment costs, as well as limited scalability and migration. Additionally, the method based on offensive and defensive experiments typically represents results through programming languages, which by themselves cannot provide a unified security metric directly.

On the other hand, the experimental schemes based on simulation focus on capturing the details during the network attack as well as the interconnectedness of attack behaviors. It involves collecting fine-grained details of both attack and defense for experimental reproduction [52]. Currently, most methods for evaluating the performance of ACD mechanisms rely on simulation experiments. These methods are more cost-effective compared to the schemes based on real experiments and offer higher flexibility and credibility than modeling analysis methods when it comes to portraying specific attack behaviors.

Theoretical Evaluation Schemes

ACD mechanisms can be applied to build different secure systems in various scenarios. As the fundamental idea behind ACD is to transform passive defense into active defense and enhance system security by reducing the available attack surface, there are certain commonalities in the anti-attack process of these systems.

For theoretical evaluation schemes, such as model-based evaluation schemes, they begin with the design of the entire system and focus on the commonalities of the ACD process to evaluate security in a higher dimension. This type of research usually abstracts the offensive and defensive details, collects more coarse-grained information, and represents the active defense process as a specific mathematical or security problem.

Various evaluation models are commonly used, such as security models like attack trees and attack graphs typically used in static defense network evaluation, Petri nets and their variant models as well as mathematical models represented by Markov chains and probability theory [53].

11.7.2 Overview of Common Quantitative Evaluation Models

In the field of network security, evaluation schemes based on mathematical-based quantitative evaluation models are widely utilized.

Attack Graph

The concept of attack graph was officially proposed in 1998. It takes an attack-centric perspective and illustrates the vulnerabilities that may be exposed and the existing attack processes under a specific network configuration. The attack graph represents this information in the form of an attack path. This graph-based approach provides an intuitive representation of the relationships between vulnerability points and various parts of the network's configuration. Furthermore, since the network topology itself can be represented as a graph structure, the attack graph accurately depicts the possible attack paths and node relationships from the attack entry point to the attack target.

Petri Net

The Petri net, proposed by Carl Adam Petri in 1962, is a modeling tool used to describe the asynchronous and parallel operation modes of a system. It provides an effective means of modeling and analyzing complex systems, starting from the development process of objects. The Petri net excels in describing system process characteristics such as sequential execution, concurrency, conflict, synchronization, competition, conditionality, merging, priority, and suppression. By establishing graphical models, it mathematically expresses discrete parallel systems. The Petri net offers an intuitive graphical representation, enables rigorous mathematical analysis, and provides the technical advantage of easy programming.

Over time, the Petri net and its concepts have expanded and developed, finding applications in various fields such as automation, workflow, hardware architecture, protocols and networks, real-time systems, embedded systems, defense systems, and more. Presently, the Petri net has evolved into various variant models. When evaluating the safety and effectiveness of active defense, different modeling schemes are employed based on the characteristics of the target system. Common ones include the basic Petri net, stochastic Petri net, generalized stochastic Petri net, and other modeling schemes [54].

As shown in Fig. 11.53, the basic Petri net mainly contains the following three basic elements, where: $N = (P, T, F)$.

- P stands for place, which describes possible local state of the system, such as queues, buffers, resources of computers and communication systems.
- T stands for transition, which describes events that modify the state of the system, such as information processing, transmission, and access to resources in computers and communication systems.
- F stands for arc, which describes the relationship between states and events, and has two main functions: indicating the local state conditions that need to be met for an event to occur, and transitions among states caused by events.

This triplet constitutes a Petri net if and only if:

- $P \cup T \neq \varnothing$: the net is not empty;
- $P \cap T \neq \varnothing$: that is duality;
- $F \subseteq (P \times T) \cup (T \times P)$: the flow relationship is only between the P and T elements;
- $dom(F) \cup cod(F) = P \cup T$: $dom(F)$ represents the input elements of arc F, and $cod(F)$ represents the output elements of arc F.

A token is a dynamic object that resides within a place in a Petri net. It represents the presence or availability of a resource, and it can move from one place to another within the net. Tokens are used to model the flow of entities, resources, or events in a Petri net, and their movement between places represents the occurrence of transitions or events in the modeled system. By tracking the movement and distribution of tokens in a Petri net, we can analyze the behavior and state changes of the modeled system.

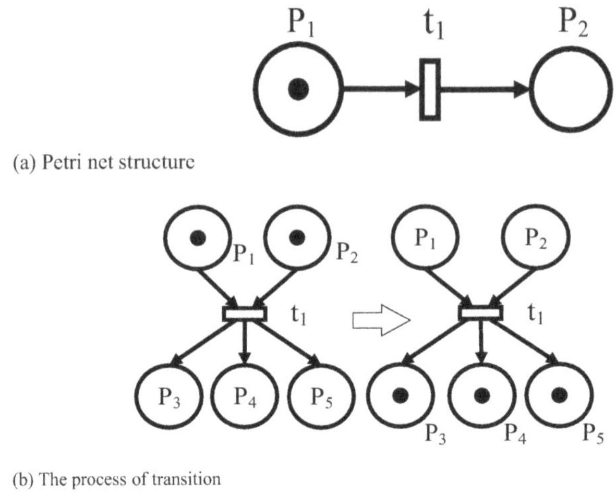

Fig. 11.52 Basic Petri net. (**a**) Petri net structure. (**b**) The process of transition

If each input place of a transition in a Petri net has a sufficient number of tokens, the transition is said to be enabled. When a transition is enabled, it can fire. Firing a transition involves consuming tokens from the input places and producing tokens for the output places.

Token movement is controlled by the transition implementation principles of Petri nets. When the incoming arc weight of a transition is greater than or equal to 1, each input position must contain a number of tokens greater than or equal to the arc weight to trigger the transition. Once the transition is executed, the outgoing arcs generate a corresponding number of tokens in each output position, while the input positions absorb the corresponding number of tokens.

Figure 11.52 illustrates a transition implementation process in a basic Petri net.

In a Petri net, as tokens move between different locations, they represent different system states. Based on the movement of tokens within a Petri net, we can derive the entire set of reachable states of the system, forming the state space of the Petri net. Furthermore, it is possible to map the Petri net to an equivalent Markov chain model. This allows for the calculation of performance metrics such as reliability, availability, and other key indicators. The complete reachability graph of the Petri net is isomorphic to the state space of the Markov chain.

Using the obtained Markov chain and its transition rate matrix parameters, the steady-state probabilities of each state can be calculated. These probabilities provide various system performance indicators, such as the time spent in each state (M), the probability density function of markers, the average number of markers in a specific location, and the marker flow rate of transitions. When the Petri net is used to describe an active defense system, these indicators can be further analyzed to obtain safety and performance metrics such as average failure time, average failure probability, number of failures, and task execution time of the system.

The probability density of tokens in useful locations commonly used in the Petri net reflects the utilization rate of system components. The average number of tokens in a specific location represents the probability of system failure, while the utilization rate of transitions indicates the throughput or delay of the system. These metrics provide insights into the system's performance and can be used to evaluate the effectiveness of ACD mechanisms.

Stochastic Petri Nets

Stochastic Petri nets (SPNs) extend the basic model of Petri nets by associating transitions with implementation delays that follow a random exponential distribution. Additionally, each transition in the SPNs is associated with an implementation rate, also known as the firing rate. This means that the execution of a transition is completed after a certain delay, and the delay time is inversely proportional to the implementation rate.

That is to say, the variations of an SPN can be associated with an implementation rate obeying an exponential distribution, indicating that the corresponding action is completed after a certain time delay, which is inversely proportional to the implementation rate. After adding the ability to describe time, each SPN is isomorphic to a continuous-time Markov chain whose state transfer matrix Q element q_{ij} is obtained based on the arcs between states M_i to M_j and the corresponding rates. Specifically, if $i \neq j$, then the value of q_{ij} is equal to the rate of the arcs between states M_i to M_j; if $i = j$, then the value of q_{ij} is equal to the negative of the sum of the rates of the arcs output from state M_i.

Generalized Stochastic Petri Nets

Generalized Stochastic Petri Nets (GSPNs) are an extension of SPNs that address the issue of state space explosion when dealing with complex problems. GSPNs introduce two types of transitions: immediate transitions and timed transitions. Immediate transitions have a real-time rate of zero. When both immediate and timed transitions satisfy their implementation conditions, immediate transitions take precedence over timed transitions.

The reachable state set in GSPNs can be divided into two subsets based on the type of transition that triggers them: the set of vanishing states that trigger transient transitions and the set of real states that trigger timed transitions.

When solving problems with GSPNs, the first step is to construct the underlying Markov chain. Then, the vanishing states can be removed or compressed using techniques such as stochastically discontinuous finite state Markov process (SDFSMP) or embedded Markov chains. This compression helps reduce the complexity of the model by eliminating unnecessary states. Finally, the steady-state probability distribution and other characteristic indicators of the real states can be determined.

By categorizing transitions and managing the state space, GSPNs provide a more efficient way to model and analyze complex systems with stochastic behavior.

Stochastic Reward Nets

Stochastic Reward Nets (SRNs) enhance the expressive power of SPNs and generalized stochastic Petri nets (GSPNs) by allowing the specification of output indices as reward-based functions. This expansion is mainly achieved through three key aspects: variable arcs, guard functions, and changeable priorities.

Variable arcs in SRNs enable the specification of reward-based functions that determine the flow of tokens based on certain criteria. These functions can depend on various factors such as the current state of the system, token distributions, or other relevant parameters.

Guard functions, utilized in SRNs, are expressed using a C-based SPN language. They represent Boolean expressions that evaluate based on the current token distribution of the network. Each transition in the SRN can be associated with a corresponding guard function. The guard function must return true for the transition to be executable. If the guard function returns false, all related transitions are disabled, meaning they cannot be fired or executed.

The use of guard functions allows for the modeling of interaction and behavior triggers between system states with active defense mechanisms. These functions play a crucial role in controlling the firing sequence of transitions based on token distribution. By incorporating variable arcs and guard functions, SRNs provide a flexible and expressive framework for modeling and analyzing complex systems. They enable the specification of reward-based functions and the dynamic control of transition execution based on system state and token distribution.

Markov Chain

Consider a stochastic process X_n that takes values at a finite or countable number of possible values, and the process is said to be in state i at moment n if $X_n = i$. Suppose that whenever the process is in state i, there exists a fixed probability P_{ij} such that the process is in state j at the next moment. Suppose that for all states $i_0, i_1, \ldots, i_{n-1}, i, j$ and $n \geq 0$:

$$\begin{aligned} P\left(X_{n+1} = j | X_n = i, X_{n-1} = i_{n-1}, \ldots, X_1 = i_1, X_0 = i_0\right) \\ = P\left(X_{n+1} = j | X_n = i\right) \\ = P_{ij} \end{aligned} \tag{11.2}$$

Such a sequence of random variables is a Markov chain X_n, and X_i as the countable set of possible values is called the state space of the chain represents the probability of the next transition to state j when the process is in state i. Since the probabilities are non-negative, and the process must transition to a specific state, so $P_{i,j}$:

$$P_{i,j} \geq 0, i, j \geq 0; \sum_{j=0}^{\infty} P_{i,j} = 1, i = 0, 1, \ldots \tag{11.3}$$

A matrix of one-step transfer probabilities written in P, there is $P_{i,j}$:

$$P = \begin{matrix} P_{00} & \cdots & P_{0i} & \cdots \\ \vdots & \ddots & \vdots & \cdots \\ P_{i0} & \cdots & P_{ii} & \cdots \\ \vdots & \vdots & \vdots & \ddots \end{matrix} \tag{11.4}$$

In a continuous-time Markov chain with time homogeneity, the transition probability of the system from state i to state j depends only on the length of its time interval, independent of the start time. Described in formal language, that is:

$$P\left(X_{n+m} = j | X_n = i\right) = P\left(X_{n+m+k} = j | X_{n+k} = i\right) \tag{11.5}$$

Due to its flexible and easy calculation characteristics, Markov chain has been widely used in security analysis. In active network defense, the system can be abstractly divided into different states, and a state set with Markov nature can be constructed, so as to establish a Markov chain, and calculate security parameters such as defense cost, system performance, attack success rate, and attack success time can be calculated. Its portability and dynamics make the research based on Markov chain an important method for active defense security assessment.

In total, compared to real attack and defense experiments, the mathematical-based method focuses on the commonalities among different ACD systems. It establishes an explicit relationship between evaluation indicators and system configuration, enabling high-sensitivity analysis in general scenarios.

The mathematical model can be employed to analyze the abstract processing network, assess the impact of attacks, and provide quantitative outcomes. In other words, it is possible to establish a hierarchical model, where a more optimal mathematical approach can be applied to the upper layer. Simultaneously, simulation, experimentation, and other methods can be utilized in the lower layer for data collection and initial calculations. The upper model then utilizes the preliminary results to generate high-dimensional quantitative evaluation after conducting further calculations.

The hybrid evaluation method is a combination of the above methods, generally using a hierarchical analysis method to evaluate the effectiveness of ACD-based systems.

11.7.3 Hierarchical Model for Evaluating the Effectiveness of Combined ACDs

The dynamic characteristics of ACDs provide defenders with a tactical advantage against threats. However, when assessing the effectiveness of ACDs, the structure of traditional security evaluation methods becomes unstable, especially when combining multiple ACD techniques. Therefore, there is still a lack of standard methods to quantitatively evaluate the effectiveness of ACDs.

CoG-MIN establishes a hierarchical model named SPM [55] for evaluating the effectiveness of ACDs. SPM consists of three layers integrating Stochastic Reward net (SRN), Poisson process, and Martingale theory incorporated in the Markov chain. The SPM model enables comprehensive and modular evaluation of ACD effectiveness in a hierarchical manner. This hierarchical structure provides greater flexibility in analyzing the security of the entire network using the three-layer analysis models. Additionally, each layer can be independently used to assess the effectiveness of individual ACD methods.

In the SPM model, the bottom level establishes an SRN model to evaluate the security effectiveness of a single node with NVP technology, while the top level employs a Markov and martingale model to analyze the migration effectiveness of VMs [56]. The Poisson model serves as an intermediate layer connecting the two levels of the model.

It is important to clarify that although the underlying SRN model can be viewed as isomorphic to a Markov process in the three-layer model mentioned earlier, this specific layer of modeling is not directly connected to the Markov chain at the top level of the SPM model. The SRN model primarily focuses on the internal structure of the node, and its steady-state distribution characterizes the potential outcomes that follow an attack on an ACD node. Conversely, the top-level Markov model illustrates the attacker's position changes within the attack chain, and its steady-state distribution represents the total number of breached nodes in the attack chain, signifying the possible locations where the attacker may be present.

Each of these three layers of the model concentrates on an attack phase, with the output of the lower layer serving as the input for the upper layer. The selection of SRN, Poisson process, Markov, and Martingale evaluation methods is based on the characteristics of NVP and VM migration defense processes.

The reasons for choosing the corresponding modeling method for each layer are provided below.

- Firstly, the single-step attack process of a single ACD node focuses on analyzing the detailed attack and defense processes within the node after the implementation of NVP technology. The offensive and defensive processes within a single node involve numerous intricate behaviors and interactions between attackers and defenders. Describing these detailed interaction behaviors using other more mathematical methods, such as Markov or probabilistic methods, increases the complexity. Therefore, for this process, the modeling approach based on SRN is selected. A single-step attack evaluation model based on SRN is established to characterize the individual attack process within a single node, providing quantitative calculation results and graphical representations. At this layer, the defensive capability is quantitatively measured by the success rate of a single-step attack.
- Then, during multiple migrations, the attacks by attackers on a single node are memoryless. The Poisson distribution is the most suitable type of random distri-

bution for simulating the timing of critical, memoryless events. Therefore, the Poisson distribution is used to describe the number of attacks during each migration.

- Finally, it is necessary to analyze the movement of the attacker's position throughout the entire attack chain under the VM migration strategy. This refers to the changes in the attacker's attack node position in each migration cycle. In comparison to the previous migration cycle, each migration cycle offers three possible directions for the attacker's position on the attack chain: attacking the next node, returning to the previous node, or staying on the same node. Regardless of how the attacker arrived at the current position, their position in the next migration cycle depends solely on their current position and the probabilities of transferring in different directions. This exhibits Markov characteristics. Therefore, in the third layer of SPM, a homogeneous discrete-time Markov chain (DTMC) is constructed to describe this process [57]. The DTMC model can calculate the steady-state probability of failure of the target node and lays the foundation for the application of Martingale theory. Based on this, the established Martingale model can calculate the failure time and repair time of the entire network.

The attack chain is illustrated in Fig. 11.53.

Let's assume an attacker has compromised k nodes.

Next, Martingale theory is utilized to calculate the expected time for the attacker to move to the next L node or return to the previous L node.

Martingale is formally defined as:

Definition 11.1 [58]: A stochastic process Z_n, $n \geq 1$ is a martingale process if, for all n, $E[|Z_n|] < \infty$ and $E[Z_{n+1}|Z_1, Z_2, \ldots, Z_n] = Z_n$.

When the attacker is located on the node k at the beginning of the nth migration period, the attack status can be speculated as follows in the next migration period:

$$P\{X_{n+1} = k + 1X_n = k\} = (1 - \omega)\mu \tag{11.6}$$

$$P\{X_{n+1} = kX_n = k\} = (1 - \omega)(1 - \mu) \tag{11.7}$$

$$P\{X_{n+1} = k - 1X_n = k\} = \omega \tag{11.8}$$

Therefore,

$$E[X_{n+1}X_n = k] = k + (1 - \omega)\mu - \omega = X_n + (1 - \omega)\mu - \omega \tag{11.9}$$

Next, establish a martingale sequence.

Theorem 1 [58]: Let M_0, M_1, ..., M_n be independent random variables, where $M_i = X_i - [(1 - \omega)\mu - \omega] \bullet i$, then the sequence M_n is a Martingale with respect to $X_0, X_1, \ldots, X_n$.

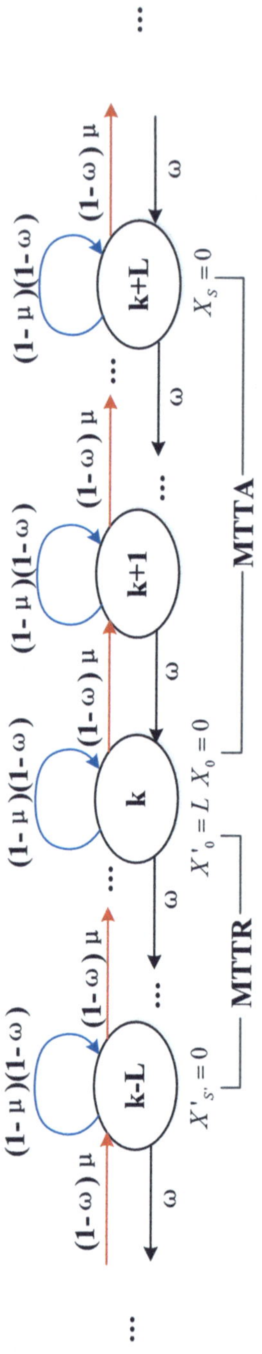

Fig. 11.53 Markov chain of the stochastic walk [58]

$$
\begin{aligned}
&E\left[M_{n+1}|X_0, X_1, X_2, \ldots, X_n\right] \\
&= E\left[M_{n+1}|X_n\right] \\
&= E\left[X_{n+1} - \left[(1-\omega)\mu - \omega\right]\cdot(n+1)|X_n\right] \\
&= E\left[X_{n+1}|X_n\right] - \left[(1-\omega)\mu - \omega\right]\cdot(n+1) \\
&= X_n + (1-\omega)\mu - \omega - \left[(1-\omega)\mu - \omega\right]\cdot(n+1) \\
&= X_n - \left[(1-\omega)\mu - \omega\right]\cdot n = M_n
\end{aligned} \tag{11.10}
$$

After establishing a martingale sequence, in order to calculate the attacking time, it is necessary to first address the stochastic stopping time.

Definition 11.2 [58]: The positive inter-valued, possibly infinite, random variable N is said to be a random time for the process $\{Z_n, n \geq 1\}$ if the event $\{N = n\}$ is determined by the random variables $Z_1, \ldots, Z_n$. That is, $Z_1, \ldots, Z_n$ determines whether or not $N = n$. If $P\{N < \infty\} = 1$, then the random time N is said to be a stopping time.

The overall movement direction of the attacker on the attack chain can be affected by the different relative strengths between defending and attacking abilities. For example, in case the attacking ability ($(1 - \omega)\mu$) is stronger than the defensive ability (ω), then the attacker is getting closer to his target and vice versa. This means that when $E[X_{n+1}|X_n] > X_n$, i.e., $\omega < \mu/(\mu + 1)$, the time to approach the target node L hop along the attack chain tends to be positive. On the contrary, when $E[X_{n+1}|X_n] < X_n$, i.e., $\omega > \mu/(\mu + 1)$, the probability of moving to the next node is smaller than the probability of the attacker returning to the previous node. The time to reach the Lth node in the direction of the target node has a "negative" tendency.

In this case, the discussion of the "negative" time of the downstream L-hop loses its meaning, but the time of the upstream L-hop can be calculated similarly. Therefore, based on the relative magnitude of ω and $\mu/(\mu + 1)$, we can analyze the time of the first arrival at different specific nodes in the corresponding scenarios.

$$\omega < \mu/(\mu+1)$$

In this case, the position at which an attack starts is denoted as the initial position: $A_0 = 0$.

Definition 11.3 [58]: When $\omega < \mu/(\mu + 1)$, the stopping time of the martingale sequence S is the minimum value of i:

$$\mathrm{E}\left[\mathrm{X_i}\right] = \mathrm{L} \tag{11.11}$$

In order to derive the number of steps for the attacker to reach the target node by L hops down the attack chain, the martingale stopping time theorem, that is, Lemma 11.1, is introduced.

Lemma 11.1 [58]: When S is a stopping time of *a* martingale sequence Z_n, $n \geq 1$ satisfies any of the following conditions.

The stopping process $\overline{Z_n}$ is uniformly bounded, or S is bounded, or, $E[S] \leq \infty$and there is an $M \leq \infty$ such that:

$$E\left[\left|Z_{n+1} - Z_n\right|\left|Z_1, \ldots Z_n\right.\right] < M \tag{11.12}$$

Then,

$$E\left[Z_S\right] = E\left[Z_0\right] \tag{11.13}$$

Theorem 11.2 [58]: For an ACD game, there is a probability μ that the attack on a single node is successful, and every T time each node is migrated and reconfigured with probability ω, if there are L nodes on the attack chain, the attacker wins, that is, the expected number of migration periods until the attacker arrives at the next Lth node is:

$$E\left[S\right] = \frac{L}{(1-\omega)\mu - \omega}, \omega < \frac{\mu}{\mu + 1} \tag{11.14}$$

Proof When $(1 - \omega)\mu > \omega$, the condition of stopping time S is $X_S = L$. The arrival time of the next L^{th} node tends to be positive. The last n rounds can determine whether n and S are equal. So, the time S is the stopping time of Martingale. To show that Lemma 11.1 is applicable, we verify the third condition.

$$\begin{aligned} &E\left[\left|M_{n+1} - M_n\right|M_0, \ldots, M_n\right] \\ &= E\left[\left|X_{n+1} - X_n\right|M_0, \ldots, M_n\right] \\ &= E\left[\left|X_{n+1} - X_n\right|\right] \\ &\leq 2E\left[\left|X_n\right|\right] \end{aligned} \tag{11.15}$$

Therefore, the step expectation to reach node L can be calculated based on Lemma 11.1:

$$E\left[M_S\right] = E\left[X_S - \left[(1-\omega)\mu - \omega\right] \cdot S\right] \tag{11.16}$$

And,

$$E\left[X_S\right] = L \tag{11.17}$$

So,

$$L-\left[(1-\omega)\mu-\omega\right]\cdot E[S]=0 \tag{11.18}$$

$$E[S]=\frac{L}{\left[(1-\omega)\mu-\omega\right]} \tag{11.19}$$

$$\omega=\mu/(\mu+1)$$

In this case, the downlink probability and upside probability of the attacker were equal, the state of the Markov obeys a uniform distribution, and the position of the attacker remained stable over time, that is $E[X_{n+1}|X_n] = X_n$. Therefore, the time it takes for the attacker to reach any other node tends to be positive and infinite.

$$\omega>\mu/(\mu+1)$$

In this case, the expected time to reach the next L node tended to be "negative" and had no practical significance. However, in this case, over time, the attacker will gradually move away from the target and be pushed out of the network. The expectation of how long it will take to expel the attacker can then be calculated, which reflects the network's ability to repair itself from the worst-case scenario.

In this scenario, it is assumed that the attack has been successful at the very beginning, that is $X_0^{'} = L$. The $X_i^{'}$ means the same distribution as X_i, but the initial position of the attacker is different, starting from node L instead of $X_0 = 0$. The attacker's location at the beginning of the ith migration cycle is indicated by a random variable. Next, the expected time to return to the attack entry before expelling the attacker back to L nodes is analyzed.

Definition 11.4 [58]: When $\omega \geq \mu/(\mu + 1)$, the stopping time $S^{'}$ of the martingale sequence is the minimum value of i making:

$$E\left[X_i^{'}\right]=0 \tag{11.20}$$

The conditions of stopping time are $X_{S'}^{'}=0$. The corresponding sequence is $M_i^{'}=X_i^{'}-\left[(1-\omega)\mu-\omega\right]\cdot i$ still about the martingale of $X_0^{'},X_i^{'},\ldots,X_n^{'}$. The different magnitude relationship of $(1-\omega)\mu$ and ω only affects the subjective choice of the stopping time and does not affect the objectively existing sequence X_n and sequence M_n. And $X_i^{'}$ and $M_i^{'}$ can be considered as a sequence X_i and M_i of starting from other nodes.

Theorem 11.3 [58]: For an ACD game, there is a probability μ that the attack on a single node is successful, and each node is migrated and reconfigured with probability ω every period T, and when the attacker has conquered L nodes, the expected number of migration cycles to expel the attacker back to the entry node is:

$$E[S'] = \frac{L}{\omega - (1-\omega)\mu}, \omega > \frac{\mu}{\mu+1} \tag{11.21}$$

According to the Lemma 11.1, the number of migration cycles of the repair network satisfies: $E\left[M'_{S'}\right] = E\left[M'_0\right] = E\left[X'_0\right] = L$.

Then the number of steps required to reach node L can be calculated according to the Lemma 11.1 and $E\left[X_{s'}\right] = 0$:

$$E\left[M'_{S'}\right] = E\left[X'_{S'}\right] - \left[(1-\omega)\mu - \omega\right] \cdot E[S'] = L \tag{11.22}$$

$$E[S'] = \frac{L}{\omega - (1-\omega)\mu} \tag{11.23}$$

Corollary 11.1 For the ACD game that considers the probability μ of a single node being compromised and the probability ω of the node being migrated in each period T, the expected time of the attacker along the downstream or upstream L nodes of the attack chain is:

$$E\left[T_A\right] = \begin{cases} \dfrac{LT}{\omega - (1-\omega)\mu} & \omega > \dfrac{\mu}{\mu+1} \\ \infty & \omega = \dfrac{\mu}{\mu+1} \\ \dfrac{LT}{(1-\omega)\mu - \omega} & \omega < \dfrac{\mu}{\mu+1} \end{cases} \tag{11.24}$$

According to the analysis above, when attackers and defenders compete with varying relative strengths, attackers may gradually approach the target over time or lose the privileges they have gained and be expelled from the system. Therefore, different defensive strengths can be employed based on different scenarios to achieve corresponding defensive objectives.

Firstly, two scenarios are defined:

- Ordinary defense scenario: The attacker's daily defense activities go undetected, and the defender tends to utilize lower defense costs in exchange for a certain level of security. Attackers can assess the system's resilience by means of the Mean Time to Attack (MTTA).
- Crisis scenario defense: The system may have detected the presence of an attacker or has higher security protection requirements. In such situations, defenders are willing to invest in more expensive defensive measures to achieve higher levels of security. More frequent and large-scale VM migration operations make it challenging for attackers to approach the target, but they gradually lose unauthorized privileges. The Mean Time to Repair (MTTR) is employed as an evaluation metric for attack resistance.

Given the system parameters L,ω,T,r,M,N, MTTA and MTTR can be calculated, respectively, as follows:

$$\text{MTTA} = \frac{LT}{(1-\omega)\left(1-e^{-Trp_A}\right)-\omega}, \omega < \frac{1-e^{-Trp_A}}{2-e^{-Trp_A}} \tag{11.25}$$

$$\text{MTTR} = \frac{LT}{\omega-(1-\omega)\left(1-e^{-Trp_A}\right)}, \omega > \frac{1-e^{-Trp_A}}{2-e^{-Trp_A}} \tag{11.26}$$

11.7.4 Reliability Analysis of CoG-MIN

CoG-MIN itself has various security guarantees. In CoG-MIN, each packet undergoes a process of signing and verification, which enhances the security of the network layer. This approach effectively addresses the challenges associated with packet spoofing and tampering that are commonly encountered in IP networks.

Moreover, since CoG-MIN itself is based on identity identifier and identity authentication, it can conveniently establish secure transmission channels. In CoG-MIN, user identity contains various information, such as the user's device and certificate, which are stored in MIS. Identity-based management renders many network attacks ineffective in CoG-MIN, such as identity theft, account blasting, unauthorized access/operation, and so on.

The hierarchical security defense scheme of CoG-MIN is depicted in Fig. 11.54.

- In the network layer, CoG-MIN is designed with multiple identifier coexistence centered on the identity identifier. This ensures the independence, management, and control of the network, providing architectural security.
- The routing scheme incorporates underlying identity authentication and packet signature, allowing to trace the source of each packet, hold network content accountable, and establish trust in the identity of entities entering the network.
- To address unknown vulnerability threats, MIN introduces a weighted centrality algorithm: Weighted Network Centrality Measure (WNCM) algorithm to identify important nodes in the network [59]. Mimic defense is deployed based on this algorithm, establishing an endogenous security system that enhances data security and service reliability.

Regarding reliability, we compare the reliability of the network using four important node selection strategies: WNCM, Network Centrality Measure (NCM), Stochastic Strategy, and Exhaustive Strategy. The Exhaustive Strategy involves iterating through all available solutions, comparing their anti-attack performance, and selecting the best one.

External users would like to access the data stored on Storage Server 1 and Storage Server 2 through the MIN network. Through the test, when the above four algorithms are used to select nodes with the same proportion to deploy mimic

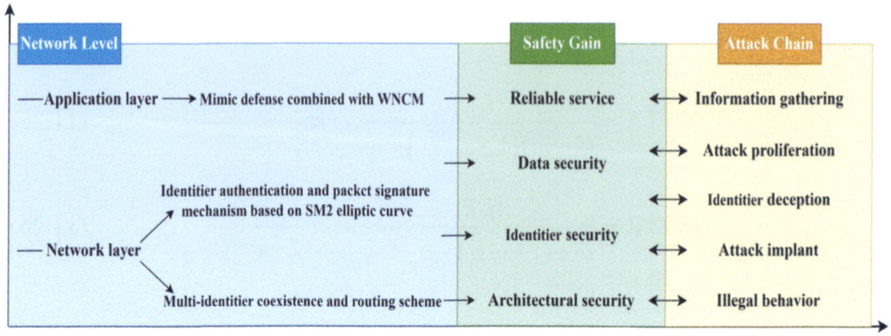

Fig. 11.54 Security defence scheme in CoG-MIN

Table 11.1 Nodes that fail 30% randomly

The number of protection nodes		1	2	3
P_f	NCM	2/15	1/10	0
	WNCM	1/15	0	0
	Random	2/21	2/21	2/21
	Exhaustive	1/15	0	0

Table 11.2 Nodes that randomly fail 40%

The number of protection nodes		1	2	3
P_f	NCM	8/20	3/10	0
	WNCM	7/20	2/10	0
	Random	3/7	3/7	3/7
	Exhaustive	7/20	2/10	0

Table 11.3 Probability of user access failure

The number of failed nodes		2	3	4	5
P_f	NCM	1/10	3/10	3/5	1
	WNCM	0	2/10	3/5	1
	Random	2/21	3/7	4/5	1
	Exhaustive	0	2/10	3/5	1

defense, and other nodes fail randomly, the user cannot obtain the probability of access failure.

Tables 11.1 and 11.2 describe the probability p_f of user access failure when the MIN network randomly fails 30% of the nodes and 40% of the nodes under the four selection strategies.

Table 11.3 describes when the protection ratio $\delta = 30\%$, the probability of user access failure under different failure ratios.

The overall trend is that the effect of WNCM is similar to that of the exhaustive scheme, and both outperform NCM and the random scheme. The defensive effect of

WNCM and NCM improves significantly with an increase in the protection ratio. When the protection ratio reaches 40%, which means protecting three nodes, both schemes establish a complete information propagation chain and can withstand failures in other nodes. The resistance of the random scheme to attacks remains unchanged with an increase in the protection ratio since its node protection and failure are independent random strategies. According to the conditional probability formula and the full probability formula, when employing a random protection strategy, the average access failure probability is only related to the number of failed nodes and is not influenced by the defender's selection of key protection nodes.

Only when the network randomly fails by 30% and only one key node is selected for protection (as shown in the first column of Table 11.1), the failure probability of the NCM scheme is higher than that of the random scheme. This occurs because both the WNCM and NCM schemes differ from exhaustive solutions, which aim to provide the optimal solution. The centrality algorithm selects relatively important nodes based on multiple indicators, but it may not always yield the optimal solution in every scenario. In this scenario, the NCM scheme tends to protect important central nodes. However, the optimal strategy would be to select four end nodes for protection, which explains why the failure probability of the NCM scheme is higher than that of the random scheme. The data in the three tables demonstrate that the WNCM algorithm in the MIN network adjusts the weights of different devices based on the characteristics of the MIN network, producing results that closely align with the optimal strategy.

In terms of computational complexity, exhaustive solutions can provide the optimal protection strategy but come with exponentially increasing computational overhead as the network size grows. Both the WNCM and NCM schemes have polynomial complexity. In summary, at the same protection ratio, WNCM can offer a node selection strategy that is quite close to the optimal solution with lower computational complexity, which translates to lower defense costs.

11.8 Large-Scale Security Testing and Practical Verification

11.8.1 Crowd Security Testing—International Elite Security Competition

The security of the MIN network has been widely demonstrated in various practical verifications. For example, for four consecutive years, the MIN network has been regarded as a standalone attack target in the Information Security and Countermeasures Contest (ISCC).

In the 18th ISCC competition in 2021, the security verification test based on the MIN network involves two challenges. The first one aimed to challenge participants to penetrate the server host within the MIN network by exploiting a server that had already been compromised. The second one utilized HS-VPN as an upper layer application, aiming to bypass the identity management mechanism in the MIN network and achieve unauthorized access. The detailed topology of the two challenges is shown in Fig. 11.55.

The competition lasted for 25 days, and the final statistical for the practical questions are given in Table 11.4. During the competition, the MIN network security verification challenges were accessed approximately 10.41 million times by participants. A total of 3156 files were uploaded, including 496 malicious files, generating 34.14GB of attack traffic. The attacks originated from 1725 different IP sources.

Figure 11.56 shows the statistics of uploaded files per day during the 25-day participation period. This demonstrates the large scale of the competition and the high enthusiasm of the participants. Until the end of the competition, no participant passed the challenges.

In the 19th Information Security and Countermeasures Contest in 2022, the number of participants for the challenge based on MIN networks is approximately 718, generating 14,713,579 access logs and successfully executing 12,216 commands. The access data are shown in Fig. 11.57, and the IP sources of the accesses are shown in Fig. 11.58. During the competition, a total of 148 participants completed the first stage of the challenge, but no participants were able to complete the second and third stage of the challenge, the data are given in Table 11.5.

In the 2022 ISCC, the practical challenge based on the MIN network was designed to test the participants' ability to first penetrate the IP network (thus demonstrating the MIN network's immunity to IP-based penetration) and then focus on attacking and cracking the MIN network protocol (verifying the reliability of the MIN network). The final data results align with these two expectations.

In the 4th "Qiangwang" International Elite Challenge On Cyber Mimic Defense in 2021, a security verification question based on the MIN network is provided as a MISC-type topic (the same challenges as those provided in the ISCC competitions).

As one of the practical shooting targets of the 4th "Qiangwang" International Elite Challenge On Cyber Mimic Defense, the MIN network was provided to participants for security attack testing.

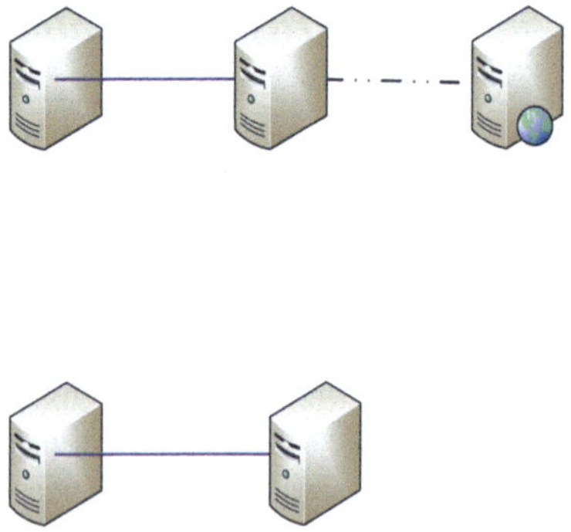

Fig. 11.55 The topology for the security verification test based on the MIN network

Table 11.4 The security verification competition data

Statistical items	Description
Total number of visited pages (including CSS and other files)	10,417,598 times
The number of uploaded files	3156
Number of malicious backdoors	4,96
The total size of the resulting traffic	34.14GB
Total number of visitors (measured by IP)	1725 IPs

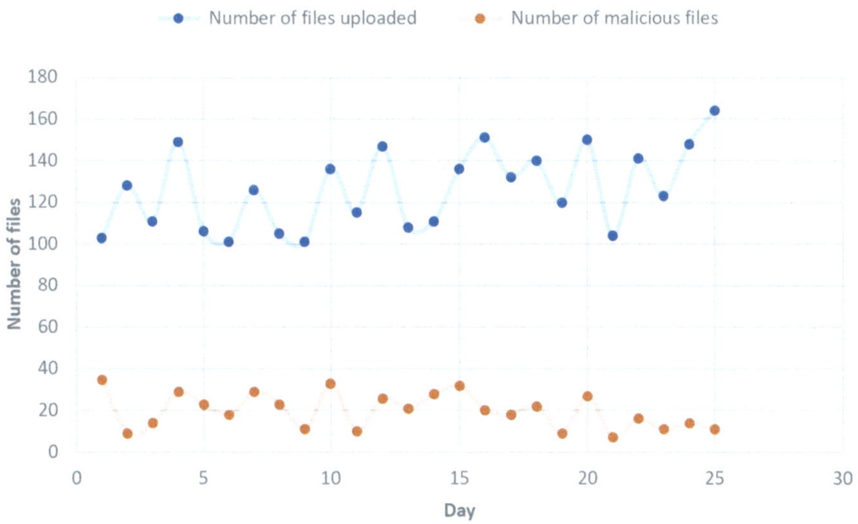

Fig. 11.56 2021 Classic file distribution

After 72 h of continuous attack testing by 48 elite teams from both domestic and international backgrounds, the MIN network experienced over 5000 access and attack attempts, with more than 100 malicious files uploaded to the servers.

As shown in Fig. 11.59, each target within the MIN network experienced different attack scenarios. The system protected by this security architecture continued to operate normally and provide services until the end of the game. The MIN network security verification question (called HS-VPN) has still not been successfully solved after experiencing various attacks from many top teams, which further proves the effectiveness of this solution.

The high security of MIN network enables it to be applied in various scenarios, such as the rapidly developing field of Internet of Vehicles (IoV). The MIN-V2X (Vehicle-To-Everything), a high-security private network based on MIN networks, can provide excellent solutions to communication security, data security, and privacy protection in V2X.

In the 2021/2022 "Qiangwang" International Elite Challenge On Cyber Mimic Defense, the MIN network is regarded as a real combat target, competing with

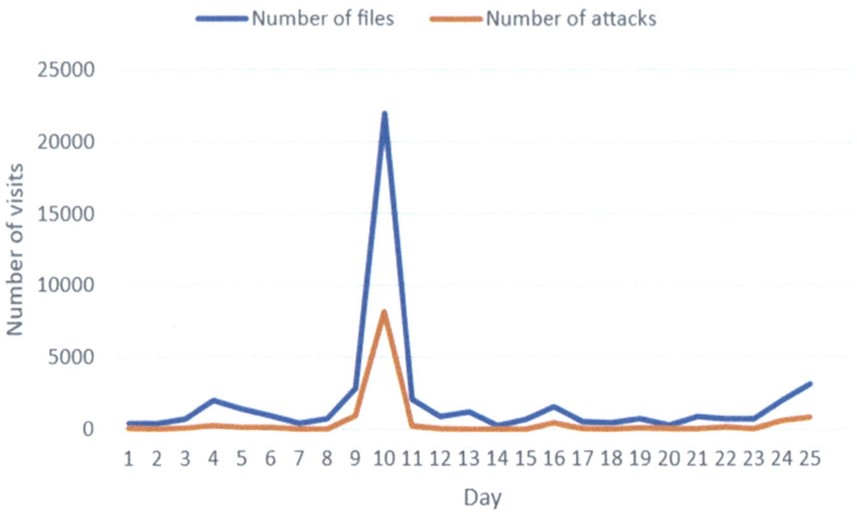

Fig. 11.57 Classic malicious access distribution

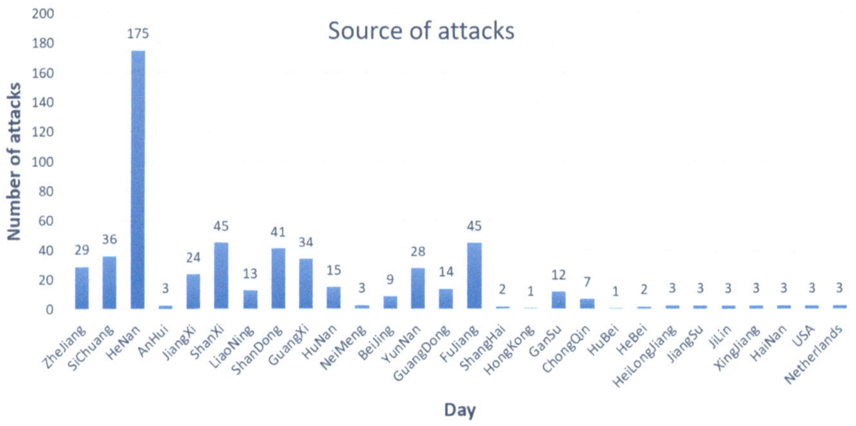

Fig. 11.58 IP address statistics of attack sources

T-Box/ADAS from international players. In the end, through online pre-selection and special invitations, a total of 48 teams participated in the final competition. These teams have achieved outstanding results in the Capture The Flag (CTF) competitions around the world and have rich practical experience.

After 72 hours of continuous attack testing by 48 teams, more than 100 malicious files were uploaded by the players on the servers of the HS-VPN high-security system based on the MIN network. Until the end of the competition, no participant was able to breach the system and solves the question based on HS-VPN.

The 2023 World Intelligent Drive Challenge (WIDC) took place successfully at DongLi Lake in Tianjin from May 17th to 19th (Fig. 11.60). In 2023, WIDC includes

Table 11.5 Overview of the data

Statistical items	Description
Total number of VPN logs	14,713,579
Orders executed by players	12,216
Number of VPN enrollments	416
Access the source IP	554
Client downloads	718
The number of packets downloaded	303
Number of people who passed the first stage	148
Number of people who passed the second stage	0
Number of people who passed the third stage	0

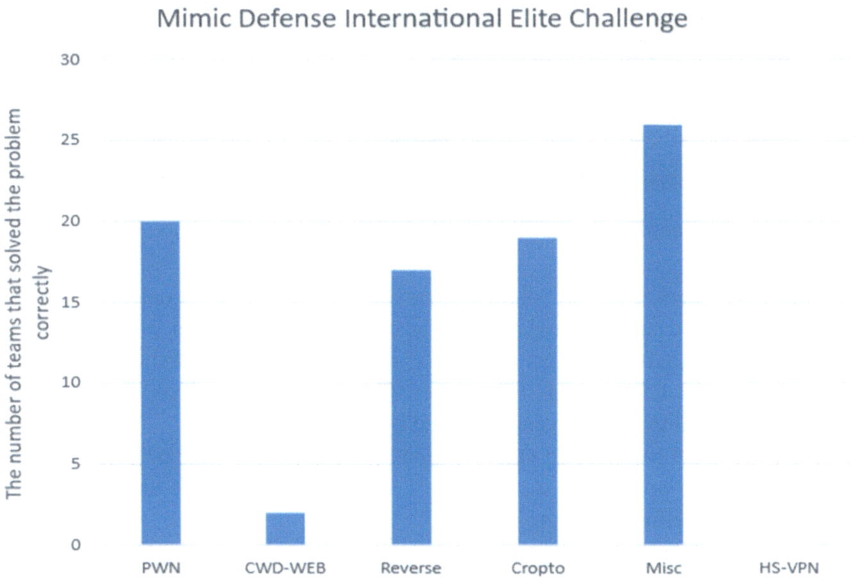

Fig. 11.59 Number of puzzles solved by teams in the 4th "Qiangwang" International Elite Challenge On Cyber Mimic Defense in 2021

four major competitions, including the metaverse virtual simulation competition, the "TianRongXin Cup" information security attack-defence competition, the intelligent driving mass production competition, and the intelligent connected real car competition. Additionally, there was a Smart Transportation Sandbox Race held concurrently.

In the final of the "TianRongXin Cup" information security attack and defense competition, the HS-V2X high security private network showed high security in practical applications. The unmanned automatic sweeper and the unmanned jeep were both remotely controlled via the HS-V2X APP by the owner, allowing remote operation of their power systems, including start, stop, steering, and speed control, through mobile public operator's network. During the final, given account and basic

Fig. 11.60 The “TianRongXin Cup” information security attack-defence competition [60]

password to all hacker teams, ask them enter the vehicle and try to control the power system to the three targets vehicles. Until the end of the competition, no hacker team was able to successfully control the power system of the two automatic sweepers and one jeep remotely through the Internet. The prize money offered by the target owner remained intact and was not claimed by any team.

This successful real vehicle target competition shows that the MIN network has high security and provides a solid network security guarantee for the widespread application of intelligent driving vehicles.

In summary, the results of these competitions indicate that the MIN network can prevent the spread of intranet attacks, ensure the confidentiality and integrity of network communications, and facilitate identity tracking and attack traceability.

11.8.2 Third-Party Security Testing

In 2021, The Peking University Laboratory of Future Network in Peking University Shenzhen Graduate School, together with many universities including the Macau University of Science and Technology (M.U.S.T.), the Hong Kong University of Science and Technology (HKUST), the University of Sheffield, the University of Surrey, the University of Waterloo, and the Universiti Tunku Abdul Rahman, launched cross-border deployments. The deployments involved technical tests such as consensus mechanism, transmission control, and situational awareness, as well as

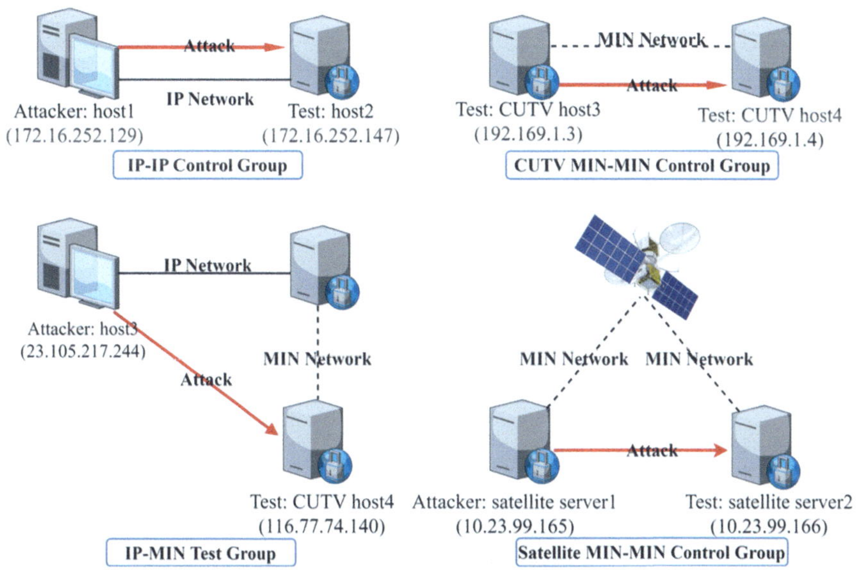

Fig. 11.61 Comparative test topology for cyber-attack resistance

functionality testing for identity management, video-on-demand, and video conferencing.

Among them, the comparative test topology of IP and MIN against cyberattacks is shown in Fig. 11.61, and the test covers the main links of the classic attack chain of the current cyber forces (Red Hat Hackers) and hackers (Fig. 11.62). The test result is given in Table 11.6. The results show that the MIN network can effectively defend against network attacks at various stages of the classic attack chain in the scenarios of IP-MIN and MIN-MIN.

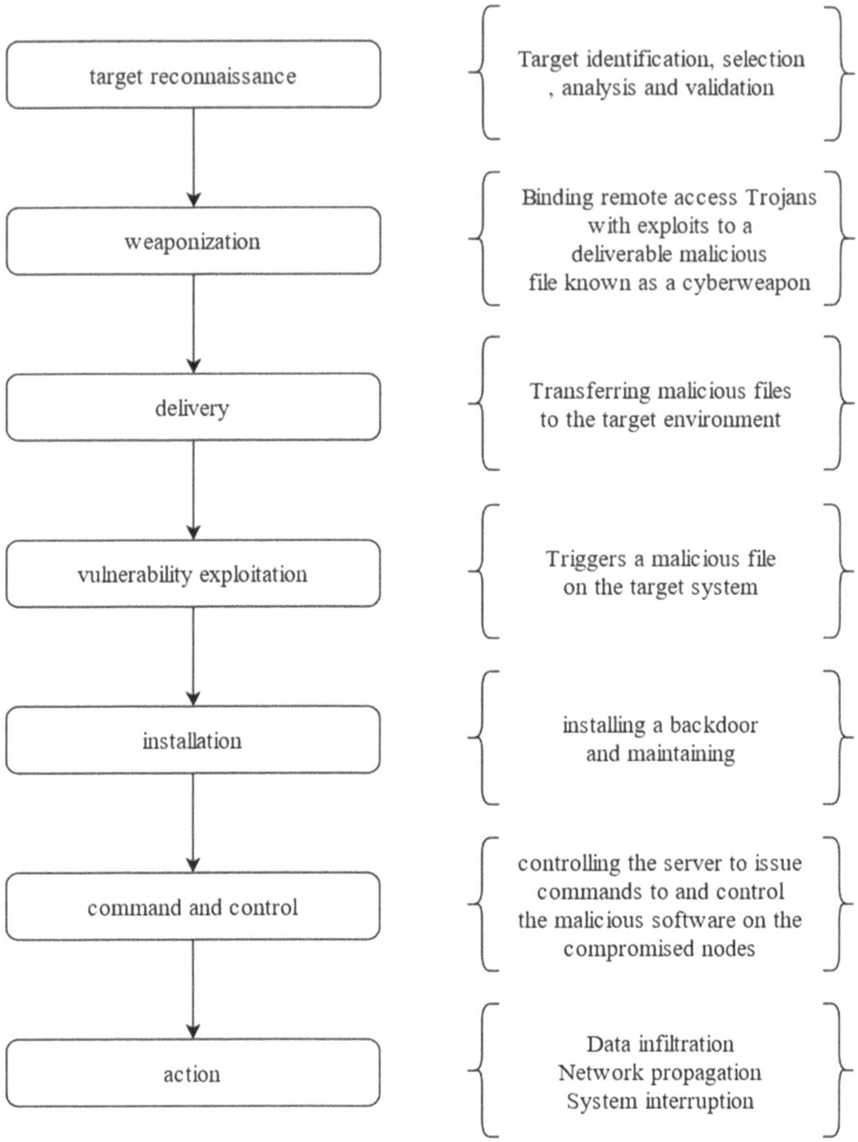

Fig. 11.62 Classical network attack chain

11.9 Quantum Security

11.9.1 Overview of Quantum Communication

As human society continues to progress, there is an increasing need for communication in people's daily lives and work. With the continuous advancement of technology, the means of communication have also been innovating and progressing. From

Table 11.6 The test result against network attacks

Attack phase	Attack means	IP-IP test result	IP-MIN test result	CUTV MIN-MIN test result	Satcom MIN-MIN test result
Reconnaissance	Host discovery	Can be discovered	Discover hosts that are not CUTV's	Nothing found	Nothing found
	Ping scan	Can be detected	Undetectable	Undetectable	Undetectable
	Operating system identification	System fingerprint can be obtained	Nothing found	Nothing found	Nothing found
	Post scan	Can detect all port service	Can't found any port information	Nothing found	Nothing found
Exploitation	Trojan implantation	TCP trojan	Connected	Can't connect	Can't connect
		UDP trojan	Connected	Can't connect	Can't connect
		ICMP trojan	Connected	Can't connect	Can't connect
	Web shell	Connected	Can't connect	Can't connect	Can't connect
Actions	ARP poisoning	Sniff	Sniff successfully	Non-intranet	Sniff failed
		Forced disconnection	Disconnected	Non-intranet	Failed

the initial use of objects and sounds, to the use of writing and electronic information technology, and now the widespread use of the internet for transmitting information, these developments have not only made communication more efficient but also expanded the scope of information storage and transmission in terms of time and space. This has brought unprecedented convenience to social development.

However, while meeting the communication needs of people's daily lives, there is also increasing concern about effectively ensuring communication security. The development of communication technology necessitates better protection of communication security to prevent information leakage and other security issues. Consequently, more and more people are paying attention to communication security, seeking more efficient, secure, and reliable methods of communication.

In 1949, Claude Shannon, the father of information theory, proposed the communication theory of secrecy systems which laid the foundation for modern cryptography. Encryption algorithms based on mathematical theories such as RSA and elliptic curves offer very high security. However, this security is limited. Particularly with the advent and maturation of quantum computing theory and practice, the security of classical encryption methods based on mathematics faces severe threats. Quantum computers will solve encryption algorithms in a short time that would take traditional computers thousands of years to crack, posing significant challenges to modern communication and information security. Therefore, the research on new encryption technologies and algorithms has become a hot topic in the fields of cryptography and information security.

Quantum communication [61] is a method of secure information transmission that leverages the fundamental principles of quantum mechanics. Unlike any classical communication security technologies, quantum communication can theoretically ensure unconditional security and is the only communication technology that has been rigorously proven in theory. Its theoretical research includes directions such as quantum key distribution, quantum secure direct communication, quantum teleportation, and quantum secret sharing. Quantum communication has sparked a global surge of interest. It not only addresses the issues of insecurity and unreliability in traditional communication methods but also brings new challenges and opportunities to disciplines such as physics, materials science, mathematics, cryptography, and computer science. In recent years, countries around the world have placed high importance on quantum communication technology, conducting extensive experiments and promoting its industrialization, leading to its rapid development.

Quantum communication generally achieves secure network communication based on the principles of quantum uncertainty and quantum no-cloning. Quantum states cannot be precisely measured and thus cannot be cloned; moreover, quantum states change when observed by a quantum system, making eavesdropping detectable. Quantum key distribution (QKD) is based on this concept, using the transmission of the quantum states to obtain secure quantum keys. Currently, QKD technology includes multiple types, mainly divided into discrete variable protocols and continuous variable protocols. The most well-developed theoretical approach involves using non-entangled single photons for key distribution and negotiation under discrete variable protocols. It is generally believed that the proposal of the BB84 protocol for QKD in 1984 can be regarded as the starting point of quantum communication.

The BB84 protocol is a QKD protocol that employs the principles of quantum no-cloning and quantum uncertainty to ensure the security of the quantum keys. This protocol is based on the polarization of discrete single photons, using four polarization states: $0^\circ |\leftrightarrow\rangle$, $45^\circ |\nearrow\rangle$, $90^\circ |\updownarrow\rangle$ and $135^\circ|\searrow\rangle$, divided into two bases: the rectilinear basis $\langle\leftrightarrow|\updownarrow\rangle(\langle\leftrightarrow|\updownarrow\rangle = 0)$ and the diagonal basis $\langle\nearrow|\searrow\rangle(\langle\nearrow|\searrow\rangle = 0)$. Both the sender and the receiver can choose different preparation and measurement bases to send and receive the contents of the quantum channel. Later, verification, error correction and other processing steps are performed in a classical channel. The types of classical channels include coaxial cables, twisted pairs and optical fibers. The quantum channel used for transmitting single photons typically employs optical fibers.

The specific steps to realize the transmission of quantum states through quantum channels are as follows: (1) The sender randomly prepares the quantum state, setting its polarization to one of the four possible polarization states and sends this quantum state to the receiver; (2) Upon receiving the quantum state, the receiver randomly selects either the rectilinear basis or the diagonal basis for measurement. For each measurement, the receiver records the measurement result and the basis used, and communicates the basis used for each measurement to the sender through a classical channel; (3) The sender compares the preparation bases with the receiver's measurement bases and informs the receiver which measurement bases match the preparation bases. Theoretically, when the bases chosen by both parties are identical, their results should also be identical; (4) Based on a pre-agreed encoding rule, the sender and receiver derive the key. For example, polarizations at 0° and 45° might represent 0, while polarizations at 90° and 135° represent 1. Table 11.7 illustrates the principle of this protocol process.

The BB84 protocol process must be carried out before each communication, which conforms to the principle of one-time pad in information theory, so it is absolutely safe in theory. The distributed quantum states and classical information to be encrypted are transmitted in their respective channels without interfering with each other.

The BB84 protocol process requires the preparation and detection of single photons. There are currently three common types of single-photon sources: the first type is quantum dot-based single-photon sources; the second type involves generating photon pairs and using one photon as a trigger for another; the third type attenuates laser light to the single-photon level, typically using the combination of semiconductor lasers and optical attenuators, which is most commonly used in QKD. Chinese quantum research teams have made breakthroughs in various aspects of these directions and are currently leading globally in the preparation of single photons. Single photons require preparation in quantum polarization states, often achieved using multiple lasers, passive polarization beam splitters and polarization-independent beam splitters to prepare four quantum polarization states. There are many types of devices capable of detecting single photons, with the most widely used being indium gallium arsenide avalanche photodiodes and superconducting nanowire single-photon detectors.

The BB84 protocol was later developed into a simplified version known as the B92 protocol, which shares the core principles of BB84. In practical systems, single-photon sources are typically prepared using weak coherent light sources obtained by attenuating laser light sources. Photons from weak coherent light sources follow a Poisson distribution of photon numbers, which includes a non-negligible multi-photon component. Eavesdroppers can exploit this multi-photon component through photon-number-splitting attacks. This problem is addressed by

Table 11.7 BB84 protocol principle

Preparation basis of the sender	Data sent by the sender	Measurement basis of the receiver	Measurement result of the receiver	Shared secret key after comparison
+	0	+	0	0
+	1	×	0	–
×	1	×	1	1
+	0	×	1	–
×	1	+	0	–
×	0	×	0	0
×	0	+	1	–
+	1	+	1	1

the decoy-state protocol, where the sender randomly prepares weak coherent pulses with phase randomization at different intensities, one as the signal state for generating the key and the others as decoy states. After phase randomization, weak coherent pulses can be viewed as mixed states of different photon number states that satisfy the Poisson distribution. The proportions of vacuum states, single-photon states, and multi-photon states vary across weak coherent pulses of different intensities. Eavesdroppers adjusting the transmittance of multi-photon states to maintain consistency in the photon distribution of intercepted light pulses at the receiver end depend on the intensity of the weak coherent light source used by the sender and channel losses. However, eavesdroppers cannot distinguish which intensity of coherent light modulated by the sender corresponds to intercepted light pulses, making it impossible to adjust the efficiency of photon transmission based on intensity and ensure consistency in the photon distribution at the receiver end compared to non-eavesdropped conditions. Therefore, by mixing decoy states into the signal state, receivers can detect eavesdropping based on statistical anomalies in detected coherent states of various intensities. Quantum communication using the decoy-state scheme can achieve information transmission rates of several thousand bits per second per hundred kilometers.

The quantum key distribution schemes mentioned above are all initiated unilaterally. For greater efficiency and longer transmission distances, entangled quantum pairs are necessary for key distribution. The BBM92 protocol, equivalent to the BB84 protocol, uses an entangled source to send a pair of entangled photon pairs to parties separated in different locations, who then measure them to establish the key. A more secure scheme, measurement-device-independent quantum key distribution (MDI-QKD), reverses the process of BBM92: both the sender and receiver send quantum states to an untrusted third party for Bell state measurements. The secure key is established based on the Bell state measurement results announced by the third party. Subsequently, scientists have further proposed twin-field QKD protocols, phase-matching QKD protocols and mode-matching QKD protocols based on other properties of photon, building upon the foundation of MDI-QKD.

Quantum communication networks have evolved over many years and now encompass several main approaches: quantum relay schemes, which involve dividing a complete channel routed path into segments, entangling these segments with each other to transmit entangled states, ultimately achieving direct transmission of quantum states between sender and receiver across the entire channel; trusted-node-based trusted relay networks, where QKD and one-time pad message transmission occur between all intermediate nodes, requiring absolute trustworthiness of all intermediate nodes; a further advancement, integrating trusted relays with optical switch functionality, proposing a centralized control station approach, which is currently the most effective solution for wide-area optical fiber quantum communication.

According to the requirements of the MIN network, devices in the network need to communicate extensively with the MIS. This distinguishes it from any known quantum communication network: MIS uses blockchain technology to carry and manage information about all users and devices in the network, ensuring the trustworthiness of all users and devices. Therefore, the MIN system inherently meets the premise of trusted-node-based trusted relay networks. Building upon the excellent network architecture of MIN, quantum technology can expand new types of physical identifiers in MIN networks, enhancing network security. Without altering existing quantum communication network physical devices, this expands the applicability of quantum communication networks while ensuring security, making communication more flexible and freer. For ease of description and understanding, this section uses single-photon quantum to describe the entire process, employing weak coherent light sources following a Poisson distribution, which operates on the same principles. This utilizes existing hardware devices that support preparation and detection of single-photon polarization states, managed and controlled by software systems, similar to current quantum communication practices. Specific technical solutions will be detailed below.

11.9.2 Quantum Identifier

In the MIN network, irrespective of the type or semantic representation of the network identifier, they share a fundamental condition: an identifier contains a piece of definitive information. Quantum states possess properties of uncertainty and non-clonability [61], accurately expressing their content only when the preparation and measurement bases (hereafter referred to as quantum bases) align. Quantum identifiers [62] in the MIN network leverage these properties by defining accurate content expressed through the combination of quantum states and bases: while quantum states and bases individually may vary, their combination yields a precise and unique result. Considering the one-to-one relationship between quantum states and bases, they can convey limited information, thus requiring representation in a sequential form to constitute a definitive and comprehensive set of information. Quantum identifiers are defined as deterministic identity information stored in the MIS, decipherable by MIRs, represented jointly by variable quantum sequences and variable quantum basis sequences. Positioned at the network layer in MIN, quantum identifiers are implemented in communication by dividing this precise, immutable information into its variable quantum and basis components, presenting an innovative solution to the quantum storage and forwarding problem. This approach maximizes the use of quantum uncertainty and non-clonability properties, ensuring the communication security.

Considering that the identifier area of MIN can only carry traditional information, quantum bases are written into MIN network packets as a type of identifier, referred to as quantum basis identifiers. During information transmission, complete information can only be obtained by combining quantum basis identifiers with quantum states. Quantum bases correspond to the polarization angles chosen for the preparation and detection of single photons. Therefore, quantum basis identifiers include polarization angle identifiers for quantum states. When expressing longer information, multiple quantum bases are combined into sequences of states, requiring the formation of quantum basis sequences in communication, which include polarization angle data for multiple quantum bases. In this process, each individual quantum basis represents 0 or 1, and multiple quantum bases are combined to form quantum basis sequences composed of 0 and 1, similar in form to 0101. The content of quantum basis sequences is variable and typically generated randomly by default.

The network packets of MIN are based on the TLV encoding scheme, consisting of three parts: Type, Length, and Value. The TLV encoding scheme is highly extensible as it allows arbitrary additional padding content, and different TLV packets can be combined and overlaid to form more comprehensive information expressions. This section focuses on the improvement of quantum identifiers in the network packets of MIN, primarily in the Identifier area and Signature area. According to the requirements of MIN, the Identifier area must contain one or more network identifiers, which MIRs can use for network packet processing. Leveraging this feature, a new type of quantum basis identifier is proposed to be added to the Identifier area, with the type determined based on practical network conditions, such as 128, 256, and so on, and the value randomly selected within the constraints of length.

According to the requirements of MIN, the Signature area includes one or more digital signatures, typically covering the Identifier area and the Read-Only area. Each signature consists of two TLV groups: metadata information for the signature and the signature result itself. Leveraging this feature, the following improvements are proposed: separate signatures for the Identifier area and Read-Only area, then integrate all signature TLV groups to form the signature area within the MIN packet. No changes are made to the Variable area within the MIN packet. These enhancements to the Identifier area and Signature area align with the basic principles of applying for new types of identifiers in MIN and ensuring router storage and forwarding capabilities, ensuring they can be effectively read, identified and processed by both MIS and MIR.

The MIN network evolves from traditional network architecture and differs physically from quantum communication implementations. As they are not fully compatible, simple integration using existing technologies is not feasible; support for dual channels is necessary. Additionally, deployment requires the combined use of existing communication devices and quantum physical hardware, as illustrated in Table 11.8, integrating both the MIN network and quantum communication systems to enable routing and addressing support for quantum identifiers at the network layer.

Based on the four conditions mentioned above, all of which are already present in existing technology, it is feasible to implement a highly secure communication method that supports quantum identifiers for network layer routing without increasing physical equipment or costs. This approach saves significant software and hardware expenses. Building upon these conditions ensures seamless communication between quantum systems and the MIN network during the communication process, allowing them to function properly as required. Moreover, these conditions enable each router in the path of the MIN network supporting optical quantum

Table 11.8 Software and hardware conditions

Hardware Condition 1: Hardware devices capable of preparing and detecting single-photon quantum polarization states.
Software Condition 1: Software systems capable of managing and controlling Hardware Condition 1.
Hardware Condition 2: Communication devices supporting the MIN network.
Software Condition 2: The MIN network, including MIS and MIR software systems.

technology to interpret and forward content received from previous routers, thereby achieving joint routing of quantum and conventional information.

Among the requirements of MIN, MIR needs to communicate with MIS to verify the source of data for each MIN packet and whether there is tampering and falsification. Distributed MIS systems also need to synchronize to ensure timely updates of various information. Additionally, it is also necessary to support dual-channel communication between MIRs capable of quantum identifier resolution, communication between regular MIRs and those supporting quantum identifier resolution, and ultimately enable communication among all MIRs to achieve fully compatible communication within MIN supporting quantum identifiers.

The deployment example can be seen in Fig. 11.63. It supports progressive deployment on the existing MIN network, and the enhanced quantum communication does not interfere with communication in the existing MIN network.

The routing functionality of MIN maintains the traditional routing methods and does not route quantum states. The quantum identifier information formed by the quantum states and quantum basis sequences is considered accurate information, which is the fundamental reason it can be routed. In practical applications, the use of quantum properties hides the identity information of the sender and receiver, as well as the content of the transmitted information. When using quantum identifiers for network communication, each MIR that supports quantum identifier resolution along the way must read the quantum basis identifier information, parse and generate the quantum identifier, and regenerate the quantum states and quantum basis sequences. This process allows the accurate information of the quantum identifier to bypass the non-cloning restriction of quantum states and enables storage forwarding and routing. Since the transmission of quantum states and traditional information cannot be compatible simultaneously, a dual-channel approach is required. Considering the issue of timing, the stop-and-wait method is used in this dual-channel transmission process: first, the sender transmits all the contents of the MIN packet in the classical channel, and after receiving the acknowledgment from the receiver, the quantum states are prepared and sent.

The network equipment supporting quantum communication essentially combines both MIN and quantum communication devices, and therefore still supports basic MIN communication. The software and hardware supporting quantum communication are only activated when quantum communication is needed, using the stop-and-wait method. The deployment of quantum communication software and hardware can be tailored to actual needs, using existing equipment or implementing

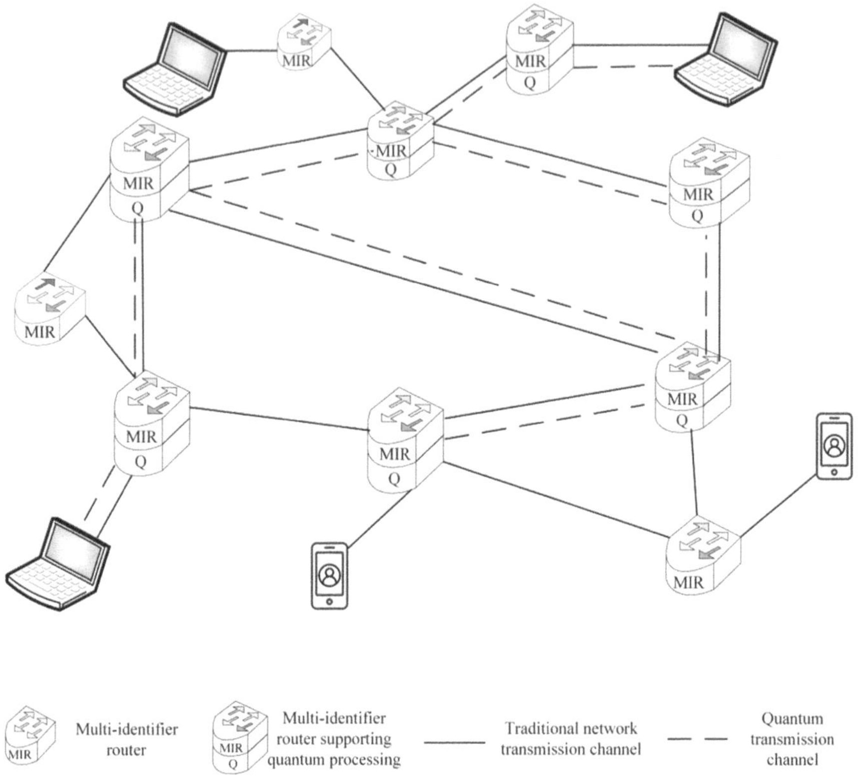

Fig. 11.63 Deployment example

communication schemes of varying ranges and security levels based on specific requirements.

11.9.3 Quantum Communication in the MIN Network

Next, the MIN communication scheme based on quantum identifiers [62] is introduced. Note that the related aspects of quantum state transmission and reception only involve the usage of existing technologies without any modifications, and thus will not be described in detail.

In the process of transmitting and receiving quantum states, the MIN communication scheme based on quantum identifiers preferably adopts the non-entangled single-photon scheme under the most theoretically mature discrete variable protocol. The scheme fully utilizes the characteristics of the BB84 protocol, by default using single-photon quantum, the vertical polarization basis and the diagonal polarization basis for preparation and detection, as well as four different polarization states for transmitting and receiving quantum states. The preparation and reception of quanta use the same purely random process as in the BB84 protocol. Based on the basic concepts described in the previous section, the communication steps are described as follows:

Step 1: (Optional, newly added users apply for their quantum identifier information from MIS) The sender packages the information to be sent. During the generation of the MIN network packet, the current sender first randomly generates the required quantum basis sequence as the quantum basis identifier and records it. Then the original sender must use their private key to sign the content of the quantum basis and the content of the Read-Only area separately. Intermediate routers, acting as new senders, will re-sign the modified Identifier area. Finally, the current sender packages the quantum basis identifier, signature content and other information together to generate the MIN network packet and then sends it to the receiver.

Step 2: After the current receiver receives the MIN network packet, they determine from the type value in the Identifier area that this communication uses quantum identifiers. They then verify the signature of the previous sender. If the verification passes, they activate the quantum receiving device and send a message back to the current sender: "MIN network packet received, please send the quantum state information." If the verification fails, they report the communication error to MIS for processing and terminate the current communication.

Step 3: The current sender uses a quantum device to generate discrete single-photon quantum states corresponding to the quantum basis sequence according to the quantum identity of the original sender and the currently existing quantum basis sequence, and sends it to the receiver.

Step 4: The current receiver decodes the quantum identifier information based on the quantum basis information in the received MIN network packet. The current receiver then checks whether the public key of the original sender exists. If not, the current receiver requests the information from MIS. If the public key already exists, the current receiver uses it to verify the signature. If the verification fails, the current communication error is submitted to the MIS for processing, and the current communication is terminated. If the verification succeeds, the process proceeds to the next step. The specific communication process can be seen in Fig. 11.64.

An example is given here to help readers understand the process. If a certain bit of the quantum identifier is 1, corresponding to a quantum state, within the vertical basis $(0^\circ, 90^\circ)$ and the diagonal basis $(45^\circ, 135^\circ)$, the polarization states of 0° and 45° represent 0, while 90° and 135° represent 1. In the quantum basis sequence, 0 represents the vertical basis and 1 represents the diagonal basis. After randomly generating the quantum basis sequence, it is only necessary for the sender and receiver to have matching angles. If the 0 basis is randomly used, both parties will be at 90°; if the 1 basis is randomly used, both parties will be at 135°. If an error occurs, it indicates a problem with the link. After the receiver receives the quantum identifier information, they use their routing table or request the MIS to

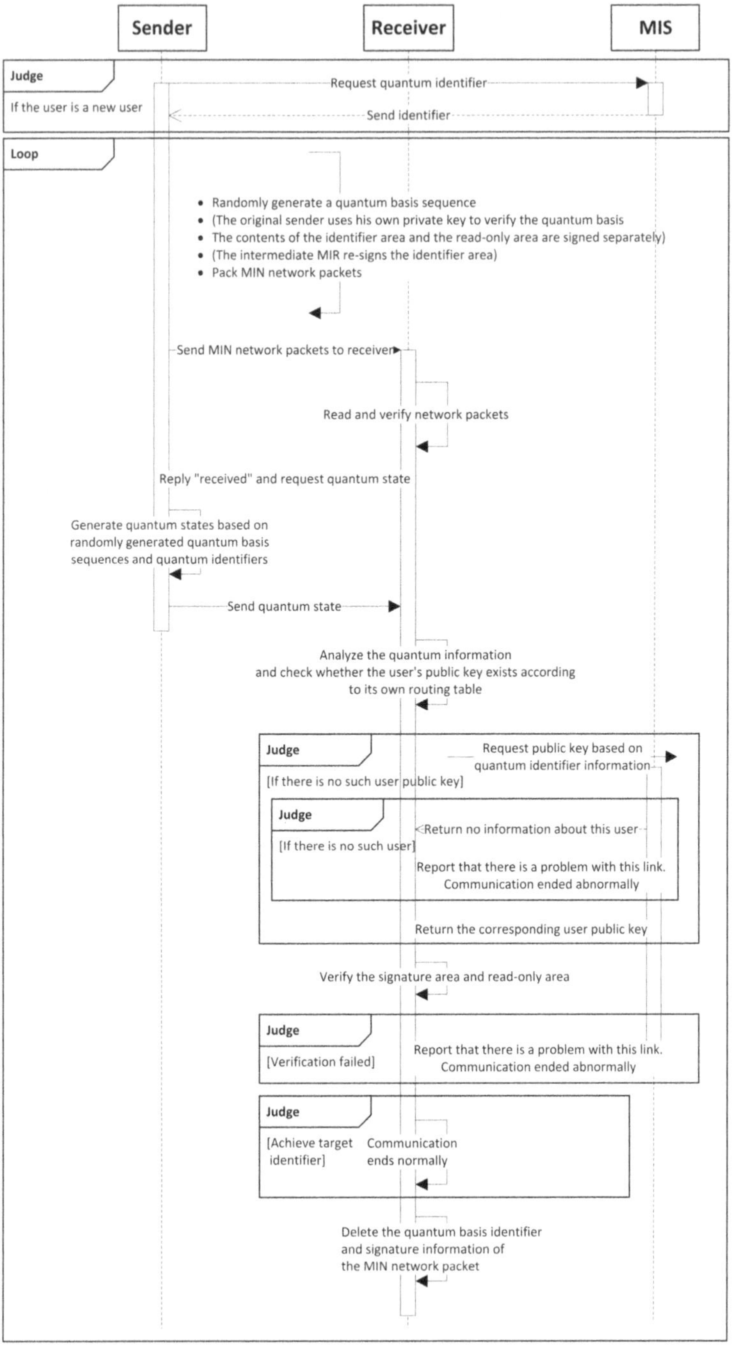

Fig. 11.64 Communication process

find the original sender's public key to verify the MIN network packet. The verification reveals the reliability of the previous MIR's information which indicates the reliability of all MIRs in the link, the integrity of the original sender's quantum basis identifier, the real quantum identifier information and the integrity of the read-only area information.

Step 5: After the current receiver successfully verifies the signature in the Identifier area where the current sender's signature is verified and the Read-Only area where the original sender's signature is verified, it determines whether it can provide the required content or serve as the destination address. If so, the communication ends, and the router handles the relevant services and content. If not, the receiver acts as the new sender, removes the previous sender's quantum basis identifier and its signature from the MIN network packet, and returns to step 1, repeating steps 1–5 until the complete information reaches the final receiver.

In addition to the original sender and the final receiver, each MIR along the path has dual attributes of sender and receiver to relay communication until completion. Regarding security, the system addresses channel interference and eavesdropping concerns by employing dual-channel operation simultaneously. The difficulty of simultaneous monitoring of both channels is significantly greater than for single-channel operations. Using the stop-and-wait mode enhances security further, making it difficult for eavesdroppers to capture complete information from both channels simultaneously. If communication issues arise, the receiver can promptly detect problems in step 4 and report them to MIS for handling by administrators. Quantum states are highly susceptible to interference; hence, any tampering by eavesdroppers can be quickly detected by MIR, prompting immediate security checks on the line. Moreover, if an eavesdropper attempts to forge information without the corresponding user identity, MIR can swiftly identify such attempts and notify administrators for investigation. For enhanced security, consideration can be given to encrypting the Read-Only area using QKD protocols for key negotiation during communication. This ensures that the content in the Read-Only area meets the requirement of one-time pad encryption, further enhancing security measures.

This section also presents a method to achieve one-time pad communication. Firstly, the original sender empties the value content in the Read-Only area of the MIN packet. Secondly, during the communication process, each current receiver, upon successfully receiving the quantum state, obtaining the complete quantum identifier and verifying the signature, checks that the content in the Read-Only area is empty. Upon confirmation, the current receiver immediately initiates the QKD process with the original sender. Finally, after both parties confirm the quantum key used, the current sender sends the information encrypted with the quantum key, including the entire content of the Read-Only area. This encrypted information continues through the whole routing process.

Therefore, the security of MIN communication scheme based on quantum identifiers can fully meet the principle of one-time pad in information theory. Firstly, it utilizes the quantum properties to conceal the true information of both senders and receivers in the communication channel. Secondly, by employing quantum key distribution technology to encrypt the actual transmitted content, it effectively applies one-time pad in both processes. This ensures that any communication conducted in this manner remains secure, achieving a high-security communication method where both information theory and quantum mechanics guarantee its security.

In summary, the MIN communication scheme based on quantum identifiers integrates advanced technologies from both the MIN network and existing quantum communication. It proposes a high-security communication method supporting quantum identifier routing at the network layer, thereby enabling communication methods based on quantum and MIN networks. Through this technological approach, MIN is poised to adapt to the era of future quantum communication. On the one hand, it leverages the unique properties of quantum mechanics such as non-cloning and uncertainty for enhanced network security. On the other hand, it applies the distinctive features of MIN and advanced network communication methods to quantum communication, addressing challenges such as quantum storage forwarding and routing impossibilities. This advancement significantly improves the usability of quantum communication without increasing physical equipment and costs, enabling flexible routing and expanding its applicability.

The MIN communication scheme based on quantum identifiers combines the advantages of MIN communication with existing technologies, significantly saving on software and hardware costs. This integration enriches the application ecosystem within new secure private networks, thereby catalyzing the continuous evolution of secure private networks and development of quantum communication. It promotes their convergence and mutual advancement, allowing overlapping deployment of their respective technological solutions without interference during communication. Therefore, based on practical needs, it supports the deployment of quantum devices on existing network equipment, thereby establishing higher security secure private networks. The scheme integrates different physical media suitable for communication, evolves existing network systems with quantum technology, and expands the application scope of existing quantum communication technologies.

Additionally, based on the specifications and foundation of MIN, the scheme optimizes the network packet structure to better suit quantum communication methods without altering the original packet structure and communication methods of MIN. The optimized structure can separately process information of different physical quantities, providing clear advantages for future network evolution, particularly in compatibility with other networks using different physical quantities. Through organic integration and rational design, it supports both traditional MIN communication and quantum communication, and the fusion of two approaches meets the needs of MIN communication based on discrete single-photon quantum technology.

References

1. Meichuang Technology. Speculation on Traditional Network Security (boundary) and New Security. https://www.freebuf.com/news/235236.html.
2. Borkar A. When implementing zero trust, context is everything. https://securityintelligence.com/posts/when-implementing-zero-trust-context-is-everything.
3. Ramcomminc. Traditional-vs-cloud-based-firewall. https://www.ramcomminc.com/traditional-vs-cloud-based-firewall-2/.
4. Mailtolaozhao. Network Engineer - Case study of network planning and design. https://blog.csdn.net/mailtolaozhao/article/details/124066082.
5. Purplesec. Intrusion-detection-vs-intrusion-prevention-systems. https://purplesec.us/intrusion-detection-vs-intrusion-prevention-systems/.
6. Wujiudun Network. What is the difference between IPS and IDS. https://www.59dun.com/notice_view/zx/2136.html.
7. Ping An Safety Lab. SQL injection for WAF attack and defense. https://www.freebuf.com/column/163469.html.
8. Cloudflare. Web-application-firewall-waf. https://www.cloudflare.com/learning/ddos/glossary/web-application-firewall-waf/.
9. DigApis. Summary of WAF mechanism and bypass methods: injection section. https://www.freebuf.com/articles/web/229982.html.
10. Count the movie stars. How does DLP prevent data leakage? https://zhuanlan.zhihu.com/p/556431723.
11. Educba. Data-loss-prevention. https://www.educba.com/data-loss-prevention/.
12. Zunliang L. The contemplation between traditional network security (boundaries) and new security. https://www.freebuf.com/news/235236.html.
13. Wenyu W. Prediction and analysis of the Data Leakage Prevention (DLP) Market in China in 2016. https://cloud.tencent.com/developer/article/1793075.
14. CyberOne. Endpoint Protection EPP vs EDR: What's the difference? https://cyberone.security/endpoint-protection-epp-vs-edr-whats-the-difference/.
15. Xiejava1018. Brief analysis of SIEM, situation awareness platform, security operations center. https://blog.csdn.net/fullbug/article/details/104620037.
16. Number Shadow Planet How DLP prevents data leakage. https://blog.csdn.net/Dsphere_shuying/article/details/126471411.
17. Spiceworks. What is SIEM? https://www.spiceworks.com/it-security/vulnerability-management/articles/what-is-siem/.
18. China News Net. 360 launched the first industrial Internet security situation awareness system in China. https://www.chinanews.com/it/2017/02-20/8154722.shtml.
19. Cybersecurity-101. Situational Awareness. https://www.linkedin.com/pulse/cybersecurity-101-situational-awareness-john-d-johnson-ph-d-.
20. Peng ye. On the origin of SOC. https://blog.51cto.com/yepeng/571114.
21. Paloaltone. What is a SOC? https://www.paloaltonetworks.com/cyberpedia/what-is-a-soc.
22. Nsfocus Technologies Group Co., Ltd. Data Security Frontier technology research report. https://partner2020.nsfocus.com.cn/html/2021/137_0705/159.html.
23. Radware. UEBA. https://www.radware.com/cyberpedia/cloud-security/ueba/.
24. Sharon Shea. Software-defined perimeter (SDP). https://www.techtarget.com/searchcloudcomputing/definition/software-defined-perimeter-SDP.
25. Xie Java. Analysis of SIEM, Situation Awareness Platform, and Security Operations Center. https://www.cnblogs.com/xiejava/p/12398240.html.
26. Reed J. How zero trust changed the course of cybersecurity. https://securityintelligence.com/articles/how-zero-trust-changed-cybersecurity/.
27. Safety reference How capable is zero trust SDP technology. https://www.secrss.com/articles/24371.
28. AnQuan NeiCan. SDP. https://www.secrss.com/articles/24371.

29. A code is a person's life Information Security - Zero Trust Technology - What is SDP and what security threats can SDP defend against. https://blog.csdn.net/philip502/article/details/127150442.
30. Gartner. Gartner Magic Quadrant for Network Firewalls. https://www.gartner.com/en/documents/4022346.
31. Netmateit. Sangfor NGAF. https://netmateit.com/product/sangfor-ngaf-next-generation-firewall-price/.
32. Sangfor. Sangfor-security NGFW. https://www.sangfor.com.cn/product-and-solution/sangfor-security/ngfw.
33. TopsecGroup. Firewall. https://www.topsecgroup.com/products/Firewall.
34. Topsec. Topsec-security NGTOS. https://max.book118.com/html/2021/0916/5223331311004004.shtm.
35. Qi Anxin. The new generation of smart firewalls. https://www.qianxin.com/product/detail/pid/341.
36. Hu H, Wu J, Wang Z, et al. Mimic defense: a designed-in cybersecurity defense frame-work[J]. IET Inf Secur. 2018;12(3):226–37.
37. Wang Z, Jiang D, Lv Z. AI-assisted trustworthy architecture for industrial IoT based on dynamic heterogeneous redundancy[J]. IEEE Trans Industr Inform. 2022;19(2):2019–27.
38. Yang X, Li H, Que JM, Ma ZT, et al. Efficient secure architecture for future network [J]. Comput Sci. 2023;50(03):360–70.
39. Lin ZL, Li KJ, Hou HX, et al. MDFS: a mimic defense theory based architecture for distributed file system[C]//2017 IEEE International Conference on Big Data (Big Data). IEEE. 2017:2670–5.
40. Yu H, Li H, Yang X, et al. On distributed object storage architecture based on mimic defense[J]. China Commun. 2021;18(8):109–20.
41. Zhang JY, Hou HX, Li KJ, et al. On the implementation of BRS codes in Ceph[C]//2017 IEEE international conference on big data (big data). IEEE; 2017. p. 2676–81.
42. Yang X, Li GX, Li H. EHFM: an efficient hierarchical filtering method for multi-source Network malicious alerts[J]. Computer Science. 2023;50(02):324–32.
43. Husák M, Sadlek L, Špaček S, et al. CRUSOE: a toolset for cyber situational awareness and decision support in incident handling[J]. Comput Secur. 2022;115:102609.
44. Ma X, Afanasyev A, Zhang L. A type-theoretic model on NDN-TLV encoding[C]//Proceedings of the 9th ACM Conference on Information-Centric Networking. 2022: 91–102.
45. Wang YM, Li H, et al. Scalable identifier system for industrial internet based on multi-identifier network architecture[J]. IEEE Internet Things J. 2021;10:1919–32.
46. Wang YM, Abla S, Zhang HY, Li H. Towards double defense network security based on multi-identifier network architecture[J]. Sensors. 2022;22(3):747.
47. Da Silva SS, Cardoso M, Nardo L, et al. A new chaos-based PRNG hardware architecture using the HUB fixed-point format[J]. IEEE Trans Instrum Meas. 2023;72:1–8.
48. Ferguson N, Schneier B, Kohno T. Chapter 9: Generating randomness cryptography engineering design principles and practical applications. Wiley Publishing, Inc. ISBN 978-0-470-47424-2. 2010.
49. Ferguson N, Schneier B. Practical cryptography[M]. Wiley; 2003.
50. Schneier B. Questions & answers about yarrow. Schneier on Security. https://www.schneier.com/academic/yarrow/
51. Torquato M, Maciel P, Vieira M. Security and availability modeling of VM migration as moving target defense[C]// Proceedings of the IEEE 25th Pacific Rim International Symposium on Dependable Comput. 2020: 50–59.
52. Levitin G, Xing L, Xiang Y. Reliability vs. vulnerability of N-version programming cloud service component with dynamic decision time under co-resident attacks[J]. IEEE Trans Serv Comput. 2020:1–12.
53. Najm M, Tamarapalli V. Towards cost-aware VM migration to maximize the profit in federated clouds[J]. Futur Gener Comput Syst. 2022;134:53–65.

54. Ross SM, Kelly JJ, Sullivan RJ, et al. Stochastic processes[M]. New York: Wiley; 1983.
55. van der Meulen R. Build adaptive security architecture into your organization, 30 June 2017.
56. Wang YM, Huang T, Wei GH, Li H, et al. Scalable name identifier lookup for industrial internet[J]. Comput Commun. 2022;186:102–9.
57. Que JM, Li H, Bai H, et al. A Network architecture containing both push and pull semantics[C]//2021 7th international conference on computer and communications (ICCC). IEEE. 2021:2211–6.
58. Yang X, Smahi A, Li H, et al. SPM: a novel hierarchical model for evaluating the effectiveness of combined ACDs in a blockchain-based cloud environment[J]. Appl Sci. 2022;12(18):9230.
59. Yang X, Li H, et al. Efficiently secure architecture for future network[J]. Comput Sci. 2023;50(3):360–70. https://doi.org/10.11896/jsjkx.220600265.
60. Topsec. The "TianRongXin Cup" information security attack-defence competition. https://www.topsec.com.cn/newsx/4234.html.
61. Zhou H, Lv K, Huang L, et al. Quantum network: security assessment and key management[J]. IEEE/ACM Trans Network. 2022;30(3):1328–39.
62. Li H, Meng XZ, et al. A high-security communication method and system supporting quantum identifier routing and addressing at the network layer[P]. CN116527248A, August 1, 2023

Chapter 12
Network Evolvable Scheme

As the core component of modern information technology, computer network technology is closely related to social production and daily life. This chapter analyzes the key challenges in network evolution and introduces the identifier extension mechanism based on identifier fallback. Furthermore, it discusses the theoretical foundation of complex networks and the role of artificial intelligence technology in network evolution at a macro level.

12.1 Overview

The progressive evolution of the network [1] refers to the method of expanding network layer protocols and functionalities, as well as ensuring compatibility between new and old network protocols, without replacing or updating all existing network equipment such as routers and switches at the same time.

In response to the challenges of network evolution, CoG-MIN [2] implements an identifier extension mechanism [3]. In contrast to traditional overlay-based solutions and protocol conversion schemes, such as Plutarch and COIN, the identifier extension mechanism aims to incorporate the ease of deployment advantages of overlay-based solutions while attempting to provide a universal solution for enabling communication between different network architectures.

The identifier extension mechanism utilizes the idea of identifier translation in MIN networks, combined with the basic technical approach of new network identifier fallback to old network identifiers. By allowing new network packets to carry old network identifiers, it addresses routing, forwarding, and processing issues of new network packets on old network devices. This enables a progressive extension and evolution of network functionality in MIN networks.

To overview the core idea of the identifier extension mechanism, several simple communication scenarios are introduced below.

H. Li, H. Bai, *Principle of Architecture, Protocol, and Algorithms for CoG-MIN*,
https://doi.org/10.1007/978-981-96-3596-2_12

As shown in Fig. 12.1, a network topology consists of both IPv6 and IPv4 networks. Suppose that router R0 in the IPv6 network sends a network packet to router R5 in the IPv4 network. R0 encapsulates R5's IPv6 address into an IPv6 network packet and sends it out. The IPv6 network packet sent by R0 can be correctly forwarded from R0 to R2, and then from R2 to R3. However, when the IPv6 network packet arrives at router R3, it is discarded because R3 does not support the IPv6 protocol. Based on the idea of the identifier extension mechanism, an IPv4 address is added to the IPv6 network packet sent by R0, as shown in the right subgraph of Fig. 12.1. When the IPv6 network packet arrives at router R3, R3 can correctly forward the network packet to R5 by using the IPv4 address in the IPv6 packet.

To achieve the aforementioned operations, the identifier extension mechanism proposes three design principles:

Design Principle 12.1 The format of the network packet is uniform, meaning that both old and new routers can parse certain fields of the network packet.

For instance, in Fig. 12.1, as an IPv4 router, R3 can parse the IPv4 address carried in the IPv6 network packet, to use the IPv4 address for forwarding network packets.

Design Principle 12.2 The structure of the network packet is extensible, meaning that the field types and lengths of the network packet can be changed.

In the scenario described in Fig. 12.1, an IPv4 address can be add into the IPv6 network packet.

Design Principle 12.3 Routers can attempt to use multiple kinds of destination addresses or identifiers to forward network packets.

Similarly, if a network packet is sent from an IPv4 network to an IPv6 network, as long as the IPv4 network packet carries an IPv6 address, the packet can be sent to the correct node in the IPv6 network, which enables communication between two different network identifiers.

Another scenario is shown in Fig. 12.2, by carrying an IPv4 address in an NDN network packet, the NDN packet can be forwarded from the NDN network's R0 router to the IPv4 network's R5 router. However, if an NDN address is carried in an IPv4 network packet, as shown in the right subfigure of Fig. 12.2, the packet cannot

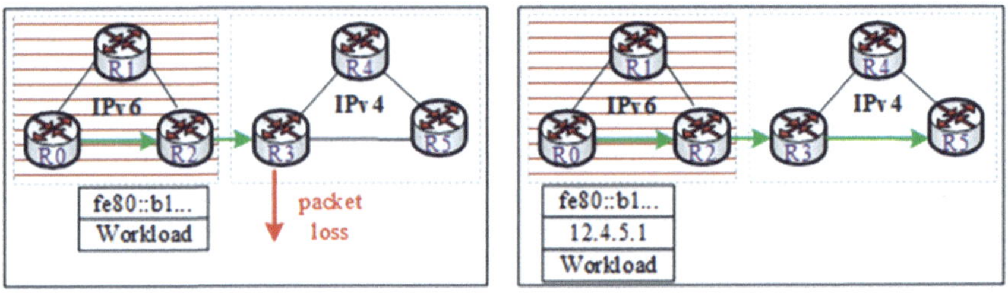

Fig. 12.1 Diagram of communication between IPv4 and IPv6

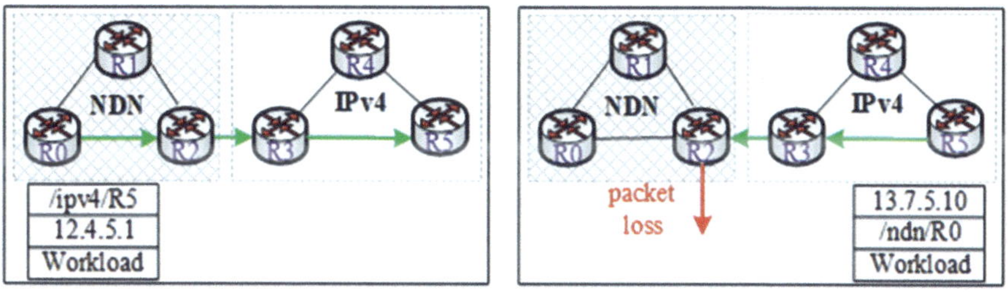

Fig. 12.2 Diagram of communication between IPv4 and NDN

be forwarded to the correct node in the NDN network from the IPv4 network. This is because the processing of NDN network packets is more complicated than that of IPv4 networks. For example, Interest packets in NDN cannot carry data, and Data packets in NDN can only be forwarded to the network in response to Interest packets. When the IPv4 network packet reaches router R2, R2 can resolve the address "/ ndn/R0" because the packet carries data. R2 cannot send the packet as an Interest packet, nor can it forward the packet as a Data packet because R2 did not receive a request for the Data packet.

Figure 12.2 illustrates that communication between NDN and IPv4 network architectures is unidirectional rather than bidirectional due to the differences in the processing of network packets. To support the forwarding of all new network packets with old network identifiers in old routers, the identifier extension mechanism requires that routers in the network support a certain identifier, referred to as the basic identifier.

Based on the example shown in Fig. 12.2, it can be concluded that the identifiers used in the NDN network cannot serve as the basic identifier. The example shows that IP packets carrying NDN identifiers cannot be forwarded to the NDN network. IPv4 addresses, IPv6 addresses, and some other identifiers whose processing flows in routers are the same as these two identifiers can serve as the basic identifier of the network. Only when a certain unified basic identifier is supported throughout the network, can the network evolve progressively based on this anchor point through the identifier extension mechanism. This leads to the fourth design principle of the identifier extension mechanism.

Design Principle 12.4 In MIN networks, there should exist a kind of basic identifier, any new type of packet with new identifier carrying this basic identifier can be addressed and forwarded by old network devices.

12.2 Identifier Extension Based on Identifier Fallback

12.2.1 Identifier Fallback and Recovery

The idea of identifier fallback is to carry multiple destination identifiers in network packets so that the packets can be forwarded using the candidate identifiers carried in different network identifier spaces.

In MIN networks, all network devices support identity identifiers, and all network identifiers can be fall backed to identity identifiers. Therefore, each network packet is supposed to carry an identity identifier (or other basic identifier supported by the entire network) as one of its destination identifiers in general, which ensures that the packet can be forwarded by all devices in the network. The process of identifier fallback refers to the communication process where users utilize new network identifiers to communicate with old network devices.

Taking Fig. 12.3 as an example, let's consider a scenario where an organization registers a new communication identifier X in MIS and uses this new identifier X to build two small networks at the edge of MIN, forming two new X identifier spaces as shown in Fig. 12.3. Users within each identifier space are capable of communicate directly using the new identifier X, while communication between the two X identifier spaces necessitate the use of identifier fallback mechanism. The basic process for a user to send a network packet from one X identifier space to another X identifier space is as follows:

1. The user queries the MIS for the target user's all identifier records using either the target user' new identifier X1 or username.

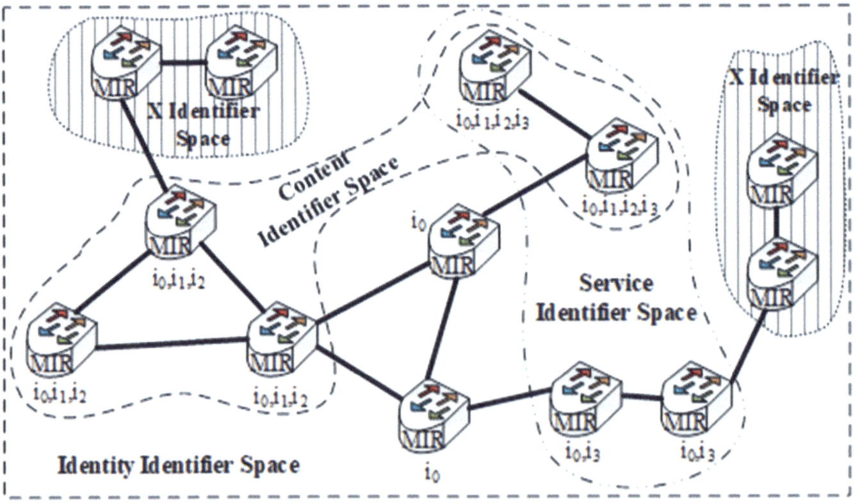

Fig. 12.3 An example for identifier extension mechanism

2. The user adds the new identifier X1, the corresponding identity identifier for X1, and other identifiers associated with X1 that have the same communication semantics or can serve as fallback identifiers for X1, into the destination identifier field of the MIN network packet. The identifiers in the destination identifier field are sorted based on the user's preferred addressing priority, with higher priority given to identifiers at the beginning of the list.
3. Intermediate routers that receive the network packet extract all the identifiers from the destination identifier field. Routers examine the Type field of each identifier in sequential order and determine whether they can resolve and process identifiers with a specific Type value. The router selects the highest priority identifier that it supports in terms of semantics for processing and forwarding the network packet. If the chosen identifier is not the new identifier X1, then it means that X1 has fallen back to an old identifier, and the forwarding process involves identifier fallback.
4. If a router selects a higher priority identifier for addressing and forwarding but is unsuccessful, it continues to select lower-priority identifiers for addressing and forwarding. When all the identifiers in the network packet's identifier field have been attempted for forwarding but none of them are successful, the network packet is discarded.
5. When the network packet reaches the destination identifier space, routers within the destination identifier space naturally select the new identifier X1, for processing, addressing, and forwarding the network packet. Finally, the network packet is forwarded to the network communication entity (such as a host, router, or application) associated with that identifier. This process is referred to as the recovery of the new identifier X1.

12.2.2 Identifier Space Detection

Before sending out a network packet, the selection of identifiers with fallback relationships to the original identifier needs to be done through an identifier relationship graph. These selected identifiers are considered as candidate identifiers and are included in the destination identifier field of the network packet. The identifier relationship graph is stored in MIS and describes whether there are fallback relationships between each pair of identifiers in the MIN network. Additionally, the identifier extension mechanism code specifies a maximum limit of six identifiers in the identifier field. However, if only the identifier relationship graph is used to select candidate identifiers, it may lead to exceeding the predefined limit. Moreover, there may be certain candidate identifiers that are not used throughout the entire network communication process, resulting in unnecessary overhead in the network packet header.

To address the issue of identifier selection, an Identifier Space Detection Protocol (ISDP) [4] can be utilized. This protocol, similar to the ICMP protocol in IP network architecture, can be considered as part of the network layer protocol. The

ISDP protocol employs an ISDP request packet and an ISDP response packet to explore network identifier spaces.

The basic method of the ISDP protocol for exploring the identifier spaces traversed by a communication path is as follows: An ISDP request packet is sent from the source of the path to the destination. The Intermediate router that forward the ISDP request packet will records the ID type supported by itself and has a fallback relationship with the ID recorded in the read-only data area field into the variable data area of the ISDP request packet.

Since "recording identifier types in the network packet" is an operation performed by network routers on the network packet, an identifier type needs to be assigned to the ISDP request packet, known as the ISDP request identifier. The ISDP response packet, on the other hand, can use the identity identifier to identify network packets directly. The identifier form of the ISDP request identifier is the same as the identity identifier, while its semantics are {record the identifier type in the variable field of the network packet, look up the forwarding table, and forward the packet}.

Let's assume that User A needs to communicate with User B using the new identifier X1. User A follows the following steps to explore the identifier spaces traversed from A to B:

1. User A queries the identity identifier, IDB, of User B using either User B's username or the new identifier X1. User A then sends an ISDP request packet to the network, including IDB in the destination identifier field and setting the identifier type of IDB to the Type value of the ISDP request identifier. The identifier type of X1 is also stored in the read-only data field of the ISDP.
2. When an intermediate router receives the ISDP request packet, it reads the identifier type number in the read-only data field. If the router supports that identifier type, it directly forward the packet. Otherwise, the router records in the variable data field of the ISDP request packet the identifier types it supports and that have fallback relationships with X1. The format of the record is "(100,2), (150,3)," indicating that a router supporting identifier type number 100 appears twice in the communication path, while a router supporting identifier type number 150 appears three times. If a router supports multiple identifier types with fallback relationships to X1, only the identifier closest in semantics to X1 (the identifier type number closest to X1 in the identifier semantics relationship graph) will be recorded in the detection packet.
3. When the ISDP request packet reaches User B's host, the ISDP protocol in User B's host automatically extracts the recorded identifier types from the variable data field of the ISDP request packet, encapsulates them into the read-only data field of a response packet, and includes User A's identity identifier in the destination identifier field. Finally, the response packet is sent back to User A's host.
4. Upon receiving the ISDP response packet, User A extracts the identifier records from the read-only data field of the response packet and can sort the identifiers based on the number of occurrences following the identifier type.

12.2.3 *Candidate Identifier Sorting and Selection*

The selection of candidate identifiers is based on the results obtained from the identifier space detection mechanism and the path distance between the original identifier and the candidate identifiers in the identifier relationship graph. The probability of selecting a certain type of identifier as a candidate identifier follows two principles:

1. It is directly proportional to the count of the identifier in the results of the identifier space detection mechanism. The count of an identifier in the exploration results represents the number of routers supporting that identifier in the communication path. A higher count indicates a greater chance of that identifier being used in the communication path, thus increasing the probability of selecting it as a candidate identifier.
2. It is inversely proportional to the semantic distance between the original identifier and the candidate identifier. If the semantic distance between the candidate identifier and the original identifier is large, it indicates a significant difference in router operations between the candidate identifier and the original identifier in the intermediate routers. This difference can lead to varying network service effects. Therefore, the farther the semantic distance between an identifier and the original identifier, the lower the probability of selecting that identifier as a candidate identifier.

The sorting algorithm for candidate identifiers follows these two principles, and the priority of candidate identifiers in this algorithm is calculated based on the above rules, as shown in Eq. 12.1.

$$p_i = \begin{cases} \dfrac{\alpha c_i}{C} + \beta\left(1 - \dfrac{d_i}{D}\right), & D > 0, C > 0 \\ \dfrac{\alpha c_i}{C} + \beta, & D = 0, C > 0 \\ 0, & C = 0 \end{cases} \tag{12.1}$$

Here, p_i represents the priority of identifier i, where a higher value of p_i indicates a higher priority and a greater probability of selecting identifier i as a candidate identifier. c_i represents the number of routers that support identifier i on the communication path between two communication parties. C represents the total sum of c_i. d_i represents the semantic distance between identifier i and the original identifier in the semantic relationship graph. D represents the sum of the weights of all edges in the multi-branch tree generated from the semantic graph with the original identifier as the root node. α and β are two important coefficient constants that represent the weights of the two principles for selecting candidate identifiers in priority calculation.

Therefore, when selecting candidate identifiers, the following steps should be followed as outlined in Algorithm 12.1, should be performed:

1. Generate a minimum spanning tree using the identifier semantic relationship graph, starting from the original identifier and selecting the path with the minimum sum of weights. This can be achieved using algorithms like Kruskal algorithm or Prim algorithm, with the original identifier as the root node of the tree.
2. Calculate the semantic distance (d_i) between each identifier and the original identifier by determining the path length from the root node to each identifier node in the generated tree. Additionally, calculate the sum of path lengths in the tree (D).
3. Obtain the statistical count of identifiers in the communication path using ISDP.

Iterate through the set of identifiers returned in the ISDP response packet, calculate the p_i value for each identifier, and select an appropriate number of candidate identifiers in descending order of their p_i values.

Algorithm 12.1: Candidate Identifier Sorting Algorithm
Input: idSemanticMap, detectList, α, β, originalIdType, idList.
Output: candidateIdList.

```
function chooseCandidateIdentifier (...)
   start from originalIdType generate idSemanticTree from idSemanticMap;
   int D = calculate the all path len in idSemanticTree;
   int C = 0;
   for i = 0; i < detectList. size(); i + + ; do
   C = C + detectList[i]. count;
   done
   List < double, ID> candidateIdList;
   for i = 0; i < detectList. size(); i + + ;do
   double p_i = 0;
   if C = = 0 then
   p_i = 0;
   else if D = = 0 & & C > 0 then
   p_i = α * detectList[i]. count/C + β;
   else if D > 0 & & C > 0 then
   int d_i = detectList[i]. idType path len in idSemanticTree;
   p_i = α * detectList[i]. count/C + β * (1 − d_i/D);
   end if
   ID_i = get id from idList, where id's type equal to detectList[i]. idType;
   candidateIdList.add(p_i, ID_i);
   done
   sort candidateIdList by p_i;
   return candidateIdList;
     end function
```

12.3 Complexity Science and Artificial Intelligence in Network Evolution

12.3.1 Complexity Science: The Theoretical Foundation of Network Evolution

In the 1960s, humans began using computers for data processing, which led to the need for connecting computers together for data sharing and collaboration. The initial computer network structures were relatively simple, connecting multiple computers together through shared cables or telephone lines. In the 1970s and 1980s, the precursor to the internet emerged. With the widespread use and improved performance of computers, people started researching new network technologies and protocols, leading to the development of layered network architectures and increased complexity in network systems. In the 1990s, with the gradual improvement and rapid popularization of the Internet, computer network structures became even more complex. The Internet, primarily based on the TCP/IP protocol, facilitated convenient and fast communication between computers. The complexity of computer networks surpassed the capacity of a single organization or institution, requiring the establishment of more distributed and automated network structures. Today, computer network architectures continue to evolve, with various new network structures emerging, and network technologies and protocols continuously advancing and improving. The trend of network development has always been towards more distributed, autonomous, and complex systems.

The increasing complexity of computer network architectures is a necessary condition to meet the demands of networks and address various challenges. It is also an inevitable outcome of network development. Complex network structures enable efficient and convenient communication between computers while enhancing network security and robustness. Therefore, the complexity of computer network architectures is unavoidable. It drives the continuous progress and improvement of network technologies and provides a solid foundation for the wide-ranging development of network applications. Although the complexity of network architectures contributes to improved network performance and efficiency, it also presents obstacles for scientific research and engineering implementation of network structures.

Complexity science [5] was introduced in the 1980s and initially focused on studying the patterns and behaviors of natural, social, and economic systems, as shown in Fig. 12.4. With advancements in computer science, physics, biology, and other fields, complexity science experienced rapid development in the 1990s. Researchers started applying various theories and methods of complexity science to studying complex systems in different domains. Applying the theories and methods of complexity science to the study of network architecture evolution may provide

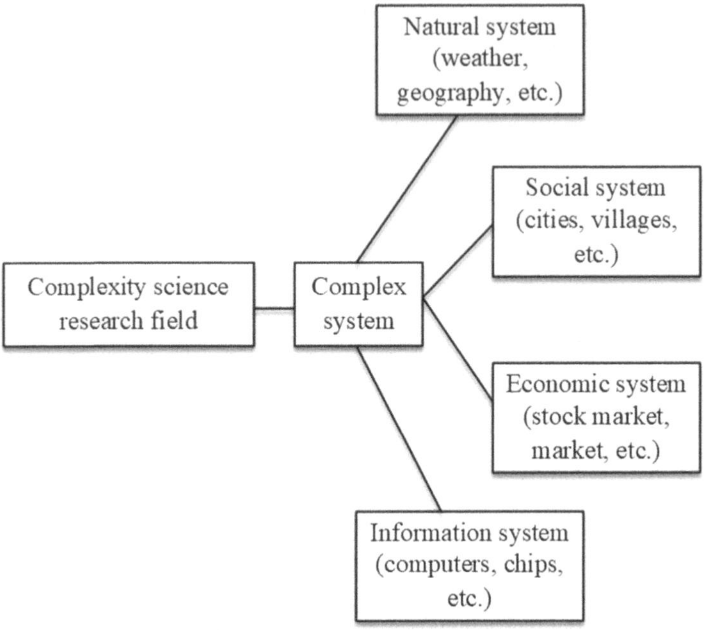

Fig. 12.4 The research fields of complexity science

insights and assistance in overcoming the current obstacles in network architecture evolution. Such research can enhance the scientific rigor and accuracy of network architecture evolution while promoting its development and progress. The application of complexity science in the field of computer networks holds great potential for future advancements.

Complexity science, as an interdisciplinary field, primarily studies the characteristics and behaviors of complex systems in various domains such as physics, mathematics, computer science, biology, sociology, engineering, anthropology, and more. Computer networks, as systems composed of interconnected and interdependent components, exhibit typical characteristics of complex systems, such as nonlinearity and unpredictability. Therefore, complexity science is highly suitable as the foundational theory for studying the evolution of computer network architectures.

Complexity science helps uncover the intrinsic patterns of complex systems like computer network architectures. By utilizing the theories and methods of complexity science to delve into aspects such as network topology, dynamic evolution, and information transmission, one can reveal the internal behaviors and evolutionary trends of networks, providing crucial guidance for the evolution of network architectures. Moreover, complexity science can be used to simulate the behavior and performance of complex network systems, enabling the evaluation of different network structures and communication strategies. This offers solutions to the challenges of testing and promoting network structure evolution that are difficult to address otherwise. The principles of complexity science emphasize self-organization and adaptivity, which will drive network architectures towards greater automation. This development will enable networks to achieve higher performance and stronger stability, adapting to ever-changing environments and demands. Lastly, as a multidisciplinary theory, complexity science bridges different fields and serves as a platform for scholars and experts from various domains to exchange ideas and collaborate. This provides new perspectives and approaches for the entire network architecture evolution.

Complexity science plays a positive role in the evolution of computer network architectures by providing theoretical support and methodologies for technological innovation and development. It promotes the efficient, secure, reliable, and sustainable development of networks.

12.3.2 Artificial Intelligence: The Important Driving Force for Network Development

Traditional computer networks are no longer able to meet the growing volume of data, increasing communication demands, and the ever-increasing complexity of network structures. Therefore, the application of artificial intelligence (AI) technology to computer networks is imperative. As one of the hottest research directions in the field of computer science, using AI technology in computer network architectures to advance network intelligence and improve performance has become a major focus [6–8].

The rapid development of AI technology can be attributed to its unique advantages in the field of computer science. Firstly, certain AI models possess self-learning capabilities, allowing them to continuously gather data and improve while performing tasks, thereby enhancing their performance during runtime. Additionally, AI technology has the ability to handle "unexpected" situations to some extent through fuzzy processing. This is due to the powerful feature extraction capabilities of AI technology. Moreover, certain AI technologies can achieve green computing, as although the training process may consume significant computational resources, the computational requirements of AI models are significantly reduced during actual usage, which helps conserve operational resources.

While AI technology possesses these excellent characteristics, it may not be applicable to all network functionalities. To determine whether AI technology can be integrated with a particular network functionality, the "network problem abstraction" method can be employed for assessment. The process involves several steps. Since the correctness of problem mapping determines whether AI models can be integrated with a network functionality, the network space problem is initially mapped to categories that can be solved by AI technology. Next, the difficulty of data acquisition, overall quality of the dataset (including information such as types and quantity distribution), and similar relevant metrics are evaluated to analyze whether the data can meet the training and testing requirements of AI models. Lastly, suitable training methods and model evaluation strategies can further improve the performance of AI models.

Taking the example of malicious webpage detection, the "network problem abstraction" method can be used to assess the feasibility of utilizing AI technology for detecting malicious webpages. Firstly, all webpages can be classified into two categories: malicious and non-malicious, which falls under the classification problem in AI technology. In daily browsing, webpage types (malicious and non-malicious) can be recorded to construct a dataset, or existing open-source datasets can be utilized. Data collection is not difficult, and the dataset exhibits reasonable content distribution and rich variety. During training, the collected data can be divided into training, testing, and validation sets, and appropriate training methods such as K-fold cross-validation can be employed. The accuracy can be analyzed. Multiple training iterations can be conducted using a range of optimization and hyperparameter tuning methods to select the AI model with the best performance. Finally, the malicious webpage detection model can be integrated into the current network architecture for detecting malicious webpages.

AI modularization refers to embedding AI technology as a module within the corresponding network hierarchy to assist or extend partial functionalities of the original network. In the field of network security, there have been numerous relevant studies [9, 10].

For instance, the user authentication module is one of the earliest modules that applied AI technology to computer networks. This module primarily employs techniques such as fingerprint recognition and iris recognition, utilizing deep learning methods such as artificial neural networks (ANNs) and convolutional neural networks (CNNs).

The network security situational awareness module is used to assess the overall security of the network structure. In the process of network situational awareness, complex networks need to be modeled, network features need to be extracted, and network states need to be determined. Classical AI technologies such as Bayesian networks, fuzzy neural networks (FNNs), and random forest provide powerful feature extraction capabilities.

The malicious behavior detection module is used to detect various attacks targeted at the network. This module combines deep feature extraction with support vector machines (SVM), utilizing deep belief networks (DBNs) for dimensionality reduction of large-scale network traffic datasets to detect anomalous behavior.

The anomaly traffic recognition module is commonly used to detect illegal data within the network, which may cause accidents by disrupting the proper transmission of network nodes and links, leading to service unavailability or even information loss.

12.3.3 Evolution Trend of CoG-MIN

CoG-MIN, as a novel computer network, aims to provide more flexible, efficient, and secure network support for various network application scenarios. However, this flexibility also introduces complexity into the network architecture itself. For instance, components such as identifier domain partitioning, communication between identifier domains, resource management within identifier domains, selection of security policies, system integration and management are interconnected and will impact the challenges associated with the further evolution of CoG-MIN.

Complexity science offers a comprehensive and unified theoretical framework for the study and development of complex systems. This framework can be utilized to mitigate the challenges associated with the development and evolution of CoG-MIN.

Drawing from complexity science theory, network systems can be conceptualized as intricate systems comprised of multiple interacting and interdependent components, where the complexity among these components dictates the overall system performance.

Complexity science theory can be employed to analyze the interactions and behavioral patterns among different network components within MIN networks, thereby enhancing network system efficiency. For instance, complexity science theory can be applied to scrutinize and investigate the network topology structure in CoG-MIN, which significantly influences information transmission paths and efficiency within networks. By leveraging complexity science theory, it is possible to simulate and compare various network topology structures' strengths and weaknesses while offering instructive insights for optimizing such structures.

On the other hand, integrating artificial intelligence technology into CoG-MIN can drive the intelligence of the network. Various functions within CoG-MIN can be made intelligent by leveraging artificial intelligence technology, such as intelligent domain partitioning and resource management. Similarly, security assurance is particularly crucial in CoG-MIN. The diversity of identifiers and complexity of the network architecture often pose challenges for screening malicious network traffic and attacks. Manual handling of various abnormal situations in the MIN network is time-consuming and labor-intensive. Utilizing artificial intelligence technology for intelligent detection and processing can save human resources and computing power required for detection while modularly embedding this function into the network system, providing convenience for subsequent maintenance and evolution of the network structure. Furthermore, during subsequent module iteration upgrades, only replacing that specific module will not impact on overall layout of the network's structural design.

The evolution of CoG-MIN is a complex issue that requires the comprehensive application of complexity science and network intelligence theories and technologies. Within the theoretical framework of complexity science, research can be conducted to optimize the network topology structure and relationships between components in order to enhance the performance and stability of CoG-MIN. The use of artificial intelligence technology can drive the evolution of network intelligence, thereby improving system efficiency and resource conservation within CoG-MIN. Further exploration can be conducted in these two aspects for the future evolution of CoG-MIN.

References

1. Li H, Yang X, Qi JH. Multilateral co-management of the sovereign internet: an introduction to the legal basis, its architecture system and prototype[M]. Tsinghua University Press; 2020. p. 1–8.
2. Wang YM, Li H, Huang T, et al. Scalable identifier system for industrial internet based on multi-identifier network architecture[J]. IEEE Internet Things J. 2021:1–22.
3. Li H, Wu JX, Wei GH, et al. Method and system for general packet network addressing routing and identifier evolution (in Chinese). Sci Sin Inform. 2023;53:1629–44.
4. Wei GH, Li H, Bai YJ, et al. Space-terrestrial integrated multi-Identifier network with endogenous security [J]. Space Integ Ground Info Netw. 2020;1(2):66–72.
5. Huang G. On the overall structure of the eight principles of systems theory - comment on "system theory - philosophy of systems science" [J]. J Syst Sci. 2022;30(01):1–13.
6. Zhang Z, Ning H, Shi F, et al. Artificial intelligence in cyber security: research advances, challenges, and opportunities[J]. Artif Intell Rev. 2022:1–25.
7. Wang H, Fu T, Du Y, et al. Scientific discovery in the age of artificial intelligence[J]. Nature. 2023;620(7972):47–60.
8. Zador A, Escola S, Richards B, et al. Catalyzing next-generation artificial intelligence through neuroai[J]. Nat Commun. 2023;14(1):1597.
9. Sarker IH. Machine learning for intelligent data analysis and automation in cybersecurity: current and future prospects[J]. Ann Data Sci. 2023;10(6):1473–98.
10. Mijwil M, Salem IE, Ismaeel MM. The significance of machine learning and deep learning techniques in cybersecurity: a comprehensive review[J]. Iraqi J Comp Sci Maths. 2023;4(1):87–101.

Chapter 13
Secure Private Network Based on CoG-MIN

A private network, commonly known as an enterprise or dedicated network, is a customized network infrastructure designed for organizations. The services and resources within a private network are inaccessible to external networks, with access granted only to authorized personnel within the organization. Due to the high importance of the services and resources within a private network, ensuring network security is of utmost importance.

The secure private network based on CoG-MIN utilizes the inherent security advantages of the CoG-MIN architecture to improve the security of the private network.

This chapter introduces the overall architecture and communication process of the secure private network based on CoG-MIN and provides detailed explanations of its applications.

13.1 Overview of Secure Private Network Based on CoG-MIN

13.1.1 Overall Architecture

The secure private network based on CoG-MIN, also referred to as the "internal network" or "MIN private network," represents a highly secure private network built on the CoG-MIN architecture. It utilizes a dedicated MIN link for communication and incorporates a robust security mechanism that effectively mitigates network attacks commonly encountered in IP-based networks. Moreover, the MIN private network incorporates an integrated virtual private network (VPN) system, enabling users to access the network services and resources remotely. From an architectural perspective, the MIN private network is mainly divided into several modules, and their relationships are shown in Fig. 13.1.

H. Li, H. Bai, *Principle of Architecture, Protocol, and Algorithms for CoG-MIN*,
https://doi.org/10.1007/978-981-96-3596-2_13

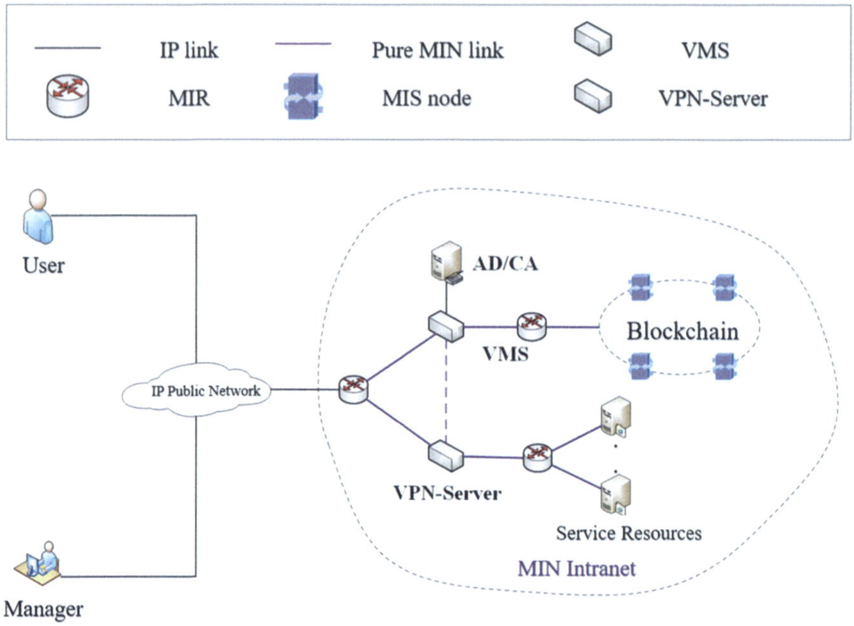

Fig. 13.1 Overall architecture of the MIN private network

VPN Client (MIN-VPN)

MIN-VPN is located on the user side. It directly interacts with the user and is responsible for authenticating the user identity, interacting with the backend to forward network packets, and determining the type of website being accessed (whether it belongs to an internal or external network).

VPN Server

VPN Server is deployed on the internal network server, acting as a network proxy together with the SOCKS proxy. It is responsible for forwarding network packets generated by users, parsing accessed domain names, enforcing access permissions, and generating corresponding access logs based on permissions.

Multi-identifier System (MIS)

MIS includes the client and server. The client is located on the administrator side. Administrators can use MIS to manage identifiers and logs in the MIN private network. The MIS server is deployed on the internal network server. The MIS server is responsible for storing identifiers and logs and providing interfaces for client calls [1].

VPN Management Service (VMS)

VMS includes the VMS client and server. The client is deployed on the administrator side. Administrators can use the client to assign corresponding permissions to user groups and view user access logs. The VMS server is deployed on the internal network server. The server is responsible for storing user group information, permission information, assisting MIN-VPN in user identity authentication, and providing interfaces for client calls.

MIN-Proxy

MIN-Proxy is located on the boundary server between the external network and internal network. It is responsible for converting external IP communication into MIN communication to achieve compatibility between IP and MIN networks.

Windows Server 2016

MIN-VPN uses the active directory (AD) and certificate authority (CA) services provided by Windows Server 2016. The AD service is used to manage users and user groups, and the CA service serves as a certificate authority and authentication machine.

Multi-identifier Router (MIR) [2]

MIR is the router in the MIN private network. MIR supports network packet forwarding, routing, translation, in-network caching, recording operation logs, and other necessary functions. It also supports optional modules such as multi-hop signing and network packet verification.

Service Resources

The currently implemented service resources in the MIN private network include file sharing service, email service, and video conferencing service.

13.1.2 Communication Process

The complete invocation chain for users accessing service resources within the MIN private network via MIN-VPN can be summarized into the following steps, as illustrated in Fig. 13.2.

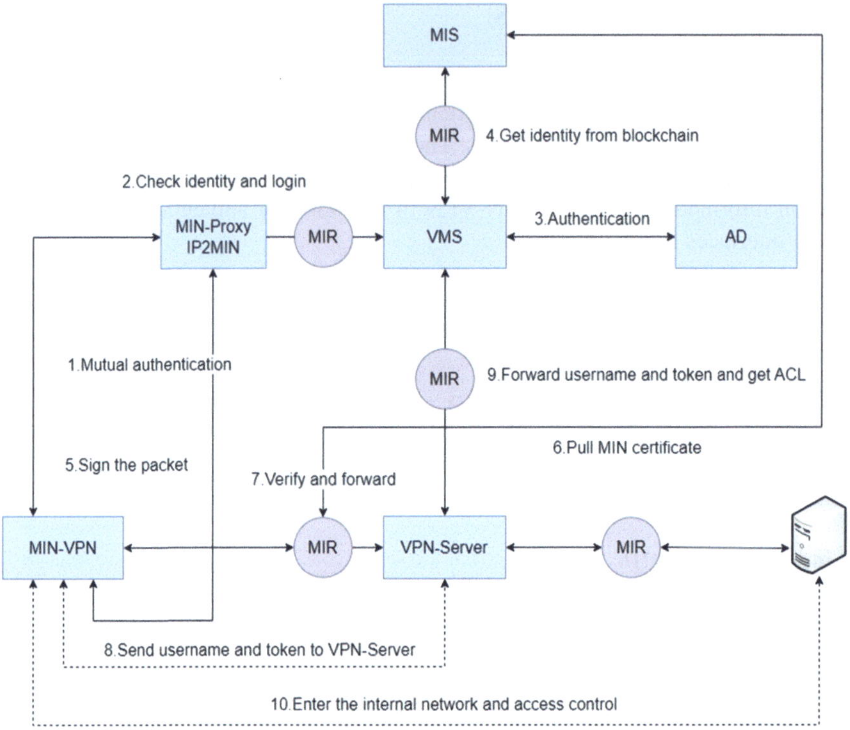

Fig. 13.2 The complete invocation chain of the MIN private network

1. MIN-VPN is started and mutual authentication between MIN-VPN and MIN-Proxy (replacing VPN Server, which is operated in a pure MIN environment within the internal network where IP communication is not supported, and mutual authentication is based on IP communication). If the authentication is successful, the startup is successful. If the authentication fails, the startup fails.
2. On the MIN-VPN login screen, the user enters the account and password, and clicks “Login.” MIN-VPN checks whether there is a corresponding MIN identity for the user locally. If it exists, MIN-VPN sends the user’s account password and the flag indicating the existence of the MIN identity to the VMS server. If it does not exist, MIN-VPN generates a pair of public and private keys and sends the user’s account password, the flag indicating the non-existence of the identity, and the public key to the VMS server.
3. After receiving the information, the VMS server forward the user’s account and password to the AD for user authentication. If the authentication fails, a login failure message is returned to MIN-VPN.
4. If the authentication is successful and the MIN identity flag indicates non-existence, MIN-VPN sends the user’s public key to MIS to register the MIN identity, and MIS returns the MIN identity and token (or if the identity has already been registered, MIS directly returns the MIN identity and token).

5. MIN-VPN receives the login success message, constructs a network packet containing the user's account name and token, reads the private key, and signs the network packet.
6. MIN-VPN establishes a connection with VPN Server and sends the signed network packet. During this process, MIR requests the user's MIN certificate from MIS based on the obtained username.
7. Before forwarding the network packet to VPN Server, MIR verifies the signature of the network packet.
8. If the signature verification passes, the username and token are successfully sent to VPN Server.
9. VPN Server receives the username and token, sends them to VMS, VMS verifies the token successfully, and retrieves the user's ACL and returns it to VPN Server.
10. MIN-VPN successfully connects to VPN Server, and when the user clicks on a website to access it, VPN Server retrieves the user's ACL for permission control.

13.2 MIN-VPN

13.2.1 System Architecture

The MIN-VPN architecture can be divided into two parts based on the programming languages used. One part is written in Java, while the other part is written in Golang.

The modules written in Golang form the core components at a lower level within the system. They include communication functionalities with MIS, VMS, and VPN Server, as well as core functionalities such as starting, stopping, and reading/writing to the virtual network card.

On the other hand, the Java code primarily focuses on application-level functionalities, including user interface for interaction, SOCKS5, Proxy Automated Config (PAC), and other features.

To enable communication between Java and Golang, the Golang functions that Java needs to invoke are compiled into dynamic link libraries. The Java code and the dynamic link libraries communicate with each other via Java Native Access (JNA), acting as a bridge for code integration.

The specific architecture is depicted in Fig. 13.3.

MIN-VPN employs a two-tier architecture for its proxy functionality. At the lower level, it utilizes a virtual network card (TUN) as the foundation of the VPN, enabling the creation of an IP-MIN-IP tunnel. However, using a virtual network card requires modifying the routing table extensively (or redirecting all traffic through the VPN) to access the external network. This approach does not achieve precise traffic routing between domestic and international destinations. To address this limitation, an application layer SOCKS proxy is added on top of the

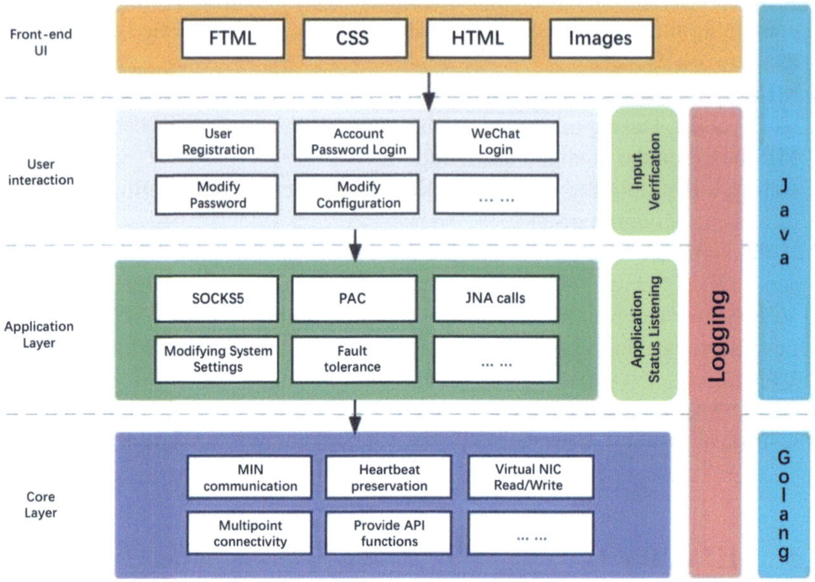

Fig. 13.3 Architecture diagram of MIN-VPN

TUN-based setup. This combination allows for accurate traffic routing and enables decryption of HTTPS traffic. By incorporating the SOCKS proxy, MIN-VPN achieves both precise traffic routing and the ability to decrypt HTTPS traffic.

13.2.2 Detailed Design

Front-End UI

The front-end user interface (UI) refers to the visible pages and elements that users interact with directly. It includes menu bar pages and other pages such as registration and login. The menu bar refers to the menu that appears when the application is minimized to the system tray. It currently consists of four different menu items: "Upgrade," "Open," "View log," and "Exit." Clicking on each menu item triggers a specific functionality. Figure 13.4 illustrates the class diagram for the menu bar, and Table 13.1 provides detailed explanations for each class within the diagram.

In the design of MIN-VPN, the registration, login, configuration modification, and post-start pages are implemented using the classic MVC design architecture.

In the classic MVC pattern, the View (V) refers to the user interface that users see and interact with. The UI functionality is achieved through a combination of FXML, CSS, and Java code. One of the advantages of MVC is its ability to handle various

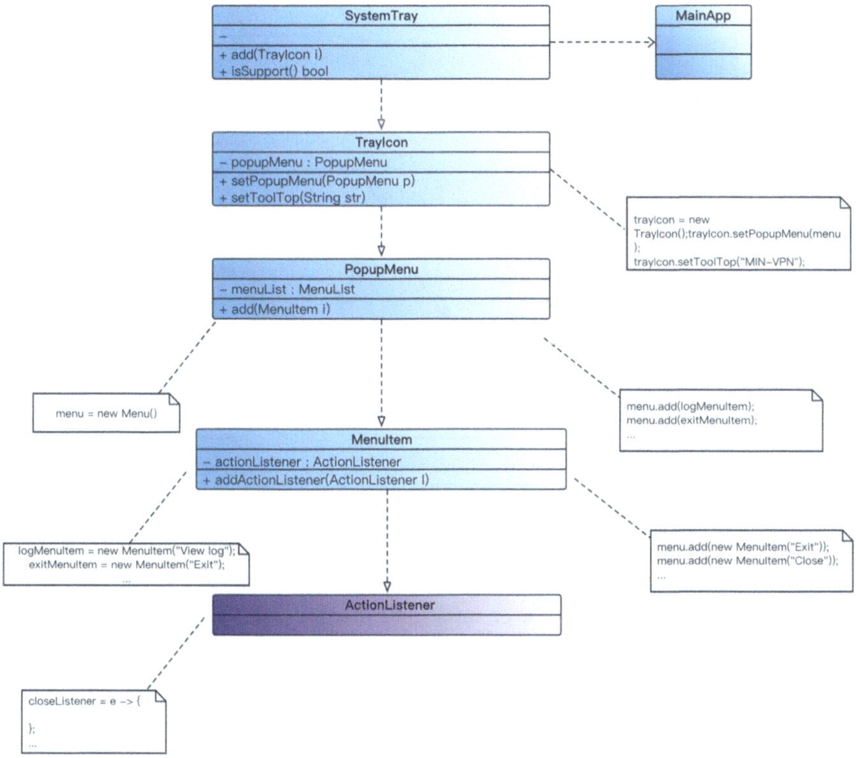

Fig. 13.4 Class diagram for the menu bar

Table 13.1 Class descriptions for the menu

Class Name	Description
SystemTray	A system-level tray object. After adding a TrayIcon to it, related icons can be displayed in the system tray
TrayIcon	An icon in the system tray. A PopupMenu can be added to it, and it will pop up when right-clicked
PopupMenu	The entire menu, which is also the container for MenuItems, and can contain multiple MenuItems
MenuItem	A single menu item displayed in a separate row. It contains an ActionListener, and when the mouse clicks on it, the function saved in the ActionListener is triggered
ActionListener	A listener that can customize the triggering function

views within an application. In the view, there is no actual processing taking place; it serves as a means to display data and allow user interactions.

The Model (M) represents the business rules and logic. Among the three components of MVC, the model handles the majority of the processing tasks. The data returned by the model is neutral and independent of the data format, allowing a

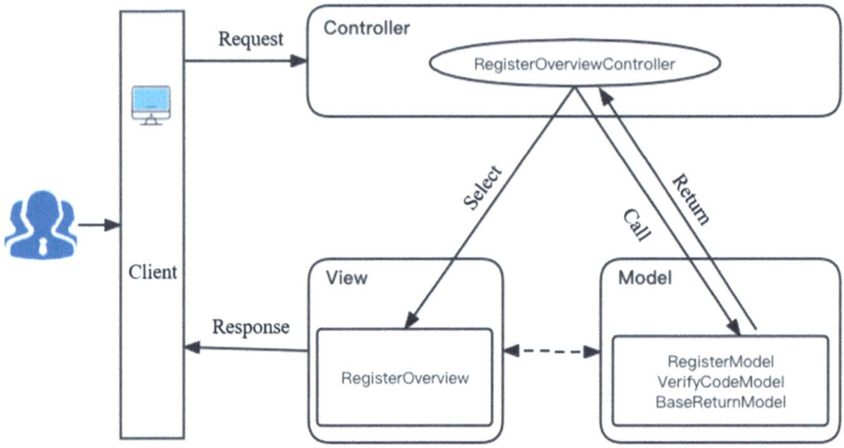

Fig. 13.5 MVC architecture of the registration module

single model to provide data to multiple views. This reduces code duplication as the model code can be reused by multiple views.

The Controller (C) accepts user input and invokes the appropriate model and view to achieve user requirements. The Controller itself does not output any data or perform any processing. Its primary role is to receive user requests, determine which model component to invoke for processing the request, and then decide which view to use to display the returned data.

Next, taking the registration function as an example, the implementation of the MVC architecture in MIN-VPN is explained. In the registration module, M includes a "RegisterModel" for sending registration requests, a "VerifyCodeModel" for sending verification code requests, a "UserIdentityModel" for pulling identity, and a general model "BaseReturnModel" for processing server-returned data. V only includes one page, "RegisterOverview.fxml", and C only includes one controller, "RegisterOverviewController."

The architecture diagram of the registration function is shown in Fig. 13.5.

The controller mainly includes three related functions for interacting with MIS and VMS, which are "handleGetVerificationCode()" for obtaining the verification code, "handleIdregister()" for identity registration, and "handleRegister()" for user registration.

User Interaction

The user interactions in MIN-VPN include user registration, user login, pulling user identity, and MIN-VPN startup.

The user registration process consists of three important steps, namely obtaining the verification code, identity registration, and user registration.

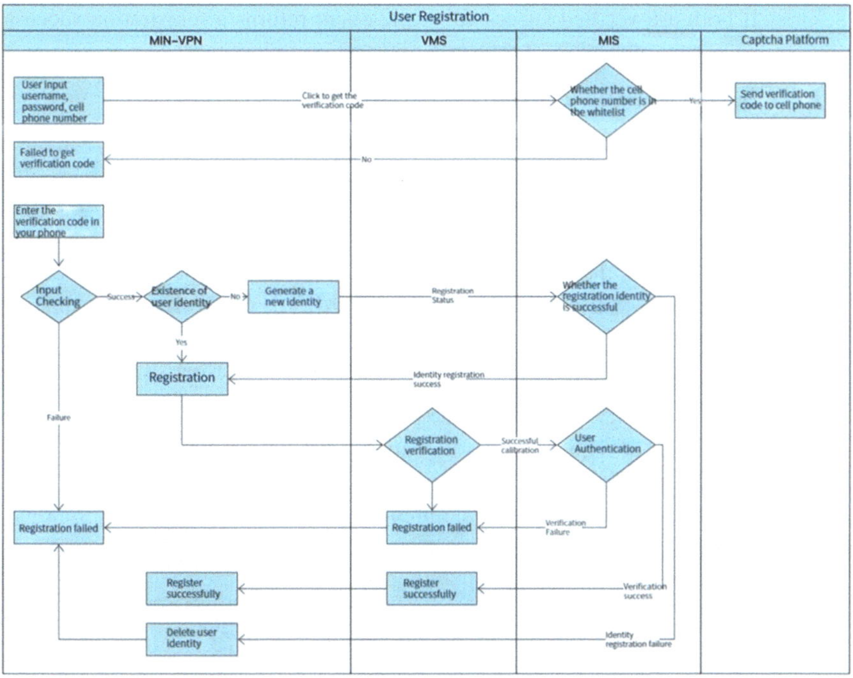

Fig. 13.6 Swimlane diagram of user registration

The swimlane diagram is shown in Fig. 13.6, and the specific process is as follows:

1. The user enters the account, password, and mobile phone number and clicks to obtain the verification code.
2. The client sends a request to MIS to obtain the verification code.
   (a) MIS verifies whether the mobile phone number is on the whitelist. If so, it requests the verification code platform to send the verification code to the mobile phone.
   (b) Otherwise, the user fails to obtain the verification code and the registration fails.
3. After the user obtains the verification code, the user enters the verification code and clicks to register.
4. The local machine searches for the existence of the user's identity.
   (a) If the user's identity exists locally,
      - A registration request is sent to VMS.
      - VMS verifies the registration request.
      - After successful verification, it requests MIS to verify the user's identity information.

- If both are verified successfully, the client returns a registration success message; otherwise, it returns a registration failure message.

(b) If the user's identity does not exist,

- A request is sent to MIS to register the identity. User registration can only be performed after the identity registration is successful; otherwise, the registration fails.
- A registration request is sent to VMS.
- VMS verifies the registration request.
- After successful verification, it requests MIS to verify the user's identity information.
- If both are verified successfully, the client returns a registration success message; otherwise, it returns a registration failure message.

The user login process encompasses two main methods: account password login and WeChat QR code login.

Figure 13.7 presents a swimlane diagram illustrating the account password login procedure.

The detailed process of this login method is as follows:

1. The user enters the account and password and clicks to login.
2. MIN-VPN verifies whether the user's identity exists locally.

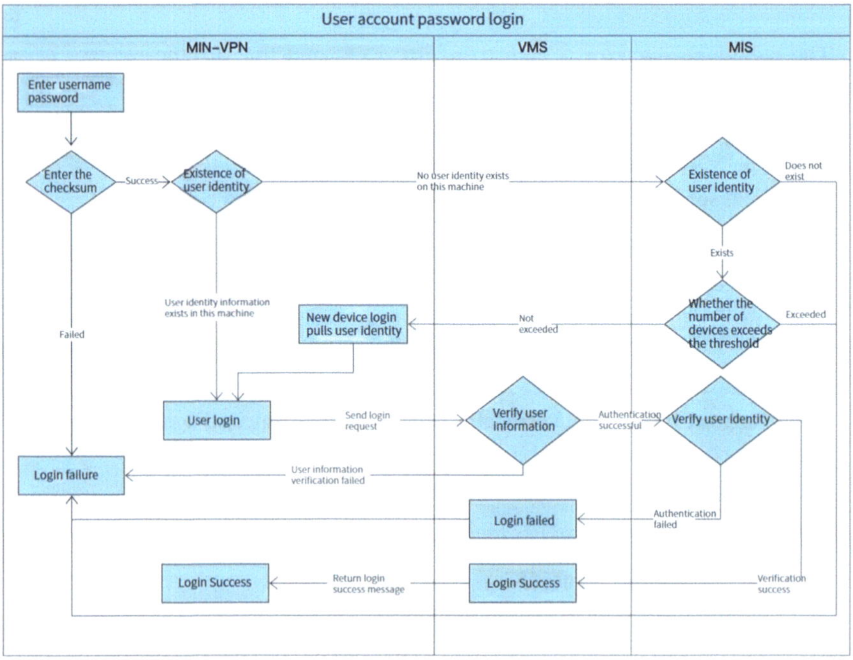

Fig. 13.7 Swimlane diagram of account password login

(a) If it exists, a login request is sent to VMS.

- VMS verifies the user's account information.
- VMS requests MIS to verify the user's identity information.
- If both verifications are successful, the login is successful; otherwise, the login fails.

(b) If it does not exist, a request is sent to MIS to pull the identity.

- If the identity exists and the number of devices is less than the threshold, the identity can be pulled.
  - The client pulls the identity.
  - VMS verifies the user's account information.
  - VMS requests MIS to verify the user's identity information.
  - If both verifications are successful, the login is successful; otherwise, the login fails.
- Otherwise, the identity cannot be pulled, and the login fails.

The swimlane diagram of WeChat QR code login is shown in Fig. 13.8, and the detailed process is as follows:

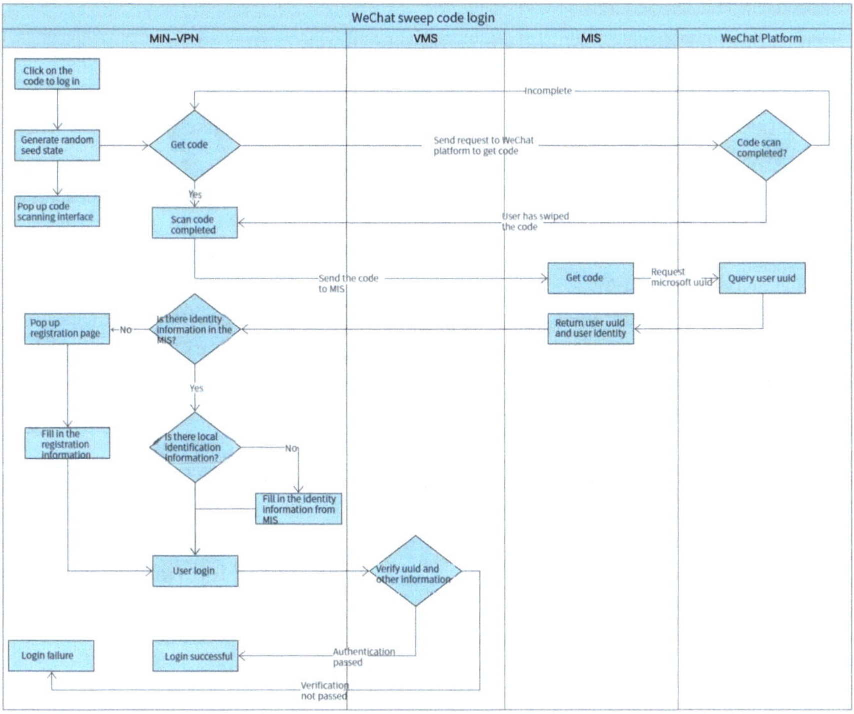

Fig. 13.8 Swimlane diagram of WeChat QR code login

1. The user clicks to login with QR code. The client generates a random seed state and pops up the WeChat QR code based on the state.
2. The client backend cyclically requests the code for this scan result from the WeChat platform.
3. When the user scans the code, the client obtains the corresponding code from the WeChat platform.
4. The client sends the code to MIS to request the corresponding WeChat scan result and user identity information.
5. After receiving the code, MIS requests the user's WeChat uuid from the WeChat platform and returns the user's information to the client.

   (a) If the user's identity information does not exist,

   - A mobile phone registration window pops up, prompting the user to register with the mobile phone and verification code.
   - A random username + mobile phone number suffix is generated for user registration.

   (b) If the user's identity information exists, proceed to the next step directly.

6. The user sends a login request to VMS based on the obtained WeChat uuid.
7. After VMS verifies the username and MIS verifies the identity, the login is completed.

The swimlane diagram of pulling identity is shown in Fig. 13.9.

The startup process of MIN-VPN after login is as follows:

1. First, MIN-VPN checks whether the user is banned. If the user is banned, MIN-VPN is not allowed to be used by this user.
2. Obtain relevant information about the VPN Server. There may be multiple VPN Servers.
3. Establish a LogicFace connection with and register the identity to the first VPN Server between them.
4. After generating the encryption seed, handshake with the VPN Server, negotiate encryption communication, and allocate a virtual network interface card IP for the client.
5. Start the TUN network interface card and use the IP allocated during the handshake as the IP of the virtual network interface card.
6. Wait for the network interface card to start. If it does not start for a long time, a prompt will be given.
7. If there is a second VPN Server, perform the second handshake with it (the client carries the allocated virtual network interface card IP for handshake instead of the VPN Server allocating IP).
8. Start the SOCKS5 thread to implement the SOCKS5 proxy function.
9. Start the PAC thread to implement PAC script pre-filtering.
10. Modify the routing table.
11. Record the startup process in the log.
12. Start the heartbeat coroutine and maintain heartbeat with multiple VPN Servers.

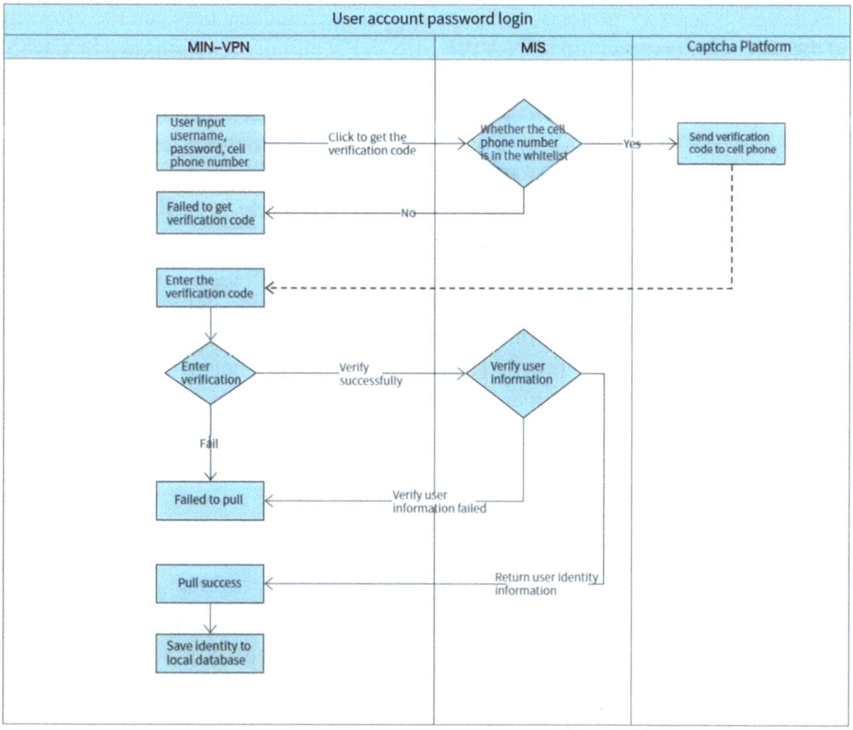

Fig. 13.9 Swimlane diagram of pulling identity

13. Start the receive thread and write the information received from the VPN Server to the receive buffer.
14. Start the write network interface card thread and write the contents of the receive buffer to the virtual network interface card.
15. Start the read network interface card thread and read IP packets from the virtual network interface card, and write them to the TUN packet buffer.
16. Start the send packet thread, read data from the TUN packet buffer, query the VPN Server corresponding to the destination IP based on the network segment and package the data into MIN packets to end to the VPN Server.

Any failure in the above steps will result in the failure of MIN-VPN startup.

Application Layer

The application layer encompasses various functions essential to the system such as SOCKS5 proxy, PAC proxy, JNA call, system settings modification, and fault tolerance, primarily implemented using the Java programming language.

SOCKS5 is a proxy protocol that serves as an intermediary between the browser and the SOCKS-Server within MIN-VPN. MIN-VPN initially functions as a SOCKS5 server, receiving requests from the browser front-end. It then executes the necessary operations on the request and forward it to the actual target server, known as the SOCKS-Server. The communication between the browser front-end and the SOCKS5 server occurs through the TCP/IP protocol. The browser front-end sends the request, originally intended for the real server SOCKS-Server, to the SOCKS5 server. Subsequently, the SOCKS5 server forward this request to the SOCKS-Server, ensuring that the request is appropriately processed and responded to by the target server.

A PAC file contains a JavaScript function "FindProxyForURL (url, host)." The function returns a string containing one or more access rules. The user agent applies a specific proxy or accesses directly based on these rules. When a proxy server cannot respond, multiple access rules provide other alternative access methods. The browser accesses this PAC file before accessing other pages. In MIN-VPN, the URL in the PAC file is manually configured.

Core Layer

The core layer of the system handles the underlying functionality of the entire system, including MIN communication, heartbeat maintenance, virtual network card read/write operations, and providing API functions.

13.3 VPN Server

13.3.1 VPN Server Architecture

The VPN Server plays a crucial role as it handles all the network traffic passing through the MIN-VPN. It establishes a network tunnel by utilizing a virtual network interface card, effectively encapsulating and encrypting the packets for secure transmission. It also works with MIS and VMS to further ensure the security of user access requests. The architecture of the VPN Server is shown in Fig. 13.10:

The code components of the VPN Server mainly include the TUN adapter module, packet receiving module, connection module, packet sending module, and logging module.

13.3.2 VPN Server Design

TUN Adapter Module

TUN virtual network interface card is supported by Linux, Windows, and Android systems.

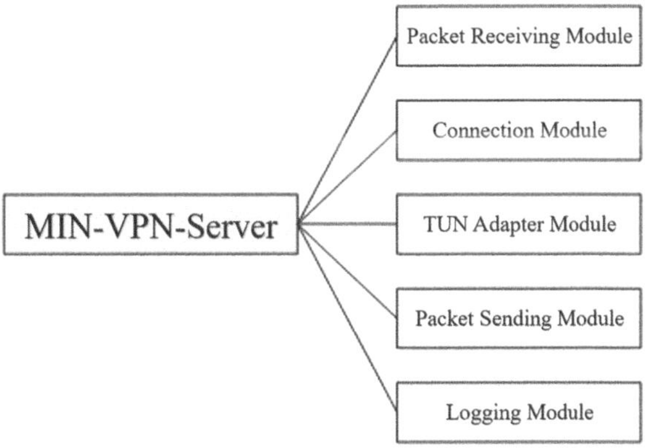

Fig. 13.10 Architecture of VPN Server

Figure 13.11 provides an illustration of the working principle of TUN, comparing it to the operation of a physical network interface card. When a TUN device is opened on a host, both a physical network interface card and a virtual network interface card coexist simultaneously. Both physical and virtual network interface cards have a send buffer and a receive buffer.

The TUN virtual network interface card and physical network interface card serve similar functions but interact with different entities. In the case of a physical network interface card, the entities involved are the network cable and the network protocol stack of the operating system. On the other hand, for a TUN virtual network interface card, the entities are the network protocol stack of the operating system and a specific application program.

In practical applications, network packets generated by upper-layer applications (such as browsers) enter the operating system's network protocol stack, which determines the network interface (including physical and virtual network interfaces) to which the packets should be sent. If a packet is forwarded to the TUN virtual network interface, it is copied into the sending buffer of the TUN interface. When there is a packet in the sending buffer of the TUN virtual network interface, it notifies a specific upper-layer application, which is the MIN-VPN program, to read the network packet.

For reverse communication, the upper-layer application can write a network packet to the receiving buffer of the TUN virtual network interface using the write function. When the TUN virtual network interface detects the presence of a network packet in its receiving buffer, it delivers the packet to the operating system's network protocol stack, which then forward it to the appropriate application program.

Connection Module

1. Processing Logic

   (a) Establishing Connection: When the backend receives the first data packet from the frontend, it checks the first byte to determine if it is a handshake packet. If the first byte is 0, it indicates non-encrypted communication,

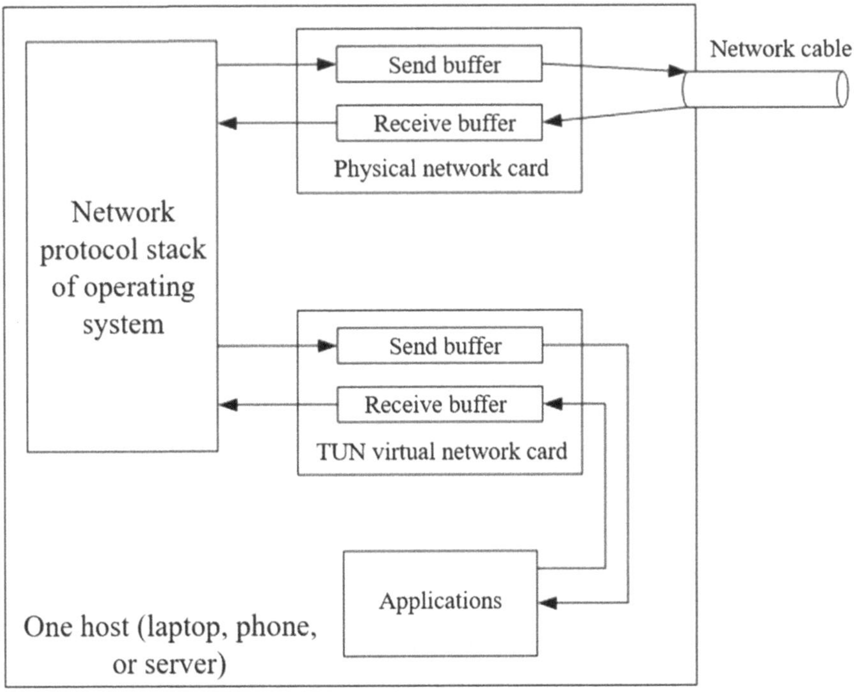

Fig. 13.11 Schematic diagram of TUN adapter principle

while 1 indicates encrypted communication. For encrypted communication, the backend decrypts the data packet using the private key of asymmetric encryption to obtain the client's symmetric key and stores it. For non-encrypted communication, an empty string is stored. An IP address is assigned to each client, and their user prefix, permission set, symmetric key, and connection time are stored accordingly. Finally, the allocated IP address and connection information are returned to the client.

(b) Disconnecting Connection: A separate thread continuously monitors the connection time for each user. If a client has not performed any operation for more than 10 min, the connection is terminated. The server sends a data packet filled with zeros to notify the corresponding client of the disconnection and deletes all information stored for that client on the backend.

2. Interfaces

The formats of handshake packets from the frontend are shown in Figs. 13.12 and 13.13.

The format of a disconnection packet sent by the backend is shown in Fig. 13.14.

Fig. 13.12 Handshake packet for non-encrypted communication

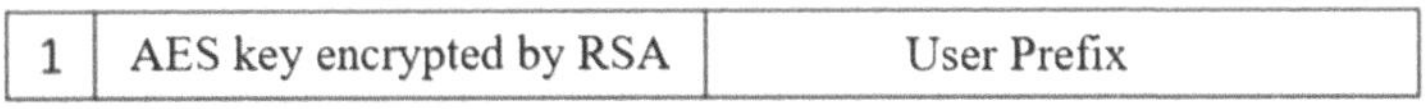

Fig. 13.13 Handshake packet for encrypted communication

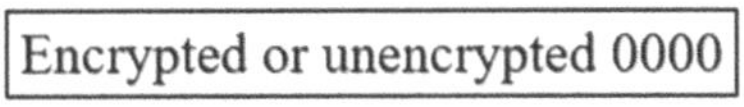

Fig. 13.14 The notification packet for disconnecting a connection from the backend

Packet Receiving Module

The backend analyses packets received from the frontend to identify normal packets. This determination is made by examining the first byte of each packet. Normal packets are identified as those with a first byte value that is neither 0 nor 1. Once a normal packet is detected, the dataRequest thread, which is specifically designed to handle normal packets, is notified. Subsequently, this thread retrieves the appropriate symmetric key associated with the IP address, decrypts the data, and transmits it to the network interface card.

Packet Sending Module

The process logic of the packet sending module is shown in Fig. 13.15.

The server actively receives packets from the network interface card in a continuous manner. Upon receiving a packet, it triggers the business coroutine responsible for packet transmission. This coroutine retrieves relevant information such as the user prefix, symmetric key, and other data stored in the backend associated with the client's IP address. It then proceeds to perform encryption, encapsulation, updates the connection time, and ultimately sends the packet to the intended client.

Logging Module

The logging module primarily functions to capture and store user behavior data. Upon a user establishing a connection using a handshake packet, the relevant thread within the logging module generates and transmits a packet containing the user's login log information. Similarly, during the processing of normal packets, the logging module logs and transmits relevant information based on whether the user's behavior exceeds the authorized parameters.

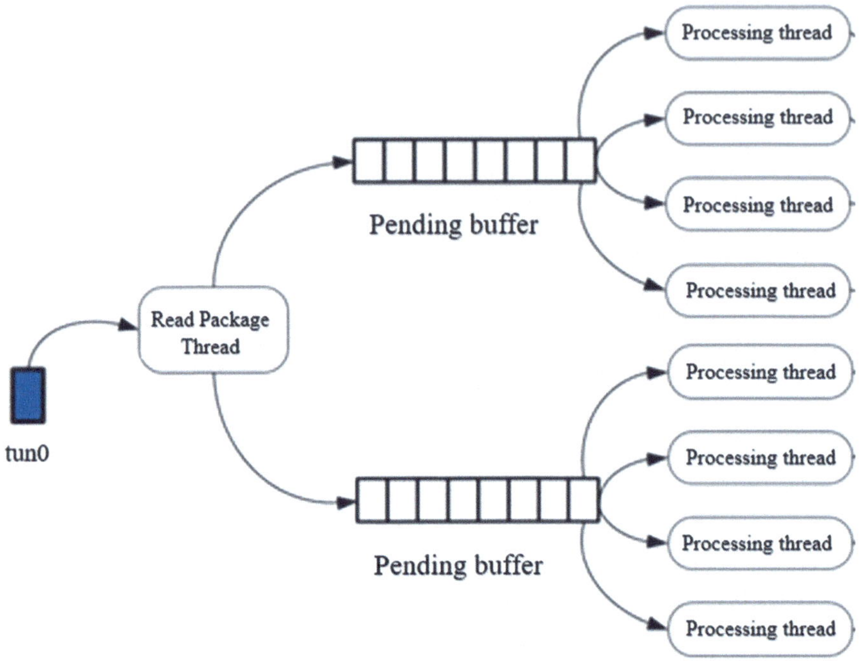

Fig. 13.15 Process logic of packet sending module

13.4 VMS

13.4.1 VMS Architecture

VPN Management Server (VMS) manages VPN users and their activities. The VMS system consists of two main components: the frontend and the backend. The frontend is developed using JavaScript, while the backend comprises the application layer and the core layer, which are implemented in Golang. The architecture of VMS is illustrated in Fig. 13.16.

13.4.2 VMS Design

Frontend

1. Login Interface
   The login interface of the VMS incorporates fields where users can input their login account, password, and verification code, as shown in Fig. 13.17.
2. Functional Interface
   The functional interface of VMS consists of a list of functions on the left and a detailed interface for each function on the right, as shown in Fig. 13.18.

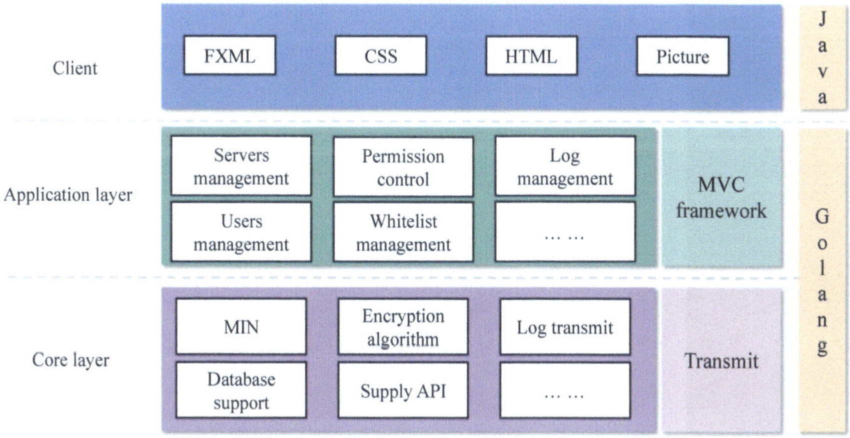

Fig. 13.16 Architecture of VMS

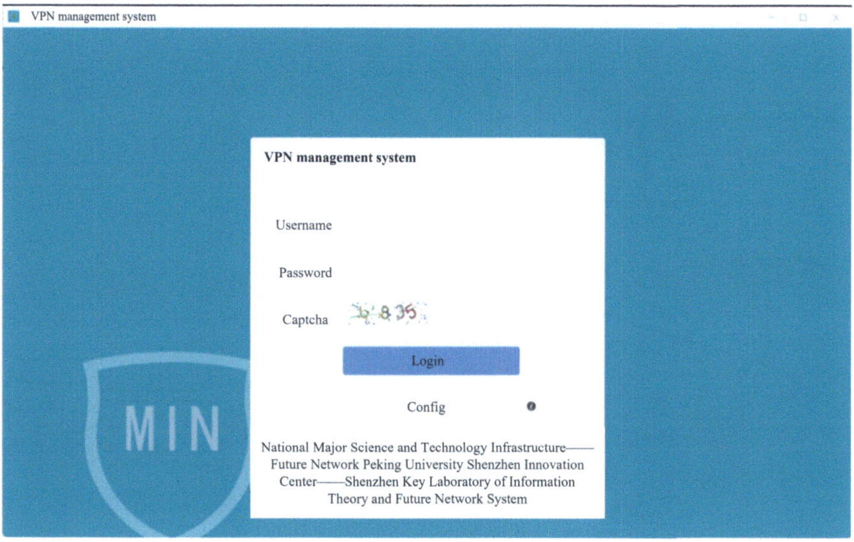

Fig. 13.17 Login interface

Application Layer

The application layer of VMS is accountable for the service functionalities and adopts the MVC framework. From a code design standpoint, the implementation of this architecture can be categorized into six modules, namely: Controller, Database Access Object (DAO), Interceptor, Model, Router, and Service. These modules correspond to the functionalities of controller, database interface, interceptor, model, router, and service interface, respectively, as depicted in Fig. 13.19. Each request from the frontend is received by the corresponding route in the router, which binds

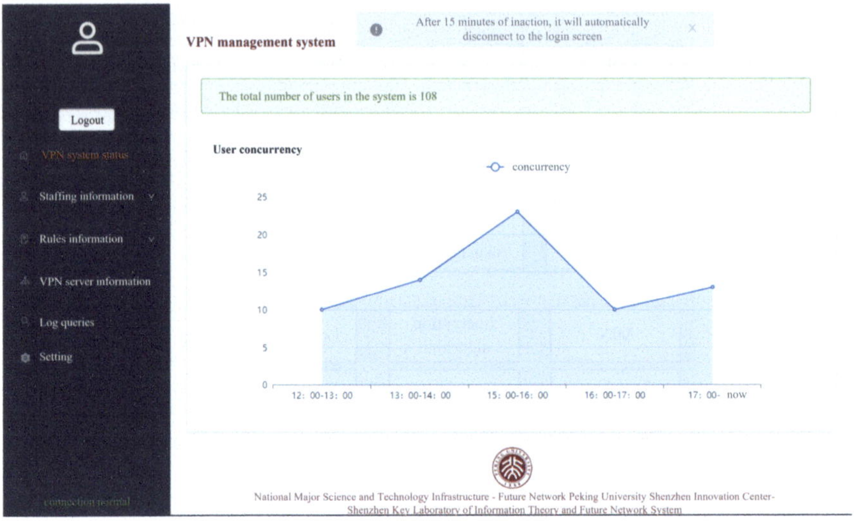

Fig. 13.18 VPN status information interface

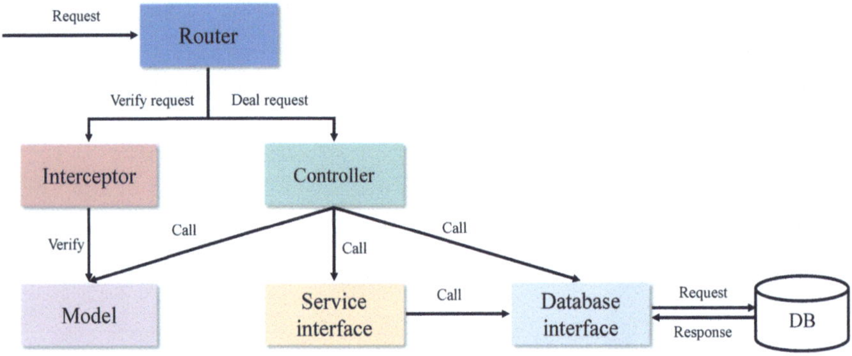

Fig. 13.19 Module composition relationships in the VMS architecture

a set of interceptors and controller functions to validate the request and process the business logic. At the same time, the interceptor also checks the correctness of the structure of the request, and the controller operates on the correct structure, which requires the support of the model. In order to reduce the coupling of the controller and increase the reusability of functions, there are corresponding service interfaces to implement the business processes of the controller. Additionally, database interfaces are available within the controller and service interfaces to handle requests to the database.

The functions corresponding to each module are given in Table 13.2.

Table 13.2 Composition and functions of core modules

Module name	Function description
Controller	The core processing function, which has the corresponding functions based on the received requests
DAO	The interface that directly interacts with the MySQL database
Interceptor	Intercepts and verifies the legality of various users and operations
Model	Defines various structures and operation objects
Router	Initializes and binds various interfaces
Service	Services provided to the controller

The main functions contained in each module are shown below:

1. Controller
    (a) admincontroller: functions for adding, deleting, modifying, logging in, and verifying administrators.
    (b) adminlogcontroller: function for obtaining and querying administrator logs.
    (c) analysiscontroller: functions for generating analysis pie charts and bar charts based on user and user group logs.
    (d) rgroupcontroller: functions for adding, deleting, modifying, authorizing, and distributing rules for rule groups.
    (e) rulecontroller: functions for adding, deleting, and modifying rules.
    (f) ugroupcontroller: functions for adding, deleting, modifying user groups and managing users within a group.
    (g) usercontroller: functions for adding, deleting, modifying, logging in, verifying, and resetting passwords for users.
    (h) userlogcontroller: functions for obtaining and querying user's ordinary logs, alarm logs, etc.
    (i) vpncontroller: functions for adding, deleting, and modifying VPN information.
    (j) whitelistcontroller: functions for adding, deleting, and modifying whitelists.
2. DAO
    (a) admindao: interfaces for interacting directly with the MySQL database for administrator-related functions.
    (b) adminlogdao: interfaces for interacting directly with the MySQL database for administrator log-related functions.
    (c) rgroupdao: interfaces for interacting directly with the MySQL database for rule group-related functions.
    (d) ruledao: interfaces for interacting directly with the MySQL database for rule-related functions.
    (e) ugroupdao: interfaces for interacting directly with the MySQL database for user group-related functions.

(f) userdao: interfaces for interacting directly with the MySQL database for user-related functions.
(g) vpndao: interfaces for interacting directly with the MySQL database for VPN-related functions.
(h) whilelistdao: interfaces for interacting directly with the MySQL database for whitelist-related functions.

3. Interceptor

(a) admininterceptor: request validation for administrator-related functions.
(b) adminloginterceptor: request validation for administrator log-related functions.
(c) analysisinterceptor: request validation for log analysis-related functions.
(d) authinterceptor: request validation for permission-related functions.
(e) rgroupinterceptor: request validation for rule group-related functions.
(f) ruleinterceptor: request validation for rule-related functions.
(g) ugroupinterceptor: request validation for user group-related functions.
(h) userinterceptor: request validation for user-related functions.
(i) userloginterceptor: request validation for user log-related functions.
(j) vpninterceptor: request validation for VPN-related functions.
(k) whitelistinterceptor: request validation for whitelist-related functions.

4. Model

(a) adminmodel: structure for administrator-related functions.
(b) adminlogmodel: structure for administrator log-related functions.
(c) analysismodel: structure for log analysis-related functions.
(d) authmodel: structure for permission-related functions.
(e) identitymodel: structure for identity-related functions.
(f) rgroupmodel: structure for rule group-related functions.
(g) rulemodel: structure for rule-related functions.
(h) ugroupmodel: structure for user group-related functions.
(i) usermodel: structure for user-related functions.
(j) userlogmodel: structure for user log-related functions.
(k) vpnmodel: structure for VPN-related functions.
(l) whitelismodel: structure for whitelist-related functions.

5. Router

(a) adminrouter: initialization and binding of interfaces for administrator-related functions.
(b) adminlogrouter: initialization and binding of interfaces for administrator log-related functions.
(c) analysisrouter: initialization and binding of interfaces for log analysis-related functions.
(d) rgrouprouter: initialization and binding of interfaces for rule group-related functions.
(e) rulerouter: initialization and binding of interfaces for rule-related functions.

(f) ugrouprouter: initialization and binding of interfaces for user group-related functions.
(g) userrouter: initialization and binding of interfaces for user-related functions.
(h) userlogrouter: initialization and binding of interfaces for user log-related functions.
(i) vpnrouter: initialization and binding of interfaces for VPN-related functions.
(j) whitelistrouter: initialization and binding of interfaces for whitelist-related functions.

6. Service

(a) adminservice: administrator-related services.
(b) adminlogservice: administrator log-related services.
(c) authservice: permission-related services.
(d) rgroupservice: rule group-related services.
(e) ruleservice: rule-related services.
(f) ugroupservice: user group-related services.
(g) userservice: user-related services.
(h) userlogservice: user log-related services.
(i) vpnservice: VPN-related services.
(j) whitelisservice: whitelist-related services.

The aforementioned modules encompass all the functions within the VMS application layer. Functionally, these modules can be categorized as follows: administrator module, administrator log module, user group module, rule module, user module, user log module, VPN module, and whitelist module.

For a comprehensive understanding of the functions, please refer to Table 13.3, which provides a detailed description of each module's functionalities.

Next, taking the "Add Administrator" function as an example.

As shown in Fig. 13.20, it explains the use of the MVC architecture in VMS and the relationship and process of each module. The "Add Administrator" function

Table 13.3 Modules divided by functions and their descriptions

Module name	Function description
Admin module	Includes functions related to administrators such as adding, deleting, modifying, and querying
Admin log module	Provides the ability to retrieve and query administrator logs
Rule group module	Allows for adding, deleting, modifying, and querying rule groups as well as authorizing and assigning rules
Rule module	Provides functions for adding, deleting, modifying, and querying rules
User module	Includes functions for adding, deleting, modifying, and querying users, as well as login, verification, password resetting, and other related functions
User group module	Allows for adding, deleting, modifying, and querying user groups, as well as managing users within the group

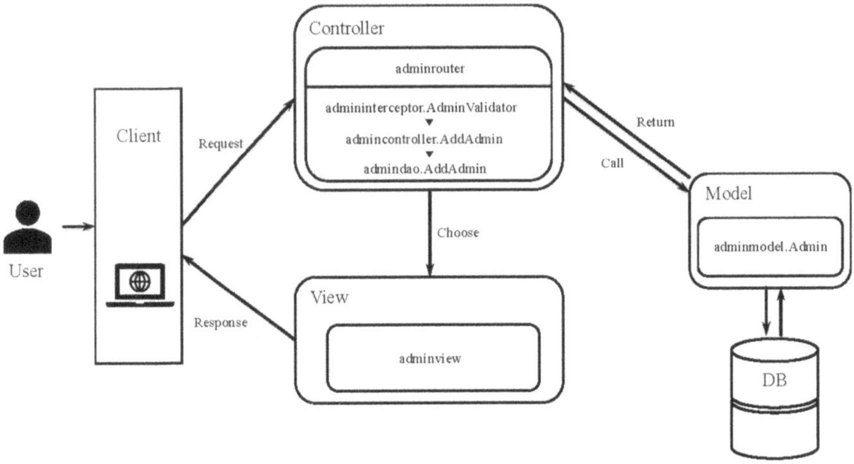

Fig. 13.20 An example of "Add Administrator"

belongs to the Admin module. When a user initiates an "addAdmin" request on the client side, it is transmitted to the VMS backend. Within the MVC framework, the request is received by the Controller class. Specifically, it is directed to the "adminrouter" route within the router module. This route is associated with both an interceptor and a core processing function. In this example, they are "admininterceptor. AdminValidator" and "admincontroller.AddAdmin," respectively, belonging to the interceptor and controller. The former is used to verify the correctness of the request and the data it carries, and the latter will handle the request formally after passing through the interceptor. In the controller, "adminmodel.Admin" is used, which defines the relevant structure of this request. This request involves operations on the database, which are handled by the function "admindao.AddAdmin" from the database interface. This function executes the necessary database operations and returns the corresponding results. In certain cases, a core processing function may involve multiple logical operations. To maintain a concise code structure, corresponding service functions are implemented to assist the core processing function in handling business operations. Once the controller component within the MVC architecture completes its processing, it selects the appropriate View interface, "adminview" in this instance, and returns it to the client along with the corresponding data. At this stage, a request within the MVC architecture is considered complete.

Core Layer

The core layer includes the cache module, database files, encryption module, log module, and network module. The architecture of the modules is shown in Fig. 13.21.

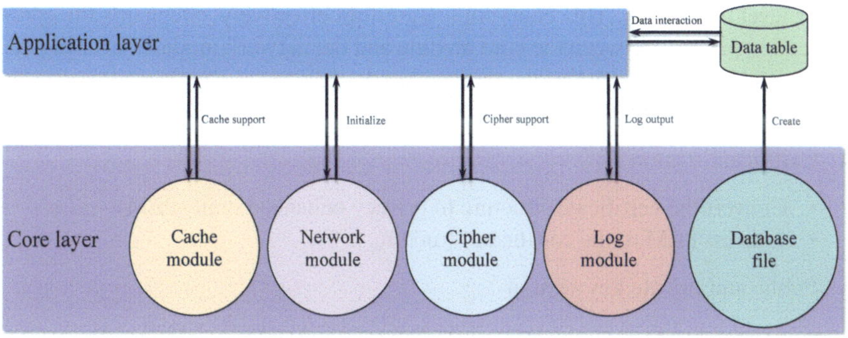

Fig. 13.21 The core layer module architecture

Cache Module

The cache module in the system relies on the memory cache library called go-cache, which is provided by the Go language. It employs the least recently used (LRU) algorithm to manage the cache, ensuring that the most frequently accessed data is retained in the cache. This approach enhances system performance by providing quick access to frequently used data. The cache module offers functions to create new caches for both the network module and core module.

The main components of the module include:

- Creating a new cache and creating a path.

Database Files

The database files contain SQL statements responsible for creating various tables within the database. These statements define the table structures, data types, and relationships between different data tables. By utilizing these files, it becomes feasible to efficiently establish the required relational database for VMS on a new server. This allows for a streamlined setup process, ensuring that the database is configured correctly and ready for use in the VMS system.

Encryption Module

The encryption module in VMS primarily focuses on generating and verifying certificates required by the system, managing public and private keys, and implementing various encryption algorithms such as MD5, SHA256, SHA512, as well as Chinese national encryption algorithms like SM2, SM3, and SM4. In particular, the SM2 algorithm utilizes an elliptic curve encryption algorithm (ECC) [3] and employs a specific elliptic curve known as the SM2 curve. Compared to algorithms like RSA and DSA, SM2 algorithm offers shorter key length while maintaining a higher level of security. This encryption algorithm effectively safeguards the communication process between the core module and the network module, ensuring the confidentiality and integrity of the transmitted data.

The main components of the module include:

(a) Certificate section

- Convert the certificate structure to privacy enhanced mail (PEM).
- Convert PEM to the certificate structure.

(b) Public and private key section

- Create/initialize public and private keys.
- Verify public and private keys.
- Public and private key structure conversion.
- Create a digital signature.
- Verify the digital signature.

(c) Encryption section

- Register encryption algorithm.
- Encrypt.
- Decrypt.
- Verify the key.

Log Module

The log module defines various types of module logs, including ordinary, alarm, and error logs, as well as their output formats, storage locations, etc., which can be used in VMS modules to effectively provide feedback on program execution status and steps.

The main components of the module include:

- Initialize the log.
- Set the log.
- Bind the host.
- Locate the calling function name.
- Get the calling function pointer.

Network Module

The network module in VMS primarily handles the listening functionality of TCP network, MIN network, and SSL certificates. It is bound and initialized within the router module.

The main components of the module include:

(a) MIN network section.

- Listen.
- Key setting.

(b) TCP network section.

- Listen.
- Read TCP packets.
- Write TCP packets.

(c) SSL section.

- Start SSL service.
- Establish SSL.
- Process SSL.

13.5 Secure Applications Based on MIN-VPN

13.5.1 File Sharing

MIN-File is a web application based on the MIN-VPN. It is designed for managing files and folders. The application allows users to manage files and folders in the local storage repository located on the server's hard disk drive or connect to other storage adapters.

MIN-File allows users and administrators to have different access permissions. Each role is granted access only to the folders and files corresponding to their assigned permissions. The application supports all essential file operations, including copying, moving, renaming, creating, deleting, compressing, decompressing, downloading, and uploading files.

To access and use MIN-File, users need to log in to both MIN-VPN and MIN-File. Once logged in, they can enter the system and make use of the various functionalities offered by MIN-File (Fig. 13.22).

To access the MIN-File, users must first enable MIN-VPN. They need to apply for whitelist access from the VMS and obtain authorization. Once authorized, an account will be issued to users for logging in to MIN-VPN. Additionally, users are required to apply for an account in MIN-File, which will restrict their access to specific file directories and control read and write operations. After the account application is successfully processed and users have logged into MIN-VPN, they can enter and use MIN-File. The MIN-File interface is shown in Fig. 13.23.

MIN-File can create folders, copy, move, compress, rename, and delete files. It also allows for file search operations, as shown in Fig. 13.24.

By default, MIN-File requires users to log in to view and download files. However, it is possible to configure guest user permissions in the user management

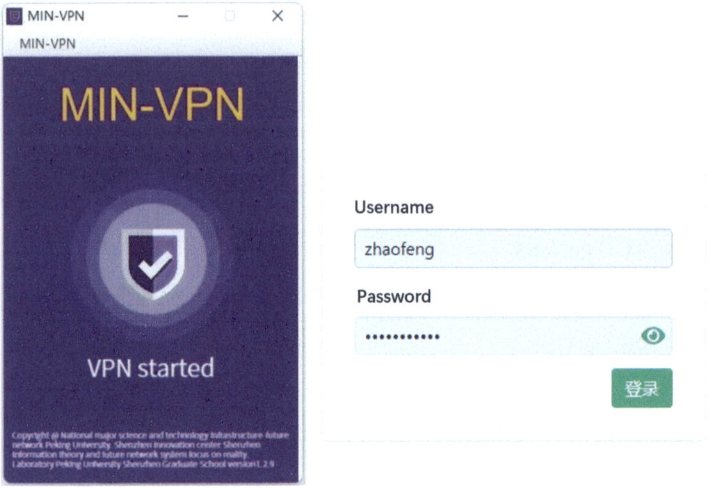

Fig. 13.22 The user logs in to MIN-VPN

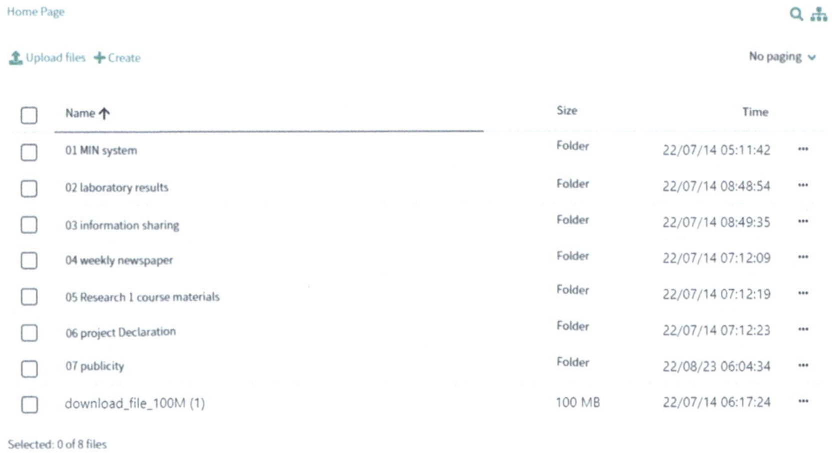
Home Page
Upload files
Create
No paging
Name
Size
Time
01 MIN system
Folder
22/07/14 05:11:42
02 laboratory results
Folder
22/07/14 08:48:54
03 information sharing
Folder
22/07/14 08:49:35
04 weekly newspaper
Folder
22/07/14 07:12:09
05 Research 1 course materials
Folder
22/07/14 07:12:19
06 project Declaration
Folder
22/07/14 07:12:23
07 publicity
Folder
22/08/23 06:04:34
download_file_100M (1)
100 MB
22/07/14 06:17:24
Selected: 0 of 8 files

Fig. 13.23 MIN-File interface

section of MIN-File. This allows for options such as enabling anonymous users to upload, download, or view files, as shown in Fig. 13.25.

13.5.2 Email

MIN-Mail is a system based on the MIN-VPN that provides electronic information services for transmitting mail, documents, and other data over the network. After logging in to MIN-VPN, users can access the functionalities of the MIN-Mail upon authorization by the administrator.

Fig. 13.24 File operations

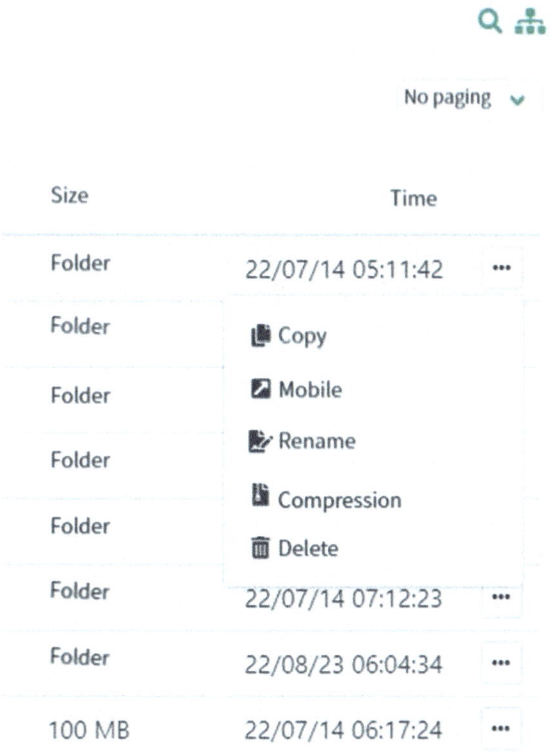

Fig. 13.25 Viewing files using the guest user

MIN-Mail utilizes encrypted communication protocols by default. Users are required to establish encrypted connections, such as TLS-based POP3/IMAP/SMTP services or HTTPS. The transmission between mail servers is also encrypted, and user passwords are stored using strong encryption algorithms like SSHA512 or BCRYPT (available only on BSD systems).

MIN-Mail allows users to create multiple email domains and accounts. MIN-Mail has comprehensive anti-spam and anti-virus functions. It integrates SpamAssassin (anti-spam system) and ClamAV (anti-virus software), supports Sender Policy Framework (SPF), DomainKeys Identified Mail (DKIM) [4], gray/white/black lists, and Domain Name System Blacklists (DNSBL) [5] services. It supports isolating detected spam and virus emails into an SQL database for later management.

To access MIN-Mail services, users must obtain authorization from the administrator and register their account through the administrator. During registration, users are required to provide the desired email account to the administrator. Subsequently, the administrator will generate a random password and assign the account to the user, who will receive the account details. Upon logging in to the email account, users can change the password independently and it is strongly advised to avoid using the default password for security reasons.

To access the login page, enter the corresponding URL in a web browser, as shown in Fig. 13.26.

Users can login using the account granted by the administrator, as shown in Fig. 13.27.

After logging in, click "Compose" to write a new email. Users can add attachments on the right side, as shown in Fig. 13.28.

To modify the password, users should log in to their email account and navigate to the "Settings" section. Within the settings, there will be an option to change the password. It is important for users who are accessing their account for the first time

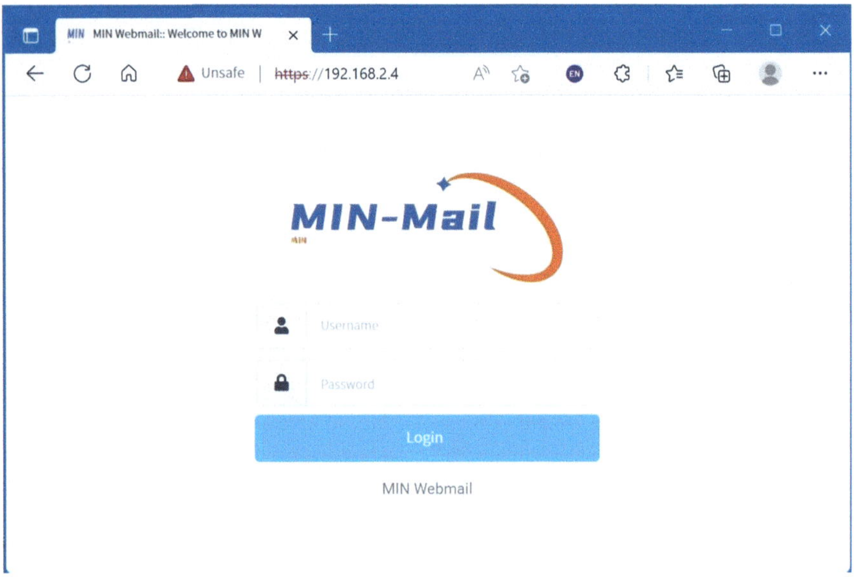

Fig. 13.26 Login page

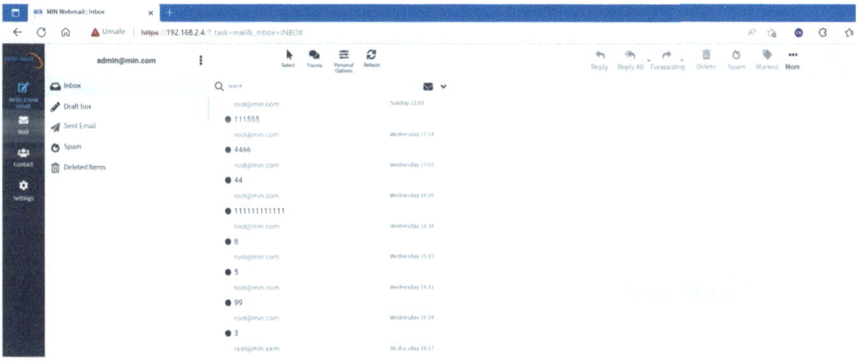

Fig. 13.27 Account interface

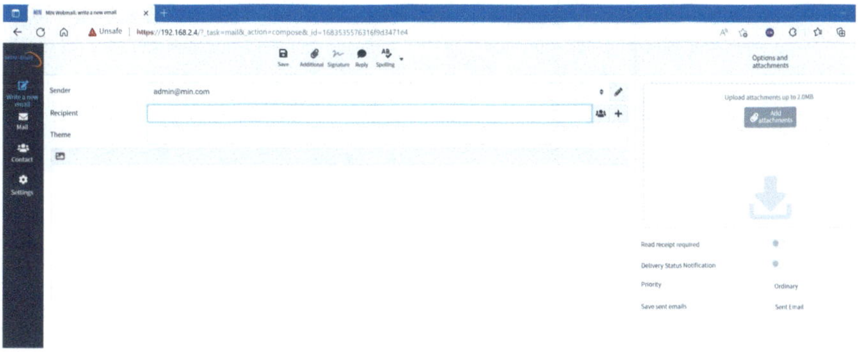

Fig. 13.28 Email composition interface

to remember to change the initial password provided. Figure 13.29 illustrates the page where users can proceed with the password modification process.

13.5.3 Video Conference

MIN-Meeting is a system built on the MIN-VPN and provides services for voice and video conferencing as well as instant messaging. Upon logging into MIN-VPN, users gain access to the functionalities offered by MIN-Meeting.

System Homepage

The system homepage is shown in Fig. 13.30.

1. This is the system settings module where users can perform device debugging for their camera, microphone, and other equipment before entering a meeting.

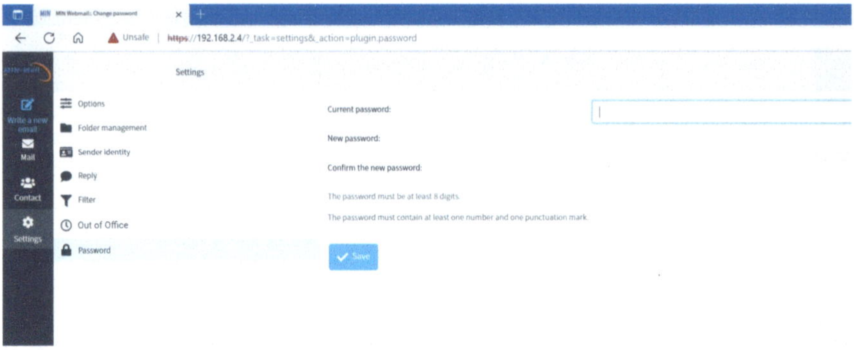

Fig. 13.29 Password modification interface

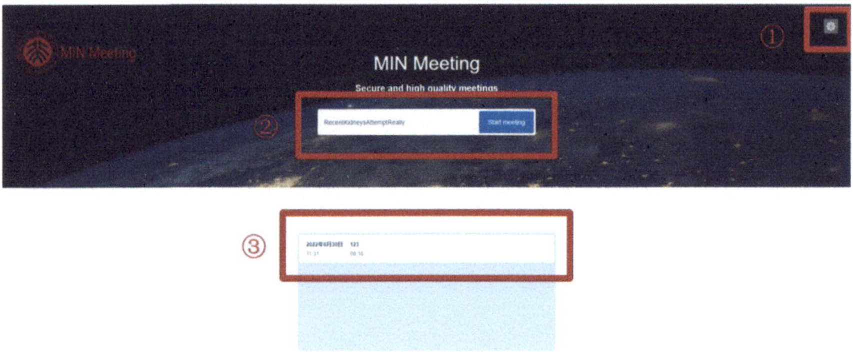

Fig. 13.30 MIN-Meeting homepage

Users can also configure their display name and other relevant settings. The system also supports device debugging after entering a meeting.

The specific information is shown in Fig. 13.31.

2. This displays a list of past meetings, recording the names, times, and durations of meetings that the user has previously participated in. If a meeting is still ongoing or if the meeting name has not changed, clicking on the respective meeting allows the user to re-enter that meeting.
3. Here, users can enter the meeting name into the designated white text box. Afterward, by clicking the blue "Start Meeting" button, users will be directed to enter the respective meeting room and initiate the meeting session.

MIN-Meeting Login Page

After clicking "Start Meeting" on the homepage, users are directed to the pre-meeting preparation page. This page allows users to customize their display name, test their devices, and adjust various settings. The red boxes highlight the following

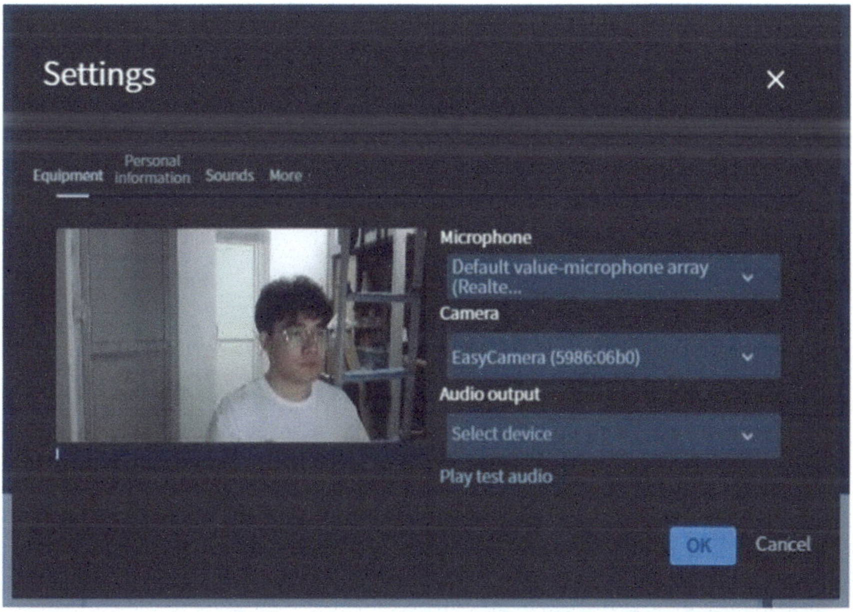

Fig. 13.31 MIN-Meeting settings

sections from left to right: microphone settings, camera settings, screen sharing link configuration, virtual background options, and additional settings.

After testing the devices, click the blue button "Join Meeting" to enter the meeting room, as shown in Fig. 13.32.

The MIN-Meeting

Meeting interface is shown in Fig. 13.33.

(1)–(4) are the four modules of the video system, which include the chat interface, main screen, meeting participants, and member list.

The (5) section is the settings module. From left to right, it includes the microphone, camera, screen sharing, chat interface, raise hand, member list, video list, and more settings (such as setting a password), as shown in Fig. 13.34.

Set Meeting Password

To set the meeting password, the meeting host, who is typically the first user to enter the room, has the authority to do so. By clicking on "More Actions" in the settings menu, the host can select "Security Options" and then enter the desired password in the provided pop-up box. Subsequently, any users wishing to join the meeting room will be required to enter the corresponding password.

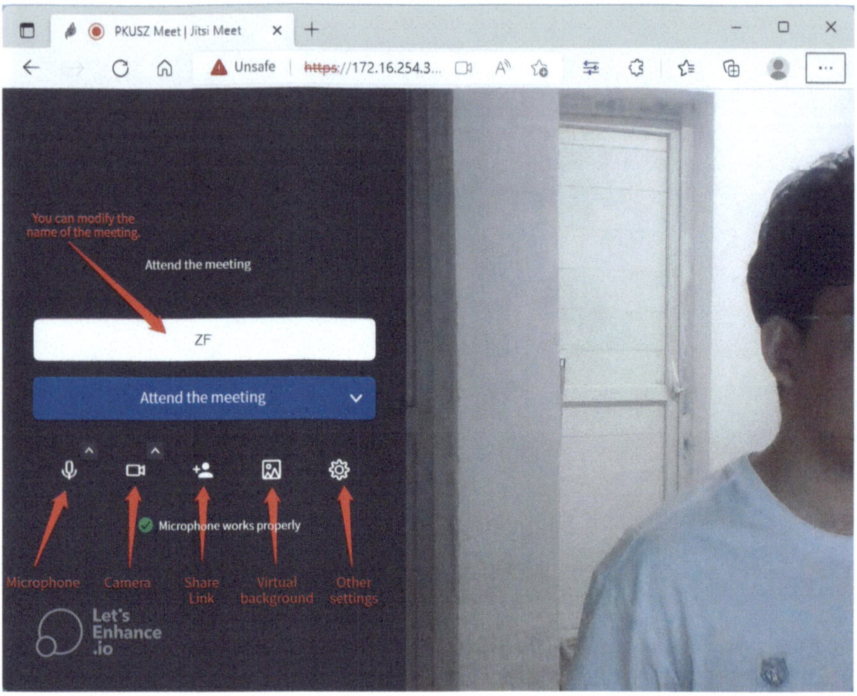

Fig. 13.32 Joining a meeting

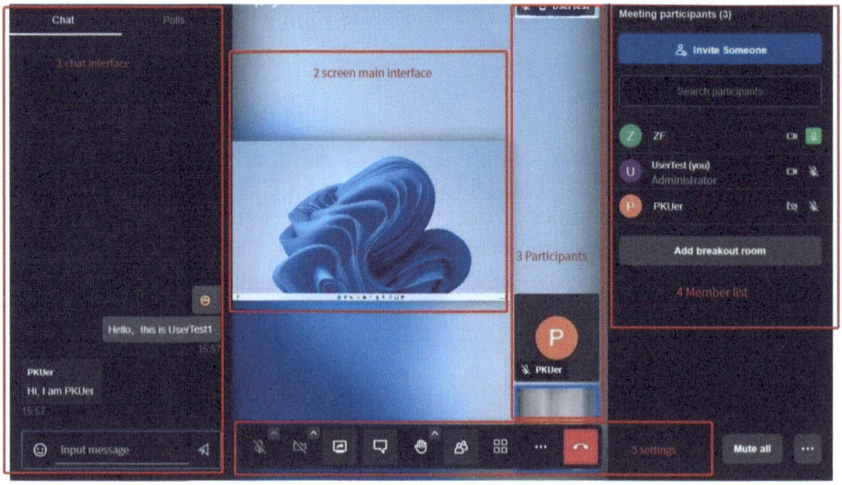

Fig. 13.33 Meeting interface

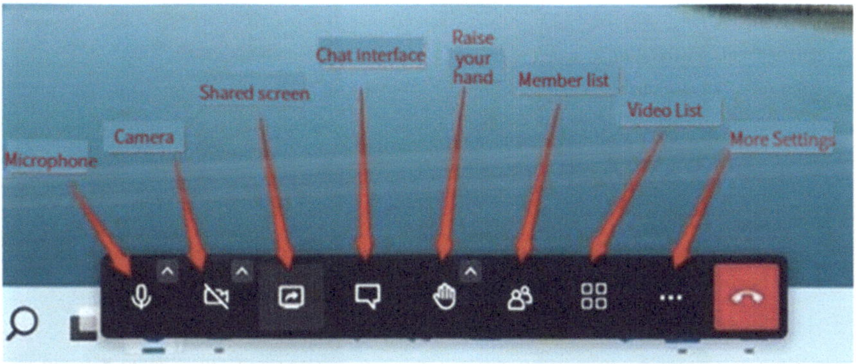

Fig. 13.34 MIN-Meeting settings module

This process is depicted in Fig. 13.35, illustrating the interface where the password is entered to access the meeting room.

13.6 MIN-SSH

The multi-identifier Network-SSH (MIN-SSH) protocol is an SSH (Secure Shell) protocol specially developed for the MIN Network. It supports remote login, command execution, and remote computer management within the MIN network. MIN-SSH incorporates encryption communication and identity authentication mechanisms, which effectively mitigate risks such as man-in-the-middle attacks and data leaks [6]. It can also securely transfer files and other data.

By leveraging the advantages of the MIN network, MIN-SSH facilitates efficient, secure, and reliable remote management. It enables communication between different network architectures and offers better scalability and flexibility. Within the MIN secure private network, system administrators can utilize MIN-SSH to remotely log in to and maintain the backend systems of the secure private network, ensuring the security of the infrastructure.

13.6.1 MIN-SSH Architecture

The overall communication architecture of MIN-SSH is depicted in Fig. 13.36. At the application layer, MIN-SSH implements the basic functionalities of the SSH protocol, which divides the user's remote login into five stages: version negotiation, algorithm negotiation, key exchange, user authentication, and session interaction. Each stage employs corresponding key exchange algorithms or encryption algorithms to ensure the confidentiality and integrity of user accounts, passwords, and

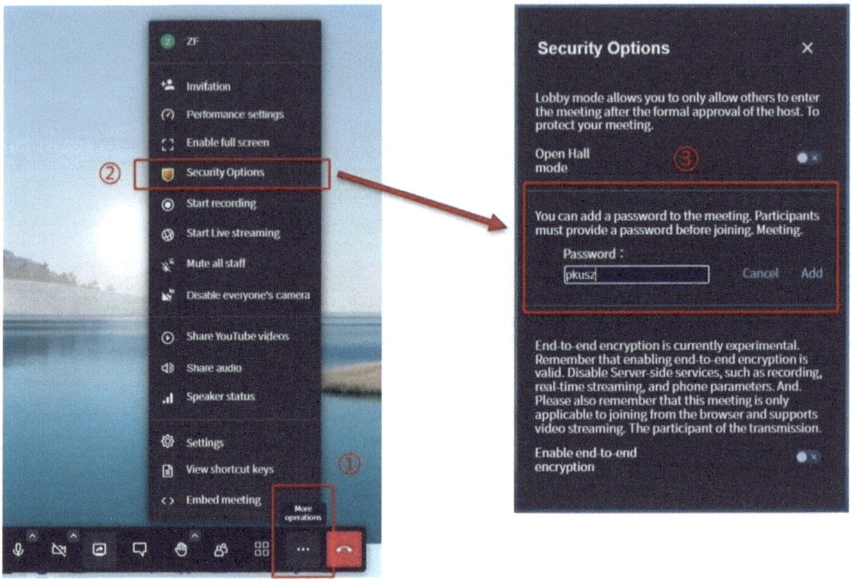

Fig. 13.35 Set meeting password

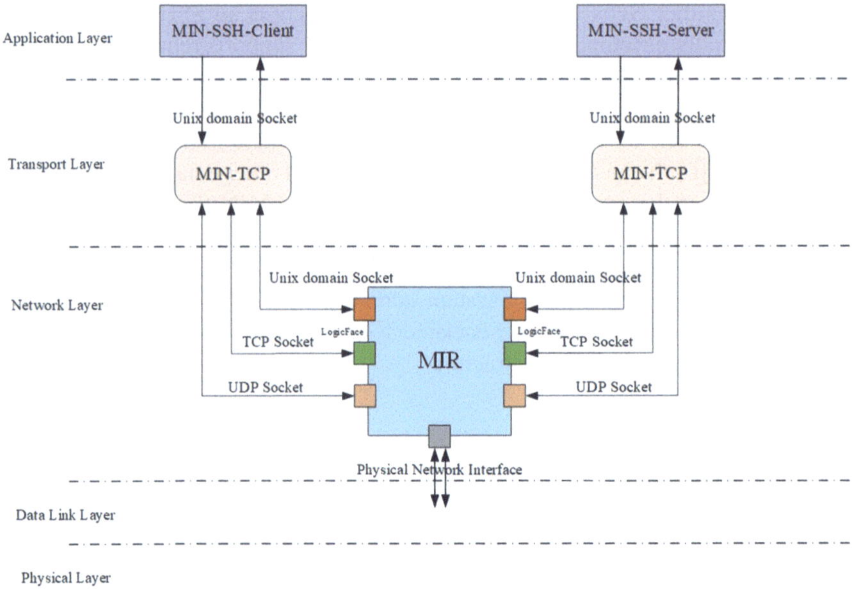

Fig. 13.36 MIN-SSH communication architecture

transmitted data, protecting them from eavesdropping or tampering by intermediaries.

MIN-SSH utilizes MIN-TCP as the transport layer protocol. MIN-TCP is responsible for encapsulating and transmitting application layer packets to the network layer, as well as parsing and delivering packets received from the network layer to the application layer. MIN-TCP handles essential aspects of network communication such as flow control, congestion control, and reliable transmission.

At the network layer, MIR encapsulates MIN-TCP packets into MIN network packets (GPPkt) and handles their reception, routing, and forwarding. This ensures that user data can traverse the network links and reach the destination. MIR is responsible for routing and forwarding within the network, ensuring the correctness of MIN-SSH communication.

The MIN-TCP protocol supports both TCP socket and UDP socket communication methods. This enables the MIR to receive IP packets and extract MIN network packets. As a result, the MIN-SSH protocol can operate in both MIN networks and IP networks. This cross-network communication capability aligns with the prevalent IP network architecture of today's Internet environment, and it holds significant importance for the development of the MIN-SSH protocol and the promotion of the MIN network.

13.6.2 MIN-SSH Design

The MIN-SSH protocol is designed with the following considerations:

1. User-friendly interface: Provide an intuitive, concise, and easy-to-use user interface that allows users to conveniently authenticate, connect, and manage remote hosts.
2. Security and privacy protection: Ensure that the communication process of the MIN-SSH protocol in the MIN network has a high degree of security, including mechanisms such as encrypted transmission, identity authentication [7], and prevention of man-in-the-middle attacks. At the same time, protect the user's privacy information and do not disclose sensitive data.
3. Connection stability: Consider several unstable network conditions, design the protocol to ensure connection stability and reliability, and reduce connection interruption or data loss caused by network jitter or disconnection [8].
4. Exception handling and error prompts: When there are connection problems, authentication failures, or other exceptional situations, provide clear error prompts to help users quickly identify problems and take appropriate action.
5. User configuration: Provide necessary configuration file settings, allowing users to set relevant information for the MIN-SSH and MIN-TCP protocols.

The design principles of the MIN-SSH protocol prioritize user experience and security, providing a convenient operational approach, stable and reliable connections, and efficient functionalities. This aims to meet users' needs for remote access and host management, enabling them to accomplish their tasks more easily.

Currently, the SSH protocol is recognized as a basic secure transmission protocol by various operating systems. It is registered as a system service by default during system installation, allowing users to use SSH protocol commands for remote connection and command transmission [9].

MIN-SSH references the design of the SSH protocol and registers MIN-SSH as a Linux system service, allowing Linux systems to recognize MIN-SSH commands and use them for remote connections. Users can use MIN-SSH smoothly without changing their usage habits.

MIN-SSH-Server is the server-side component of the MIN-SSH protocol. Its role is to initiate the MIN-SSH protocol and listen on a specified port for user connections. For the server side, users only need to run the program, so there are no complex command parameters in the server's system service. The MIN-SSH-Server commands should cover the entire lifecycle of the MIN-SSH protocol, from installation to uninstallation by the user. The five core commands of MIN-SSH-Server are given in Table 13.4. These five MIN-SSH-Server commands span its lifecycle, allowing users to quickly, conveniently, and efficiently perform specific operations on the MIN-SSH protocol.

MIN-SSH-Client is the client-side component of the MIN-SSH protocol. Its role is to connect to remote hosts for remote login, information transfer, and executing user commands. Since the MIN-SSH protocol allows operation in IP networks and supports connections to remote hosts identified by IP addresses, and considering that users may configure their own user identities flexibly, the MIN-SSH-Client is designed with different commands from the server side. This allows users to use the MIN-SSH protocol in a flexible manner. To ensure the user-friendliness and reasonable utilization of system resources, the MIN-SSH-Client is not designed with a set of five commands similar to MIN-SSH-Server to keep it running at all times. Instead, the program is designed to start when the user wants to use MIN-SSH-Client and remains stopped at other times.

The MIN-SSH-Client commands are given in Table 13.5.

The -f command is used to specify the MIN-SSH-Client configuration file, allowing users to set their MIN network identity and password. The -tcpf command is used to specify the MIN-TCP protocol configuration file, completing some basic transport layer protocol configuration information. The (IP network identifier)

Table 13.4 MINSSH-Server commands

Command	Description
install	Registers the MIN-SSH-Server service into the Linux system
start	Starts the service, listens on the specified port, and allows user connections
stop	Pauses the service, preventing remote user connections
status	Checks the current status of the service, indicating whether it is running or paused
remove	Uninstalls the service. After removal, the service can only be used again after reinstallation with the install command

Table 13.5 MINSSH-Client commands

Command	Description
-f	Specify MIN-SSH-Client configuration file
-tcpf	Specify MIN-TCP protocol configuration file
(IP network identifier)	Connect to a remote host in the IP network

```
ubuntu@VM-12-5-ubuntu: /
root@ubuntu:/usr/local/etc/mir# minssh ubuntu@119.91.238.8
Password:
2023-05-15 09:01:31     DEBUG    /home/guozhan/MIN/MINTCP/channel/MessageChannel.
go:92   WriteMessage: 102
2023-05-15 09:01:32     DEBUG    /home/guozhan/MIN/MINTCP/channel/MessageChannel.
go:110  ReadMessage: 203
2023-05-15 09:01:32     DEBUG    /home/guozhan/MIN/MINTCP/socket/PushConn.go:164o
penBytesChannel: 06730309-ba1b-4818-be88-21f7783a4387
ubuntu@VM-12-5-ubuntu:/$ netstat -tunlp | grep 22
(Not all processes could be identified, non-owned process info
 will not be shown, you would have to be root to see it all.)
tcp        0      0 0.0.0.0:22              0.0.0.0:*               LISTEN
-
tcp6       0      0 :::22                   :::*                    LISTEN
-
ubuntu@VM-12-5-ubuntu:/$ free -mh
              total        used        free      shared  buff/cache   available
Mem:          3.3Gi       2.1Gi       112Mi       1.0Mi       1.2Gi       1.0Gi
Swap:         4.0Gi       1.8Gi       2.2Gi
ubuntu@VM-12-5-ubuntu:/$ █
```

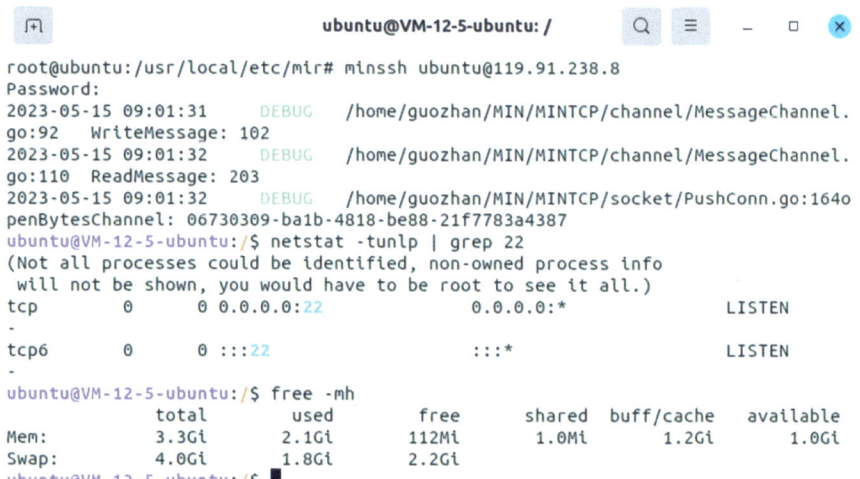

Fig. 13.37 MIN-SSH-Client example—network command and system information command

command is used to specify the remote host IP address that MIN-SSH-Client will connect to. The MIN-SSH protocol sends MIN network packets to the IP network in the form of an IP tunnel and route them to the final destination host. These three commands allow users to use MIN-SSH-Client quickly, efficiently, and conveniently, and only start MIN-SSH when the user needs it, without occupying system resources all the time.

As shown in Figs. 13.37 and 13.38, MIN-SSH protocol supports basic commands, file handling commands, system management commands, network commands, pipeline and redirection commands, compression and decompression commands, permission and user management commands, and system information commands, just like the SSH protocol.

```
ubuntu@VM-12-5-ubuntu: /
top - 00:10:51 up 162 days,  4:54,  2 users,  load average: 0.16, 0.16, 0.12
Tasks: 126 total,   1 running, 122 sleeping,   0 stopped,   3 zombie
%Cpu(s):  9.4 us,  3.1 sy,  0.0 ni, 87.5 id,  0.0 wa,  0.0 hi,  0.0 si,  0.0 st
MiB Mem :  3419.2 total,   118.4 free,  2136.8 used,  1164.0 buff/cache
MiB Swap:  4096.0 total,  2227.5 free,  1868.4 used.  1034.3 avail Mem

    PID USER      PR  NI    VIRT    RES    SHR S  %CPU  %MEM     TIME+ COMMAND
    362 root      19  -1  158676  74228  73360 S   6.2   2.1  35:55.27 systemd+
  18679 root      20   0 2541112 356880  12964 S   6.2  10.2  12017:17 mird
1229105 root      20   0 9016628   1.5g   7664 S   6.2  44.8 724:35.89 7DaysTo+
      1 root      20   0  171088   8712   5880 S   0.0   0.2   5:59.94 systemd
      2 root      20   0       0      0      0 S   0.0   0.0   0:04.63 kthreadd
      3 root       0 -20       0      0      0 I   0.0   0.0   0:00.00 rcu_gp
      4 root       0 -20       0      0      0 I   0.0   0.0   0:00.00 rcu_par+
      6 root       0 -20       0      0      0 I   0.0   0.0   0:00.00 kworker+
      8 root       0 -20       0      0      0 I   0.0   0.0   5:26.06 kworker+
      9 root       0 -20       0      0      0 I   0.0   0.0   0:00.00 mm_perc+
     10 root      20   0       0      0      0 S   0.0   0.0   1:31.65 ksoftir+
     11 root      20   0       0      0      0 I   0.0   0.0 126:29.39 rcu_sch+
     12 root      rt   0       0      0      0 S   0.0   0.0   0:34.15 migrati+
     13 root     -51   0       0      0      0 S   0.0   0.0   0:00.00 idle_in+
     15 root      20   0       0      0      0 S   0.0   0.0   0:00.00 cpuhp/0
     16 root      20   0       0      0      0 S   0.0   0.0   0:00.00 cpuhp/1
     17 root     -51   0       0      0      0 S   0.0   0.0   0:00.00 idle_in+
```

Fig. 13.38 MIN-SSH-Client example—system management command

13.6.3 MIN-SSH Communication

The communication diagram for MIN-SSH protocol in the MIN network is depicted in Fig. 13.39. The MIN-SSH protocol communication in the MIN network is similar to SSH protocol communication in IP networks.

The MIN-SSH protocol packets are encapsulated based on the five-layer network protocol model and ultimately delivered to the physical layer, transmitted as bit streams to the MIR. On the MIR, the network layer packets are extracted from the physical layer and data link layer. The packet's source identifier, destination identifier, signature value, congestion flag, and time-to-live are examined to validate the packet's legitimacy. MIR also coordinates congestion control and performs loop-back detection. Once the packet passes these checks, MIR forward the packet through routing until it reaches the destination host. Upon receiving the packet, the destination host verifies its legitimacy by checking the destination identifier to determine if it is intended for itself. The host then retrieves the corresponding public key from the MIS system based on the signature area and performs signature validation [10]. In this way, a MIN-SSH communication is completed, and the data successfully travels from the sender through intermediate routers to the receiver.

The current Internet is predominantly based on IP-based network architecture; therefore, the integration of MIN network with IP network was considered from the inception of MIN. To establish MIN network testing within the existing IP network environment, MIN-SSH can use IP tunnels to forward MIN network packets across the IP network to another MIN network, as shown in Fig. 13.40.

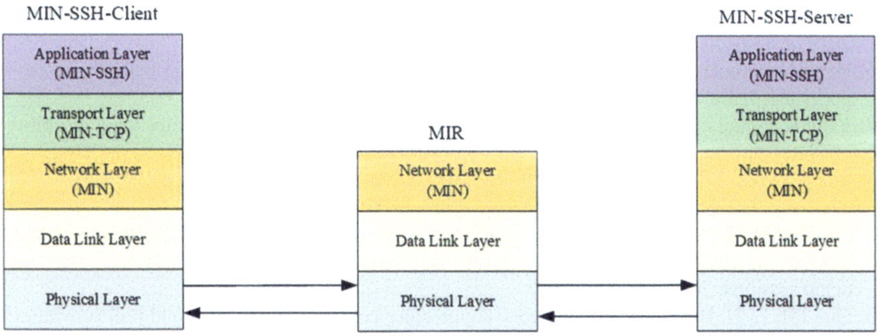

Fig. 13.39 The communication diagram for MIN-SSH protocol in the MIN network

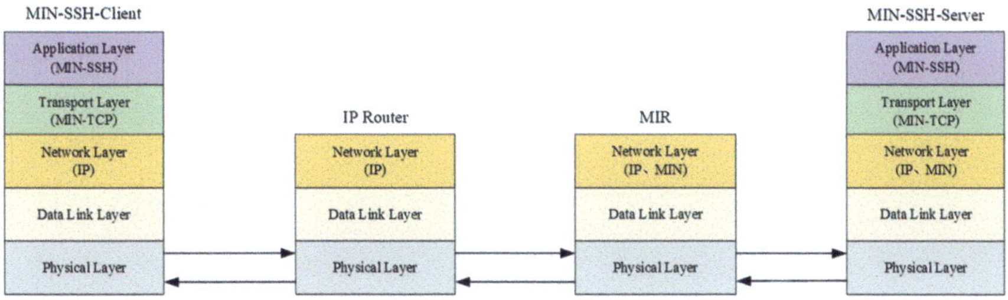

Fig. 13.40 The communication diagram for MIN-SSH protocol in the IP-based network

The compatibility with IP networks allows the MIN-SSH protocol to have a broader application scope, meeting the requirements of various use cases. Additionally, it enables smooth migration and utilization of the MIN-SSH protocol during network upgrades and transitions. This compatibility also helps in reducing the network hardware costs associated with the replacement of network devices.

References

1. Wang H, Li H, Smahi A, et al. MIS: a multi-identifier management and resolution system in the metaverse. ACM Trans Multimed Comput Commun Appl. 2023;20:1–28.
2. Zhang XC, Chen QS, Li H. MIR: multi-identifier router and its prototype. In: Proceedings of the 8th international conference on computer and communications management, 2020. p. 103–7.
3. Patel C, Doshi N. Secure lightweight key exchange using ECC for user-gateway para-digm. IEEE Trans Comput. 2020;70(11):1789–803.
4. Chauhan PD, Shah AM. Effectiveness of anti-spoofing protocols for email authentication. In: 2023 3rd international conference on intelligent communication and computational techniques (ICCT). Piscataway: IEEE; 2023. p. 1–5.
5. Al Mugni A, Herdiansah MF, Andhika MG, et al. DNSBL for internet content filtering utilizing pfSense as the next generation of opensource firewall. In: 2019 6th international confer-

ence on electrical engineering, computer science and informatics (EECSI). Piscataway: IEEE; 2019. p. 117–21.
6. Hahn C, Yoon H, Hur J. Multi-key similar data search on encrypted storage with secure pay-per-query. IEEE Trans Inf Forensics Secur. 2023;18:1169–81.
7. Yang K, Zhang Z, Tian Y, et al. A secure authentication framework to guarantee the traceability of avatars in metaverse. IEEE Trans Inf Forensics Secur. 2023;18:3817–32.
8. Wu F, Song HH, Yin J, et al. NEMA: automatic integration of large network management databases. IEEE Trans Netw Serv Manag. 2020;18(3):3783–97.
9. Groshev M, Sacido J, Martín-Pérez J. FoReCo: a forecast-based recovery mechanism for real-time remote control of robotic manipulators. In: Proceedings of the SIGCOMM'22 poster and demo sessions, 2022. p. 7–9.
10. Que JM, Li H, Bai H, et al. A network architecture containing both push and pull semantics. In: 2021 7th international conference on computer and communications (ICCC). Piscataway: IEEE; 2021. p. 2211–6.

Chapter 14
MIN-Web

Web technology has become one of the primary methods for accessing information and facilitating communication in today's digital age [1–3]. With the continuous advancement of the Internet, web technology provides users with convenient, efficient, and secure online experiences. It allows individuals and businesses to create and publish content, interact with others through various platforms and applications, and access a vast array of resources and services seamlessly.

MIN-Web, based on the MIN network, combines various technologies such as Web 3.0, artificial intelligence, blockchain, and big data. It introduces a novel architecture that not only ensures secure and reliable network services but also enhances data transmission efficiency. MIN-Web provides a new direction for the development of next-generation network technologies.

14.1 Overview of MIN-Web

Web, short for World Wide Web, refers to a global wide-area network. It is a worldwide information system composed of interconnected hypertext documents and other resources that can be accessed and linked through Uniform Resource Locators (URLs) and hyperlinks. The emergence of the Web has made information retrieval easier and faster, while reducing the cost and barriers associated with information dissemination. It has enabled more people to participate in the production and dissemination of information, and has provided new channels and opportunities for various commercial activities, thereby driving economic development and global trade growth.

MIN-Web is built upon the MIN network, which has already established reliable and stable network layer and transport layer protocols. The application layer protocol is the main focus of MIN research for the next phase. As an emerging architecture for future networks, the MIN network is currently transitioning from the experimental phase to the commercial phase. To accomplish this transition,

H. Li, H. Bai, *Principle of Architecture, Protocol, and Algorithms for CoG-MIN*,
https://doi.org/10.1007/978-981-96-3596-2_14

simplified, efficient, and visually accessible network resource access technologies are crucial. The MIN-Web project has emerged to meet these requirements.

In MIN-Web, various network resources are globally shared. These resources exist within a pure MIN network and are located and accessed through the unified MIN network resource locator. The MIN network ensures the legitimacy, accuracy, and traceability of network resource access.

MIN-Web has the following characteristics and advantages:

- Cross-platform and openness: It enables cross-platform and open network services, providing more flexibility and diversity in applications.
- Data sharing and collaborative work: It facilitates data sharing and collaborative work, supporting collaboration and interaction among multiple users.
- Intelligent and high-security applications: It offers intelligent and personalized services and support while ensuring user privacy and security.

The MIN-Web project holds significant importance in the development and transformation of the MIN network. It serves as a crucial means for the dissemination and promotion of the MIN network and paves the way for its diversified development.

14.2 Architecture of MIN-Web

MIN-Web is built on the MIN network and utilizes the MIN-HTTP protocol to define the data exchange and communication between clients and servers, providing users with access to MIN websites and other web services. MIN-Web consists of the following three components:

- MIN-Web-Server: It is the entity that provides web services in the MIN-Web project. The MIN-Web-Server is not restricted to any specific form; it only requires MIN-HTTP as the application layer protocol to serve as a web service provider.
- Browser-Client: It is the communication library used by the MIN-Browser. Since MIN network implementations are primarily based on the Go programming language, which differs from mainstream browser implementations, the Browser-Client addresses this language difference by providing communication capabilities in the form of a dynamic link library (DLL) for use by the MIN-Browser.
- MIN-Browser: It is the entity that uses web services in the MIN-Web project, typically referring to a web browser. The users of MIN-Browser consist of all users who use the MIN network.

Figure 14.1 shows the overall architecture of MIN-Web.

In MIN-Web, MIN-Web-Server serves as the server-side component that provides MIN network web services. Its main role is to receive client requests, process them, and return responses as well as manage and maintain resources on the server.

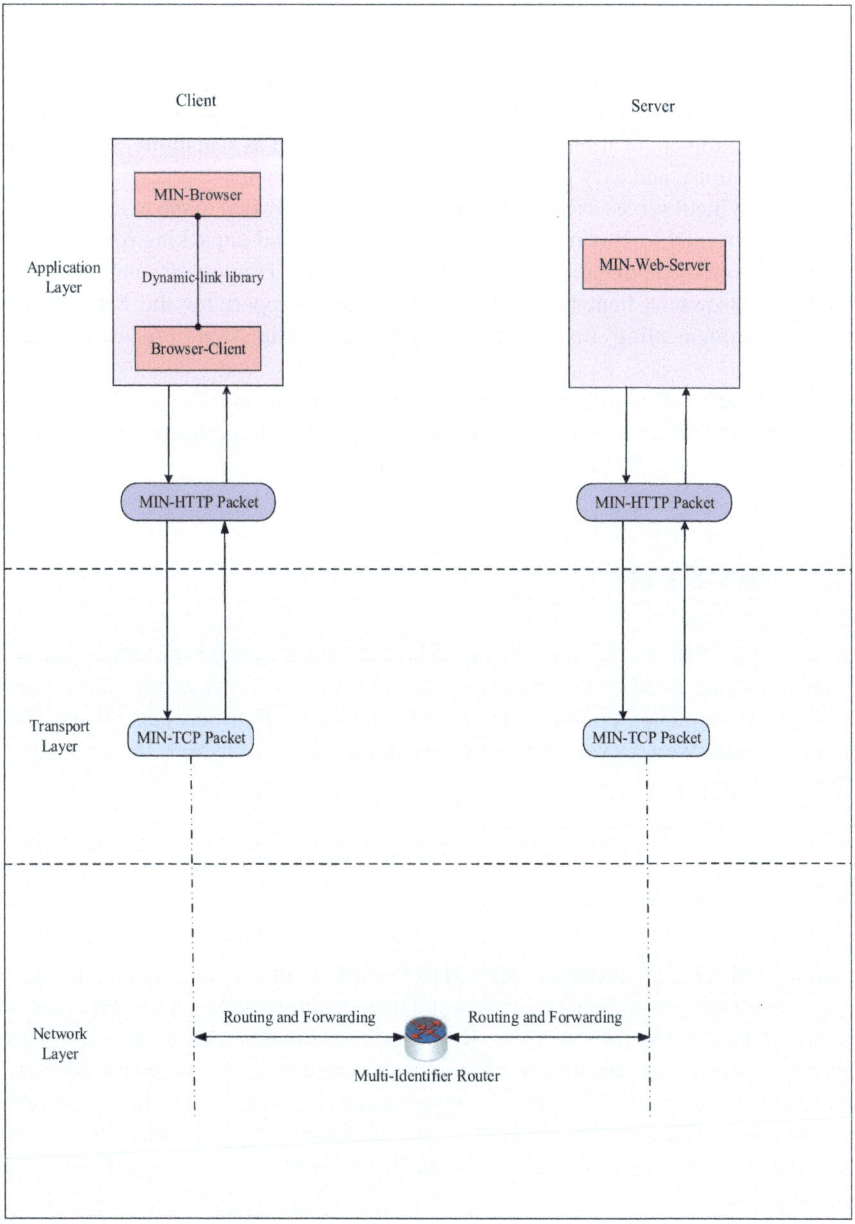

Fig. 14.1 The overall architecture of MIN-Web

At the application layer, it utilizes the MIN-HTTP protocol, which inherits the statelessness, flexibility, and scalability of the HTTP protocol. This allows service providers to create corresponding HTTP request handling methods. At the transport layer, it employs the MIN-TCP protocol to ensure secure and reliable transmission of web requests and responses within the MIN network.

MIN-Browser is implemented using the Electron framework, based on the open-source projects Chromium and Node.js. It enables the development of cross-platform desktop application browsers with features such as scalability, support for local applications, and easy packaging and distribution.

Browser-Client serves as a communication library provided to the MIN-Browser in the form of a DLL. It is responsible for packetizing and unpacking requests and responses from the application layer, initiating MIN-HTTP requests, and receiving responses. Browser-Client provides communication support for the MIN-HTTP protocol, implementing functions such as data transmission, processing, and parsing.

As MIN network continues to evolve and MIN-Web undergoes updates and iterations, the MIN-Web architecture will be optimized and upgraded to ensure the provision of better MIN network web services.

14.3 MIN-HTTP

The MIN-HTTP protocol is an application layer protocol used for transmitting communication data in MIN-Web. Developed using the Go programming language, MIN-HTTP facilitates communication and data interaction between clients and servers in MIN-Web. Developers can easily implement various web services using MIN-HTTP.

14.3.1 Interaction Logic

Similar to the HTTP protocol, MIN-HTTP consists of requests and responses. Requests are sent from clients to servers and include information such as the request method, URL, and request headers. Responses, on the other hand, are sent from servers to clients and contain information such as status codes, response headers, and response bodies. In MIN-HTTP, the protocol type used to identify requested resources is "MIN-HTTP://" instead of the traditional "http://". The interaction logic between the client and server in the MIN-HTTP protocol is illustrated in Fig. 14.2.

The communication between the client and server in the MIN-HTTP protocol has the following steps:

1. Client initiates the request: The client initiates a Get() or Post() request (in the first version of MIN-HTTP, only these two requests are supported). The request method retrieves a Request object, which includes the protocol type, request method, request headers, request body, and other information.

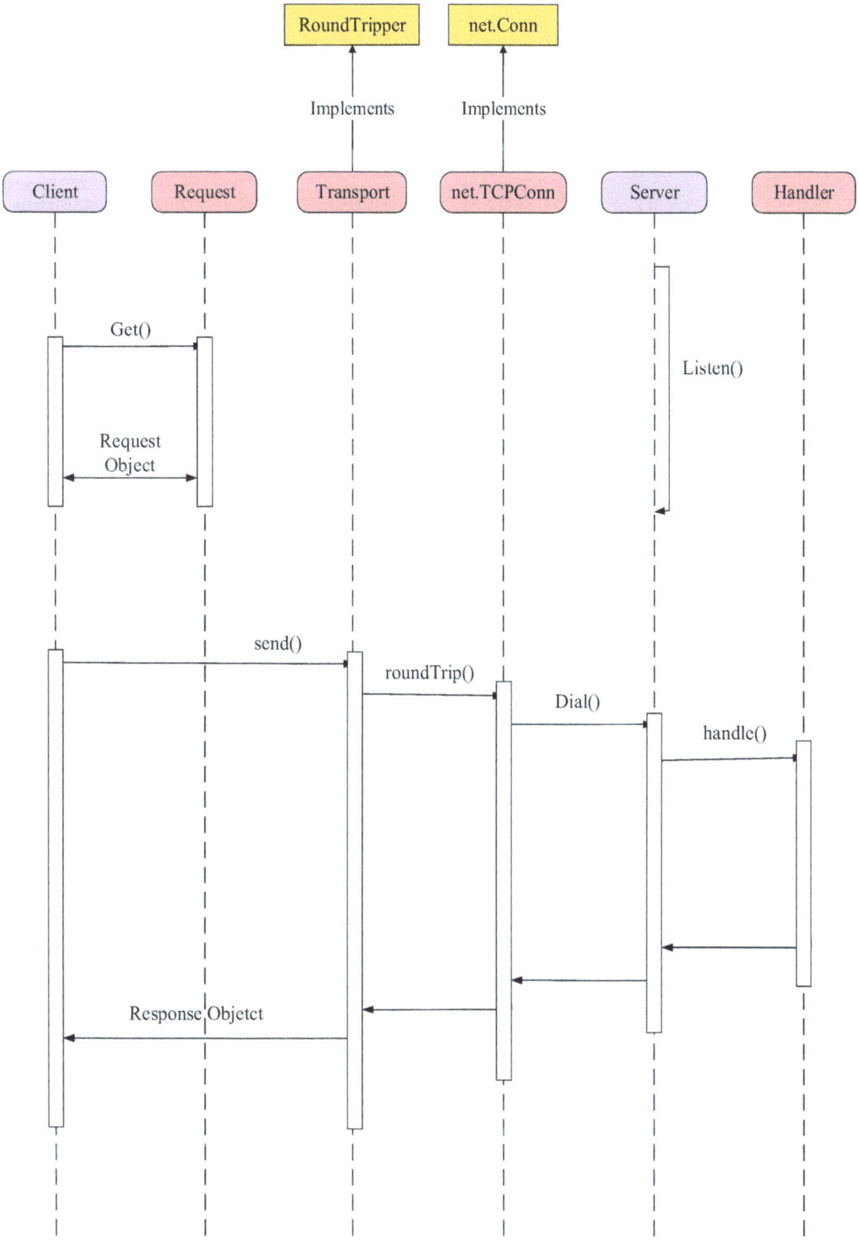

Fig. 14.2 MIN-HTTP interaction logic

2. Sending the request to the server: After the client obtains the request object using the Get() method, it calls the sent() method to send the request. The request object is handed over to the Transport class, which is responsible for handling

the MIN-HTTP transaction. The Transport class processes the client's request connection and waits for the server's response. It calls the roundTrip() method to obtain the Conn connection. In MIN-HTTP, the Conn connection is implemented based on the net.Conn library and represents a TCPConn connection responsible for implementing the MIN-TCP connection. It delivers the application layer transport tasks to the transport layer.
3. Server receives the request: The server remains in the Listen() state, continuously listening for incoming MIN-HTTP connections. Upon receiving a connection, it calls the handle() method to deliver the request to the Handler class for processing and obtains the processing result.
4. Server sends the response: The server returns the processing result from the Handler class to the client. The client receives the Response object, and thus completes one round of communication in MIN-HTTP.

14.3.2 Optimization Strategy

To enhance the performance and user experience of MIN-Web services, reduce network latency and resource consumption, and improve system scalability and stability, the MIN-HTTP protocol has established a series of optimization strategies. These strategies include the following aspects:

1. Persistent connections: After the client sends a MIN-HTTP request, the connection with the server is kept open instead of being closed. This allows multiple requests to be sent and multiple responses to be received over the same connection, eliminating the overhead of establishing and closing connections for each request.
2. IO buffer pool: In MIN-HTTP, data transmission and processing are required for network requests and responses, utilizing IO objects. By using an IO buffer pool, the frequency of IO object creation can be reduced, thereby improving network transmission efficiency. Additionally, the IO buffer pool reduces the number of memory allocations and deallocations, reducing CPU burden and enhancing program performance.
3. Timeout mechanism: The timeout mechanism prevents blocking issues caused by unexpected situations during network transmission, ensuring the reliability and stability of network communication. Without a timeout mechanism, if a network connection fails, both the client and server will wait indefinitely for a response, resulting in resource waste and service unavailability. The introduction of a timeout mechanism allows for timely detection and handling of such situations, improving system robustness and reliability. Moreover, the timeout duration can be adjusted based on specific application scenarios and performance requirements to achieve optimal network communication effectiveness.

14.3.3 *File Transmission*

The MIN-HTTP protocol is based on the MIN network for data transmission. The MIN network supports two modes of data transmission: push-based and pull-based. Pull-based transmission is primarily utilized for file transfer services. It leverages caching nodes within the network to expedite file data access, reduce network resource consumption, and better accommodate largescale file transmission requirements.

Figure 14.3 illustrates the process of pull-based file transmission in MIN-HTTP, which consists of three steps:

1. Client requests file metadata: The client initiates a request for file metadata, and the server responds with the metadata content. The metadata is used for subsequent file fragment reassembly.
2. Client requests file content: The client sends multiple requests for data fragments, and the server, utilizing the IO module, reads, parses, and responds with the corresponding file data fragments.
3. Client reassembles the file: Upon receiving multiple file data fragments, the client utilizes the metadata information to reassemble the fragments into a single file, completing the file retrieval process.

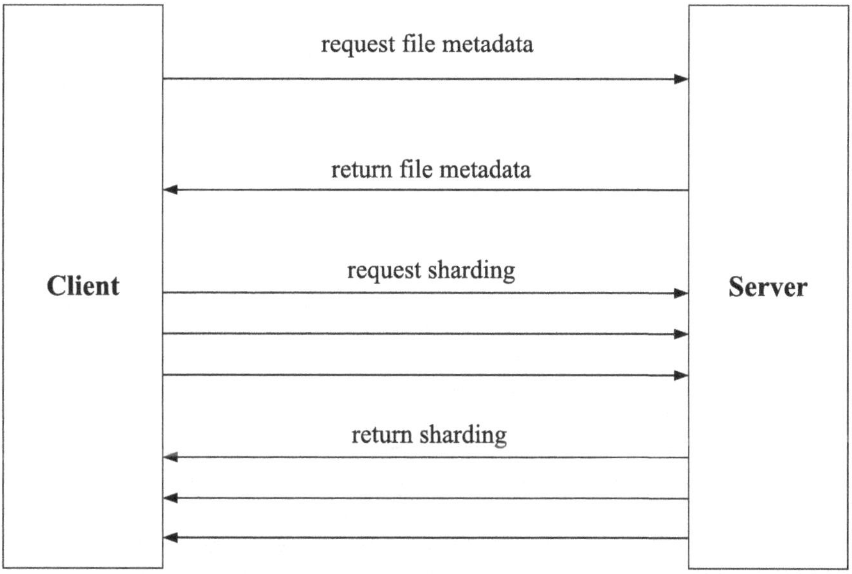

Fig. 14.3 MIN-HTTP file transmission

14.4 MIN-Browser

MIN-Browser is a browser application based on the MIN network. It serves as the client in MIN-Web. It utilizes MIN-HTTP to request HTML files from the MIN-Web-Server and then parses and renders these HTML files to present them to the user. Implemented based on the open-source projects Chromium and Electron framework with Node.js, MIN-Browser offers scalability, support for local applications, and ease of packaging and distribution.

The frontend interface of MIN-Browser follows the design of mainstream browsers, including components such as a navigation bar, tabbed browsing, bookmarks, favorites, settings, and a console. Additionally, MIN-Browser provides a console specifically designed for developers to facilitate debugging.

The user interface of MIN-Browser is depicted in Figs. 14.4 and 14.5. It supports both the HTTP and HTTPS protocols in IP networks and the MIN-HTTP protocol in the MIN network. By default, MIN-Browser employs the MIN-HTTP protocol for MIN network requests when the protocol is not specified. MIN-Browser supports the transmission of various types of content, including websites, text, images, videos, and audio.

During runtime, MIN-Browser operates with multiple threads, including a Main Process and multiple Renderer Processes. The Main Process is a Node.js process responsible for managing the entire lifecycle of the application. Its tasks include creating Renderer Processes, establishing browser windows, handling system events, accessing the local file system, and performing network requests. On the other hand, the Renderer Process is a Chromium rendering process dedicated to rendering web content. Each browser window corresponds to a Renderer Process, which can utilize most browser-provided APIs like DOM API and Canvas

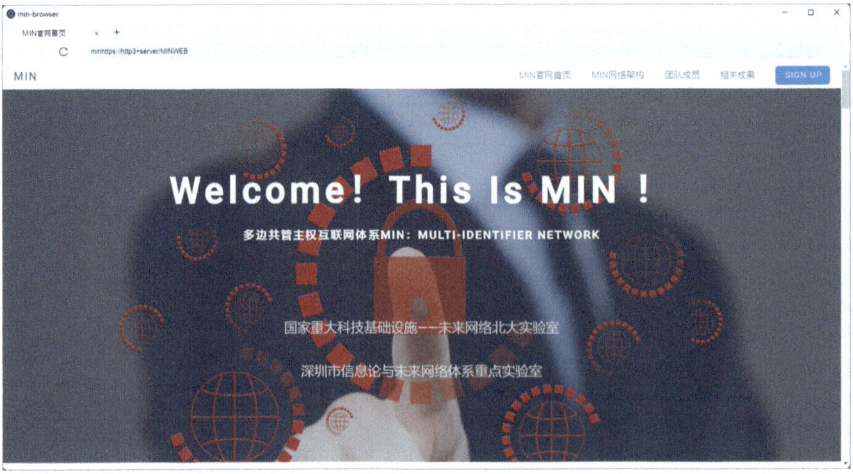

Fig. 14.4 An example of a website in MIN-Browser

Fig. 14.5 An example of a video in MIN-Browser

API. However, it cannot directly access Node.js APIs. If there is a need to employ Node.js APIs within the Renderer Process, communication with the Main Process is required to facilitate the implementation.

MIN-Browser uses the MIN-HTTP protocol for communication. In the Electron framework, all HTTP communication is conducted through the HTTP and HTTPS modules provided by Node.js. MIN-Browser modifies this segment by intercepting and filtering the HTTP requests, identifying the requests that require processing. These requests are then handled and encapsulated as MIN-HTTP protocol datagrams by the Browser-Client. The encapsulated data is subsequently sent to the MIN-Web-Server to request content and obtain a response. The communication process is illustrated in Fig. 14.6.

14.5 MIN-Web 3.0

14.5.1 Overview of Web 3.0

Web 3.0 refers to the decentralized Internet based on blockchain technology, also known as the "Intelligent Internet" or "Distributed Internet. Web 3.0 integrates new technologies such as Artificial Intelligence, Big Data, and Blockchain. The goal of Web 3.0 is to achieve the intelligence, decentralization, security, and transparency of the Internet, making it more trustworthy, programmable, and decentralized [4–6]. The Web 3.0 era places greater emphasis on the development of user privacy protection, decentralization, and intelligence, which will have a profound impact on the future development of the Internet. This transformation will not only change people's way of living but also give rise to new emerging industries and business models.

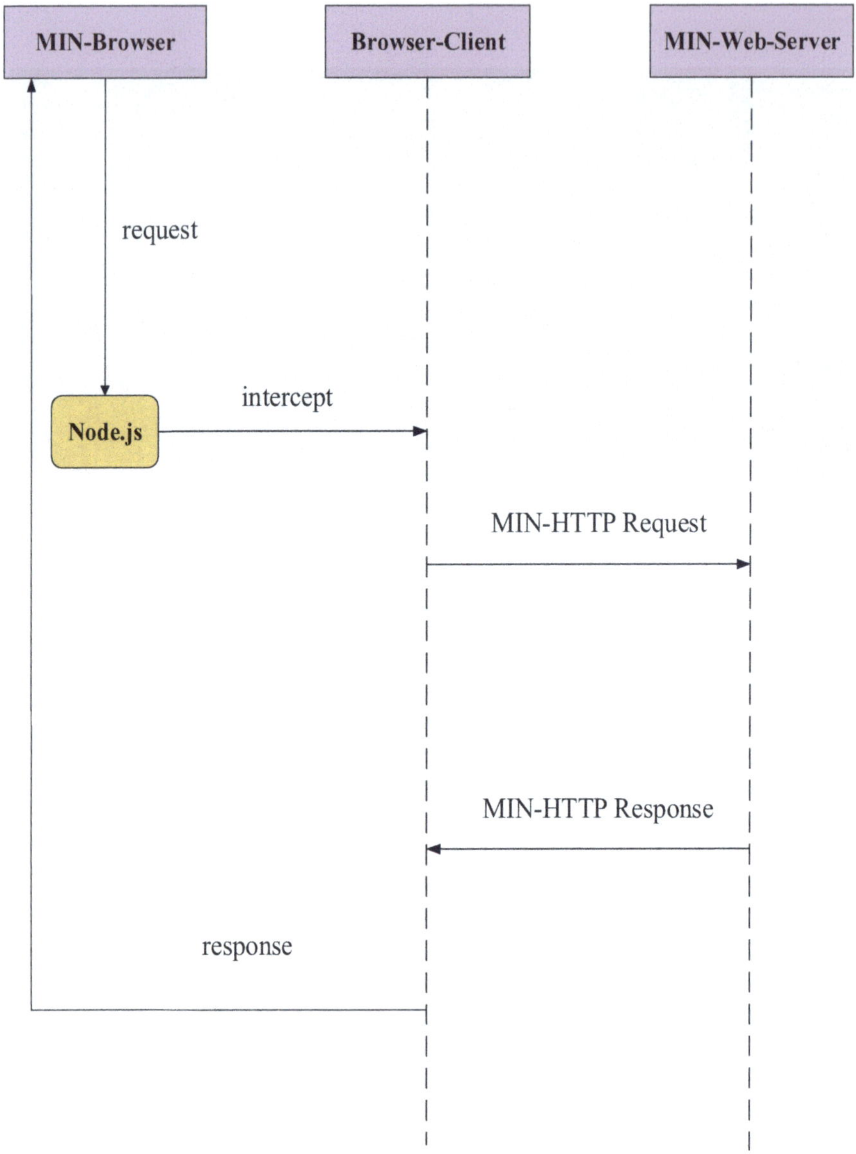

Fig. 14.6 MIN-Browser communication diagram

Web 3.0 has the following characteristics:

- Decentralization: Web 3.0 is a decentralized Internet that utilizes technologies like blockchain, making data and transactions more secure and transparent, and avoiding the monopoly and misconduct of a single institution.
- Data Privacy Protection: Web 3.0 prioritizes the protection of user data privacy, using encryption technology and decentralized storage to protect personal information, thereby avoiding the risk of data abuse.

- Smart Contracts: Smart contract technology is an important technical feature of Web 3.0. Smart contracts can be executed automatically without human intervention, making transactions more efficient and secure. At the same time, smart contracts also have a high degree of programmability, allowing them to be customized according to specific business requirements, bringing more efficient, secure, and transparent transaction methods to various industries.
- Artificial Intelligence: Artificial intelligence technology, by analyzing and learning from large amounts of data, provides more intelligent services for Web 3.0, thereby enhancing the user experience. Additionally, it can also provide more secure and reliable data privacy protection and related services for Web 3.0 platforms.
- Cross-Platform Interconnectivity: Web 3.0 can achieve seamless connection and interoperability between different platforms and devices. This interconnectivity is not limited to traditional computers and mobile devices, but also includes IoT devices, smart homes, connected vehicles, and various other intelligent devices. Web 3.0 uses open standards and protocols, allowing these devices to communicate and interact with each other, thereby achieving more intelligent, efficient, and convenient services and applications.

The MIN-Web 3.0 project aims to build a more secure, reliable, open, and interoperable Internet environment by integrating the MIN network and the Web 3.0 technology.

14.5.2 Designs of MIN-Web 3.0

Blockchain Network

In MIN-Web 3.0, blockchain technology is used to build a secure and reliable value transmission network, ensuring the consistency of the ledger through encryption algorithms and consensus mechanisms, and introducing smart contract functionality to expand the application boundaries of the blockchain. The blockchain infrastructure of MIN-Web 3.0 relies on the technical support of CoG-MIN in the communication module, adopts the Proof of Vote (PoV) [7] and the Parallel Proof of Vote (PPoV) consensus algorithm [8] in the consensus algorithm module, and provides an identifier management system based on the consortium chain.

Data Assets

In MIN-Web 3.0, data can circulate and trade freely among users. The data trading market based on blockchain technology provides a platform for the circulation and monetization of data assets. Users can obtain income by selling their own data or purchase the required data resources, forming a new data economic model.

MIN-Web 3.0 supports users' control and management of their own data. Through encryption technology and distributed storage, users can securely store their digital assets, personal information and other data in a decentralized network, rather than concentrated in a few centralized platforms. In addition, unified data standards and protocols are crucial. This includes data format specifications, metadata definitions, identity authentication, and other standardization work. By implementing these foundational standards, the MIN-Web 3.0 ecosystem can develop in a robust and healthy manner, ensuring interoperability and facilitating seamless data exchange among different participants.

Decentralized Applications

MIN-Web 3.0 supports various decentralized applications (DApps). These applications are built on the underlying blockchain infrastructure and use smart contracts to implement complex business logic. Examples include decentralized finance (DeFi), metaverse, decentralized games, and other innovative application scenarios.

Identity Management

MIN-Web 3.0 supports digital identity authentication based on zero-knowledge proof, which realizes fine-grained attribute-based non-interactive credential encryption verification, allowing users to complete digital identity authentication without revealing personal privacy information. This mechanism can greatly improve user data security and avoid the potential privacy leakage issues in traditional verification processes.

Identifier Management

Relying on blockchain technology, MIN-Web 3.0 provides a decentralized identifier management. MIN-Web 3.0 has redefined and classified various types of identifiers within the network. Identifiers are no longer limited to traditional forms such as personal accounts or domain names, but cover various digital assets, such as personal assets and organizational assets. MIN-Web 3.0 supports identifier registration, deletion, and other management functions. With the automatic execution feature of smart contracts, users can conveniently complete identifier creation, update, and cancelation operations without relying on centralized management agencies. This not only improves management efficiency, but also enhances users' autonomous control over their own digital assets. In addition, MIN-Web 3.0 also combines distributed storage technology to record the off-chain resources associated with identifiers. This means that users can not only manage their digital identifiers on the blockchain, but also bind these identifiers with actual digital assets, such as personal information and digital works.

14.6 Metaverse Application in MIN-Web 3.0

14.6.1 Overview of Metaverse

The concept of the metaverse was first proposed by Neil Stephenson in his 1992 science fiction novel "Snow Crash," which described a universe running in parallel with the real world, created by humans. The metaverse is considered a fully immersive, transcendent, and self-sustaining virtual shared space. Currently, the metaverse is regarded as the next generation of the Internet, following the mobile Internet [9].

As shown in Fig. 14.7, in the metaverse, users in the physical world are represented as avatars in the virtual world. Users can interact with other avatars in the virtual world and associate with digital twins of real objects, virtual objects, applications, and other available entities, such as generating content or minting digital items as non-fungible tokens (NFTs). The virtual world consists of a series of interconnected sub-metaverses, each of which can provide specific types of services to users' avatars, including games, social dating, online museums, and online concerts.

The vision of the metaverse is to connect everything in the world, not only including the digital twins of physical entities and systems, but also the vast amount of data generated, such as content, services, and asset resources, thereby forming a new type of virtual world. For example, in the decentralized virtual world Decentraland, users can trade parcels and equipment in the marketplace, and build

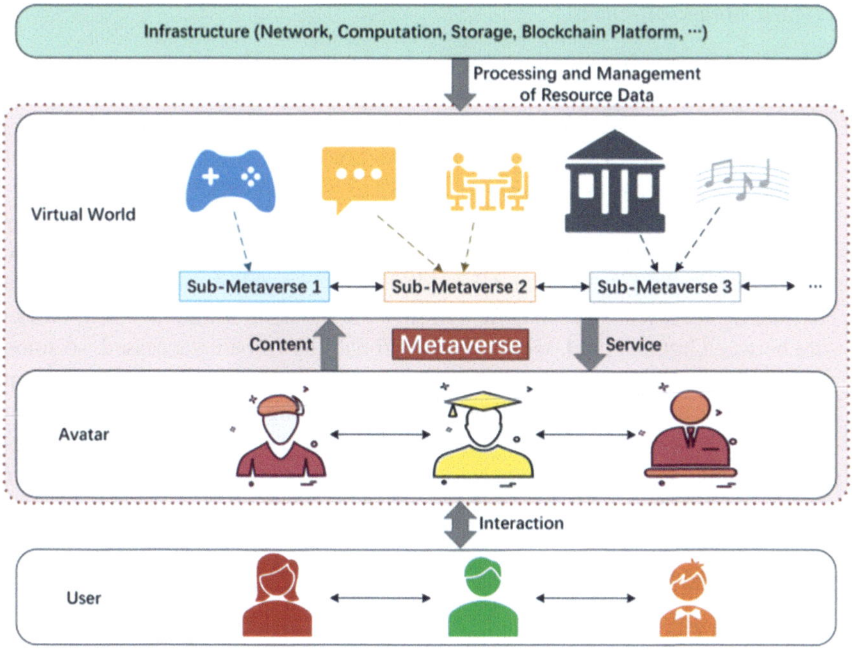

Fig. 14.7 Examples of Metaverse Application Illustrations

their own architecture and social games. In the blockchain game Cryptovoxels, users can trade land in the virtual world "Origin City" and establish virtual stores and art galleries, where they can display and trade their digital assets such as artwork. The ownership and transaction details of these digital resources are recorded on the Ethereum blockchain, which can be authenticated and audited at any time. Therefore, reliable identity and resource data are crucial for the sustained existence of the virtual world.

14.6.2 *Multi-Identifier Management System for Metaverse*

The multi-identifier management system (MIS) for the metaverse is built on a consortium blockchain, aiming to fundamentally maintain the global state of various types of identifiers and related resource data among the trusted core nodes in the metaverse context.

The four-layer architecture of MIS for the metaverse is shown in Fig. 14.8.

In the lower two layers, the candidate nodes need to compete to participate in the consensus process to be elected as core nodes. The core nodes then run a lightweight deterministic consensus algorithm and record the state changes of resources in the form of transactions.

Meanwhile, in the upper two layers, the metadata and complete data of the resources are indexed in a layered manner, ultimately achieving distributed encrypted storage off-chain.

- **The First Layer**: Network layer of blockchain nodes. This layer is mainly composed of nodes responsible for managing identifiers at the same level, forming the core network. They process messages at different levels of priority.
- **The Second Layer**: Lightweight consensus layer. This layer adopts an efficient parallel voting consensus algorithm (PPoV) to write and verify relevant transactions, and implements a lightweight storage timeline strategy. This strategy divides all blocks into three states based on their height: hot, warm, and cold. The newest blocks are set as hot, and the oldest blocks are set as cold. Hot blocks are frequently accessed, so each node will save the block information. Warm blocks are between hot and cold, with a certain probability of being accessed, so some nodes will cache the full block information. When a block's state changes from hot to warm, the node first needs to use erasure coding to encode it into a certain number of data chunks and parity chunks, and then each node saves one erasure-coded chunk. If an erasure-coded chunk has an error, the node can request other chunks to help decode the original data chunk. Cold blocks have a relatively low probability of being accessed. At this stage, nodes only save the block headers and erasure-coded chunks generated from the warm blocks, without the need for caching.
- **The Third Layer**: Indexing layer. This layer maintains the global state of the basic MIS and manages these identifiers. For example, these identifiers can be

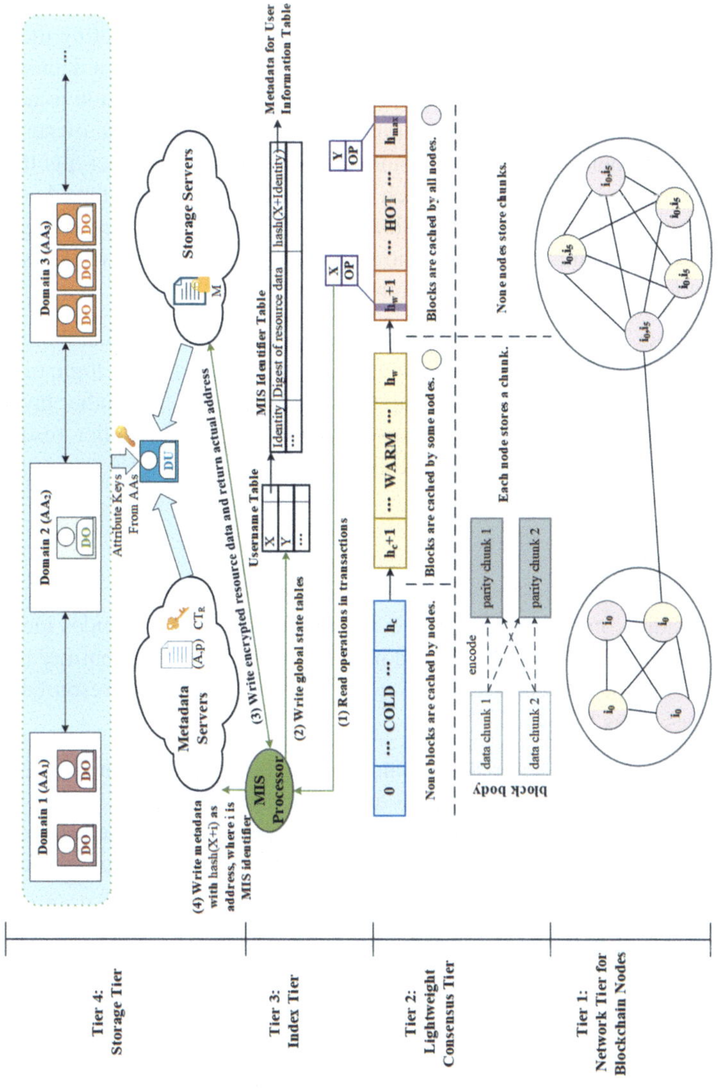

Fig. 14.8 Four-layer architecture diagram of the MIS system for the Metaverse [10]

dynamically added, updated or deleted as the network changes. The MIS uses a non-relational database, using key-value pairs to store the user name table and identifier tables. Each username corresponds to an MIS identifier table, which includes the binding records of multiple identifiers, the hashes of the identifiers (as the metadata addresses of the associated resources), and other relevant information.
- **The Fourth Layer**: Storage layer. This layer is responsible for storing the complete off-chain resource data related to identifiers. And it designs a data storage and access scheme with multi-permission attribute-based encryption to achieve secure and controllable off-chain storage. In this scheme, the data owner (DO) encrypts the resource data using a symmetric key, and then re-encrypts the key based on the access control policy. Each sub-metaverse has an Attribute Authority (AA) responsible for user authentication and generating the corresponding attribute keys, ensuring that only users who meet the policy and have the corresponding attribute keys can decrypt the resource data.

The four-layer architecture of MIS for the metaverse has good scalability. The different layers maintain a loosely coupled relationship, allowing the logic of a single layer to be modified without changing the operation logic of the other layers.

In addition, the MIS for the metaverse provides various identifier resolution function services, mainly including the following:

Identifier Resolution

When there is only one identifier space in the network, the MIS provides identifier resolution services similar to the domain name system. When the identifier resolution is successful, the user can access the storage server or associated resources. The specific process is as follows:

- **Step 1**: The user queries the global state table of the MIS to obtain the metadata address and the summary information of the associated resources.
- **Step 2**: The user accesses the metadata server and receives a metadata file. This file contains the location of the storage server and other information, such as the access control policy and symmetric key.
- **Step 3**: The user accesses the resource data server according to the information stored in the metadata file.
- **Step 4**: The user needs to decrypt resource and verify the integrity. If the verification passes, the identifier resolution is considered successful.

Identifier Translation

The future network architecture requires many different types of identifiers and corresponding communication modes to meet new functionalities or demands.

For example, content identifier has advantages in accessing resources such as videos and web pages. Service identifier improves the flexibility, loose coupling, and reusability of services. Identity and location identifiers are suitable for mobile devices that are constantly switching locations.

Through the identifier translation service, the MIS can help users resolve various types of identifiers and access the relevant resources, as shown in the process depicted in Fig. 14.9.

As shown in the above diagram, each terminal user needs to register an identity identifier, so they are all located in the identity identifier space. When a user wants to resolve resources in other identifier spaces, they need to query the global state table first. If the information is recorded, the relevant data will be returned to the user. If the query fails, the system needs to perform the aforementioned resolution process and then return the translation result to the user.

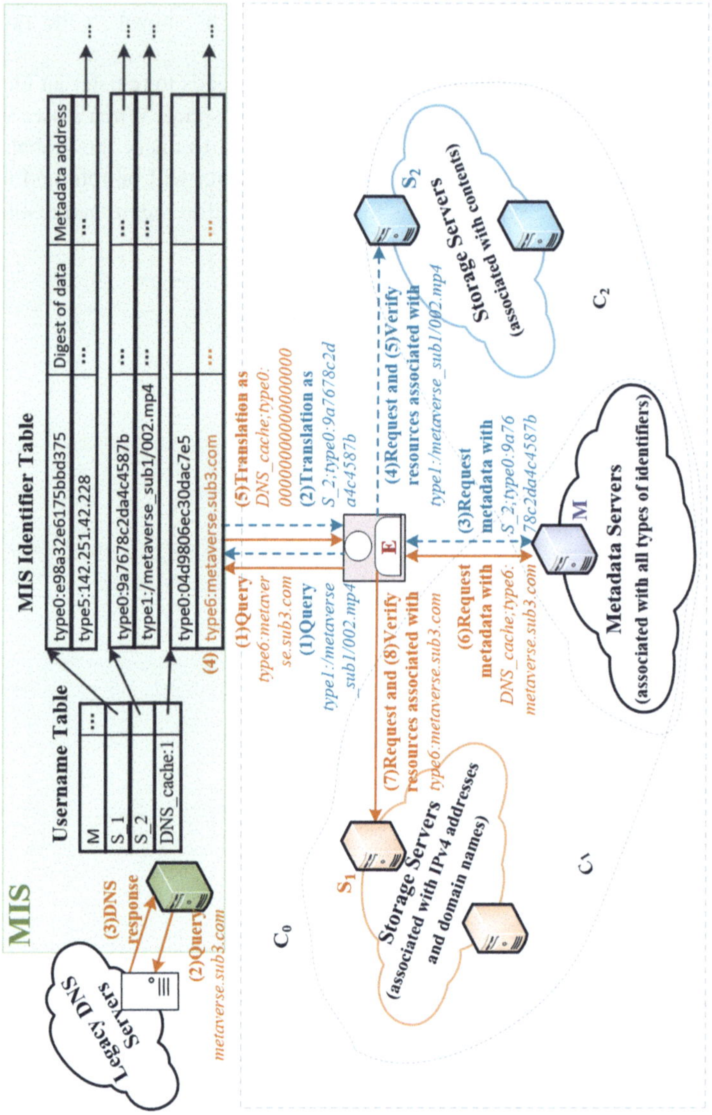

Fig. 14.9 An example of identifier translation [10]

References

1. Berners-Lee T, Cailliau R, Luotonen A, et al. The world-wide web[M]//Linking the World's information. In: Essays on Tim Berners-Lee's invention of the World Wide Web. ACM Books; 2023. p. 51–65.
2. Patel A, Jain S. Present and future of semantic web technologies: a research statement[J]. Int J Comput Appl. 2021;43(5):413–22.
3. Amara FZ, Hemam M, Djezzar M, et al. Semantic web and internet of things: challenges, applications and perspectives[J]. J ICT Standard. 2022;10(2):261–91.
4. Liu Z, Xiang Y, Shi J, et al. Make web3. 0 connected[J]. IEEE Trans Depend Secure Comput. 2021;19(5):2965–81.
5. Guan C, Ding D, Guo J. Web3.0: a review and research agenda[C]//2022 RIVF international conference on computing and communication technologies (RIVF). IEEE. 2022:653–8.
6. Chen C, Zhang L, Li Y, et al. When digital economy meets web3. 0: applications and challenges[J]. IEEE Open J Comput Soc. 2022;3:233–45.
7. Li KJ, Li H, Hou HX, et al. Proof of vote: a high-performance consensus protocol based on vote mechanism & consortium blockchain[C]//2017 IEEE 19th international conference on high performance computing and communications; IEEE 15th international conference on Smart City; IEEE 3rd international conference on data science and systems (HPCC/SmartCity/DSS). IEEE. 2017:466–73.
8. Wang ZX, Li H, Wang H, et al. A data lightweight scheme for parallel proof of vote consensus[C]//2021 IEEE international conference on big data (big data). IEEE. 2021:3656–62.
9. Wang H, Ning H, Lin Y, et al. A survey on the metaverse: the state-of-the-art, technologies, applications, and challenges[J]. IEEE Internet Things J. 2023;10(16):14671–88.
10. Wang H, Li H, Smahi A, et al. MIS: a multi-identifier management and resolution system in the Metaverse[J]. ACM Trans Multimed Comput Commun Appl. 2023;20:1–25.

Chapter 15
Application Scenarios of CoG-MIN

This chapter introduces the application scenarios based on CoG-MIN, including industrial internet of things (IIoT), internet of vehicles (IoV), space-terrestrial integrated networks (STIN), digital asset management and trading, and a community with a shared future in cyberspace.

15.1 Industrial Internet of Things

15.1.1 Overview of Industrial Internet of Things

With the rapid development of information and communication technology, as well as the increased collaboration and integration with operational technology in the industrial manufacturing field, the Industrial Internet of Things (IIoT) has become a research hotspot, garnering widespread attention within academia and industry [1].

IIoT utilizes cyber-physical systems to facilitate two-way communication between human, machine, physical, and digital systems within the industrial environment [2]. This enables the organic integration and deep collaboration of real-time sensing, dynamic control, and information services in intelligent manufacturing systems, as shown in Fig. 15.1.

Through network connectivity, the IIoT enables intelligent decision-making and optimized operations in industrial systems. Furthermore, it unlocks the potential of machines and enables high-end manufacturing, heralding a seamless connection between the physical world and cyberspace, making them ubiquitous within enterprises. It also promotes the transition of the entire lifecycle from products to services, triggering innovation in products, services, and business models, which has long-lasting and profound effects on value chains, supply chains, and ecosystems.

Building a system that allows for multiple network access methods, provides stable and reliable service quality, and enables intelligent network connectivity is

H. Li, H. Bai, *Principle of Architecture, Protocol, and Algorithms for CoG-MIN*,
https://doi.org/10.1007/978-981-96-3596-2_15

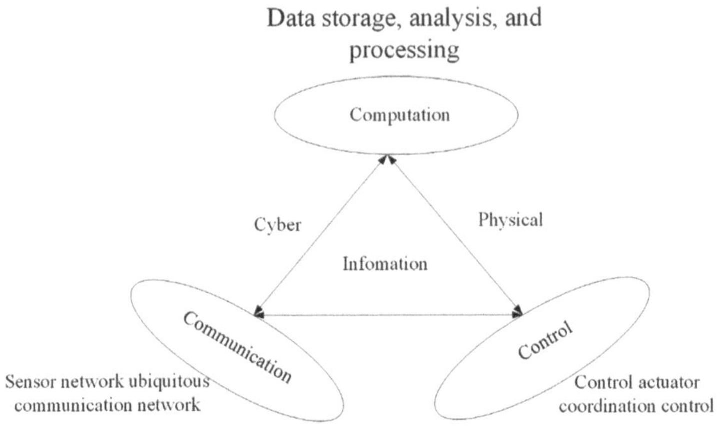

Fig. 15.1 Information physical system for sensing and control

the foundation for achieving the integration of IIoT objects into the ubiquitous Internet.

Numerous new network technologies and protocols are emerging in the realm of the IIoT, such as Software-Defined Networking (SDN), Time-Sensitive Networking (TSN), Network Function Virtualization (NFV), and Segment Routing over IPv6 (SRv6). These technologies can enhance the performance of the IIoT, bring offline industrial production elements online and achieve interconnectedness among online production elements. The collection, decision-making, and utilization of data are achieved through the bottom-up flow of intelligent connection, conversion, and cyber transmission to the top-level processes of cognition and configuration.

In addition, the IIoT identifier system serves as both the basic element of network interconnection and the medium for data transmission [3]. IIoT objects include not only the physical resources of industrial manufacturing enterprises, such as humans, machines, components, materials, and products, but also digital resources such as algorithms, processes, blueprints, and data [4]. Identifier serves as the unique symbol of an IIoT object within the IIoT. It permeates throughout the entire lifecycle of IIoT objects, serving as the link to enable data sharing and interconnectedness among different objects. This forms an intelligent closed-loop for bidirectional data exchange between the physical world and the digital space. The construction of the IIoT identifier system can break the information silos caused by the chaotic information structure and levels of differentiation among different regions, industries, companies, departments, and individuals. It establishes connections, information querying, and sharing, as well as interactive interoperability among different IIoT objects. Therefore, the IIoT identifier system can be considered as the central nervous system of the IIoT [5].

15.1.2 Industrial Internet of Things Based on CoG-MIN

In IIoT, an identifier acts as a unified and immutable ID card of the managed and controlled object (a physical or virtual digital object) throughout the entire lifecycle. The encoding and parsing of identifier aid in the management and interaction of identifiable data objects, enabling connectivity and data sharing in the IIoT. Identifier technology can refine the resource granularity from host to commodity, information, and services. On the other hand, it facilitates intelligent associations of heterogeneous information over different hosts, locations, and types in the IIoT.

Due to the rapid advancement of digital transformation in businesses, the scale of IIoT identifiers has exceeded billions, along with millions of parallel parsing requests. Such a large-scale demand for identifier parsing puts higher requirements on identifier management and system security. To address this issue, several solutions have been proposed, such as the Handle Identifier System [6], Global System 1 (GS1) [7], and Object Identifiers (OID) [8]. However, different identifier systems have different encoding and decoding schemes. The incompatibility of identifier systems across different industries leads to communication disruptions, hindering the large-scale development of the IIoT.

To address the aforementioned issues, Multi-Identifier Network for Industrial Internet of Things (MIN-IIoT) is proposed [9, 10]. MIN-IIoT aims to solve the challenges of routing, forwarding, parsing applications, security, and support for heterogeneous identifier systems in large-scale deployments of IIoT.

The main characteristics of MIN-IIoT are as follows:

MIN-IIoT supports the coexistence of various types of identifiers in IIoT scenarios, such as identity identifier, content identifier, service identifier, geographic location identifier, and IP identifier. It also supports identifier extension and interconnection with existing heterogeneous identifier systems in IIoT.

MIN-IIoT has a comprehensive set of identifier management strategies, including identifier management, translation, addressing, routing, and forwarding.

MIN-IIoT establishes a unified security mechanism. The information of all IIoT identifiers is stored in a layered consortium blockchain after undergoing identity verification, ensuring its authenticity and integrity without being illegally modified. Based on an independently developed Parallel Proof of Vote (PPoV) consensus algorithm, which separates voting rights and bookkeeping rights in the blockchain, the identifier system of MIN-IIoT can resist security risks. Besides, identity authentication and trusted computing technologies further ensure data security.

The Overall Architecture of MIN-IIoT

In IIoT, there are numerous resource-constrained heterogeneous devices with a massive number of connectivity requirements. The off-site network of IIoT is an optimized and upgraded Internet, with low latency, high bandwidth, and comprehensive coverage as its basic requirements. On the other hand, the on-site network IIoT is a network that integrates information and production, demanding high reliability and customizability.

In the complex and diverse industrial environment, there are various network communication protocols, such as MQTT, CoAP, LoRaWAN, and NB-IoT. The compatibility of various heterogeneous bus connections and the coexistence of multiple industrial Ethernet connection modes should be considered.

In industrial manufacturing enterprises, network construction primarily focuses on bringing offline devices online and establishing interconnectivity between online devices. From the perspectives of the workshop, network construction aims to achieve horizontal interconnection between underlying devices and vertical interconnection with upper-level systems.

At the enterprise and external level, network construction focuses on achieving interconnectivity between production devices, control systems, industrial information systems, and IIoT applications through cloud platforms.

The overall architecture of MIN-IIoT [10] is shown in Fig. 15.2. MIN-IIoT enables the widespread connectivity, flexible supply, and efficient configuration of IIoT resources and supports various identifiers in IIoT scenarios.

MIN-IIoT can achieve real-time control and hierarchical management in IIoT. MIN-IIoT supports commonly used protocols in IIoT scenarios, such as NB-IoT, TSN, ZigBee, 6LoWPAN, PON 2.0, as given in Table 15.1.

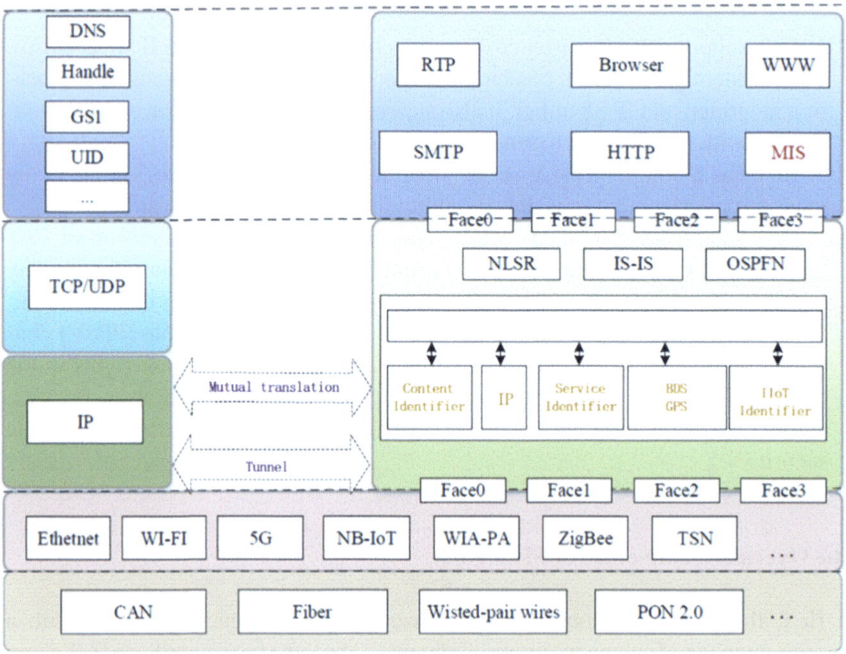

Fig. 15.2 The overall architecture of MIN-IIoT [10]

Table 15.1 Partial network protocols supported in MIN-IIoT [10]

Protocols	Protocol position in network protocol stack	Description
IS-IS	Network layer	Routing protocol
BGP	Application layer	Routing protocol
NLSR	Network layer	Routing protocol, generates FIB
DNS	Application layer	Store different identifier relationships
PON 2.0	Physical layer	Passive optical network
NB-IoT	Physical layer	Narrowband Internet of Things
WIA-PA	Data link layer	Industrial wireless network specifically designed for industrial process automation
TSN	Data link layer	Time-sensitive networking
EVPN	Data link layer	Ethernet virtual private network
…	…	…

Table 15.2 Identifiers supported in MIN-IIoT [10]

Identifier type	Type number	Form	Example
Identity identifier	101	128-bit hash value	d98a342e615bd263
Content interest identifier	102	Hierarchical structure	/min-iiot/pku/svr1/movie.mp4
Content data identifier	103	Hierarchical structure	/min-iiot/pku/movie.mp4
Service request identifier	104	Hierarchical structure	/min-iiot/pku/website1
Service response identifier	105	Hierarchical structure	/min-iiot/pku/website1
Geographical location identifier	106	Hierarchical structure	(114.196, 222.33)
IIoT identifier	107	Hierarchical structure	88.126.6/AB08.16001

MIN-IIoT also supports dedicated protocols like OPC, Modbus, and CAN bus to meet the high-density and low-latency connectivity requirements of various industrial IoT devices. MIN-IIoT can be easily installed and deployed in industrial field networks, facilitating the upgrade and migration.

Encoding Format for IIoT Identifiers

The MIN network inherently supports multiple types of identifiers such as identity, content, service, and location, as given in Table 15.2. For resource-constrained IIoT objects, MIN-IIoT has designed IIoT identifiers to facilitate interconnection between identifiers, reduce storage space, and support identifier expansion.

IIoT identifiers consist of two hierarchical parts separated by a forward slash ("/"). The first part represents the identifier prefix assigned by the MIN-IIoT system, while the second part represents the identifier suffix defined by the industry or enterprise. The specific encoding format of the IIoT identifier is given in Table 15.3.

The prefix of the IIoT Identifier is divided into three parts by a dot ("."). The first part consists of 1–3 digits representing the country code; the next part consists of 3–4 digits representing the region code; and the last part consists of 1–8 digits representing the enterprise code.

MIN-IIoT follows a unified approach for assigning identifier prefixes. Users who have been allocated identifier prefixes have the privilege to enable MIN-IIoT identifier resolution services for their identifiers. Industries and enterprises interested in customizing and distributing identifiers are required to apply through the Multi-Identifier System (MIS) within MIN-IIoT.

When users apply for a prefix, the MIS first verifies their certificate. Upon successful verification, the MIS allocates the prefix within the system. It ensures that the format of the custom identifier complies with the requirements of the MIN network and follows the corresponding specifications.

Enterprises have the flexibility to customize the identifier suffix for different encoded objects based on their specific needs and business requirements. They can choose to retain their existing coding systems and rules within the identifier suffix. Enterprises can use a dot (or enable other forms of separators) to define the format and length of the identifier suffix. However, it is important to ensure the uniqueness of the internal coding within the enterprise while keeping the overall length of the identifier as short as possible. The length of the suffix should not exceed 128 characters. After allocating the identifier suffix, the enterprise needs to register it with MIN-IIoT. These identifiers are then stored in MIS for addressing, resolution, and forwarding purposes.

An example of a specific IIoT identifier is shown in Fig. 15.3. The suffix is separated by a dot (".") into two parts. The first part (AB08) represents a specific IIoT application identifier used to differentiate different types of identifier applications. The second part (16001) is a unique code for an IIoT object, which could be a physical or digital entity.

For physical entities such as IIoT devices, materials, and products, the encoded identifiers need to be represented in the form of tags to facilitate the perception and collection of identifier information and coding resources for subsequent communication and interaction operations.

The identifier carriers can be passive or active. Common passive identifier carriers include one-dimensional barcodes for item coding, two-dimensional barcodes

Table 15.3 Encoding format for the IIoT identifier

Types	Identifier prefix					Separator	Identifier suffix
	Country code	Separator	Region code	Separator	Enterprise code		
length	1–3	.	3–4	.	1–8	/	0–128

Fig. 15.3 Example of IIoT identifier in MIN-IIoT [10]

Table 15.4 Identifier type number allocation for IIoT identifiers [10]

Tag interval	Description
0x00-0x63	Reserve
0x64-0x7F	Assign to MIS
0x100-0x1FF	Assign to other identifier systems, such as Handle, GS1, etc.
0x200-0x7FF	Reserved for future new identifier systems

for payment applications, RFID sensors for logistics and identity recognition, and near field communication (NFC). Active identifier carriers are commonly found in universal integrated circuit cards (UICCs) or smart chips, which have bidirectional communication and easy modification capabilities.

To facilitate the management of IIoT identifiers, MIN-IIoT assigns different identifier type numbers for different IIoT identifier systems according to the rules given in Table 15.4. This allows for providing corresponding identifier resolution services based on the coding methods and parsing protocols associated with each identifier system. It ensures compatibility with existing identifier systems and facilitates support for future innovative identifier systems.

15.2 Internet of Vehicles

15.2.1 Architecture of MIN-V2X

Currently, automotive technology is undergoing rapid changes, with electrification, intelligence, connectivity, and sharing being important development directions. Intelligent connected V2X (Vehicle to Everything) is one of the significant directions for future automobiles, and it holds great importance in reshaping the automotive industry chain and value chain.

However, the rapid development of intelligent connected vehicle technology also brings various network security issues, such as signal or data eavesdropping and tampering.

The security risks faced by V2X include terminal spoofing, fake base stations, signal/data eavesdropping, and signal/data tampering/replay. Without protection, unauthorized terminals can impersonate legitimate terminals to access cellular networks, occupy network resources, obtain network services, or send forged network signals or business data, thereby affecting the normal operation of the system.

To address the security risks of V2X, the multi-identifier network for vehicle to everything (MIN-V2X) has emerged as a high-security dedicated network [11] for intelligent connected vehicles based on CoG-MIN. It effectively ensures network security and communication efficiency in the connected vehicle environment.

The overall architecture of MIN-V2X is illustrated in Fig. 15.4.

In MIN-V2X, communication through the antenna interface and Uu interface is divided into the access layer, network layer, and application layer. Communication [7, 8] through the PC5 interface is divided into the access layer and security application layer.

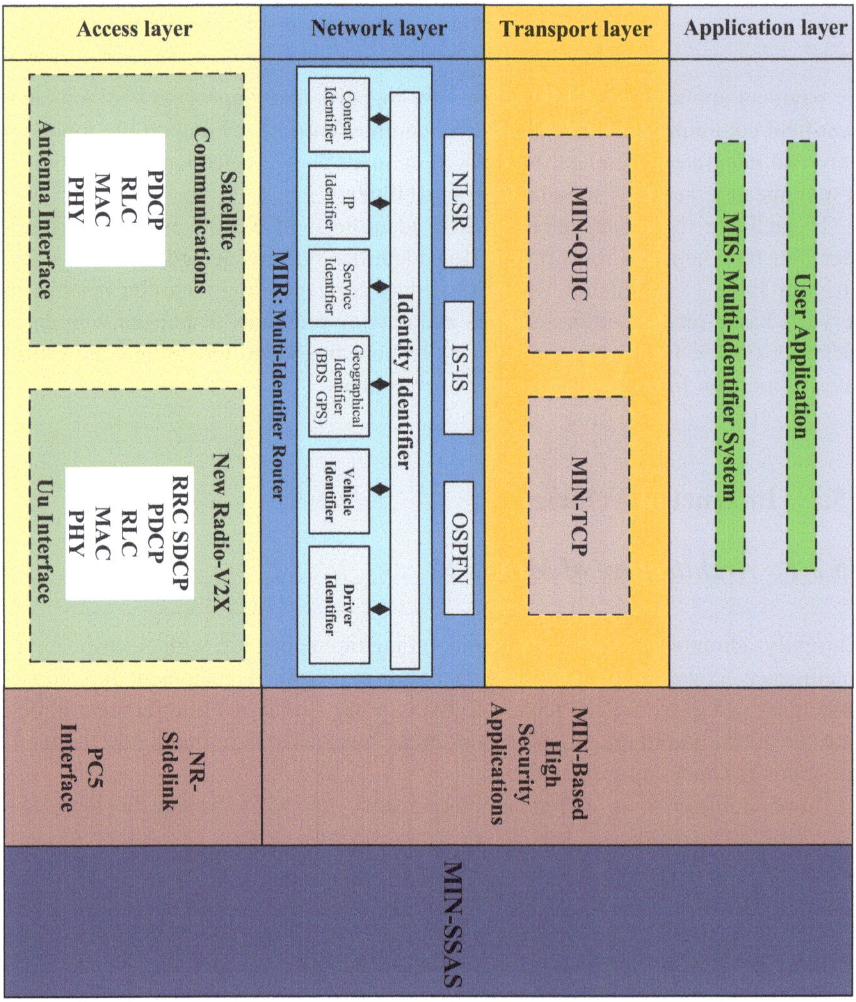

Fig. 15.4 MIN-V2X protocol stack

The architecture is further supported by the Security Situational Awareness System (MIN-SSAS), which is based on CoG-MIN and covers all levels. In this context, the Uu interface refers to the interface between the On-Board Unit (OBU) or Road-Side Unit (RSU) and the base station. The PC5 interface represents the direct communication interface between OBUs or between OBUs and RSUs.

In the access layer, MIN-V2X includes the Uu interface, PC5 interface, and satellite antenna interface, all of which support V2X communication. The Uu interface and satellite antenna interface are both based on network communication, while the PC5 interface uses direct communication mode. Therefore, the Uu interface and satellite antenna interface are categorized together and interface with the network layer. The PC5 interface directly interfaces with the security application layer developed for PC5 communication.

In the network layer, MIN-V2X utilizes the Multi-Identifier Router (MIR) [12] to perform identifier translation, routing, content filtering, and data protection functions. MIR performs routing addressing based on various types of identifiers, including identity, content, IP, service, geographic information, vehicle information, and driver information. Furthermore, all identifier-based communications require binding with authenticated unique identity identifiers and carry their corresponding private key signatures when sending packets to ensure security and traceability.

In the application layer, MIN-V2X consists of the User Application Interface and the Multi-Identifier System (MIS) [13, 14]. The MIS is primarily responsible for managing identifiers and its associated tasks include maintaining V2X network node, managing user registrations, and managing generation, querying, and parsing of identifiers.

The Security Situation Awareness System (MIN-SSAS) is responsible for monitoring the traffic at various levels of the network, perceiving and recording abnormal network behaviors. MIN-SSAS locks all abnormal events in the blockchain to ensure network security. It also provides real-time assessment and prediction of the system's security situation, sets thresholds for security situations, and provides feedback to administrators regarding critical security information that exceeds the threshold for adjusting defense strategies.

Taking the example of remote vehicle control protection scenario under MIN-V2X, the interaction process is depicted in Fig. 15.5.

The implementation of remote vehicle control is based on the V2X platform. Users send remote control commands through a mobile app, and the cloud server receives the control commands and forward them to the Intelligent Vehicle Terminal (TBOX) via 4G/5G networks. If the TBOX is in a sleep state, the V2X platform sends a wake-up message to the TBOX. If the TBOX is in an active state, it directly receives the remote control commands and transmits the signals to the vehicle's actuators. The Electronic Control Unit (ECU) executes the commands and provides feedback to the TBOX, which is then sent back to the mobile app through the V2X platform, completing the closed-loop process and realizing the entire remote control interaction flow.

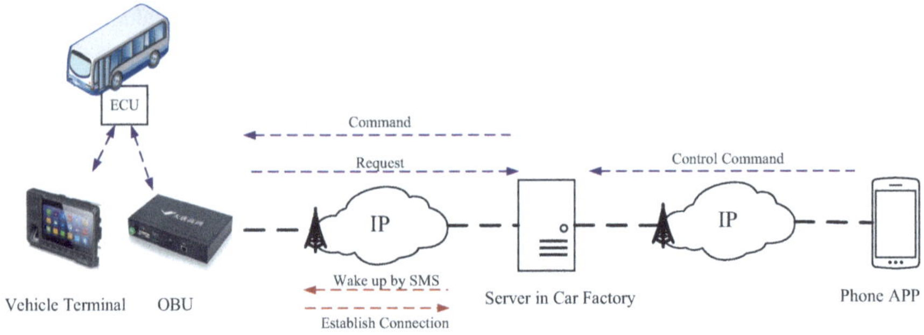

Fig. 15.5 Remote vehicle control process

15.2.2 Application Scenarios of MIN-V2X

MIN-V2X can effectively safeguard the security of networks and communications. Its main application scenarios include complete network scenarios, base station network scenarios, satellite network scenarios, and no-network scenarios.

In the complete network scenario, vehicles have good communication with both base stations and satellites in their operating areas. Vehicles can simultaneously transmit information with base stations, satellites, and other vehicles.

As shown in Fig. 15.6, vehicles communicate with cellular base stations through the Uu interface. They utilize satellites for real-time positioning and inter-vehicle network communication. High-orbit satellites provide real-time positioning services, while low-orbit communication satellites offer comprehensive communication support for V2X. Vehicles communicate directly with each other through the PC5 interface, enabling direct communication.

In the base station network scenario, vehicles have good communication only with base stations in their operating areas and cannot communicate with satellites. In this scenario, vehicles can simultaneously transmit information with base stations and other vehicles.

As shown in Fig. 15.7, vehicles communicate with cellular base stations through the Uu interface. Vehicles directly connect to each other for communication through the PC5 interface.

In the satellite network scenario, vehicles have good communication only with satellites in their operating areas and cannot communicate with base stations. In this scenario, vehicles can simultaneously transmit information with satellites and other vehicles.

As shown in Figs. 15.8 and 15.9, vehicles utilize satellites for real-time positioning and inter-vehicle network communication. High-orbit satellites provide real-time positioning services, while low-orbit communication satellites offer comprehensive communication support for V2X. Vehicles directly connect to each other for communication through the PC5 interface.

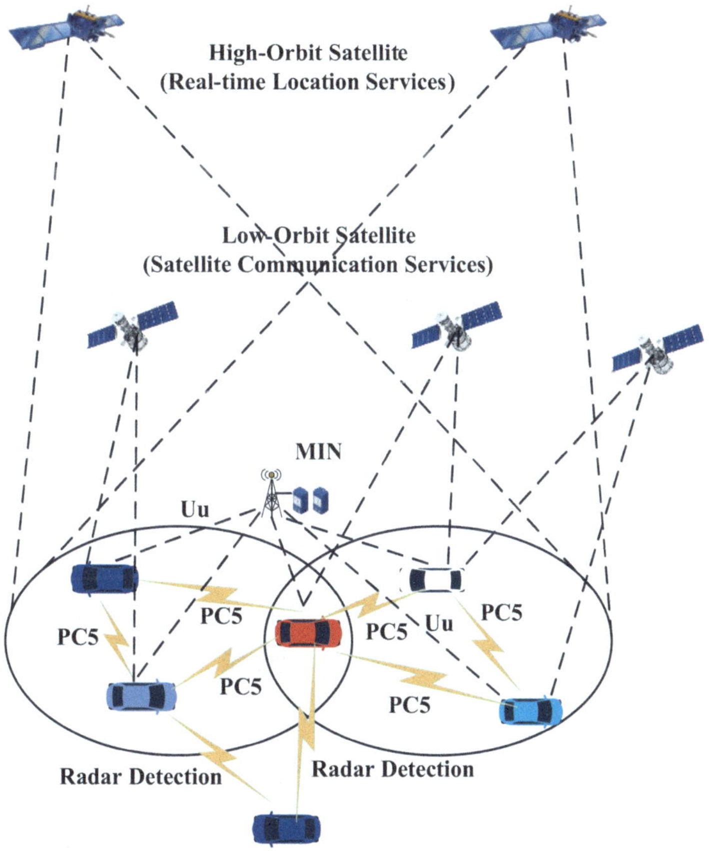

Fig. 15.6 Communication in the complete network scenario

In scenarios without network coverage, vehicles in the operating area are unable to directly communicate with base stations and satellites. However, they can still communicate with other vehicles.

As shown in Fig. 15.10, vehicles can establish short-range communication with each other using the PC5 interface. This allows for direct communication between vehicles in the absence of network connectivity.

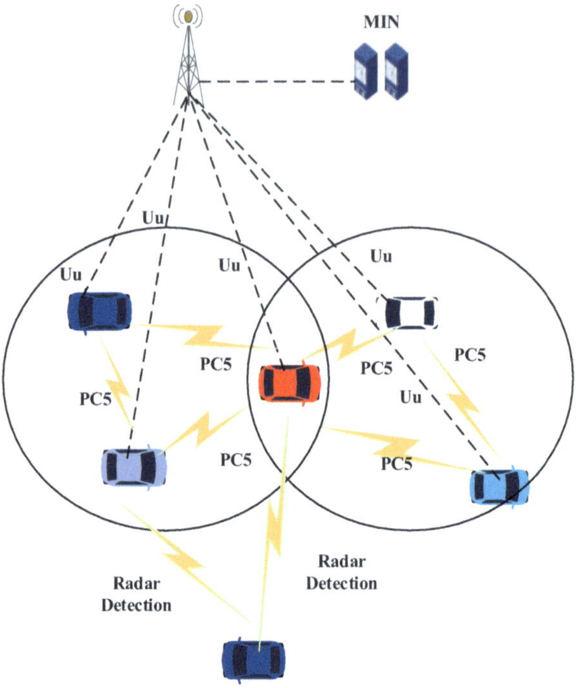

Fig. 15.7 Communication in the base station network scenario

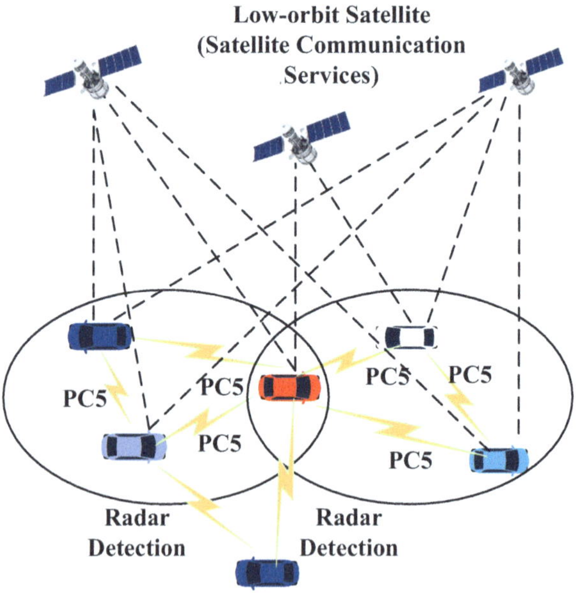

Fig. 15.8 Communication in the low-orbit satellite network scenario

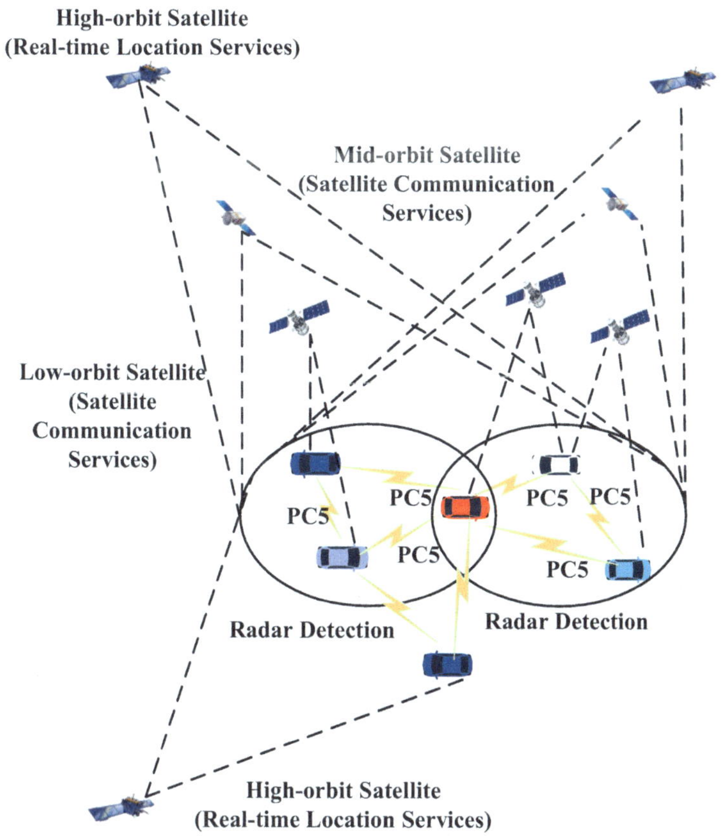

Fig. 15.9 Communication in the high-orbit satellite network scenario

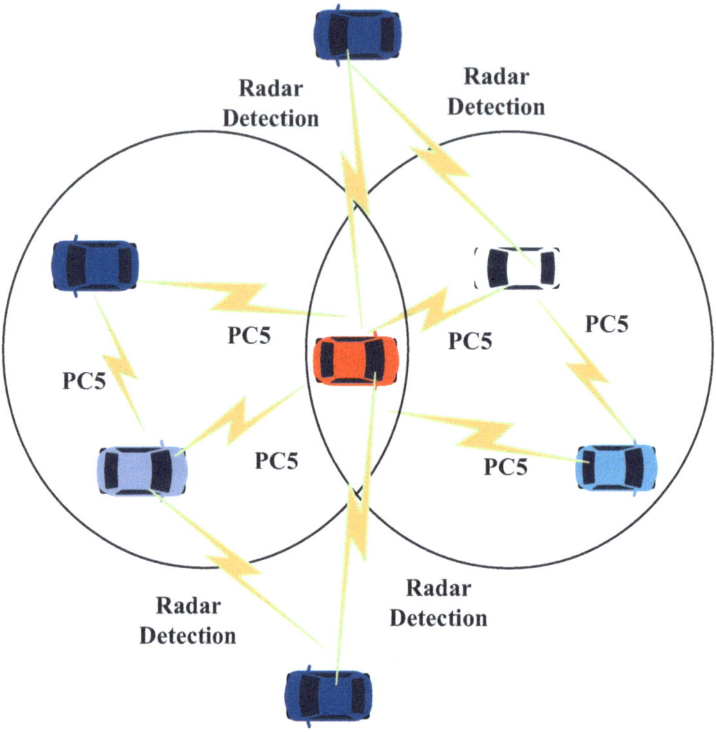

Fig. 15.10 Communication in the scenarios without network coverage

15.3 Space-Terrestrial Integrated Networks

With the rapid development of science and technology, humanity has progressed from the industrial society to the information society. Concurrently, the leaps and bounds in aerospace technology have made space a critical strategic domain for nations. The demand for global internet services in remote terrestrial regions, oceans, and airspace has been growing year by year. Space-Terrestrial Integrated Networks (STINs), which can meet the communication coverage requirements across the globe, have emerged as a trend in the development of future networks, attracting widespread attention from various countries.

15.3.1 Overview of Space-Terrestrial Integrated Networks

Research on STIN has been underway for many years and has seen widespread application. In 2000, the U.S. Department of Defense proposed the Global Information Grid (GIG) project, which is primarily composed of four layers: ground, aerospace, near-space, and satellite. The GIG integrates communication networks, sensor networks, and operational networks to achieve seamless global communication and information resource sharing, with plans to establish end-to-end connectivity by 2020. Subsequently, the USA, the United Kingdom, and various European countries have successively developed and launched a series of satellite constellation systems, such as Geostationary Earth Orbit (GEO) satellite systems and Transformable Satellite (TSAT), as well as Non-Geostationary Orbit (NGEO) satellite systems, including Iridium, GlobalStar, OneWeb, and SpaceX's StarLink.

Space-based networks have an exceptionally broad coverage range and clear advantages for communication in remote mountainous areas, deserts, oceans, and airspace that are difficult for terrestrial systems to cover. However, since the majority of human activities still primarily take place on the ground, the research and application of various satellite systems must always be closely integrated with terrestrial systems. The development direction of STIN is to achieve efficient information transmission and sharing among users in the maritime, land, and air domains through the fusion of space-based networks and terrestrial networks.

The construction of STIN faces many challenges, including the design of a reasonable network architecture, satellite constellation orbits, networking technologies, transmission technologies, network management, and security technologies. Networking technology is the foundation for achieving the interoperability between satellite networks in the space segment and the terrestrial internet. One of the key challenges in building an effective STIN is the routing problem.

STIN support a diverse range of services and applications. Traditional routing approaches typically rely on running routing protocols within the network to obtain the status of network nodes and links, thereby deriving the overall network topology and computing optimal paths across the entire network to populate the routing tables. This approach requires handling large-scale routing tables and massive data forwarding loads. As the network scale grows rapidly, the number of routing table entries experiences dramatic inflation. This forces network operators to invest significant resources in addressing the various problems caused by the immense routing tables, such as communication interruptions that can severely impact the performance and stability of the STIN.

Furthermore, the nodes and links in STIN are not in a fixed and unchanging state. Satellite nodes and links have a certain probability of failure, and the dynamic nature of space nodes like satellites and drones leads to constant changes in the topology of the space-based network segment. When such situations occur, traditional routing approaches lack the necessary adaptive capabilities. They require notifying all network nodes of the topology changes and then re-calculating the optimal routing paths, resulting in substantial routing overhead. STIN needs to perform space-based data transmission tasks efficiently, robustly, quickly, and accurately to ensure the reliability of diverse communication requirements.

To facilitate the development of STIN, CoG-MIN research team has designed a practical and scalable routing solution for STIN. Leveraging the unique characteristics of each layer in the STIN architecture, this approach effectively utilizes space network resources and provides efficient and robust routing and forwarding services.

15.3.2 *Routing Scheme for Space-Terrestrial Integrated Networks Based on CoG-MIN*

Satellite Network Routing Algorithm

For polar orbit satellite constellation systems, all satellites are in polar orbits, and the number of satellites and constellation parameters on each orbital plane are identical, with the satellites uniformly distributed within each orbital plane. Each satellite has four inter-satellite links, with two connecting to the previous and next satellites on the same orbital plane, and the other two connecting to the left and right satellites on adjacent planes.

Figure 15.11 is a schematic of the polar orbit constellation, observed from the north polar direction.

The satellites on the left side of the seam move from south to north, while the satellites on the right side of the seam move from north to south. This opposing direction of satellite movement gives rise to the region known as the reverse seam. Due to the high-speed movement of satellites on either side of the reverse seam, it is difficult to establish reliable inter-satellite links in this area. As the satellites reach the polar regions, the distance between adjacent satellites on different planes decreases dramatically, making it challenging to maintain proper antenna alignment and establish reliable inter-satellite links.

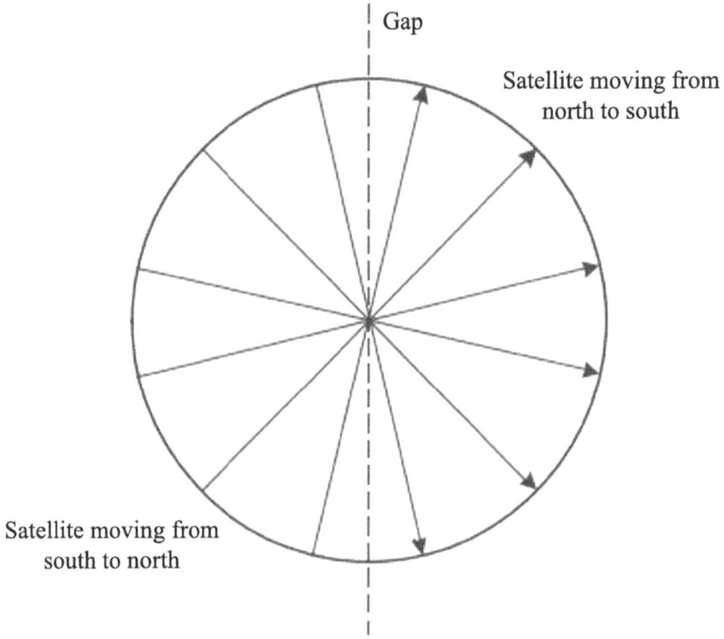

Fig. 15.11 Schematic diagram of polar orbit constellation in the north pole direction

To implement geolocation-based distributed routing for satellite networks, the space-terrestrial integrated routing scheme based on CoG-MIN requires each satellite to establish an access information table and a status information table. In the access information table, the AIT_s entry records the user and gateway information connected to the current satellite, while the AIT_u, AIT_d, AIT_l, and AIT_r entries record the user and gateway information for the satellite connections in the up, down, left, and right directions, respectively. In the status information table, the SIT_u, SIT_d, SIT_l, and SIT_r entries record the link status, buffer queue packet size q_i, buffer queue load L_i, and channel attenuation factor ε for the satellites in the up, down, left, and right directions, respectively. Each satellite node periodically sends a notification message to its neighbor nodes, which includes the current satellite's access information table AIT_s, the packet size q_i in the buffer queue, the buffer queue load L_i, and the channel attenuation factor ε_i.

When a satellite node receives a data packet, it needs to query the access information table and status information table based on the destination identity and location information in the packet header to obtain the potential next-hop node. First, it queries the access information table, if the destination identity information is in AIT_s, the satellite node directly forward the packet to the ground user device. If the destination identity is in AIT_u, AIT_d, AIT_l, or AIT_r, it forward the packet to the corresponding satellite. Otherwise, it uses the destination location information and the status information table to obtain the candidate next hop.

Depending on the different orbits and intra-orbital positions of the current satellite node and the destination satellite node, the number of candidate next hops is typically one or two. If there is only one candidate next hop, the probability of that node being the next hop is 100%. If there are two or more optional next-hop nodes, the probabilities of selecting each node need to be calculated. Assuming the choice of the next hop is between a vertical direction and a horizontal direction, and the paths converge completely two hops later, the probability calculation only considers the delay of the last two hops. Let the vertical next hop be N_v and the horizontal next hop be N_h; the probability of selecting the next hop depends on the inverse of the sum of the total delays for the two paths from the current node to the second-hop node via N_v and N_h, respectively. The total delay includes both transmission delay and queuing delay.

The satellite network routing algorithm calculates the propagation delay and queuing delay of each candidate next hop to obtain the probability of selecting the next hop, and then forward the data packet according to the probability. When the satellite network load is low and the link status is good, data transmission between satellite network devices is prioritized through the satellite network; when the satellite network experiences high load or link failures, data will be offloaded to gateways and relayed through the terrestrial network. A further introduction to the satellite network routing algorithm can be found in [15].

Terrestrial Network Routing Algorithm

As described in Chap. 5, hyperbolic routing is a routing mechanism based on hyperbolic space embedding, which is essentially a greedy routing that guarantees reachability for each node. In this routing process, each node does not need to query and maintain the next-hop node of the optimal path through a routing table. It can dynamically determine the next-hop node based solely on its own hyperbolic coordinates, the hyperbolic coordinates of its neighbor nodes, and the hyperbolic coordinates of the destination node.

Hyperbolic identifiers are used to guide the greedy routing between different network domains. The network identifier domain can be divided into k levels, assuming each level of routers can support N network identifiers. Hyperbolic embedding is performed on the network topology of each level sequentially, obtaining the hyperbolic coordinate sets (R_i, θ_i), $i = 1, 2, \ldots, k$, for the nodes at each level. The hyperbolic coordinates of the nodes are used as a new network identifier—the hyperbolic identifier—to guide the hyperbolic routing in the terrestrial network.

For example, in a three-level network domain, the network topology of the first-level autonomous domain is embedded into the hyperbolic space, obtaining the hyperbolic coordinates (R_1, θ_1) for each node in the first-level autonomous domain, which are used as the hyperbolic identifiers to guide the hyperbolic routing between nodes in the terrestrial network. The network topology of each second-level autonomous domain under the first-level domain is also embedded into the hyperbolic space, obtaining the hyperbolic coordinates (R_2, θ_2) for each node in the second-level domains, which are used as the hyperbolic identifiers to guide the hyperbolic routing, with the complete hyperbolic identifier of a second-level domain node defined as "$(R_1, \theta_1) : (R_2, \theta_2)$". This process can be extended to further hierarchical levels. Within a third-level domain, where the topology changes frequently, an intra-domain routing protocol is used, with routers selecting the path with the lowest cost based on the link state.

The greedy routing process based on hyperbolic identifiers in the terrestrial network domains is as follows:

Step 1: Assuming the hyperbolic coordinates of the source node are (r_s, θ_s), and the hyperbolic coordinates of the destination node are (r_d, θ_d), the destination node's hyperbolic coordinates are encapsulated in the packet and forwarded by the source node through the intermediate nodes.

Step 2: When an intermediate node receives the packet, it calculates the hyperbolic distance of each of its neighbor nodes (r_i, θ_i) to the destination node (r_d, θ_d) using the hyperbolic distance formula $x_{id} = \text{arccosh}(\cosh r_i \cosh r_j - \sinh r_i \sinh r_j \cos \theta_{id})$. The intermediate node then selects the neighbor node with the shortest hyperbolic distance to the destination as the next hop and forward the packet to that neighbor.

Step 3: Through the process described in step 2, the packet eventually reaches the destination node (r_d, θ_d).

Step 4: If an AS node experiences a temporary failure, a backtracking mechanism can be added to the above simple greedy routing algorithm to find an alternative path to the destination, in which case the nodes' hyperbolic coordinates do not need to be changed.

A further introduction to the hyperbolic routing algorithm can be found in Chap. 5.

Example of Space-Terrestrial Routing

As shown in Fig. 15.12, when User 1 located in Urumqi establishes communication with User 2 in Beijing via a satellite network, the communication establishment process is as follows:

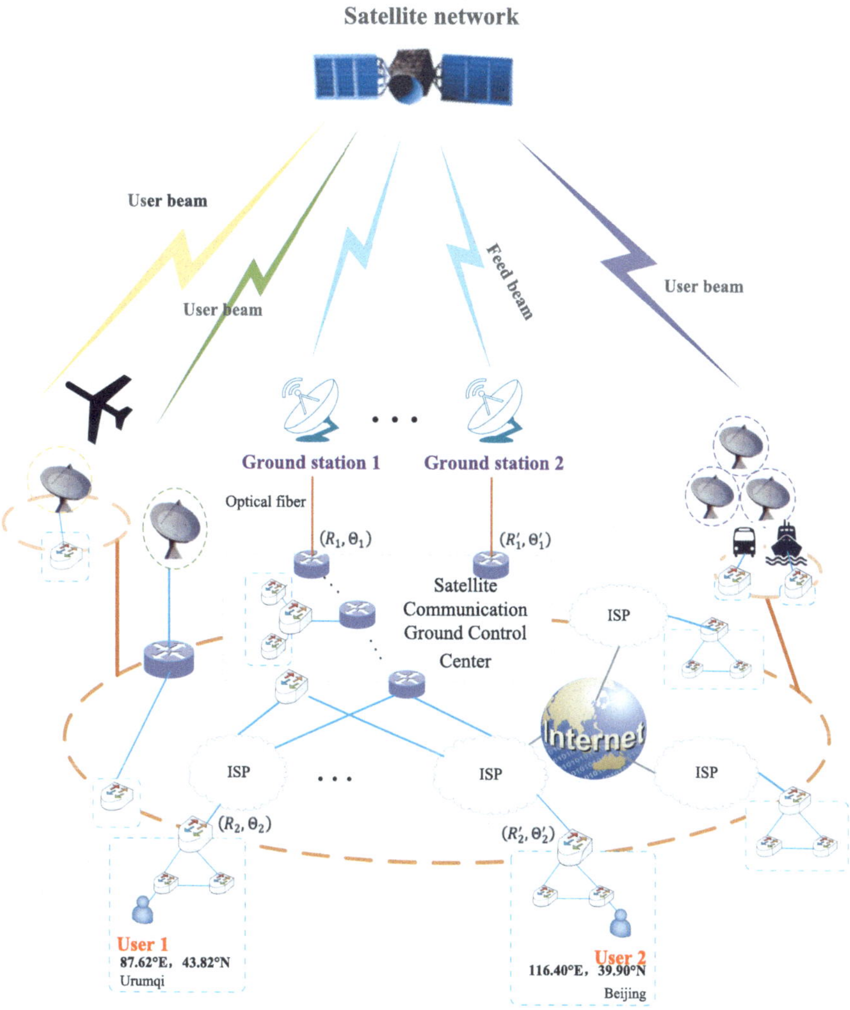

Fig. 15.12 The example for space-terrestrial routing

User 1 requests information about User 2 through the terrestrial domain name resolution system and obtains the hyperbolic coordinates and geographical location of the gateway station closest to User 2's location.

Using the greedy routing algorithm based on hyperbolic geometry, User 1 calculates the hyperbolic distances from multiple neighboring gateway stations of the domain border router to the destination gateway station, and selects the nearest gateway station 1 as the next hop to forward the data packets.

Gateway station 1 then transmits the data packets to the connected satellite 1.

The satellite network runs its routing algorithm and routes the data packets from satellite 1 to the destination satellite 2 based on the destination geographical information encapsulated in the data packets.

Satellite 2 then disseminates the data packets to the destination gateway station 2.

Gateway station 2 forward the data packets to User 2 through the hyperbolic routing in the terrestrial network.

15.4 Digital Asset Management and Trading

With the swift advancement of digital technology, digital assets have emerged as a prominent topic in current economic and financial domains. Digital assets involve utilizing digital technology to convert traditional physical assets into tradable digital assets [16]. This process transforms conventional physical assets into divisible, transferable, tradable, storable, and traceable digital forms, consequently expanding the liquidity and reach of assets. In the future, digital assets will assume an increasingly pivotal role in financial activities, driving improvements in asset efficiency and liquidity, optimizing the financial system, and facilitating economic transformation and upgrading.

The global market for digital assets is seeing tremendous growth [17]. According to statistics, the global digital asset market size reached $2.3 trillion in 2022 and is projected to hit $5.6 trillion by 2027 [18].

Figure 15.13 illustrates the scale of the digital asset market over the past decade. The advent and implementation of blockchain technology has enabled secure, reliable, and efficient trading and management of digital assets, while also fostering exploration and innovation in the field of digital assets [18]. Initially confined to finance, digital assets' applications now extend to the non-financial sector. Consequently, digital assets have become a focal point for governments and financial institutions worldwide, given the prevailing market landscape.

The emergence and adoption of blockchain technology have significantly accelerated the advancement of digital assets [19]. Blockchain, a decentralized distributed ledger technology, facilitates secure and reliable exchange of information and storage of data [20]. This innovation has rendered recording and trading of traditional physical assets in digital form practicable. Due to its decentralized nature, immutability, and data transparency, blockchain offers robust technical support and security for digital assets [21].

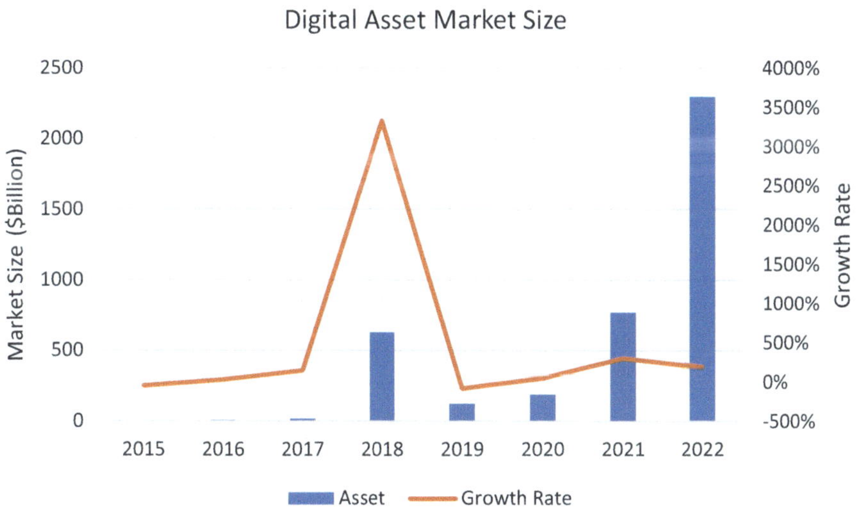

Fig. 15.13 Digital asset market size [18]

The Digital Asset Management and Trading System is a blockchain-based platform over CoG-MIN. It aims to offer a comprehensive solution for the digitization, management, and trading of diverse asset types. This system ensures the secure, transparent, and efficient circulation of assets while providing convenient services for investors, issuers, and regulatory agencies. The overall architecture of Digital Asset Management and Trading System is depicted in Fig. 15.14.

15.4.1 Core Components

The core components of the system are as follows:

PPoV (parallel proof of vote) consensus algorithm: The system leverages distributed ledger technology and incorporates the PPoV consensus algorithm, which is self-developed, efficient, and dependable. This algorithm underpins asset decentralization, immutability, and data transparency.

Smart contract: A self-executing contract within the blockchain ecosystem, designed to handle business logic such as asset issuance, trading, and clearing.

Asset digitization module: Transform traditional assets into digital formats that are readily tradable on the blockchain, including asset tokenization, issuance, and registration.

Transaction matching engine: Handles user transaction requests and facilitates real-time matching of buy and sell.

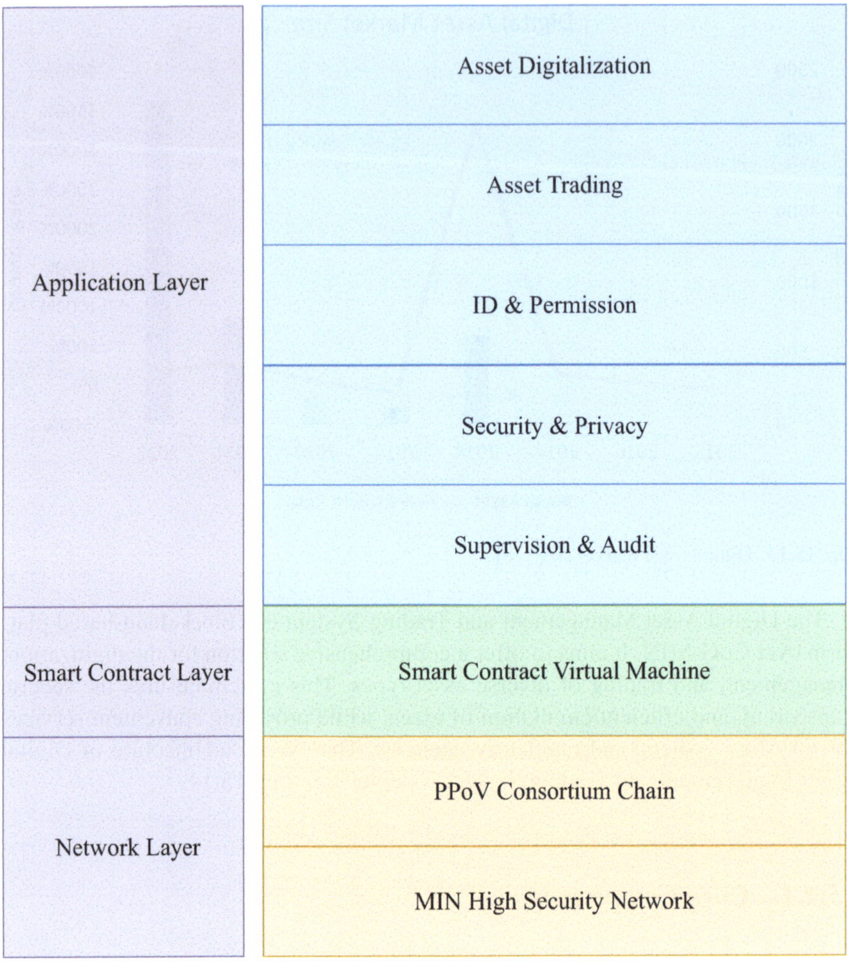

Fig. 15.14 The architecture of digital asset management and trading system

Identity authentication and permission management: Verifies the authenticity of platform users' identities, performs compliance checks in line with relevant laws and regulations, and grants user-specific permissions based on their roles.

Data security and privacy protection: Utilizes cryptography and the highly secure MIN network to protect the confidentiality and integrity of user data.

Supervision and auditing module: Offers real-time data surveillance and audit features for regulatory bodies to ensure the compliance and reliability of the platform.

15.4.2 System Advantages

The system advantages are as follows:

High security: Leveraging the decentralized foundation of blockchain technology coupled with the robust security protocols of the MIN network, the system guarantees the security of assets and transaction data.

Transparency and trustworthiness: All transaction records are stored on the blockchain, ensuring data transparency and traceability, which bolsters confidence among participants.

Cost reduction: The utilization of smart contracts automates business processes, slashing intermediary costs and operational expenses.

Enhanced efficiency: Real-time transaction matching minimizes the settlement cycle, resulting in improved efficiency in fund utilization.

Increased liquidity: By overcoming the physical limitations of traditional assets, the system enables the flow of previously idle capital, thus enhancing liquidity.

The architecture of the Digital Asset Management and Trading System is crafted to deliver a comprehensive, secure, and efficient solution, facilitating the digitization, trade, and global circulation of diverse asset classes. The system not only aids in the value discovery of assets and the utilization of funds but also erects a reliable and compliant trading environment for investors, issuers, and regulatory agencies [22].

15.4.3 Business Functions

The business functions of the system are as follows:

Asset tokenization: Leveraging smart contract technology within the PPoV blockchain, physical assets can be digitized and represented as tokens, streamlining asset tokenization. Typical assets for tokenization include commodities like gold, properties such as real estate, and art pieces. Token issuance and management are efficiently conducted via smart contracts on the PPoV blockchain, enabling the trade and circulation of digital assets on the blockchain. This approach ensures a secure and fluid exchange between digital and physical assets under distributed management.

Asset information registration: Asset ownership confirmation is crucial to ensure the legality and security of digital assets during the asset digitization process. The system utilizes identity management on the MIN network to ensure the authenticity and legality of user identities. Through smart contract technology and integration with regulatory agencies, the system verifies the authenticity and integrity of assets in real time, safeguarding legal ownership and minimizing disputes.

Asset issuance and management: During digital asset issuance, it is necessary to consider the issues asset fundraising and custody. The system offers various fundraising methods and channels, such as public and private fundraising, and ensures asset custody and fund security. The system can utilize centralized or decentralized custody solutions based on the issuer's preference, reinforcing the security and trustworthiness of the digital assets. Post-issuance, all pertinent transaction data is recorded on the PPoV-based blockchain. After digital asset issuance, equity management and dividend distribution to digital asset holders become imperative. Holders of digital asset stake ownership and corresponding rights to digital assets, which need to be properly managed and allocated. Equity management, including equity records and changes, is updated and managed in real-time on the PPoV-based blockchain. Dividends are managed efficiently and transparently through smart contracts on the PPoV-based blockchain, offering distribution methodologies like proportional allocation and time-specific distribution, guaranteeing equitable and transparent oversight of digital asset entitlements.

Asset trading: The trading platform records and updates user buying and selling order information through its self-developed high-performance PPoV-based blockchain. The platform ensures the security and reliability of orders through the high-security MIN network, safeguarding against the alteration or misuse of trade orders.

The platform utilizes real-time matching based on order specifics to cater to the demands and intents of both purchasers and vendors. Real-time matching accounts for variables such as price, volume, and urgency to secure equitable, unbiased, and efficient transaction pairings. This trading concordance is orchestrated via on-chain smart contracts, enabling an automated and decentralized trading process. The security of user accounts is underpinned by the MIN network, while the high-performance PPoV-based blockchain ensures the swiftness, dependability, and integrity of the digital asset trading records.

15.5 A Community with a Shared Future in Cyberspace

Cyber sovereignty is the embodiment and extension of national sovereignty in cyberspace. Building a national sovereignty network and realizing multilateral management and co-governance of the Internet is a key step in building a community with a shared future in cyberspace. CoG-MIN supports the joint construction of peaceful, secure, development and cooperation of cyberspace, and has great application value in the IoV, IIoT, cyberspace United States and other scenarios. It can provide a solution for global demand of cyberspace management and governance.

15.5.1 Overview of a Community with a Shared Future in Cyberspace

Since the inception of ARPANET in the 1960s, the Internet has undergone significant advancements driven by scientific and technological progress. It has expanded from its initial military applications to encompass all aspects of people's social lives, including areas such as daily life, economy, and education. As a result, human society has gradually transitioned into the digital age. In recent years, the rapid development of Internet technologies, such as big data, cloud computing, blockchain, and artificial intelligence, along with the flourishing digital economy, has fostered international cooperation in cyberspace. The Internet has increasingly transformed the global community into an interconnected network, uniting everyone in a shared future. However, certain challenges have emerged alongside these developments. Issues such as the exportation of ideological conflicts through online platforms, the slow progress in network governance, and the compromise of personal information have surfaced. Cyberspace has now become a crucial factor influencing national strength and international relations [23].

On December 16, 2015, during his speech at the World Internet Conference held in Wuzhen Town, China, Chinese President Xi Jinping introduced the significant proposal of establishing a community with a shared future in cyberspace.

The concept of a community with a shared future in cyberspace represents a collective space for human activities that has been formed through the Internet. In order to promote a mutually beneficial and inclusive cyberspace, international legal treaties like the Convention on Cybercrime have been adopted. However, certain countries still impose restrictions on the development of their respective cyberspaces. The initiative to establish a community with a shared future in cyberspace encourages outstanding local Internet companies from all nations to expand globally. Simultaneously, it supports the technological advancement of cyberspace for all countries. This approach aims to transcend the Cold War mentality and zero-sum game mindset, address issues related to cyberspace governance, foster consensus among nations regarding equal participation in cyberspace, and provide a framework for advancing the modernization of the global governance system [24].

15.5.2 Challenges in Building a Community with a Shared Future in Cyberspace

With the rapid growth of the digital economy, the value of Internet data has soared, but it has also brought about significant data security risks. Currently, the development of the global Internet is uneven, resulting in a digital divide.

Regarding the challenges existing in international cyberspace, countries hold varying governance concepts and strategies. The debates surrounding cyberspace sovereignty persist. Consequently, there is a shared global demand to develop a new network architecture with multilateral management and governance. This approach seeks to address the congenital defects in the existing Internet system and is an essential step toward collectively building a community with a shared future in cyberspace.

National sovereignty serves as a fundamental concept in contemporary state law theory and practice. However, cyberspace, often referred to as the fifth frontier alongside land, sea, air, and space, currently lacks an internationally agreed-upon code of conduct. The emergence of malicious cyber activities has brought heightened attention to the matter of cyberspace sovereignty.

The characteristics of cyberspace, including its virtuality, sharing, openness, and susceptibility to attacks, may seem to weaken the notion of national sovereignty in this realm. However, it is important to recognize that cyberspace is not a lawless environment. Just like any other domain governed by sovereignty, adherence to the law remains the fundamental norm, and there are certain boundaries that cannot be crossed. Respecting legal principles and abiding by regulations are essential in maintaining order and security in cyberspace [25].

The crucial foundation for establishing a community with a shared future in cyberspace lies in recognizing, respecting, and safeguarding the cyber sovereignty of all nations. The principle of cyber sovereignty is an inevitable choice for global cyber governance. As early as 2013, the United Nations clearly stated that the principle of sovereign equality enshrined in the UN Charter extends to cyberspace. This signifies that within a country, the state holds dominion over cyberspace and is not subject to external constraints. In the community with a shared future in cyberspace, all countries hold equal status, rights, and responsibilities. They have an equal obligation to fulfill their commitments in this realm. Upholding the principle of cyber sovereignty ensures that each nation is empowered to govern its own cyberspace and contribute to the collective development and security of the global digital landscape.

At present, organizations with significant influence on international Internet governance include the Internet Governance Forum (IGF), the European Internet Forum (EIF), and the Georgia Institute of Technology's Internet Governance Project (IGP). All countries can further formulate fair and transparent international cyberspace governance rules through these international organizations and conferences, continuously improve the cooperation mechanism of international cyberspace governance entities, and build a community with a shared future in cyberspace that is mutually beneficial and peaceful.

The Internet is a huge international interconnection network based on the interweaving of global standardized data communication protocols. It is imperative to develop a novel network architecture with inherent "resilience." The consensus within the scientific and technological community is that the future network should support identity, content, services, and IP addresses. This novel network architecture should be designed to address the shortcomings of the current network architecture and meet the future evolving needs. This effort will pave the way for a more robust and adaptable network infrastructure in the future.

15.5.3 Building a Community with a Shared Future in Cyberspace Based on CoG-MIN

To effectively respond to the above challenges and global demands, it is essential to construct a Community with a Shared Future in Cyberspace based on CoG-MIN.

Furthermore, a Community with a Shared Future in Cyberspace based on CoG-MIN will enable the network system to adapt to the evolving technological landscape and leverage its potential for enhanced economic growth and innovation.

In 2021, CoG-MIN research team conducted a large-scale testing based on CoG-MIN in the existing operators' network environment. The large-scale testing deployed 150 nodes in the five continents of the world with more than ten universities, allowing the coexistence of MIN network and IP network. Technology tests such as consensus mechanism, transmission control, situation awareness, and functional tests such as identifier management, video on demand, and video conferencing were successfully conducted. CoG-MIN achieves efficient network access and orderly supervision through various technologies.

Figure 15.15 shows the large-scale international testbed.

Over the past 3 years, CoG-MIN has undergone numerous professional penetration attack tests and nearly ten large-scale attack and defense tests, all of which it has successfully passed. These tests have included challenging scenarios such as the real car attack and defense competition for IoVs, where CoG-MIN served as a robust defense system that remained impervious to breaches.

Both theoretical analysis and practical tests have demonstrated that CoG-MIN is highly effective in immunizing against attacks originating from various methodologies, attack toolchains, and attack software chains within the existing network system. Its capabilities have proven to be reliable in safeguarding against potential threats.

In general, CoG-MIN ensures compatibility with existing IP networks and supports progressive deployment. This eliminates concerns about the need for radical network architecture reconstruction when new communication requirements arise. CoG-MIN's flexibility is exemplified by its seamless adaptation to evolving network layer addressing and routing patterns without the need for extensive rebuilding. This adaptability extends to future expansions involving diverse identifiers, including IoT, IoV, IIoV, mobile communication, and other emerging technologies. As the world progresses toward economic globalization, cultural diversity, and widespread information technology applications, CoG-MIN is well-positioned to keep pace with these rapid advancements.

CoG-MIN's ability to adapt to the changing times is crucial for fostering the progress of human civilization. By providing a secure and evolvable framework for network communication, it supports the development and integration of various technologies, contributing to the advancement of society [15].

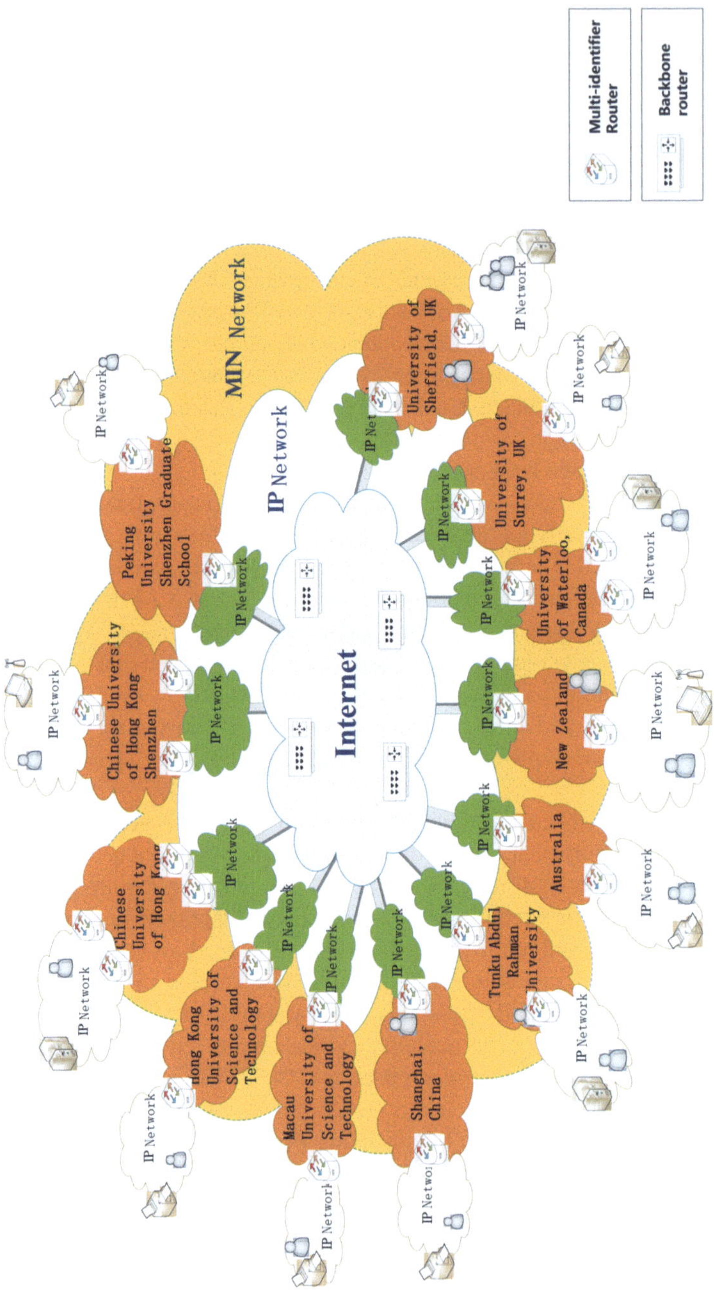

Fig. 15.15 The large-scale international testbed

References

1. Evans PC, Annunziata M. Industrial internet: pushing the boundaries of minds and machines. General Electric Reports, 2012, p. 488–508.
2. Malik PK, Sharma R, Singh R, et al. Industrial Internet of Things and its applications in industry 4.0: state of the art. Comput Commun. 2021;166:125–39.
3. Li JQ, Yu FR, Deng G, et al. Industrial internet: A survey on the enabling technologies, applications, and challenges. IEEE Commun Surv Tutor. 2017;19(3):1504–26.
4. Qin W, Chen S, Peng M. Recent advances in industrial internet: insights and challenges. Digit Commun Netw. 2020;6(1):1–13.
5. Yang C, Shen W, Wang X. The internet of things in manufacturing: key issues and potential applications. IEEE Syst Man Cybernet Magaz. 2018;4(1):6–15.
6. Fu Q, Liu J. Generalized multi-hop NR Sidelink relay for future V2X communication. IEEE/ACM Trans Networking. 2023;32:1691–706.
7. Chen S, Hu J, Shi Y, et al. A vision of C-V2X: technologies, field testing, and challenges with Chinese development. IEEE Internet Things J. 2020;7(5):3872–81.
8. Khan MJ, Khan MA, Malik S, et al. Advancing C-V2X for level 5 autonomous driving from the perspective of 3GPP standards. Sensors. 2023;23(4):2261.
9. Wang YM, Huang T, Wei GH, et al. scalable name identifier lookup for industrial internet. Comput Commun. 2022;186:102–9.
10. Wang YM, Li H, Huang T, et al. Scalable identifier system for industrial internet based on multi-identifier network architecture. IEEE Internet Things J. 2021;10(3):1919–32.
11. Smahi A, Li H, Yang Y, et al. BV-ICVs: a privacy-preserving and verifiable federated learning framework for V2X environments using blockchain and zkSNARKs. J King Saud Univ Comput Inf Sci. 2023;35(6):101542.
12. Zhang XC, Chen QS, Li H. MIR: multi-identifier router and its prototype. In: Proceedings of the 8th international conference on computer and communications management; 2020, p. 103–107.
13. Wang H, Li H, Smahi A, et al. MIS: a multi-identifier management and resolution system in the metaverse. ACM Trans Multimed Comput Commun Appl. 2023;20(7):1–25.
14. Wang ZX, Li H, Wang H, et al. A data lightweight scheme for parallel proof of vote consensus. In: 2021 IEEE international conference on big data (big data). Piscataway: IEEE; 2021. p. 3656–62.
15. Li H, Yang X. Co-governed sovereignty network: legal basis and its prototype & applications with MIN architecture. Cham: Springer; 2021.
16. Sazandrishvili G. Asset tokenization in plain English. J Corp Acc Financ. 2020;31(2):68–73.
17. Mahmoudi A, Sadeghi M, Naeni LM. Blockchain and supply chain finance for sustainable construction industry: ensemble ranking using ordinal priority approach. Oper Manag Res. 2023;17:809.
18. Wątorek M, Drożdż S, Kwapień J, et al. Multiscale characteristics of the emerging global cryptocurrency market. Phys Rep. 2021;901:1–82.
19. Du M, Chen Q, Xiao J, et al. Supply chain finance innovation using blockchain. IEEE Trans Eng Manag. 2020;67(4):1045–58.
20. Asante Boakye E, Zhao H, Coffie CPK, et al. Seizing technological advancement; determinants of blockchain supply chain finance adoption in Ghanaian SMEs. Tech Anal Strat Manag. 2023;36:2774–90.
21. Li D, Han D, Crespi N, et al. A blockchain-based secure storage and access control scheme for supply chain finance. J Supercomput. 2023;79(1):109–38.
22. Sun W. Application of blockchain technology in the supply chain finance. In: 2022 7th international conference on cloud computing and big data analytics (ICCCBDA). Piscataway: IEEE; 2022. p. 205–9.
23. Haber E, Topor L. Sovereignty, cyberspace, and the emergence of internet bubbles. J Adv Military Stud. 2023;14(1):144–65.

24. Hong Y, Goodnight GT. How to think about cyber sovereignty: the case of China. Chin J Commun. 2020;13(1):8–26.
25. Johnson DR, Post D. Law and borders: the rise of law in cyberspace. Stanford Law Rev. 1996;48:1367–402.

The manufacturer's authorised representative in the EU is Springer Nature Customer Service Centre GmbH, Europaplatz 3, 69115 Heidelberg, Germany. If you have any concerns regarding our products, please contact ProductSafety@springernature.com

Printed and bound by CPI Group (UK) Ltd, Croydon, CR0 4YY
26/03/2026
02078939-0010